WHAT
HAPPENED
WHEN

WHAT HAPPENED WHEN

A chronology of Australia
from 1788

Anthony Barker

ALLEN & UNWIN

First published as *When was that?* in 1988
This edition first published 1996
This revised edition 2000

Allen & Unwin
9 Atchison Street
St Leonards NSW 2065
Australia
Phone: (61 2) 8425 0100
Fax: (61 2) 9906 2218
Email: frontdesk@allen-unwin.com.au
Web: http://www.allenandunwin.com

National Library of Australia
Cataloguing-in-Publication entry:

Barker, A. W. (Anthony Wilhelm), 1930– .
What happened when: a chronology of Australia from 1788

  3rd ed.
  Includes index.
  ISBN 1 86508 426 3.

  1. Australia – History – Chronology. I. Title.

994

Set in 10/11pt Times by DOCUPRO, Sydney
Printed by SRM Production Services Sdn Bhd, Malaysia

10 9 8 7 6 5 4 3 2

CONTENTS

For David Elder

PREFACE

The idea for this book originated many years ago. As a publisher's editor, frequently working on books of Australian history, biography, art, sport, entertainment, social history, and general Australiana, I was required to check facts and dates that were often not readily accessible. For my own future use I recorded these details on index cards and filed them away in chronological order in cardboard boxes. Gradually I got into the habit of noting down details of any event or achievement that I came across, not only in the manuscripts I was working on but in books, magazines, and newspapers, in guidebooks and leaflets from historic places, in pamphlets and advertisements published in celebration of some anniversary, and on plaques attached to buildings and memorials.

Eventually I decided to gather the material systematically, with the object of producing a chronology of Australia for publication. I started to read through *The Australian Encyclopaedia* and collections of historical documents as well as specialized histories, noting down every date and fact of significance and filing the cards away in the ever-increasing number of cardboard boxes. The work became a time-consuming occupation.

To my great good fortune, the publisher of the original edition, John Ferguson, put me in touch with a fellow chronologist, David Elder, who had recently retired after a lifetime in publishing. David Elder had amassed an enormous amount of chronological information from prodigious reading, patient investigation, and years of travelling round Australia as a publisher's representative. The extent of his research was matched by the extent of his generosity; he graciously put all of his material at my disposal to use as I thought fit.

The amount of material was several times as much as I had gathered, even though its cut-off point was 1950, and far more than I could fit into a manageable single volume. But if I could not use it all, I could select freely from it. It allowed me to fill in many blank spaces in years where little of note seemed before to have happened, and it provided me with precise dates for innumerable events for which I and many reference works could

PREFACE

supply only the year or at best the month. It also often provided me with the answer to a recurring question: Which of the two or more conflicting dates or facts obtained from accepted authoritative sources was the right one?

Despite this help, the project still took much longer than I had expected. Even when I called a halt to the gathering of information, there still remained the editing of the cards—deciding what to include and what to leave out, compressing each piece of information into a line or two, sorting out the remaining inconsistencies—and then the typing of the manuscript and the huge job of preparing the index. Meanwhile, other books of a similar nature were published—it seems ideas float in the air like viruses and infect various authors and publishers at the same time. But I was convinced that my book, with its emphasis on precise dates and its detailed index, was sufficiently different to make its publication worth while.

When the text was eventually set in type, David Elder kindly read through the proofs, tactfully drawing my attention to misconceptions or ambiguities caused by compression, making helpful comments, answering queries, and suggesting useful additions. I am deeply indebted to him for his generous help at every stage of the book's long gestation, and the book is infinitely the better for it. He should not, of course be held responsible for whatever faults the book may have; the selection of events and their presentation are mine, and responsibility for any shortcomings is mine alone.

Anthony Barker

NOTE TO THE FOURTH EDITION

In the twelve years since the first edition was published, I have continued to gather information, not only for the purpose of updating the book—now to the end of 1999—but to correct or amend entries and make additions in the light of recent research. This has been done for each new edition. The index has been correspondingly amended and overhauled, and the deaths of notable people over the past twelve years have been recorded in the index and in the Births and Deaths section as appropriate. I would like to acknowledge my debt to the new volumes of the *Australian Dictionary of Biography*, which have provided me with the full names of a number of people and enabled me to include or correct missing and erroneous birth and death dates.

A.B.

INTRODUCTION

What Happened When is a guide to events in Australia's history and the achievements of notable Australians from the beginning of European settlement to the present day. It is arranged chronologically, each year beginning with a list of political and general events against precise dates, followed by the year's achievements and other information listed under the following seven categories:

A Architecture, Building
B Science, Technology, Discovery, etc.
C Arts and Entertainment
D Books and Writing
E Sport and Recreation
F Statistics, Social Change, the Environment
G Births and Deaths

The book also contains a comprehensive index which uses references to the relevant year and month (**1** to **12**) or classification (A to G) rather than to a page. For example, the reader will find the reference to Gough Whitlam's dismissal as "1975 **11**" (i.e., under November in the general chronological list of 1975) and the reference to his birth as "1916 G" (under Births and Deaths in the classified section of 1916). The book thus enables the reader to find out readily when any important event happened and also to see at a glance what was going on at the one time in various fields of activity.

The General Chronological List

In the first section of each year, the general chronological list, an event with no date or symbol alongside it can be assumed to have taken place on the day of the event immediately above it. Where the precise day of the month on which an event occurred is unknown, the entry is placed at the end of the month with a dash in place of the date. An event for which a month cannot be assigned is placed at the end of the section and indicated by an asterisk in place of a date (in the index, the reference to such an event—say, the drought of 1919—would be "1919*").

Establishing the correct date of an event has often been difficult, as works of reference are surprisingly inconsistent. To resolve problems of inconsistency, original sources have been

INTRODUCTION

sought to verify dates and facts. Despite all the care taken to avoid perpetuating errors, there are bound to be slips in a book containing so many facts and dates and covering such a wide range, and it is hoped that readers will inform the publisher of any inaccuracy or serious omission so that amendments can be made in subsequent printings.

Some of the date inconsistencies in reference works are understandable. Acts of parliament, for example, present a confusing choice of date—when a bill was introduced, when the act was passed, when it was given royal assent, and when the legislation (or the authority established by the legislation) came into operation. Where practicable, the date an act was assented to has been used; at times, however, one of the other dates was more relevant or accessible and has been used.

For reasons of space, only rare references have been made to outside world events that had no direct bearing on Australia, and events that occurred before the arrival of the First Fleet have not been included. The arrival of all convict transports is noted up to 1800, after which only those carrying some noteworthy person or involved in some noteworthy incident have been listed.

The Classified Section

In the classified section of each year, precise dates are given only in the Births and Deaths classification and occasionally to note some historic event in the arts or science or sport. Unless otherwise noted, architectural works are entered in the year the work was begun, together with the architect's name where appropriate, with the year of completion and other details given in brackets—for example, in 1858: "Leonard Terry, Melbourne Club (–1859; extended in 1879)." Plays are entered in the year they were first produced, films when first released, books when first published, and art works when first exhibited.

In classification G, birth entries include the year of death if the person is no longer living, and death entries include the age of the person at death. Thus in 1882 we have "Jul 8 Percy Grainger b. (–1961)" and "Aug 1 Henry Kendall d. (43)".

Estimated population numbers are as calculated by the Australian Bureau of Statistics to 31 December each year. Before 1961 they do not include full-blood Aborigines.

Some entries could just as well have been placed in a different classification from the one in which they appear or in the general chronological section. Where inconsistencies occur or any doubt arises, reference to the index will direct the reader to the right place.

INTRODUCTION

The Index

The index is in itself a handy reference source. Entries for persons almost always contain full name, occupation or claim to fame, and birth and death years; for notable individuals there are chronologically arranged sub-entries which provide a potted biography. Titles of books are listed with their author's name in brackets. Places are assigned their state; entries for the various states contain sub-entries relating to such matters as the foundation, exploration, granting of self-government and franchise, boundaries, and education system, followed by chronological lists of Governors and Premiers; capital cities have sub-entries relating to major events, structures, services, and institutions. Prime Ministers are listed in chronological order, as are Governors-General and Chief Justices of the High Court. Subjects covered in detail in the chronology have extensive entries appropriately subdivided.

For the most part, the subdivisions of a main entry are arranged chronologically and run on, separated from one another by a semicolon. Certain subject entries, however, have been arranged by states alphabetically and then, within states, chronologically. Other large main entries, such as "Aborigines", also lend themselves to initial alphabetical subdivision. Where sub-entries are arranged alphabetically, they begin on separate, indented lines for easy recognition. Other examples of alphabetical subdivision are the entry "Shipwrecks and Shipping Disasters" and the list of Melbourne Cup winners, which enables the reader to establish readily the year in which any given horse won the race (the winner in any year being obtainable from the main text).

In many cases the index will in fact provide the answers to questions without the need to refer to the main text. What was Ben Chifley's full name? When did Nellie Melba die? When was *Summer of the Seventeenth Doll* filmed? Who wrote *Such Is Life?* Who was Premier of South Australia after Sir Thomas Playford? Who was Governor of Tasmania in 1817? How many times was Alfred Deakin Prime Minister? Who succeeded Sir Isaac Isaacs as Chief Justice? And as Governor-General? When was it that Delta won the Melbourne Cup? The answers to questions such as these can all be found in the index.

1788

Jan 18 *Supply*, carrying Capt. Arthur Phillip, arrives at Botany Bay.

19 Convict transports *Alexander*, *Scarborough*, and *Friendship* arrive.

20 Remainder of the First Fleet—HMS *Sirius* (Capt. John Hunter); transports *Lady Penrhyn*, *Charlotte*, and *Prince of Wales*; and storeships *Fishburn*, *Golden Grove*, and *Borrowdale*—reach Botany Bay.

22 Phillip and Hunter investigate Port Jackson as a better site for settlement.

24 French frigates *La Boussole* and *L'Astrolabe*, commanded by the Comte de la Pérouse, arrive off Botany Bay.

26 Settlement established at Sydney Cove, Port Jackson.

Feb 3 Rev. Richard Johnson conducts the first Christian service in the colony.

6 Female convicts landed; debauchery and riot follow. At night, during a violent thunderstorm, lightning kills six sheep and a pig.

7 Colony of New South Wales formally proclaimed; Judge-Advocate David Collins reads the commission appointing Phillip Captain-General and Governor-in-Chief of NSW.

10 First marriages solemnized in Australia, including those of William Bryant and Mary Broad, and Henry Kable and Susannah Holmes.

11 First sitting of the Court of Criminal Jurisdiction (Judge-Advocate and six/seven military or naval officers).

14 *Supply* (Lt Henry Lidgbird Ball) sails for Norfolk Is. with a party of 23 led by Lt Philip Gidley King to found a settlement there.

17 Ball discovers Lord Howe Is.

27 Convict Thomas Barrett sentenced to death for robbing public store; executed in evening (first death sentence imposed in the colony).

– Farm established at Farm Cove under the direction of Henry Dodd.

Mar 2 Phillip explores Broken Bay (to 9th).

6 King takes formal possession of Norfolk Is.

10 *La Boussole* and *L'Astrolabe* leave Botany Bay, never to be seen again (wrecked on Vanikoro Is., Vanuatu, and all lives lost).

13 Ball explores Lord Howe Is. on way back to Port Jackson in *Supply*.

Apr 15 Phillip leads an expedition from Manly (to 18th); sights Blue Mountains.

23 On another expedition, Phillip discovers the site of Parramatta.

– Dingoes kill five ewes and a lamb at Farm Cove.

May 5 *Scarborough*, *Charlotte*, and *Lady Penrhyn* are discharged and leave for England via China.

29 Aborigines kill two convicts at Rushcutters Bay. (Phillip leads a punitive expedition against them on 31st.)

Jun 5 All the cattle brought from Cape Town stray from the settlement. (Found, with their progeny, in Nov. 1795.)

Jul 1 First sitting of the Court of Civil Jurisdiction (Collins, Johnson, and Surgeon-General John White).

14 *Alexander*, *Prince of Wales*, *Friendship*, and *Borrowdale* sail for UK.

Aug 12 White and Asst Surgeon William Balmain fight a duel; both slightly wounded.

Sep – Sydney's first road—a cleared track from the Governor's residence to Dawes Point—completed.

Oct 2 Hunter sails for Cape Town in the *Sirius* to obtain provisions.

1788

More convicts and marines sent to Norfolk Is. in the *Golden Grove*.

25 HMS Bounty (Capt. William Bligh) arrives at Tahiti to procure breadfruit plants for the West Indies.

Nov 2 Settlement established at Rose Hill (Parramatta).

10 Golden Grove returns to Port Jackson and (19th) sails for England with Fishburn.

Dec 31 Phillip secures the capture of an Aboriginal named Arabanoo to train as an interpreter.

A Architecture, Building

Phillip instructs surveyor Augustus Alt to draw up a plan for Sydney (Apr.). (Plan sent to Lord Sydney, 9 July.)

Government House foundation stone laid (15 May).

Battery, fitted with two guns, erected by Lt William Dawes on eastern side of Sydney Cove.

B Science, Technology, Discovery, etc.

Observatory erected by Dawes on Point Maskelyne (Dawes Point).

C Arts and Entertainment

First named piece of music performed in Australia—"The Rogue's March"—played at drumming-out of soldier caught in the convict women's tents (9 Feb.).

D Books and Writing

E Sport and Recreation

F Statistics, Social Change, the Environment

Number of persons landed from First Fleet (excluding RN and merchant seamen): about 1,030, including an estimated 736 convicts (548 male and 188 female) and 13 of their children, 211 marines, and about 27 wives and 16 children of marines and officials; livestock: 2 bulls, 4 cows, 2 stallions, 4 mares, 19 goats, 74 pigs, 29 sheep, 5 rabbits, 18 turkeys, 29 geese, 35 ducks, 209 fowls.

Estimated Aboriginal population of Australia: 750,000.

G Births and Deaths

Feb 17 Father Laurent Receveur (of La Pérouse's expedition) d.

May 22 William Grant Broughton b. (–1853).

1789

Jan – Planned convict uprising on Norfolk Is. suppressed.

Feb 20 Gov. Phillip informs Under-Secretary Evan Nepean in England of the non-cooperation of Maj. Robert Ross.

Mar 25 Seven marines tried for systematic robbery of stores. (Six executed on 27th.)

– Henry Dodd takes charge of a farm established at Rose Hill.

Apr 4 *Bounty* leaves Tahiti. (Stops at Cook Islands on 11th.)

27 Capt. James Campbell and other marine officers challenge Phillip's authority to make them sit as members of the Criminal Court.

29 Mutineers led by Fletcher Christian seize the *Bounty* and cast adrift Captain William Bligh and 18 others in the ship's launch.

– Outbreak of a disease resembling smallpox at Sydney Cove causes the death of many Aborigines, including Arabanoo (May).

May 8 *Sirius* arrives back at Port Jackson with supplies from the Cape, having completed a voyage round the world.

13 Convict John Caesar—"Black Caesar"—escapes to the bush with arms and ammunition. (Recaptured 6 June.)

28 Bligh lands on and names (29th) Restoration Is., off the east coast of Cape York Peninsula, then sails on through the Barrier Reef and Torres Strait.

Jun 6 Phillip leads an expedition to Broken Bay (to 16th), where he discovers the Hawkesbury River (12th).

14 Bligh arrives at Kupang, Timor, after a voyage of 5,800 km in the open boat.

27 Capt. Watkin Tench and party discover the Nepean River.

29 Phillip makes another expedition to the Hawkesbury (to 14 July), exploring its tributaries the Colo and the Macdonald, and climbs Richmond Hill.

Jul 3 Brig *Mercury* (Capt. John Cox) arrives at Oyster Bay, Maria Is., having visited and named Cox Bight, Van Diemen's Land.

Aug 7 Police force composed of 12 of the best-behaved convicts formed to carry out a night watch in Sydney.

20 Colonial Office instructs Phillip to make land grants to marines and to assign convicts as servants.

Sep 20 Hunter explores and charts Botany Bay (to 30th).

Oct 5 *Rose Hill Packet*, the first vessel built in the colony, launched for the Parramatta River trade.

Nov 1 Rations reduced by one-third.

21 Time-expired convict James Ruse established on land at Rose Hill (Experiment Farm) to see if and when he could support himself.

25 Aborigines Bennelong and Colbee captured by Phillip. (Colbee escapes 12 Dec.)

Dec 9 Dawes and a small party make an unsuccessful attempt (to 17th) to climb the Carmarthen Hills (Blue Mountains).

22 Black Caesar takes to the bush again. (Surrenders at Parramatta on 30 Jan. 1790.)

24 HMS *Guardian* (Lt Edward Riou), bound for NSW with stores for the colony, strikes an iceberg 12 days out from Cape Town and is forced to return to the Cape (21 Feb.).

 * First school in the colony—a dame school—established, with Isabella Rosson as teacher.

A Architecture, Building
Phillip's first Government House completed (by 4 June).

B Science, Technology, Discovery, etc.

C Arts and Entertainment
George Farquhar's comedy *The Recruiting Officer* performed by convicts on the occasion of King George III's birthday (4 June)—first theatrical performance in Australia.

D Books and Writing
The Voyage of Governor Phillip to Botany Bay; with an Account of the Establishment of the Colonies of Port Jackson and Norfolk Island.
Watkin Tench, *Narrative of an Expedition to Botany Bay.*

1789

E Sport and Recreation

F Statistics, Social Change, the Environment

Estimated population at Port Jackson: 645.

More than 200 bushels of wheat harvested at Rose Hill (Dec.), as well as 35 bushels of barley and some maize, oats, and flax; 25 bushels of barley harvested at Farm Cove.

G Births and Deaths

May 1 George Fife Angas b. (–1879).

Nov 5 William Bland b. (–1868).

1790

Jan 15 Eight *Bounty* mutineers, led by Fletcher Christian, and a number of natives arrive at Pitcairn Is. from Tahiti and (23rd) burn the *Bounty*.

– "Famine . . . approaching with gigantic strides" at Sydney Cove, Capt. Watkin Tench records.

Feb 28 Hospital assistant John Irving becomes the first convict emancipated.

Mar 6 *Sirius* (Hunter) and *Supply* leave Port Jackson for Norfolk Is. with a detachment of marines and over 200 convicts, under Major Robert Ross.

19 *Sirius*, having landed passengers on Norfolk Is., runs aground on a reef and is completely wrecked; Ross proclaims martial law.

24 P. G. King leaves Norfolk Is. in *Supply*; Ross takes over as commandant.

Apr 1 Rations further reduced at Sydney.

5 *Supply* returns to Sydney with news of the wreck of the *Sirius*; Phillip announces a further cut in rations.

15 Phillip writes to Lord Sydney asking permission to return to England.

17 *Supply* (Ball) sails for Batavia to obtain provisions; King leaves on it to return to England to report on conditions in the colony.

May 3 Bennelong escapes.

Jun 3 Transport *Lady Juliana*, carrying 221 female convicts and 11 children, arrives at Port Jackson.

20 Food shortage relieved by the arrival of the *Justinian*, storeship of the Second Fleet; rations restored next day.

26 Second Fleet transports *Surprize* and (on 28th) *Neptune* and *Scarborough* arrive at Port Jackson with 759 convicts, including 486 sick, and the first detachment (100 men) of the New South Wales Corps, under Capt. Nicholas Nepean; others aboard include Lt John Macarthur, his wife, Elizabeth, and their infant son Edward, Surgeon John Harris, and D'Arcy Wentworth (assistant surgeon on *Neptune*).

– Phillip instructs Dawes to lay out a regular town at Rose Hill; two streets (the present George and Church Streets, Parramatta) are marked out.

Jul 6 *Supply* arrives at Batavia, where Ball hires the Dutch snow *Waaksamheyd*.

Aug 1 D'Arcy Wentworth sails for Norfolk Is. in the *Surprize;* with him is the convict Catherine Crowley, who gives birth to their son William [W. C. Wentworth] in Cascade Bay before disembarkation.

Sep 7 Phillip is speared by an Aboriginal at Manly, where he had gone to speak to Bennelong and Colbee.

26 Five convicts steal a boat and set out for Tahiti. (Boat wrecked at Port Stephens, where four survivors live with Aborigines for five years.)

Oct 18 *Supply* returns from Batavia with a small cargo of provisions.

Dec 10 Phillip's gamekeeper, John Macintyre, is speared by the Aboriginal Pemulwy; Tench leads a punitive party (14th); none captured or shot.

17 *Waaksamheyd* arrives from Batavia with supplies of beef, pork, flour, sugar, and rice.

A Architecture, Building

Look-out post and signal station established on Port Jackson's South Head (Jan.).

Portable hospital brought out in the *Justinian* erected at Dawes Point (7 July).

Brick hut built for Bennelong on the eastern point of Sydney Cove (Nov; demolished in 1795).

B Science, Technology, Discovery, etc.

C Arts and Entertainment

Unidentified "Port Jackson painter" produces some of the 250 drawings now in the British Museum.

D Books and Writing

John White, *Journal of a Voyage to New South Wales.*

E Sport and Recreation

F Statistics, Social Change, the Environment

Population at census taken on 25 July: NSW, 1,715; Norfolk Is., 524.

Deaths during year: 2 seamen, 1 soldier, 123 male convicts, 7 female convicts, and 10 children die of sickness; 4 male convicts executed; 1 midshipman, 2 soldiers, and 6 male convicts drown; 1 male convict dies in the bush.

G Births and Deaths

May 1 James Hurtle Fisher b. (–1875).

Aug 13 William Charles Wentworth b. (–1872).

— – Saxe Bannister b. (–1877).

— – Isaac Nathan b. (–1864).

— – John Joseph Therry b. (–1864).

1791

Feb 22 James Ruse having declared himself self-supporting, the deed of the first land grant made in Australia—30 acres (12 ha) at Rose Hill (Experiment Farm)—is signed. (Ruse receives title to the land in April.)

27 *Supply* returns from Norfolk Is. with Capt. John Hunter and the rest of *Sirius*'s company.

Mar 16 First land grants made to free men (two sailors from *Sirius*).

23 HMS *Pandora* (Capt. Edward Edwards), dispatched from England in Nov. 1790 to search for *Bounty* mutineers, reaches Tahiti; 14 mutineers arrested.

28 *Waaksamheyd* sails for England, carrying Hunter and officers and crew of the *Sirius*.

Convict William Bryant and his wife, Mary, their two children, and seven other convicts escape from Port Jackson in the Governor's six-oared cutter.

30 Bryant's party go ashore near present-day Newcastle and find coal.

Apr 2 Bryant's party enters and examines Port Stephens.

1791

May 24   Capt. Watkin Tench and Lt William Dawes set out from Prospect Hill on an expedition that establishes the Hawkesbury and Nepean as the one river.

Jun   2   Rose Hill renamed Parramatta.

     5   Bryant's party reaches Kupang, Timor, posing as survivors of a shipwreck.

Jul   9   Transport *Mary Ann* arrives at Port Jackson with 141 female convicts.

     –   John McCluer, in the *Panther*, with the *Endeavour* (Lt Proctor) begins a two-month survey of the north-west coast of New Guinea during which he discovers McCluer Gulf.

Aug   1   *Matilda*, first of the Third Fleet transports, arrives at Port Jackson with 205 convicts.

     3   Captain William Bligh leaves England in HMS *Providence* with the brig *Assistant* (Lt Nathaniel Portlock) on a second voyage to obtain breadfruit and to explore Torres Strait.

    18   Jervis Bay entered and named by Lt Richard Bowen in the transport *Atlantic*.

    20   *Atlantic* arrives at Port Jackson with 202 convicts, including Simeon Lord.

    21   Salamander arrives at Port Jackson with 155 convicts.

    28   *William and Ann* (Eber Bunker) arrives at Port Jackson with 181 convicts. HMS *Pandora* wrecked on the Great Barrier Reef near Torres Strait; 35 drowned, including 4 *Bounty* mutineers; 99 set out in four open boats to sail to Timor.

Sep 17   Capt. Edwards and *Pandora* shipwreck survivors arrive at Kupang.

    21   Storeship HMS *Gorgon* arrives at Port Jackson with 30 convicts and a large quantity of provisions, livestock, and seed; on board is Philip Gidley King, with the colony's seal.

    26   HMS *Discovery* (Capt. George Vancouver) and the brig *Chatham* (Lt W. R. Broughton), on way to Nootka Sound, arrive off the south-west coast of WA. *Active* and *Queen* arrive at Port Jackson with 302 convicts, including the first Irish prisoners (from Cork).

    28   Vancouver discovers and names King George Sound.

Oct   5   Capt. Edwards of the *Pandora* arrests Bryant's party and sails next day with them and fellow survivors and prisoners to Batavia (where William Bryant and one child die).

    13   *Albermarle* arrives at Port Jackson with 256 convicts.

    14   *Britannia* (Thomas Melville) arrives at Port Jackson with 129 convicts; Thomas Reibey one of the officers.

    16   *Admiral Barrington*, last of the Third Fleet transports, arrives at Port Jackson with 264 convicts, including James Underwood and Isaac Nichols; on board is Capt. William Paterson of the NSW Corps.

    21   Vancouver leaves the WA coast at Termination Is. to continue his voyage into the Pacific.

    24   *Britannia* and *William and Ann* leave to make the first whaling expedition. (Return 10 Nov.)

    26   King leaves for Norfolk Is. in *Atlantic*. (Replaces Ross as commandant, 4 Nov.)

Nov   1   Party of convicts (20 male and 1 female) escape from Parramatta and attempt to walk to China. (Some die; others captured.)

    26   *Supply* sails from Port Jackson for England.

Dec   5   Ross returns to Sydney from Norfolk Is.

    18   HMS *Gorgon* leaves Port Jackson for England carrying returning marines (including Ross, Tench, and Dawes).

31 New arrivals among convicts protest at Parramatta following changes to the issuing of rations.

– *Salamander* visits Port Stephens and makes a rough survey of the harbour.

* Colony experiences its third year of drought.

A Architecture, Building
New fortification built at Dawes Point; battery transferred there from Bennelong Point.

B Science, Technology, Discovery, etc.

C Arts and Entertainment

D Books and Writing

E Sport and Recreation

F Statistics, Social Change, the Environment
Estimated population of NSW: 2,873, including 2,350 convicts and 87 free settlers (1 original, 44 former convicts, 11 seamen, 31 discharged marines).
Livestock, public (Nov.): 1 ram, 50 ewes, 6 lambs.

G Births and Deaths
Jan 28 Henry Dodd d.
Jan – James Stirling b. (–1865).
Apr 26 John Lee Archer b. (–1852).
Jul 13 Allan Cunningham b. (–1839).
Aug 4 Henry Savery b. (–1842)
Dec 13 Phillip Parker King b. (–1856)
— – George Gipps b. (–1847)

Feb 14 *Pitt* arrives at Port Jackson carrying 368 convicts and the second detachment of the NSW Corps, commanded by Major Francis Grose, Lt-Governor of the colony; also on board are Lt John Piper and Richard Atkins.
Sydney's first retail shop opens.

Mar 11 HMS *Gorgon*, en route to England, arrives at the Cape of Good Hope, where the *Bounty* mutineers and Mary Bryant and the surviving members of her party, having been brought from Batavia in Dutch ships, are taken aboard.

Apr 10 *Providence* (Bligh) and *Assistant* (Portlock) at Tahiti (to 19 July).
21 French ships *Recherche* (Adm. Bruni d'Entrecasteaux) and *Espérance* (Capt. Huon de Kermadec), on their way to the Pacific to investigate the fate of La Pérouse's ships, arrive at Recherche Bay, Van Diemen's Land.
23 D'Entrecasteaux explores the coast of south-east Van Diemen's Land (to 28 May), then sails on to Amboina.

May 12 Flour ration reduced.

Jun 18 *Gorgon* arrives at Portsmouth; Mary Bryant and her surviving fellow absconders gaoled indefinitely.
20 *Atlantic* returns to Port Jackson from Calcutta with supplies and 20 Bengal sheep; rations increased.

Jul 14 Home Secretary Henry Dundas authorizes Phillip to make land grants to civil and military officers.

1792

25 Storeship *Britannia* (William Raven) arrives at Port Jackson.

Sep 1 Bligh discovers Portlock Reef.
2 *Providence* and *Assistant* successfully pass through Torres Strait (to 18th).

Oct 7 *Royal Admiral* arrives at Sydney with 336 convicts, including artist Thomas Watling and Mary Haydock (Reibey).
24 *Britannia* (Raven) leaves Sydney for the Cape of Good Hope on a speculative voyage for officers of the NSW Corps. (Some crew members are left at Dusky Sound, NZ, to hunt seals.)

Nov 1 American brigantine *Philadelphia*, the first foreign trading vessel to visit Sydney, arrives with a speculative cargo, which Phillip buys.
18 *Kitty* arrives at Port Jackson with 29 convicts and £1,000 in silver dollars.

Dec 5 D'Entrecasteaux arrives off Cape Leeuwin, WA, from Amboina, and enters and names Esperence Bay (9th).
10 Phillip sails for England in the *Atlantic*, taking Bennelong and another Aboriginal, Yemmerrawannie.
11 Grose becomes administrator of the colony.
24 American trading vessel *Hope* arrives in Sydney; Grose is obliged to buy 34,095 litres of spirits in order to obtain other cargo.
– Civil magistrates' powers suspended and transferred to NSW Corps officers.

A Architecture, Building
Water tank of 36,000 litres capacity constructed on the Tank Stream in Sydney near present-day Hamilton Street (completed 3 May).
Work begins on George Street (Wynyard) Barracks (Sept.).

B Science, Technology, Discovery, etc.

C Arts and Entertainment
Les Emigrés aux Terres Australes, the first play having reference to Australia, has its première in Paris.

D Books and Writing

E Sport and Recreation

F Statistics, Social Change, the Environment
Estimated population of NSW: 3,264, plus 1,115 on Norfolk Is.

G Births and Deaths
Jun 15 Thomas Livingstone Mitchell b. (–1855).
Oct 20 John Pascoe Fawkner b. (–1869).
— – Fletcher Christian d. (*c.* 29).

1793

Jan 1 Samuel Marsden appointed assistant to the chaplain of NSW.
16 *Bellona* arrives at Port Jackson with the first immigrant free settlers (five men, one with wife and children) and 17 women convicts.
21 D'Entrecasteaux arrives back at Van Diemen's Land, anchoring in Recherche Bay, having circumnavigated Australia.

Feb 7 Land grants made to free settlers at Liberty Plains (Strathfield–Homebush).
12 John Macarthur receives grant of 100 acres at Parramatta, which he names Elizabeth Farm; other grants made to Capt. George Johnston (100 acres,

Annandale), Commissary-General John Palmer (100 acres, Woolloomooloo), Quartermaster Thomas Laycock (80 acres, Vaucluse), Surgeon John White (100 acres, Petersham), and Rev. Richard Johnson (100 acres, Canterbury).

16 Macarthur appointed Inspector of Public Works.

18 School opened in an unfinished church building in Sydney; teacher is Johnson's clerk, Stephen Barnes.

25 William Bampton's *Shah Hormuzear* arrives at Port Jackson with a cargo of goods and livestock, including about a hundred Bengal sheep.

28 D'Entrecasteaux sails from Van Diemen's Land for Tonga after charting bays and islands in the south-east.

Mar 13 Spanish expedition led by Alessandro Malaspina visits Sydney in the ships *Descubierta* and *Atrevida* (to 20 Apr.).

Apr 20 Storeship *Daedalus* arrives at Port Jackson with two young Maori chiefs carried off from NZ to assist in flax dressing on Norfolk Is.

26 Lt John Hayes, with the *Duke of Clarence* and *Duchess of Bengal*, arrives at the Derwent River (which he names) and carries out a survey of the area (to 9 June).

May 2 Mary Bryant granted an unconditional pardon in England after the intercession of James Boswell.

Jun 20 *Britannia* returns from Cape Town, having picked up en route the sealing party from NZ and 4,500 sealskins.

– Home Secretary Henry Dundas authorizes Lt-Gov. Grose to assign convicts as servants to civil and military officers and instructs him to prevent "secret and clandestine sale of spirits" in the colony.

Jul 1 *Shah Hormuzear* and the whaler *Chesterfield* (M.B. Alt), the first merchant vessels to sail through Torres Strait, anchor at Darnley Is., where some crew members are killed by natives; others sail in a ship's boat to Timor.

20 D'Entrecasteaux dies of fever off the coast of New Guinea.

24 Schooner *Francis*, the first ocean-going vessel to be built in the colony, launched at Sydney.

– Phillip, in England, resigns from the governorship of NSW.

Aug 7 Bligh arrives back in England with *Providence* and *Assistant*.
Boddingtons arrives at Port Jackson with 144 Irish convicts.

Sep 8 Britannia, chartered by Grose, leaves Port Jackson for India via Norfolk Is.

15 Grose River, NSW, discovered and named by William Paterson during an unsuccessful attempt to cross the Blue Mountains.

17 *Sugar Cane* arrives at Port Jackson with 159 Irish convicts.

Oct 25 Hayes annexes part of New Guinea at Dore Bay, which he names New Albion, and forms a settlement.

Nov 8 P. G. King takes the two Maori chiefs back to NZ in the *Britannia*. (Returns to Norfolk Is. on 18th and is later reprimanded by Grose for leaving his post without permission.)

* Regular ferry service begins on the Parramatta River.

A Architecture, Building

Sydney's first church, of wattle-and-daub with thatched roof, built by Rev. R. Johnson at his own expense. (Opens for divine service on 25 Aug.)
John Macarthur's Elizabeth Farm House, Parramatta (–1794)

B Science, Technology, Discovery, etc.

1793

C Arts and Entertainment
P. G. King sanctions regular performance of plays on Norfolk Is.

D Books and Writing
John Hunter, *Historical Journal of the Transactions at Port Jackson and Norfolk Island.*
Watkin Tench, *A Complete Account of the Settlement at Port Jackson.*

E Sport and Recreation

F Statistics, Social Change, the Environment
Estimated population of NSW: 3,514.

G Births and Deaths
Mar　8　David Jones b. (–1873).
Jun　1　Augustus Earle b. (–1838).

1794

Jan　2　James Ruse given a land grant at Green Hills (Windsor), on the Hawkesbury River. (Others settle there during the month.)
　　18　Members of the NSW Corps on Norfolk Is. riot following a play held for the Queen's Birthday; Commandant P. G. King is forced to take stern measures to keep the peace.

Feb　6　Capt. John Hunter appointed Governor of NSW to succeed Phillip.

Mar 10　Rev. Samuel Marsden arrives at Port Jackson in the storeship William.

Apr　1　Macarthur receives a further grant of 100 acres in the Parramatta district.

May 18　Yemmerrawannie dies in England.

Jun　1　Britannia (Raven) returns from India and Batavia with supplies; crew member Thomas Reibey settles in Sydney.

Jul　1　Hunter is given his commission as Governor and his instructions, including permission to assign convicts as servants to landowners.
　　4　Marsden moves to Parramatta to become chaplain there.
　　8　American ships *Indispensable* and *Halcyon* leave Port Jackson with an escaping convict on each ship.

Aug 20　Henry Hacking leads an expedition to try to find a way over the Blue Mountains. (Returns 27th.)

Sep　1　*Britannia*, chartered by civil and military officers, leaves Port Jackson for the Cape of Good Hope to purchase trade goods.
　　7　Thomas Reibey marries Mary Haydock.

Oct 25　Four of the five "Scottish Martyrs"—Thomas Muir, Thomas Fyshe Palmer, William Skirving, and Maurice Margarot—sentenced to 14 years' transportation for sedition, arrive in Sydney in the *Surprize*.
　　29　Marsden receives a grant of 100 acres at Hunters Hill.

Nov　9　Storeship *Resolution* sails from Port Jackson with 14 escaping convicts.

Dec 12　William Paterson replaces Francis Grose as commander of the NSW Corps and administrator of the colony.
　　17　Grose and Surgeon John White sail for England in the *Daedalus*.
　　*　Road cleared between Sydney and Parramatta.

A Architecture, Building

B Science, Technology, Discovery, etc.
George Shaw, *Zoology of New Holland* (contains the term *Australia* to apply to the whole continent, probably the first time in a printed book).

C Arts and Entertainment
Thomas Watling, A Direct North General View of Sydney Cove.

D Books and Writing
Rev. Richard Johnson, *An Address to the Inhabitants of the Colonies Established in New South Wales and Norfolk Island.*

E Sport and Recreation

F Statistics, Social Change, the Environment
Estimated population of NSW: 3,579.

G Births and Deaths
Nov 10   Robert Towns b. (–1873).

1795

Feb 15   HMS *Reliance*, with the *Supply*, leaves England carrying John Hunter to take up his appointment as Governor of NSW; also aboard are Henry Waterhouse (second captain), Matthew Flinders (master's mate), George Bass (surgeon), with the boat *Tom Thumb*, and a repatriating Bennelong.

Mar 4   *Britannia* returns from the Cape with goods and livestock.

May –   New Albion settlement abandoned and settlers evacuated in *Duke of Clarence*.

Jun 18   *Britannia* leaves on another voyage to India chartered by Lt-Gov. Paterson to procure provisions for the colony.

Jul 25   James Squire granted 30 acres at Eastern Farms (Ryde), on which he later builds a brewery.

Aug 26   HMS *Providence* (W. R. Broughton), bound for survey work in the Pacific, arrives at Port Jackson with four survivors of the party of convicts who escaped in Sept. 1790, picked up at Port Stephens.

Sep 7   *Reliance* arrives at Port Jackson with Hunter, Waterhouse, Flinders, Bass and Bennelong.
11   Hunter takes up his position as Governor of NSW and its dependencies.
–   Floods occur on the Hawkesbury.

Oct 26   Bass and Flinders in the *Tom Thumb* explore Botany Bay and Georges River (to 4 Nov.).

Nov 5   Joseph Gerrald, the fifth of the Scottish Martyrs, arrives in Sydney in the storeship *Sovereign*.
28   First export consignment of cedar from NSW sent to India in *Experiment*.
–   Cattle that strayed from Port Jackson in June 1788 are found, with their progeny, at the Cowpastures (Camden).
–   Convict George Hughes does the first printing in the colony (government orders, etc.) on a small press brought out in the First Fleet.

Dec –   Black Caesar absconds again and joins up with other runaways.

1795

A Architecture, Building

B Science, Technology, Discovery, etc.

C Arts and Entertainment

D Books and Writing

E Sport and Recreation

F Statistics, Social Change, the Environment
Estimated population of NSW: 3,466.

G Births and Deaths
Apr 28 Charles Sturt b. (–1869).
Jul 21 George Gawler b. (–1869).

1796

Jan 23 General order issued prohibiting distilling of spirits.

Feb 4 NSW Corps soldiers wreck the house of carpenter John Baughan.
10 Magistrate William Balmain challenges Macarthur over the Baughan incident; in return, all NSW Corps officers offer to fight Balmain.
11 *Marquis Cornwallis* arrives at Port Jackson with 222 Irish convicts, a mutiny having been put down during the voyage.
15 Black Caesar is shot and killed by a settler at Liberty Plains.
18 Thomas Muir, one of the Scottish Martyrs, escapes in the American vessel *Otter* (eventually reaching Paris).
29 Macarthur resigns as Inspector of Public Works and is replaced by Richard Atkins.

Mar 19 William Skirving dies, three days after the death of his fellow Scottish Martyr Joseph Gerrald.
24 Bass and Flinders in the second *Tom Thumb* explore the coast south of Botany Bay (to 2 Apr.); discover Lake Illawarra (27 Mar.); examine Port Hacking (1 Apr.).

Apr 7 D'Arcy Wentworth, back in Sydney from Norfolk Is., is appointed assistant surgeon.
30 *Indispensable* arrives at Port Jackson with 131 female convicts.
– In an attempt to control the sale of spirits, Gov. Hunter issues the first 10 licences to run public houses.

May 11 *Britannia* (Raven) returns from Calcutta with provisions.

Jun – Fishermen find coal near Port Stephens.
– Bass makes an unsuccessful attempt to cross the Blue Mountains.

Aug – Balmain's appointment as principal surgeon (to replace White) confirmed.
– William Paterson returns to England on sick leave.

Sep 14 Hunter writes to the Colonial Secretary, the Duke of Portland, complaining of Macarthur's behaviour.
15 Macarthur writes to Portland complaining of Hunter's governorship.
29 *Reliance* (Waterhouse) and *Supply* sail for the Cape of Good Hope for supplies. *Britannia* sails for England via Norfolk Is., carrying David Collins home on leave of absence; his position as Judge-Advocate is taken by Atkins.

Oct 22 P. G. King sails from Norfolk Is. for England in *Britannia*; Capt. John Townson of the NSW Corps replaces him as commandant.

Nov 9 Hunter disbands the convict night watch and divides Sydney into four districts whose inhabitants choose three residents to act as watchmen; also orders houses to be numbered.

* First beer brewed in Australia by John Boston.

A Architecture, Building

B Science, Technology, Discovery, etc.

C Arts and Entertainment
Australia's first theatre opened by Robert Sidaway in Sydney (16 Jan.); Edward Young's *The Revenge* and a farce, *The Hotel*, first performance.
William Shield's ballad opera *The Poor Soldier* performed in Sydney.

D Books and Writing
"A Society of Gentlemen", *A New and Correct History of New Holland*.

E Sport and Recreation

F Statistics, Social Change, the Environment
Estimated population: 4,100.

G Births and Deaths
Mar 20   Edward Gibbon Wakefield b. (–1862).

1797

Feb 9 *Sydney Cove*, en route from Calcutta to Port Jackson, is beached on Preservation Is. in the Furneaux Group; 17 men set out in the ship's longboat to sail to Sydney for help (28th).

Mar 11 *Sydney Cove* longboat is wrecked on the southern coast near present-day Cape Everard; the survivors continue their journey to Port Jackson on foot (15th).

May 15 Three survivors of the *Sydney Cove* are picked up by fishermen about 22 km south of Botany Bay; they report finding coal further south and the probable existence of a strait between the mainland and Van Diemen's Land.

27 *Britannia* (Thomas Dennott) arrives at Port Jackson with 177 Irish convicts, 11 deaths having occurred on the voyage from harsh treatment.

30 Gov. Hunter sends the schooner *Francis* and longboat *Eliza* to the stranded *Sydney Cove*. (Arrive Preservation Is. 11 June.)

Jun 2 *Ganges* arrives at Port Jackson with 190 convicts, including Joseph Wild, and a detachment of the NSW Corps.

21 *Francis* and *Eliza* leave Preservation Is. for Port Jackson with the survivors of the *Sydney Cove*; *Francis* arrives at Sydney on 6 July; *Eliza* is never seen again.

26 *Reliance* (Waterhouse) returns to Port Jackson with stores and some merino sheep from the Cape of Good Hope, some of which are bought by John Macarthur (2 rams, 4 ewes) and Samuel Marsden (1 ram, 1 ewe).

Jul 3 Hunter sends a party of soldiers to protect settlers in the Hawkesbury area following the killing of a number of settlers by Aborigines.

Aug 1 Soldiers aboard the transport *Lady Shore* (carrying 66 female and two male convicts as well as three officers and 70 men of the NSW Corps) mutiny,

1797

kill the captain and mate, set "loyalists" adrift, and sail the ship to Montevideo (where the ship is impounded).

5 George Bass makes a voyage to the south coast (to 13th) with one of the *Sydney Cove* survivors to examine the reported coal seams; finds coal at present-day Coalcliff.

Sep 5 Convicts steal the government boat *Cumberland* from the Hawkesbury and sail north; Hunter sends Lt John Shortland in pursuit in a whaleboat.
9 Shortland discovers the Hunter River estuary and an abundance of coal.

Oct 2 Fourteen convicts seize a boat and escape from Port Jackson. (Later abandon seven of their number on Glennie Is., off Wilsons Promontory.)

Dec 3 Bass sets out from Port Jackson in a whaleboat with six oarsmen to explore the southern coast of NSW.
6 Bass discovers the Blowhole at Kiama and (7th) names the Shoalhaven River.
10 Bass examines Jervis Bay.
19 Bass enters and names Twofold Bay.

A Architecture, Building

Foundation stone of St John's Church, Parramatta, laid by Gov. Hunter (5 Apr; another foundation stone laid in 1799; church opened 1803; twin steeples added 1818–20; new church built 1852–58, incorporating twin steeples; transepts added 1883–85).

Construction of Australia's first windmill—on Observatory Hill, Sydney—completed.

B Science, Technology, Discovery, etc.

Platypus first observed, at the Hawkesbury River.

C Arts and Entertainment

D Books and Writing

E Sport and Recreation

F Statistics, Social Change, the Environment

Estimated population: 4,344.

G Births and Deaths

May   8 John Septimus Roe b. (–1878).
Jun 19 Hamilton Hume b. (–1873).
Jul 20 Paul Edmond de Strzelecki b. (–1873).

1798

Jan 2 George Bass sights Wilsons Promontory.
3 Bass finds the seven escaped convicts abandoned on Glennie Is.
5 Bass discovers and names Western Port (now Westernport, Vic.).
14 Party guided by the ex-convict and "wild white man" John Wilson explores to the south-west of Sydney as far as the junction of the Wingecarribee and Wollondilly rivers (to 9 Feb.).
26 Bass transfers five of the stranded convicts from Glennie Is. to the mainland to walk to Sydney. (Not seen again.)

Feb 1 *Francis*, with Matthew Flinders aboard, leaves Port Jackson again to retrieve stores from the wreck of the *Sydney Cove*.
8 *Francis* discovers the Kent group of islands.

1798

	12	Flinders explores the Furneaux Is.

Mar 9 Wilson leads another party, which includes Henry Hacking, to the south-west of Sydney, penetrating as far as the vicinity of present-day Goulburn.

12 Flinders explores the Furneaux Is.
25 Bass returns to Port Jackson convinced of the existence of a strait at the south of the continent, which Hunter names in his honour.

Mar 9 Wilson leads another party, which includes Henry Hacking, to the south-west of Sydney, penetrating as far as the vicinity of present-day Goulburn.

May 14 *Nautilus* (Charles Bishop) arrives at Port Jackson from a trading cruise in the Pacific carrying missionaries of the London Missionary Society from Tahiti, including Rowland Hassall.
18 Transport *Barwell* arrives at Port Jackson with 287 convicts, including the lawyer/poet Michael Massey Robinson; passengers include Richard Dore.

Jun 8 Dore appointed Judge-Advocate, to succeed David Collins.
10 Calcutta merchant Robert Campbell arrives at Port Jackson in the *Hunter* on a trading visit and buys land at Dawes Point.
15 *Norfolk*, a sloop built on Norfolk Is., arrives at Port Jackson.
22 Dore appointed Hunter's secretary.

Jul 18 *Britannia* (Robert Turnbull) arrives at Port Jackson with 94 convicts.

Sep – Simeon Lord acquires a warehouse from which to retail goods and spirits bought from NSW Corps officers.

Oct 1 Sydney's first church destroyed by fire, apparently deliberately.
7 Bass and Flinders leave Port Jackson in the *Norfolk* on an exploratory trip to Van Diemen's Land, accompanied by the brig *Nautilus* (Charles Bishop) on a sealing expedition to Cape Barren Is.

Nov 3 Bass and Flinders discover and explore the Tamar estuary (to 20th).
8 Nauru discovered by Capt. John Fearn in the *Hunter*.

Dec 9 Bass and Flinders ascertain the existence of Bass Strait.
22 *Norfolk* enters the mouth of the Derwent River.
25 Bass climbs Mount Wellington.
Bishop returns to Port Jackson in the *Nautilus* with 9,000 sealskins.

* Capt. William Reed in the sealer *Martha* discovers King Is. in Bass Strait.

A Architecture, Building
Foundation stone of St Phillip's, Church Hill, Sydney, laid by Gov. Hunter (7 Oct; church opened Aug. 1809, consecrated 25 Dec. 1810, demolished 1856).

B Science, Technology, Discovery, etc.
Lyrebird and koala first observed, by John Price, one of John Wilson's party (26 Jan.).

C Arts and Entertainment
Robert Sidaway's theatre closed by order of the Governor because of the number of robberies occurring on theatre nights.

D Books and Writing
David Collins, *An Account of the English Colony in New South Wales,* vol. 1 (vol. 2 in 1802).

E Sport and Recreation

F Statistics, Social Change, the Environment
Estimated population: 4,588.
Opening of licensed premises prohibited during church hours (Aug.).

G Births and Deaths

1799

Jan 7 Bass and Flinders complete their circumnavigation of Van Diemen's Land. (Return to Port Jackson on 12th.)

23 Gov. Hunter dispenses with the services of Richard Dore as his secretary.

Feb 11 Public gaol in Sydney deliberately burnt down.

28 Hunter issues another general order prohibiting the distilling of spirits.

Mar 3 Hawkesbury River floods after torrential rains break the drought; grain stores destroyed and one man drowned.

6 William Paterson ordered to return to NSW from leave in England and put an immediate end to trading by the NSW Corps officers, especially in spirits.

12 Isaac Nichols charged with receiving stolen goods and sentenced (16th) to 14 years on Norfolk Is.

Apr 1 Hunter orders an inquiry into the verdict of the Nichols case and (3rd) suspends sentence. (Refers case to UK on 30th.)

24 Spanish ship *Nuestra Senora de Bethlehem*, captured by whalers off Peru, arrives at Port Jackson and (1 May) is declared a lawful prize (bought by Simeon Lord and renamed *Hunter*).

May 3 Storeship *Buffalo* (W. Raven) arrives at Port Jackson as a replacement for HMS *Supply*.

16 D'Arcy Wentworth becomes surgeon at Parramatta.

29 *Nautilus* (Bishop) sails for England via China with Bass aboard.

Jun 4 Violent storms in Sydney (to 6th) cause much damage.

29 Capt. Eber Bunker arrives at Port Jackson in the storeship *Albion* and subsequently goes whaling.

Jul 8 Flinders leaves Port Jackson in the *Norfolk* to examine the coast to the north. (Explores the Moreton Bay area, 15th to 31st.)

26 *Hillsborough* arrives at Port Jackson with 205 convicts, 95 having died, mostly of typhoid fever, on the way; prisoners include lawyer George Crossley.

Aug 2 Flinders examines and charts Hervey Bay (to 7th). (Returns to Sydney 20th.)

Oct 18 Five settlers on the Hawkesbury found guilty of murdering two Aborigines. (Subsequently pardoned.)

Nov 3 Paterson arrives back in Sydney and resumes command of the NSW Corps.

5 Dispatch sent recalling Hunter and naming Philip Gidley King as his successor.

12 Capt. Thomas Rowley replaces John Townson as commandant on Norfolk Is.

Dec 2 Spanish ship *El Plumier*, captured by whalers off the South American coast, arrives at Port Jackson and (7th) is sold as a prize.

28 Gaol at Parramatta deliberately burnt down.

A Architecture, Building

Old Government House, Parramatta, erected on the site of an earlier house built by Gov. Arthur Phillip which had collapsed.

B Science, Technology, Discovery, etc.

C Arts and Entertainment

D Books and Writing

E Sport and Recreation

F Statistics, Social Change, the Environment
Estimated population: 5,088, including 1,724 convicts.
Albion makes the voyage from England to Port Jackson in a record 93 days.

G Births and Deaths
Jan 26 Thomas Muir d. (33).
Aug 25 John Dunmore Lang b. (−1878).
Oct   2 William Lonsdale b. (−1864).
Oct 15 Archibald Mosman b. (−1863).

1800

Jan 11 *Minerva* arrives at Port Jackson with 188 convicts, including Father James Harold and "General" Joseph Holt; passengers include Lt William Cox. *Thynne*, under charter to officers of the NSW Corps, arrives from Bengal with large quantity of spirits.

Feb 14 Robert Campbell returns to Sydney from Calcutta to establish a trading and importing business.

      16 *Friendship* arrives at Port Jackson with 114 convicts, including Father James Dixon and James Meehan.

Mar   3 *Reliance* (Henry Waterhouse) leaves Port Jackson for England with Matthew Flinders aboard.

Apr 15 Capt. Philip Gidley King arrives at Port Jackson in the *Speedy* to replace John Hunter as Governor; also aboard are George Caley, Francis Barrallier, and 50 convicts.

      26 William Balmain receives a land grant of 550 acres on the west side of Cockle Bay (Balmain).

Jun 26 Maj. Joseph Foveaux appointed Lt-Governor of Norfolk Is., replacing Thomas Rowley.

Jul 16 Revs Richard Johnson and Samuel Marsden open a Church school at Kissing Point (Ryde).

       – Henry Kable and James Underwood establish a business partnership for manufacturing, sealing, shipbuilding, etc.

Sep   7 Holt arrested on suspicion of being involved in a planned insurrection of Irish political prisoners. (Later released.)
Concerned about the possible insurrection, Hunter forms Loyal Associations—the first volunteer corps in the colony—in Sydney (commanded by Balmain) and Parramatta (Richard Atkins).

      28 King takes over from Hunter as Governor.

      29 Col. William Paterson appointed Lt-Governor.

Oct   1 King issues a general order aimed at ending monopolies in trade and forbids traffic in spirits without permission.

      10 Import duties imposed on liquor; ships required to pay entry and victualling charges.

      17 Balmain appointed Naval Officer (i.e., harbourmaster).
Paterson arrests George Johnston on charges of paying spirits to a sergeant as part of his pay.

1800

21 *Buffalo* leaves for England carrying Hunter, Rev. Richard Johnson, George Johnston (under arrest), and eight sample merino fleeces from John Macarthur's farm.

Nov 6 *Porpoise* (with John Murray as master's mate) arrives at Port Jackson with four tons of copper coins.

19 King fixes the value of coinage in circulation.

21 *Royal Admiral* arrives at Port Jackson with 257 convicts, including the West Indian George Howe (subsequently Government Printer), 43 having died of typhoid fever on the voyage; passengers include Ensign William Lawson.

Dec 3 *Lady Nelson* (Lt James Grant) arrives in southern Australian waters to begin survey work; Grant names Cape Northumberland, Cape Banks, Mt Schanck, and Mt Gambier.

7 Grant names Portland Bay and Cape Otway, then passes through Bass Strait, the first to do so from the west. (Arrives Port Jackson 16 Dec.)

14 Foveaux suppresses an incipient rebellion on Norfolk Is; hangs two Irish prisoners.

18 Atkins appointed deputy Judge-Advocate following the death of Dore.

A Architecture, Building

Sydney's first customs house built.

James Larra's inn, the Freemasons Arms (later the Woolpack Inn), erected at Parramatta.

B Science, Technology, Discovery, etc.

George Caley establishes a botanical garden at Parramatta and begins collecting Australian plants for Joseph Banks.

C Arts and Entertainment

After allowing Robert Sidaway to again present plays in Sydney's first theatre, Gov. King changes his mind and has the playhouse razed to the ground.

D Books and Writing

E Sport and Recreation

F Statistics, Social Change, the Environment

Estimated population: 5,217.

General order (31 Oct.) decrees that assigned convicts are to be clothed, fed, and housed at the expense of their masters (without wages).

G Births and Deaths

Apr 22 Roger Therry b. (–1874).

Jun 1 Edward Deas Thomson b. (–1879).

Dec 13 Richard Dore d. (51).

1801

Jan 1 King Is., Bass Strait, named by Capt. John Black of the brig *Harbinger.*

5 T. F. Palmer, his sentence expired, leaves Sydney in *El Plumier.* (Detained as prisoner of war in Guam, where he dies in June 1802.)

18 Simeon Lord appointed public auctioneer.

21 US ship *Follensbe* arrives at Port Jackson with a huge cargo of liquor, which Gov. King refuses to allow to be landed.

1801

Feb 10 Ticket-of-leave system introduced by King, enabling convicts to work for wages and choose their own master.

21 Transport *Ann* arrives at Port Jackson with 251 convicts, including 137 Irish political prisoners.

Mar 21 Lt James Grant in the *Lady Nelson* surveys Westernport Bay (to 29 Apr.).

May 1 King orders Aborigines to be driven out of Parramatta, Prospect, and Georges River districts.

2 US ship *Missouri* arrives at Port Jackson; King refuses to allow the landing of a cargo of spirits.

30 French mariner Nicolas Baudin, with the ships *Le Géographe* and *Le Naturaliste* (Emmanuel Hamelin), arrives at Geographe Bay, WA, on a voyage of scientific discovery. (Ships there part company.)

Jun 10 King sends Lt-Gov. Paterson in the *Lady Nelson* (Grant) to examine the Hunter River.

12 *Earl Cornwallis* arrives at Port Jackson with 253 convicts.

16 Paterson founds a settlement on the Hunter. (Abandoned in 1802.)

Jul 4 Survey party finds seams of coal at the Hunter.

14 Hamelin at Rottnest Is. (to 28th); explores Swan River.

18 Flinders leaves England in *Investigator* to explore Australian coastline.

20 Baudin explores De Witt's Land and names Monte Bello Is. (to 10 Aug.).

27 King disbands the Loyal Associations.

Aug 8 Female Orphan School opened in Sydney by Samuel Marsden under Gov. King's patronage.

26 Balmain leaves Sydney in the *Albion* to return to England; Surgeon John Harris replaces him as Naval Officer.

28 *Venus* (Charles Bishop) arrives at Port Jackson, carrying part-owner George Bass.

Sep 14 Paterson and Macarthur fight a duel; Paterson wounded; Macarthur arrested.

Oct 4 Consignment of coal exported to Bengal in the *Earl Cornwallis*.

Nov 12 Lt John Murray, who replaced Grant as commander of *Lady Nelson*, leaves Port Jackson to explore in southern waters.

15 Macarthur leaves Sydney for court martial in England. (Arrives London 21 Dec. 1802.)

21 Bass sails in the *Venus* on a commercial voyage in the Pacific.

Dec 6 Flinders in the *Investigator* arrives off the coast of WA, names Cape Leeuwin (7th), and enters King George Sound (8th).

7 Murray surveys Westernport (to 2 Jan. 1802).

14 Transports *Minorca*, *Canada*, and *Nile* arrive at Port Jackson with 296 convicts, including James Hardy Vaux, Dr William Redfern, artist John Eyre, and Margaret Catchpole; passengers include Richard Rouse.

– Female convicts at the Parramatta gaol begin making rough blankets from locally produced wool.

* Schooner *Cumberland* (28 tons), the first armed vessel belonging to the colony, launched at Sydney.

A Architecture, Building
King installs a battery on Georges Head, Port Jackson.

1801

B Science, Technology, Discovery, etc.

Hamelin finds and restores (16 July) the metal plate left by Dutch navigator Willem de Vlamingh on Dirk Hartog Is. (WA) in 1697.

C Arts and Entertainment

D Books and Writing

Matthew Flinders, *Observations on the Coasts of Van Diemen's Land, on Bass's Strait, etc.*

E Sport and Recreation

F Statistics, Social Change, the Environment

Estimated population: 5,945.

G Births and Deaths

Jan   21   John Batman b. (–1839).
Mar 20   Charles Joseph La Trobe b. (–1875).
Mar 21   Conrad Martens b. (–1878).
Aug 21   Benjamin Boyd b. (–1851).

1802

Jan   4   Lt John Murray discovers the entrance to Port Phillip.
5   Matthew Flinders in the *Investigator* leaves King George Sound, sights Stirling Range.
10   Murray examines King Is. (to 27th).
13   Nicolas Baudin's expedition in D'Entrecasteaux Channel (to 7 Mar.); explores Derwent.
29   Flinders surveys Nuyts Archipelago, the Investigator Group, and the coast as far as Cape Catastrophe (to 21 Feb.).
31   J. Bowen, mate of *Lady Nelson*, examines Port Phillip (to 4 Feb; *Lady Nelson* enters on 14th).

Feb   21   Boat crew of eight from *Investigator* drown at Cape Catastrophe.
25   Flinders surveys Port Lincoln and Spencer Gulf (to 20 Mar.).

Mar   8   Murray takes formal possession of Port Phillip area.
Baudin's two ships are separated in a gale off Van Diemen's Land.
21   Flinders discovers Kangaroo Is., observes a high hill on the mainland (23rd) which he later names Mount Lofty, and explores Gulf St Vincent (to 1 Apr.).

Apr   8   Flinders and Baudin meet at Encounter Bay.
9   Emmanuel Hamelin in *Le Naturaliste* examines Westernport (to 17th).
24   *Le Naturaliste* arrives at Port Jackson.
26   Flinders examines Port Phillip (to 3 May; returns to Sydney on 9th).

May   –   Rations reduced in Sydney owing to food shortage.

Jun   2   Aboriginal leader Pemulwy shot and killed following the killing of four white men by Aborigines at Parramatta and Toongabbie.
13   *Coromandel* arrives at Port Jackson with 137 convicts and 10 free settlers; Surgeon Charles Throsby settles.
14   Duty of 5% imposed on all goods imported from east of Cape Town.
20   *Le Géographe* (Baudin) arrives at Port Jackson.
26   Arrival of US ship *General Boyd* with cargo of salted meat eases food shortage. *Hercules* arrives with 121 convicts, 14 having been killed during a mutiny and 30 others having died of sickness.

Jul 6 *Atlas* (1) arrives with 111 convicts (65 having died), including Sir Henry Browne Hayes.

22 Flinders leaves Sydney in the *Investigator*, with Murray in the *Lady Nelson*, to explore and chart the northern coastline of Australia.

23 Colony divided into two parishes—St Phillip's (Sydney) and St John's (Parramatta).

Aug 5 Flinders discovers Port Curtis and (21st) Port Bowen.

Sep 17 First properly assembled masonic lodge in Australia (held by officers of *Le Naturaliste*) admits Capt. Anthony Fenn Kemp of the NSW Corps into masonry.

Oct 16 Maj. George Johnston returns to Sydney in HMS *Buffalo*, his trial in England having been quashed; also aboard are John Oxley, G. W. Evans, and Garnham Blaxcell.

18 Flinders, at Cumberland Is., orders *Lady Nelson* back to Sydney.

30 *Atlas* (2) arrives at Port Jackson with 188 Irish rebel prisoners.

Nov 3 Flinders enters the Gulf of Carpentaria, having passed through Torres Strait, and begins a running survey of the gulf.

5 Francis Barrallier makes an attempt to cross the Blue Mountains (to 23 Dec.), reaching about 25 km south of Jenolan Caves.

18 *Le Géographe*, *Le Naturaliste*, and a purchased vessel, *Casuarina* (Louis de Freycinet), leave Port Jackson for Bass Strait.

23 Gov. King sends Lt Charles Robbins in *Cumberland* to examine Bass Strait (Surveyor-Gen. Charles Grimes also aboard) and to thwart any colonizing attempts by the French.

24 Flinders careens *Investigator* and finds it unfit to return to Sydney the way he came.

Dec 6 Baudin's expedition at King Is. (*Le Naturaliste* sails for Mauritius on 9th.)

7 Flinders names Mornington Is.

13 Robbins hoists the British flag near Baudin's tents on King Is. and fires a volley over them.

A Architecture, Building

B Science, Technology, Discovery, etc.

C Arts and Entertainment

D Books and Writing
New South Wales General Standing Orders, printed by George Howe—the first book printed in Australia.

E Sport and Recreation

F Statistics, Social Change, the Environment
Estimated population: 7,014.
Some 25,660 fur seal skins and 34 tons of elephant seal oil obtained from Bass Strait (most skins exported to China).

G Births and Deaths
Jun 2 Thomas Fyshe Palmer d. (54).

1803

Jan 2 *Le Géographe* and *Casuarina* at Kangaroo Is. (to 1 Feb.); de Freycinet explores mainland gulfs.

    8 Capt. A. F. Kemp arrested (with Lts Hobby and Bayly) for being involved in scurrilous attacks on Gov. King.

  10 "Pipe" (scurrilous verse) lampooning King found in barracks.

  20 *Cumberland* (Robbins) in Port Phillip (to 27 Feb.) to enable Charles Grimes to make a survey.

Feb 2 Grimes discovers the Yarra River and (3rd) navigates to the site of Melbourne.

    5 George Bass leaves Port Jackson in the *Venus* and is never heard of again.

  12 Robert Campbell's ship *Castle of Good Hope* arrives in Port Jackson with 307 Bengal cows and 64,000 litres of spirits. (King allows only 18,000 litres to be landed.)

  17 Matthew Flinders in the *Investigator* meets a fleet of Macassan praus off Arnhem Land.
      Nicolas Baudin's expedition in King George Sound (to 1 Mar.).

  23 Maj. George Johnston, president of the court martial of Capt. Kemp, stops proceedings by arresting deputy Judge-Advocate John Harris for revealing votes at Hobby's trial.

Mar 1 Flinders charts Arnhem Bay (to 5th) and then sails for Timor to repair the *Investigator.*

    5 Kemp acquitted on resumption of his court martial.
      George Howe publishes the first issue of the weekly *Sydney Gazette and New South Wales Advertiser*, Australia's first newspaper.

  11 Harris acquitted by court martial.
      HMS *Glatton* arrives at Port Jackson carrying 387 convicts, some free settlers, and Lt John Bowen.

Apr 8 Flinders leaves Kupang to sail west about to Port Jackson.

  10 St John's Church, Parramatta, opened; Samuel Marsden conducts the inaugural service.

  19 Father James Dixon given conditional emancipation.

  27 Lt-Col. David Collins leaves UK in HMS *Calcutta*, accompanied by storeship *Ocean*, with an expedition to settle Port Phillip; 307 convicts with 30 of their wives and children (including John Fawkner and his 11-year-old son John Pascoe Fawkner), 49 free settlers, 60 marines, and 17 civil establishment, including Rev. Robert Knopwood.

  30 Baudin leaves the Australian coast and sails for Timor.

May 9 Gov. King applies for leave to return to England.

  14 Meeting of freemasons held in Sydney at the home of Sgt Thomas Whittle; participants arrested for unlawful assembly, including Sir H. B. Hayes.

  15 First authorized public Roman Catholic mass in Australia and first Catholic marriage celebrated in Sydney by Father Dixon.

Jun 9 *Investigator* arrives back in Port Jackson, Flinders having circumnavigated Australia in one voyage.

  19 William Redfern, assistant surgeon at Norfolk Is., is granted a free pardon.

Aug 10 Flinders sails for England as a passenger in the *Porpoise.*

  17 *Porpoise* runs aground on Wreck Reef.

  26 Flinders sails from Wreck Reef for Sydney in a ship's cutter.

1803

Sep 11 Lt John Bowen in the *Albion* (preceded by *Lady Nelson*) arrives at the Derwent with a party of 48 to found the first settlement in Van Diemen's Land. (Settles at Risdon Cove.)

26 Convicted murderer Joseph Samuels reprieved after three attempts to hang him fail.

Oct 7 Flinders returns to Wreck Reef in the *Cumberland* with *Francis* and *Rolla* to pick up maroons. (*Cumberland* sails for England 10 Oct.).

9 Collins in the *Calcutta* (preceded by *Ocean*, 7 Oct.), arrives at Port Phillip and (10th) founds a settlement on the site of the present-day Sorrento.

23 Rev. R. Knopwood conducts the first Christian church service at Port Phillip.

Nov 5 Collins seeks King's permission to move the settlement from Port Phillip.

25 First white child (William James Hobart Thorne) born at Sullivan Bay.

Dec 8 King calls for volunteers for the Loyal Associations, re-formed because of the resumption of war between Britain and France.

12 Collins receives King's authorization to move from Port Phillip to the Derwent.

15 *Cumberland*, leaking, stops at Mauritius, and Flinders is interned by the French (17th).

27 Convict William Buckley escapes from Port Phillip and lives for the next 32 years with a tribe of Aborigines.

A Architecture, Building
Campbell's Wharf completed in Sydney.

B Science, Technology, Discovery, etc.

C Arts and Entertainment

D Books and Writing
James Grant, *Narrative of a Voyage . . . in H.M. Vessel the Lady Nelson.*

E Sport and Recreation
First record of cricket being played in Australia—by officers of HMS *Calcutta* in Sydney (arr. 26 Dec. on way back to UK).

F Statistics, Social Change, the Environment
Estimated population: NSW, 7,016; Van Dieman's Land, 177.
Estimated Aboriginal Tasmanian population; 3,000–4,000.
Dr John Harris imports deer for his property near Blackwattle Swamp, Sydney.

G Births and Deaths
Sep 16 Nicolas Baudin d. (*c.* 53).
Nov 17 William Balmain d. (41).
— – George Bass d. (32).

1804

Jan 9 William Collins, sent from Port Phillip to examine Port Dalrymple and the Tamar River, discovers the site of Launceston.

Feb 15 David Collins and party in the *Ocean* arrive at the Derwent from Port Phillip. (Collins becomes Lt-Governor of Van Diemen's Land, 16th.)

19 Collins decides on Sullivan Cove (not Bowen's site at Risdon Cove) as settlement site, takes possession, and (20th) lands a party there.

26 First church service in Tas. conducted by Robert Knopwood on the site of Hobart Town Hall.

1804

Mar 4 Irish convicts at Castle Hill launch a full-scale rebellion.

5 Gov. King declares martial law in Parramatta, Castle Hill, and adjacent districts; Maj. George Johnston and a force from the NSW Corps march to Parramatta, and the rising is quickly put down at Vinegar Hill (Kellyville); 12 rebels are killed and 26 captured; leader Philip Cunningham hanged without trial.

8 Principal Castle Hill rebels tried and condemned; three hanged forthwith at Parramatta (another three at Castle Hill, 9th; two at Sydney, 10th).

10 Martial law revoked.

30 Lt Charles Menzies arrives at the Hunter River to re-establish a settlement, which is named Newcastle.

Apr 22 Soldiers refuse guard duties at Risdon Cove; fears are held of a convict uprising.

May 3 Aborigines approach Risdon Cove settlement and are fired upon; 50 killed—the first casualties in Tasmania's "Black War".

7 *Coromandel* arrives at Port Jackson with 200 convicts and a consignment of smallpox vaccine.

8 Bowen relinquishes command at the Derwent to Collins.

20 Last of the Sorrento settlement leave Port Phillip for the Derwent.

Jun 15 Hobart Town adopted by Collins as the name of the Sullivan Cove settlement.

24 *Experiment* arrives at Port Jackson with 132 convicts (130 females, including Molly Morgan for the second time) and Alexander Riley as a free settler.

Aug 9 Settlement at Risdon Cove abandoned; most of the establishment, including Bowen, return to Sydney in the *Ocean*.

Sep 9 Capt. John Piper replaces Joseph Foveaux as Lt-Governor of Norfolk Is., most of the convicts and half the military detachment having been withdrawn; Foveaux sails for UK in the *Albion* on leave.

16 Government brewery at Parramatta begins producing beer.

– G. W. Evans discovers the Warragamba River, NSW.

Oct 15 Col. William Paterson in HMS *Buffalo* leaves Port Jackson to establish a settlement at Port Dalrymple; Johnston takes over as commander of the NSW Corps.

Nov 4 *Buffalo* arrives at Port Dalrymple, and (11th) Paterson officially takes possession at Outer Cove on the eastern side of the Tamar (now George Town). George Caley makes an attempt to cross the Blue Mountains. (Reaches Mount Banks; returns 23rd.)

9 Crew of the *Union*, under charter to Simeon Lord, massacred by Koro Is. natives.

26 Guards at Port Dalrymple fire on a band of unfriendly Aborigines, killing one and wounding another.

Dec 27 Paterson moves the Port Dalrymple settlement to the West Arm of the Tamar, which he names York Town.

A Architecture, Building

Stone bridge across the Tank Stream in Sydney completed (27 Mar.).

B Science, Technology, Discovery, etc.

Asst Surgeon John Savage carries out the first successful inoculation against smallpox in Australia (9 May).

Australia's first medical treatise—*General Observations of the Smallpox*, by Principal Surgeon Thomas Jamison—published in the *Sydney Gazette* (14 Oct.).

C Arts and Entertainment

John Eyre (pardoned on 4 June) advertises in the *Sydney Gazette* for a box of watercolours.

D Books and Writing

E Sport and Recreation

Chuck-farthing (two-up) referred to in the *Sydney Gazette* of 15 Apr.

F Statistics, Social Change, the Environment

Estimated population: NSW, 7,040; Van Diemen's Land, 558.
Assigned convicts entitled to claim wages from their masters (from Jan.).

G Births and Deaths

May 3 William Denison b. (–1871).
Sep 14 John Gould b. (–1881).

1805

Jan 21 Robert Campbell's ship *Lady Barlow* leaves Port Jackson with the first all-colonial cargo (sealskins, seal oil, and timber) to be shipped directly to UK, defying the East India Co. monopoly.

– Simeon Lord enters into partnership with Henry Kable and James Underwood.

Feb 23 Surveyor-General G. W. Evans discharged for fraud.

Mar 21 Colonial schooner *Francis* wrecked on Oyster Bank, Newcastle.

30 In an attempt to stop convicts escaping in ships, Gov. King decrees that all ships' captains will be required to put up bonds before communicating with the settlement.

Apr 27 King orders troops to be sent to the Hawkesbury following the killing of several settlers by Aborigines.

30 Kable and Underwood launch their 185-ton deep-sea whaler *King George*, the largest vessel thus far built in Sydney.

May 24 Capt. William Bligh commissioned in London as Governor of NSW.

Jun 7 John Macarthur, having resigned from the army and received permission to return as a private citizen to NSW, arrives at Port Jackson in his own ship, the *Argo*, accompanied by his nephew Hannibal, with eight merino sheep from King George III's flock, and a letter ordering King to grant him 5,000 acres of land.

24 Lt-Gov. Collins notifies King of an extreme shortage of food in Hobart.

Jul 5 Judge-Advocate Atkins states that since Aborigines have neither religion nor morals they cannot give evidence.

13 *Lady Barlow* arrested on arrival in England for infringing East India Co. charter (but allowed to leave on condition the cargo would be sold outside Britain).

Oct 13 Macarthur is given conditional occupancy of land in the Cowpastures area subject to Colonial Office confirmation. (Receives grant on 15 Jan. 1806.)

Nov 28 Food and settlers from Norfolk Is. arrive at the Derwent.

Dec 12 Four convicts escape from Newcastle; recaptured near Castle Hill, they and their pursuers become the first white overlanders from Newcastle to Sydney.

1805

18 First land grants made in Van Diemen's Land, including 10 acres to Rev. Robert Knopwood.

A Architecture, Building

B Science, Technology, Discovery, etc.
John Lewin, *Prodromus Entomology: Natural History of the Lepidopterous Insects of New South Wales.*

C Arts and Entertainment
Lewin's engravings of butterflies and moths in *Prodromus Entomology* are the first engravings done in Australia.

D Books and Writing
James Tuckey, *An Account of a Voyage to Port Phillip.*

E Sport and Recreation

F Statistics, Social Change, the Environment
General muster of settlements: NSW, 6,980 (3,863 men, 1,370 women, 1,747 children); Van Diemen's Land, 760; Norfolk Is., approx. 700.
Tasmanian tiger shot near York Town (30 Mar.).

G Births and Deaths
Feb   7 Alexander Harris b. (–1874).
Oct 24 John Fairfax b. (–1877).
Dec 19 John Skinner Prout b. (–1876).

1806

Mar 15 Hawkesbury River rises to an unprecedented level, causing great loss of crops, stock, and houses and reducing the colony almost to starvation; seven drown in floods (to 20th).
    – William Paterson begins transferring his settlement on the Tamar from York Town to "Patersonia" (Launceston).

Apr 11 *William Pitt* arrives at Port Jackson with 117 convicts and news of the Battle of Trafalgar; passengers include Gregory Blaxland and family, as free settlers, and Charles Grimes returning from leave.
    22 Colonial schooner *Governor King* wrecked on Oyster Bank, Newcastle.

Jun 16 Convicts at Port Dalrymple seize the brig *Venus* and sail to NZ.
    – Sydney's first girls' school opened by a Mrs Williams.

Aug   6 *Lady Madelaine Sinclair*, carrying William Bligh as Captain-General and Governor-in-Chief, and William Gore as Provost-Marshal, arrives at Port Jackson, escorted by HMS *Porpoise*.
    13 Bligh assumes office as Governor, replacing Philip Gidley King.
    15 King embarks on the *Buffalo* but collapses, and his departure is delayed for six months.
    20 *Alexander* arrives at Port Jackson with 56 convicts, including Solomon Wiseman.
    21 With provisions at Hobart almost exhausted, prisoners are permitted to hunt kangaroos.

Sep 22 Sydney's free inhabitants present an address of welcome to Bligh, repudiating an earlier address signed by Macarthur on their behalf.

Oct 4 Bligh issues new and stricter port regulations.

21 Food shortage at Hobart relieved by the arrival of the *Royal George* with provisions.

Dec 4 Bligh proclaims that all able-bodied people are liable to work to bring in the harvest and stipulates wages and conditions for the various tasks.

* Maori chief Te Pehi and four of his sons visit Sydney and are entertained by King and Rev. Samuel Marsden.

* William Collins sets up Australia's first bay whaling station at Ralphs Bay, on the Derwent estuary.

* Formal Roman Catholic education begins in Australia with the opening of a Catholic school in Sydney, apparently run by a Jeremy Cavanagh (mentioned in a dispatch by King on 12 Aug.).

A Architecture, Building

B Science, Technology, Discovery, etc.

C Arts and Entertainment
John Eyre, *View of Sydney from West Side of Cove.*

D Books and Writing
George Howe, *New South Wales Pocket Almanack and Colonial Remembrancer.*

E Sport and Recreation

F Statistics, Social Change, the Environment
Estimated population: NSW, 7,162; Van Diemen's Land, 748.

G Births and Deaths
Jan 14 Charles Hotham b. (–1855).
Mar 29 James Matra d. (60?).
May 26 John Ridley b. (–1877).

1807

Jan 24 Ship *Perseverance* launched at Robert Campbell's yard. (Sails for China via Norfolk Is., 9 Feb.)

Feb 3 Lt Thomas Laycock and four others walk from Port Dalrymple to Hobart (arr. 11th) to try to obtain provisions for the settlement.

8 Laycock discovers the Clyde River, Tas.

10 P. G. King sails for England in command of HMS *Buffalo*; also aboard are Samuel Marsden, going to England to recruit clergy for the colony and taking with him the first consignment of Australian wool large enough to weave into a length of cloth, and J. H. Vaux as King's unofficial secretary.

14 Gov. Bligh prohibits the use of spirits to barter for food and clothing.

Mar 9 *Dart*, part-owned by John Macarthur, arrives at Port Jackson carrying two stills, one for Macarthur and the other for Capt. Edward Abbott. (Confiscated and held in government stores awaiting re-exportation; Naval Officer John Harris allows Macarthur to remove the two boilers belonging to the stills.)

Apr 4 John Blaxland arrives at Port Jackson in his ship, *Brothers*.

May 2 Robert Campbell is appointed Naval Officer in place of Harris.

Jun 16 Russian corvette *Neva* (Capt. Leontii Hagemeister), the first Russian vessel to call at Port Jackson, arrives on a voyage of exploration (to 1 July).

1807

18   *Sydney Cove* arrives at Port Jackson with 114 convicts; passengers include Joseph Underwood and his brother James (returning from England).

27   Public notice in Sydney announces that a convict transported for life had escaped from the colony in the *Parramatta*, a schooner owned by Macarthur and Garnham Blaxcell, bound for Tahiti.

Jul 25   Bligh suspends D'Arcy Wentworth for alleged misconduct in administering Parramatta Hospital.

Aug 2   William Blue advertises in the *Sydney Gazette* as a licensed ferryman on Sydney Harbour.

11   Simeon Lord, Henry Kable, and James Underwood are fined and gaoled for a month by Bligh for "writing a letter in improper terms" seeking permission to tranship goods without unloading them.

Oct 22   Bligh orders the confiscation of the boilers imported on the *Dart*.

24   Macarthur institutes proceedings for unlawful seizure of the boilers.

Nov 15   *Parramatta* returns to Port Jackson from Tahiti and is placed under arrest and its bond of £800 forfeited.

Dec 7   Macarthur notifies the captain of the *Parramatta* that he has abandoned the ship and will not be responsible for pay or rations.

14   Captain and crew of the *Parramatta* go ashore and are charged with violating regulations. Judge-Advocate Richard Atkins summons Macarthur to come to Sydney to "show cause" for his conduct over the *Parramatta* affair. (Macarthur refuses.)

15   Atkins issues a warrant for Macarthur's arrest; Macarthur gives the arresting officer a defiant written refusal to comply.

16   Macarthur arrested on a second warrant; granted bail.

17   Macarthur committed for trial before the Criminal Court.

21   Macarthur demands payment of a 15-year-old debt from Atkins.

A Architecture, Building

B Science, Technology, Discovery, etc.

C Arts and Entertainment

D Books and Writing

E Sport and Recreation

F Statistics, Social Change, the Environment
Estimated population: NSW, 7,948; Van Diemen's Land, 846.

G Births and Deaths
Apr 26 Charles Cowper b. (–1875).

1808

Jan 12   *City of Edinburgh*, carrying 100,000 litres of whisky, arrives at Port Jackson with part-owner Alexander Berry aboard.

25   John Macarthur comes before court on a charge of sedition; he challenges the right of Judge-Advocate Richard Atkins to try him; the court adjourns in confusion.

26   Macarthur arrested and gaoled; military officers forming the court ask Gov. Bligh to restore bail and replace Atkins; Bligh summons them to appear

before him next day; Maj. George Johnston signs an order for the release of Macarthur, proclaims martial law, and arrests Bligh.

27 Johnston suspends Atkins and several other officials; martial law repealed.

30 Charles Grimes becomes acting Judge-Advocate.

Feb 2 Johnston reports the arrest of Bligh to Lt-Gov. William Paterson (his senior officer) in Port Dalrymple; Paterson subsequently orders HMS *Porpoise* to be sent to convey him to Sydney.
Macarthur faces a new trial and (6th) is acquitted.

6 Capt. Mayhew Folger of the US whaler *Topaz* discovers, on Pitcairn Is., the last survivor of the *Bounty* mutineers, John Adams (alias Alexander Smith), with a small community of the mutineers' descendants.

12 Macarthur appointed magistrate and "Secretary to the Colony"—its virtual administrator.

17 D'Arcy Wentworth exonerated by court martial.

Mar 21 Former Provost-Marshal William Gore charged with perjury and held in gaol. (Sentenced to seven years at Newcastle on 30 May.)

Apr 3 Grimes resigns as acting Judge-Advocate and (20th) is sent to England with dispatches.

May 15 Brig *Harrington* seized by 50 convicts, led by Robert Stewart, in Farm Cove and sailed for the Philippines. (Captured three months later and Stewart hanged in Sydney in August.)

24 Floods on the Hawkesbury and Georges rivers (to 27th).

28 Anthony Fenn Kemp appointed acting Judge-Advocate.

Jul 28 Lt-Col. Joseph Foveaux arrives from England on his way to resume administration of Norfolk Is. and, being senior to Johnston, takes over next day as administrator of NSW.

29 Further flooding on the Hawkesbury and Georges rivers.

30 Foveaux refuses Bligh's request to be reinstated.

Aug 16 Foveaux asks Paterson to come to Sydney immediately or send a plan for the government of the colony.

Sep 1 William Redfern is examined by tribunal of surgeons and given a certificate of competence—the first medical diploma issued in Australia.

Oct 18 Bligh refuses to leave Government House to make way for Paterson.

Nov 1 *Porpoise* leaves Port Jackson to bring Paterson from Port Dalrymple.

16 *Speke* arrives in Port Jackson with 97 convicts; passengers include Lt John Oxley.

Dec 13 Kemp resigns as acting Judge-Advocate; Foveaux reinstates Atkins.

A Architecture, Building

B Science, Technology, Discovery, etc.
Tasmanian Devil (*Sarcophilus harrisi*) first described by G. P. R. Harris (published by Linnean Society in London).

C Arts and Entertainment

D Books and Writing
J. W. Lewin, *Birds of New Holland with Their Natural History*.

E Sport and Recreation

F Statistics, Social Change, the Environment
Estimated population: NSW, 9,105; Van Diemen's Land, 1,158.

1808

Number of liquor licences in NSW increased to 112.

G Births and Deaths
May –   Caroline Chisholm b. (–1877).
Sep   3   Philip Gidley King d. (50).

1809

Jan 1   William Paterson arrives at Port Jackson in HMS *Porpoise* and (9th) assumes governorship of NSW.
26   John Hosking and Isaac Lyons, the first trained teachers in the colony, arrive in the *Aeolus* (carrying 79 convicts), Hosking to take charge of the Female Orphan School.

Feb 20   Deposed Governor William Bligh boards the *Porpoise*, agreeing to proceed to England and not return to any part of the colony or interfere with the government. (For various reasons, sailing is delayed.)

Mar 17   *Porpoise* leaves Port Jackson, but instead of proceeding to UK, Bligh sails for Hobart.
29   John Macarthur (with his sons James and William) and Maj. George Johnston (bound for England to put his version of events before the British government) sail from Port Jackson in the returning transport *Admiral Gambier*.
31   Bligh arrives at Hobart and subsequently moves into the government cottage with his daughter, Mrs Putland.

Apr 25   Isaac Nichols, assistant to the Naval Officer, is appointed Sydney's first postmaster. (Post office opened in Nichols's house on 28th.)

May 8   Lt-Col. Lachlan Macquarie officially appointed Governor of NSW.
21   Lt-Gov. David Collins makes public in Hobart a proclamation by Paterson forbidding communication with Bligh.
22   Macquarie leaves England in HMS *Dromedary* escorted by HMS *Hindostan*; with him is Ellis Bent, to become Judge-Advocate (appointed 6 May); *Hindostan* carries Lt-Col. Maurice O'Connell with headquarters of Macquarie's own regiment, the 73rd, which is to replace the NSW Corps.
25   Hawkesbury River in flood (to 27th), rising to a higher level than the great flood of Mar. 1806.

Jun 6   "General" Holt given conditional pardon (officially confirmed 1 Jan. 1811).

Jul 30   Floods on the Hawkesbury yet again (to Aug; eight lives lost, as well as much grain) and on the Derwent, Tas.

Aug 14   *Boyd* arrives at Port Jackson with 134 Irish convicts and a detachment of the 73rd Regiment.
18   *Indispensable* arrives at Port Jackson with 61 female convicts; passengers include asst. chaplain William Cowper and family (including son Charles).

Oct 29   G. W. Evans appointed assistant surveyor at Port Dalrymple.

Dec 28   *Dromedary* and *Hindostan* arrive at Port Jackson. (Macquarie lands on 31st.)
–   *Boyd*, chartered by Simeon Lord, is attacked and burnt by Maoris at Whangaroa, NZ, and about 60 persons on board are massacred; only a woman and three children survive.

A Architecture, Building

Ebenezer Church, on the Hawkesbury River near Windsor, NSW—the oldest existing church in Australia—opens (completed in 1817).

B Science, Technology, Discovery, etc.

C Arts and Entertainment

D Books and Writing

E Sport and Recreation

F Statistics, Social Change, the Environment

Estimated population: NSW, 10,263; Van Diemen's Land, 1,298.

In one week, three vessels arrive in Port Jackson with 45,000 seal skins caught in the region of Foveaux Strait, NZ.

G Births and Deaths

Jan 17 John West b. (–1873).

Oct 13 Robert Sidaway d. (*c.* 52).

1810

Jan 1 Lt-Col. Lachlan Macquarie takes over as Governor of NSW.

4 Macquarie dismisses all persons appointed to official positions since Gov. Bligh's removal, restores those previously in office, and nullifies all trials and land grants, gifts, etc., made to members of the NSW Corps.

8 *Derwent Star and Van Diemen's Land Intelligencer*, Australia's second newspaper and the first in Tas., begins publication.

12 Macquarie appoints emancipist Andrew Thompson a JP and chief magistrate at the Hawkesbury (the first emancipist magistrate appointed).

17 Bligh returns to Sydney from Hobart in HMS *Porpoise*.

Feb 24 Macquarie issues a proclamation condemning cohabitation and immorality.

27 Rev. Samuel Marsden returns to Sydney in the transport *Anne* (197 convicts), accompanied by Rev. Robert Cartwright and Maori chief Ruatara, who had been taken to England.

Mar 22 Charity School opened in Parramatta by Macquarie; John Eyre appointed teacher.

24 David Collins dies suddenly in Hobart.

– W. C. Wentworth, aged 19, returns to NSW after schooling in England.

Apr 10 Lt T. A. Crane replaces John Piper as commandant at Norfolk Is.

– Macquarie enunciates his policy on emancipation to Secretary of State Lord Castlereagh.

May 8 Lt-Col. Maurice O'Connell marries Bligh's widowed daughter, Mary Putland.

12 Bligh sails for England in HMS *Hindostan*, accompanied by HMS *Dromedary* and *Porpoise*; aboard are officers (including William Paterson) and other ranks of the NSW Corps, as well as Richard Atkins and William Gore as Bligh's witnesses at the court martial of George Johnston.

Jun 13 Matthew Flinders is released from internment on Mauritius. (Arrives in England on 24 Oct.)

Jul 11 Capt. Frederick Hasselburg, on a sealing voyage in Robert Campbell's ship *Perseverance*, discovers Macquarie Is.

1810

Aug – William Pascoe Crook, a missionary, organizes Australia's first Congregational Church in Sydney.

Oct 6 Macquarie divides Sydney into five police districts, seven constables being allotted to each, and names four major streets as well as Hyde Park, Macquarie Place, etc.

Nov 6 Alexander Riley and Garnham Blaxcell (and, later, D'Arcy Wentworth) sign a contract with Macquarie giving them a monopoly on the import of rum (i.e., 205,000 litres of all spirits) in return for their undertaking to build a hospital in Sydney (the "Rum Hospital").
Macquarie, his wife, and party set out from Sydney to visit all the inhabited inland districts. (Return 15 Jan. 1811.)

7 Macquarie fixes the site of Liverpool and orders James Meehan to begin a survey.

Dec 6 Macquarie names five township sites: Windsor, Richmond, Castlereagh, Pitt Town, and Wilberforce.

16 *Indian* arrives at Port Jackson with 192 convicts, including James Hardy Vaux for the second time.

29 D'Arcy Wentworth appointed Superintendent of Police in Sydney.

A Architecture, Building

B Science, Tehnology, Discovery, etc.
Robert Brown publishes vol. 1 of his *Prodromus Florae Novae Hollandiae et Insulae Van-Diemen.*

C Arts and Entertainment
Public fair held on St George's Fields (cricket ground) on Easter Monday, and Subscribers' Ball held during Race Week in Oct.

D Books and Writing
Michael Massey Robinson's "Ode on His Majesty's Birthday" published in the *Sydney Gazette* (first of a series of similar odes published until 1821).

E Sport and Recreation
First recorded horse-race in Australia held at Parramatta on 21 Apr.
Race Week held in Hyde Park, Sydney, on 15, 17, and 19 Oct.

F Statistics, Social Change, the Environment
Estimated population: NSW, 10,096 (Sydney, 6,160); Van Diemen's Land, 1,470.
Number of public houses in Sydney reduced by Macquarie from 75 to 20.
Caterpillar plague destroys wheat and other crops in the Hawkesbury River area (Sept.).

G Births and Deaths
Mar 24 David Collins d. (54).
Jun 21 William Paterson d. (54).
Aug 14 Angus McMillan b. (–1865).

1811

Jan 1 Gov. Macquarie's police regulations for Sydney (issued 6 Oct. 1810) come into effect; Sydney Police Court established.

Apr 10 Toll bars come into operation on the newly completed turnpike road from Sydney to Parramatta (one in George St, Haymarket; the other at Boundary St, Parramatta).

Jun 5 At his court martial in London, George Johnston is convicted of mutiny and sentenced to be cashiered from the army (but allowed to return to NSW); Macarthur is ordered to remain in England.

Jul 2 *Providence* arrives at Port Jackson with 174 convicts, including Edward Eagar.
– D'Arcy Wentworth appointed Principal Surgeon following the death of Thomas Jamison in England (27 Jan.).

Sep 1 Maj. Thomas Davey commissioned as Lt-Governor of Van Diemen's Land.

Oct 8 Brig *Governor Macquarie* launched in Sydney.
10 *Friends* arrives at Port Jackson with 100 female convicts; Edward Smith Hall also on board as passenger.
26 Macquarie appoints W. C. Wentworth acting Provost-Marshal (the first native-born Australian to hold an important official position).

Nov 4 Macquarie leaves Port Jackson in the *Lady Nelson* to visit Van Diemen's Land and the Hunter River.
23 Macquarie arrives at Hobart, visits New Norfolk and fixes the site for the town of Elizabeth (27th), and crosses overland to Port Dalrymple (2–8 Dec.).

Dec 2 Samuel Marsden exports 1,800 kg of wool to England in the returning transport *Admiral Gambier.*
16 Macquarie decides to move the settlement at Port Dalrymple back to the George Town site on Outer Cove (renamed York Cove).
20 Macquarie sails from Port Dalrymple in the *Lady Nelson* for Port Stephens (arrives 31st).

* Mental asylum established at Castle Hill.

A Architecture, Building
Foundation stone of Rum Hospital laid by Macquarie, 23 Oct. (completed 1816; central block demolished in 1879; the two surviving wings now form Parliament House and the Mint Museum).
Bridge rebuilt over the Tank Stream.

B Science, Tehnology, Discovery, etc.

C Arts and Entertainment
John Lewin opens a painting academy in Sydney.

D Books and Writing

E Sport and Recreation

F Statistics, Social Change, the Environment
Estimated population: NSW, 10,287; Van Diemen's Land, 1,588.

G Births and Deaths
Apr 5 Thomas Reibey d. (42).
Jun 13 Owen Stanley b. (–1850).
Nov 17 Eugen von Guérard b. (–1901).

1812

Jan 1 John Oxley (in England) appointed Surveyor-General of NSW.
3 Gov. Macquarie visits Newcastle (to 5th) and inspects coalmines, lime pits, and cedar camps.

1812

18   *Guildford* arrives at Port Jackson with 199 convicts, including Andrew Bent (who continues to Hobart, 2 Feb.).

Feb 12   House of Commons appoints a select committee to consider transportation.

Mar 6   Methodist laymen meet in Sydney and resolve to form two fellowship classes.
9   Private John Gould of the 73rd Regt hanged for the murder of the wife of a fellow private.
25   G. W. Evans sails in the *Lady Nelson* to survey Jervis Bay.

Apr 4   Returning overland from Jervis Bay, Evans traverses the sites of Nowra, Port Kembla, and Wollongong (to 11th; arrives Appin 15th).

Jun 19   USA declares war on Britain, bringing the Australian colonies also into conflict with America.

Jul 10   Select committee of the House of Commons reports on transportation to NSW.

Sep 12   Macquarie orders the branding of all cattle.

Oct 19   *Indefatigable*, the first convict transport to sail direct to Van Diemen's Land, arrives at the Derwent with 199 convicts, including Michael Howe.
25   *Minstrel* arrives at Port Jackson with 125 female convicts; passengers include Thomas Davey and John Oxley.

Nov 26   *Samarang* arrives at Port Jackson from India with £10,000 in Spanish dollars.
30   Armed brig *Emu*, en route to Hobart with 49 female convicts, is captured by US privateer *Holkar* and taken to New York as a prize. (Captain and convicts released at Cape Verde Is. on 17 Jan. 1813.)

A Architecture, Building
Site for St Andrew's Cathedral in Sydney chosen by Gov. Macquarie and Rev. Samuel Marsden (5 June).

B Science, Tehnology, Discovery, etc.

C Arts and Entertainment

D Books and Writing

E Sport and Recreation
First record of a hunt with hounds in Australia (after a kangaroo) at the Cowpastures (8 Oct.).

F Statistics, Social Change, the Environment
Estimated population: NSW, 10,936; Van Diemen's Land, 1,694.

G Births and Deaths
Apr 14   George Grey b. (–1898).
Jul   27   Henry Waterhouse d. (42).
Dec 16   Stuart Donaldson b. (–1867).
—   –   John Lort Stokes b. (±1885).

1813

Feb 7   *Isabella*, bound for London from Sydney with Macquarie's first dispatches, is wrecked on a reef off the Falkland Is. (Crew and passengers —including Sir Henry Browne Hayes and Joseph Holt—rescued by HMS *Nancy*, 17 May.)

10 Col. Thomas Davey leaves Port Jackson for Hobart and (20th) takes up his post as Lt-Governor of Van Diemen's Land.

Mar 30 George Johnston returns to Sydney in the *James Hay* as a private citizen and takes up residence at his Annandale property.

Apr 23 Schooner *Unity* seized by convicts in the Derwent and is not heard of again.

May 8 New South Wales Society for Promoting Christian Knowledge and Benevolence in these Territories and Neighbouring Islands established at a meeting chaired by Edward Smith Hall. (Reorganized as the Benevolent Society of NSW on 6 May 1818.)

11 Gregory Blaxland, Lt William Lawson, and W. C. Wentworth set out on an expedition to find a way across the Blue Mountains.

15 Gov. Macquarie issues an order restricting Sunday trading.

28 Blaxland, Lawson, and Wentworth reach Mount York and (31st) arrive at Mount Blaxland, beyond the Cox River, where they turn back, having found a way across the mountains and sighted the plains beyond.

– First Sunday school in Australia established by Thomas Hassall on the Parramatta property of his father, Rowland Hassall.

Jun 28 Macquarie again sets forth his emancipist policy to the Colonial Office.

Jul 1 Proclamation issued regarding the introduction and design of the "holey dollar": "ring" worth 5s, "dump" worth 1s 3d, to become legal tender on 30 Sept. (but not in fact issued until Jan. 1814).

16 Two officers of the 73rd Regt who killed a settler are convicted only of manslaughter and given a six-month gaol sentence by the Court of Criminal Jurisdiction (Judge-Advocate and seven of their fellow officers); public outcry ensues.

31 Macquarie informs the Colonial Office of his dissatisfaction with the 73rd Regt and asks that no officer be allowed to remain in the colony after the regiment's withdrawal.

Sep – Road to Botany completed.

Oct 9 *Earl Spencer* arrives at Port Jackson with 196 convicts and some free settlers, including William Hovell.

Nov 19 G. W. Evans crosses the main range of the Blue Mountains (to 18 Dec.) and discovers and names the Fish and Macquarie rivers and the Bathurst Plains. (Returns to Nepean, 8 Jan. 1814.)

27 Macquarie prohibits meetings of more than six persons without notice to the Provost-Marshal and any attempts to influence rates of exchange through the issue of promissory notes.

Dec 20 Public meeting held in Sydney to form a society for the protection of Pacific Island natives.

– Convict Michael Howe escapes and joins a bushranging gang in Van Diemen's Land. (Later becomes its leader.)

* Turnpike road completed to Windsor.

A Architecture, Building

Foundation stone of Female Orphan School, Parramatta, laid. (Completed by Francis Greenway in 1818; now part of the University of Western Sydney's Parramatta campus.)

B Science, Tehnology, Discovery, etc.

C Arts and Entertainment

1813

D Books and Writing

J. H. Clark, *Field Sports . . . of the Native Inhabitants of New South Wales.*
John Lewin, *Birds of New South Wales* (the first illustrated book published in Australia).

E Sport and Recreation

F Statistics, Social Change, the Environment

Estimated population: NSW, 12,157; Van Diemen's Land, 1,800.

G Births and Deaths

Jan   3   Bennelong d. (*c.* 50).
Jan 23   Charles Harpur b. (−1868).
Jun   7   Redmond Barry b. (−1880).
Aug 16   P. E. Warburton b. (−1889).
Oct 23   Ludwig Leichhardt b. (−1848).

1814

Jan 31   Margaret Catchpole given a conditional pardon.
    –   "Holey dollar" and "dump" go into circulation.

Feb   4   Second Charter of Justice provides for the establishment of three new civil courts—Governor's Court and Supreme Court in NSW, Lt-Governor's Court in Van Diemen's Land.

    7   *General Hewitt* arrives at Port Jackson with 266 convicts, including Francis Greenway and Joseph Lycett, and a detachment of the 46th Regt to replace the 73rd Regt; passengers include Capt. John Piper, returning to become Naval Officer and Collector of Customs.

  11   Lt-Col. George Molle, commander of the 46th Regt and Lt-Governor of NSW (appointed 20 June 1813), arrives in the *Windham* with headquarters of the regiment.

  28   Last inhabitants leave Norfolk Is. (which remains unoccupied for next 11 years).

Mar 22   Road from Sydney to Liverpool opened.

Apr   5   Lt-Col. Maurice O'Connell and members of the 73rd Regt leave Sydney for Ceylon.

May 14   First issue of the fortnightly *Van Diemen's Land Gazette and General Advertiser* appears. (Ceases publication, 24 Sept.)
        Macquarie offers an amnesty to bushrangers in Van Diemen's Land who surrender before 1 Dec.

  20   *Three Bees* (arr. 6 May with 210 convicts) catches fire in Sydney Cove and explodes, some shot landing in Bridge Street.

Jun 14   *Argo* seized by convicts in the Derwent and not seen again.

Jul 14   Macquarie authorizes William Cox to build a road across the Blue Mountains along the Blaxland-Evans track.

  28   Jeffery Hart Bent, bringing with him the Charter of Justice, arrives in Sydney on the transport *Broxbornebury* to take up his post as judge of the NSW Supreme Court (appointed in Feb.).

Aug   2   Court of Civil Jurisdiction dissolved and (12th) Governor's Court and Supreme Court established.

  22   Russian ship *General Suvorov* at Port Jackson (to 11 Sept.).

23 J. P. Fawkner sentenced to 500 lashes and three years' gaol for helping convicts to escape from Hobart.

Oct 1 "Common stage cart" service begins between Sydney and Parramatta–Richmond–Windsor.

Nov 28 Rev. Samuel Marsden leaves for New Zealand to take Christianity to the Maoris.

Dec 28 Macquarie calls a conference of Aborigines at Parramatta to try to induce them to settle.

31 Ellis Bent withdraws from the Bench without informing Macquarie, following the Governor's criticism of the magistracy.

Rum Hospital contractors' monopoly on the sale of spirits expires; government order allows importation of spirits and imposes a duty.

A Architecture, Building

Francis Greenway advertises in the *Sydney Gazette* (17 Dec.) his services as an architect.

Officers' Quarters (part of Anglesea Barracks), Hobart (–1819).

B Science, Technology, Discovery, etc.

C Arts and Entertainment

D Books and Writing

Matthew Flinders, *A Voyage to Terra Australis* (in which he advocates the adoption of the name *Australia* for the continent).

E Sport and Recreation

First recorded prize fight in Australia takes place on 7 Jan. between John Berringer (winner) and Charles Lifton, over 56 rounds.

F Statistics, Social Change, the Environment

Estimated population: NSW, 12,183; Van Diemen's Land, 1,903.

G Births and Deaths

Mar 3 Louis Buvelot b. (–1888).

May 8 Francis Grose d. (55?).

Jul 19 Matthew Flinders d. (40).

Aug 31 Arthur Phillip d. (75).

— – Robert Richard Torrens b. (–1884).

1815

Jan 4 *Frances and Eliza*, en route to Australia with 123 convicts, is captured by US privateer *Warrior* and pillaged. (Later allowed to continue.)

14 Road over the Blue Mountains completed to the Macquarie River.

18 Residential school for Aboriginal children opened at Parramatta.

27 Attorney W. H. Moore, the first free solicitor in NSW, arrives in Sydney as a passenger in the transport *Marquis of Wellington.*

Mar 23 Samuel Marsden returns to Sydney from NZ with several Maori chiefs.

Apr 24 Michael Howe's bushranging gang raid New Norfolk, Van Diemen's Land; two settlers killed.

25 Lt-Gov. Davey proclaims martial law throughout Van Diemen's Land to check

1815

bushranging. (Revoked in Oct. following censure by Gov. Macquarie.) Macquarie and party journey west of the Blue Mountains (to 19 May).

May 1 Jeffery Bent opens the Supreme Court and swears in William Broughton and Alexander Riley, Macquarie's nominees, as magistrates.

5 Jeffery Bent rejects applications from emancipist attorneys George Crossley and Edward Eagar to appear before the Supreme Court and subsequently adjourns the court until a ruling can be obtained from the UK government on the matter.

7 Macquarie selects the site of and names Bathurst.

8 First sitting of the Governor's Court, presided over by Judge-Advocate Ellis Bent and two assistants, who (15th) refuse to permit emancipist attorneys to appear before the court.

13 G. W. Evans begins an exploring trip south from Bathurst and (25th) discovers the Lachlan River.

Jul 1 Macquarie complains to the Colonial Office about the conduct of the Bent brothers and says he will resign if they are not recalled.

Aug 8 Crown Solicitor Frederick Garling arrives in Sydney in the *Frances and Eliza*.

10 First Wesleyan minister in Australia, Rev. Samuel Leigh, arrives in Sydney in the *Hebe* to organize the Methodist Church in Australia.

Oct 27 Dr William Bland receives a pardon and establishes a private medical practice in Sydney.

Nov 10 Ellis Bent dies before the arrival of the letter recalling him.

Dec 9 Garling appointed deputy Judge-Advocate.

12 James Kelly and four others circumnavigate Van Diemen's Land (to 30 Jan. 1816), discovering Port Davey (17 Dec.) and Macquarie Harbour (28th).

– NSW Sunday School Institution opened on a non-denominational basis, by Rowland Hassall and John Eyre.

* Simeon Lord establishes a woollen mill at Botany Bay.

A Architecture, Building

John Watts, Military Hospital on Observatory Hill, Sydney (later Fort Street School, now the National Trust headquarters).

Macquarie Arms Inn, Windsor, NSW (opened by Macquarie 26 July).

B Science, Technology, Discovery, etc.

First steam engine in Australia begins operating at John Dickson's flour mill on Cockle Bay, Sydney (29 May).

C Arts and Entertainment

D Books and Writing

E Sport and Recreation

F Statistics, Social Change, the Environment

Estimated population: NSW, 13,116; Van Diemen's Land, 1,947.

G Births and Deaths

Jan 9 Augustus Alt d. (83?).

May 27 Henry Parkes b. (–1896).

Aug 5 Edward John Eyre b. (–1901).

Sep 7 John McDouall Stuart b. (–1866).

Nov 10 Ellis Bent d. (32?).

Nov 11 Maurice Margarot d. (70?).

1816

Jan 18 *Fanny* arrives at Port Jackson with 171 convicts and news of the Battle of Waterloo (18 June 1815).

19 Colonial schooner *Estramina* (captured as a Spanish prize in 1805) wrecked on Oyster Bank, Newcastle.

Mar 3 Aborigines kill four whites near the Nepean River, NSW.

25 W. C. Wentworth sails for England to study law.

30 Gov. Macquarie appoints Francis Greenway as the government's Civil Architect.

Apr 10 Macquarie sends out three punitive expeditions against Aborigines along the Nepean, Grose, and Hawkesbury rivers; one party kills 14 Aborigines and captures several others.

Jun 1 Andrew Bent's *Hobart Town Gazette and Southern Reporter* begins regular publication (trial issue published 11 May).

Sep 12 Convicts seize Simeon Lord's brig *Trial* in Port Jackson and escape. (Vessel found wrecked north of Port Stephens—Trial Bay—in Jan. 1817.)

20 First free migrants arrive in Hobart in the *Adamante*.

Oct 5 John Wylde arrives in Sydney as a passenger in the transport *Elizabeth* to succeed Ellis Bent as Judge-Advocate; ship also brings dispatches recalling Jeffery Bent. (Macquarie stops Bent's salary as Supreme Court justice.)

Nov 20 Macquarie calls a meeting of 14 people to discuss plans for opening a bank. (Public meetings for subscribers held on 5 and 18 Dec.)

30 Advertisement in the *Sydney Gazette* calls for horses for export to India (beginning of export trade in horses for Indian army).

Dec 2 First land grants in the Illawarra district, NSW, allotted by Surveyor-General John Oxley on the site of present-day Wollongong. (Deeds issued on 24 Jan. 1817.)

11 Macquarie announces the recall of Jeffery Bent and proclaims that Bent no longer has any authority in NSW.

A Architecture, Building

Francis Greenway, Macquarie Tower (Lighthouse), South Head, Sydney (completed 1817; light installed Nov. 1818; lighthouse replaced with a replica in 1883).

Old Government House, Parramatta, enlarged by John Watts and Francis Greenway for Macquarie.

Cadman's Cottage, on the shore of Sydney Cove—the oldest residence still standing in Sydney—probably built this year.

B Science, Technology, Discovery, etc.

Road completed to Mrs Macquarie's Chair, Sydney, on 13 June, the date traditionally observed as the foundation of the Sydney Botanic Gardens, with Charles Frazer as superintendent.

Botanist Allan Cunningham arrives in Sydney as a passenger in the transport *Surry* (20 Dec.).

C Arts and Entertainment

D Books and Writing

E Sport and Recreation

1816

F Statistics, Social Change, the Environment
Estimated population: NSW, 15,518; Van Diemen's Land, 2,035.

G Births and Deaths
Apr 12 Charles Gavan Duffy b. (–1903).
Oct 7 Edward Hammond Hargraves b. (–1891).
Oct 15 John Robertson b. (–1891).
Dec 23 Thomas Sutcliffe Mort b. (–1878).

1817————————————————————

Jan 4 Gov. Macquarie's secretary, J. T. Campbell, under the name of "Philo Free", attacks Samuel Marsden in the *Sydney Gazette*.

Feb 21 Hawkesbury River in high flood; two lives lost.
     24 Barron Field arrives in Sydney as a passenger on the transport *Lord Melville* to replace J. H. Bent as judge of the Supreme Court.

Mar 7 Bible Society of NSW (auxiliary of the British and Foreign Bible Society) formed in Sydney.

Apr 8 Australia's first bank, the Bank of New South Wales (now Westpac) opens for business in Mary Reibey's house in Macquarie Place.
       Col. William Sorell arrives at Hobart in the *Cochin* and next day takes office as Lt-Governor of Van Diemen's Land, replacing Thomas Davey.
     20 John Oxley and party set out from Bathurst to explore the inland plains and trace the Lachlan River.

May 18 J. H. Bent leaves Sydney to return to England.

Jul 9 Oxley turns back after meeting swamps about 60 km from the Murrumbidgee River and (25th) discovers Lake Cargelligo.
     25 Macquarie requests the withdrawal of the 46th Regt, which he has criticized for insubordinate conduct.
     26 Transport *Chapman* arrives at Port Jackson with 186 convicts, 12 having been killed and 30 wounded during threatened uprisings en route; inquiry held immediately; military involved subsequently acquitted.
     28 Charles Throsby explores south-west of Moss Vale (to 10 Aug.).

Aug 3 First detachment of 48th (Northamptonshire) Regt, under Lt-Col. James Erskine, arrives in Sydney to replace the 46th Regt.
     19 Oxley reaches the locality of Wellington and names it Wellington Valley. (Returns along Macquarie River to Bathurst, 29 Aug.)

Sep 3 Lt Phillip Parker King and John Septimus Roe arrive at Port Jackson in the *Dick* to conduct hydrographic surveys.
     17 Lt-Gov. George Molle brings charges against D'Arcy Wentworth consequent on a "pipe" by W. C. Wentworth lampooning Molle and demands a court martial. (Judge-Advocate John Wylde rules the court cannot try him.)
     30 John Macarthur returns to Sydney as a passenger on the transport *Lord Eldon*, after an "exile" of eight years, on condition that he take no further part in public affairs.

Oct 7 First Methodist church in Australia, at Castlereagh, NSW, opened by Rev. Samuel Leigh.
     10 Bushranger Michael Howe captured but escapes after stabbing and shooting his two captors.

21   Marsden brings a libel action in the Criminal Court against Campbell for his "Philo Free" letter in *Sydney Gazette*. (Action fails.)

Nov 9   Father Jeremiah O'Flynn, appointed Prefect Apostolic of New Holland but without official sanction of the British government, arrives in Sydney and is allowed to stay temporarily. (Subsequently avoids orders to leave.)

Dec 1   Marsden awarded £200 damages in a civil case against Campbell before Justice Barron Field in the Supreme Court.
Macquarie tenders his resignation to Earl Bathurst.
John Beamont leads an expedition to explore the interior of Van Diemen's Land (to 10th).

16   Francis Greenway given conditional pardon.

21   Macquarie recommends the adoption of the name *Australia* for the continent instead of New Holland.

22   P. P. King, with botanist Allan Cunningham and J. S. Roe, leave Port Jackson in the cutter *Mermaid* to survey the north-western coast of the continent.

*   Jewish burial society formed in Sydney. (Early Jewish burial services and memorial prayers conducted by German-born convict Joseph Marcus.)

A Architecture, Building
Francis Greenway, Hyde Park Barracks (−1824); Government House stables (−1821; become the NSW State Conservatorium of Music in 1914); Fort Macquarie (−1819; demolished 1903 and replaced by tram depot; replaced by Sydney Opera House 1973); St Matthew's Church, Windsor (work demolished and restarted 1818, completed 1822).
St David's Church, Hobart (−1823; demolished 1874).

B Science, Technology, Discovery, etc.

C Arts and Entertainment
James Wallis, *Corroboree at Newcastle* (painting).

D Books and Writing

E Sport and Recreation

F Statistics, Social Change, the Environment
Estimated population: NSW, 17,848; Van Diemen's Land, 2,344.

G Births and Deaths
Jul   8   James Bonwick b. (−1906).
Aug 25   Edmund Blacket b. (−1883).
Dec   7   William Bligh d. (63).

1818

Jan 8   Gov. Macquarie accuses Samuel Marsden of conspiracy against him and forbids him to come to Government House.

18   Great Western Road between Parramatta and Emu Ford (Plains) opened.

26   First Australia Day celebrations held.

Mar 3   Charles Throsby, Hamilton Hume, and James Meehan set out from Liverpool to find an overland route to Jervis Bay. (Throsby reaches Jervis Bay on 2 Apr.)

28   Samuel Marsden removed as JP and magistrate.

1818

Apr 6 Prosper de Mestre arrives at Port Jackson from Calcutta as supercargo in the *Magnet*.

19 P. P. King discovers Port Essington and (8 May) the (East) Alligator River.

May 15 Father Jeremiah O'Flynn arrested and gaoled and (20th) deported because he lacked credentials.

20 King names Bathurst Is. and (21st) Melville Is.

28 John Oxley sets out from Bathurst with a party including G. W. Evans to explore along the Macquarie River.

29 First regular mail service between Hobart and Launceston begins, a road having been recently built between the towns.

Jun 19 King names Barrow Is. (Returns to Port Jackson, 29 July.)

30 Female orphans moved to a new orphanage at Parramatta.

Jul 8 Oxley sends Evans off to the north-east, where he discovers the Castlereagh River (12th).

Aug 8 Oxley reaches the Warrumbungle Ranges, discovers the Liverpool Plains (26th), and crosses the Peel River near site of Tamworth (2 Sept.).

Sep 12 Louis de Freycinet in the French naval corvette *L'Uranie* surveys Shark Bay, WA (to 26th) and at Dirk Hartog Is. finds de Vlamingh's plate (which he takes to Paris).

15 Oxley crosses the Macleay River and (25th) reaches the Hastings River, which he follows to the sea, discovering and naming Port Macquarie (8 Oct.)

Oct 21 Bushranger Michael Howe killed by Private William Pugh and convict Thomas Worrall on the banks of the Shannon River.

Nov 21 Macquarie issues a proclamation giving magistrates jurisdiction in wages disputes between master and servant.

Dec 24 King leaves Port Jackson in the *Mermaid* to survey Macquarie Harbour, Van Diemen's Land. (Completed 24 Jan. 1819.)

* Thomas Raine establishes a whaling station at Twofold Bay, the first in NSW.

* Paper mill established at present-day Waterloo, Sydney, by Messrs Warren and Duncan.

A Architecture, Building

Francis Greenway, Female Factory, Parramatta (–1821; demolished in 1844); St Luke's Church, Liverpool (–1824); and obelisk in Macquarie Place, Sydney, from which all distances from Sydney to be measured.

B Science, Technology, Discovery, etc.

C Arts and Entertainment

D Books and Writing

Thomas Wells, *Michael Howe, the Last and Worst of the Bush Rangers of Van Diemen's Land*, published by Andrew Bent.

E Sport and Recreation

Four-oared gig stroked by John Piper wins a rowing race from Bradley's Head to Sydney Cove.

F Statistics, Social Change, the Environment

Estimated population: NSW, 22,438; Van Diemen's Land, 3,421.

G Births and Deaths

May 21 S. T. Gill b. (–1880).

Sep 5 Edmund Kennedy b. (–1848).

— – Eliza Winstanley b. (–1882).
— – Thomas Elder b. (–1897).

1819

Jan 1 Male Orphan School opened in Sydney in the former female orphan institution.

5 J. T. Bigge commissioned by Colonial Secretary Lord Bathurst to inquire into conditions in NSW and the administration of the colony.

Feb 27 Schooner *Young Lachlan* seized by convicts in the Derwent. (Apprehended in Java.)

Mar 6 William Gore suspended as Provost-Marshal and J. T. Campbell appointed in his place.

22 Macquarie forwards to the Colonial Office a petition by 1,260 colonists requesting a new legal system, including trial by jury, and the removal of restrictions on trade and the distillation of liquor.

Apr 25 Charles Throsby makes an exploratory journey from Moss Vale to Bathurst (to 9 May).

May 8 P. P. King in the *Mermaid* leaves Port Jackson to resume his survey of the north-west coast of Australia. (Returns, 12 Jan. 1820.)

22 Headquarters at Port Dalrymple transferred from Launceston to George Town.

Jun 4 Hyde Park Barracks officially opened by Macquarie.

5 Public meeting chaired by Macquarie decides to establish a savings bank.

25 Road from Hobart to New Norfolk completed.

26 Rev. L. H. Halloran arrives as a convict on the transport *Baring*. (Given a ticket-of-leave, he opens a private school in Sydney on 10 Jan. 1820.)

Jul 17 First savings bank in Australia, founded by Barron Field and Robert Campbell and popularly known as Campbell's Bank, opens in Sydney, Parramatta, Liverpool, and Windsor.

Sep 26 Commissioner Bigge arrives in Sydney in the transport *John Barry*; with him are his secretary, T. H. Scott, and Dr James Bowman.

Oct 24 John Howe finds an overland route to the Hunter River (arr. 5 Nov.).

25 Bowman succeeds D'Arcy Wentworth as Principal Surgeon. (Redfern resigns from the medical service as a result of being overlooked.)

Nov 1 Macquarie appoints Redfern a magistrate. (Appointment subsequently overruled by Lord Bathurst.)

18 Capt. Louis de Freycinet in Port Jackson (to 25 Dec.) after survey in *L'Uranie* from WA to Timor, New Guinea, and the Marianas.

Dec 13 Henry Rice leads an expedition from the Coal River settlement (Richmond, Tas.) to St Patrick's Head and thence to Port Dalrymple.

* The 210-ton ship *Frederick* wrecked near Bathurst Bay (Qld) with the loss of 22 lives; five saved. (Wreck found by King in the *Mermaid*.)

A Architecture, Building
Francis Greenway, St James's Church, Sydney (–1824). (Intended originally as a courthouse but changed on Bigge's direction to a church.)

1819

Foundation stone of St Andrew's Cathedral, Sydney, laid by Gov. Macquarie (1 Sept.). (Commissioner Bigge orders work to stop soon after.)

B Science, Technology, Discovery, etc.

Thomas Kent develops a method of extracting tannin from wattle bark.

C Arts and Entertainment

D Books and Writing

Barron Field, *First Fruits of Australian Poetry* (first book of Australian verse).
William Charles Wentworth, *A Statistical, Historical and Political Description of the Colony of New South Wales* (first book by an Australian-born author).
Memoirs of James Hardy Vaux: Written by Himself, with an appendix: *Vocabulary of the Flash Language*.

E Sport and Recreation

F Statistics, Social Change, the Environment

Estimated population: NSW, 26,059; Van Diemen's Land, 5,413.

G Births and Deaths

Apr 8   George Coppin b. (–1906).
May 13   Margaret Catchpole d. (57).
Aug 1   A. C. Gregory b. (–1905).
Aug 27   John Lewin d. (49).
Nov 8   Isaac Nichols d. (49).

1820

Jan 26   James Hardy Vaux given conditional pardon.
     27   Consecration of Sydney Burial Ground (Sandhills Cemetery) on the site of Central Station.

Feb 29   Gov. Macquarie again asks Earl Bathurst for permission to resign as Governor. (Granted, 15 July.)

Mar 2   Russian exploration ships *Blagonamerenny* and *Otkrytie*, en route to Alaska, sojourn in Port Jackson (to 27th).

Apr 1   William Minchin (holder of a land grant, Minchinbury, at Rooty Hill) appointed Superintendent of Police.
     11   Russian ship *Vostok*, commanded by F. F. Bellingshausen, arrives at Port Jackson on a voyage of scientific discovery to the Antarctic, followed by the *Mirnyi* on 19 Apr.

May 3   John Joseph Therry and Philip Conolly, the first Catholic priests officially appointed to Australia, arrive at Port Jackson in the convict transport *Janus*.
     19   *Vostok* and *Mirnyi* leave for the Antarctic.

Jun 14   P. P. King sets out again in the *Mermaid*, proceeding via Torres Strait to Brunswick Bay, WA, naming York Sound and Prince Regent River. (Returns 9 Dec.)

Jul 29   Supplementary issue of *Sydney Gazette* printed on paper made at a mill established at Waterloo in 1818.

Aug 12   Australian Social Lodge, the first permanent masonic lodge in Australia, established in Sydney.
     15   Macquarie issues an order enforcing left-hand driving.

19 Joseph Wild discovers Lake George and (21st) sights mountains he calls Snowy.

Sep 21 *Vostok* and *Mirnyi* return to Port Jackson for a stay of seven weeks.

Nov 25 Macquarie issues a government order permitting limited grazing outside the Cumberland Plains and (9 Dec.) allows grazing on the Goulburn and Breadalbane Plains—marking the beginning of the movement of graziers inland.

Dec 1 Campbelltown, NSW, marked out and named by Macquarie.

31 Frederick Goulburn arrives in Sydney to become Colonial Secretary, replacing J. T. Campbell.

* John Macarthur establishes a vineyard at Camden with cuttings brought from France in 1817.

* Benevolent Asylum—for the poor, blind, aged, and infirm—erected in Sydney under Macquarie's direction and run by the Benevolent Society. (Opens 12 Oct. 1821.)

A Architecture, Building
John Watts, Lancer Barracks, Parramatta, NSW, completed.

B Science, Technology, Discovery, etc.

C Arts and Entertainment

D Books and Writing
John Oxley, *Journals of Two Expeditions into the Interior of New South Wales.*

E Sport and Recreation

F Statistics, Social Change, the Environment
Estimated population of Australia: 33,543, including 4,969 emancipists (1,352 pardoned convicts and 3,617 expirees).

G Births and Deaths
May 14 James Martin b. (–1886).
Jun 13 W. J. Macleay b. (–1891).
Jun 19 Sir Joseph Banks d. (77).
Nov 21 Richard Atkins d. (75?).

1821

Jan 23 Meeting of emancipists in Sydney to prepare a petition to the king. (Petition forwarded to UK by Macquarie on 22 Oct.)

Feb 1 Frederick Goulburn assumes duty as Australia's first officially appointed Colonial Secretary.

3 Lt-Gen. Sir Thomas Brisbane commissioned as Governor to succeed Macquarie.

14 Commissioner Bigge leaves Sydney in HMS *Dromedary* to return to the UK.

17 Solomon Wiseman granted a licence for the Packet Inn on the Hawkesbury (Wiseman's Ferry).

– New, self-contained Female Factory at Parramatta opens for 200 convicts.

Mar 4 Stage coach begins operating between Sydney and Richmond.

17 Capt. Francis Allman and a party of soldiers and convicts sail from Sydney

1821

in the *Prince Regent* and *Lady Nelson* to found a penal settlement at Port Macquarie, NSW.

Apr – Charles Throsby discovers the Murrumbidgee River.

May 1 Australia's first periodical, the *Australian Magazine*, begins publication.
26 P. P. King in the brig *Bathurst* leaves on his final survey voyage to the west coast.
30 Macquarie, on a visit to Van Diemen's Land, selects the site of Perth, then Campbell Town (31 May), Ross (2 June), Oatlands (3 June) and Brighton (4 June).

Aug – King surveys Collier Bay and names Roebuck Bay and then sails to Mauritius to rest his crew.

Oct 25 William Redfern and Edward Eagar sail for England to present the emancipists' petition to the king.
29 Macquarie lays the foundation stone of St Mary's Chapel (Cathedral) in Sydney, the first Catholic church built in Australia.

Nov 7 Sir Thomas Brisbane arrives in Sydney to take over from Macquarie as Governor; with him are astronomers Carl Rümker and James Dunlop.
12 Site of Mudgee, NSW, traversed by Lt William Lawson.

Dec 1 Brisbane sworn in as Governor.
Clyde River, NSW, discovered by Lt Robert Johnston in the *Snapper.*
18 Barnett Levey arrives in Sydney as a free settler.
23 *Bathurst* arrives back on the WA coast near Rottnest Island; King then resumes his survey from North-West Cape to King Sound. (Returns to Sydney 25 Apr. 1822.)

* Turon River discovered by James Blackman.
* Father J. J. Therry establishes a Catholic school at Parramatta (now Parramatta Marist High School).

A Architecture, Building
St Mary's Cathedral, Sydney (consecrated 1836; destroyed by fire 1865).
Francis Greenway, Windsor Courthouse (–1822).

B Science, Technology, Discovery, etc.
Philosophical Society of Australasia, the country's first scientific body, holds its first meeting in Sydney on 27 June. (Disbanded 1823.)
Observatory established by Gov. Brisbane at Parramatta begins operation by observing the solstice (21 Dec.).

C Arts and Entertainment

D Books and Writing

E Sport and Recreation

F Statistics, Social Change, the Environment
Estimated population: NSW, 29,665; Van Diemen's Land, 5,827.
In one month (Aug.) 26 prisoners are condemned to death at Sydney criminal sessions and 19 executed.

G Births and Deaths
Mar 13 John Hunter d. (83).
May 11 George Howe d. (51?).
Nov 2 George Bowen b. (–1899).
— – Robert O'Hara Burke b. (–1861).

1822

Jan 1 Van Diemen's Land Agricultural Society formed in Hobart, with Edward Lord as president.

2 Penal settlement established at Macquarie Harbour, Van Diemen's Land, for twice-convicted prisoners.

6 First service held in the unfinished St James's Church, Sydney.

Feb 15 Macquarie sails for England in the *Surry*.

Mar 1 Brisbane reinstates Samuel Marsden as magistrate.

25 Magistrates meet in Parramatta to discuss claims by Judge Wylde that laws effected by the Governor which are contrary to British laws are invalid.

May 6 Commissioner Bigge's first report, "On the State of the Colony of NSW" (i.e., the convict system), submitted to Lord Bathurst.

Jul 5 Agricultural Society of NSW (later the Royal Agricultural Society of NSW) founded at a public meeting in Sydney.

Aug 2 Marsden and Dr James Hall try to induce convict servant Ann Rumsby to leave the house of Dr J. H. Douglass; she refuses; magistrates at Parramatta subsequently refuse to sit on the Bench with Douglass.

8 First sale of Australian-grown tobacco leaf held in Sydney.

19 Parramatta magistrates convict Ann Rumsby of perjury against Hall (superintendent surgeon of the ship on which she was transported) and sentence her to gaol at Port Macquarie.

23 Brisbane dismisses Marsden, Hannibal Macarthur, and other magistrates and remits Rumsby's sentence.

31 First part of Bigge's second report (on judicial system) submitted. (Second part submitted 2 Oct.)

– Henry Dangar begins a survey of the town of Newcastle.

Sep 25 P. P. King sails for England in the *Bathurst*.

Nov 15 Greenway dismissed as Civil Architect following a series of disagreements with his superiors.

Dec 24 Rev. Archibald Macarthur, the first Presbyterian minister in Australia, arrives in Hobart.

A Architecture, Building
Darlinghurst Gaol, Sydney (not completed until 1885).

B Science, Technology, Discovery, etc.
Carl Rümker, Gov. Brisbane's private astronomer, verifies the reappearance of Encke's Comet (2 June).

C Arts and Entertainment
Richard Read's portrait of Governor Macquarie.
Musician John Phillip Deane arrives in Hobart (19 June).

D Books and Writing

E Sport and Recreation

F Statistics, Social Change, the Environment
Estimated population: NSW, 29,680; Van Diemen's Land, 7,684.
Assigned convict James Straiter is given 500 lashes and a month's solitary

1822

confinement on bread and water for inciting his master's servants to combine for higher wages and better rations.

Honey bees successfully introduced and acclimatized.

G Births and Deaths

Feb   9   Francis Cadell b. (–1879).

Aug 28   Graham Berry b. (–1904).

1823

Jan   1   Distilling of spirits permitted.

     10   Commissioner Bigge's third and final report on NSW issued.

Feb   9   St David's Church, Hobart, consecrated (but opened on 25 Dec. 1819).

    15   Gold discovered by surveyor James McBrien at the Fish River near Bathurst—the first known discovery, though not made public.

    24   Lt Percy Simpson arrives at Wellington Valley, NSW, with a party of convicts and soldiers to establish an agricultural depot.

Mar   5   Road from Richmond, NSW, to Wallis Plains (Maitland) opened for droving.

    21   Convict Thomas Pamphlett and three others leave Port Jackson in an open boat and are driven north for several days by a gale, eventually being wrecked at Moreton Bay, where Pamphlett and two surviving companions settle with Aborigines.

Apr 15   Allan Cunningham leaves Bathurst to explore north to Liverpool Plains.

    21   Cunningham discovers and names Blaxland's River.

May 12   Samuel Marsden comes before magistrate H. G. Douglass on a charge of having allowed his assigned servant to be at large contrary to regulations and is fined but refuses to pay. (Fine eventually remitted.)

    22   Capt. Mark Currie, accompanied by Maj. John Ovens, explores beyond Lake George to the upper Murrumbidgee (to 4 June) and discovers the Monaro district.

    23   Rev. John Dunmore Lang arrives in Sydney in the *Brixton*.

Jun   5   Cunningham finds an opening through the Liverpool Range (Pandora's Pass) leading into the Liverpool Plains.

Jul 14   Board of inquiry begins investigation into the behaviour of Douglass following charges by Marsden; Douglass is exonerated.

    19   New South Wales Judicature Act receives royal assent, enabling the establishment of a nominated Legislative Council, a Supreme Court with full independence, courts of quarter sessions, the appointment of a Chief Justice to replace the Judge-Advocate and Supreme Court judge, and trial by jury in civil cases under certain conditions.

Aug 29   Headquarters and final detachment of the 3rd Regt (Buffs) arrives in the *Commodore Hayes* to replace the 48th Regt.

    –   Archibald Bell pioneers a shorter and less rugged route across the Blue Mountains (Bell's Line).

Sep 24   Royal Veteran Company (formed from former members of NSW Corps) disbanded.

    –   Australian Religious Tract Society established.

Oct 13   Supreme Court of NSW constituted under the Third Charter of Justice.

23 John Oxley leaves Port Jackson in the cutter *Mermaid* to examine Port Bowen, Port Curtis, and Moreton Bay.

31 Oxley discovers and names the Tweed River.

Nov 13 Band of Tasmanian Aborigines led by Musquito (transported from NSW) and Black Jack kill two stock-keepers at Grindstone Bay.

29 Oxley, at Moreton Bay, finds Pamphlett (and next day one of his companions, John Finnegan).

Dec 2 Oxley explores and names the Brisbane River (to 4th), which Pamphlett and Finnegan direct him to.

* Cutter *Eclipse* begins a regular service between Sydney and Newcastle.

A Architecture, Building

B Science, Technology, Discovery, etc.

C Arts and Entertainment

D Books and Writing

Gregory Blaxland, *Journal of a Tour of Discovery across the Blue Mountains in New South Wales.*

B. Godwin, *Emigrant's Guide to Van Diemen's Land, More Properly Called Tasmania.*

W. C. Wentworth, *Australasia.*

E Sport and Recreation

F Statistics, Social Change, the Environment

Estimated population: NSW, 30,623; Tas., 10,009.

The treadmill adopted for punishment of convicts and other offenders.

G Births and Deaths

Jan   5 George Johnston d. (58).

May   2 Thomas Davey d. (64?).

1824

Feb 11 St James's Church, Sydney, consecrated by Samuel Marsden.

Mar 5 Francis Forbes arrives in Sydney to take up his position as first Chief Justice of the Supreme Court.

15 Bank of Van Diemen's Land opens for business in Hobart.

May 10 Supreme Court of Van Diemen's Land opened; John Lewes Pedder Chief Justice; Joseph Tice Gellibrand Attorney-General.

12 Meeting held in London to form the Van Diemen's Land Co., with Edward Curr as secretary.

Col. George Arthur arrives in Hobart and (14th) replaces William Sorell as Lt-Governor of Van Diemen's Land.

17 New Charter of Justice proclaimed in Sydney; Francis Forbes installed as Chief Justice, Saxe Bannister as Attorney-General.

Jun 9 Convict Matthew Brady escapes from Macquarie Harbour and begins bushranging career.

21 Australian Agricultural Co. incorporated by an act of the British Parliament. (Royal charter issued on 1 Nov.)

Jul 15 W. C. Wentworth returns to Sydney with Robert Wardell to start a newspaper.

1824

24   Gov. Brisbane initiates a system for the sale of Crown land.

Aug   5   Convict Alexander Pearce, who escaped twice from Macquarie Harbour and survived by eating his companions, is hanged in Hobart.

14   Brisbane proclaims martial law in the Bathurst district following attacks by Aborigines. (Revoked, 11 Dec.)

24   Capt. J. J. G. Bremer in HMS *Tamar* leaves Sydney to establish a settlement in northern Australia.

25   First meeting of Legislative Council of NSW.

 –   Musquito and Black Jack captured near Little Swanport River.

Sep   1   Brisbane sends John Oxley with a party of convicts and soldiers under Lt Henry Miller in the *Amity* to found a penal settlement at Moreton Bay.

10   Wentworth and Wardell admitted as barristers.

11   Oxley arrives at Moreton Bay and finds Richard Parsons, companion of Pamphlett and Finnegan; Redcliffe chosen as site of settlement.

20   Bremer lands at Port Essington and takes formal possession of the coast from 135°E to 129°E; finding no fresh water at Port Essington, he chooses a site on Melville Island which he names Fort Dundas (30th).

28   Oxley recommends an alternative settlement site on the Brisbane River.

Oct   2   NSW raised to the status of archdeaconry within Anglican diocese of Calcutta; T. H. Scott appointed Archdeacon.

       Hamilton Hume and William Hovell leave Appin, NSW, to find an overland route to Port Phillip.

14   Wentworth and Wardell begin publication of the *Australian*, the first independent newspaper in Australia.

15   Freedom of press recognized; censorship of *Sydney Gazette* ends.

Nov   2   First civil jury empanelled at first court of quarter sessions.

       Hume and Hovell discover the Tumut River, then sight and name the Australian Alps (8th) and discover the Murray (16th), Ovens (24th), and Goulburn (3 Dec.) rivers.

Dec 16   Hume and Hovell reach Corio Bay, Port Phillip, which they mistake for Westernport.

A Architecture, Building

St John's Church, Launceston (–1825).

Scots Church, Sydney (–1826).

B Science, Technology, Discovery, etc.

Sugar first made by T. A. Scott from cane grown at Port Macquarie (Sept.).

C Arts and Entertainment

Joseph Lycett, *Views in Australia.*

Artist Thomas Bock arrives in Hobart.

Robert Campbell opens Sydney's first music shop in George Street.

D Books and Writing

E Sport and Recreation

"Young" Kable, of Windsor, NSW, knocks out visiting English pugilist Sam Clark in 10 minutes (Feb.).

F Statistics, Social Change, the Environment

Estimated population: NSW, 35,769; Tas., 12,303.

Dysentery the most common disease in NSW.

G Births and Deaths
Jul   1   Lachlan Macquarie d. (62).

1825

Feb 17   Ship *Almorah*, chartered to bring "rice, flour, etc." from Batavia, arrested in Sydney for carrying tea contrary to East India Co. charter.
19   *Lady Nelson* sails from Fort Dundas and is subsequently captured by Malay pirates and her crew murdered.
25   Aboriginal outlaws Musquito and Black Jack hanged in Hobart.
28   Gov. Brisbane orders the removal of the Moreton Bay settlement from Redcliffe to the site of Brisbane. (Move made in May–June.)

Mar 4   Penal settlement established on Maria Is., Tas.
24   Brisbane issues regulations for the sale of Crown land (from 5 shillings to 10 shillings per acre).

May 19   F. N. Rossi succeeds D'Arcy Wentworth as Superintendent of Police in NSW.
20   Andrew Bent prosecuted for libelling Gov. Arthur in the *Hobart Town Gazette*. (Subsequently fined and gaoled.)

Jun 6   Norfolk Is. reopened as a penal settlement for incorrigibles.
14   Van Diemen's Land administratively separated from NSW by order in council.
–   Van Diemen's Land Co. established by act of parliament to operate pastoral and agricultural interests. (Charter and 250,000 acres granted in Nov.)

Jul 16   Lt-Gen. Ralph Darling given separate commissions as Governor of NSW and Tas., the area of NSW (with its western boundary extended from 135°E to 129°E, to include Fort Dundas) to extend south to Wilsons Promontory; south of that to be Tas.
17   Warrant issued in London for the appointment of three non-official members to the NSW Legislative Council.
21   Australian Agricultural Co. promised a 31-year lease of Newcastle coalmines.

Sep 6   Maj. Edmund Lockyer in the *Mermaid* explores 195 km up the Brisbane River (to 6 Oct.).
29   *Sydney Gazette* changes from weekly to twice-weekly publication.
Licence issued for the Bush Inn (later Bush Hotel) at New Norfolk, Van Diemen's Land, the oldest continuously licensed house in Australia.

Oct 21   At a public meeting in Sydney to frame a farewell address to Gov. Brisbane, W. C. Wentworth makes his first important move in a campaign for representative government.

Nov 4   Sydney Free Grammar School opens; L. H. Halloran headmaster. (Closes late 1826.)
24   Darling arrives at Hobart in the *Catherine Stewart*.

Dec 3   Darling sworn in as Governor of Van Diemen's Land, proclaims the colony's independence from NSW, establishes the Legislative Council, and then hands over control to Lt-Governor Authur.
17   Darling arrives at Port Jackson in the *Catherine Stewart* and (19th) takes over from Brisbane as Governor.
20   New Legislative Council of NSW sworn in. Members: Lt-Gov. William Stewart, Chief Justice Francis Forbes, Archdeacon T. H. Scott, Colonial Secretary Alexander Macleay (arr. 3 Jan. 1826), and the three non-official members, John Macarthur, Robert Campbell, and Charles Throsby.

1825

A Architecture, Building

Richmond Bridge, Tas. (oldest existing bridge in Australia) opened 1 Jan.

B Science, Technology, Discovery, etc.

C Arts and Entertainment

Artist Augustus Earle arrives in Hobart from Tristan da Cunha, where he had been accidentally marooned.

First church organ in Australia installed at St David's Church, Hobart; J. P. Deane appointed organist.

D Books and Writing

Barron Field, ed., *Geographical Memoirs on New South Wales.*

E Sport and Recreation

Sydney Turf Club (Australian Turf Club) formed, 18 Mar; holds its first meeting at Bellevue Hill on 25–26 May.

F Statistics, Social Change, the Environment

Estimated population: NSW, 38,313; Tas., 14,192.

Livestock in NSW: 237,600 sheep, 134,500 cattle; 18,500 hectares of land under cultivation; 186,600 kg of wool exported during year.

Buffaloes imported from Timor and acclimatized at Fort Dundas.

G Births and Deaths

Jun 30   F. J. H. von Mueller b. (–1896).

Oct 31   Catherine Helen Spence b. (–1910).

Nov 15   Andrew Garran b. (–1901).

1826

Jan 3   Alexander Macleay arrives in Sydney to replace Frederick Goulburn as Colonial Secretary.

–   Fr Philip Conolly opens the first Catholic school in Van Diemen's Land at Hobart.

Feb 8   Gov. Arthur suspends J. T. Gellibrand as Attorney-General.

Mar 9   Letters Patent issued in London to form a Church and School Corporation, giving the Anglican Church the status of an established religion in NSW with the right to vast areas of Crown land and control of the school system.

16   Australian Subscription Library, forerunner of the State Library of NSW, founded. (Opens, 1 Dec. 1827.)

17   Bushranger Matthew Brady captured by John Batman near Launceston. (Hanged, 4 May.)

Capt. Patrick Logan takes command of the Moreton Bay settlement.

Apr 8   First street lamp in Australia lit in Macquarie Place, Sydney. (General lighting in Sydney turned on, 13 Mar. 1827.)

12   Tasmania's Legislative Council meets for the first time.

–   Female School of Industry opened in Sydney to train girls as domestics.

May 19   Edward Smith Hall's *Monitor* newspaper begins publication in Sydney.

Jun 3   Chamber of Commerce founded in Sydney.

12   Gas lighting installed by shopkeeper J. T. Wilson of Pitt Street, Sydney (first recorded use of gas light in Australia).

17   Frederick Fisher (of "Fisher's Ghost" fame) murdered at Campbelltown.

Jul 3 Bank of Australia opens in Sydney.

Aug 21 Logan discovers the Logan River (Qld).

29 Darling cancels tickets of occupation of land (from 1 Mar. 1827) and substitutes grazing licences at £1 per 100 acres.

– Sydney Dispensary (renamed Sydney Infirmary and Dispensary in 1843) opens in Macquarie Street for the care of the free pauper sick.

Sep 5 Darling issues a "Limits of Location" order restricting settlement to certain areas.

25 Convict insurrection on Norfolk Is. savagely suppressed.

Oct 7 French navigator J. S. C. Dumont d'Urville in *L'Astrolabe* at King George Sound (to 25th).

13 W. H. Moore replaces Saxe Bannister as NSW Attorney-General.

21 Bannister fights a duel with Robert Wardell at Pyrmont.

27 Van Diemen's Land Co. lands settlers and livestock at Circular Head.

Nov 8 Privates Joseph Sudds and Patrick Thompson openly commit a robbery to get convicted, considering a convict's life better than a soldier's; Darling orders that they serve seven years' hard labour in irons.

12 Dumont d'Urville at Westernport (to 19th).

27 Joseph Sudds dies, giving rise to public criticism of Darling.

– Fr J. J. Therry deprived of his official status and salary as chaplain. (Restored, Apr. 1837.)

– Influenza epidemic causes 37 deaths in two days in Sydney.

Dec 12 Settlement established by Capt. Samuel Wright at Westernport as a precaution against French colonization. (Abandoned, Jan. 1828.)

20 Convicts bound for Norfolk Is. in the brig *Wellington* seize the ship and sail it to NZ (where they are captured by the whaler *Sisters*).

25 Maj. Edmund Lockyer and a party of soldiers and convicts in the brig *Amity* arrive at King George Sound to take possession of the western part of the continent and establish a settlement there. (Settlement established on the site of Albany.)

* Aboriginal mission established on Lake Macquarie, NSW, under the charge of L. E. Threlkeld.

A Architecture, Building

B Science, Technology, Discovery, etc.
Carl Rümker discovers a new comet in the constellation Orion.

C Arts and Entertainment
Augustus Earle publishes his *Views in Australia*, printed on his own lithographic press.
Sydney Amateur Concerts launched (7 June).

D Books and Writing
P. P. King, *Narrative of a Survey of the Intertropical and Western Coasts of Australia.*
Charles Tompson, *Wild Notes from the Lyre of a Native Minstrel* (first book of poetry from an Australian-born writer).

E Sport and Recreation

F Statistics, Social Change, the Environment
Estimated population: NSW, 38,890; Tas., 14,992.
Fifty-three persons executed in Tas. during year.

1826

Registration of births, deaths, and marriages required to be kept in each parish (from 1 Jan.).

Burials no longer allowed within church walls but in burial grounds at least one mile from town.

G Births and Deaths

May 6 George Dalrymple b. (–1876).
May 16 Joseph Holt d. (69?).
Jun 24 George Goyder b. (–1898).
Aug 6 T. A. Browne ("Rolf Boldrewood") b. (–1915).

1827

Jan 1 *Sydney Gazette* begins daily publication (until 10 Feb., when reduced to three times a week).
9 L. H. Halloran opens his own private school in Sydney.
26 Public meeting held in Sydney to demand trial by jury, taxation by representation, and a Legislative Assembly elected on manhood suffrage; W. C. Wentworth the main speaker.

Feb 7 Henry Helyer, exploring for the Van Diemen's Land Co. (to 4 Mar.), discovers the Helyer River, the Surrey Hills, and the Arthur River.

Mar 3 G. T. Howe publishes the first edition of the *Tasmanian* in Hobart.
5 Capt. James Stirling in HMS *Success* examines the Swan River district (to 22nd) with a view to establishing a settlement there.
16 *Monitor* attacks the government of Darling on 24 charges.
19 Darling's private secretary Henry Dumaresq fights a duel with Robert Wardell over an article in the *Australian* attacking him and his brother.

Apr 11 Darling introduces two bills into the Legislative Council to stifle criticism by licensing newspapers and imposing a tax of fourpence a copy. (Chief Justice Forbes refuses to certify the legislation.)
30 Allan Cunningham sets out from the Hunter River to explore to the north.

May 12 Cunningham crosses the Namoi River and discovers the Gwydir (21st), the Macintyre, and the Dumaresq (28th) rivers.
18 Lt Nathaniel Lowe arraigned before the Supreme Court for the murder of an Aboriginal while in custody. (Subsequently acquitted.)
23 Capt. Charles Sturt arrives in Sydney on the transport *Mariner*.

Jun 5 Cunningham reaches the Condamine River and discovers the Darling Downs.
8 Patrick Logan discovers coal at Limestone (Ipswich).
Cunningham sights the Canning Downs from Mt Dumaresq.
18 Stirling establishes a settlement at Raffles Bay (NT).
– Sturt appointed military secretary to Gov. Darling.

Jul 17 First lecture delivered at the Van Diemen's Land Mechanics' Institute in Hobart, the first mechanics' institute in Australia.

Sep 15 Lt-Gov. Arthur passes acts to restrict the press and impose duties on newspapers.
23 T. L. Mitchell arrives in Sydney to become Asst Surveyor-General.
29 Robert Wardell tried for seditious libel for referring to Darling in the *Australian* as "ignorant and obstinate". (Discharged by jury.)
– Work begins on "Busby's bore", John Busby's tunnel scheme to bring water from the Lachlan Swamps (Centennial Park) into Sydney.

Dec 14 John ("Bold Jack") Donohoe and gang rob carts on the Sydney–Windsor road. (Subsequently caught and condemned, gang members are hanged except for Donohoe, who escapes and begins terrorizing the countryside.)

    * John Clunies Ross establishes a settlement on the Cocos (Keeling) Is.

A Architecture, Building
Vaucluse House, Sydney, probably begun.
Old Windmill, Brisbane.
John Lee Archer takes up his post as Colonial Architect in Tas. (2 Aug.).
Building regulations issued in Sydney to control alignment of buildings.

B Science, Technology, Discovery, etc.
Colonial Office sanctions the establishment of the Colonial Museum in Sydney. (Becomes the Australian Museum in 1834.)

C Arts and Entertainment

D Books and Writing
Peter Cunningham, *Two Years in New South Wales.*
Rev. L. E. Threlkeld, *Specimens of a Dialect.*

E Sport and Recreation
Regattas held on the Derwent at Hobart on 3 Jan. and on Sydney Harbour (arranged by officers of HMS *Success* and HMS *Rainbow*) on 28 April.

F Statistics, Social Change, the Environment
Estimated population: NSW, 39,467; Tas., 16,833.
Colonial Times, Hobart (11 May), reports the "common rabbit" running about in thousands on some estates.

G Births and Deaths
Feb 5 Peter Lalor b. (–1889).
Mar 13 Rev. Richard Johnson d. (73?).
Jul   7 D'Arcy Wentworth d. (65?).
Oct 2 David Syme b. (–1908).

1828

Jan 24 Gov. Darling sends the schooner *Isabella* to withdraw the settlers from Westernport. (Schooner returns with settlers, 7 Apr.)

Feb 6 R. L. Murray founds *Murray's Austral-Asiatic Review* (in Hobart).

    – Orders issued against the practice of "squatting" in Tas.

Mar 1 Post offices opened at Parramatta, Windsor, Liverpool, Campbelltown, Penrith, Bathurst, and Newcastle; Australia's first postman appointed in Sydney, a twice-weekly horse post established between principal towns, and a regular sea postal service started between Sydney, Newcastle, Port Macquarie, and Hobart.

    3 Transport *Morley* arrives at Port Jackson carrying whooping cough (first time in Sydney); several deaths occur, including that of Gov. Darling's son.

    – Visiting Malays form a trepang-fishing establishment at Raffles Bay.

Apr 15 Lt-Gov. Arthur issues a proclamation excluding all Aborigines from settled areas in Tas.

1828

May 28   T. L. Mitchell becomes Surveyor-General of NSW following the death of John Oxley.

Jul   17   First Masters' and Servants' Act passed in NSW.

      24   Allan Cunningham and Patrick Logan set out from Brisbane to establish a route to the Darling Downs.

      25   Judicature Act of 1823 amended in UK to increase the NSW Legislative Council to 15 members (7 official and 7 non-official, plus the Governor), a majority of whom being able to overrule the Governor's proposals; a week's notice to be given of proposed bills.

      30   Capt. James Stirling, back in England, urges the Colonial Office to form a colony on the Swan River.

Aug   3   Logan and Cunningham climb Mount Lindesay (now Mount Barney) and sight and name the Macpherson Range.

      25   Cunningham determines access to the Darling Downs through Cunningham's Gap.

      26   Capt. Henry Rous in the *Rainbow* discovers and names the Richmond River, NSW.

Sep 13   Capt. Collet Barker arrives at Raffles Bay to take over command of the settlement.

      14   Bank of Australia in Sydney robbed of a large amount by a gang who break into the strongroom by a tunnel from a water drain. (Bank never recovers from the loss.)

      17   "Holey dollars" withdrawn from circulation.

Nov   1   Martial law proclaimed by Lt-Gov. Arthur in the settled districts of Tas; roving parties hunt Aborigines.

      10   Charles Sturt with Hamilton Hume and a party leave Sydney to trace the course of the Macquarie River.

      14   Thomas Peel in Britain puts forward a proposal to the Colonial Office for the colonization of WA.

Dec 30   Stirling given instructions to occupy the Swan River area and officially appointed Lt-Governor of WA.

      *   Female convict factory opened at the Cascades, near Hobart.
      *   NSW in the third year of drought.
      *   Widespread floods in Tas.
      *   The Netherlands claims the south-west coast of New Guinea.

A   Architecture, Building
    John Verge arrives in Sydney (Dec.).

B   Science, Technology, Discovery, etc.
    Sir Thomas Brisbane awarded the gold medal of the Royal Astronomical Society for his work at Parramatta.
    Charles Frazer begins laying out Brisbane's Botanic Gardens (3 July).

C   Arts and Entertainment

D   Books and Writing

E   Sport and Recreation
    Australian Racing and Jockey Club formed in Sydney. (First meeting held at Parramatta on 1 and 3 Oct.).

F Statistics, Social Change, the Environment

First regular census taken in NSW in Nov: population, 36,598 (including 15,728 convicts).

New legislation provides for forfeiture of wages and six months' imprisonment for any servant or workman leaving a job in breach of contract.

G Births and Deaths

Apr 2 Charles Throsby d. (50?).

May 9 Nicholas Chevalier b. (–1902).

May 26 John Oxley d. (42).

1829

Jan 1 Charles Sturt's party reaches the Bogan River.

Feb 2 Sturt discovers the Darling River, near the present site of Bourke (then traces the Castlereagh River before returning to Sydney, 27 Apr.).

9 *Launceston Advertiser* founded by J. P. Fawkner.

Mar 1 W. C. Wentworth, in a letter to the Colonial Office, impeaches Darling.

25 G. A. Robinson appointed guardian of Aborigines at Bruny Is., Tas.

31 Fort Dundas, Melville Is., is abandoned; settlers move to Raffles Bay.

Apr 10 Edward Smith Hall found guilty of seditious libel of Darling in the *Monitor* of 22 Nov. 1928. (Sentenced to 12 months' gaol, 15 Sept.).

14 A. E. Hayes, editor of the *Australian*, fined and gaoled for six months for libelling Darling.

– James Hardy Vaux absconds to Ireland.

May 2 Capt. Charles Fremantle of HMS *Challenger* lands at the site of Fremantle and takes formal possession of the western third of Australia (i.e., all of the mainland not included in NSW).

31 Capt. (later Sir) James Stirling in HMS *Parmelia* arrives at Cockburn Sound to form a settlement on the Swan River. (Forms temporary settlement on Garden Is., 7 June.)

– Ship *Governor Ready* wrecked in Torres Strait; crew in ship's boats sail 2,400 km to Timor in 14 days.

Jun 18 Colony of Western Australia proclaimed, with Stirling as Lt-Governor. (Becomes Governor and Commander-in-Chief on 28 Apr. 1831.)

Aug 12 Site of Perth chosen. (Land sales in Perth and Fremantle begin on 5 Sept.)

14 Convicts seize the brig *Cyprus* at Recherche Bay, Tas., and sail it to China.

15 Foreign coins no longer accepted by the government.

21 Legislative Council of NSW meets for the first time in the present Parliament House.

31 Settlement at Raffles Bay closes down. (Most of the settlers move to the Swan River settlement.)

Sep 13 Archdeacon William Grant Broughton (later Bishop Broughton, the first Anglican bishop in Australia) arrives in Sydney.

– Lt William Preston and Surgeon Alexander Collie follow the Canning River, WA, to its source and examine part of the Darling Range.

Oct 9 Emancipists become eligible for jury service, such juries to consist of 12 men.

1829

14   Gov. Darling proclaims the Nineteen Counties of NSW, redefining the "Limits of Location", beyond which settlement is prohibited.

  –   NSW's four-year drought breaks.

Nov **3**   Sturt leaves Sydney on an expedition to determine the course of the Murrumbidgee.

  30   Compositors on the *Australian* newspaper strike over a reduction in wages owing to currency depreciation.

  –   Preston and Collie discover the Preston and Collie rivers, WA.

Dec **3**   Capt. Collet Barker, transferred from Raffles Bay, takes command of the settlement at King George Sound.

  15   Thomas Peel arrives at the Swan River with 300 settlers, too late to be eligible for the land grant for his colonization scheme.

  *   Shipwrights' Society ʻof Sydney formed—believed to be the first trade association in NSW.

A Architecture, Building

Commissariat Store, Brisbane.

B Science, Technology, Discovery, etc.

C Arts and Entertainment

Barnett Levey given a licence to hold balls and concerts in the Assembly Room of his Royal Hotel, Sydney.

David Burn's play, *The Bushrangers*, performed in Scotland.

D Books and Writing

"Simon Stukeley" (Henry Savery), *The Hermit in Van Diemen's Land* appears in the *Colonial Times*.

Edward Gibbon Wakefield, *Sketch of a Proposal for Colonizing Australia* (published anonymously).

Robert Gouger, ed., *A Letter from Sydney* (written by E. G. Wakefield in prison).

E Sport and Recreation

First record of a football game being played in Australia (noted in the Sydney *Monitor* of 25 July).

F Statistics, Social Change, the Environment

Estimated population: NSW, 40,916; Tas., 20,015; WA, 1,003.

Fifty-two persons hanged in NSW during the year.

Tickets-of-leave granted to female convicts (from 19 Mar.).

G Births and Deaths

Mar   5   John Adams (last survivor of Bounty mutineers) d. (*c.* 62).

May 23   George Caley d. (58).

1830

Jan **7**   Charles Sturt begins his journey by whaleboat down the Murrumbidgee and (14th) enters "a broad and noble river" which he names the Murray.

  23   Following a dangerous encounter with Aborigines, Sturt passes the junction of the Murray and Darling.

  26   Foundation stone of Sydney College (now Sydney Grammar School) laid by Francis Forbes.

27 G. A. Robinson sets out from Hobart for Port Davey to conciliate the Aborigines. (Continues up west coast to Circular Head.)

29 Legislation to restrict the press passed by the NSW Legislative Council. (Disallowed by Colonial Office, Jan. 1831.)

Feb 9 Public meeting held in Sydney to consider a petition prepared by Sir John Jamison calling for trial by jury and more representative government.

Sturt arrives at Lake Alexandrina and, after crossing the lake to Encounter Bay, begins (13th) the return journey up the Murray, against the current.

27 *Fremantle Journal and General Advertiser*, a manuscript newspaper, begins publication.

Mar 6 Edward Smith Hall sentenced to 25 months' gaol for libel.

23 Sturt's boat party arrive back at their depot on the Murrumbidgee and find it abandoned; they continue to row up the river in flood.

26 Foundation stone laid of a Congregational church in Pitt Street, Sydney.

Apr 11 Sturt abandons the whaleboat near the site of Narrandera and sends two men to obtain relief supplies. (Continues return journey overland, arriving at Sydney on 25 May.)

21 NSW Bushranging Act authorizes arrest on suspicion.

Australian Agricultural Co. given permission to select more than 400,000 acres (162,000 hectares) in two locations.

– Destructive floods on the Hunter and Hawkesbury rivers, NSW.

May – Swan River in flood at Perth (to June).

Jun 28 Order in council empowers Legislative Council to extend trial by jury to criminal cases if "advantageous to the community".

Jul 13 Port Macquarie opened to free settlers. (Most convicts moved to Moreton Bay and Norfolk Is.)

31 Ensign Robert Dale explores the Avon River, WA (to 15 Aug.). (Returns with Stirling in Oct. to examine the Avon Valley.)

Sep 1 "Bold Jack" Donohoe shot dead by police near Campbelltown, NSW.

– Port Arthur, Tas., penal station founded.

Oct 7 Lt-Gov. Arthur organizes a drive by police, soldiers, and settlers—the Black Line—to capture and confine all Tasmanian Aborigines (to 26 Nov.). (Only two captured; two others shot.)

17 Capt. Patrick Logan killed (apparently by Aborigines) during a survey of the upper Brisbane River.

Nov 1 Order in council constitutes WA as a separate Crown colony and authorizes the establishment of a Legislative Council.

15 First hackney coach begins operating in Sydney.

Dec 14 Capt. Thomas Bannister and party make an overland expedition from Fremantle to King George Sound (to 4 Feb. 1831).

* James Busby establishes the Kirkton vineyard in the Hunter Valley, NSW.

A Architecture, Building

Architect Mortimer Lewis arrives in Sydney.

B Science, Technology, Discovery, etc.

T. L. Mitchell finds Pleistocene vertebrate fossils in the Wellington Caves, NSW.

C Arts and Entertainment

Augustus Earle, *Views in New South Wales and Van Diemen's Land.*

Officers of HMS *Crocodile* and HMS *Zebra* present the plays *Agnes, or the*

1830

Bleeding Nun and *The Miller and His Men* under canvas at Fort Macquarie, Sydney.

D Books and Writing

E Sport and Recreation

Cornwall Turf Club holds its first meeting in Launceston (9 Mar.).

F Statistics, Social Change, the Environment

Estimated population: NSW, 44,588; Tas., 24,279; WA, 1,172.

G Births and Deaths

Jan 2 Henry Kingsley b. (–1876).
Sep 16 Patrick Francis Moran b. (–1911).
— – Frank Gardiner b. (–1903?).

1831

Jan 14 Janet Templeton and her nine children, with her brother John Forlonge and family and a flock of merino sheep, arrive at Launceston in the brig *Czar.* (Forlonges remain in Van Diemen's Land; Templetons continue to NSW.)

Mar 7 Control of King George Sound settlement transferred from NSW to WA. (Capt. Collet Barker and garrison relieved and convict station closed on 29th.)
15 Colonial Office recalls Gov. Darling.
31 *Surprise*, the first steamer built in Australia, launched at Sydney. (Makes trial run 1 June; begins regular service to Parramatta in July.)

Apr 13 Barker arrives at Gulf St Vincent in the *Isabella* to make a survey.
16 Darling issues a proclamation prohibiting trade in Maori heads (the schooner *Prince of Denmark* having arrived at Port Jackson with 14 Maori heads on 29 Mar.).
18 *Sydney Herald* begins publication (as a weekly).
19 Barker ascends Mount Lofty and views the opening to present-day Port Adelaide.
24 John McKaeg conducts the first Baptist service in Sydney.
30 Barker disappears while tracing the connection between Lake Alexandrina and Encounter Bay (presumed killed by Aborigines).
James Hardy Vaux arrives in Sydney for the third time as a transportee.
– Serious floods on the Hunter and Hawkesbury rivers.

May 14 *Sophia Jane*, the first steamship to operate in Australian waters, arrives at Port Jackson from UK under sail. (Begins Sydney–Newcastle service, 13 June.)
28 Agricultural Society formed in Perth.
31 Robert Hoddle's plan for Berrima, NSW, approved.

Jun 25 Regular coach service between Hobart and Launceston begins.

Aug 1 Free land grants discontinued in NSW and sale by auction introduced, with a minimum price of five shillings per acre—the Ripon regulations. (Implemented in Tas. in June 1831 and in WA in Jan. 1832.)
Guards on the convict transport *Eleanor* in Sydney Harbour fire on the heavily ironed prisoners, killing two and wounding two.
– Party of Aborigines led by Midgegoroo and Yagan kill a European near Melville Water, WA, in retaliation for the shooting of an Aboriginal. (No attempt is made to punish them.)

1831

Oct 13 *Stirling Castle* arrives at Port Jackson with a large number of skilled Presbyterian workmen, two ministers, and three schoolmasters to build and staff Rev. J. D. Lang's Australian College.

22 Darling sails for England in the *Hoogly* (Col. Patrick Lindesay replacing him as administrator); W. C. Wentworth holds a huge celebration at Vaucluse.

– Australian Agricultural Co. takes over completely the mining of coal in the Newcastle area.

Nov 15 Australian College classes begin (in a hired hall).

24 T. L. Mitchell leaves Sydney to explore the Castlereagh–Gwydir area. (Returns, March 1832.)

Dec 2 Maj.-Gen. Sir Richard Bourke arrives at Port Jackson in the *Margaret* and is installed next day as Governor of NSW.

A Architecture, Building
Henry Reveley, the Round House gaol, Fremantle, WA.
Ross Bridge, Tas. (–1836).

B Science, Technology, Discovery, etc.

C Arts and Entertainment
Artist John Glover arrives at Launceston (1 Apr.).
Thomas Bock opens an art studio in Hobart.

D Books and Writing
Jorgen Jorgenson, *Observations on the Funded System.*
Henry Savery, *Quintus Servinton* (the first novel written, printed and published in Australia).

E Sport and Recreation

F Statistics, Social Change, the Environment
Estimated population: NSW, 48,000; Tas., 26,640; WA, 1,341.
Boat builders in Sydney establish a benefit society providing medical treatment and sickness, unemployment, and funeral benefits.
First honey bees to survive in Tas. introduced.

G Births and Deaths
Jul 5 William Bede Dalley b. (–1888).
Jul 21 Henry Hacking d. (81).
Nov 8 Alfred Felton b. (–1904).
Nov 17 Adelaide Ironside b. (–1867).

1832

Jan 7 G. A. Robinson arrives in Hobart with Aborigines from Oyster Bay and Big River tribes—the last of the Aborigines from the settled districts—to be resettled on Bass Strait islands.

Feb 7 WA Legislative Council and Executive Council meet for the first time.

8 Quakers James Backhouse and G. W. Walker arrive in Hobart and (12th) hold the first Australian meeting of the Society of Friends.

13 King's School, Parramatta, opens.

Mar 7 *Government Gazette* first issued (as part of *Sydney Gazette*).

– Hunter River flooded; six or seven lives lost.

1832

Apr 6   Soldier Thomas Brennan executed by firing squad at Dawes Battery, Sydney, for "discharging his piece at a sergeant".

Jun –   Party of Aborigines led by Yagan kill a settler on the Canning River, WA. (Yagan later captured, but reprieved.)

Aug 5   Large number of vine cuttings obtained by James Busby in France, Spain, and Portugal arrive in Sydney in the transport *Lady Harewood.*

     10   *Red Rover* arrives at Port Jackson with 202 female assisted migrants from Irish charitable institutions.

     12   Gov. Stirling leaves for London to place WA's problems before the British government.

     18   Savings Bank of New South Wales, established as a public concern by act of parliament (and taking over from Campbell's Bank) opens to receive deposits.

     –   John Macarthur formally declared insane.

Sep –   Truganini saves G. A. Robinson from pursuing hostile Aborigines by ferrying him across a river on a log.

Oct 11   Sydney receives news of the passing of the Reform Bill in UK.

Dec 14   Presbytery of NSW formed in Sydney, thus beginning ordered Presbyterian Church government in Australia.

     *   Cascade Brewery established in Hobart by Peter Degraves.

     *   Charles Macfaull plants first grape vines in WA—on Hamilton Hill, near Fremantle.

A Architecture, Building
John Verge, Camden Park House, NSW (–1835); included in its design is Australia's first authenticated bathroom.

B Science, Technology, Discovery, etc.
Experiment, a paddle-boat driven by horses moving a capstan (later converted to steam), begins service between Sydney and Parramatta.
Rudimentary washing machines (agitating devices in barrel or cradle form) become available.

C Arts and Entertainment
Charles Rodius, *Sydney Harbour from Dawes Point* (painting).
Sydney's first professional theatrical performance—the melodrama *Black-Eyed Susan* and the farce *Monsieur Tonson*—presented by Barnett Levey in the converted saloon of the Royal Hotel (26 Dec.).

D Books and Writing

E Sport and Recreation
Ned Chalker beats Young Kable in a bare-knuckle fight over 28 rounds at Baulkham Hills, Sydney (19 Oct.).

F Statistics, Social Change, the Environment
Estimated population: NSW, 53,524; Tas., 28,903; WA, 1,510.
Assisted-migrant arrivals during year: NSW, 782; Tas., 550.

G Births and Deaths
Jan   4   E. W. Cole b. (–1918).
Feb 20   John White d. (75?).

1833

Jan 5 Charles Macfaull launches the *Perth Gazette and West Australian Journal*, forerunner of the *West Australian* (published under that title in 1879).

23 Bathurst, NSW, gazetted as a town. (First land sales, 9 Aug.)

Feb 4 Order in council issued in London abolishing the Church and School Corporation, ending Anglican monopoly in NSW.

5 *Hibernia*, bound for NSW from Ireland, catches fire off the coast of America; 153 people burnt to death.

18 William Ullathorne arrives in Sydney as Vicar-General of the Catholic Church in Australia.

Mar 22 Sydney Mechanics' School of Arts formally constituted. (Lectures begin, 13 June.)

27 Goulburn, NSW, gazetted as a town.

Apr 12 Australian Steam Navigation Co. founded.

21 James Busby leaves Sydney to become Government Resident in New Zealand. (Arrives at the Bay of Islands, 16 May.)

May 1 Yagan and Midgegoroo proclaimed outlaws for killing two whites on the Canning River, WA, in revenge for hostile acts towards Aborigines.

Jun – Edward Henty explores Portland Bay area en route from Port Lincoln to Launceston.

Jul 11 Yagan and another Aboriginal shot dead near the Swan River. (Yagan's head is severed and sent to Britain.)

Aug 28 Legislation passed in NSW providing for trial by jury in criminal cases. Legislation passed authorizing the appointment of land commissioners to prevent unauthorized occupation of outlying Crown land by "squatters".

30 *Amphitrite*, bound for Australia with 106 female convicts and 12 children, is driven ashore on the coast of France and 134 lives are lost, only three being saved.

Sep 13 Sir Richard Spencer arrives at Albany, WA, to become Government Resident at King George Sound.

Oct 23 Township of Muscle Brook (Muswellbrook), NSW, proclaimed.

Nov 1 Convict John Graham returns to Moreton Bay after living with the Aborigines since his escape in July 1827.

5 Assigned convicts of James Mudie in the Hunter Valley abscond and return to rob Mudie's house and attempt to kill his son-in-law John Larnach. (Captured and hanged, 21 Dec.)

30 Brig *Ann Jamieson* explodes at King's Wharf, Sydney; eight people killed.

– Macquarie Habour penal settlement closed down.

Dec 26 South Australian Association founded by Robert Gouger and other followers of E. G. Wakefield.

A Architecture, Building

Lennox Bridge, Lapstone Hill, NSW—the oldest existing bridge on the Australian mainland—completed (28 June).

Robert Campbell's house Duntroon (now part of Royal Military College).

Mortimer Lewis, Hartley Courthouse (opened 1837).

1833

B Science, Technology, Discovery, etc.

Dr George Bennett establishes that kangaroos conceive in the womb and not in the pouch.

C Arts and Entertainment

Philharmonic Society of Sydney formed.

Theatre Royal, Sydney, opened by Barnett Levey (5 Oct.).

First professional theatrical performance in Hobart staged at the Freemasons Tavern by Samson Cameron's company in Kotzebue's *The Stranger* and a farce, *The Married Bachelor* (17 Dec.).

D Books and Writing

Charles Sturt, *Two Expeditions into the Interior of Southern Australia.*

E Sport and Recreation

First race meeting held at Randwick Racecourse, Sydney (17 Apr.)

F Statistics, Social Change, the Environment

Estimated population: NSW, 62,112 (census, 2 Sept: 60,794); Tas., 34,328; WA, 1,655.

A total of 53,038 lashes given in 1,149 floggings; 247 convicts in NSW receive 9,909 lashes between them.

Police Act prohibits bathing in Sydney Cove and Darling Harbour between 6 a.m. and 8 p.m. as well as the flying of kites and the beating of carpets in the streets.

G Births and Deaths

May 7   Watkin Tench d. (74?).

Jul   –   William Redfern d. (59?).

Oct 19   Adam Lindsay Gordon b. (–1870).

1834

Jan 10   John Lhotsky leaves Sydney to explore the Monaro district and the Australian Alps (to 12 Mar.). (Names the Snowy River, 27 Jan.)

13   Convicts evacuating Macquarie Harbour seize the brig *Frederick* and sail it to Chile.

14   Convict servants Sarah McGregor and Mary Maloney kill their tyrannical employer in the Illawarra district. (Their death sentences are commuted to three years' imprisonment following public sympathy.)

15   Insurrection on Norfolk Is; nine convicts shot dead. (Thirteen others executed, 22–25 Sept.)

Feb 8   Gov. Arthur informs the Colonial Office that he has set up a separate establishment at Port Arthur, Tas., for boy convicts, which he names Point Puer.

Apr 4   Australian Union Benefit Society formed in Sydney.

–   First land sale at Albany, WA.

May 5   NSW Temperance Society holds its first meeting in Sydney (Francis Forbes chairman).

Jun 19   Gov. Stirling returns to WA. (Arrives at Perth, 19 Aug.)

Aug 1   Passenger coach service begins between Sydney and Bathurst.

5   Forbes Act passed in NSW, limiting and defining the rate of interest recoverable on borrowed money.

15 Act for the establishment of the province of South Australia receives royal assent; land to be sold to finance migration; board of commissioners to be appointed.

Barque *Charles Eaton* wrecked on the Barrier Reef. (Four men make their way in a boat to Amboina; natives murder remaining 27 except for the ship's boy, John Ireland, and a passenger's two-year-old child, William D'Oyley, whom they keep.)

17 Five of the "Tolpuddle Martyrs"—James Loveless, Thomas and John Standfield, James Hammett, and James Brine—arrive in Sydney after being sentenced to seven years' transportation for conspiring to raise wages "by administering unlawful oaths".

25 Barque *Edward Lombe* wrecked on Middle Head when entering Sydney Harbour; 12 lives lost, 17 saved.

Sep 4 George Loveless, the sixth of the Tolpuddle Martyrs, arrives at Hobart.
  7 Robert Wardell shot dead by one of three runaway convicts he encountered on his land near Cooks River, Sydney.

Oct 28 "Battle of Pinjarra", WA—an armed party of police, soldiers, and civilians led by Gov. Stirling clash with a band of Aborigines; at least 14 Aborigines killed; police superintendent dies from spear wounds.

Nov 1 Commercial Banking Company of Sydney opens for business.
  19 Edward Henty and party in the schooner *Thistle* arrive at Portland Bay to establish an agricultural settlement.
  28 Wollongong, NSW, notified as a town site. (Laid out by T. L. Mitchell in July.)

Dec 11 Blacktrackers (Migo and Mollydobbin) used for the first time in WA, to find a lost boy in bush near Fremantle.
  – First wool exported from WA—3,440 kg to UK.

A Architecture, Building
John Lee Archer, St John's Church, New Town, Tas. (–1835).
Peter Degraves, Theatre Royal, Hobart (–1837).
Edward Hallen, Lindesay, Sydney.
David Lennox, Lansdowne Bridge, NSW (–1836).
Throsby Park, Moss Vale, NSW.

B Science, Technology, Discovery, etc.

C Arts and Entertainment
Eliza Winstanley makes her debut in Henry Bishop's *Clari, or the Maid of Milan* at the Theatre Royal, Sydney (31 Oct.).
John Phillip Deane presents concerts and plays at the Argyle Rooms (later the Argyle Theatre), Hobart.

D Books and Writing
John Dunmore Lang, *An Historical and Statistical Account of New South Wales.*
L. E. Threlkeld, *An Australian Grammar . . . of the Language as Spoken by the Aborigines . . . of Hunter's River.*

E Sport and Recreation

F Statistics, Social Change, the Environment
Estimated population: NSW, 66,068; Tas., 37,688; WA, 1,800.

G Births and Deaths
Jan 5 William Wills b. (–1861).
Apr 11 John Macarthur d. (66).
Oct 12 George Dibbs b. (–1904).

1835

Jan 1 J. D. Lang's *Colonist* newspaper begins publication in Sydney.

19 Sydney College opens, with W. T. Cape as headmaster.

– Almost all the remaining Tasmanian Aborigines surrender to G. A. Robinson and are placed on Flinders Is.

Feb 8 Board of Commissioners for SA appointed, with Col. Robert Torrens as chairman. (Gazetted, 5 May.)

Mar 9 T. L. Mitchell and party leave Parramatta on an expedition down the Bogan and Darling rivers.

Apr 12 Convict ship *George III* wrecked in D'Entrecasteaux Channel; 133 lives lost.

May 12 John Batman in the *Rebecca* sails from Launceston for Port Phillip to acquire land for the nascent Port Phillip Association.

14 Convict ship *Neva* wrecked off King Is. with the loss of 225 lives; 22 survive.

25 Mitchell reaches the junction of the Bogan and Darling rivers and (29th) completes the building of a stockade he names Fort Bourke.

28 John Hindmarsh appointed Governor of SA.

29 Australian Patriotic Association formed in Sydney to obtain representative government for NSW (Sir John Jamison president, W. C. Wentworth vice-president).
Batman arrives at Port Phillip and (6 June) makes a treaty with the Aborigines to acquire 242,800 hectares of land near the site of Melbourne. (Leaves party at Indented Head and returns to Launceston.)

Jul 6 William Buckley, after living with the Aborigines for almost 32 years, meets Batman's party at Indented Head, Port Phillip.

9 Mitchell reaches the site of Menindee but turns back before reaching the Murray owing to the hostility of the natives.

17 Emigrant ship *Enchantress* wrecked in D'Entrecasteaux Channel, with the loss of 16 lives.

21 J. P. Fawkner and a party in the *Enterprise* leave Launceston to investigate the mainland for the purposes of settlement. (Fawkner, sick, is left at George Town.)

Aug 8 *Enterprise* at Westernport (to 16th).

26 Gov. Bourke declares Batman's treaty invalid and the settlers at Port Phillip to be trespassers.

29 *Enterprise* sails up the Yarra River and anchors at the site of Melbourne (an advance party having pitched tents there on 23 Aug.).

Sep 13 John Bede Polding, first bishop of the Catholic Church in Australia (consecrated 29 June 1834) arrives in Sydney.

Oct 5 Tooth's Kent Brewery established in Sydney by John Tooth and Charles Newnham.

16 Fawkner and family, with cattle, arrive at the Yarra camp in the *Enterprise*. (Fawkner subsequently opens a store and a hotel.)

28 Regulations issued for the "bounty system" of emigration-settlers introducing labourers to be paid a per capita bounty equal to the cost of the passage.

Nov 9 Batman and party land with 500 sheep and 20 cattle at site of Williamstown.

26 Foundation stone laid for first Baptist church in Australia, in Bathurst Street, Sydney. (Opens 23 Sept. 1836.)

1835

Dec 14 Bank of Australasia opens in Sydney.

* George Wyndham produces wine from his Dalwood estate in the Hunter Valley.

A Architecture, Building
John Lee Archer, Parliament House, Hobart (–1840).
Mortimer Lewis, Berrima courthouse, NSW (–1838).
John Verge, Elizabeth Bay House, Sydney (–1838).

B Science, Technology, Discovery, etc.
Publication of the Parramatta Catalogue of 7,385 stars observed by Gov. Brisbane's observatory in 1825.

C Arts and Entertainment
Artist Conrad Martens arrives in Sydney (17 Apr.).
First performance of a self-contained ballet in Australia—*The Fair Maid of Perth*, at the Theatre Royal, Sydney.
E. H. Thomas, *The Bandit of the Rhine* (first Australian play published as a book).

D Books and Writing
Henry Melville, *The History of the Island of Van Diemen's Land*.

E Sport and Recreation

F Statistics, Social Change, the Environment
Estimated population: NSW, 71,304; Tas., 40,172; WA, 1,878.
Stocks and pillories "with comfortable accommodation for five couples" erected at the corner of Bathurst Street, Sydney.

G Births and Deaths
May 17 Thomas McIlwraith b. (–1900).
Jun 17 James Brunton Stephens b. (–1902)
Jul 20 Ernest Giles b. (–1897).

1836

Jan 12 HMS *Beagle*, carrying Charles Darwin, at Sydney (to 30th).
22 South Australian Company constituted; George Fife Angas chairman.
– Land sales at Singleton, NSW (beginnings of town).

Feb 14 William Grant Broughton consecrated as bishop of the newly created Anglican diocese of Australia. (Enthroned in Sydney on 5 June.)
24 Independent Order of Odd Fellows formed in Sydney.
– Australian Gas Light Co. issues its first prospectus. (Company formed 7 Sept. 1837.)

Mar 10 Free pardons ordered for the Tolpuddle Martyrs. (Reach Sydney in June.)
15 T. L. Mitchell leaves a site near Orange on an expedition to check Sturt's findings on the junction of the Murray and Darling rivers.
16 Wooden-railed tramway, with trucks hauled by convicts, completed between Port Arthur and Norfolk Bay, Tas.

Apr 13 Gov. Bourke sends opposing petitions from "exclusives" and "emancipists" to the Colonial Office.
20 John Batman and family arrive at Port Phillip and occupy Batman Hill.

May 21 Brig *Stirling Castle* wrecked on Swain Reefs; Capt. James Fraser, his wife,

1836

Eliza, and crew take to the boats and eventually reach Great Sandy (now Fraser) Is.

27 Mitchell's party ambush about 180 Aborigines on the Murray near present-day Euston, killing eight and wounding many others.

31 Mitchell examines the junction of the Murray and Darling (to 2 June).

Jun **1** First public meeting at Port Phillip requests a resident magistrate.

   13 Mitchell crosses the Murray near its junction with the Murrumbidgee, follows its southern bank to the site of Swan Hill (20th) and Cohuna (25th), then strikes south through "Australia Felix".

   18 First number of the *South Australian Gazette* published in London.

Boy survivors of the *Charles Eaton* wreck in 1834 found on Murray Is.

   28 Snow falls in Sydney.

   29 St Mary's Cathedral, Sydney, consecrated by Bishop Polding.

Jul **11** Thomas Petty opens Petty's Hotel in York Steet, Sydney.

   27 First SA settlers arrive at Kangaroo Is. with the South Australian Co.'s whaling expedition.

   29 Church Act places all religious bodies on an equal footing and provides for state aid to principal Christian denominations in NSW.

   31 Mitchell reaches the Glenelg River, and then follows it to the sea.

Aug **3** Bishop Broughton at a meeting of Protestants attacks Bourke's proposal for a national system of education favouring no Church.

   11 Rescue party, including "wild white man" John Graham, leave Moreton Bay to look for survivors of the *Stirling Castle*; Graham finds two ship boys (13th) and the second mate (15th) and rescues Mrs Fraser (Capt. Fraser having died) from Aborigines (17th).

   20 Col. William Light, Surveyor-General of SA, arrives at Kangaroo Is. to choose a site for the SA settlement.

   29 Mitchell arrives at Portland Bay and finds the Hentys there.

Sep **9** Port Phillip district declared open for settlement.

   29 Capt. William Lonsdale arrives at Port Phillip as police magistrate.

   30 Mitchell climbs Mt Macedon and sees Port Phillip.

Oct **1** Gov. Bourke grants squatters grazing rights beyond the "Limits of Location" subject to payment of a £10 licence fee (to operate from 1 Jan. 1837).

   5 Mitchell discovers and names the Campaspe River, reaches the Goulburn River (8th) and Ovens River (15th). (Returns to Sydney 3 Nov.)

   – John Gardiner, Joseph Hawdon, and John Hepburn set out from the Murrumbidgee with the first stock to be overlanded to Port Phillip (arr. Dec.).

Nov **6** Torrens River discovered by G. S. Kingston and named by Light.

Dec **28** Gov. Hindmarsh arrives at Holdfast Bay in HMS *Buffalo*, with Resident Commissioner J. H. Fisher, and proclaims the province of SA.

   31 Light confirms his choice of site of Adelaide, despite Hindmarsh's objections.

   * "Mahogany Ship", an ancient wreck of unknown origin, discovered by shipwrecked sealers in "The Hummocks"—sand dunes in the Port Fairy–Warrnambool district. (Last seen in 1880.)

A Architecture, Building

David Lennox, Lennox Bridge, Parramatta (–1839).
Mortimer Lewis, Darlinghurst Courthouse, Sydney.
Henry Reveley, Old Courthouse, Perth (–1837).

B Science, Technology, Discovery, etc.

Charles Darwin makes geological and botanical observations in Australia.
First recorded meeting of Australian Museum committee in Sydney (June).

C Arts and Entertainment

John Glover, *The Last Muster of Tasmanian Aborigines at Risdon* (painting).
Irish musician W. V. Wallace and his brother and sister arrive in Sydney.
J. P. Deane comes to Sydney from Hobart and sets up a music school.

D Books and Writing

E Sport and Recreation

F Statistics, Social Change, the Environment

Estimated population: NSW, 78,929 (census, 2 Sept: 77,096, incl. 27,831 convicts;
Port Phillip District, Nov. census: 364); Tas., 43,689; WA, 1,956; SA, 546.
Supreme Court of NSW rules that Aborigines within the colony are subject to
the colony's laws.

G Births and Deaths

Jan 14 William Saumarez Smith b. (–1909).
Mar 19 David Scott Mitchell b. (–1907).
Aug 27 W. C. Piguenit b. (–1914).
—   –   William Dawes d. (74?).

1837

Jan 2 Edward Deas Thomson succeeds Alexander Macleay as Colonial Secretary
of NSW.

5 Sir John Franklin arrives in Hobart to take up his appointment as Governor
of Tas. (Sworn in on 6th.)

11 Col. William Light surveys and lays out Adelaide (to 10 Mar.)

Feb 26 Migrant ship *Lady McNaghten* arrives at Port Jackson, 44 children having
died of measles and whooping cough and 10 adults from typhus on the way;
a further 80 arrivals subsequently die.

Mar 1 Gov. Bourke visits the Port Phillip settlement and (8th) approves Robert
Hoddle's plan of a town, which he names Melbourne.

2 Charles Bonney leaves C. H. Ebden's station on the Murray for the Goulburn
River with 9,000 sheep, the first to be overlanded.

4 Yass, NSW, gazetted as a town. (First land sale 12 July.)

27 First land sales held in Adelaide (holders of preliminary land orders having
made their selection on 23 Mar.).

Apr 7 House of Commons select committee appointed to inquire into transportation.

21 Sir John Jeffcott arrives in Adelaide to become first Chief Justice of the
Supreme Court.

– Fremantle Whaling Co. begins operations.

May 20 Prison reformer Alexander Maconochie submits to Franklin a new system
for the treatment of convicts.

Jun 1 First sale of town allotments in Melbourne and Williamstown.
Bank of Western Australia opens for business in Perth.

3 *South Australian Gazette and Colonial Register* begins publication in Adelaide.

– Busby's bore completed and begins providing Sydney's water supply.

1837

- – Busselton, WA, declared a town site, and first land sold.
- **Jul** 3 Gov. Bourke's resignation accepted by the Colonial Office.
- **Aug** 21 Gov. Hindmarsh suspends Robert Gouger as Colonial Secretary of SA following a street fight between Gouger and Treasurer Gilles.
- **Sep** 5 Scone, NSW, gazetted as a village.
- **Oct** 2 WA Governor Sir James Stirling submits his resignation.
  - 8 News reaches Sydney of the death of King William IV and the accession to the throne of Queen Victoria.
  - 27 Police station and gaol erected in Bourke Street West, Melbourne.
- **Nov** 15 *Beagle* (Commander J. C. Wickham) arrives at Fremantle to begin a 5½-year survey, mainly in Torres Strait and Bass Strait.
- **Dec** 2 Lt George Grey and a small party arrive at Hanover Bay, WA, to begin an exploratory journey.
  - 5 Bourke leaves Sydney to return to England. (Lt-Col. Kenneth Snodgrass becomes administrator.)
  - 11 Dr J. D. Lang separates from the Church of Scotland Presbytery of NSW and forms a separate Church court known as the Synod of NSW.
  - 30 Overland mail service by coach and packhorse begins between Sydney and Melbourne.

  - * St Mary's Seminary, Australia's first Catholic secondary school for boys, established in Bishop Polding's residence in Woolloomooloo, Sydney.
  - * J. B. Hack plants the first grape vines in SA.

A Architecture, Building

Edward Blore, Government House, Sydney (–1845).
Foundation stone relaid and work begins on St Andrew's Cathedral, Sydney. (Completed by Edmund Blacket 1846–74.)
Semi-circular quay built at Sydney Cove (–1844).
John Lee Archer, Treasury Building, Hobart (–1842).

B Science, Technology, Discovery, etc.

Tasmanian Natural History Society formed (Nov.)

C Arts and Entertainment

Royal Victorian Theatre (subsequently the Theatre Royal), Hobart, opens (6 Mar.).
W. V. Wallace and members of the Deane family form a chamber music ensemble in Sydney.

D Books and Writing

James Macarthur, *New South Wales: Its Present State and Future Prospects*.
James Mudie, *The Felonry of New South Wales*.

E Sport and Recreation

F Statistics, Social Change, the Environment

Estimated population: NSW, 86,482; Tas., 42,698; WA, 2,035; SA, 3,273.
Between 1830 and 1837, 42,000 convicts received 1.8 million lashes.

G Births and Deaths

Feb – Ben Hall b. (–1865).
Mar 15 William Cox d. (72).
Sep 5 James Ruse d. (77?).
Sep 26 Francis Greenway buried (59).
Oct 2 Barnett Levey d. (39).

1838

Jan 1 J. P. Fawkner's *Melbourne Advertiser* begins publication (first copies hand-written; suppressed after 17 issues for being unlicensed).

12 Mudgee, NSW, gazetted as a village.

31 G. A. Robinson appointed Chief Protector of Aborigines, with headquarters at Port Phillip.

Feb 23 Sir George Gipps arrives in Sydney and next day takes up his duties as Governor of NSW.

26 Fitzroy River, WA, discovered by the *Beagle*.

Mar 2 George Grey discovers the Glenelg River, WA.

25 Site of Geelong determined by Robert Hoddle. (Proclaimed town site, 26 Oct; first land sales, Feb. 1839.)

30 Party of Lutheran missionaries arrive at Moreton Bay—the first free settlers there—and establish a mission at Nundah.

Apr 3 Joseph Hawdon, accompanied by Charles Bonney, arrives at Adelaide with cattle overlanded from Howlong, NSW, having discovered and named Lake Victoria and Lake Bonney on the way.

11 Aborigines attack a party of men and cattle belonging to George and William Faithfull near present-day Benalla; at least eight whites killed.

Jun 9 Station hands on Henry Dangar's Myall Creek station near present-day Inverell, NSW, massacre 28 Aborigines.

22 William Light resigns as Surveyor-General of SA after being refused additional staff and being ordered to use an inexact method of survey.

Jul 12 E. J. Eyre arrives at Adelaide with a herd of cattle overlanded from Sydney by way of the Port Phillip district.

14 Gov. Hindmarsh leaves Adelaide, having been recalled.

Aug 3 Final report of the select committee on transportation criticizes all forms of transportation and condemns assignment.

28 Charles Sturt and party arrive at Adelaide with a mob of 300 cattle overlanded from NSW.

Oct 10 Site of Gundagai gazetted. (First land sales, 2 Dec. 1842.)

12 Lt-Col. George Gawler arrives in Adelaide and (17th) is sworn in as Governor of SA, also replacing Fisher as Resident Commissioner.

19 Public market opened in Sydney.

26 Capt. Sir J. Gordon Bremer in HMS *Alligator*, together with Lt Owen Stanley in the *Britomart*, arrives at Port Essington to establish a new settlement there (named Victoria).

27 *Port Phillip Gazette* begins publication.

Nov 18 Some 200 German migrants under the guidance of Lutheran pastor Augustus Kavel arrive at Adelaide in the *Prince George*.

29 Seven of the men involved in the Myall Creek massacre, previously tried and acquitted on a technicality, are charged again and found guilty. (Sentenced to death, 5 Dec; hanged, 18 Dec.)

Dec 31 William Ullathorne returns to Sydney with a group of priests, students, and teachers, as well as five Sisters of Charity, the first nuns in Australia, and the first two trained nurses.

* David Jones opens a retail store in Sydney.

1838

* John Reynell establishes Reynella farm south of Adelaide, SA. (Plants first vineyard in 1841.)
* Commercial vineyard established by William Ryrie at Yarra Glen, Vic.
* Drought in NSW and WA.

A Architecture, Building
Trinity Church, Adelaide.

B Science, Technology, Discovery, etc.
Sydney Botanic Gardens opened to the public.

Ornithologist John Gould and his family, with field assistant John Gilbert, arrive in Hobart (18 Sept.).

Natural History Society of SA founded in Adelaide.

Prepaid stamped letter sheet—the first in the world—introduced by PMG James Raymond for the Sydney delivery area (1 Nov.).

C Arts and Entertainment
Augustus Earle, *A Bivouac of Travellers in Australia in a Cabbage Tree Forest, Day Break,* exhibited at the Royal Academy, London.

Conrad Martens, *Elizabeth Bay and Elizabeth Bay House* (watercolour).

Aboriginal wandjina paintings discovered by George Grey in a cave near the Glenelg River, WA.

Music festival held in St Mary's Cathedral, Sydney (31 Jan.).

Barnett Levey's Theatre Royal, Sydney, closes down (22 Mar.), and Joseph Wyatt's Royal Victoria Theatre opens (26 Mar.).

Adelaide's first playhouse, the Theatre Royal, opens with the play *The Mountaineers, or Love and Madness*, and the farce *The Lancers*.

D Books and Writing
Anna Maria Bunn, *The Guardian* (first novel printed and published on the Australian mainland).

James Maclehose, *Picture of Sydney.*

James Martin, *The Australian Sketch Book.*

T. L. Mitchell, *Three Expeditions into the Interior of Eastern Australia.*

E Sport and Recreation
Melbourne Cricket Club founded (15 Nov.).

First race meetings held in Adelaide (1 Jan.) and Melbourne (6 Mar.).

F Statistics, Social Change, the Environment
Estimated population: NSW, 98,176; Tas., 45,764; WA, 1,928, SA, 6,000.

Assigned convict's entitlements: 5.5 kg wheat, 3.2 kg mutton or beef or 2 kg salt pork, 57 g salt, and 57 g soap per week; and two jackets, three shirts, two pairs of trousers, three pairs of shoes, and a hat or cap each year.

Asylum opened (29 Nov.) at Tarban Creek, Sydney (later part of Gladesville Mental Hospital).

G Births and Deaths
May 12   Samuel Marsden d. (73).
Sep 18   Robert Knopwood d. (75).
Dec 10   Augustus Earle d. (45).

1839

Jan   1   Assignment of male convicts for service in town ends.

3 John Hutt replaces Sir James Stirling as Governor of WA. (Stirling leaves for UK on 4 Jan.).

15 First US consul in Sydney, J. H. Williams, takes up office.

17 Minimum price for Crown land in NSW increased from five to twelve shillings an acre.

Feb 6 J. P. Fawkner launches the *Port Phillip Patriot* and *Melbourne Advertiser*.

16 Kiama, NSW, proclaimed a town.

25 George Grey leads an expedition from Shark Bay to Perth (to Apr.).

Mar 19 Settlement begins at Port Lincoln, SA.

22 Legislation passed requiring squatters in NSW to pay a variable tax on the number of stock grazed as well as the £10 annual licence fee.

31 Joseph Forbes ("Timor Joe") rescued by the schooner *Essington* from Timorlaut Is., where he had been held captive for 14 years.

Apr 3 Charles Sturt replaces William Light as Surveyor-General of SA.

6 French corvettes *Astrolabe* and *Zélée*, commanded by Commodore Dumont d'Urville, at Port Essington (to 9th).

13 Albury gazetted as a village. (First land sales, 10 Oct.)

24 Braidwood gazetted as a town. (First land sale, 9 July 1840.)

May 1 E. J. Eyre explores to the north of Adelaide (to 25 June) and discovers Lake Torrens. (Returns, 29 June.)

20 Moreton Bay penal settlement closes down.

Angus McMillan begins his first exploration of Gippsland. (Reaches site of Omeo, 11 June.)

– Drought in NSW ends.

Jun 15 Boundaries of NSW extended to include "such portions of New Zealand as the Crown might acquire".

20 R. W. Newland and party begin a settlement at Victor Harbour, SA.

Jul 27 Adelaide River, NT, discovered by L. R. Fitzmaurice of the *Beagle*.

Aug 1 Hunter River Steam Navigation Co. formed.

5 Eyre leaves Port Lincoln to explore Eyre Peninsula. (Reaches Streaky Bay and returns to the head of Spencer Gulf.)

Sep 9 Lt J. L. Stokes of the *Beagle* examines and names Port Darwin.

20 Military juries abolished in NSW.

30 C. J. La Trobe arrives at Port Phillip to take up his post as Superintendent of the Port Phillip district.

Oct 16 J. C. Wickham of the *Beagle* discovers the Victoria River, NT.

27 First shipload of assisted immigrants (mainly Scots) arrive at Port Phillip in the *David Clark*.

Nov 24 Cyclone hits Port Essington; HMS *Pelorus* wrecked; 12 lives lost.

28 SA Agricultural Society formed.

29 Two frigates of a US scientific expedition commanded by Capt. Charles Wilkes enter Port Jackson at night and anchor in Sydney Cove, causing near panic when discovered next morning. (Incident leads to construction of Fort Denison.)

Dec – Floods on the Yarra and Saltwater rivers, Victoria.

* Drought in SA.

1839

A Architecture, Building
Robert Russell, St James' Church (Old Cathedral), Melbourne (opened 1842; completed 1851; moved to present site 1913).

G. S. Kingston, Government House, Adelaide (–1840; central portion erected 1855; additions 1863–78).

All Saints Church, Upper Swan, the oldest standing church in WA (–1841).

Berrima Gaol (NSW) completed.

B Science, Technology, Discovery, etc.

C Arts and Entertainment
First theatrical performance in WA—the play *Love à la Militaire* in Perth (9 July).

Marines from HMS *Britomart* at Port Essington stage the first theatrical performance in NT—the play *Cheap Living* (24 Aug.).

Samson Cameron's Royal Victoria Theatre opens in Adelaide (27 Nov.).

D Books and Writing
George Grey, *Vocabulary of the Aboriginal Language of Western Australia*.

Alexander Maconochie, *Thoughts on Convict Management*.

E Sport and Recreation

F Statistics, Social Change, the Environment
Estimated population: NSW, 113,437; Tas., 44,033; WA, 2,154; SA, 10,315.

Registration of births, deaths, and marriages begins in Tas. (WA in 1841, SA in 1842, Vic. in 1853, NSW [incl. Qld] in 1856).

G Births and Deaths
Mar 14   George Adams b. (–1904).
Apr 18   Henry Kendall b. (–1882).
May 6   John Batman d. (38).
Jun 27   Allan Cunningham d. (47).
Oct 6   William Light d. (54?).
—   –   George Rignold b. (–1912).

1840

Jan 3   *Port Phillip Herald* (later the Melbourne *Herald*) first published.
11   Angus McMillan and party set out from the Tambo River to explore into Gippsland.
16   McMillan discovers Lake Victoria (Lake King), the Nicholson River (17th), the Mitchell (18th), and the Avon and Macalister rivers (22nd).
19   William Hobson leaves Sydney to become Lt-Governor of NZ.

Feb 2   P. E. de Strzelecki and James Macarthur begin an exploratory journey to Port Phillip (alt. date 2 Mar.).
6   Hobson signs the Treaty of Waitangi with Maori chiefs.
15   Strzelecki climbs and names Mount Kosciuszko (alt. date 12 Mar.).
26   HMS *Buffalo* arrives at Port Jackson with 58 French-Canadian political exiles (others disembarked at Hobart) to be interned near present-day Concord (hence Canada Bay, French Bay, Exile Bay).

Mar 2   Patrick Leslie overlands sheep from New England to the Darling Downs (to 4 June), the first overlanding of stock from NSW to the Moreton Bay district.
6   Alexander Maconochie becomes superintendent at Norfolk Is.
18   Royal Hotel and theatre, Sydney, destroyed by fire.

May 5 Public meeting in Melbourne to petition for separation from NSW.

12 Strzelecki and party reach Westernport. (Arrive Melbourne 28 May.)

21 Hobson proclaims British sovereignty over all of NZ.

22 Transportation of convicts to NSW abolished by order in council (effective from 1 Aug.).

31 Surveyor G. C. Stapylton and assistant killed by Aborigines near the McPherson Range, Queensland.

Jun 18 E. J. Eyre and party leave Adelaide to explore to the north.

– Brigantine *Maria* wrecked on the Coorong, SA; 27 passengers and crew killed by Aborigines. (Two natives hanged in reprisal, 25 Aug.).

Aug 4 Runaway convict John Storry Baker ("Booralsha") gives himself up at Moreton Bay after living with Aborigines for 14 years.

14 Eyre discovers Lake Eyre (thinking it to be part of Lake Torrens).

19 Adelaide incorporated as Australia's first municipality.

– Tailors in Sydney and carpenters in Melbourne strike for higher wages.

Sep 2 Eyre reaches Mt Hopeless, then turns back towards the coast.

28 Mass meeting of workers in Sydney protests against amendments to the Masters and Servants Act which make conspiring to increase wages or improve conditions illegal. (Legislation passed, 20 Oct.)

Oct 1 *Sydney Herald* begins daily publication.

5 NSW's two Presbyterian synods unite to form the Synod of Australia.

14 Road from Adelaide to Port Adelaide completed.

15 First sale of land at Portland.

31 Adelaide municipal election held (Australia's first political election); J. H. Fisher elected mayor.

Nov 17 Eyre sets up base at Fowler's Bay.

18 *Eden*, the last convict transport to unload in Sydney, arrives with 267 male convicts.

21 *Geelong Advertiser* established by J. P. Fawkner.

Dec 23 Bushranger Edward Davis ("Teddy the Jewboy") and five of his gang captured and sentenced to death. (Hanged 16 Mar. 1841.)

A Architecture, Building

Holy Trinity Church (the Garrison Church) Miller's Point, Sydney (–1843).

Christ Church St Laurence, Sydney (consecrated 10 Sept. 1845; spire, by Edmund Blacket, added in 1856).

Causeway over the Swan River near Perth (–1843).

B Science, Technology, Discovery, etc.

Meteorological records begin in Sydney, Port Macquarie, and Melbourne.

C Arts and Entertainment

D Books and Writing

John Gould, *The Birds of Australia* (–1848).

E Sport and Recreation

First race meeting held at Flemington, Port Phillip district (3 Mar.).

F Statistics, Social Change, the Environment

Estimated population: NSW, 127,468; Tas., 45,999; WA, 2,311; SA, 14,630.

Total number of convicts transported to NSW and Van Diemen's Land between 1788 and 1840: 111,500 (16,000 of whom were women).

1840

Two compositors sentenced (in Feb.) to two months on the treadmill for absenting themselves from work on a Saturday.

Camels first introduced (a pair landed at Hobart on 10 Dec.)

Bathurst burr introduced into NSW during the 1840s (possibly from the tails of horses imported from Chile). '

G Births and Deaths

Jan 29   Simeon Lord d. (69?).

1841

Jan 3   Sydney–Melbourne steamer *Clonmel*, on its second voyage, is wrecked near Corner Inlet, Vic.

17   Brisbane River in high flood.

Feb 8   John Fairfax and Charles Kemp buy the *Sydney Herald*.

9   Angus McMillan makes an expedition to Port Albert, near Corner Inlet (to 14th).

25   E. J. Eyre, with John Baxter and three Aborigines, leaves Fowler's Bay to attempt a crossing of the Great Australian Bight.

–   Bunbury, WA, surveyed as town site. (First land sales in June.)

Mar 18   *Parkfield* arrives at Leschenault Inlet, WA, with the first settlers for the Australind colony.

–   John Lort Stokes replaces J. C. Wickham as commander of the *Beagle*.

Apr 6   Hunter River SN Co.'s first vessel, the iron paddle-steamer *Rose*, arrives in Port Jackson from the UK.

12   First sitting of the Supreme Court in Melbourne.

29   Two of Eyre's Aborigines murder Baxter, steal much of the stores and run away; Eyre and Wylie continue their journey westward.

–   Rev. W. B. Clarke discovers gold near Hassan's Walls in the Hartley Valley, NSW.

May 3   New Zealand proclaimed a colony independent of NSW from 1 July.

15   Capt. George Grey replaces George Gawler as Governor of SA.

24   Gas lighting in Sydney (the first gas lighting scheme in Australia) turned on during celebrations for Queen Victoria's birthday.

Jun 2   Eyre and Wylie receive succour from the French whaler *Mississippi* (Capt. Rossiter) at Thistle Cove, near Esperance.

20   First land sales at Jervis Bay.

Jul 1   Assignment of convict labour to private employers abolished in NSW. Bounty system of assisted migration suspended.

7   Eyre and Wylie reach Albany.

28   J. L. Stokes, surveying the Gulf of Carpentaria in the *Beagle*, discovers the Flinders River and the Albert River (1 Aug.) and names a nearby fertile area the Plains of Promise.

Aug 27   Police and volunteers kill about 50 Aborigines in an encounter near the Rufus River, south-western NSW.

Sep 1   Savings Bank of Port Phillip established.

Oct 6   Five Tasmanian Aborigines (Truganini among them), absconders from G. A. Robinson's Port Phillip establishment, kill two whalers near Westernport. (Arrested 20 Oct.)

18 Hunter River SN Co.'s *Shamrock* begins service between Sydney, Melbourne, and Launceston.

Sheriff of NSW Supreme Court suicides over money difficulties.

Dec 11 *Hunter River Gazette*, the first mainland country newspaper, begins publication in Maitland.

– Caroline Chisholm establishes a Female Immigrants Home in Sydney.

– Registrar of NSW Supreme Court suspended following discovery of his embezzlement of large sums of money.

* Silver-lead deposits found at Glen Osmond, near Adelaide.

A Architecture, Building

George Barney, Victoria Barracks, Sydney (–1848).

John Bibb, Pitt Street Congregational Church, Sydney (–1846).

St John's Church, ACT (–1845).

Work begun on Fort Denison, Sydney Harbour, but abandoned until 1855.

B Science, Technology, Discovery, etc.

First known Australian photograph (a daguerreotype)—of Bridge and George Streets, Sydney—taken by a visiting Frenchman (reported in *Australian*, 15 May).

C Arts and Entertainment

English composer Isaac Nathan arrives in Sydney (6 Apr.) and becomes choirmaster at St Mary's Cathedral.

Pavilion (later the Royal Victoria Theatre) opens in Melbourne.

Queen's Theatre opens in Adelaide. (Closes Nov. 1842.)

D Books and Writing

[Lady Bremer? Charlotte Barton?], *A Mother's Offering to Her Children: By a Lady Long Resident in New South Wales*.

George Grey, *Journals of Two Expeditions of Discovery in North-West and Western Australia*.

E Sport and Recreation

Port Phillip Turf Club holds its first meeting (13 Apr.)

Australia's oldest classic horse race, the St Leger, is run for the first time (at Homebush Racecourse, Sydney).

Legislation prohibits sport, for profit or pleasure, on Sundays in NSW.

F Statistics, Social Change, the Environment

Estimated population: NSW, 145,303 (census, 2 Mar: 130,856 [87,298 males, 43,558 females], incl. 11,738 in the Port Phillip District); Tas., 57,420 (first official census, 27 Sept., 50,216); WA, 2,760; SA, 15,485.

Legislation passed in WA allowing Aborigines to give evidence. (Similar legislation passed in SA in 1844, Vic. in 1854, NSW in 1876, Qld in 1884.)

G Births and Deaths

Jan   20   Jorgen Jorgenson d. (60).

Aug 13?   Johnny Mullagh (Muarrinim) b. (–1891).

Nov   8   Sir Francis Forbes d. (57?).

1842

Jan 21   First public execution in Melbourne—the hanging of two male Tasmanian

1842

Aborigines involved in the murder of two whalers on 6 Oct. 1841. (Truganini and two other females acquitted.)

Feb 10 Gov. Gipps proclaims the Moreton Bay district open to free settlers.

24 Native police force of 25 Aborigines formed at Narre Warren, near Dandenong, under command of Henry Dana.

Mar 12 *Launceston Examiner, Commercial and Agricultural Adviser* first published (as a weekly; daily publication begins 21 Dec. 1877).

Apr 5 Australian Roman Catholic hierarchy established; John Bede Polding becomes Archbishop of Sydney and Metropolitan of Australia (9th).

19 Foundation stone laid for a permanent synagogue in Sydney. (Consecrated 2 Apr. 1844.)

May 4 German settlement established at Lobethal, SA.

7 Andrew Petrie, exploring to the north from Moreton Bay, finds David Bracewell ("Wandi") and (20th) James Davis ("Duramboi"), escaped convicts who lived with Wide Bay Aborigines for many years.

17 Petrie discovers the Mary River.

Jun 21 Convicts at Norfolk Is. attempt to escape in the brig *Governor Phillip*; six killed in fray and four later executed.

22 Imperial Waste Lands Act increases the minimum price of land in the colonies to £1 an acre, half the proceeds to be used to encourage migration.

Jul 14 First sale of Brisbane building allotments.

18 Benjamin Boyd arrives at Port Jackson in his yacht *Wanderer.* (Opens the Royal Bank in Sydney soon after.)

20 Sydney incorporated as a city.

30 Act for the Government of NSW and Van Diemen's Land introduces representative government for NSW, creating a Legislative Council of 36 members, 24 elected (franchise dependent on property and rent qualifications) and 12 nominated (6 chosen by Governor; 6 officials appointed by British government); district councils to be established.
SA becomes a Crown colony, losing its semi-independent status, with a nominated Legislative Council; self-government to be granted on population reaching 50,000.

Aug 1 *Sydney Herald* becomes the *Sydney Morning Herald.*

12 Melbourne officially incorporated as a town.

20 *Portland Guardian* (later *Portland Observer*) first published.

27 Boys from Parkhurst Prison, UK, arrive at Perth as migrants.

– Vehicular ferry begins across Sydney Harbour from Dawes Pt to Blues Pt.

Sep – W. C. Wentworth forms a Coolie Association to investigate uses of Asian labour.

Oct 15 HM Corvette *Fly* (Capt. F. P. Blackwood) and the cutter *Bramble* arrive at Port Jackson to begin a survey of the Barrier Reef and Torres Strait.

20 *Sydney Gazette* published for the last time.

Nov 1 Election held for Sydney's first municipal council—the first popular election in NSW. (John Hosking elected mayor, 9 Nov.)

Dec 1 Melbourne's first municipal council elected (Henry Condell elected mayor, 9 Dec.).

– George B. Goodman, Australia's first professional photographer, opens a studio in Sydney.

* Hunter River SN Co. begins a regular Sydney–Brisbane service.

1842

* Copper discovered at Kapunda, SA, by C. H. Bagot and Francis Dutton.
* Falling wool prices, higher cost of labour, and drought cause a slump.

A Architecture, Building
Edmund Blacket arrives in Sydney (3 Nov.)

B Science, Technology, Discovery, etc.
Tasmanian Journal of Natural Science, Australia's first scholarly scientific journal, first published.

C Arts and Entertainment
First statue erected in Australia—of Sir Richard Bourke, near the present State Library of NSW in Sydney—unveiled (11 Apr.)
Complete performance of Handel's *Messiah* presented for the first time at Sydney's Royal Victoria Theatre.
Sir Joseph Banks Hotel opens in Botany and becomes a favourite resort and pleasure gardens.

D Books and Writing
David Burn, *Plays and Fugitive Pieces in Verse.*
John Skinner Prout, *Sydney Illustrated* (–1844).

E Sport and Recreation
Australian Jockey Club founded (Jan.) and holds its first meeting at Homebush Racecourse (29 Sept.)

F Statistics, Social Change, the Environment
Estimated population: NSW, 162,317; Tas., 58,851; WA, 3,476; SA, 16,340.
Some 600 people in NSW declared bankrupt.
Tasmania receives 4,334 convicts during year.

G Births and Deaths
Jan 15 Mary MacKillop b. (–1909).
Feb 6 Henry Savery d. (50).

1843

Jan 7 *Maitland Mercury*, the oldest surviving provincial newspaper in NSW, first published.
17 J. C. Wickham arrives in Brisbane as police magistrate. (Appointed Government Resident on 1 Jan. 1853.)

Feb 1 Riots in Parramatta Female Factory; 80 arrested after military called in.
14 Foundation stone of the Australian Subscription Library's new building in Macquarie St, Sydney, laid by Alexander Macleay.
23 Old (nominated) Legislative Council of NSW meets for the last time.

Mar 1 Great Comet makes its appearance in southern skies.

Apr 1 Bank of Australia fails.

May 1 Rush on Sydney Savings Bank.

Jun 4 Sydney Banking Co. fails.
15 First election for the NSW Legislative Council begins. (Those elected include W. C. Wentworth, William Bland, Hannibal Macarthur, Charles Cowper, William Lawson, Alexander Macleay, Roger Therry, and J. D. Lang.)
17 Gov. Gipps orders the removal from office of Justice J. W. Willis, resident

1843

judge in the Port Phillip district, after powerful interests in Melbourne petition for his recall.

- Yass pastoralist Henry O'Brien begins boiling down sheep for their tallow, thus establishing a standard minimum value for sheep.

Jul 1 *Adelaide Observer* first published.
15 Assisted migration resumed by British government.
26 Maitland, NSW, proclaimed the first district council area.
- Consignment of horses shipped to India as cavalry remounts and polo ponies.

Aug 1 New Legislative Council meets for the first time (ceremonial opening by Gipps on 3 Aug.); Alexander Macleay elected Speaker; W. C. Wentworth becomes natural leader of the non-official majority.
21 Sir John Eardley-Wilmot arrives in Hobart to take office as Lt-Governor of Tas., Franklin having been recalled.
22 Bushranger Martin Cash caught in Hobart. (Given death sentence, later commuted; pardoned in 1853.)
- Unemployed mechanics and labourers, thrown out of work as a result of the economic crisis, given relief work on roads by NSW government.

Sep 3 Thomas Sutcliffe Mort establishes his wool-auctioning agency in Sydney.
5 Australian Mutual Protection Association formed in Sydney to ameliorate conditions of disadvantaged and unemployed.

Oct 10 SA Legislative Council (of seven nominees) meets for the first time.
11 First Ipswich (Qld) land sales.

Dec - Australind scheme collapses. (Land sales cease and surveyors discharged, 10th.)

* Benjamin Boyd takes up 259 hectares of land at Twofold Bay.
* H. J. Lindeman establishes the Cawarra vineyard on the Paterson River in the Hunter Valley, NSW.

A Architecture, Building

Argyle Cut, Sydney, begun, partly to provide filling for Circular Quay, still under construction.
Hero of Waterloo Hotel, Sydney (–1844).
Seahorse Hotel, Boydtown, NSW.
Present NSW Legislative Assembly chamber (designed by Mortimer Lewis) added to the north wing of the Rum Hospital.

B Science, Technology, Discovery, etc.

Botanical and Horticultural Society of Van Diemen's Land (later Royal Society of Tasmania) founded (14 Oct.).
John Ridley's wheat stripper successfully tested in Adelaide (14 Nov.).

C Arts and Entertainment

Charles Abrahams, marble bust of Sir Thomas Mitchell (first sculpture carved from Australian marble).
First Italian opera—*The Barber of Seville*—performed in Sydney (19 June).
George Coppin arrives in Sydney and performs with his wife in *The Stranger* at the Royal Victoria Theatre (18 Mar.).

D Books and Writing

Richard Hengist Horne, *Orion* (epic poem).

E Sport and Recreation

First horse-race meeting held in Brisbane (17 July).

Launceston Cricket Club formed.

F Statistics, Social Change, the Environment
Estimated population: NSW, 169,135; Tas., 60,664; WA, 3,853; SA, 17,196.
Register of unemployed set up in Sydney in Sept; 700 register in ten days.
More than 5,000 people leave NSW, mainly for Valparaiso, Chile.
Lunacy Act passed (12 Dec.), making it compulsory for certification to be carried out by two qualified medical practitioners.
Introduced blackberry bushes thrive in Tas.

G Births and Deaths
Sep 26 Joseph Furphy b. (–1912).
Dec   4 Harry Rickards b. (–1911).

1844

Jan 1 Crowd of unemployed threaten Gov. Gipps in Hyde Park, Sydney.

Feb 1 Regular monthly sea mail service begins between UK and Sydney.
       7 Maj. Joseph Childs arrives at Norfolk Is. to replace Alexander Maconochie as commandant.
      13 John Knatchbull hanged outside Darlinghurst Gaol for the murder of Ellen Jamieson on 6 Jan.

Mar 20 First sale of land at Seymour (Vic.).

Apr 2 Occupation regulations issued limiting area and stock-carrying capacity of squatters' runs and making it obligatory to hold a separate licence for each run.
          First permanent Hebrew synagogue opened in York Street, Sydney.
       9 Public meeting of pastoralists in Sydney protests against occupation regulations and forms the Pastoralist Association.

Jun 1 Squatters meet in Melbourne to protest against new land regulations.

Aug 13 Ludwig Leichhardt and party leave Sydney in the *Sovereign* for Moreton Bay to begin an overland expedition to the far north.
      15 Charles Sturt sets out from Adelaide to explore inland Australia and investigate the existence of an inland sea.
       – Smelting of copper begins in Adelaide.

Sep 29 Norfolk Is. annexed to Tas.

Oct 1 Leichhardt's party leave Jimbour station, on the Darling Downs, at the start of their expedition to Port Essington.
      10 Sturt's party reach the site of Menindee on the Darling River.

Nov 5 Leichhardt discovers and names the Dawson River.
      16 *Royal George* arrives in Port Phillip from London with 21 "exiles"— convicted criminals given conditional pardons on landing.
      28 Public meeting in Melbourne demands separation from NSW and appoints a representative to take a petition to England.

Dec 17 Public meeting of squatters in Melbourne supports the continued arrival of "exiles".
      28 Leichhardt discovers and names the Comet River.

       * Dr C. R. Penfold establishes a vineyard at Magill, SA, with cuttings from France and Spain.

1844

* South Australian Subscription Library formed.
* Ben Boyd establishes a whaling station at Twofold Bay.

A Architecture, Building

B Science, Technology, Discovery, etc.
Charles Sturt, exploring the Broken Range near the site of Broken Hill, gathers the desert pea that bears his name (23 Oct.).

C Arts and Entertainment
Convict Edward Geoghegan's musical play *The Currency Lass* and his melodrama *The Hibernian Father* performed at Sydney's Royal Victoria Theatre during May.
Isaac Nathan conducts the first concert of the Australian Philharmonic Society in Sydney.

D Books and Writing
Louisa Anne Meredith, *Notes and Sketches of New South Wales.*

E Sport and Recreation
Swimming baths opened on the south bank of the Yarra in Melbourne.
Bowling green established at Sandy Bay, Tas.

F Statistics, Social Change, the Environment
Estimated population: NSW, 178,460; Tas., 62,478; WA, 4,350; SA, 18,999 (first official census, 26 Feb: 17,366).

G Births and Deaths
Apr 6 W. J. Lyne b. (–1913).
Jun 29 Sir John Jamison d. (67?).
Nov 21 Ada Cambridge b. (–1926).

1845

Jan 4 Weekly newspaper *Bell's Life in Sydney* begins publication.
10 Ludwig Leichhardt discovers the Mackenzie River.
27 Charles Sturt's party reach Depot Glen (site of Milparinka), where they are forced to remain for six months owing to lack of rain.

Feb 13 Leichhardt discovers and names the Isaac River.

Mar 1 Hobart Savings Bank opens.

Apr 2 Leichhardt discovers and names the Burdekin River.
4 Cutter *America* wrecked in Torres Strait. (Sole survivor Barbara Thompson lives with Aborigines until rescued in 1849.)

May 19 Copper discovered at Burra Burra, SA.
23 Leichhardt reaches the Lynd River, his first encounter with a stream flowing into the Gulf of Carpentaria.
24 *Mary* wrecked off Flinders Is., Bass Strait, with the loss of 17 lives.

Jun 15 Leichhardt discovers the Mitchell River.
28 Aborigines attack Leichhardt's party, killing one man (John Gilbert) and wounding two others (John Roper and J. S. Calvert).

Jul 3 Sydney Infirmary and Dispensary reopened in the south wing of the Rum Hospital.

1845

5 Leichhardt reaches the Gulf of Carpentaria and (12th) discovers and names the Gilbert River.

14 Sturt divides his party, sending most back to Adelaide under James Poole (who dies on 16th); Sturt moves on to a new depot at Fort Grey (15th).

Aug 4 Emigrant ship *Cataraqui* wrecked off King Is; only 9 of the 415 aboard survive.

18 Sturt discovers and names Strzelecki Creek.

20 Leichhardt discovers and names the Nicholson River.
Sturt crosses Cooper's Creek, which he later names.

Sep 8 Sturt turns back after reaching Sturt's Stony Desert and retreats to his depot at Fort Grey (2 Oct.).

21 Leichhardt discovers and names the Macarthur River.

Oct 9 Sturt moves north again from Fort Grey.

19 Leichhardt names the Roper River (sighted by Roper on 17 Oct.).

21 Sturt again forced to turn back from the Stony Desert.

25 Maj. F. H. Robe replaces George Grey as Governor of SA. (Grey leaves for NZ to become Lt-Governor.)

31 "The patriotic six" unofficial members of Tasmania's Legislative Council walk out in protest over taxes to pay for police and judicial establishments.

Nov 14 Sir Thomas Mitchell leaves Sydney on his last expedition, to lead a party overland to Port Essington.

Dec 6 Sturt's party set off from Depot Glen to return to Adelaide; Sturt, too ill to ride, is carried on a dray.

17 Leichhardt's party reach Port Essington, after a journey of 14½ months. (They return to Sydney by sea, arriving 25 Mar. 1846.)

A Architecture, Building

All Saints Church (now the Anglican cathedral), Bathurst (–1848).

B Science, Technology, Discovery, etc.

Sizar Elliott of Sydney begins experimenting with large-scale preservation of food in tins.

Leichhardt discovers the barramundi in the Mackenzie River.

C Arts and Entertainment

First known exhibition of pictures in Australia held in Hobart (6 Jan.), organized by John Skinner Prout.

Carandini Opera Company performs in Sydney, Madame Carandini appearing in Auber's *The Fairy Lake* and in *Fra Diavolo*.

First civilian brass band in Australia formed at Launceston by the St Joseph's Total Abstinence Society.

Queen's Theatre Royal, Melbourne, opens (21 Apr.).

George Coppin opens Launceston's first regular theatre, the Royal Victoria.

D Books and Writing

E. J. Eyre, *Journals of Expeditions of Discovery into Central Australia and Overland from Adelaide to King George's Sound*.

P. E. de Strzelecki, *Physical Description of New South Wales and Van Diemen's Land*.

E Sport and Recreation

F Statistics, Social Change, the Environment

Estimated population: NSW, 187,918; Tas., 64,291; WA, 4,479; SA, 22,460.

1845

G Births and Deaths
    Feb 25   George Reid b. (–1918).
    Apr 3   William Farrer b. (–1906).
    Jun 21   Samuel Griffith b. (–1920).
    Aug 26   J. C. Williamson b. (–1913).
    Sep 16   Robert Logan Jack b. (–1921).

1846

Jan 19   Charles Sturt's party arrive back at Adelaide.
     21   Wellington, NSW, gazetted as a village.
     27   Lt-Col. Andrew Clarke succeeds John Hutt as Governor of WA.

Feb 16   Spanish Benedictine monks Dom Rosendo Salvado and Dom Joseph Serra leave Perth for the Victoria Plains to found an Aboriginal mission (New Norcia).

Mar 5   Lt-Gov. Robe imposes a royalty on minerals recovered in SA, which leads to a public outcry.
      8   Barque *Peruvian* wrecked on the Barrier Reef; sole survivor of the 22 on board, James Murrell, lives with the Aborigines for 17 years.
      –   *Orwell* arrives at Moreton Bay with 51 coolies from India to work for Robert Towns, Ben Boyd, and others.

Apr 30   Sir John Eardley-Wilmot dismissed as Governor of Tas., allegedly for not suppressing homosexuality among convicts.

May –   Convict transportation to Tas. suspended for two years.

Jun 1   Sir Thomas Mitchell makes a depot on the Maranoa River, from there making expeditions to the Warrego (28 June) and Belyando (20 July) rivers.
      2   *Argus* begins publication in Melbourne (published by William Kerr and named *Melbourne Argus* until 1852).
     20   Brisbane's first newspaper, the *Moreton Bay Courier* (later *Brisbane Courier* and then *Courier-Mail*) begins publication.
     29   Paddle-steamer *Experiment*, brought from Sydney, begins running on the Brisbane River between Brisbane and Ipswich.

Jul 1   Four guards killed during a riot on Norfolk Is; 12 convicts subsequently executed.
          Launceston Church Grammar School opens.
     11   Sir George Gipps leaves Sydney to return to UK; Lt-Gen. Sir Maurice O'Connell becomes acting Governor.
     12   Riot in Melbourne between Orangemen and Roman Catholic members of the Irish community; shots fired; martial law proclaimed for one night.
     21   Public meeting in Adelaide opposes state aid for religion proposed by Gov. Robe.

Aug 2   Sir Charles FitzRoy arrives in Sydney and next day takes up his appointment as Governor of NSW.
      3   Hutchins School opens in Hobart.
      6   John Price replaces Joseph Childs as commandant on Norfolk Is.
     18   Alexander Berry's ship *Coolangatta* wrecked on the coast south of Moreton Bay which now bears the ship's name.
     28   Sale of Waste Lands Act passed in UK, offering squatters long leases in unsettled districts and other privileges.

Sep 15 Mitchell discovers a river he thinks flows north-west to the Gulf, which he names the Victoria (later found to be the Barcoo).

24 Mitchell turns back and returns to Sydney (29 Dec.).

Oct 1 Christ's College, near Longford, Tas., opens.

10 Breakaway group of "Free Presbyterians" forms the Synod of Eastern Australia in Sydney.

22 First of several public meetings held in Sydney to protest against the proposed resumption of transportation to NSW.

Nov 18 Orange, NSW, proclaimed as a site for a village. (First land sales Dec. 1848.)

Dec 2 Ludwig Leichhardt sets out again from the Darling Downs, this time to cross to the west coast. (Returns unsuccessful on 31 July 1847.)

22 Anti-Transportation Committee founded at meeting in Sydney.

A Architecture, Building

Mortimer Lewis, Australian Museum, Sydney (north wing completed in 1849; additions carried out in 1861, 1892, and 1909).

Samuel Jackson, Melbourne Hospital (–1848).

David Lennox, Princes Bridge, Melbourne (–1850; demolished 1884).

Corrugated iron used as roofing for Walwa homestead at Walwa in the Port Phillip district—first known building to use the material.

B Science, Technology, Discovery, etc.

C Arts and Entertainment

Royal Adelaide Theatre opens (22 June).

D Books and Writing

John Lort Stokes, *Discoveries in Australia*.

E Sport and Recreation

First recorded swimming championship in Australia held at Sydney Domain baths on 14 Feb.—won by W. Redman over 440 yards.

F Statistics, Social Change, the Environment

Estimated population: NSW, 196,704 (census, 2 Mar: 189,609, incl. 25,781 over the age of 13 unable to read or write); Tas., 66,105; WA, 4,547; SA, 25,893 (census, 26 Feb: 22,390).

"Pushes" such as the Cabbage Tree Mob (mentioned in Col. G. C. Mundy's journal in Aug.) make a nuisance of themselves in Sydney.

G Births and Deaths

Feb 10 James Burns b. (–1923).

Mar 16 Henry Kable d. (82?).

Mar 20 Joseph Foveaux d. (80?).

Apr 11 Barron Field d. (59).

Apr 15 Robert Campbell d. (76).

Apr 24 Marcus Clarke b. (–1881).

Jul 7 Livingston Hopkins ("Hop") b. (–1927).

Jul 17 Nikolai Mikluho-Maclay b. (–1888).

1847

Jan 8 Lt-Col. George Barney and party leave Sydney in the barque *Lord Auckland*

1847

to found the "Gladstone Colony" in northern Australia centred on Port Curtis. (Colony proclaimed 30 Jan.)

26 Sir William Denison takes up his appointment as Lt-Governor of Tas.

30 Warrnambool (Vic.) proclaimed a town site. (First land sale 22 July.)

Feb 12 Lt-Col. F. C. Irwin becomes Governor of WA following the death of Andrew Clarke on 11 Feb.

Mar 9 Order in council implementing the Sale of Waste Lands Act divides land in NSW into settled, intermediate, and unsettled areas; 8- and 14-year leaseholds available to squatters in intermediate and unsettled areas with subsequent right of purchase; a scramble for land follows.

11 Paddle-steamer *Sovereign* wrecked in Rous Channel, between Moreton and Stradbroke islands, with a loss of 44 lives.

13 E. B. Kennedy sets out to investigate whether Mitchell's Victoria River flows into the Gulf of Carpentaria.

Apr 9 Ben Boyd's ship *Velocity* arrives at Twofold Bay with 65 Melanesian labourers to work on his estates.

15 Gladstone Colony disbanded on instructions from the Colonial Office. (Evacuation completed by July.)

May 4 Earl Grey orders the closing of the convict establishment in NSW and the transfer of the remaining convicts to Tas.

6 Large anti-transportation meeting in Hobart petitions the Queen for abolition.

Jun 25 Melbourne proclaimed a city. (Gazetted 5 Feb. 1848.)

Anglican diocese of Australia subdivided into dioceses of Sydney (Bishop Broughton), Newcastle, Melbourne, and Adelaide.

29 Three new bishops, William Tyrrell (Newcastle), Charles Perry (Melbourne), and Augustus Short (Adelaide) consecrated in London.

Jul 9 J. A. Goold appointed first Catholic Bishop of Melbourne.

15 Collegiate School (later St Peter's College) opens in Trinity Church, Adelaide, schoolrooms. (College building erected 1849–51.)

16 HMS *Rattlesnake* (Capt. Owen Stanley) with English biologist T. H. Huxley aboard, arrives in Sydney to begin a three-year survey in Australian waters.

Aug – Kennedy establishes that Mitchell's Victoria River is the upper course of Cooper's Creek, which he names the Barcoo River. (Returns to Sydney 7 Feb. 1848.)

Oct 18 Aboriginal station at Flinders Is. (Wybalenna) closes down, and the 47 survivors are taken to Oyster Cove, south of Hobart.

Dec 7 Lady Mary FitzRoy, wife of the NSW Governor, and the Governor's aide-de-camp are killed when thrown from a carriage at Parramatta.

* Johann Gramp establishes his Orlando vineyard, the first in the Barossa Valley, SA, at Jacob's Creek near Rowland's Flat.

* Henry and William Dangar set up a meat-canning works at Newcastle, NSW.

* Paddle-steamer *The Brothers* begins the Manly ferry service in Sydney.

A Architecture, Building

W. P. Kay, Lands Department Building, Hobart (–1848).

New Norcia monastery, WA (foundation stone laid 1 Mar.).

Richard Lambeth, Supreme Court, Adelaide (–1851).

B Science, Technology, Discovery, etc.

Ether first used as a general anaesthetic in Australia—by Dr W. R. Pugh at

St John's Hospital in Launceston and by dental surgeon John Belisario in Sydney.

C Arts and Entertainment

Society for the Promotion of Fine Arts founded in Sydney. (Holds its first exhibition 22 June.)

Isaac Nathan's opera *Don John of Austria* (first opera written, composed, and produced in Australia) given its first performance at Sydney's Royal Victoria Theatre on 3 May.

D Books and Writing

Alexander Harris, *Settlers and Convicts.*

J. B. Jukes, *Narrative of the Surveying Voyage of H.M.S. Fly.*

Ludwig Leichhardt, *Journey of an Overland Expedition in Australia.*

E Sport and Recreation

Golf first played in Melbourne on the site of Flagstaff Gardens.

First interstate race meeting held in Melbourne (Apr.).

F Statistics, Social Change, the Environment

Estimated population: NSW, 205,009; Tas., 67,918 (census, 31 Dec: 70,164 incl. 29,000 convicts); WA, 4,717; SA, 31,153.

G Births and Deaths

Feb   3   Sir John Eardley-Wilmot d. (63).

Feb 28   Sir George Gipps d. (55?).

Aug 22   John Forrest b. (−1918).

Oct   8   Rose Scott b. (−1925).

1848

Jan   4   Dual system of education introduced in NSW, with the appointment of two boards of education, one national, one denominational.

–   Female Factory at Parramatta closed.

Feb 25   Ludwig Leichhardt sets out from Canning station on the Darling Downs in a second attempt to cross Australia from east to west. (Fate of the party remains unknown; last communication from Cogoon on 4 Apr.).

Mar 15   Melbourne Hospital opens.

Apr   7   Benalla (Vic.) proclaimed a town site. (First land sale 28 June 1849.)

Jun   4   E. B. Kennedy and 12 others set out from Rockingham Bay to find a route through Cape York Peninsula.

Jul 26   Electors in Port Phillip district, in protest against an absentee government in Sydney, refuse to nominate representatives to the NSW Legislative Council (and elect Earl Grey as the member for Melbourne).

–   Netherlands Indies government claims all of west New Guinea from the 141st parallel.

–   Some 120 Chinese shipped from Amoy to become shepherds in NSW under an indenture scheme.

Aug   2   Sir Henry Fox Young replaces F. H. Robe as Governor of SA.

12   Capt. Charles Fitzgerald replaces F. C. Irwin as Governor of WA.

Sep   4   British government revokes the order in council abolishing convict transportation to NSW.

1848

8 J. S. Roe explores south-east of Perth and north-east of Albany, WA (to 2 Feb. 1849).

9 A. C. Gregory leads an expedition to the Murchison district, WA, and discovers good pastoral land as well as lead in the Murchison River. (Returns to Perth 12 Nov.)

28 *Australian* newspaper published for the last time.

– Richard Goldsbrough founds a wool auction in Melbourne.

Oct 9 *Port Phillip Patriot* becomes the Melbourne *Daily News.*

27 Convict ship *Governor Phillip* wrecked off Cape Barren Is; 16 die from drowning or starvation before rescue arrives.

Nov 7 First sale of land in Colac (Vic.)

13 Kennedy, having reached Weymouth Bay, leaves eight of the party there and pushes on with Aboriginal Jacky Jacky and three others.

24 Kennedy leaves three men at Shelbourne Bay and continues with Jacky Jacky.

Dec 11 Gov. Fitzgerald wounded by Aborigines while exploring with Gregory near Champion Bay, WA.

13 Kennedy fatally speared by Aborigines; Jacky Jacky continues alone to Cape York.

First government-assisted immigrants arrive at Moreton Bay.

15 Australian Mutual Provident Society founded.

20 Constitutional Association formed in Sydney to effect electoral and land reforms. (Subsequently publishes the *People's Advocate.*)

24 *Ariel* rescues Jacky Jacky at Port Albany and (30th) the two other survivors of the Kennedy expedition at Weymouth Bay.

* Australia's first iron smelting works opened at Mittagong, NSW.

* Port Phillip Farmers' Society (later Royal Agricultural Society) formed.

A Architecture, Building

Edmund Blacket, St Phillip's, Church Hill, Sydney (–1857) and St Mark's, Darling Point (–1864; tower and spire added 1875).

B Science, Technology, Discovery, etc.

Chloroform first used as an anaesthetic in Australia.

W. L. Morton demonstrates his swing gate for drafting sheep.

C Arts and Entertainment

D Books and Writing

T. L. Mitchell, *Journal of an Expedition into the Interior of Tropical Australia.*

E Sport and Recreation

Port Phillip Turf Club obtains a lease of Flemington Racecourse site.

First meeting at Ascot Racecourse, Perth.

W. F. King ("the Flying Pieman") races a coach from Windsor to Sydney, winning by seven minutes.

F Statistics, Social Change, the Environment

Estimated population: NSW, 220,805; Tas., 68,235; WA (first official census, 10 Oct.), 4,622; SA, 38,666.

Hobart reaches its peak as a deep-sea whaling port, with 37 whaling ships manned by 1,046 men.

SA Destitute Board established for the welfare of immigrants.

Jenolan Caves first described (in the *Bathurst Advocate*, 30 Dec.).

G Births and Deaths

Jan 28 George Chaffey b. (–1932).

Feb 17 Louisa Lawson b. (–1920).
Jun 4 William Sorell d. (72?).
Jul 18 Alexander Macleay d. (81).
Oct 15 John Langdon Bonython b. (–1939).
Oct 28 Jessie Couvreur ("Tasma") b. (–1897).
Dec 13 Edmund Kennedy d. (30).
— – Ludwig Leichhardt d. (*c.* 35).

1849

Jan 1 *Port Phillip Herald* becomes the *Melbourne Morning Herald.*
    2 Mortgaged estates of the Bank of Australia liquidated by public lottery.
    8 *Plymouth*, the first of several ships carrying people to the California gold-fields, leaves Port Jackson for San Francisco.
  20 *Fortitude* arrives at Moreton Bay with 253 immigrants from Britain for J. D. Lang's Cooksland cotton-growing scheme. (Temporary headquarters set up in an area of Brisbane that becomes known as Fortitude Valley.)

Feb 11 First batch of German migrants arrive in Melbourne in the *Godeffroy*.
  23 Public meeting in Perth requests that WA be converted into a penal settlement to aid the flagging state of the colony.

Mar 23 Armidale, NSW, town site gazetted. (First land sale 14 June.)
  – Mass meetings held in Sydney and Melbourne opposing reintroduction of convict transportation.

Jun 8 Convict ship *Hashemy*, carrying 212 convicts "of the better class", arrives at Port Jackson, La Trobe having refused it permission to land convicts at Port Phillip.
  11 Protest meeting held at Circular Quay, Sydney, against the landing of convicts from the *Hashemy.*
  28 Plan of Grafton, NSW, approved. (First sale of land 22 Jan. 1851.)
      First sale of land at Wangaratta (Vic.).
  – Aborigines kill two brothers from Gregory Blaxland's Gin Gin station (near Bundaberg), leading to the massacre by whites of a huge number of Aborigines.

Jul 21 *Phoenician*, the first clipper ship to come to Australia, arrives at Port Jackson from Britain after a 91-day voyage (compared with an average of 140 days).

Aug 8 Convict ship *Randolph* arrives at Port Phillip; La Trobe orders it to sail on to Sydney.
  20 *Randolph* arrives at Port Jackson; FitzRoy sends the convicts to Moreton Bay. (All subsequent convict ships sent direct to Moreton Bay.)
  24 Cooma, NSW, proclaimed a village site.
  – Ben Boyd's Royal Bank closes. (Subsequently liquidated.)

Oct 10 Sydney Railway and Tramway Co. incorporated by act of parliament.
  12 Town of Geelong (Vic.) incorporated.
  16 Castaway Barbara Thompson, after living with Aborigines for five years, is rescued by HMS *Rattlesnake* at Evans Bay, Cape York Peninsula.

Nov 23 Wagga Wagga, NSW, proclaimed a town, Dubbo a village site.
  – Geraldton, WA, laid out as a town site. (First town lots sold in June 1850.)
  – Yarra and Saltwater rivers in high flood.

Dec 1 Port Essington again abandoned and settlers returned to Sydney.

1849

13 *Adelaide* arrives at Port Phillip with 281 "exiles"; refused entry and sails on to Port Jackson (last ship to bring "exiles" to NSW).

14 Cowra, NSW, gazetted as a town site.

* Caroline Chisholm establishes the Family Colonization Loan Society in London to help families migrate.

* Tasmanian apples exported to New Zealand and California.

* Tokens, used as currency, issued for the first time in Australia by Melbourne grocers Annand, Smith & Co.

A Architecture, Building
Mortimer Lewis, Treasury Building, Sydney (opened 1851; now incorporated in the Inter-Continental Hotel), and Richmond Villa, Sydney.

B Science, Technology, Discovery, etc.
Australian Museum opens a small zoo in Hyde Park, Sydney.

C Arts and Entertainment

D Books and Writing
Alexander Harris, *The Emigrant Family.*
Charles Sturt, *Narrative of an Expedition into Central Australia.*

E Sport and Recreation

F Statistics, Social Change, the Environment
Estimated population: NSW, 247,260; Tas., 68,553; WA, 4,645; SA, 52,904.
Livestock in NSW: 12.1 million sheep, 1.8 million cattle, 122,000 horses, 59,000 pigs.
Secondary industry in NSW: 95 boiling-down works, 168 mills, 19 soap and candle factories, 6 woollen cloth manufacturers, 72 tanneries, 7 meatpreserving factories, 31 breweries, 2 distilleries.

G Births and Deaths
Jan 18 Edmund Barton b. (–1920).

1850

Jan 1 Adhesive postage stamps issued in NSW (first in Australia).

3 Vic. issues its first adhesive postage stamps.

Feb 19 Railway between Adelaide and Port Adelaide authorized by the SA Legislative Council.

Mar 12 Deniliquin, NSW, gazetted as a town.

Apr 1 Rev. J. D. Lang, recently returned to Sydney from the UK, reopens his Australian College and (3rd) separates the Synod of NSW from the Synod of Australia.

30 *Bangalore*, the last convict ship to Moreton Bay, arrives with 392 "exiles".

May 9 Horsham (Vic.) notified as a village site.

Jun 1 Transportation of convicts to WA begins with the arrival of the *Scindian* carrying 75 convicts together with 54 prison guards, a number of officials, and their families.
Tamworth, NSW, gazetted as a town.

27 *Freeman's Journal* founded in Sydney. (Merges with *Catholic Worker* in 1942.)

30 First Unitarian congregation in Australia formed in Sydney.

Jul 3 Work begins on NSW's first railway line, from Sydney to Parramatta.

31 First land sales at Warwick, on the Darling Downs.

Aug 5 Australian Colonies Government Act receives royal assent in Britain—provides for the separation from NSW of the Port Phillip district, to be known as Victoria, and for the eventual self-government of the Australian colonies.

Sep 28 *Slain's Castle*, first of the ships to sail under Caroline Chisholm's Family Colonization Loan Society scheme, leaves England with 150 migrants.

Oct 1 Act to incorporate and endow the University of Sydney receives royal assent. NSW Legislative Council resolves that no more transported convicts will be received under any conditions.

29 Anglican bishops of Australia and NZ, meeting in Sydney, establish the Australian Board of Missions.

Nov 11 Ship *Lysander* brings news to Melbourne of the passing of the Australian Colonies Government Act, which sets off four days of general rejoicing.

14 Bank of NSW opens a branch in Brisbane, the first bank there.

15 Princes Bridge opened in Melbourne. (Demolished in 1884.)

16 United Operative Masons' Society formed in Melbourne. (Held to be the precursor of all labour organizations in Aust.)

Dec 5 Pentridge Gaol, recently completed, receives its first prisoners.

18 First Australian branch of the YMCA formed in Adelaide.

28 Henry Parkes's *Empire* newspaper founded in Sydney. (Suspended 1858– 59; incorporated in *Evening News* 1875.)

* Measles first reported in Australia.

* Model School (later Fort Street School) opens in Sydney, inaugurating teacher training in Australia.

A Architecture, Building

Constitution Dock, Hobart, officially opened (1 Dec.).

A. W. N. Pugin, old St Stephen's Church ("Pugin's Chapel"), Brisbane, opened (12 May).

B Science, Technology, Discovery, etc.

Australian Philosophical Society (later the Royal Society of NSW) formed in Sydney (19 Jan.).

T. L. Mitchell reads a paper to the Philosophical Society applying the principle of the boomerang to a ship's propeller (3 Dec.).

C Arts and Entertainment

Joseph Wilkie opens a music shop (later Allans) in Collins Street, Melbourne.

A new Royal Victoria Theatre opens in the old Queen's Theatre, Adelaide.

"Grand Fete" held by William Beaumont and James Waller at their Sir Joseph Banks Hotel, Botany, to inaugurate their zoological gardens (26 Dec.).

D Books and Writing

E Sport and Recreation

Game of "Australian Rules Football"—12 players to a side—played in Melbourne as part of the Separation celebrations (18 Nov.).

F Statistics, Social Change, the Environment

Estimated population: NSW, 266,900; Tas., 68,870; WA, 5,886; SA, 63,700.

G Births and Deaths

Jan 29 Lawrence Hargrave b. (–1915).

1850

Feb 9 Elizabeth Macarthur d. (82?).
Mar 13 Owen Stanley d. (38).
May 12 F. W. Holder b. (–1909).
Jun 16 William Lawson d. (76).
—   – Quong Tart b. (–1903).

1851

Jan 2 Sir Charles FitzRoy appointed Governor-General of all the Australian colonies.

Feb 1 Australasian League, originated by John West in Launceston to secure the abolition of transportation, constituted in Melbourne.
2 Maryborough (Qld) proclaimed a town site.
6 "Black Thursday"—bushfires rage from near Melbourne, where shade temperature reaches 47°C at 11 a.m., to Mount Gambier in SA; at least 10 people killed.
12 E. H. Hargraves discovers gold at Lewis Ponds Creek, near Bathurst.

Mar 29 Sydney Chamber of Commerce revived.

Apr 1 Melbourne Chamber of Commerce founded.
Balranald, NSW, proclaimed a town site. (First land sales 14 Jan. 1852.)
7 John Lister and William Tom find gold at Ophir, NSW.
24 J. D. Lang sentenced to four months' gaol and fined £100 for the libel of Thomas Icely in Lang's *Press* in Feb.
– Earl Grey's revocation of the order in council abolishing transportation is rescinded.

May 15 *Sydney Morning Herald* carries news of gold discovery; rush to the Ophir goldfield begins.
22 Proclamation issued in NSW declaring all gold found on private or Crown land to be the property of the Crown; licence to dig required after 1 June (fee 30s per month).
26 Hamilton (Vic.) notified as a town site.

Jun 19 Goldfield discovered on the Turon River, NSW.
26 Sale (Vic.) gazetted as a village site.

Jul 1 Port Phillip district officially becomes the colony of Victoria; C. J. La Trobe becomes Lt-Governor (15 July).
2 Election held for SA Legislative Council (to 12th).
7 James Esmond's discovery of gold at Clunes, Vic., announced.
8 First great nugget found in Australia, the Kerr Hundredweight, yielding 1,272 oz of gold, discovered on the Turon River.
20 Gold discovered near Castlemaine, Vic. (Mount Alexander).

Aug 8 Gold discovered in the Buninyong Range, near Ballarat.
20 New SA Legislative Council, with 16 of the 24 members elected, meets for the first time. (Discontinues state aid to religion, 29th.)
– Most extensive flooding of the Torrens since the founding of SA.
– Gold discovered at Araluen, NSW, and near Daylesford and Bendigo, Vic., and a rush begins to Hill End, NSW.

Sep 1 Gold-digging licences (fee 30s per month) required in Vic.
11 Election held for Vic. Legislative Council (to 18th).

27 Sir Thomas Mitchell and politician Stuart Donaldson fight a duel over allegations of extravagance in the Surveyor-General's Dept.
–   Goldfield discovered near Creswick, Vic.

Oct 6 Melbourne Academy (later Scotch College) opens in Spring Street.
7 Tenterfield, NSW, gazetted as a town. (First land sale 9 Mar. 1854.)
15 Ben Boyd disappears, presumed killed by natives, after going ashore at Guadalcanal Is. from his yacht *Wanderer.*
24 Election held for Tasmania's Legislative Council.
30 First official Mormon missionaries to Australia arrive in Sydney.

Nov 13 Victoria's Legislative Council formally opened in St Patrick's Hall, Bourke Street, Melbourne.
Boyd's yacht *Wanderer* wrecked at Port Macquarie.

Dec 29 Education Act in SA ends state grants to denominational schools.
30 Bega, NSW, town site gazetted.

* J. E. Seppelt establishes a vineyard near Tanunda, SA.
* Influenza epidemic in all colonies.

A Architecture, Building
Work begins on the Convict Establishment, Fremantle (commissariat stores and offices completed 1852; gaol built 1852–58; lunatic asylum 1861–65).

B Science, Technology, Discovery, etc.
Dr William Bland sends to the Great Exhibition in London designs for an "atmotic ship", a precursor of the airship.

C Arts and Entertainment

D Books and Writing

E Sport and Recreation
Aboriginal runner Manuello beats Tom McLeod, acknowledged as the fastest runner in Australia, over 100 yards in Melbourne.
Thomas Spencer opens the first billiard saloon in Sydney.

F Statistics, Social Change, the Environment
Estimated population: NSW, 197,265 (census, 1 Mar; 268,334 [includes Port Phillip District]); Tas., 69,187 (census, 1 Mar: 70,130); WA, 7,186; SA, 66,538 (census, 1 Jan: 63,700); Vic., 97,489.

G Births and Deaths
Jan 27 Julian Ashton b. (–1942).
Mar 27 Rosa Caroline Murray-Prior (Mrs Campbell Praed) b. (–1935).
Jun 8 John Piper d. (78).
Jun 30 Henry Bournes Higgins b. (–1929).
Oct 15 Benjamin Boyd d. (50).
Dec 28 Robert Philp b. (–1922).

1852

Jan 28 SA passes the Bullion Act which allows for the stamping of gold ingots to be used as legal tender for one year.

Feb 10 Supreme Court of Vic. established (William à Beckett Chief Justice).

1852

19 Hovenden Hely and party leave Brisbane to search for Leichhardt's missing expedition.

– Gold discovered at Beechworth, Vic.

Mar 19 First gold escort from Mount Alexander to Adelaide arrives with 5,119 oz of gold.

21 *Isabella Watson* wrecked off Port Phillip; nine lives lost.

Apr 2 Gang of 22 men raid the barque *Nelson* at anchor off Williamstown, Vic., and get away with 8,000 oz of gold (not recovered).

30 Wodonga (then known as Belvoir), Vic., notified as a town site.

May 9 Schooner *Favourite* leaves Melbourne for Sydney and is lost with all hands (13 passengers, 8 crew).

24 Port Augusta, SA, named by exploring party under A. L. Elder and J. Grainger in the government yacht *Yatala*. (First land sales in 1854.)

Jun 24 Murrumbidgee River in flood washes away most of Gundagai; 89 lives lost out of a population of 250.

Jul 29 P & O mail steamer *Chusan* arrives at Port Phillip (continues to Sydney, arriving 3 Aug.) to inaugurate a two-monthly mail and passenger service between Sydney and London (overland at Egypt).

Aug 3 Gold discovered in the Ovens Valley, Vic.

10 Glen Innes, NSW, proclaimed a town site. (First land sales June 1855.)

25 First sale of land at Ballarat, Vic. (Proclaimed a municipality 17 Dec. 1855.)

Sep 15 SS *Conside* wrecked off Point Lonsdale, Vic; 10 of its 200 passengers drown.

18 Clipper *Marco Polo*, first of the Black Ball Line's emigrant ships, arrives at Port Phillip after a record 68-day run from Liverpool with 930 government-assisted migrants, 53 of whom die on the way (all but two of them children).

Oct 8 Amalgamated Society of Engineers formed by a shipboard group en route to Sydney.

11 Australia's first university, the University of Sydney, inaugurated.

16 Crew of the migrant ship *Georgiana*, anchored in Port Phillip, mutiny, kill one of the ship's officers, and make off for the goldfields.

Nov 12 SS *Great Britain*, then the largest iron passenger steamer in the world, arrives in Melbourne with 615 passengers and 137 crew.

24 Transportation to eastern Australia ends with the dispatch of the last convict ship (*St Vincent*) to Tasmania.

Dec 9 "Adelaide sovereigns"—gold pound tokens minted by the Adelaide Assay Office—first issued.

15 Colonial Secretary Sir John Pakington authorizes NSW, Vic., SA, and Tas. to draft new separate constitutions providing for an elected lower house and a nominated upper house.

22 Clipper *Ticonderoga* arrives at Port Phillip with 646 migrants, 96 having died from typhus on the way; another 82 die while at the new Point Nepean quarantine station.

A Architecture, Building

B Science, Technology, Discovery, etc.
Joseph Bosisto begins distilling eucalyptus oil near Dandenong, Vic.

C Arts and Entertainment
S. T. Gill, *A Series of Sketches of the Victorian Gold Diggings and Diggers As They Are* (published as lithographs).

D Books and Writing

James Bonwick, *Notes of a Gold Digger.*
John MacGillivray, *Narrative of the Voyage of H.M.S. Rattlesnake.*
G. C. Mundy, *Our Antipodes.*
John West, *The History of Tasmania.*
Melbourne bookseller and publisher George Robertson opens his first bookshop in Russell Street.

E Sport and Recreation

Western Australian Turf Club founded (22 Oct.).

F Statistics, Social Change, the Environment

Estimated population: NSW, 204,656; Tas., 63,445; WA, 8,711; SA, 68,663; Vic., 168,321.
Vic. receives 94,644 immigrants (mainly gold-diggers), doubling its population.

G Births and Deaths

Jan 19 Thomas Price b. (–1909).
Apr 14 John Quick b. (–1932).
Sep 4 E. J. Banfield b. (–1923).
Oct 16 George W. Evans d. (72).
Dec 4 John Lee Archer d. (61).

1853

Jan 3 Bank of Victoria opens in Melbourne.
 5 Hobart Municipal Council meets for the first time; mayor elected.

Feb 3 Bushranger "Captain Melville" (Frank McCallum) sentenced to 32 years' gaol at Geelong.
 19 HMS *Herald* (Capt. H. M. Denham) arrives in Sydney to begin nine years of survey work on the Australian coast.

Apr 6 La Trobe's resignation as Governor of Vic. accepted by the Colonial Office.
 29 Barque *Rebecca* wrecked off the west coast of Tas; nine lives lost.

May 7 Operative Stonemasons' Society formed in Sydney.
 15 *Monumental City*, the first screw steamer to cross the Pacific, runs aground near Gabo Is., Vic., with a loss of 33 lives.
 20 Select committee chaired by W. C. Wentworth appointed by the NSW Legislative Council to draft a new constitution.
 26 *St Vincent*, the last convict transport to Tas., arrives at Hobart.
 31 Ship *Sea* wrecked near Point Nepean when leaving Port Phillip; 16 lives lost.

Jun 5 Rabbi Herman Hoelzel, the first qualified Jewish minister in Australia, inducted as minister of the Hobart Synagogue.
 6 Miners at Bendigo form an Anti-Gold Licence Association.

Jul 1 Beechworth, Vic., proclaimed a town.
 20 Bushrangers hold up the gold escort from the McIvor field, Vic., killing three troopers and the driver and taking 2,320 oz of gold and cash. (Five later captured; three hanged.)
 28 Wentworth's select committee makes its recommendations, which include an upper house whose members would constitute a colonial peerage.
 – Australia's first government-maintained free public library established in Melbourne.
 – Severe flooding on the Murrumbidgee (higher than previous year).

1853

- Gold discovered at Buckland River, Vic.

Aug 1 Vic. miners petition La Trobe for a reduction of licence fee, representation on Legislative Council, and release of land.

10 Meeting held at the Royal Hotel, Sydney, to protest against Wentworth's proposal for a hereditary nobility.

11 Frigate *Madagascar* leaves Melbourne for London with 70,000 oz of gold and is not seen again.

15 At a public meeting in Sydney, Henry Parkes makes his first public speech to denounce Wentworth's Constitution Bill, and Daniel Deniehy ridicules the proposed "bunyip aristocracy".

- Murray River navigated by steamer from Goolwa to Swan Hill (arr. 17 Sept.) by Francis Cadell in his *Lady Augusta* and from Mannum to Echuca (arr. 24 Sept.) by William Randell in the *Mary Ann.*

Sep 24 New Caledonia annexed by France.

Oct 1 Gold licence fee in NSW reduced to 10 shillings per month.

8 *Illustrated Sydney News* first published. (Ceases publication 1894.)

Nov 1 Tas. issues its first adhesive postage stamps.

Dec 9 *Bendigo Advertiser* first published. (Absorbed in *Independent*, 1918.)

21 Town site at Gladstone (Qld) gazetted. (Land sales Feb. 1854.)

* Freeman Cobb establishes a coaching service (Cobb & Co.) in Melbourne.

A Architecture, Building

W. P. Kay, Government House, Hobart (–1858).

B Science, Technology, Discovery, etc.

Australian Museum incorporated by act of parliament.

Baron Ferdinand von Mueller appointed Victorian Government Botanist.

Observatory established at Williamstown (Melb.). (Moved to Domain park in 1863.)

Adelaide Philosophical Society (later Royal Society of SA) holds its first meeting (21 Feb.).

C Arts and Entertainment

Victorian Fine Arts Society, recently formed, holds its first exhibition in Melbourne (Aug.).

Dutch violinist W. H. Paling arrives in Sydney.

Melbourne Philharmonic Society founded (15 Oct.).

Cremorne Gardens amusement park founded in Melbourne by James Ellis. (Closes in 1862.)

D Books and Writing

J. E. Erskine, *Journal of a Cruise among the Islands of the Western Pacific.*

Charles Harpur, *The Bushrangers* (play).

E Sport and Recreation

F Statistics, Social Change, the Environment

Estimated population: NSW, 224,324; Tas., 65,954; WA, 9,334; SA, 78,944; Vic., 222,436.

Gold becomes Australia's major export (surpassing wool).

Public hangings abolished in NSW.

G Births and Deaths

Jan 1 Gregory Blaxland d. (74).

Feb 20 William Grant Broughton d. (64).

Jun 11 Francis Barrallier d. (80?).
Sep 9 Fred Spofforth b. (–1926).

1854

Jan 13 Fire destroys three stores and five houses in Elizabeth Street, Melbourne.
20 Fire destroys a city block in Hobart.
30 Cobb & Co. extend operations to the Victorian goldfields.

Feb 25 T. S. Mort begins building a dry dock (Mort's Dock) at Balmain, Sydney (completed 1855).

Mar 3 Australia's first telegraph line begins operating between Melbourne and Williamstown.
5 St Vincent de Paul Society established in Australia.
13 Dalby (Qld) proclaimed a town.
30 M. C. O'Connell arrives at Gladstone to become Government Resident.

May 5 C. J. La Trobe relinquishes his post as Lt-Governor of Vic. and next day leaves the colony.
18 Horse-drawn railway opened between Goolwa and Port Elliot, SA.
21 *Brahmin* wrecked on King Is; 15 lives lost.

Jun 22 Sir Charles Hotham installed as Governor of Vic.
News received of the outbreak of the Crimean War (28 Mar.), which gives rise to fears of an attack on Australia by the Russian navy.
24 First sales of land at Toowoomba (Qld.)
– Goldfields discovered at Ararat and Maryborough, Vic.

Jul 5 John Davies founds the bi-weekly *Hobarton Mercury* (later the Hobart *Mercury*; daily publication from 1 Jan. 1860).

Aug 1 Adhesive postage stamps first issued in WA.
18 SS *Great Britain* arrives at Port Phillip with several cases of smallpox on board. (Fireworks to indicate its discharge from quarantine give false alarm that the Russians have invaded.)
25 Surveyor Robert Austin discovers Mount Magnet during his exploration of the Murchison district, WA.
– First land sales at Bendigo, Vic.

Sep 12 Australia's first steam railway, from Flinders Street, Melbourne, to Sandridge (now Port Melbourne) opens.
13 Gov. Hotham orders a twice-weekly inspection of miners' licences instead of once a month as before.

Oct 17 Melbourne *Age* first published.
Melbourne Exhibition opens (to 12 Dec.).
– Francis Cadell in the *Lady Augusta* reaches Howlong on the Murray.

Nov 11 Ballarat Reform League formed at a meeting of aggrieved miners.
29 At a mass meeting at Bakery Hill, Ballarat, miners burn their licences, fly the Southern Cross flag, and swear to resist any attempt to arrest them.
30 Shots fired during a licence check at Ballarat; Riot Act read; Peter Lalor appointed leader of the rebellious miners, who begin to build a stockade at the Eureka Lead.

Dec 3 Military and police attack the Eureka Stockade and quickly overcome the miners; five troopers and 35 to 40 miners killed; Lalor, badly wounded,

1854

escapes; Raffaello Carboni and 12 others captured; martial law proclaimed (revoked 9th).

8 Carboni and the other captured diggers charged with high treason.
– First land sales at Taree, NSW, a town having been laid out.

* SA and Vic. legislate to raise volunteer defence forces.

A Architecture, Building

Edmund Blacket, main building of the University of Sydney (–c. 1860).
Kirribilli House, Sydney.
Joseph Reed, Melbourne Public Library (now State Library of Vic; opened 1856; domed reading room added 1909–13; La Trobe wing and long façade, 1951–61).
Foundation stone of University of Melbourne laid (3 July).
Old Legislative Council Building, Adelaide (–1855).

B Science, Technology, Discovery, etc.

National Museum, Melbourne, established.
Victorian Institute for the Advancement of Science and the Philosophical Society of Victoria founded. (Amalgamated in 1855; become the Royal Society of Vic. in 1859.)
Two masses (3½ tons and 1½ tons) of an iron meteorite found near Cranbourne, Vic.

C Arts and Entertainment

Nicholas Chevalier arrives in Melbourne (25 Dec.).
Irish soprano Catherine Hayes gives concert performances in Sydney, Melbourne, and other centres.

D Books and Writing

Catherine Helen Spence, *Clara Morison: A Tale of South Australia during the Gold Fever.*

E Sport and Recreation

F Statistics, Social Change, the Environment

Estimated population: NSW, 241,813; Tas., 64,874; WA, 11,743 (census, 30 Sept.); SA, 92,545; Vic., 283,942 (first census as a separate colony, 26 Apr; 234,298).
Public hangings abolished in Vic.
The crinoline introduced in Australia.
Royal Park, Melbourne, permanently reserved.

G Births and Deaths

Jan 21 George Musgrove b. (–1916).
Sep 19 Sir George Arthur d. (70).
Oct 22 Walter Withers b. (–1914).

1855

Jan 1 Colonial Sugar Refining Co. founded in Sydney to take over the insolvent Australasian Sugar Co.

8 Sir Henry Fox Young becomes Governor of Tas., replacing Sir William Denison, who succeeds Sir Charles FitzRoy as Governor of NSW and becomes Governor-General of the five colonies (20 Jan.).

– Adhesive postage stamps first issued in SA.

1855

Feb 22   Trials of the 13 charged with treason at Eureka (to 27 Mar.); all acquitted.

Apr 4   Armed ketch *Spitfire* (65 tons), first warship built in NSW, launched in Sydney.

    12   Sandhurst (Bendigo), Vic., proclaimed a municipality.

    13   University of Melbourne, established by act of parliament in Jan. 1853, officially opened. (First permanent buildings opened 30 Oct.)

    23   Castlemaine, Vic., proclaimed a municipality.

    27   First land sales at Echuca, Vic.

May 1   Coalminers begin an unsuccessful ten-week strike at the Australian Agricultural Co.'s mines at Newcastle.

       Tas. Constitution Act assented to in UK.

    14   Branch of the Royal Mint opened in the south wing of the Rum Hospital, Sydney (to coin sovereigns and half-sovereigns).

Jun 8   Sir Richard MacDonnell becomes Governor of SA.

    –   Chinese Immigration Restriction Act in Vic. imposes a head tax of £10 on every new arrival and limits the number of Chinese immigrants to one for every ten tons of shipping.

Jul 13   Site of Shepparton, Vic., surveyed. (First land sales 13 Mar. 1856.)

    16   NSW and Vic. constitution bills assented to in UK.

    18   A. C. Gregory and party (including Ferdinand von Mueller) leave Sydney by ship for the Victoria River (NT) to search for Leichhardt.

    23   A. E. (later Sir Arthur) Kennedy becomes Governor of WA.

Aug 2   Australia's first illustrated popular magazine, *Melbourne Punch* (shortened to *Punch* in 1900), begins publication.

Sep 26   NSW's first railway—the first government-owned steam railway in the British Empire—opens between the Sydney station (Redfern) and Parramatta Junction (Granville).

Oct 1   Diocesan school—the origins of Geelong Church of England Grammar School—opens in a private house in Newtown, Vic. (School building officially opened in Geelong on 24 June 1858; moves to Corio in 1914.)

    2   G. B. Johnston takes Cadell's river steamer *Albury* up the Murray as far as Albury.

    8   *Illawarra Mercury* founded in Wollongong. (Becomes a daily in 1950.)

    24   Constitution Act, granting responsible government, proclaimed in Tas.

Nov 23   Constitution Act proclaimed in Vic.

    24   Constitution Act proclaimed in NSW.

    28   First Vic. ministry formed; W. C. Haines becomes Premier.

Dec 7   Warrnambool, Vic., gazetted as a municipality.

    17   Portland, Vic., proclaimed a municipality.

    18   William Nicholson moves and carries a motion in the Vic. Legislative Council providing for votes by secret ballot in elections.

    21   Haines government resigns over ballot motion; Nicholson deputed to form a government but is unable to.

A Architecture, Building

     George Barney, Fort Denison, Sydney Harbour (–1857).

     Joseph Reed, Geelong Town Hall, foundation stone laid (9 Apr.).

     Corio Villa, Geelong, assembled from prefabricated cast-iron parts (–1856).

     Present NSW Legislative Council chamber added to the north wing of the Rum Hospital.

1855

Como, in South Yarra, Melbourne, completed. (Ballroom wing added in 1874.)

B Science, Technology, Discovery, etc.

Brisbane Museum (later Queensland Museum) founded.

C Arts and Entertainment

S. T. Gill's series of lithographs *The Diggers, Diggings of Victoria as They Are in 1855.*

English soprano Anna Bishop (wife of Sir Henry Bishop) arrives in Sydney with harpist Nicholas Bochsa, who dies after giving one concert.

Lola Montez entertains Sydney, Melbourne, and Adelaide with her "Spider Dance".

Joseph Wyatt's Prince of Wales Theatre opens in Sydney (12 Mar.).

George Coppin opens the prefabricated Olympic Theatre in Melbourne (June).

John Black's Theatre Royal, Melb., opens (6 July) with *School for Scandal.*

D Books and Writing

Edward Hammond Hargraves, *Australia and Its Gold Fields.*

John Lang, *The Forger's Wife.*

E Sport and Recreation

James Kelly and Jonathan Smith fight with bare knuckles for 6 hours at Fiery Creek, near Daylesford Vic. (3 Dec.)—the longest fight on record.

F Statistics, Social Change, the Environment

Estimated population: NSW, 266,001; Tas., 69,962; WA, 12,605; SA, 97,387 (census, 31 Mar: 85,821); Vic., 347,305.

G Births and Deaths

Feb 25 Frederick McCubbin b. (–1917).
May 30 Mary Reibey d. (78).
Jun 18 Louis Becke b. (–1913).
Jun – Ned Kelly b. (–1880).
Aug 6 Isaac Isaacs b. (–1948).
Aug 12 Sir Richard Bourke d. (78).
Aug 13 William Astley (Price Warung) b. (–1911).
Oct   5 Sir Thomas Mitchell d. (63).
Dec 31 Sir Charles Hotham d. (49).

1856

Jan 1 Tasmania officially adopted as a name in place of Van Diemen's Land.
5 Melbourne weekly the *Leader* first published. (Last issue 26 Jan. 1957.)

Feb 11 Melbourne Public Library opened.

Mar 1 Moore Theological College opened at Liverpool, NSW. (Moves to Sydney in 1891.)
11 Elections held for NSW's first Legislative Assembly (to 19 Apr.).
19 Voting by secret ballot introduced in Australia with Vic.'s passing of the first ballot law.
– Sydney stonemasons achieve the eight-hour working day.

Apr 2 Voting by secret ballot becomes law in SA.
19 SA's first steam railway, from Adelaide to Port Adelaide, opens.
21 Building workers in Melbourne begin working an eight-hour day; large demonstration held by workers not granted the shorter hours.

25 Eight Hours Labour League established in Melbourne.

May 1 Victorian Railways established, the government having taken over the privately owned Melbourne, Mt Alexander and Murray River Railway Co.

2 Lismore, NSW, gazetted as a village. (First land sales Apr. 1858.)

22 First representative parliament of NSW assembles.

31 Vic.'s first warship, the steam sloop *Victoria*, arrives at Port Phillip from Britain.

Jun 6 NSW's first ministry under responsible government appointed, with Stuart Donaldson as Prime Minister (Premier).

Ebenezer Syme buys the Melbourne *Age*. (His brother David becomes a partner on 27 Sept., manager and editor on Ebenezer's death in 1860, sole owner in 1891.)

8 Pitcairn Island's entire community of 194 arrive at Norfolk Is. for resettlement. (Some return to Pitcairn in 1858 and 1863.)

21 A. C. Gregory and party, having explored the Victoria River, set out to traverse northern Australia from west to east. (Arrive Port Curtis 22 Nov.)

24 Norfolk Is. separates from Tas. and becomes an individual settlement under the NSW Governor's administration.

Jul 1 Belfast (now Port Fairy), Vic., declared a town site.

Aug 26 Charles Cowper replaces Donaldson as Premier of NSW.

Sep 23 Perth constituted a city, and a bishopric created.

Oct 3 H. W. Parker replaces Cowper as Premier of NSW.

17 Election held for Tasmania's first House of Assembly.

24 SA Constitution Act proclaimed; first ministry appointed.

Election held for Vic.'s first Legislative Assembly. (Results gazetted 6 Nov; Peter Lalor one of those elected.)

Nov 1 Tasmania's first ministry under responsible government appointed; W. T. N. Champ becomes Premier.

21 First Vic. parliament under responsible government meets.

– *Hansard* reporting of parliament begins in Vic. (by the *Argus*). (Introduced in SA in 1857, Qld in 1864, NSW in 1879, WA in 1890, Commonwealth in 1901, NT in 1948, Tas. in 1979.)

Dec 2 First Tas. parliament under responsible government opens.

26 Sir Henry Barkly becomes Vic.'s first constitutional Governor.

* Melbourne Trades Hall Committee formed.

* Chinese begin to land in SA and walk overland to Vic. to circumvent immigration regulations.

A Architecture, Building

J. G. Knight and Peter Kerr, Parliament House, Melbourne (Legislative Assembly and Legislative Council chambers; additions in 1860, 1879, and 1892).

B Science, Technology, Discovery, etc.

South Australian Museum established. (Available to public in 1862.)

James Harrison patents an ice-making process employing the evaporation of ether.

C Arts and Entertainment

SA Society of Fine Arts founded in Adelaide.

Lola Montez attacks Henry Seekamp, editor of the *Ballarat Times*, with a horsewhip following an article critical of her (19 Feb.).

1856

D Books and Writing

James Bonwick, *The Bushrangers* and *The Discovery and Settlement of Port Phillip*.

E Sport and Recreation

First intercolonial cricket match, between NSW and Vic., played in Melbourne (26–27 Mar.).

Victorian Yacht Club formed (later Royal Yacht Club of Vic.).

SA Jockey Club holds its first meeting (24 Jan.).

A crowd of 10,000, gathered in the Sydney Domain to watch a balloon ascent by Pierre Maigre, riot when the attempt is unsuccessful, and a boy is killed in the crush (15 Dec.).

F Statistics, Social Change, the Environment

Estimated population: NSW, 288,361 (census, 1 Mar: 269,722); Tas., 76,940; WA, 13,158; SA, 107,886; Vic., 390,384.

SA leads the world with the granting of adult male suffrage; constitution also provides for triennial parliaments, no property qualifications for lower house members, and no plural voting.

American cooking stoves become popular in Australia.

G Births and Deaths

Jan 14 J. F. Archibald b. (–1919).
Feb 26 Phillip Parker King d. (64).
Mar 9 Tom Roberts b. (–1931).
Aug 3 Alfred Deakin b. (–1919).

1857

Jan 11 First sale of town land at Nowra, NSW.
16 Charles Gavan Duffy obtains the appointment of a Vic. select committee to inquire into federation of the Australian colonies.
– *Bell's Life in Victoria* first published (–1868).

Feb 26 T. G. Gregson replaces William Champ as Premier of Tas.

Mar 9 Hobart lit by gas.
Elections held for SA's first parliament under responsible government. (Opens 22 Apr; B. T. Finniss becomes Premier.)
11 John O'Shanassy replaces W. C. Haines as Premier of Vic.
Supreme Court of Moreton Bay established.
26 Convicts from the prison hulk *Success* attack and kill Inspector-General John Price at Gellibrand Point, near Williamstown, Vic.
28 Maryborough, Vic., proclaimed a municipality.
30 Railway opened between Newcastle and East Maitland.

Apr 1 Brig *Sea Belle* wrecked off Fraser Is; only survivors, a woman and two children, not rescued for two years.
25 W. P. Weston succeeds Gregson as Premier of Tas.
29 W. C. Haines replaces O'Shanassy as Premier of Vic.

May 12 F. V. Smith becomes the fourth Tas. Premier in less than a year.
– Chinese driven off the Ararat, Vic., goldfield.

Jun 25 Railway line opened from Williamstown to Geelong.
30 Dutch barque *Koenig Willem II* wrecked at Guichen Bay, SA, with the loss of 16 lives.

1857

Jul 4 European miners drive some 2,000 Chinese from the Buckland River gold-field, burning their tents and looting their equipment.

15 National convention meets in Melbourne (to 6 Aug.) to press for the "unlocking" of the land.

23 First sale of town land at Gunnedah, NSW.

Aug 3 Sydney Grammar School opens (in the buildings of Sydney College).

10 Melbourne streets lit by gas.

Telegraph line between Hobart and Launceston officially opened.

20 *Dunbar* wrecked at the Gap, Sydney, with the loss of 121 lives and only one survivor.

21 John Baker, MLC, forms a ministry in SA after the resignation of the Finniss government.

24 SS *Champion* collides with SS *Lady Bird* off Cape Otway, Vic., and sinks with a loss of 32 lives.

25 St Vincent's Hospital, Sydney, opens in temporary premises.

Sep 1 R. R. Torrens replaces Baker as Premier of SA.

7 Charles Cowper again becomes Premier of NSW.

30 R. D. Hanson replaces Torrens as Premier of SA.

– W. Masson takes the riverboat *Mosquito* as far as Balranald on the Murrumbidgee.

Oct 5 Railway from Adelaide to Gawler completed.

24 Clipper *Catharine Adamson* wrecked on inner North Head, Sydney Harbour, with a loss of 21 lives.

27 Aborigines murder Martha Fraser, of Hornet Bank station, central Qld, and seven of her children.

Nov 19 SA imposes a head tax of £10 on Chinese arrivals.

24 Manhood suffrage granted for Vic. lower house elections.

Dec 1 Fitzroy Dock on Cockatoo Is., Sydney, opens.

22 Hobart incorporated.

31 Melbourne's Yan Yean water supply turned on.

* Cocos Islands proclaimed a British possession.

A Architecture, Building

J. J. Clark, old Treasury Building, Melbourne (–1862).

Alexander Dawson, Sydney Observatory (–1858).

Wesley Church, Lonsdale Street, Melbourne (–1858).

B Science, Technology, Discovery, etc.

Ferdinand von Mueller appointed director of Melbourne Botanic Gardens.

Zoological Society formed in Melbourne.

Sir Charles Nicholson presents his collection of Egyptian, Greek, Roman, and Etruscan antiquities to the University of Sydney.

John Carter obtains a patent for the manufacture of corrugated-iron water tanks.

C Arts and Entertainment

J. A. Gilfillan, *Captain Cook Taking Possession of New South Wales*, shown at Vic. Society of Fine Arts exhibition.

Carl Linger forms the Adelaide Liedertafel.

D Books and Writing

Caroline Atkinson, *Gertrude the Emigrant* (the first novel by an Australian-born woman).

1857

F. de B. Cooper, *Wild Adventures in Australia* (contains the first use in print of the term *Never-Never*).

Charles Thatcher, *Colonial Songster.*

E Sport and Recreation

First bathing machine in Australia "launched" at Wollongong, for female bathers only.

F Statistics, Social Change, the Environment

Estimated population: NSW, 306,562; Tas., 83,918 (census, 31 Mar: 81,492); WA, 13,368; SA, 109,917; Vic., 456,522 (census, 29 Mar: 408,998).

G Births and Deaths

May 9 Sidney Kidman b. (–1935).

May 10 John Busby d. (91?).

Dec 21 Nat Gould b. (–1919).

1858

Jan 26 First telephone line in NSW opened between Sydney GPO and South Head.

Feb 1 "Captain" William Dean in his balloon *Australasian* makes the first balloon ascent in Australia at Cremorne Gardens, Melbourne.

25 Voting by secret ballot adopted in Tas.

Mar 1 Eight-hour working day granted to some stonemasons in Qld. (Granted to others on 5 Apr.)

B. H. Babbage explores to the west of Lake Torrens, SA (to 29 Aug.).

10 John O'Shanassy becomes Premier of Vic. for the second time.

24 A. C. Gregory and party set out from the Dawson River (Qld) to search for Leichhardt traces.

Apr 7 Melbourne Church of England Grammar School opens.

14 F. T. Gregory explores and discovers pastoral land in the Murchison–Gascoyne–Lyons rivers area, WA (to 22 June).

17 A. C. Gregory reaches the Barcoo River and (21st) finds a tree marked "L".

May 14 J. M. Stuart and a companion set out to follow up Babbage's expedition into country west of Lake Torrens.

– Australia's first Agent-General in London appointed—G. S. Walters (SA).

Jun 1 A. C. Gregory passes Kennedy's furthest point on Cooper's Creek and (9th) passes the point from which Sturt returned. (Reaches Adelaide 21 July.)

9 Welcome nugget, weighing 2,217 oz and containing an estimated 2,195 oz of pure gold, found at Bakery Hill, Ballarat.

11 Township of Stawell, Vic., proclaimed.

– Inverell, NSW, approved as a town site. (First land sales Mar. 1859.)

Jul 2 Torrens system of land conveyancing and registration comes into operation in SA (adopted in Qld. in 1861; NSW, Vic., Tas. in 1862; WA in 1874).

10 Two killed in a train derailment at Haslem's Creek (Lidcombe), NSW.

12 *South Australian Advertiser* first published in Adelaide. (Renamed the *Advertiser* 3 Mar. 1899.)

21 First intercolonial telegraph line officially opened between Melbourne and Adelaide.

Aug 16 Francis Cadell takes the steamer *Albury* up the Murrumbidgee as far as Gundagai.

28 Stuart and his companion reach Streaky Bay in a state of near starvation after travelling more than 1,600 km.
- *Newcastle Chronicle* (later *Newcastle Morning Herald*) first published.

Sep 20 Ararat, Vic., becomes a municipality.
- Rush begins to Canoona, north of Gladstone, following the discovery of gold in July.

Oct 7 W. S. Jevons publishes a shocking report on the state of the Rocks area of Sydney ("a social cesspool").
National Bank of Australasia opens.
8 Rockhampton proclaimed a port of entry. (First land sale 17 Nov.)
22 Lying-in Hospital (later Royal Women's Hospital) opens in Melbourne.
29 Sydney linked by telegraph with Melbourne (and thus with Adelaide).
Launceston, Tas., incorporated.

Nov 24 Secret ballot and manhood suffrage granted in NSW for the Legislative Assembly; property qualifications abolished for candidates.

Dec 9 Royal commission on the defence of NSW names Russia as a possible aggressor.
13 Balloonist William Dean makes the first balloon ascent over Sydney.

* Carlton Brewery established in Melbourne.

A Architecture, Building
William Wardell, St Patrick's Cathedral, Melbourne (consecrated 1897; spires not completed until 1939).
Leonard Terry, Melbourne Club (–1859; extended in 1879).
Pyrmont Bridge, Sydney, opened (17 Mar.)
Knight, Kemp, and Kerr, Customs House, Melbourne (modified and completed 1876).

B Science, Technology, Discovery etc.

C Arts and Entertainment
W. H. Paling opens a music centre in Wynyard Square, Sydney.

D Books and Writing
Richard Rowe, *Peter 'Possum's Portfolio*.

E Sport and Recreation
Football match played between Scotch College and Church of England Grammar in Melbourne (7 Aug.) considered to be the foundation of Australian Rules football.
Melbourne Football Club formed.

F Statistics, Social Change, the Environment
Estimated population: NSW, 335,990; Tas., 85,484; WA, 14,543; SA, 118,665; Vic., 496,146; total population of the five colonies passes one million.
Diphtheria recorded for the first time in Australia.

G Births and Deaths
Jan 25 John Norton b. (–1916).
Jan 28 T. W. Edgeworth David b. (–1934).
Feb 26 Sir Charles FitzRoy d. (61).
Apr   2 Sir Ralph Darling d. (86?).
Jul   4? King O'Malley b. (–1953).
Sep   5 Victor Daley b. (–1905).
Nov 20 Nellie Stewart b. (–1931).

1859

Jan 13 Railway line from Geelong to Williamstown extended to Melbourne (Spencer Street).
    – Tariff League of Victoria formed, the first of many such leagues for the promotion of the protection movement.
    – Francis Cadell takes the paddle-steamer *Albury* up the Darling River and reaches Mount Murchison, near Wilcannia (Feb.).

Feb 4 Corowa, NSW, gazetted as a town site.
    24 Paddle-steamer *Gemini* reaches Brewarrina on the Darling.

Mar 25 Australian naval station established as a separate command of the Royal Navy under Captain William Loring (who takes up his post on 1 July).

Apr 2 J. M. Stuart explores central SA (to 3 July), discovering Hergott Springs (Marree) and the Neales River.

May 24 Melbourne Trades Hall opened.

Jun 14 Wentworth, NSW, gazetted as a town. (First land sales in Mar. 1860.)
    15 First NSW election under secret ballot. (J. D. Lang elected for West Sydney.)

Aug 6 SS *Admella*, en route from Adelaide to Melbourne, strikes a reef near Cape Northumberland and breaks into three; only 24 of the 113 on board saved in rescue attempts made over a week.
    16 G. E. Dalrymple and party leave Rockhampton to look for pastoral land to the north. (Discover Bowen and Bogie rivers.)
    – Stonemason C. J. Don, considered to be Australia's first "Labour" MP, elected to the Vic. Legislative Assembly (to represent Collingwood) in the colony's first election under manhood suffrage.

Sep 7 Brisbane proclaimed a municipality.
    23 Ship *Sapphire* wrecked near Raine Is., Barrier Reef; all but one of the crew of 18 killed by natives on reaching Hammond Is.
    – Submarine cable between Cape Otway, Vic., and Circular Head, Tas., completed. (Breaks down within a few weeks.)

Oct 3 Hay, NSW, proclaimed a town. (First land sale 11 Oct.)
    27 William Forster replaces Charles Cowper as Premier of NSW.
    William Nicholson replaces John O'Shanassy as Premier of Vic.

Nov 30 Traralgon, Vic., proclaimed a township. (First land sale 27 Dec.)
    Condobolin, NSW, proclaimed a town. (First land sale 3 Jan. 1860.)
    – J. M. Stuart makes another expedition in the vicinity of Lake Eyre.
    – Gold found at Kiandra, NSW. (Rush begins in Dec.)

Dec 10 Queensland proclaimed a colony separate from NSW; Sir George Ferguson Bowen becomes Governor; R. G. W. Herbert becomes Premier.
    17 Copper discovered on Yorke Peninsula, SA, leading to the opening of the Wallaroo mine.
    20 Manhood suffrage and secret ballot granted in Qld.

A Architecture, Building
Government House, Perth (–1863).
State Public Offices, Melbourne (–1876).

B Science, Technology, Discovery, etc.

Queensland Philosophical Society formed (1 Mar.)

Joseph Hooker's *Introductory Essay to the Flora of Tasmania* supports Darwin's theory on the mutability of species.

C Arts and Entertainment

Charles Parker's oratorio *The Second Advent* performed in Melbourne.

"Song of Australia" (words by Caroline Carleton, music by Carl Linger) wins the Gawler Institute's national song competition. (First public performance 12 Dec.)

D Books and Writing

Richard Hengist Horne, *Australian Facts and Prospects.*

Henry Kingsley, *The Recollections of Geoffry Hamlyn.*

John Lang, *Botany Bay.*

Caroline Leakey, *The Broad Arrow.*

E Sport and Recreation

Tasmanian Jockey Club founded in Hobart.

First meeting held on a primitive Caulfield, Vic., Racecourse.

F Statistics, Social Change, the Environment

Estimated population: NSW, 327,459; Tas., 87,682; WA, 14,837 (census, 31 Dec.); SA, 122,735; Vic., 521,072; Qld, 23,520.

Chinese on the Vic. goldfields reach a peak of 42,000.

Rabbits released in Vic. by Thomas Austin of Barwon Park, near Geelong, who imported 72 partridges, 5 hares, and 24 wild rabbits on the clipper *Lightning* on 25 Dec.

G Births and Deaths

Jun 19   Ethel Pedley b. (–1898).

Oct 16   Daisy Bates b. (–1951)

Dec 27   William Lister Lister b. (–1943).

1860

Jan 6   Melbourne Trades Hall Committee and Operatives' Board of Trade merge to form the Trades Hall Council.

Feb 15   Volunteer corps formed in Qld.

Mar 2   J. M. Stuart and two companions leave Chambers Creek, SA, in an attempt to cross the continent from south to north.

9   John Robertson forms his first government in NSW.

16   John Mackay begins an expedition north from Rockhampton during which he discovers the Pioneer River.

Apr 4   Stuart discovers the Finke River and (12th) reaches the MacDonnell Range, which he names.

9   Launceston Mechanics' Institute (later Public Library) opens.

16   NSW parliamentary select committee reports on the Condition of the Working Classes of the Metropolis (large number unemployed; many living in overcrowded and insanitary conditions).

22   Stuart reaches the centre of the Australian continent and next day ascends and names Central Mount Sturt (later changed to Stuart).

24   HMCS *Victoria* sails from Hobart for NZ with British troops for the war in Taranaki between the Maoris and colonists.

1860

May 9 Thomas Reynolds replaces R. D. Hanson as Premier of SA.
22 First Qld parliament meets. (Officially opened 29th.)

Jun 6 Stuart discovers Tennant Creek.
25 Twenty-five camels landed in Melbourne for the use of the Burke and Wills expedition.
26 Aborigines attack Stuart's party at Attack Creek; Stuart decides to turn back. (Arrives back at Chambers Creek 3 Sept.)

Jul 7 *Sydney Mail* begins publication (−1938).

Aug 4 Gold discovery at Lambing Flat (Young), NSW, reported; rush begins.
20 Expedition led by Robert O'Hara Burke, with William Wills, sets out from Melbourne to attempt to cross the continent to the north.
28 Melbourne's Parliament House attacked and stoned by a crowd of irate citizens during a debate on a controversial land bill.

Sep 18 Nicholson Land Act passed in Vic. (free selection after survey).
– State aid to religion ceases in Qld.

Oct 3 Prince of Wales Theatre, Sydney, destroyed by fire; three killed.
9 Qld's first Agent-General, Henry Jordan, assumes duty in London.
– First sale of town land at Bairnsdale, Vic.

Nov 1 W. P. Weston succeeds F. V. Smith as Premier of Tas.
Qld issues its first adhesive postage stamps.
11 Burke and Wills reach Cooper's Creek.
Maryborough Chronicle (Qld) founded by C. H. Buzacott.
26 Richard Heales replaces William Nicholson as Premier of Vic.

Dec 12 Vigilance committee of miners at Lambing Flat burn grog shanties and attack Chinese miners; two reported killed.
16 Burke and Wills, with Charles Gray and John King, leave Cooper's Creek in a bid to reach the Gulf of Carpentaria.
28 Adelaide gets a domestic water supply from Thorndon Park reservoir.

A Architecture, Building
Charles Tiffin, old Government House, Brisbane (−1862; becomes part of University of Queensland in 1909).

B Science, Technology, Discovery, etc.
Terracotta roofing tiles manufactured in Melbourne to a patent awarded to Charles Curet.

C Arts and Entertainment
S. T. Gill, *Sketches in Victoria*.

D Books and Writing

E Sport and Recreation
Victorian pugilist Tom Curran beats Harry Sellers for the championship of Australia in a bout lasting 2½ hours (13 Mar.).
AJC transfers race meetings from Homebush to Randwick (which had been closed since 1838).
Skiing believed to have been introduced into Australia by Norwegian gold miners at Kiandra.

F Statistics, Social Change, the Environment
Estimated population: NSW, 348,546; Tas., 89,821; WA, 15,346; SA, 125,582; Vic., 538,234; Qld, 28,056.
Kerosene lamps introduced into Australia by the American Thomas W. Stanford.

G Births and Deaths

Jan 27 Sir Thomas Brisbane d. (86).
Jun 10 Edmund Lockyer d. (76).
Jun 23 Walter Baldwin Spencer b. (–1929).
Jun 30 Sir John Hindmarsh d. (78?).
Dec 7 Joseph Cook b. (–1947).

1861

Jan 1 J. M. Stuart sets out again from Chambers Creek, SA, to try to cross the continent from south to north. (Returns 23 Sept., having reached as far as Bonney Creek.)
10 Charles Cowper becomes Premier of NSW for the third time.

Feb 11 Burke and Wills, with King and Gray, reach the tidal waters of the Flinders River at the Gulf of Carpentaria. (Begin return journey two days later.)
25 G. E. Dalrymple leads an expedition from Rockhampton to found Bowen, Qld. (Town proclaimed 12 Apr.)

Mar 22 Sir John Young becomes Governor of NSW.

Apr 21 Burke, Wills, and King (Gray having died 17 Apr.) arrive back at Cooper's Creek to find the depot party had left earlier in the day; they decide to make for Mt Hopeless.

May 13 *Moreton Bay Courier* becomes a daily.
25 F. T. Gregory explores country inland from Nickol Bay, WA (to 17 Oct.), and discovers and names the Ashburton, Fortescue, De Grey, and Oakover rivers and the Hamersley Range.
– Copper discovered at Moonta, on Yorke Peninsula, SA.

Jun 25 Supreme Court established in WA.
30 Miners attack the Chinese tent township at Lambing Flat. (Five leaders arrested next day.)

Jul 4 A. W. Howitt leaves Melbourne to search for Burke and Wills. (Other relief parties subsequently set out: John McKinlay from Adelaide; William Landsborough from the Gulf of Carpentaria; Frederick Walker from Rockhampton.)
8 Geelong College founded.
14 Miners attack police camp at Lambing Flat in an attempt to release those arrested. (Order restored when military arrive on 31st.)

Aug 2 T. D. Chapman becomes Premier of Tas.
13 Cootamundra, NSW, gazetted as a town site.
17 Coalminers in NSW refuse to accept a 20% wage cut and walk out. (Locked out until 14 Oct.)

Sep 2 First bridge across the Murray River at Albury officially opened.
15 Howitt finds King, alive, and the remains of Wills (18th) and Burke (21st). (McKinlay finds Gray's grave 21 Oct.)
– Rush begins to Forbes, NSW, following discovery of gold in July.

Oct 8 G. M. Waterhouse becomes Premier of SA.
17 Aborigines massacre 19 whites at Cullin-la-ringo station, near Springsure, Qld.

1861

18 Legislation passed in NSW—Robertson Land Acts—providing for free selection before survey. (Comes into force 1 Jan. 1862.)

26 Stuart's third transcontinental expedition sets out from Adelaide. (Stuart, ill, does not leave Adelaide to join until 5 Dec.)

Nov 6 Brisbane and Sydney linked by telegraph.

14 John O'Shanassy becomes Premier of Vic. for the third time.

27 NSW act restricting Chinese immigration becomes law.

Dec 6 Landsborough discovers the Barkly Tableland.

10 Western boundary of SA extended to coincide with the eastern boundary of WA—i.e., the 129th meridian. (Legislation passed 22 July.)

23 First trams (horse-drawn) run in Sydney, along Pitt Street from Circular Quay to the railway station at Redfern. (Cease in 1866.)

* Pearling begins in WA, at Nickol Bay.

A Architecture, Building

B Science, Technology, Discovery, etc.

John Tebbutt discovers the great comet of 1861 (Tebbutt's Comet) (13 May).

Peppin family of Wanganella station in the Riverina begin a sheep stud that develops the Peppin merino types.

Eugene Nicolle takes out a patent for ice-making by the liquefaction of ammonia.

C Arts and Entertainment

Museum of Art opens in Melbourne's Public Library.

Irish-American impresario W. S. Lyster brings his opera company to Australia for a seven-year period of opera presentations.

Liedertafel established in Tanunda, SA.

D Books and Writing

E Sport and Recreation

First English cricket team to visit Australia arrives in Melbourne on 23 Dec.

Melbourne Cup run for the first time (7 Nov.); won by Archer.

Brisbane Turf Club formed.

F Statistics, Social Change, the Environment

Population (census, 7 Apr.): Vic. 538,628 (Melbourne, 139,916); NSW, 350,860 (Sydney, 95,789); SA, 126,830; Tas., 89,977; Qld (first official census as separate colony), 30,059.

Acclimatization Society of Vic. formed to introduce exotic animals, fish, birds, plants, and insects (depot at Royal Park, Melb.).

G Births and Deaths

Mar 10 John Longstaff b. (–1941).

May 19 Nellie Melba b. (–1931).

Jun 29? William Wills d. (27).

Jun 30? Robert O'Hara Burke d. (40?).

Jul 9 John Verge d. (79?).

Sep 6 William Lane b. (–1917).

Dec 29 Hubert Murray b. (–1940).

1862

Jan 1 *Bendigo Independent* first published (–1918).

1862

Feb 21 Moree, NSW, gazetted as a town site. (First land sale 21 June.)

28 J. S. Hampton becomes Governor of WA.

Mar 1 Police Regulation Act brings organization and control of all police forces in NSW under one central administration.

4 Sir Dominick Daly becomes Governor of SA.

Apr 4 George Dill, general manager of the Melbourne *Argus*, charged with contempt of parliament and held in custody for a month.

5 J. M. Stuart reaches Newcastle Waters (his terminus of 1861) on his final transcontinental expedition.

8 John McKinlay discovers the Diamantina River.

10 Melbourne and Ballarat connected by railway via Geelong.

May 19 McKinlay's party reach tidal waters of the Gulf of Carpentaria (second to make transcontinental crossing), then head east.

21 Landsborough's party arrive at the Warrego, having discovered good pastoral land on their expedition down the Flinders and Thompson.

Jun 15 Bushranger Frank Gardiner and gang hold up the gold escort at Eugowra, NSW, and get away with gold and notes worth £14,000.

16 Col. Thomas Browne becomes Governor of Tas.

18 Charles Gavan Duffy's Land Act assented to in Vic.

Common Schools Act in Vic. replaces the national and denominational boards with a single Board of Education; state aid to be given only to designated common schools.

23 Qld's western boundary north of SA is extended from 141°E to 138°E.

– Cobb & Co. begin a coaching service in NSW from headquarters in Bathurst.

Jul 24 Stuart's party reach the sea at Chambers Bay, having crossed the continent from south to north, and two days later begin the return journey to Adelaide. (Arrive back 17 Dec.)

Aug – McKinlay's party reach Port Denison after crossing north Qld.

Sep 3 Roma, Qld, gazetted as a town.

Oct 20 Railway line from Melbourne reaches Sandhurst (Bendigo).

– Township of Mackay, Qld, founded.

Dec 4 State aid to religion abolished in NSW.

26 Gold found at Walhalla, Vic.

A Architecture, Building

B Science, Technology, Discovery, etc.

Zoological Gardens established at Royal Park, Melbourne (Mar.)

Entomological Society of NSW founded (–1873).

Sugar first made in Qld by John Buhot from cane grown in the Brisbane Botanic Gardens.

C Arts and Entertainment

Brisbane Philharmonic Society founded.

George Coppin's Haymarket Theatre opens in Melbourne (15 Sept.)

D Books and Writing

Roderick Flanagan, *History of New South Wales*.

Charles Harpur, *A Poet's Home*.

Henry Kendall, *Poems and Songs*.

1862

E Sport and Recreation

First cricket match between English and Australian teams played in Melbourne on New Year's Day.

Australian Yacht Squadron (later Royal Sydney Yacht Squadron) founded.

Archer wins the Melbourne Cup for the second time.

F Statistics, Social Change, the Environment

Estimated population: NSW, 366,009; Tas., 90,116; WA, 17,676; SA, 136,562; Vic., 551,388; Qld, 45,077.

Law of primogeniture abolished in NSW (Vic. in 1864, SA and Qld in 1867, Tas. in 1874, WA in 1893).

NSW Coal Fields Regulation Act provides for a minimum working age of 13 years.

Acclimatization societies founded in Adelaide (13 May), Brisbane (12 Aug.) and Hobart.

G Births and Deaths

Feb   4   G. E. ("Chinese") Morrison b. (–1920).

Mar   –   G. W. L. Marshall-Hall b. (–1915).

May 16   Edward Gibbon Wakefield d. (66).

Aug 29   Andrew Fisher b. (–1928).

Sep 25   William Morris Hughes b. (–1952).

1863

Jan   1   NSW's first Agent-General in London, Edward Hamilton, appointed.

18   Railway line from Sydney reaches Penrith.

20   James Whyte replaces T. D. Chapman as Premier of Tas.

21   Public funeral of Burke and Wills in Melbourne.

25   James Murrell, sole survivor from *Peruvian* wreck in 1846, makes contact with Europeans again at the Burdekin River, Qld.

Feb   –   Macleay River, NSW, floods, causing ten deaths.

Mar 25   Settlement established at Somerset, on the northern tip of Cape York Peninsula, by John Jardine.

26   Henry Manns, one of the Eugowra gold escort robbers, executed at Darlinghurst Gaol, Sydney.

Intercolonial conference held in Melbourne (to 13 Apr.) to consider uniform tariffs.

Apr   –   Walter Padbury pioneers settlement on the De Grey River, WA.

Jun 11   First public demonstration of electric light in Sydney.

22   Adelaide lit by gas.

27   James McCulloch becomes Premier of Vic.

Jul   4   F. S. Dutton replaces George Waterhouse as Premier of SA (but resigns on 15th, when Henry Ayers, MLC, forms a government).

6   Area later named the Northern Territory (hitherto part of NSW) is annexed to SA.

16   Newington College opened in Sydney. (Moves to Stanmore in 1880.)

Aug 14   Schooner *Don Juan* arrives at Brisbane with 67 indentured kanaka labourers recruited by Ross Lewin to work on Robert Towns's plantation on the Logan River.

–   NZ government offers free grants of land to volunteers from Australia to fight in the Second Taranaki War. (By the end of the year, 11 ships have

1863

sailed from Sydney, Melbourne, and Hobart with 1,475 volunteer military settlers.)

Sep 11 Sir Charles Darling becomes Governor of Vic.
    25 Ipswich Grammar School, first of the government-subsidized secondary schools under Qld's Grammar Schools Act, opens.

Oct 12 Bushrangers John Gilbert, John O'Meally, Ben Hall, Michael Burke, and John Vane occupy Canowindra, NSW (to 14th).
    16 James Martin forms a ministry in NSW following the fall of the Cowper–Robertson government.

Nov 12 SA legislates to sell 500,000 acres (202,500 ha) of land in the NT.
    19 John Vane of the Hall gang surrenders to a priest; another member, O'Meally, is shot during a raid by the gang.

    * General and serious flooding in south-east Qld during most of the year; floods also in Vic. (Oct., Dec.) and on the Derwent, Tas. (Dec.).

A Architecture, Building

Benjamin Backhouse, St Stephen's Cathedral, Brisbane (–1874).
W. H. Hunter, Tasmanian Museum and Art Gallery, Hobart.
E. W. Wright, Adelaide Town Hall (–1866).

B Science, Technology, Discovery, etc.

School of Anatomy, Physiology, and Pathology founded at Melbourne University under Prof. G. B. Halford.
Melbourne Observatory established in the Domain park, with R. L. J. Ellery as director (June).
Capt. Louis Hope, "father of Qld's sugar industry", manufactures sugar from his 8 hectares of sugarcane at Ormiston, near Brisbane (Sept.).

C Arts and Entertainment

Sydney's Prince of Wales Theatre reopens (13 May).
Charles Kean and Ellen Tree perform in Melbourne and Sydney.
Edward Reeve's declamatory tragedy *Raymond, Lord of Milan* first performed.

D Books and Writing

Roger Therry, *Reminiscences of Thirty Years' Residence in New South Wales and Victoria*.

E Sport and Recreation

First intercolonial rowing race held on the Parramatta River, Sydney.
Queensland Turf Club founded.
Banker wins the Melbourne Cup.

F Statistics, Social Change, the Environment

Estimated population: NSW, 377,084; Tas., 90,639; WA, 19,412; SA, 142,784; Vic., 567,906; Qld, 61,467.
Cartes-de-visite—photographic portraits the size of a visiting card—become popular (one photographer claiming to have taken 30,000 negatives in Melbourne during the summer).
Vic. Acclimatization Society releases 120 sparrows, 42 mynas, and 36 starlings in the Melbourne Botanic Gardens; and the NSW society recommends the planting of blackberries as feed for introduced birds.

G Births and Deaths

Jan 29 Archibald Mosman d. (63).
Jun 12 Bertram Mackennal b. (–1931).
Sep   4 Arthur W. Jose b. (–1934).

1864

Jan 13 G. E. Dalrymple leads an expedition by sea from Bowen to establish the port of Cardwell, Qld.

Feb 25 Work begins on Qld's first railway line, from Ipswich to Toowoomba.

Mar 1 NT land offered for sale in London and Adelaide. (Most taken up by speculators.)

3 Bushranger Frank Gardiner arrested near Rockhampton, Qld. (Convicted on 8 July and sentenced to 32 years' imprisonment.)

Apr 9 *Moreton Bay Courier* becomes the *Brisbane Courier.*

11 Fire burns out 14 shops in Queen Street, Brisbane.

29 B. T. Finniss, SA Government Resident for the NT, sails from Adelaide in the *Henry Ellis* to establish a permanent settlement in the north. (Chooses site at Escape Cliffs, on Adam Bay.)

May 27 *Sydney Punch* begins publication.

Jun 2 SS *Rainbow* wrecked in Seal Rocks Bay, NSW, with the loss of seven lives.

24 Bushranger Daniel ("Mad Dog") Morgan kills Sgt McGinnerty on the Tumbarumba road, NSW.

Jul 28 Adam Lindsay Gordon makes his famous horseback leap over the fence at the edge of Blue Lake, Mt Gambier, SA.

– Settlement established at the Ross River on Cleveland Bay (Qld.) on instructions from Robert Towns. (First called Castletown, later Townsville; first land sale, 31 July.)

Aug 4 Arthur Blyth forms a government in SA.

21 Official foundation of the settlement of Somerset, at Port Albany on Cape York.

Sep 19 Railway line opened between Bendigo and Echuca, bringing the Vic. railways from Melbourne to the NSW border.

Oct 1 Melbourne *Argus* launches the weekly *Australasian* (later the *Australasian Post*).

11 Frank and Alexander Jardine set out from Carpentaria Downs station, near Rockhampton, to overland 250 head of cattle and 42 horses to Somerset.

16 Stock Exchange of Melbourne formed.

Nov 3 McCulloch government re-elected in Vic. on a program of reform of the Legislative Council, amendment of the Land Acts, and protection of local industries by tariff reform.

16 Ben Hall and his gang hold up all travellers on the Gundagai–Yass road near Jugiong and rob the mail coach; police sergeant Edmund Parry is killed in the gun battle.

Dec 1 Fire sweeps through a large area in central Brisbane bounded by Queen, George, Elizabeth, and Albert streets, destroying 50 buildings.

* General Synod of the Presbyterian Church of NSW formed from the amalgamation of the Synod of Eastern Australia and the Synod of NSW.

A Architecture, Building
W. H. Hunter, Hobart Town Hall (–1866).

1864

B Science, Technology, Discovery, etc.
Steam cultivator imported by Alfred Joyce of Plaistow, Vic. (May).

C Arts and Entertainment
William Strutt, *Black Thursday* (painting begun 1862).
Nicholas Chevalier's *Buffalo Ranges* wins a £200 prize offered by the Museum of Art's new gallery (later the National Gallery of Vic.).
Brisbane's first permanent playhouse, the Victoria Theatre, opens (26 Jan.).

D Books and Writing
Adam Lindsay Gordon, *The Feud.*
Charles Thatcher, *Thatcher's Colonial Minstrel.*

E Sport and Recreation
Sydney University forms Australia's first Rugby football club.
Melbourne Bowling Club, the oldest existing bowling club in Australia, formed at Windsor.
Victoria Racing Club (VRC) formed.
Adelaide Cup first run (won by Falcon).
Lantern wins the Melbourne Cup.

F Statistics, Social Change, the Environment
Estimated population: NSW, 390,230; Tas., 92,255; WA, 20,363; SA, 150,754; Vic., 598,003; Qld, 73,578 (census, 1 Jan: 61,467).
First trout and salmon hatched at New Norfolk, Tas., from imported ova.
Foxes liberated in Vic. by the Melbourne Hunt Club.

G Births and Deaths
Jan 15   Isaac Nathan d. (73?).
Feb 17   A. B. ("Banjo") Paterson b. (–1941).
Mar   4   Daniel Mannix b. (–1963).
Mar 28   William Lonsdale d. (64).
Apr 22   Phil May b. (–1903).
May 25   John Joseph Therry d. (73?).
Sep 29   Rupert Bunny b. (–1947).

1865

Jan   4   Brisbane and Rockhampton linked by telegraph.
   11   Charleville, Qld, gazetted as a town site.
   24   SS *Star of Australia* leaves Sydney for Rockhampton and is not heard of again; 17 lives lost.
   25   Confederate cruiser *Shenandoah* arrives at Melbourne for repairs; US consul demands its seizure as a pirate, but after being slipped at Williamstown it is allowed to leave (18 Feb.).
   26   Bushrangers Ben Hall, John Gilbert, and John Dunn raid the township of Collector, NSW; Const. Samuel Nelson shot dead by Dunn.

Feb   3   Charles Cowper again becomes Premier of NSW following the defeat of the Martin government.

Mar   2   Frank and Alexander Jardine reach Somerset after an overland journey lasting five months.
   22   F. S. Dutton becomes Premier of SA for a second time.
   28   Land Act (Grant's Act) assented to in Vic.

1865

Apr 8 Felons' Apprehension Act passed in NSW, allowing bushrangers to be proclaimed outlaws and shot on sight.

9 Bushranger Dan Morgan shot dead near Wangaratta, Vic.

21 Thirty dissatisfied settlers at Escape Cliffs leave on a supply ship for Singapore. (Six others later sail a small boat to Champion Bay and proceed to Adelaide to make a report.)

May 5 Ben Hall shot dead near Forbes. (Gilbert shot dead and Dunn wounded near Binalong eight days later.)

Jun 29 St Mary's Cathedral, Sydney, destroyed by fire.

– Wooden bridge over the Brisbane River at Brisbane completed. (Central section collapses in Nov. 1867.)

Jul 25 Vic. Legislative Council rejects the Appropriation Bill because of the protective tariff bill attached to it.

31 Qld's first railway line, between Ipswich and Grandchester, opens.

Aug 7 Protectionists and Free Traders hold separate large meetings in Melbourne.

Sep 2 *Australian Journal* begins publication in Melbourne (–1962).

8 General Assembly of the Presbyterian Church formed in NSW by union of the various synods.

20 Henry Ayers replaces Dutton as Premier of SA.

25 John McKinlay leaves Adelaide in the barque *Ellen Lewis* to investigate sites for settlement in the NT.

Oct 10 Townsville, Qld, gazetted as a port of entry and named.

23 John Hart replaces Ayers as Premier of SA.

Nov 5 B. T. Finniss recalled from Escape Cliffs and replaced by J. T. Manton.

29 Brisbane lit by gas.

Dec 6 Surveyor-General G. W. Goyder completes his survey to delineate the limits of safe agriculture in SA (Goyder's Line).

11 Election held in Vic. following the Legislative Council's refusal to pass the Appropriation Bill; McCulloch government returned.

Bank of Adelaide opens for business.

* Colonial Naval Defence Act provides for the maintenance by the separate colonies of their own naval forces.

* Stamp duties on legal documents imposed in NSW.

* Scots immigrant William Arnott opens a bakery and confectionery in Newcastle, initiating the Arnott's biscuit business.

A Architecture, Building

Charles Tiffin, Parliament House, Brisbane (–1867; Alice Street wing completed in 1889).

Stow Memorial Congregational Church, Adelaide (–1867).

Fernberg, Brisbane (purchased in 1910 to become Government House).

B Science, Technology, Discovery, etc.

C Arts and Entertainment

Charles Summers's Burke and Wills memorial (bronze casting) unveiled in Melbourne (21 Apr.).

Artist Louis Buvelot arrives in Melbourne and begins work as a photographer.

S. T. Gill's album of lithographs, *The Australian Sketchbook*, published.

D Books and Writing

E. W. Cole opens a bookshop in Melbourne's Eastern Market.

E Sport and Recreation

First race meeting held at Eagle Farm, Brisbane.

Tory Boy wins the Melbourne Cup.

F Statistics, Social Change, the Environment

Estimated population: NSW, 408,506; Tas., 93,967; WA, 21,381; SA, 161,477; Vic., 617,791; Qld, 86,921.

G Births and Deaths

Mar 12   E. Phillips Fox b. (–1915).

Apr 16   Harry Chauvel b. (–1945).

Apr 22   Sir James Stirling d. (74).

May 18   Angus McMillan d. (54).

Jun 27   John Monash b. (–1931).

Aug 16   Mary Gilmore b. (–1962).

Aug 28   A. G. Stephens b. (–1933).

1866

Jan 11 SS *London*, en route to Melbourne, founders in the Bay of Biscay; 244 passengers and crew drown, including actor G. V. Brooke.

Wesley College opens in Melbourne.

22 James Martin (Premier) and Henry Parkes form a coalition in NSW.

26 Colonial Office rebukes Governor Darling of Vic. for permitting financial and constitutional irregularities by the McCulloch government.

Feb 1 Arthur Macalister becomes Premier of Qld on the resignation of R. G. W. Herbert.

3 Australian sovereigns become legal tender in the UK.

26 Gov. Darling recalled for not keeping aloof from personal conflicts. (Leaves Melbourne in May.)

Mar 2 New Vic. Tariff Bill passed by Legislative Assembly but (9th) rejected by Legislative Council; McCulloch resigns. (Recalled 13 Apr.)

20 Hugh George, publisher of the Melbourne *Argus*, called before the bar of Vic. parliament and detained in custody for three weeks because his paper accused McCulloch of lying.

28 J. P. Boucaut becomes Premier of SA.

Apr 17 Tariff Bill passes through both houses of Vic. parliament; Australia's first protective tariffs become law next day.

Jun 20 Adelaide Town Hall opened.

– Gold discovered at Crocodile Creek, near Rockhampton.

Jul 3 Brisbane's water supply from Enoggera Creek reservoir turned on.

10 News of the failure of the Agra and Masterman Bank, supplier of finance for railway construction in Qld, reaches Brisbane, causing a financial crisis.

12 SS *Cawarra* wrecked on Oyster Bank, Newcastle, during a gale; only 1 saved of the 61 aboard.

18 Emigrant ship *Netherby* wrecked on King Is., Bass Strait; all 450 aboard saved.

20 Macalister resigns as Premier of Qld when Gov. Bowen refuses to sanction the introduction of inconvertible government notes ("greenbacks"); Herbert

1866

forms a temporary administration and authorizes the issue of Treasury bonds to sustain public works.

Aug 7 Macalister resumes the premiership of Qld on the easing of the bank crisis.
15 Sir John Manners-Sutton becomes Governor of Vic.

Sep 8 "Bread or blood" riots in Brisbane (to 10th)—unemployed workers attempt to storm the Government Stores, stone police; ringleaders arrested.

Oct 24 Intercolonial Exhibition of Australasia opens in Melbourne (to 23 Feb. 1867). John Martin and Otto Peters open a store in Adelaide (later John Martin's Ltd; in business until 1998).

Nov 24 Sir Richard Dry becomes Premier of Tas.

Dec 7 Gold commissioner J. G. Grenfell killed by bushrangers near Narromine, NSW.
22 Henry Parkes's Public Schools Act of NSW assented to; dual system abolished and Council of Education established to maintain state schools; government aid to Church schools greatly reduced.

* Mary MacKillop and Father Julian Tenison-Woods found the Sisters of St Joseph of the Most Sacred Heart of Jesus at Penola, SA.

A Architecture, Building
James Barnet, General Post Office, Sydney (opened 1874; clock tower added 1886; clock and bells installed 1891).

B Science, Technology, Discovery, etc.
Philosophical Society of NSW becomes the Royal Society of NSW.
Systematic recording of tides begins at Fort Denison, Sydney.

C Arts and Entertainment
Louis Buvelot, *Summer Afternoon, Templestowe*; and Eugen von Guérard, *Mount Kosciusko Seen from the Victorian Border* (paintings).
Pianist and composer Charles E. Horsley organizes a music festival at the Melbourne Intercolonial Exhibition.

D Books and Writing

E Sport and Recreation
Code of rules adopted for Australian Rules football (drafted by Henry Harrison).
Sydney Cup and Brisbane Cup first run.
The Barb wins the Melbourne Cup and AJC Derby.

F Statistics, Social Change, the Environment
Estimated population: NSW, 428,167; Tas., 95,889; WA, 22,370; SA, 168,907 (census, 26 Mar: 163,452 [includes NT]); Vic., 633,602; Qld, 95,020.
Saturday half-day closing introduced by Farmer's department store in Sydney, the first in Australia to do so.
Jenolan Caves area in NSW created a government reserve.
St John's wort noted by von Mueller as being a serious menace.
Thomas Elder of SA imports 122 camels from India.

G Births and Deaths
Mar 26 Barcroft Boake b. (–1892).
Apr 11 Bernard O'Dowd b. (–1953).
Jun 5 John McDouall Stuart d. (50).

1867

Jan 11 Escape Cliffs settlement abandoned. (Inhabitants return to Adelaide.)
   – A. B. Weigall becomes headmaster of Sydney Grammar School (to 1912).

Feb 4 Composite (iron and teak) clipper *Sabraon* (later the training ship *Tingira*) arrives at Sydney on its maiden voyage.

Mar 2 Townsville and Bowen severely damaged by a cyclone (to 3rd).
   4 Intercolonial conference held in Melbourne (to 20th) to decide on a common policy on postal services; Henry Parkes makes a speech advocating federation, and the conference calls for the establishment of a Federal Council.

Apr 12 Railway line between Ipswich and Toowoomba completed.
   27 Bushrangers John and Thomas Clarke of Araluen, wanted for the murder of four special police constables, are captured in the Jindera Ranges. (Executed 25 June.)

May 3 Henry Ayers replaces J. P. Boucaut as Premier of SA.
   20 Ernest Henry finds copper at Cloncurry, Qld, leading to the opening of the Great Australian Copper Mine.

Jun 23 Hawkesbury River floods; six lives lost.

Jul 1 General Post Office in Elizabeth Street, Melbourne, officially opened.
   29 Samuel Bennett's *Evening News* begins publication in Sydney (to 1931).
   – Judge Benjamin Boothby of the SA Supreme Court removed from office. (Boothby had declared the Constitution Act and all the laws enacted under its provisions to be invalid.)
   – Gold discovered at Cape River, north Qld.

Aug 15 Robert Mackenzie replaces Arthur Macalister as Premier of Qld.

Oct 16 James Nash reports his discovery of gold on the Mary River, Qld. (A rush follows, leading to the founding of a settlement called Nashville, later renamed Gympie.)
   29 Newcastle lit by gas.
   30 Prince Alfred, Duke of Edinburgh, arrives at Glenelg, SA, in HMS *Galatea* to begin a tour of the Australian colonies.

Nov 6 Two constables in charge of a gold escort from Rockhampton to the Clermont goldfield murdered and robbed. (Gold commissioner Thomas Griffin convicted of their murder and hanged on 1 June 1868.)
   27 A crowd of Irish Catholics storms the Orange Lodge building in Melbourne during the Duke of Edinburgh's visit; shots fired and a youth fatally wounded.

Dec 28 Qld Constitution Act assented to.

   * Rookwood Necropolis established in Sydney.

A Architecture, Building
Joseph Reed, Collins Street Independent (Uniting) Church, Melbourne (–1868).
Reed and Barnes, Melbourne Town Hall (opened 1870; Prince Alfred clock-tower added 1869–74; portico, 1887).
E. W. Wright, General Post Office, Adelaide (–1872).
R. R. Jewell and James Manning, Perth Town Hall (–1870).

B Science, Technology, Discovery, etc.
Dr G. H. Pringle reports his successful use at Parramatta of his friend Joseph

1867

Lister's antiseptic treatment of open wounds (before Lister had published his findings).

C Arts and Entertainment

Hobart Philharmonic Society founded.

D Books and Writing

Adam Lindsay Gordon, *Sea Spray and Smoke Drift* and *Ashtaroth.*

E Sport and Recreation

Prince Alfred Yacht Club founded in Sydney (*Royal* added in 1911).
First organized open-field greyhound coursing meeting held, at Naracoorte, SA.
Tim Whiffler wins the Melbourne Cup.

F Statistics, Social Change, the Environment

Estimated population: NSW, 444,059; Tas., 96,743; WA, 23,147; SA, 172,875; Vic., 648,302; Qld, 98,722.

G Births and Deaths

Jan 11 Sir Stuart Donaldson d. (54).
Feb 10 Robert Garran b. (–1957).
Mar 18 Charles Web Gilbert b. (–1925).
Apr 8 Arthur Streeton b. (–1943).
Apr 9 J. C. Watson b. (–1941).
Apr 15 Adelaide Ironside d. (35).
Jun 17 Henry Lawson b. (–1922).
Jun 21 Ernest Scott b. (–1939).
Nov 26 Roderic Quinn b. (–1949).

1868

Jan 2 Arrival in Brisbane of the *Syren* with kanaka labourers, 12 having died on the way and another 12 quarantined, causes a public outcry.
8 Earl of Belmore becomes Governor of NSW.
10 Last convict transport to Australia, the *Hougoumont*, arrives at Fremantle, WA, with 229 convicts, including Irish revolutionary John Boyle O'Reilly and 56 other Fenians.
24 Vic.'s first woollen mill, the Woollen Cloth Manufacturing Co. of Geelong, begins production. (First sale of cloth in May.)
26 Clipper *City of Melbourne* catches fire and sinks at Williamstown.

Feb 28 Qld's Crown Lands Alienation Act opens up land for closer settlement.

Mar 4 Polynesian Labourers Act passed in Qld to control the recruiting (black-birding) of kanakas for labour in Qld.
5 Lucy Osburn, with five other trained nurses selected by Florence Nightingale, arrives in Sydney to become superintendent of Sydney Hospital and begin the training of nurses.
12 Prince Alfred shot and wounded at Clontarf, Sydney, in an assassination attempt by an Irish Australian, H. J. O'Farrell (subsequently tried, sentenced to death, and hanged).

Apr 16 Railway to Dalby, Qld, opened.

May 1 Railway over the Blue Mountains, NSW, reaches Mount Victoria.
6 Charles Sladen forms a ministry in Vic. following the resignation of James

McCulloch because of a deadlock with the upper house over a grant to Gov. Darling.

Jul 11 McCulloch resumes the premiership of Vic. following the defeat of the Sladen government.

Aug 4 Qld's Parliament House officially opened.
14 Col. Samuel Blackall becomes Governor of Qld.

Sep 17 Henry Parkes resigns as NSW Colonial Secretary in protest at the dismissal of the Collector of Customs.
24 John Hart becomes Premier of SA for the second time but is replaced after 19 days by Henry Ayers (his fourth ministry).

Oct 27 John Robertson forms a ministry in NSW with William Forster's support.
– Gold discovered at Ravenswood, Qld.

Nov 3 H. B. T. Strangways becomes Premier of SA after a succession of unstable ministries.
19 Four members of the Christian Brothers Catholic teaching order arrive in Melbourne to found the order in Australia.
25 Charles Lilley becomes Premier of Qld following the resignation of Robert Mackenzie.
28 Sydney retailer Gowings begins operations.
30 Sydney's St Andrew's Anglican cathedral consecrated and opened.

Dec 1 Vic.'s first Agent-General, G. F. Verdon, takes up his appointment in London.
28 G. W. Goyder, Surveyor-General of SA, leaves Adelaide in the *Moonta* to found a new settlement in the NT.

A Architecture, Building
Reed and Barnes, Rippon Lea, Elsternwick, Melbourne (additions completed 1887).
William Wardell, St Mary's Cathedral, Sydney (dedicated 1882; extensions built 1913–28; spires added, 1999–2000).
St David's Cathedral, Hobart (consecrated 1874; tower completed 1936).
St Vincent's Hospital, Sydney.

B Science, Technology, Discovery, etc.
J. A. B. Higham patents the first machine for shearing sheep.
Maria Smith of Eastwood, Sydney, propagates the Granny Smith apple.

C Arts and Entertainment
New Theatre Royal opens in Adelaide (Apr. 15).

D Books and Writing

E Sport and Recreation
Team of Aboriginal cricketers from the Western District of Vic., the first Australian cricket team to make an overseas tour, play matches in England.
Glencoe wins the Melbourne Cup.
W. C. Kernot (later Professor of Engineering at Melbourne University) builds a velocipede ("boneshaker" bicycle), which he rides round Melbourne.

F Statistics, Social Change, the Environment
Estimated population: NSW, 462,529; Tas., 98,738; WA, 24,292; SA, 176,568; Vic., 671,324; Qld, 106,101 (census, 2 Mar: 99,901).
Total number of British convicts sent to Australia during the period of transportation (1788–1868): 160,500 (including 24,700 women).

1868

Births and Deaths
    Jun 10   Charles Harpur d. (55).
    Jun 11   Bert Bailey b. (–1953).
    Jul 21   William Bland d. (78).
    Jul 28   Randolph Bedford b. (–1941).
    Oct 24   Charles Conder b. (–1909).
    Oct 28   Anthony Fenn Kemp d. (95?).
    Nov 14   Arthur Hoey Davis (Steele Rudd) b. (–1935).

1869

Jan 4   Melbourne *Herald* changes to evening daily publication.
       9   Clipper *Thermopylae* arrives at Port Phillip on its maiden voyage from London in the never-beaten time of 60 days (pilot to pilot).
      15   Charles du Cane becomes Governor of Tas.
      18   Prince Alfred College opened in Adelaide. (Main building inaugurated 22 June.)

Feb 1   Brisbane Grammar School officially opened.
       5   G. W. Goyder arrives at Port Darwin to survey the area for the town of Palmerston (renamed Darwin in 1911).
           Welcome Stranger nugget (2,520 oz) found near Dunolly, Vic.
      16   Sir James Fergusson becomes Governor of SA.
      18   Transported Fenian J. B. O'Reilly escapes from Fremantle in the American whaler *Gazelle*. (Subsequently taken to the United States.)

Mar 3   William Lanney (Lanny or Lanné), alias King Billy, the last surviving full-blood male Tasmanian Aboriginal, dies.
       –   Richard Daintree finds gold on the Gilbert River, Qld.

Apr 15   John Forrest leaves Perth to explore inland and search for Leichhardt's remains. (Discovers Lake Barlee and Mts Leonora, Malcolm, Margaret, Flora, and Weld; returns to Perth 6 Aug.)

May 1   Tas. connected with the mainland by a permanent telegraphic cable from Low Head, at the mouth of the Tamar, to the Mornington Peninsula, Vic.
       3   Agricultural Society of NSW holds its first show in Sydney (at Prince Alfred Park, to 6 May).
       8   "Captain Moonlite" (Andrew Scott, an Anglican lay reader) holds up the bank at Mt Egerton, Vic.
      27   Railway from Sydney to Goulburn opened.

Jun 21   Telegraph line from Perth to Fremantle inaugurated. (Privately erected; taken over by government in 1871.)

Aug 4   J. M. Wilson becomes Premier of Tas. following the death of Sir Richard Dry on 1 Aug.
      20   National Mutual Life Association of Australasia opens in Melbourne.
       –   Eight Hour Extension Committee formed in Sydney. (Merges into NSW Trades and Labor Council in 1871.)

Sep 11   Melbourne *Herald* launches the *Weekly Times*.
      20   J. A. MacPherson replaces James McCulloch as Premier of Vic.
      30   Official opening of the Sydney Free Public Library (formerly the Australian Subscription Library; taken over by the NSW government). Frederick A. Weld becomes Governor of WA.

1869

Oct 18   Railway line over the Blue Mountains reaches Bowenfels; includes the Lithgow Zigzag (abandoned in 1910 when deviation with tunnels opened).

Nov 17   Opening of the Suez Canal speeds up travel between Australia and England.

Dec 29   Public Library, Museum, and National Gallery of Vic. incorporated by act of parliament.

    *   Copper discovered at Cobar, NSW.

A   Architecture, Building
James Barnet, Mortuary Station, Sydney.
William Butterfield, St Peter's Cathedral, Adelaide (−1904).
Charles Webb, Royal Arcade, Melbourne (−1870; Elizabeth St annexe added 1889).
J. H. Wilson, Sydney Town Hall (−1880; clock tower completed 1881; large hall built 1883–89).
Alfred Hospital, Melbourne (−1870).
Royal Mint (later Civil Marriage Registry), Melbourne (−1872).

B   Science, Technology, Discovery, etc.

C   Arts and Entertainment
Louis Buvelot, *Waterpool at Coleraine* (painting).

D   Books and Writing
Henry Kendall, *Leaves from Australian Forests*.

E   Sport and Recreation
First bicycle race held by the "Boneshaker Club" on Melbourne Cricket Ground (10 July).
Professional runner Matt Higgins beats Tom Cusack in a series of races in Wangaratta for the Australian championship.
South Australian Yacht Club formed (later Royal South Australian Yacht Squadron).
Warrior wins the Melbourne Cup.

F   Statistics, Social Change, the Environment
Estimated population: NSW, 480,784; Tas., 99,190; WA, 24,653; SA, 181,607; Vic., 696,762; Qld, 109,161.
"Paterson's Curse", a Mediterranean plant said to have spread from a garden in Albury, recorded as naturalized in Vic.

G   Births and Deaths
Mar   3   William Lanney d. (34).
May   7   George Gawler d. (73).
Jun 16   Charles Sturt d. (74).
Aug   7   E. J. Brady b. (−1953).
Aug 21   Will Ogilvie b. (−1963).
Sep   4   John Pascoe Fawkner d. (76).

1870

Jan   8   *Australian Town and Country Journal* established in Sydney by Samuel Bennett. (Ceases publication in 1919.)

   13   Charles Cowper replaces John Robertson as Premier of NSW.

   30   Townsville–Bowen area severely damaged by cyclone; several ships wrecked. (Hit by another cyclone on 20 Feb; many buildings demolished.)

1870

Mar 30   John Forrest leads an expedition overland from Perth to Adelaide (to 27 Aug.).
      –   Harry Redford and four associates overland about a thousand head of cattle (stolen from Bowen Downs station, central Qld) 2,400 km to SA, pioneering the Strzelecki Track.

Apr   9   James McCulloch replaces J. A. MacPherson as Premier of Vic.
     14   Gold found near Gulgong, NSW.
     26   Clipper *Walter Hood* wrecked near Ulladulla, NSW; 13 drown, 23 saved.

May   3   Arthur Palmer becomes Premier of Qld following the resignation of Charles Lilley.
     25   "Captain Thunderbolt" (Frederick Ward) shot dead near Uralla, NSW, by Constable A. B. Walker.
     30   John Hart becomes Premier of SA for the third time, replacing H. B. T. Strangways.
          Perth Town Hall opened.

Jun   1   New constitution adopted in WA providing for a Legislative Council of 18 (12 elected on a property franchise, 6 nominated).
     17   British and Australian Telegraph Co. agrees to lay a cable from Java to Darwin on condition that a line is completed between Port Augusta and Darwin by 1 Jan. 1872.
     20   Intercolonial conference in Melbourne (to 5 July) brings out differences between protectionists (mainly Vic.) and free traders.
     21   Legislation passed in Vic. abolishing state aid to religion (to be phased out over five years).
     25   Ship *Harlech Castle* leaves Melbourne for Newcastle and is not heard of again; 23 lives lost.

Aug   9   Melbourne Town Hall opened.
     30   Intercolonial Exhibition opens in the Exhibition Building in Prince Alfred Park, Sydney (to 30 Sept.).
     31   Charles Gavan Duffy secures the appointment of a royal commission to consider federation. (Reports 30 Oct.)
      –   All British troops withdrawn from Australia.

Sep   9   Ballarat proclaimed a city.
     15   Construction begins on the Overland Telegraph Line, superintended by Charles Todd.
      –   Children's Hospital opens in Melbourne.

Oct 14   Henry Parkes resigns from NSW parliament because of insolvency.
     26   Ballarat School of Mines officially opened.

Dec   5   WA's first elected Legislative Council meets for the first time.
     16   James Martin forms a coalition ministry in NSW with Robertson.
     29   Legislation passed in Vic. providing for the payment (£300 a year) of MPs for a trial period. (Extended in 1874; made permanent in 1886).

     *   Tooheys Brewery established in Sydney.
     *   Serious and severe floods occur in all states during the year.

A Architecture, Building
Exhibition Building, Prince Alfred Park, Sydney (demolished 1954).

B Science, Technology, Discovery, etc.
Industrial and Technological Museum (now Museum of Applied Science) opens in Melbourne (8 Sept.).

Discovery of the Qld lungfish by William Forster reported by J. L. G. Krefft in a letter to the *Sydney Morning Herald* (18 Jan.).

C Arts and Entertainment

Victorian Academy of Arts founded (10 Jan.), and art classes begin at Melbourne's Public Library and Museum (later the National Gallery School).

W. S. Lyster's second opera company gives its first performance in Melbourne (5 Feb.).

D Books and Writing

Adam Lindsay Gordon, *Bush Ballads and Galloping Rhymes.*

Marcus Clarke's [*For the Term of*] *His Natural Life* begins serialization in the *Australian Journal* (–1872).

E Sport and Recreation

First Australian Rules premiership competition held in Vic. (Won by Melbourne club.)

Nimblefoot wins the Melbourne Cup.

F Statistics, Social Change, the Environment

Estimated population: NSW, 497,992; Tas., 100,886 (census, 7 Feb: 99,328); WA, 25,135 (census, 31 Mar: 24,785); SA, 184,546; Vic., 723,925; Qld, 115,272.

Free education introduced in Qld, the first of the Australian colonies to adopt this principle.

Vic. becomes the first Australian colony to allow married women to own personal property (SA in 1884, Tas. in 1885, Qld in 1890, WA in 1891, NSW in 1893).

The word *larrikin* first appears in print.

G Births and Deaths

Jan   3   Ethel Richardson (Henry Handel Richardson) b. (–1946).
Jan 24   Ethel Turner b. (–1958).
Apr 18   William Dixson b. (–1952).
Jun   5   Jeannie Taylor (Mrs Aeneas Gunn) b. (–1961).
Jun 24   Adam Lindsay Gordon d. (36).
Oct   2   Florence Young b. (–1920).
Nov   1   Christopher Brennan b. (–1932).
Dec 16   Alfred Hill b. (–1960).

1871

Jan   5   "Precious" nugget (1,621 oz) found near Dunolly, Vic., by Ah Chang.
         8   Railway reaches Warwick, Qld, from Toowoomba.

Feb 10   First steam railway in Tas., from Deloraine to Launceston, completed by a private company. (Taken over by the government on 31 Oct. 1873.)

Mar 11   Alice Springs discovered by survey party for the Overland Telegraph Line.
         –   WA's first railway (horse-drawn until Aug.), from Lockville (Busselton) to Yoganup, opened by a private timber company.

Apr   9   Vic.'s 2,108-ton iron-clad turret ship-of-war *Cerberus* arrives at Port Phillip from England.

May   4   Australian Natives' Association (originally called the Victorian Natives' Society) founded in Melbourne.
             Alfred Hospital, Melbourne, opens.
         10   Act passed in NSW enabling the raising of a permanent military force.

1871

11 Tichborne estates trial begins in London. (Arthur Orton, a butcher from Wagga, claims to be the missing heir Roger Tichborne.)

25 NSW Trades and Labor Council holds its first meeting.

– Sydney Stock Exchange founded.

Jun 19 Charles Gavan Duffy replaces James McCulloch as Premier of Vic.

Jul 21 Bendigo (then called Sandhurst) proclaimed a city.

Aug 4 Elementary Education Act passed in WA.

12 Marquis of Normanby becomes Governor of Qld.

Sep 17 Brig *Carl*, on a blackbirding voyage, kidnaps 85 Solomon Islanders, 60 to 70 of whom are shot and thrown overboard after an escape attempt. (Nine crew members subsequently charged with murder; two convicted but serve only a short prison sentence.)

22 Haymarket Theatre, Melbourne, destroyed by fire.

24 Mary MacKillop excommunicated from the Catholic Church for protesting against a directive to break up the nuns in her order. (Absolved in Feb. 1872.)

– Russian scientist and explorer Nikolai Mikluho-Maclay begins a fifteen-month study of the "Maclay coast", east from Astrolabe Bay, New Guinea.

Oct 15 Germans in SA hold a peace festival at Tanunda to celebrate the German victory in the Franco–Prussian War.

– Government Savings Bank of NSW begins operations, through post offices.

Nov 9 Submarine cable from Java reaches Darwin. (First message transmitted 20 Nov.)

10 Arthur Blyth forms a ministry in SA following the defeat of the Hart government.

– National (later Royal) Agricultural Society of Vic. holds its first show in Melbourne (at a site on St Kilda Road).

Dec 4 One of the world's richest tin deposits discovered by James ("Philosopher") Smith at Mt Bischoff, Tas.

25 Goldfield discovered at Charters Tors (Towers), Qld, by Hugh Mosman and others. (Rush begins in Feb. 1872.)

A Architecture, Building

William Wardell, Government House, Melbourne (–1876).

General Post Office, Brisbane (–1872; central tower and southern wing added 1877–79).

Institute of Architects founded in Sydney.

B Science, Technology, Discovery, etc.

Queensland Museum opens in Brisbane.

C Arts and Entertainment

NSW Academy of Art constituted in Sydney (25 Apr.)—president, T. S. Mort; instructors, Giulio Anivitti and Achille Simonetti.

Italian opera company of Cagli and Pompei presents a season of operas in Australia.

Harry Rickards makes his first Australian stage appearance in Melbourne (9 Dec.).

D Books and Writing

James Brunton Stephens, *Convict Once* (long narrative poem).

Anthony Trollope arrives in Melbourne (27 July) to begin a year's visit to Australia.

E Sport and Recreation

Larry Foley and Sandy Ross fight a 71-round bare-knuckle match lasting 2 hours 40 minutes; declared a draw. (Foley beats Ross in a return bout.)

The Pearl wins the Melbourne Cup.

F Statistics, Social Change, the Environment

Population (censuses 2 Apr. and 1 Sept. [Qld]):

Vic: 730,198 (Melb., 206,780).

NSW: 502,998 (Syd., 137,586).

SA: 185,626 (includes NT).

Qld: 120,104.

Qld produces 3,494,000 kg of cotton.

SA becomes the first colony to allow a man to marry his deceased wife's sister (Vic., 1872; Tas., 1873; NSW, 1875; WA and Qld, 1877).

RSPCA established in Melbourne.

G Births and Deaths

Jan 19 Sir William Denison d. (66).

Jan 24 Oscar Asche b. (–1936).

Mar 3 Ada Crossley b. (–1929).

Apr 3 John Wren b. (–1953).

Jul 23 Albert Griffiths ("Young Griffo") b. (–1927).

Aug 4 W. A. Holman b. (–1934).

Aug 20 Sydney Long b. (–1955).

Sep 2 James Duhig b. (–1965).

Oct 12 Louis Stone b. (–1935).

Dec 25 Helena Rubinstein b. (–1965).

1872

Jan 6 Prince of Wales Theatre, Sydney, burnt down for the second time.

12 Tin discovered at Tenterfield, NSW.

22 Sir Henry Ayers forms a new ministry in SA following the defeat of the Blyth government.

Feb 26 Brig *Maria*, en route to New Guinea with 70 prospectors, runs onto a reef near Cardwell, north Qld; 21 drown and 14 are killed by Aborigines. (Survivors, including Lawrence Hargrave, rescued by John Moresby in HMS *Basilisk*.)

Four members of the Marist Brothers Catholic teaching order arrive in Sydney. (Open St Patrick's School 8 Apr.)

Mar 8 Tin discovered at Stanthorpe, Qld. (Town site proclaimed 26 May.)

20 Theatre Royal, Melbourne, gutted by fire.

Cyclone destroys every building in Roebourne, WA.

– Ralph Milner completes a journey from Port Augusta to the NT with a thousand sheep, the first stock overlanded from SA to NT.

May 6 General Post Office in King William Street, Adelaide, officially opened.

14 Henry Parkes, re-elected to NSW parliament in Feb. as member for East Sydney, forms his first ministry.

30 Thursday Is. and other islands in Torres Strait within 60 miles (97 km) of the mainland are annexed to Qld.

Jun 3 Sir Hercules Robinson becomes Governor of NSW.

Queensland National Bank begins business in Brisbane.

1872

7 Women at Clunes, Vic., attack Chinese miners and drive them out of town.

10 J. G. Francis replaces Charles Gavan Duffy as Premier of Vic.

12 Branch of the Royal Mint opens in Melbourne. (Ceases printing sovereigns in 1931, other coins in 1968.)

26 William Hann leads an expedition into Cape York Peninsula (to 12 Nov.) and discovers the Palmer and Normanby rivers and gold on the Palmer.

Jul 24 A. G. Scott ("Captain Moonlite") tried in Ballarat for the Egerton bank robbery and sentenced to eleven years' gaol.

Aug 4 Ernest Giles leaves Charlotte Waters, NT, to try to cross to the Indian Ocean. (Turns back at Lake Amadeus after discovering Mount Zeil, the highest mountain in the NT, and sighting Ayers Rock in the distance.)

22 Overland Telephone Line completed. (First direct messages from London to Adelaide not received till 22 Oct., after the broken Java–Darwin cable restored.)
First land sales at Bundaberg, Qld.

Oct 1 Brisbane *Telegraph* first published.

3 General Synod of the Church of England in Australia initiated.

19 Holtermann Nugget, the largest mass of gold ever found, discovered at Hill End, NSW.

Nov 4 F. M. Innes replaces J. M. Wilson as Premier of Tas.

9 Paddle-steamer *Providence* explodes soon after leaving Menindee, on the Darling River; all five crew die; two passengers saved.

Dec 5 HMS *Beagle* and HMS *Sandfly*, the first of five armed schooners built in Sydney for the NSW navy, are commissioned for anti-blackbirding duties in the Pacific.

17 Vic. Education Act assented to (see section F). (Comes into force on 1 Jan. 1873.)

18 First recorded discovery of opals, at Listowel Downs, near Adavale, Qld.

A Architecture, Building

B Science, Technology, Discovery, etc.
F. Y. Wolseley evolves a working model of a sheep-shearing machine.

C Arts and Entertainment
Theatre Royal, Melbourne, rebuilt immediately after being destroyed by fire, opens on 6 Nov.

D Books and Writing

E Sport and Recreation
First sheepdog trial held at Forbes, NSW; won by a collie named Kelpie (origin of the name of the breed).
The Quack wins the Melbourne Cup.

F Statistics, Social Change, the Environment
Estimated population: NSW, 534,194; Tas., 103,034; WA, 25,856; SA, 191,828; Vic., 759,428; Qld, 128,507.
Victoria becomes the first of the colonies to establish a free, compulsory, and secular primary education system under government control (followed by SA and Qld in 1875, NSW in 1880, Tas. in 1885, WA in 1895).
Kings Park, Perth, dedicated for public use.
Cattle tick introduced into northern Australia with cattle shipped from Java.

G Births and Deaths
    Feb 22 John Shaw Neilson b. (–1942).
    Mar 20 William Charles Wentworth d. (81).
    Sep 28 David Unaipon b. (–1967).
    Dec 1 Inigo Jones b. (–1954).

1873

Jan 1 Five Newcastle coalmining companies form "the vend" to present a common front to the miners' union, to fix a minimum price for coal, and to divide up the market.
   29 Fire in George Street, Sydney, destroys nine buildings.

Feb 10 Coalminers in NSW gain a reduction of working hours from 12 to 10½ a day after a six-week strike.
   20 Capt. John Moresby in HMS *Basilisk* discovers and names Port Moresby.

Mar 3 Sir George Ferguson Bowen becomes Administrator of Vic. (Appointed Governor 30 July.)

Apr 15 P. E. Warburton leads an expedition from Alice Springs westward in search of new pastoral areas.
   21 W. C. Gosse sets out from the Overland Telephone Line near Central Mount Stuart in an attempt to reach Perth.
   22 Arthur Orton (the Tichborne Claimant) tried for perjury in London. (Sentenced to 14 years' gaol on 28 Feb 1874; released in Oct. 1884.)
    – *Australasian Sketcher* begins publication in Melbourne (to 1889).

May 26 Legislation passed in Britain allowing Australian colonies to impose preferential and differential duties on colonial goods.

Jun 9 Sir Anthony Musgrave becomes Governor of SA.
   18 Warburton reaches Waterloo Wells, where he is pinned down through lack of water.
    – Street lighting (oil) installed in Perth.

Jul 19 Gosse discovers and names Ayers Rock and the Musgrave Ranges.
   22 Arthur Blyth becomes Premier of SA for the third time, following the resignation of Henry Ayers.

Aug 4 Ernest Giles sets out from the junction of the Alberga and Stevenson rivers, SA, to cross the continent to the west.
      Alfred Kennerley replaces F. M. Innes as Premier of Tas.

Sep 1 Eight-hour day granted in SA to building trades, the government's public works force, and certain other workers.
    3 J. V. Mulligan announces his discovery of gold on the Palmer River, north Qld, which begins a dramatic gold rush.
   17 Gosse reaches the Townsend Range, WA, and turns back. (Returns to Overland Telegraph Line 16 Dec.)
   29 G. E. Dalrymple leads an expedition by sea from Cardwell to explore the north coast of Qld to the Endeavour River.
   30 Warburton reaches Joanna Springs and decides to head for the Oakover River.

Oct 14 Giles reaches his most westerly depot (some 100 km further than Gosse had gone), then returns to Fort Mueller.

1873

24 Dalrymple reaches the Endeavour River and (26th) selects a site for a settlement (later named Cooktown). (Returns to Cardwell 22 Dec.)

Nov 7 NT's first newspaper, the *North Australian*, begins publication in Palmerston (Darwin) (to 1909).

11 Vic. passes Australia's first Factory Act, regulating employment of females in workrooms and factories.

19 Railway line from Melbourne reaches Wodonga on the NSW border.

Dec 9 Striking miners and their supporters at Clunes goldfield drive off Chinese strike-breakers and their police escort.

20 Mail-steamer service begins between Sydney and San Francisco.

29 Warburton's party, at the Oakover River, are saved by the return of one of his men (sent ahead earlier) with help and relief.

A Architecture, Building

Joseph Reed, Scots Church, Melbourne (–1874).
Bridge at Murray Bridge, SA (–1879).

B Science, Technology, Discovery, etc.

James Harrison invents a new process for freezing carcasses for export.
T. S. Mort erects a freezing works at Darling Harbour (Sydney) and Lithgow, and refrigeration begins on a commercial scale.

C Arts and Entertainment

D Books and Writing

Anthony Trollope, *Australia and New Zealand*.

E Sport and Recreation

Don Juan wins the Melbourne Cup.
Adelaide Cricket Ground formally opened (13 Dec.).
English cricket team led by W. G. Grace begins its Australian tour with a match against a Victorian XIII in Melbourne (26 Dec.).

F Statistics, Social Change, the Environment

Estimated population: NSW, 552,836; Tas., 104,311; WA, 25,952; SA, 197,685; Vic., 773,808; Qld, 139,928.

G Births and Deaths

Mar 29 David Jones d. (80).
Apr 11 Robert Towns d. (78).
Apr 19 Hamilton Hume d. (75).
Sep 13 George W. Lambert b. (–1930).
Oct 6 Sir Paul de Strzelecki d. (76).
Dec 11 John West d. (64).

1874

Jan 8 Arthur Macalister becomes Premier of Qld for the third time, following the defeat of the Palmer government.

16 Ernest Giles and party move north from Fort Mueller and (21st) reach the Rawlinson Range.

26 P. E. Warburton's expedition reaches Roebourne and then proceeds in easy stages to Fremantle (arr. 25 Mar.).

1874

Feb 6   Act passed in NSW reducing the term of the Legislative Assembly from five years to three years.

Mar 10   Giles discovers and (12th) names the Petermann Range.

     27   Henri Rochefort and five other French political prisoners arrive at Newcastle after escaping from New Caledonia in an Australian vessel. (Proceed to California 11 Apr.)

Apr 1   John Forrest leads an expedition from Geraldton, WA, across the Gibson Desert to the Peake telegraph station, SA (to 30 Sept.).

     2   Mine workers at Moonta and Wallaroo, SA, strike (to 15th) over a reduction in wages, which leads to the formation of the United Tradesmen's Society, later the Labor League of SA.

     23   Alfred Gibson, one of Giles's party, disappears in the desert that bears his name. (Giles turns back 21 May; reaches Charlotte Waters 13 July.)

May 23   Iron sailing ship *British Admiral* wrecked on King Is., Bass Strait, with the loss of 79 lives.

Jun 15   Brisbane's first Victoria Bridge officially opened. (Carried away by floods in 1893.)

     –   Amalgamated Miners' Association of Vic. formed.

Jul 20   Bushranger Frank Gardiner released from gaol (having served ten years) on condition that he leave Australia. (Sails for China on 27 July and subsequently settles in San Francisco.)

     31   G. B. Kerferd becomes Premier of Vic. on the retirement of J. G. Francis.

Sep 1   General Post Office in Martin Place, Sydney, opened.

     28   Victorian Humane Society (later the Royal Humane Society of Australasia) formed in Melbourne following the wreck of the pilot schooner *Rip* with the loss of several lives.

Oct 10   NSW Governor Sir Hercules Robinson formally accepts sovereignty of the Fiji Islands on behalf of Britain and becomes temporary Governor of Fiji.

Nov 6   University of Adelaide established by act of parliament. (Officially inaugurated 25 Apr. 1876; Letters Patent not granted until 22 Mar. 1881.)

     –   Rev. W. G. Lawes of the London Missionary Society establishes a mission at Port Moresby.

Dec 16   NSW Trades and Labor Council representative Angus Cameron elected to parliament as member for East Sydney (paid £3 a week by TLC).

     23   Fire destroys 45 houses in Windsor, NSW.

     *   Swan Brewery established in Perth.

A Architecture, Building

     A. L. Smith and A. E. Johnson, Law Courts, Melbourne (–1884).

     Central Government Offices complex, Perth, WA (–1896).

B Science, Technology, Discovery, etc.

     Transit of Venus observed in NSW by expeditions dispatched by H. C. Russell, director of Sydney Observatory, and in Vic. and SA.

     Linnean Society of NSW formed in Sydney (30 Oct.) with W. J. Macleay as president.

C Arts and Entertainment

     J. C. Williamson and his wife, Maggie Moore, tour Australia in the play *Struck Oil* (opens at Melbourne Theatre Royal 1 Aug.).

1874

French tightrope walker Charles Blondin cooks and eats an omelette on a tightrope in Sydney Domain (29 Aug.)

D Books and Writing

Marcus Clarke's [*For the Term of*] *His Natural Life* appears in book form.

E Sport and Recreation

Southern Rugby Union established. (Renamed the NSW Rugby Union in 1892.)
Joe Smith and Jack Biggs compete in a tree-felling match at Ulverstone, Tas. (regarded as the beginning of the sport).
Haricot wins the Melbourne Cup.

F Statistics, Social Change, the Environment

Estimated population of Australia: 1,849,392 (NSW, 573,979; Tas., 104,261; WA, 26,455; SA, 204,246; Vic., 786,108; Qld, 154,343).

G Births and Deaths

Feb 1 Alexander Harris d. (68).
Mar 2 Gregan McMahon b. (–1941).
May 17 Sir Roger Therry d. (74).
Sep 17 Walter Murdoch b. (–1970).
Oct 17 Lionel Lindsay b. (–1961).

1875

Jan 11 Sir William Robinson arrives in Fremantle to become Governor of WA. (With him as valet is Henri Grin, later to become notorious as the hoaxer Louis de Rougement.)
13 Sir Frederick Weld becomes Governor of Tas.
23 W. W. Cairns becomes Governor of Qld.

Feb 9 John Robertson replaces Henry Parkes as Premier of NSW.
11 Presbyterian Ladies' College, Melbourne, opens.
24 SS *Gothenburg* wrecked on the Great Barrier Reef near Flinders Passage with the loss of 102 lives; 27 survivors.

Apr 11 Narcisse Pellatier, survivor of the French ship *St Paul* (wrecked in 1858), is rescued by the schooner *John Bell* on Cape York Peninsula.
17 J. V. Mulligan leads an expedition from Cooktown, Qld, and discovers the Barron River (24 May).

May 6 Ernest Giles leads an overland expedition from Beltana, in SA, to Perth (to 10 Nov.).

Jun 3 SA Premier Arthur Blyth resigns and is replaced by J. P. Boucaut.
14 Railway from Ipswich to Brisbane completed (but rail bridge over Brisbane River at Indooroopilly not opened till 5 July 1876).

Aug 7 Graham Berry replaces G. B. Kerferd as Premier of Vic.
 – Fire at Cooktown, Qld, destroys eight stores.

Oct 1 First Australian postcards issued in Sydney (12,000 issued on first day).
9 Adelaide Steamship Co. founded in Adelaide.
20 Sir James McCulloch displaces Graham Berry to become Premier of Vic. for the fourth time.

Nov 9 Ten thousand Protestants and Orangemen march in Sydney on the occasion of the laying of the foundation stone of the Protestant Hall.

1875

Dec 16 Eskbank Ironworks begins operating in Lithgow, NSW.
24 Cyclone destroys a pearling fleet in the Exmouth Gulf, WA; 59 lives lost.

* Widespread flooding in NSW (Mar., May–Sept.), Qld (Feb.–Apr., July), SA (May), and Tas. (June, Aug., Sept., Dec.).
* Tin discovered at Herberton, Qld.

A Architecture, Building
John Horbury Hunt, St Peter's Cathedral, Armidale, NSW.
E. J. Woods, Education Department Building, Adelaide.
Titles Office, Melbourne (–1877; extensions and alterations carried out 1885–90 and 1931).
St Barnabas' Church, Norfolk Is. (–1880).

B Science, Technology, Discovery, etc.
W. J. Macleay, in the barque *Chevert*, obtains a valuable collection of zoological specimens from Torres Strait and New Guinea.

C Arts and Entertainment
Art gallery established in Sydney by the NSW government (beginnings of the Art Gallery of NSW).
William Ford, *Picnic Party at Hanging Rock near Mount Macedon* (painting).
Sydney's new Theatre Royal opens (Dec.).
Italian tragedienne Adelaide Ristori tours Australia.

D Books and Writing
Ada Cambridge's novel *Up the Murray* appears as a serial in the *Australasian*.
Alfred Deakin, *Quentin Massys*.
Ernest Giles, *Geographic Travels in Central Australia*.
Havelock Ellis (aged 16) arrives in Sydney at the beginning of his four-year stay in Australia.

E Sport and Recreation
Polo played in Australia for the first time, at Albert Park, Melbourne.
Morphettville Racecourse opened by the SA Jockey Club.
First "penny farthing" bicycles reach Melbourne from the UK.
Wollomai wins the Melbourne Cup (held on the first Tuesday in Nov. for the first time).

F Statistics, Social Change, the Environment
Estimated population of Australia: 1,898,223 (NSW, 593,367; Tas., 103,739; WA, 27,002; SA, 210,076; Vic., 794,934; Qld, 169,105).
More than three thousand Chinese arrive in Cooktown, Qld, during the year to seek gold on the Palmer River.

G Births and Deaths
Jan 28 Sir James Hurtle Fisher d. (84).
Mar 20 Benjamin Fuller b. (–1952).
Apr 29 Margaret Preston b. (–1963).
Oct 20 Sir Charles Cowper d. (68).
Nov 9 William Hovell d. (89).
Dec 2 C. J. La Trobe d. (74).
Dec 3 Max Meldrum b. (–1955).

1876

Jan 13 Ernest Giles sets out from Perth for Geraldton to make a return journey overland to SA. (Arrives Peake telegraph station 23 Aug.)

   – Quarterly *Melbourne Review* begins publication (to Oct. 1885).

Feb 8 Debate in Vic. Legislative Assembly prolonged by Graham Berry's followers without intermission until late on 10th (which introduces the term *stonewall* into the English language); Premier McCulloch finally introduces a "gag" motion.

   20 Submarine cable connected between NSW and NZ.

   23 Cyclone causes great property damage in Bowen, Qld.

Mar 3 Qld dock workers granted an eight-hour day.

   21 J. V. Mulligan reports finding gold on the Hodgkinson River, Qld.

     SS *Banshee* wrecked off Townsville with the loss of 17 lives.

   28 Academic work begins at Adelaide University, women being admitted to classes from the start.

Apr 4 Railway line reaches Bathurst, NSW.

   18 Six Fenian transportees to WA escape from Fremantle on the American whaler *Catalpa*. (Subsequently taken to the US.)

May 8 Truganini, the last surviving full-blood Tasmanian Aboriginal on the island, dies.

   18 Luigi d'Albertis in the steam launch *Neva* (with Lawrence Hargrave as engineer) leaves Somerset to explore in New Guinea. (Navigates 800 km up the Fly River; returns to Somerset 21 Nov.)

Jun 5 George Thorn becomes Premier of Qld on the resignation of Arthur Macalister.

   6 John Colton replaces J. P. Boucaut as Premier of SA.

   14 Barque *Giltwood* wrecked near Rivoli Bay, SA; 27 lives lost.

Jul 5 Opening of the railway bridge over the Brisbane River at Indooroopilly completes the rail link between Brisbane (Roma Street Station) and Ipswich.

   20 Thomas Reibey becomes Premier of Tas. following Alfred Kennerley's resignation.

Aug 1 Shipping firm Huddart Parker & Co. founded in Geelong.

   22 Intercolonial exhibition opens in Brisbane.

Sep 11 SS *Dandenong* sinks off Jervis Bay with the loss of 40 lives.

Oct – Settlers begin arriving at Trinity Bay, Qld, following the discovery of gold on the Hodgkinson. (Port and settlement later named Cairns; first town land sales, 15 Feb. 1877.)

Nov 1 Railway from Hobart to Launceston inaugurated.

   27 Legislation enacted in Qld to establish a public fire service to take over from volunteer and private fire brigades. (Similar legislation passed in SA in 1882, Tas. in 1883, NSW in 1884, Vic. in 1890, WA in 1898.)

Dec 2 SS *Georgette* runs aground near Busselton, WA; sixteen-year-old Grace Bussell, on horseback, rescues a number of passengers from the surf.

   * Barnet Glass opens a rubber factory in Footscray, Melbourne, pioneering the rubber industry in Australia.

   * SA becomes the first of the colonies to legalize trade unions by legislating to provide for registration and protection of their funds (NSW in 1881, Vic. in 1884 and 1886, Qld in 1886, Tas. in 1889, and WA in 1900).

A Architecture, Building
James Barnet, Lands Department Building, Sydney (–1890).

B Science, Technology, Discovery, etc.
Joseph Bancroft of Brisbane discovers the adult female of the parasitic worm *Filaria bancrofti* and shows how filariasis is transmitted by mosquitoes.

Robert Bowyer Smith demonstrates his working model of the first successful stumpjump plough. (Patent registered 1877.)

C Arts and Entertainment
Academy of Music (later Bijou Theatre) opens in Melbourne (5 Nov.).

Bland Holt begins his career in Australia, appearing in Sydney in the burlesque *Ixion*.

D Books and Writing
John Moresby, *Discoveries and Surveys in New Guinea.*

"The Vagabond" (J. S. James, a.k.a. Julian Thomas) begins his series of articles in the Melbourne *Argus* on conditions in gaols and institutions.

E Sport and Recreation
Onkaparinga Handicap Steeplechase (now the Great Eastern Steeplechase, Australia's biggest picnic race carnival, held each Easter at Onkaparinga, SA), first run (17 Apr.).

Edward Trickett of Sydney becomes Australia's first world sporting title-holder by beating the English champion sculler J. H. Sadler on the Thames (27 June).

Briseis wins the Melbourne Cup.

F Statistics, Social Change, the Environment
Estimated population of Australia: 1,958,679 (NSW, 613,288; Tas., 105,549; WA, 27,673; SA, 224,560 [census, 26 Mar., 213,271]; Vic., 805,424; Qld, 182,185 [census, 1 May, 173,283]).

Maximum working week of 50½ hours prescribed for boys 13 to 18 years old in NSW mines; employment of boys under 13 and females forbidden in mines.

G Births and Deaths
Jan 22 George Dalrymple d. (49).
May   8 Truganini d. (64?).
May 24 Henry Kingsley d. (46).
Aug 29 John Skinner Prout d. (70?).
Sep   7 C. J. Dennis b. (–1938).
Sep 10 Hugh D. McIntosh b. (–1942).
Sep 18 James Scullin b. (–1953).
Sep 23 Cyril Brudenell White b. (–1940).
Oct   4 Hugh McCrae b. (–1958).
Nov 24 Walter Burley Griffin b. (–1937).
Dec 21 J. T. Lang b. (–1975).

1877

Jan 16 Railway reaches Kingston via Naracoorte in SA.

Mar 8 John Douglas replaces George Thorn as Premier of Qld.
     10 Cloncurry, Qld, proclaimed a town site.

1877

16 Dr R. W. B. Vaughan becomes Catholic Archbishop of Sydney on the death of Archbishop Polding.

22 Henry Parkes forms a ministry in NSW following the defeat of the Robertson government.

Apr 1 Thursday Is. established as a coaling station for steamers, and the settlement moves there from Somerset.

Railway reaches Wellington, NSW, and Orange (19th).

May 21 Liberals win a sweeping victory in Vic; Graham Berry again becomes Premier.

Jun 4 Maj.-Gen. Sir William Jervois, appointed with Lt-Col. Peter Scratchley of the Royal Engineers to advise on defences of the various colonies, reports on NSW's defences.

8 Party of Lutheran missionaries arrive at the Finke River, NT, to found the Hermannsburg Mission.

Jul 15 Paddle-steamer *Yarra Yarra* sinks in a gale off Newcastle, NSW, with the loss of all hands. (As a result, the National Shipwreck Relief Society of NSW—later the Royal Shipwreck Relief and Humane Society of NSW—is formed.)

20 Sir Arthur Kennedy becomes Governor of Qld (having been administrator since 11 Apr.).

24 Jervois reports on Vic.'s defences.

Aug 9 P. O. Fysh replaces Thomas Reibey as Premier of Tas.

17 Sir John Robertson resumes the premiership of NSW.

20 Qld imposes a £10 poll tax on Chinese immigrants.

Sep 11 Ships *Avalanche* and *Forrest* collide and sink off Portland, Vic; 104 lives lost, only 3 being saved.

17 Port Arthur, Tas., penal establishment finally closed.

Oct 2 Sir William Jervois becomes Governor of SA.

11 Land tax imposed in Vic. (on estates over 640 acres and valued at more than £2,500) to break up large holdings.

26 J. P. Boucaut becomes Premier of SA again after the fall of the Colton ministry.

Nov 12 Maj.-Gen. Sir Harry Ord becomes Governor of WA.

Dec 8 Telegraph line from Perth to Adelaide (and hence to London) completed.

12 Jervois report on Adelaide's defences presented to SA parliament.

18 J. S. Farnell forms a ministry in NSW following the Oct. elections.

19 Railway reaches Portland, Vic.

* Drought experienced throughout Australia.

A Architecture, Building

Peter Johns installs the first hydraulic lift in Melbourne for Allans Music Warehouse.

B Science, Technology, Discovery, etc.

F. Y. Wolseley takes out his first shearing-machine patent.

Louis Brennan of Melbourne patents his invention of a self-propelling torpedo, later taken up by the British government.

Daily weather map introduced by NSW Government Astronomer H. C. Russell (first published in *Sydney Morning Herald* 5 Feb.).

C Arts and Entertainment

Alfred Dampier makes his first appearance in Sydney in *Hamlet* at the Royal Victoria Theatre (10 Feb.).

Garnet Walch's *Rainbow Revels*, performed by the Stewart family, launches Nellie Stewart as a popular stage performer.

D Books and Writing

E Sport and Recreation

A combined NSW and Vic. cricket team beats a visiting English team at Melbourne in what is regarded as the first official test match (15–17 Mar.).

Victorian Football Association formed as the controlling body of Australian Rules football (4 May).

British boxer Jem Mace visits Australia and lays the foundations of the sport in Australia under Queensberry Rules.

Chester wins the Melbourne Cup.

F Statistics, Social Change, the Environment

Population of the Australian colonies reaches two million (NSW, 642,845; Tas., 107,159; WA, 28,242; SA, 238,155; Vic., 818,935; Qld, 195,794).

Chinese on the Palmer River (Qld) goldfield number 17,000, compared with 1,400 Europeans.

Phylloxera vine pest discovered in Geelong vineyards.

G Births and Deaths

Jan 17 May Gibbs b. (–1969).

Mar 25 Caroline Chisholm d. (69?).

Apr 2 W. H. ("Bully") Hayes d. (47?).

Jun 16 John Fairfax d. (71).

Aug 25 John Latham b. (–1964).

Aug 27 Martin Cash d. (67?).

Sep 16 Saxe Bannister d. (87?).

Oct 8 Hans Heysen b. (–1968).

Nov 2? Victor Trumper b. (–1915).

Nov 14 Norman Brookes b. (–1968).

1878

Jan 8 First telephone line in Australia established in Melbourne (operated by McLean Bros and Rigg between Elizabeth and Spencer streets).

Because of the Vic. Legislative Council's refusal to pass the Appropriation Bill (with provisions for payment of MPs "tacked" on), Premier Berry orders the dismissal of more than 200 civil servants, to take effect next day—"Black Wednesday".

12 Telephone successfully tested by NSW Superintendent of Telegraphs between Sydney and Kurnell and (27th) between Sydney and Maitland.

14 Cyclone damages every building in Darwin.

30 Two goods trains collide head-on near Emu Plains, NSW; 5 killed.

Feb 10 Xavier College, Melbourne, opened.

– Long-distance telephone conversations conducted between Adelaide and Port Augusta in SA and Melbourne and Ballarat in Vic.

Mar 4 Great Synagogue in Elizabeth Street, Sydney, consecrated.

5 W. R. Giblin replaces P. O. Fysh as Premier of Tas.

8 Violent cyclone causes great damage in Cairns, Qld.

1878

Apr 15 Police constable A. Fitzpatrick is wounded while attempting to arrest Dan Kelly for horse-stealing. (Dan and Ned Kelly take to the bush, where they are joined by Steve Hart and Joe Byrne; rewards are offered for the Kellys' apprehension.)

May 16 Quorn, SA, proclaimed a town.

Jun 1 Iron clipper *Loch Ard* wrecked near Cape Otway, Vic; only two of the 54 aboard survive.

10 Horse-drawn trams begin running in Adelaide. (Tramway electrified in 1909.)

Jul 23 Barque *James Service* wrecked south of Fremantle, WA, with the loss of 24 lives.

Aug 12 Many Chinese killed in a fight between miners at Maytown, Qld.

Sep 3 Railway line from Sydney reaches Wagga Wagga.

27 William Morgan, MLC, succeeds J. P. Boucaut as Premier of SA.

Oct 15 Railway from Newcastle reaches Tamworth.

26 Kelly Gang kill three policemen at Stringybark Creek, Vic.

Nov 1 Vic. parliament passes the Felons Apprehension Act. (Three days later the Kelly Gang are declared outlaws with rewards of £500 each offered for their capture, alive or dead.)

18 Seamen in NSW, Qld, and Vic. begin a six-week strike in protest against employment of Chinese crews.

28 YMCA re-established in Adelaide.

30 Education Act in SA sets up a state education system.

Dec 6 Vic. parliament prorogued, with the deadlock over reform of the Legislative Council unresolved; Berry sails for the UK (28th) to press for reform.

10 Kelly Gang raid Euroa, Vic., and rob the bank of £2,000. (Rewards for their capture are increased to £1,000 a head.)

20 W. L. Crowther replaces Giblin as Premier of Tas.

21 Sir Henry Parkes becomes Premier of NSW for the third time, in coalition with Sir John Robertson, following the defeat of the Farnell government.

– Iron bridge across the Murray at Echuca completed.

A Architecture, Building

James Barnet, Colonial Secretary's Office, Sydney (–1880), and Bathurst Court House (–1880).

Edmund Blacket, St George's Cathedral, Perth (–1888; tower added 1902).

Lloyd Tayler, Australian Club, Melbourne (–1879).

B Science, Technology, Discovery, etc.

Zoological Society of SA founded (as the Acclimatization Society of SA).

Artesian water discovered at Kallara station, near Bourke, NSW. (First successful free-flowing bore put down in 1879.)

C Arts and Entertainment

Julian Ashton arrives in Melbourne to draw for the *Illustrated Australian News.*

"Advance Australia Fair", composed by Peter Dodds McCormick, first played and sung in Sydney on St Andrew's Day (30 Nov.).

D Books and Writing

E Sport and Recreation

Australian cricket team touring England dismisses the MCC (27 May) for a two-innings total of 52 runs, Fred Spofforth taking 10 wickets for 20 runs and

Harry Boyle 9 for 17. The successful tour launches the continuing series of first-class cricket between Australia and England.

Stawell Gift professional footrace first run, for a prize of 20 sovereigns (won by W. J. Millard).

Tennis first played in Australia at the Melbourne Cricket Club.

Melbourne Bicycle Club formed (first official bicycle club in Australia).

Callamai wins the Melbourne Cup.

F Statistics, Social Change, the Environment

Estimated population of Australia: 2,092,164 (NSW, 671,063; Tas., 109,993; WA, 28,612; SA, 252,099; Vic., 829,918; Qld, 200,479).

"Spiritualism is just now very much to the front in this city"—Melbourne *Age*.

G Births and Deaths

Feb 8   Sidney Myer b. (–1934).
May 9   Thomas Sutcliffe Mort d. (61).
May 24   Mary Grant Bruce b. (–1958).
May 28   John Septimus Roe d. (81).
Aug 8   John Dunmore Lang d. (78).
Aug 21   Conrad Martens d. (77).
Sep 23   Raymond Longford b. (–1959).

1879

Jan 21   Thomas McIlwraith becomes Premier of Qld.

Feb 5   Railway reaches Horsham, Vic.
      8   Kelly Gang raid Jerilderie, NSW, capture police, and (10th) rob the Bank of NSW of more than £2,000. (Rewards increased to £2,000 each.)
     25   Alexander Forrest leads an expedition from Roebourne, WA, to explore to the north-west through the Kimberley region. (Explores and names King Leopold Range, discovers the Ord River [24 July], and reaches Darwin on 7 Oct.)

Mar 24   Bridge at Murray Bridge, SA, opened for road traffic. (Adapted for railway 1886.)
      –   Smithfield, a settlement on the Barron River, north Qld, completely destroyed by floodwaters.

Apr 2   Railway completed to Sale from Melbourne.
     29   Marquis of Normanby becomes Governor of Vic. (having administered since 27 Feb.).

May 12   Provincial and Suburban Bank in Melbourne closes its doors after a run on its coin.

Jun 15   Tin discovered at Tinaroo Creek, north Qld, by John Atherton.
     24   Qld extends its boundary to include Torres Strait islands beyond the previous 60-mile limit.
      –   Australian and European Bank closes its doors.

Jul 1   *Daily Telegraph* (Sydney) begins publication.
     26   WA's first public railway line opens between Geraldton and Northampton.

Aug 4   Lord Loftus becomes Governor of NSW.
     15   R. L. Jack leads an expedition north from Cooktown and discovers good agricultural land.

1879

Sep 16   Steam tramway (horse-drawn until 28th because of late arrival of steam locomotives) begins in Sydney from Hunter Street to Redfern.

     17   Sydney International Exhibition opens in the newly built Garden Palace in the Domain. (Closes 20 April 1880.)

Oct 30   W. R. Giblin becomes Premier of Tas. for the second time, heading a coalition government.

     –   First Intercolonial Trade Union Congress held in Sydney.

Nov 15   "Captain Moonlite" (A. G. Scott) and gang occupy Wantabadgery station, near Wagga Wagga. (Police attack on 17th, and two bushrangers and one policeman are killed; Scott captured 18th.)

     26   R. L. Jack makes a further expedition through Cape York Peninsula to Somerset (to 3 Apr. 1880).

     29   First successful cargo of frozen meat leaves Sydney for London aboard the *Strathleven*. (Arrives London in good condition 2 Feb. 1880).

Dec 8   "Captain Moonlite" tried, found guilty, and sentenced to death. (Hanged 20 Jan. 1880.)

     *   Secret ballot introduced in WA.

     *   Working Men's College founded in Sydney, in association with the Mechanics' School of Arts.

     *   Castlemaine Brewery established in Brisbane.

A Architecture, Building

James Barnet, Garden Palace, Sydney (destroyed by fire 1882).
Reed and Barnes, Exhibition Building, Melbourne (–1880).
Charles Webb, South Melbourne Town Hall (–1880).
Jervois wing of the State Library, Adelaide (–1884).

B Science, Technology, Discovery, etc.

Zoological Society of NSW formed (originally for the purpose of acclimatizing birds and fish), with occupancy of a section of Moore Park, Sydney.

C Arts and Entertainment

Thomas Woolner's statue of Captain Cook in Sydney's Hyde Park unveiled (25 Feb.).
J. C. Williamson and Maggie Moore begin a second tour of Australia.

D Books and Writing

John Henniker Heaton, *Australian Dictionary of Dates and Men of the Time*.
John Boyle O'Reilly, *Moondyne*.
E. W. Cole publishes his *Funny Picture Book*.
Joseph Conrad visits Sydney for the first time, as an ordinary seaman on the wool clipper *Duke of Sutherland*.

E Sport and Recreation

Fred Spofforth takes 6 for 46 and 7 for 62 (including the hat-trick) against the visiting English cricket team in Melbourne (2–4 Jan.).
Larry Foley beats Abe Hicken in a bare-fist fight lasting 1 hour 20 minutes on the bank of the Murray near Echuca (20 Mar.).
Caulfield Cup first run (won by Newminster).
Darriwell wins the Melbourne Cup.
SA sanctions the use of the totalizator at race meetings.

F Statistics, Social Change, the Environment

Estimated population of Australia: 2,162,343 (NSW, 708,666; Tas., 112,506; WA, 29,139; SA, 265,055; Vic., 841,757; Qld, 205,220).

1879

Aboriginal population in Vic. reported to be declining rapidly as a result of lung disease caused by unhealthy living conditions.

(Royal) National Park, near Port Hacking, NSW—the world's first officially designated national park—established (dedicated 26 Apr.).

Riverine Grazier (5 Mar.) warns of rabbits in great numbers on the NSW side of the Murray River opposite Swan Hill.

G Births and Deaths

Feb 22 Norman Lindsay b. (–1969).
May 15 George Fife Angas d. (90).
Jul 16 Sir Edward Deas Thomson d. (79).
Sep 15 J. A. Lyons b. (–1939).
Oct 14 Miles Franklin b. (–1954).
Nov 18 C. E. W. Bean b. (–1968).

1880

Jan 1 Sydney Hospital for Sick Children (later the Royal Alexandra Hospital for Children) opens in Glebe, Sydney.
     13 Railway reaches Shepparton, Vic.
     31 J. F. Archibald and John Haynes begin publishing the *Bulletin.*

Feb 12 Sydney Town Hall (vestibule of present building) officially opened (having been in use since July 1875).
     25 NSW parliament passes Henry Parkes's Public Instruction Act, providing for the establishment of government high schools, full responsibility for primary education, and the withdrawal of all state aid to Church schools (from 31 Dec. 1882).

Mar 5 James Service forms a ministry in Vic. after the defeat of the Berry government at the polls.

Apr 10 Sir William Robinson becomes Governor of WA for the second time.
     20 William Jack and John Newell discover the Great Northern tin lode on the Wild River, north Qld.

May 12 Melbourne Telephone Exchange Co. opens the first telephone exchange in Australia in Collins Street, Melbourne.
      – Chinese find gold at the Margaret River, NT, encouraging further migration to the NT.

Jun 10 Macpherson Robertson, founder of the MacRobertson confectionery company, begins making confectionery in Fitzroy, Melbourne.
     11 First sugarcane planted on T. H. Fitzgerald's Innisfail estate, on the Johnstone River, north Qld. (Mill constructed 1881.)
     26 Joe Byrne of the Kelly Gang kills the informer Aaron Sherritt.
     27 Kelly Gang occupy the Glenrowan Hotel.
     28 Railway from Port Augusta reaches Hawker, SA.
     29 Ned Kelly captured by police and the rest of the Kelly Gang killed at Glenrowan.

Jul 22 Royal Victoria Theatre, Sydney, burns down.
     27 Service resigns the premiership of Vic. following a no-confidence motion on resumption of parliament; Berry becomes Premier again (3 Aug.).

Sep 5 First meeting of the Salvation Army in Australia held in Adelaide's Botanic Gardens by Edward Saunders and John Gore.

1880

16 Railway opened to Roma, Qld.

Oct 1 International Exhibition opens in the newly built Exhibition Buildings in Carlton Gardens, Melbourne. (Closes 30 Apr 1881.)
8 Telephone exchange opened in Brisbane.
– NSW Government Geologist Lamont Young and four others disappear mysteriously at Bermagui, NSW, and are never seen again.

Nov 1 Sydney's first telephone line opened, from the Royal Exchange to Darling Harbour. (Switchboard installed 11 Oct 1881.)
11 Ned Kelly hanged at the old Melbourne Gaol.
19 Jacob Garrard wins the seat of Balmain in the NSW Legislative Assembly to represent the interests of trade unions, which pay his salary.

* The first Young Women's Christian Association is formed in Sydney.
* St Ignatius' College (Riverview) opens in Sydney.

A Architecture, Building
William Butterfield, St Paul's Cathedral, Melbourne (–1891; spires added 1933).
Thomas Rowe, Sydney Hospital (completed to a modified design by John Kirkpatrick; opened 1894).
Last of Sydney's windmills demolished.

B Science, Technology, Discovery, etc.
Royal Society of SA formed.
A. W. Howitt and Lorimer Fison lay the foundations of scientific study of the Aborigines with their book *Kamilaroi and Kurnai*.
Sydney Technological Museum (later the Museum of Applied Arts and Sciences) founded.

C Arts and Entertainment
(Royal) Art Society of NSW founded.
Gaiety Theatre, Sydney, opens (27 Dec.).
With the death of W. S. Lyster (27 Nov.), opera presentation ceases; operetta takes its place, beginning with George Musgrove's presentation of Offenbach's *La Fille du Tambour Major* in Melbourne.

D Books and Writing
Henry Kendall, *Songs from the Mountains*.

E Sport and Recreation
Melbourne Cricket Club holds the first tennis championships of Vic.
First soccer club in Australia, the Wanderers, formed in Sydney. (Plays its first match, against King's School, Parramatta, 14 Aug.)
Grand Flaneur wins the Melbourne Cup.

F Statistics, Social Change, the Environment
Estimated population of Australia: 2,231,531 (NSW, 741,142; Tas., 114,790; WA, 29,561; SA, 276,393; Vic., 858,605; Qld, 211,040).
University of Melbourne admits female students for the first time (but not to study medicine).

G Births and Deaths
Aug 8 Earle Page b. (–1961).
Sep 3 Will Dyson b. (–1938).
Sep 20 Elizabeth Kenny b. (–1952).
Oct 27 S. T. Gill d. (62).
Nov 23 Sir Redmond Barry d. (67).
Nov 25 John Flynn ("Flynn of the Inland") b. (–1951).

1881

Jan 6 Cyclone causes great destruction to pearling vessels in north-western WA (to 7th); 16 lives lost.

13 Intercolonial conference meets in Sydney (to 24th) and decides to introduce uniform legislation to restrict Chinese immigration. (Qld, NSW, Vic., and SA subsequently pass acts based on passenger limitation in relation to tonnage of vessel carrying migrants.)

Feb 3 Railway from Sydney reaches Albury.

17 First officers of the Salvation Army, Capt. Thomas Sutherland and his wife, arrive in Adelaide. (Australian corps formed soon after.)

Mar 1 Railway opened between Fremantle and Perth, continuing to Guildford.

Apr 3 First simultaneous census of the six Australian colonies taken, as part of the first simultaneous census of the British Empire.

7 Survivors of the ill-fated New France settlement on New Ireland, organized by the Marquis de Rays, arrive in Sydney. (Later settle in the Northern Rivers area.)

– George Adams, licensee of Tattersall's Hotel in Sydney, runs a "Tattersall's Sweep" on the Sydney Cup horse race, the first of the Tattersall's lotteries.

May 17 Prince Albert and Prince George (later King George V), teenage sons of the Prince of Wales (later King Edward VII) arrive in Albany, WA, as midshipmen on HMS *Bacchante*. (Visit Adelaide, Melbourne, Sydney, Brisbane; leave Australia 20 Aug.)

25 Smallpox epidemic breaks out in the Rocks area of Sydney. (Over the next nine months, 178 cases are quarantined; 40 die.)

Jun 16 Two houses of Vic. parliament reach a compromise; number of members of Legislative Council increased, and property qualifications of members and electors reduced.

24 J. C. Bray replaces William Morgan as Premier of SA.

Jul 9 Sir Bryan O'Loghlen becomes Premier of Vic. after the fall of the Berry government.

18 "Sanitary camp" set up at Little Bay, Sydney, to deal with the smallpox epidemic. (Becomes the Coast Hospital, later Prince Henry Hospital.)

– St Joseph's College opened at Hunter's Hill, Sydney.

Aug 20 Four people killed in a train derailment at Jolimont, Vic.

Oct 3 Mrs Mary Watson, with her baby and a Chinese servant wounded in an attack by Aborigines, puts to sea from her home on Lizard Is., near Cooktown, in an iron tank; their bodies and a diary kept for 11 days are later found on an island in the Howick group.

21 SS *Balclutha*, en route from Melbourne to Sydney, last seen off Gabo Is. before apparently foundering with the loss of 22 lives.

29 Iron clipper *Loch Maree* leaves Geelong, Vic., and is not seen again.

Dec 7 Sir George Strahan becomes Governor of Tas.

A Architecture, Building

F. D. G. Stanley, Queensland National Bank head office, Brisbane (–1885).

Parliament House, Adelaide (work suspended after foundations laid; building opened in 1889; second stage built 1936–39).

1881

Farmer's department store in Sydney installs the first passenger lift using the Otis principle of a suspending cable.

B Science, Technology, Discovery, etc.

John Tebbutt discovers his second "great comet".

C Arts and Entertainment

Art Gallery of SA opens in the Public Library (18 June).

Theatre Royal, Brisbane, opens on the site of the old Queensland Theatre (18 Apr.).

J. C. Williamson becomes lessee of Coppin's Theatre Royal in Melbourne.

D Books and Writing

Mrs Campbell Praed, *Policy and Passion* (*Longleat of Kooralbyn*).

E Sport and Recreation

First six-day bike race in Australia held at Melbourne's Exhibition circuit.

Zulu wins the Melbourne Cup.

F Statistics, Social Change, the Environment

Population of Australia (census 3 Apr.): 2,250,194—Vic., 861,566 (Melb., 282,947); NSW, 749,825 (Syd., 224,939); SA, 276,414; Qld, 213,525; Tas., 115,705; WA, 29,708; NT, 3,451.

University of Sydney admits its first female students.

Legislation passed in NSW providing for Sunday closing of hotels and weekday closing at 11 p.m.

Paspalum grass, acquired from South America, introduced into Vic. by Government Botanist F. J. H. von Mueller.

G Births and Deaths

Jan 13   Essington Lewis b. (–1961).

Feb 3   John Gould d. (76).

Jul 23   J. J. Hilder b. (–1916).

Aug 2   Marcus Clarke d. (35).

1882

Jan 16   Screw-corvette *Wolverine* transferred from the Royal Navy to NSW for use as a training ship.

Cyclone hits Darwin; many buildings destroyed.

29   Russian naval vessels *Afrika*, *Vestnik*, and *Platon* visit Port Phillip (to 24 Feb.) after short visits to Sydney and Hobart. (Sensational articles subsequently appear in the press about Russian intentions.)

Feb 14   Methodist Ladies' College, Melbourne, opens in temporary premises, with W. H. Fitchett as principal.

Mar 7   Cyclone causes serious damage at Cossack and Roebourne, WA.

22   Government telephone exchange opens at the Sydney GPO.

–   J. F. Archibald and John Haynes gaoled for non-payment of costs arising from a libel action brought against them for a *Bulletin* article criticizing conduct at the Clontarf picnic grounds. (Released after six weeks when money is raised by public subscription.)

Apr 8   Agricultural Society of NSW holds its first show at Moore Park, Sydney (to 15th).

May 17   Adelaide and Port Augusta connected by rail.

1882

Jun – Australian Electric Co. exhibits electric light in Melbourne. (Illuminates Spencer Street Station in Nov.)

Jul 13 Gold found at Mount Morgan, Qld.
26 Perth *Daily News* begins publication.

Sep 8 Dedication of St Mary's Cathedral, Sydney.
22 Garden Palace in Sydney destroyed by fire.
25 (Royal) Prince Alfred Hospital opens in Sydney, and the Austin Hospital opens in Melbourne.

Oct 28 SS *Woniora* founders off Botany Bay; only one of the 16 crewmen saved.

Nov 11 Parkes ministry falls in NSW when Robertson's amending Land Bill is defeated.
SS *Austral* sinks at anchor in Neutral Bay, Sydney, with the loss of five lives.
– Wharf labourers in Sydney begin an unsuccessful four-week strike to increase their hourly rate from 1s to 1s 3d.
– Umberumberka Silver Mine opened at what is now Silverton, NSW.

Dec 2 Seven people killed when two trains collide head-on near Burnley, Vic.
4 Silver-lead discovered at Zeehan, Tas.
10 Melbourne tailoresses strike successfully over a reduction in piece-work rates and (15th) form Australia's first women's trade union—the Victorian Tailoresses Union.
12 New Australasian Mine at Creswick, Vic., floods; 22 lives lost.
– Four ministers lose their seats in NSW election.

A Architecture, Building
John Young, The Abbey, Annandale, Sydney.

B Science, Technology, Discovery, etc.

C Arts and Entertainment
J. C. Williamson, Arthur Garner, and George Musgrove form a partnership ("the Triumvirate") controlling the Theatre Royal and Princess Theatre in Melbourne and the Sydney Theatre Royal and the Adelaide Theatre Royal.
Electric light installed in the Theatre Royal, Sydney.
Wirth's Circus formed.

D Books and Writing
Rolf Boldrewood's *Robbery Under Arms* begins serialization in the *Sydney Mail* (1 July).
G. E. Morrison, in a series of articles in the Melbourne *Leader*, describes his experiences on the blackbirder *Lavinia*.

E Sport and Recreation
An Australian touring cricket team captained by W. L. Murdoch beats England at the Oval by seven runs, Spofforth taking four of the last six wickets for two runs (29 Aug.). Next day the *Sporting Times*, in a mock *in memoriam* notice lamenting the death of English cricket, reports, "The body will be cremated and the ashes taken to Australia."
NSW Soccer Association formed (Apr.).
NSW and Qld play the first intercolonial Rugby match, in Sydney (12 Aug.).
Australian Golf Club formed in Sydney.
The Assyrian wins the Melbourne Cup.

F Statistics, Social Change, the Environment
Estimated population of Australia: 2,388,082 (NSW, 809,403; Tas., 120,477; WA, 31,016; SA, 292,092; Vic., 892,765; Qld, 242,329).

1882

Fern Tree Gully, Vic., reserved.
Corriedale sheep introduced in Vic. by Henry Corbett.

G Births and Deaths

Jan 31 Peter Dawson b. (–1961).
May 5 Douglas Mawson b. (–1958).
Jul 8 Percy Grainger b. (–1961).
Aug 1 Henry Kendall d. (43).
Dec 2 Eliza Winstanley d. (64?).
Dec 16 Elioth Gruner b. (–1939).

1883

Jan 5 Alexander Stuart forms a government in NSW.
24 Aborigines ambush and kill Marcus de la Poer Beresford, officer in charge of native police at Cloncurry, Qld, and four of the police. More than a year of battles between whites and blacks ensues.
30 Premier Sir Bryan O'Loghlen loses his seat in the Vic. election. (James Service forms a coalition government 8 Mar.)

Feb 19 Sir William Robinson becomes Governor of SA.
27 Port Kembla, NSW, and Mount Kembla coalmine inaugurated.
– Irish politician J. E. Redmond and his brother arrive in Adelaide on a visit to raise funds for the Irish National League.

Mar 6 Turbulent public meeting held in the Protestant Hall, Sydney, to protest against Irish National League representatives in Australia.
24 Salvation Army newspaper *War Cry* first issued in Sydney.

Apr 4 H. M. Chester, police magistrate on Thursday Is., acting on instructions from Qld Premier Sir Thomas McIlwraith, annexes south-eastern New Guinea for the Crown. (Repudiated by Britain on 2 June.)
21 G. E. Morrison arrives in Melbourne after walking more than 3,000 km from Normanton, on the Gulf of Carpentaria, in 123 days.
– Burns Philp and Co. Ltd formed in NSW by the amalgamation of the various businesses of James Burns and Robert Philp.

May 14 Government telephone exchange opened in Adelaide. (Other exchanges opened in Hobart [6 Aug.] and Launceston [12 Dec.].)
– Durack family begin their great overlanding movement from western Qld to the Kimberleys. (Arrive at the Ord River in Sept. 1885.)

Jun 2 Sir Frederick Broome becomes Governor of WA.
David Lindsay leads a party from Palmerston (Darwin) to explore into Arnhem Land. (Arrives at Katherine in Nov.)
14 Bridge over the Murray River at Albury–Wodonga completed, linking NSW and Vic. railways. (Train service between Sydney and Melbourne—with change for break of gauge—begins 21 Aug.)
26 St John Ambulance Association formed in Melbourne.

Jul 21 G. E. Morrison leads an expedition from Port Moresby to report on New Guinea for the Melbourne *Age*. (Returns on 15 Oct., having been speared by natives and badly wounded.)

Aug 1 NSW Board of Technical Education appointed. (Takes over Working Men's College in Oct.)

1883

Sep 5 Boundary rider Charles Rasp registers the first mineral claim on what is now Broken Hill.

Oct 1 Sydney High School, first of the state-run high schools established under the Education Act of 1880, enrols its first students.

23 Ayr, Qld, proclaimed a town site.

Nov 1 Public Service Act passed in Vic., creating Australia's first Public Service Board.

6 Sir Anthony Musgrave becomes Governor of Qld.

13 Samuel Griffith replaces McIlwraith as Premier of Qld.

28 Intercolonial conference in Sydney (to 9 Dec.) calls for the creation of a Federal Council of Australasia.

– Derby and Broome, WA, declared town sites.

* Central trade union councils formed in Hobart and Brisbane.

* Alfred Thomas Bushell founds his tea business in Brisbane.

A Architecture, Building

Charles Webb, Windsor Hotel, Melbourne (–1884).

Darwin's Fanny Bay Gaol completed.

W. G. Watson, Bendigo Public Offices and Post Office (–1887).

B Science, Technology, Discovery, etc.

Zoological Gardens opened in Adelaide.

Medical School opened at Sydney University.

Time signals telegraphed from Greenwich to Australia to help determine Australia's longitude.

C Arts and Entertainment

Tomaso Sani completes his controversial carvings on Sydney's GPO.

Art Gallery of Vic. opens on Sunday (6 May) despite many protests. (Parliament votes on 5 July against Sunday opening, and galleries do not open on a Sunday until 1904.)

Livingston Hopkins ("Hop") arrives in Sydney (9 Feb.) from the US to work as a cartoonist for the *Bulletin*.

Australia's first college of music founded in Adelaide by Immanuel G. Reimann.

George Darrell stages his melodrama *The Sunny South*, starring Essie Jenyns.

D Books and Writing

Edward Curr, *Recollections of Squatting in Victoria*.

G. W. Rusden, *History of Australia*.

Cole's Book Arcade opens in Bourke Street, Melbourne (6 Nov; closes 1929).

E Sport and Recreation

Aboriginal runner Bobbie Kinnear wins the Stawell Gift.

All-round athlete "Professor" William Miller knocks down champion boxer Larry Foley in the 40th round of a challenge fight in Sydney (28 May), declared a draw after spectators rush the ring.

Martini-Henry wins the Melbourne Cup.

F Statistics, Social Change, the Environment

Estimated population of Australia: 2,505,736 (NSW, 855,398; Tas., 123,277; WA, 32,086; SA, 301,907; Vic., 912,453; Qld, 280,615).

Bella Guerin, the first woman to graduate from an Australian university, receives a BA degree from the University of Melbourne.

G Births and Death

Feb 9 Edmund Blacket d. (65).

1883

Apr 12 Dally Messenger b. (–1959).
Apr 15 S. M. Bruce b. (–1967).
Dec 4 Katharine Susannah Prichard b. (–1969).

1884

Jan 30 Cyclone severely damages Bowen, Qld, wrecking meatworks and sugar mill and unroofing nearly all houses.

31 Trades and Labor Council established in Adelaide.

Mar 21 Patrick Francis Moran appointed Roman Catholic Archbishop of Sydney. (Arrives to take up duty on 8 Sept.)

Apr 2 Two trains collide near Werribee, Vic., 3 killed, 46 injured.

May 3 Oriental Banking Corporation of London closes its doors, forcing Australian branches to do likewise. (Reopen on 6th; later reconstructed as the New Oriental Bank.)

Jun 16 John Colton replaces J. C. Bray as Premier of SA.

18 Pioneer Dairy Co., first co-operative dairy and butter factory in Australia, opens in Kiama, NSW.

22 Vic. Women's Suffrage Society formed in Melbourne by Henrietta Dugdale and Annette Bean.

Jul 15 Sir Henry Loch becomes Governor of Vic.

17 Schooner *Hopeful* arrives at the Herbert River, north Qld, with 123 island labourers; soon after, crew members are charged with kidnapping and murder. (Recruiter and bosun receive the death sentence; master and government agent sentenced to life imprisonment; other crew members receive terms of 7 to 10 years; no executions carried out.)

Aug 15 Adye Douglas becomes Premier of Tas. on the defeat of the Giblin ministry.

Sep 30 SA's first warship, the gunboat *Protector*, arrives at Port Adelaide from Britain.

– In a pitched battle at Prospector's Creek, 120 km north-west of Cloncurry, Qld, between Kalkadoon tribesmen and a punitive force of police and native police led by F. C. Urquhart, most of the Kalkadoon warriors are wiped out.

Nov 3 German warship *Elisabeth* annexes New Britain for Germany.

6 Commodore J. E. Erskine in the *Nelson* proclaims a British protectorate over south-eastern New Guinea (Papua).

14 Land and income taxes introduced in SA.

16 Germany proclaims a protectorate over north-eastern New Guinea and the Bismarck Archipelago.

22 Maj.-Gen. P. H. Scratchley appointed Special Commissioner for British New Guinea. (Dies of malaria on 2 Dec. 1885.)

– Boot factories in Melbourne lock out 1,400 employees campaigning against sweated outside labour (to Feb. 1885).

* Leaders of Sydney bakers striking for an eight-hour day imprisoned.

* Smallpox epidemics in Vic. (to 1885) and SA.

A Architecture, Building

F. D. G. Stanley, Queensland Club (opens 1 June).

Steel swing-span bridge over the Parramatta River at Gladesville, Sydney (replaced in 1964).

B Science, Technology, Discovery, etc.

C. L. Wragge establishes the Torrens Observatory at Walkerville in Adelaide (Jan.).

Royal Society of Qld founded.

Lawrence Hargrave gives his address "The Trochoided Plane", on the basic principles of flight, to the Royal Society of NSW (8 Aug.).

W. H. Caldwell establishes that monotremes lay eggs.

H. V. McKay invents his first stripper-harvester. (Patented 1885; developed about 1892–93 into the Sunshine Harvester.)

C Arts and Entertainment

Ballarat Fine Art Gallery opens, in the Academy of Music.

D Books and Writing

Rolf Boldrewood, *Old Melbourne Memories.*

E Sport and Recreation

Canterbury Racecourse opens in Sydney (19 Jan.).

Bare-fist boxing officially banned in all colonies after the death of Victorian Alex Agar in a fight with American Jimmy Lawson at Randwick Racecourse (17 Apr.).

Cyclist A. Edwards rides a penny-farthing bike from Sydney to Melbourne in 8½ days (23–31 May).

William Beach of Dapto, NSW, wins the world sculling championship, beating Canadian Edward Hanlan on the Parramatta River (16 Aug.).

Australian team captain W. L. Murdoch scores the first double century in test cricket, at the Oval.

Malua wins the Melbourne Cup.

F Statistics, Social Change, the Environment

Estimated population of Australia: 2,605,725 (NSW, 899,203; Tas., 126,665; WA, 33,546; SA, 308,947; Vic., 935,777; Qld, 301,587).

G Births and Deaths

Jan 24   Thomas Blamey b. (–1951).

Feb 8   R. L. ("Snowy") Baker b. (–1953).

Aug 31   Sir Robert Torrens d. (70?).

Nov 26   Desiderius Orban b. (–1986).

Dec 29   E. G. Theodore b. (–1950).

1885

Jan 1   NSW Crown Lands Act, aimed at promoting "closer settlement", comes into operation.

25   Train derailment near Cootamundra; 7 killed, 25 wounded.

Feb 3   Roseworthy Agricultural College, SA, opened.

11   News of General Gordon's death reaches Sydney. Next day, NSW offers a contingent of volunteer troops for service in the Sudan.

Mar 3   Troops embark from Sydney for the Sudan. (Arrive 29th.)

13   Victorian Employers' Union formed.

20   A total of 121 cities (including Armidale, Bathurst, Grafton, and Goulburn), towns, and villages in NSW proclaimed under Crown Lands Act.

28   HMQS *Gayundah*, the first of two gunboats for Qld's navy, arrives at

1885

Brisbane from Britain. (The other, *Paluma*, arrives in May, a torpedo boat, *Mosquito*, having been shipped out earlier in the year.)

Apr 14 Orbost, Vic., proclaimed a town.

May – Royal commission on island labour condemns recruiting methods.

Jun 9 First Seventh Day Adventists arrive in Melbourne.
16 J. W. Downer replaces John Colton as Premier of SA.
19 Sudan contingent returns to Sydney, having participated in only one minor skirmish. (Casualties: 3 slightly wounded in action; 7 deaths from fever or dysentery.)
20 First prospectus of the Broken Hill Proprietary Co. Ltd issued. (Company floated on 10 Aug.)
26 Weekly journal *Table Talk* founded in Melbourne (–1937).
27 Archbishop Moran becomes Australia's first cardinal.
– Boundaries between German and British New Guinea ratified.

Jul 31 NSW Chamber of Manufactures formed at a meeting at Sydney Town Hall.

Aug 10 Horse tramway begins operating in Brisbane.
– Charles Hall and Jack Slattery find gold in the Kimberley region, WA.

Sep 1 Trades and Labor Council founded in Brisbane.
18 Railway reaches Bourke, NSW.

Oct 7 George Dibbs replaces Alexander Stuart as Premier of NSW.
– Melbourne's Homeopathic Hospital (later Prince Henry's Hospital) opens in new premises in St Kilda.

Nov 10 Pacific Islanders' Act, passed by the Griffith government in Qld, prohibits the indenture of kanaka labour after 31 Dec. 1890.
11 Charles Strong, a former Presbyterian minister, founds the Australian Church. First cable tram service begins in Melbourne (to Richmond).

Dec 12 Baron Carrington becomes Governor of NSW.
18 Vic.'s new and comprehensive Factory Act regulates hours and conditions in factories employing more than six workers.
19 Weekly *Western Mail* begins publication in Perth.
22 Sir John Robertson becomes Premier of NSW for the fifth time, following the resignation of the Dibbs ministry (on the 16th).

* A. E. and J. M. Grace open a drapery store in George Street, Sydney, later to become Grace Bros. department store chain.

A Architecture, Building

James Barnet, Customs House, Sydney (–1887).
J. J. Clark, Treasury Building, Brisbane (–1928).
Sherrin and Hennessy, St Patrick's College, Manly (–1889).
Art Gallery of NSW, Sydney, opened (23 Dec; courts added 1897, 1899, southern wing 1901, central façade 1906, later additions opened 1972, 1988).
Prell's Building in Melbourne is the first to rise to ten storeys.
Grainger & D'Ebro, Fremantle Town Hall (–1887).

B Science, Technology, Discovery, etc.

C Arts and Entertainment

Tom Roberts, Frederick McCubbin, and Louis Abrahams set up an artists' camp at Box Hill, Vic., laying the foundations for the Heidelberg School.
Phil May arrives in Sydney (25 Dec.) to work for the *Bulletin* (until 1888).

Joshua Ives establishes the first (temporary) chair of music in Australia at Adelaide University.

Dion Boucicault's theatrical company brought to Australia by J. C. Williamson.

D Books and Writing

Mary Hannay Foott, *Where the Pelican Builds and Other Poems.*

Mrs Campbell Praed, *The Head Station.*

E Sport and Recreation

Rosehill Racecourse, Sydney, opens (18 Apr.).

Sheet Anchor wins the Melbourne Cup.

F Statistics, Social Change, the Environment

Estimated population of Australia: 2,694,518 (NSW, 943,867; Tas., 128,860; WA, 35,959; SA, 309,313; Vic., 959,838; Qld, 316,681).

First female medical student (Dagmar Berne) admitted to Sydney University.

G Births and Deaths

Jan   8   John Curtin b. (–1945).
Feb   7   George Sorlie b. (–1948).
Mar 28   G. J. Coles b. (–1977).
Jun 11   John Lort Stokes d. (72?).
Jul   1   Dorothea Mackellar b. (–1968).
Aug 12   Keith Murdoch b. (–1952).
Aug 18   Nettie Palmer b. (–1964).
Aug 28   Vance Palmer b. (–1959).
Sep 22   J. B. Chifley b. (–1951).
Oct 15   Frank Hurley b. (–1962).
Dec   4   David Rivett b. (–1961).

1886

Jan   1   Melbourne wharf labourers strike (to 18th) for better wages and an eight-hour day.

25   Federal Council of Australasia holds its first meeting in Hobart (to 5 Feb.).

–   First Seventh Day Adventist church in Australia opens in Melbourne.

Feb   8   Methodist Ladies' College (Oakburn College) opens in Launceston.

9   A "board of arbitration" (first of its kind) chosen by Employers' Union and Trades Hall Council settles wharf labourers' dispute; eight-hour day granted.

18   Duncan Gillies becomes Premier of Vic., replacing James Service.

26   Sir Patrick Jennings replaces Sir John Robertson as Premier of NSW.

Mar   8   J. W. Agnew becomes Premier of Tas., replacing Adye Douglas, who becomes first Tas. Agent-General in UK.

29   John Forrest leaves Fremantle to examine the Kimberley district, during which he selects the site for the port of Wyndham. (Declared a town site 2 Sept.)

–   Amalgamated Railway and Tramway Association formed in NSW.

–   Convict establishment in WA disbanded.

May   1   Railway from Adelaide to Bordertown officially opened.

22   Sydney's first cable tramway begins, from Milsons Point to Ridge Street, North Sydney. (Converts to electricity in 1900.)

30   SS *Ly-ee-moon* wrecked off Green Cape, NSW; 76 lives lost.

Jun 12   Amalgamated Shearers' Union formed at Ballarat; W. G. Spence president.

1886

Jul 7 George Clunies Ross given a grant of the Cocos Is. in perpetuity.
21 Railway reaches Gundagai, NSW.

Aug 7 Carnarvon, WA, proclaimed a town site.

Sep 2 Fourth Intercolonial Trade Union Congress meeting in Adelaide (to 7th) resolves that there should be direct representation of labour in parliament and that members should be paid.
Aboriginal Protection Act in WA provides for the setting up of a Protection Board.
16 Legislation passed granting payment of expenses for Qld MPs.
21 "The Normanby woman", a white woman speaking no English, is found living with Aborigines near Cooktown, Qld. (She dies within a few days of capture.)

Oct 1 Dookie Agricultural College, Vic., enrols its first students.
21 George Chaffey signs an agreement with the Vic. government to establish an irrigation settlement at Mildura.
– Mount Morgan Gold Mine Co. registered in Brisbane.

Nov 27 Nine young men are sentenced to death for the rape of a 16-year-old unemployed domestic servant on Mount Rennie in Moore Park, Sydney. (Five reprieved and given life sentences; other four hanged.)
30 Sydney's water supply from the Upper Nepean catchment via Prospect reservoir turned on (superseding Botany Swamps scheme).

Dec 8 SS *Keilawarra* sinks after colliding with the *Helen Nicoll* off North Solitary Is., NSW, with the loss of 40 lives.
24 Academy of Music Theatre, Adelaide, destroyed by fire for the third time in three years; three firemen killed.

* Methodist Ladies' College established in Burwood, Sydney.
* Copper (and gold) found at Mt Lyell, Tas.

A Architecture, Building
John Petrie, Customs House, Brisbane (–1889).
Princes Bridge, Melbourne (–1888).
St Francis Xavier Cathedral, Adelaide (–1926).
Terracotta Marseilles pattern roof tiles begin to take the place of slates and iron.

B Science, Technology, Discovery, etc.
Aboriginal skull 14,000–16,000 years old found at Talgai station, Qld.

C Arts and Entertainment
Tom Roberts, *Bourke Street, Melbourne* (painting).
Roberts, McCubbin, and Abrahams move their artists' camp to Mentone, where they are joined by Arthur Streeton.
Brough–Boucicault theatre company formed.
Princess Theatre, Melbourne, opens (18 Dec.).
Criterion Theatre, Sydney, opens (27 Dec.).

D Books and Writing
Andrew Garran, ed., *Picturesque Atlas of Australasia*.
Fergus Hume, *The Mystery of a Hansom Cab*.
D. M. Angus and George Robertson form a bookselling partnership in Sydney.
A. B. Paterson's first poem under the pseudonym "The Banjo" appears in the *Bulletin* (12 June).
J. F. Archibald becomes editor of the *Bulletin* (to 1902).

E Sport and Recreation

Austral Wheel Race (track cycling) inaugurated in Melbourne (30 Jan.).

Safety bicycles (i.e., with two equal-size wheels and chain drive to the rear one) introduced in Australia.

Ladies' cricket match played between the Siroccos and Fernlees on the Sydney Cricket Ground.

Arsenal wins the Melbourne Cup.

F Statistics, Social Change, the Environment

Estimated population of Australia: 2,788,050 (NSW, 983,518; Tas., 131,190; WA, 40,604; SA, 306,710; Vic., 993,717; Qld, 332,311).

Hotels in Qld close on Sundays.

Shops in Vic. close at 7 p.m. weekdays, 10 p.m. Saturdays (from 1 Mar.).

Rabbits along the Warrego River reach the Qld border. Work begins on rabbit-proof fences between NSW and SA, and NSW and Qld.

G Births and Deaths

Jan   3   Arthur Mailey b. (–1967).

Apr 28   Owen Dixon b. (–1972).

Aug   8   Ernest Fisk b. (–1965).

Sep 25   Edward Hallstrom b. (–1970).

Nov   4   Sir James Martin d. (66).

Nov 28   Margaret McIntyre b. (–1948).

1887

Jan 19   Vic. and SA railways link at Serviceton; first Adelaide–Melbourne express runs next day.

20   Sir Henry Parkes replaces Sir Patrick Jennings as Premier of NSW.

31   Quakers open the co-educational Friends' School in Hobart.

Feb   4   Qld's railways reach the NSW border at Wallangarra.

14   Chaffey Brothers make an agreement with the SA government to establish an irrigation system at Renmark. (Pumps operating by end of year.)

Mar 11   Sir Robert Hamilton becomes Governor of Tas.

23   Mine disaster at the Bulli colliery, NSW; gas explosion kills 83.

29   P. O. Fysh becomes Premier of Tas. for the second time.

Apr   4   First Colonial Conference held in London (to 9 May).

22   Twenty-two pearling vessels sink during a cyclone at Eighty Mile Beach, WA; 140 men drown.

May 5   Australian Socialist League formed in Sydney.

6   Working Men's College (later Royal Melbourne Institute of Technology) inaugurated in Melbourne. (Opens 7 June.)

11   Express train runs into a stationary train at Windsor, Melbourne; 6 killed; 154 injured.

–   Chinese investigative commission visits Australia. (Protests to Britain about restrictive legislation.)

Jun 11   Thomas Playford replaces Sir John Downer as Premier of SA.

14   Railway line from Port Pirie, SA, reaches the NSW border at Cockburn, and (16th) the line from Adelaide reaches Mt Gambier.

21   SA Intercolonial and Jubilee Exhibition opens in Adelaide (to 7 Jan. 1888). Six people killed and 73 injured in a railway accident at Peat's Ferry, NSW.

1887

Jul 16 Anti-Chinese demonstrations in Brisbane.

Sep 10 Railway from Silverton, NSW, to Broken Hill opened.

Oct 19 SS *Cheviot* wrecked near Point Nepean, Vic; 35 drown.

Nov 14 Gordon Memorial Technical College (later Gordon Institute of Technology, now Deakin University) opens in Geelong.
16 Legislation passed in SA providing for the payment of MPs.
19 *Boomerang*, a radical weekly edited by William Lane, begins publication in Brisbane (to 1892).
– Longreach, Qld, gazetted as a town.

Dec 1 Telephone exchange opens in Perth.
20 Australasian Naval Defence Act, passed in the UK, provides for an auxiliary naval squadron, partly maintained by the colonies, to supplement the British squadron in Australian waters.
31 Steam tramway begins running in Newcastle, NSW.
– Horse tramway starts in Ballarat. (Electrified between 1905 and 1913.)

* William Bede Dalley becomes a member of the Privy Council, the first Australian to be appointed.
* Smallpox epidemic in Launceston, Tas.

A Architecture, Building
Queen Victoria Museum and Art Gallery, Launceston (–1891).

B Science, Technology, Discovery, etc.

C Arts and Entertainment
John Longstaff wins the first Vic. National Gallery travelling scholarship with his painting *Breaking the News.*
Nellie Melba makes her début in grand opera in *Rigoletto* at Brussels (13 Oct.)
Francis Ormond endows a chair of music at Melbourne University.
George Rignold's Her Majesty's Theatre, Sydney, opens (10 Sept.).

D Books and Writing
John Farrell, *How He Died and Other Poems.*
John Boyle O'Reilly, *The Golden Secret: A Tale of Bush and Convict Life in Western Australia.*
Henry Lawson's first printed poem, "Song of the Republic", appears in the *Bulletin* (1 Oct.).

E Sport and Recreation
NSW Amateur Athletics Association founded (20 Apr.).
Aboriginal runner Bobby McDonald first uses a crouch start in a sprint race, initiating the start universally used today.
William Beach beats Edward Hanlan on the Nepean River (26 Nov.) to retain his world championship sculling title, then retires, having rowed unbeaten for the world championship seven times.
Dunlop wins the Melbourne Cup.

F Statistics, Social Change, the Environment
Estimated population of Australia: 2,881,362 (NSW, 1,014,607; Tas., 135,541; WA, 43,820; SA, 310,038; Vic., 1,025,476; Qld, 351,880).
Gas bath heaters begin to be used in Australian homes.

G Births and Deaths
Jan 9 Sydney Ure Smith b. (–1949).
Apr 16 H. Gordon Bennett b. (–1962).

154

Apr 17 Roland Wakelin b. (–1971).
Jun 26 Adolph Basser b. (–1964).
Nov 25 John Ridley d. (81).

1888

Jan 12 Broken Hill connected by rail to Adelaide via Silverton and Cockburn.
16 Railway line from Newcastle reaches Wallangarra on the Qld border, completing the Sydney–Brisbane rail link (though no bridge yet across Hawkesbury River).

Feb 17 Mackay, Qld, severely damaged by cyclone; 2 ships wrecked.
28 *Barrier Miner* newspaper begins publication in Broken Hill.

Mar 1 Fifth Intercolonial Trade Union Congress, held in Brisbane (to 7th), demands legislation to restrict Chinese immigration.

May 3 Mass protest meeting held in Sydney following the arrival of two ships carrying Chinese immigrants (who are prevented from landing).
15 *Dawn*, Louisa Lawson's monthly journal (edited, printed, and published by women), first issued in Sydney. (Ceases publication 1 July 1905.)
16 Chinese Exclusion Bill passed by NSW parliament in one sitting.
19 *Mildura Cultivator* begins publication. (Absorbed in *Sunraysia Daily* 2 Oct. 1920.)

Jun 6 Christmas Is. annexed by Britain. (Settlement established at Flying Fish Cove by George Clunies Ross in Nov.).
12 Intercolonial conference held in Sydney (to 14th) recommends that uniform legislation be passed to restrict Chinese immigration.
13 Sir Thomas McIlwraith forms his second ministry in Qld.

Jul 13 *Star of Greece* wrecked near Willungra, SA; 17 lives lost.

Aug 1 Centennial International Exhibition opens in Melbourne (to 31 Jan. 1889).
24 Newcastle coalminers begin a 13-week strike over a new agreement.

Sep 4 Dr (later Sir) William Macgregor arrives at Port Moresby to take up his appointment as Administrator of British New Guinea and formally annex the protectorate as a British Crown colony.

Oct 1 Nauru annexed by Germany.
3 Railway line from Sydney to Kiama completed.
4 Princes Bridge opened in Melbourne.
9 Launceston becomes a city.
13 Township of Alice Springs (originally named Stuart) surveyed by David Lindsay. (First land sales 31 Jan. 1889.)

Nov 5 Fire destroys a block of more than 60 business premises in Broken Hill's main thoroughfare.
9 Tamworth, NSW, becomes the first town in Australia (and in the Southern Hemisphere) to be lit by electricity.
30 Boyd Morehead succeeds McIlwraith as Premier of Qld.
– W. M. and R. R. Foster establish a brewery in Melbourne.

Dec 8 First demonstration of a parachute jump in Australia made by J. T. Williams from a balloon over Sydney.

* Copper discovered in the Chillagoe area, Qld, by William Atherton.

1888

* Widespread drought throughout Australia, most severe in NSW and north-west Vic.

A Architecture, Building

John Horbury Hunt, Rose Bay Convent, Sydney.

Federal Hotel, Melbourne (opened July; demolished 1972).

Pressed-metal ceilings first installed in Sydney Town Hall by Ernest Wunderlich (who begins manufacturing in 1890).

B Science, Technology, Discovery, etc.

Australasian Association for the Advancement of Science holds its first congress in Sydney (28 Aug.). (Name changed to Australian and New Zealand Association for the Advancement of Science—ANZAAS—in 1930.)

C Arts and Entertainment

Arthur Streeton, *Golden Summer* (painting).

Charles Conder, *The Departure of the S.S. Orient—Circular Quay* (bought by the Art Gallery of NSW).

Conder joins Streeton and Tom Roberts at Eaglemont, near Heidelberg, Vic.

J. E. Boehm's statue of Queen Victoria in Queen's Square, Sydney, unveiled (24 Jan.).

Brisbane's Her Majesty's Opera House (Theatre) opens (2 Apr.).

D Books and Writing

Rolf Boldrewood's *Robbery Under Arms* appears in book form.

Bulletin publishes Henry Lawson's first short story, "His Father's Mate" (22 Dec.).

E Sport and Recreation

Henry Searle—"the Clarence Comet"—wins the world sculling championship on the Parramatta River (27 Oct.).

Mentor wins the Melbourne Cup.

F Statistics, Social Change, the Environment

Estimated population of Australia: 2,981,677 (NSW, 1,044,290; Tas., 137,877; WA, 43,814; SA, 309,453; Vic., 1,079,077; Qld, 367,166).

Chinese population in Australia peaks at 50,000.

The term *White Australia* first appears in print in the *Boomerang* (2 June).

Centennial Park, Sydney, permanently reserved for the people of Sydney (26 Jan.).

Trout first released in NSW.

G Births and Deaths

Apr   2   Nikolai Mikluho-Maclay d. (41).

May 30   Louis Buvelot d. (74).

Oct 28   William Bede Dalley d. (57).

Oct 31   Hubert Wilkins b. (–1958).

1889

Jan 17   George Dibbs forms a ministry in NSW following the defeat of the Parkes government.

Feb 2   Election held in NSW; Free Traders win narrowly; new members include Charles Dickens's son Edward (Protectionist, Wilcannia).

1889

Mar 1 Longerenong Agricultural College, Vic., opens.

8 Sir Henry Parkes resumes the premiership of NSW, forming his fifth ministry.

Apr 9 Cable from Roebuck Bay, WA, to Batavia opened.

11 Earl of Kintore becomes Governor of SA.

22 Bijou Theatre, Melbourne, destroyed by fire; two firemen killed and six injured.

27 St Patrick's College, Manly, opened by Cardinal Moran.

– Liberal Political Association and Free Trade Association amalgamate to form the Free Trade and Liberal Association of NSW.

May 1 With the opening of the Hawkesbury River railway bridge, Sydney is directly connected by rail to Newcastle, and thus a rail link is formed between Adelaide and Brisbane.
Gen. Sir Henry Norman becomes Governor of Qld.

4 Sydney Church of England Grammar School (Shore) opens in Holtermann's Tower, North Sydney.

Jun 1 WA's Great Southern Railway opened, linking Perth and Albany.

11 Australian Labour Federation formed by unions in Brisbane.

22 Eleven miners killed in a fall at Hamilton Mine, Newcastle.

27 J. A. Cockburn becomes Premier of SA after the defeat of the Playford government on 22 June.

Jul 16 Qld Legislative Assembly members granted a salary of £300 a year.

Sep 13 Fire in Collins Street, Melbourne, completely destroys George's Emporium and Allan's Music Warehouse; three firemen killed and nine seriously injured.

21 Legislation passed granting payment to members of the NSW Legislative Assembly.

Oct 1 Railway completed from Darwin to Pine Creek.

14 First electric tramway in Australia begins operating between Box Hill and Doncaster, Melbourne (to Jan. 1896).

24 Parkes delivers a stirring pro-federation speech at Tenterfield, NSW, calling for a federal government and parliament in place of the ineffectual Federal Council.

Nov 27 Centennial Hall of Sydney Town Hall opened.

28 Earl of Hopetoun becomes Governor of Vic.

Dec 20 Premier Permanent Building, Land and Investment Association of Melbourne collapses, heralding the end of the "long boom".

* Opals discovered at White Cliffs, NSW.

* General flooding in Tas. (June, Oct., Nov.) and in Vic., and Murray River in flood during year.

A Architecture, Building

Cyril Blacket, Australia Hotel, Sydney (–1891; demolished in 1970 to make way for the MLC Centre).
William Pitt, Rialto Building, Melbourne (–1890).
Victoria Dock, Melbourne (–1891).

B Science, Technology, Discovery, etc.

Lawrence Hargrave invents a rotary aeroplane engine.

C Arts and Entertainment

The 9 by 5 Impression Exhibition—paintings by Roberts, Streeton, Conder, and McCubbin, many on cigar-box lids—opens in Melbourne (17 Aug.).

1889

Frederick McCubbin, *Down on His Luck.*

Cecil Sharp joins I. G. Reimann in the Adelaide School of Music (later the Elder Conservatorium).

D Books and Writing

"Tasma", *Uncle Piper of Piper's Hill.*

History of New South Wales from the Records, vol. 1 (vol. 2, 1894).

A. B. Paterson's "Clancy of the Overflow" appears in the *Bulletin* (21 Dec.).

E Sport and Recreation

Henry Searle retains his world sculling title on the Thames, London (9 Sept.), but contracts typhoid on the way home and dies in Melbourne on 10 Dec. (Crowds estimated at 170,000 line Sydney's streets to watch his funeral cortège pass after a service at St Andrew's Cathedral.)

Bravo wins the Melbourne Cup.

F Statistics, Social Change, the Environment

Population of the Australian colonies reaches three million (NSW, 1,074,140; Tas., 141,661; WA, 45,660; SA, 314,589; Vic., 1,104,938; Qld, 381,489).

Highest temperature ever recorded in Australia: 127.5°F 53.1°C) at Cloncurry, Qld, on 16 Jan.

Publication of Sunday papers prohibited in Vic. (Act repealed in 1969.)

G Births and Deaths

Jan 22 Harry Hawker b. (–1921).
Feb   9 Peter Lalor d. (62).
Feb 23 Percy Leason b. (–1959).
Apr 18 Jessie Street b. (–1970).
Sep 20 Ion L. Idriess b. (–1979).
Nov   5 P. E. Warburton d. (76).
Dec 31 Daryl Lindsay b. (–1976).

1890

Jan 1 University of Tasmania established in Hobart by act of parliament.
Sydney's North Shore railway opened between St Leonards and Hornsby.
 – Qld shearers reject an agreement made in Blackall; pastoralists subsequently make contracts with non-union labour.

Feb 4 Railway opened to Warrnambool, Vic.
 6 Representatives of all Australian colonial governments and NZ meet in Melbourne (to 14th) to discuss Parkes's federation proposals.
 28 Passenger steamer *Quetta* sinks after striking an uncharted rock near Torres Strait; more than 130 lives lost.

Mar 1 *Worker* newspaper, edited by William Lane, founded in Brisbane.
 6 Henry George arrives in Sydney to begin a lecture tour arranged by the Single Tax League.
 – Association of Marine Officers affiliates with the Melbourne Trades Hall Council; shipowners refuse to recognize the affiliation and threaten officers with dismissal.

Apr 25 Trains collide at Bathurst, NSW, killing four people.

Jun 14 Tramway (battery operated) begins operating in Bendigo, Vic. (Power inadequate; replaced by steam in 1892.)

24 William Saumarez Smith consecrated in St Paul's, London, as Anglican Bishop of Sydney and Primate of Australia.

Aug 1 Australian Labour Federation's first annual meeting in Brisbane draws up a platform of political action and socialist objective.

3 Sunday newspaper *Truth* begins publication in Sydney. (John Norton becomes associate editor in Oct., sole proprietor in 1896.)

6 Wharf labourers refuse to handle wool shorn by non-union labour.

12 Sir Samuel Griffith forms a ministry in Qld in coalition with Sir Thomas McIlwraith (the "continuous ministry").

16 Maritime Strike begins, with officers and seamen walking off their ships in Sydney (and in Melbourne on 18th).

19 Wharf labourers in Sydney withdraw their labour.
Thomas Playford forms his second ministry in SA.

25 Coalminers in NSW refuse to cut coal for local ships and are locked out by mine owners.

26 Gas workers in Melbourne called out on strike.

Sep 11 BHP locks out workers, who refuse to return to work after a week.

15 Sydney carriers refuse to convey wool from railway to wharf.

19 Riot Act read at Circular Quay in Sydney after unionists clash with volunteer carriers of non-union wool and their police escort.

24 Shearers strike (but return to work after a week).

25 BHP miners agree to return to work (but with working hours reduced from 48 to 46).

Oct 2 Fire destroys central Sydney area between Castlereagh and Pitt streets from Hosking Place to what is now Martin Place.

17 Marine officers agree to abandon affiliation with Trades Hall Council and return to work.

20 Sir William Robinson becomes Governor of WA for the third time.

21 Constitution Act Proclaimed in WA, granting responsible government.

Nov 5 James Munro becomes Premier of Vic.
Last of the unions involved in the Maritime Strike, the Newcastle coalminers, return to work.

9 Experimental electric trams begin running between Bondi Junction and Waverley in Sydney.

27 Elections held (to 12 Dec.) for WA's first Legislative Assembly.

28 Legislation enacted in Tas. providing for the payment of MPs.

Dec 29 John Forrest (commissioned Premier on 22nd) forms WA's first ministry under responsible government.

31 Importation of kanaka labour to Qld ends. (Resumed in 1892.)

* Severe floods occur on the northern rivers of NSW and along the Darling (Feb., July), in south-east and central Qld (Mar.), on the Murray in SA (Aug.–Oct.), and on the Fortescue in WA (May).

A Architecture, Building

Queen's Bridge, Melbourne, opened (14 Apr.).

Stony Creek railway bridge, built by John Robb on the line between Cairns and Atherton Tableland, completed (Apr.).

B Science, Technology, Discovery, etc.

Blue-speckle cattle dog ("blue heeler") established as a pure breed. (Standard adopted by NSW Kennel Club and Agriculture Department in 1897.)

1890

C Arts and Entertainment

Frederick McCubbin, *A Bush Burial*; Tom Roberts, *Shearing the Rams*; and Arthur Streeton, *Still Glides the Stream* (paintings).

Charterisville, a house in the Yarra Valley rented by Walter Withers, becomes the centre of an artist's colony.

G. W. L. Marshall-Hall appointed first Ormond Professor of Music at the University of Melbourne. (Gives inaugural lecture Mar. 1891.)

Florence Young makes her debut in von Suppe's *Boccaccio* at Her Majesty's Opera House, Melbourne (14 June).

Alfred Dampier presents his adaptation of *Robbery Under Arms* (melodrama).

D Books and Writing

Rolf Boldrewood, *The Miner's Right.*

Ada Cambridge, *A Marked Man.*

"Tasma", *A Sydney Sovereign and Other Tales.*

Robert Louis Stevenson visits Sydney from Samoa (13 Feb. to 10 Apr.) and while there writes *An Open Letter to the Rev. Dr Hyde of Honolulu* (a defence of Father Damien).

E Sport and Recreation

NSW Lawn Tennis Association founded.

First intercolonial women's cricket match played at the SCG (NSW v. Vic.).

Albert Griffiths ("Young Griffo") beats world featherweight champion "Torpedo" Billy Murphy in Sydney (3 Sept.), but his world championship is not recognized in the US.

Carbine wins the Melbourne Cup after winning the Sydney Cup for the second successive year.

F Statistics, Social Change, the Environment

Estimated population of Australia: 3,151,355 (NSW, 1,113,275; Tas., 144,787; WA, 48,502; SA, 318,947; Vic., 1,133,728; Qld, 392,116).

Dr Constance Stone of Melbourne becomes the first woman registered as a medical practitioner in Australia (7 Feb).

Rust disease in wheat causes huge losses.

G Births and Deaths

Jul 18 F. M. Forde b. (–1983).

Aug 10 John Boyle O'Reilly d. (56?).

Aug 29 R. G. Casey b. (–1976).

Sep 1 Arthur W. Upfield b. (–1964).

1891

Jan 6 Qld shearers' strike begins.

7 Railway from Port Augusta, SA, reaches Oodnadatta.

United Labour Party formed at a meeting in Adelaide.

15 Earl of Jersey becomes Governor of NSW.

– Great floods on the Murrumbidgee River.

Feb – Non-union labour from the south begin working in Qld shearing sheds.

– Clipper *Sobraon* becomes a reformatory ship in Port Jackson.

Mar 2 First National Australasian Convention, held in Sydney (to 9 Apr.), drafts a federal constitution.

10 Presbyterian Ladies' College opens in Croydon, Sydney (school founded in 1888).

21 Hawkesbury Agricultural College, NSW, enrols its first students.

23 Troops arrest strike leaders in union camps at Clermont and Barcaldine, Qld.

24 Sydney Trades and Labour Council draws up the platform and rules for Labour Electoral Leagues, to endorse candidates for the next election. (First league formed in Balmain on 4 Apr.)

May 1 Trial of the unionists arrested in Clermont and Barcaldine begins in Rockhampton; twelve of the strike committee gaoled for conspiracy. Workers in Barcaldine hold the first May Day procession.

2 David Lindsay leads a scientific expedition from Warrina, SA, to cover unexplored land westward to the coast of WA.

Two Aborigines murder a Pole named Murskiewicz at Dora Dora Creek, near Albury. (Culprits captured after a three-year manhunt.)

9 Two Labour candidates win seats in the SA Legislative Assembly.

30 Meeting of Vic. labour organizations in Melbourne (to 2 June) forms the Progressive Political League and draws up a platform.

– Womanhood Suffrage League formed in Sydney; Rose Scott secretary.

Jun 17 Labour candidates contest 45 seats in the NSW Legislative Assembly election and win 36, to hold the balance of power.

– Murrumbidgee again in flood.

Jul 17 Railway opened from Brisbane to Gympie (and thus to Bundaberg).

Aug 3 Bank of Van Diemen's Land, the second oldest bank in Australia, fails. (Three banks in Melbourne and one in Sydney also fail during the month.)

7 "Freedom of contract" agreement, signed by pastoralists and Shearers' Union, agrees to the employment of non-union labour.

28 SS *Gambier* sinks in Port Phillip after colliding with another ship; 21 drown.

Sep 5 Australian Auxiliary Naval Squadron—cruisers *Katoomba*, *Mildura*, *Ringarooma*, *Tauranga*, and *Wallaroo*, and torpedo gunboats *Boomerang* and *Karrakatta*—arrives in Sydney from Britain.

6 Barque *Fiji* wrecked near Moonlight Head, Vic; 12 lives lost.

28 Miners at Moonta, SA, strike for higher wages (to Feb. 1892).

– Two more banks fail in Sydney.

Oct 1 Australian colonies join the Universal Postal Union.

9 New mace presented to the Vic. Legislative Assembly by the House of Commons disappears and is never recovered.

19 Workers' journal the *Hummer* (later the *Worker*) founded in Wagga. (Moves to Sydney in 1893 and becomes the *Australian Worker* in 1913.)

23 George Dibbs becomes Premier of NSW following the resignation of Sir Henry Parkes.

– Trades and Labor Council established in Perth. (Re-formed in Jan. 1893.)

Dec – Four banks and one building society in Melbourne collapse.

– A group of 320 Italians arrive at Townsville to work on sugar plantations.

A Architecture, Building

G. H. M. Addison, Queensland Museum building, Brisbane.

J. B. Spencer, Strand Arcade, Sydney (opens 1 Apr. 1892).

Martin Place, Sydney, completed between George and Castlereagh Streets (progressively extended, reaching Macquarie Street in 1935).

B Science, Technology, Discovery, etc.

Queen Victoria Museum opened in Launceston, Tas. (Apr.).

1891

C Arts and Entertainment

Tom Roberts, *The Breakaway* (painting).

Arthur Streeton, *"Fire's On!", Lapstone Tunnel* (painting).

Roberts and Streeton establish "Curlew Camp" near Mosman, Sydney.

First South Street music competitions held in Ballarat (June).

Sarah Bernhardt performs in Melbourne, Adelaide, and Sydney in *Camille*.

D Books and Writing

The first of Nat Gould's innumerable sporting novels, *The Double Event*, published as a book.

Henry Lawson's poem "Freedom's on the Wallaby" appears in the Brisbane *Worker* (16 May) during the shearers' strike.

Rudyard Kipling makes a brief visit to Melbourne, Sydney, Adelaide, and Hobart (Nov.).

E Sport and Recreation

(Royal) Melbourne Golf Club formed (22 May).

Malvolio wins the Melbourne Cup.

F Statistics, Social Change, the Environment

Estimated population of Australia 3,240,985 (simultaneous census, 5 Apr: 3,177,823—Vic., 1,140,088 [Melb., 490,896]; NSW, 1,127,137 [Syd., 387,434]; Qld, 393,718; SA, 315,533; Tas., 146,667; WA, 49,782; NT, 4,898).

Sheep numbers in Australia exceed one hundred million.

Hotels in SA close on Sundays.

Belair Recreation Park, in the Mt Lofty Ranges, SA, reserved.

G Births and Deaths

Jan 21 J. J. Cahill b. (–1959).

Feb 15 Roy Rene ("Mo") b. (–1954).

Mar 27 A. P. Elkin b. (–1979).

Apr 7 David Low b. (–1963).

May 8 Sir John Robertson d. (74).

Aug 14 Johnny Mullagh (Muarrinim) d. (50).

Aug 24 Richard Boyer b. (–1961).

Sep 26 William McKell b. (–1985).

Sep 29 Ian Fairweather b. (–1974).

Oct 29 Edward Hammond Hargraves d. (75).

Dec 7 Sir William Macleay d. (71).

Dec 25 Clarrie Grimmett b. (–1980).

1892

Jan – Financial crisis worsens, particularly in Vic. (Twenty-three banks either suspend payment or fail before the end of June.)

Feb 4 Railway from Strahan to Zeehan, Tas., opened.

10 Run on the head office of the Savings Bank of New South Wales in Sydney (to 12th), depositors withdrawing their funds in gold.

16 William Shiels becomes Premier of Vic. after James Munro resigns and becomes Agent-General in London to escape creditors of his collapsed Real Estate Bank.

– Labour Bureau set up in NSW to provide work for the unemployed.

Mar 8 Disastrous floods on the Hunter River, NSW (to 10th).

1892

Brig *Hebe* lost near Port Stephens.

Apr 14 Prohibition on the importation of kanakas into Qld removed.
WA's first Agent-General, Sir Malcolm Fraser, appointed.
20 Labour candidates win ten seats at the general election in Vic.
27 Eight die in a train derailment near Tarana, NSW.

May 1 May Day procession inaugurated in Sydney.
23 Frederick Deeming, convicted killer of his wife and four children in England and a second wife in Melbourne, is hanged in Melbourne.

Jun 8 Melbourne *Age* accuses the Vic. railway commissioners (suspended on 17 Mar.) of mismanagement and the chairman, Richard Speight, of incompetence. (Speight sues David Syme for libel and after two prolonged trials is awarded a farthing damages in Sept. 1894.)
17 Theatre Royal, Sydney, destroyed by fire.
21 F. W. Holder replaces Thomas Playford as Premier of SA.

Jul 4 Broken Hill miners go on strike over the repudiation by the mine proprietors of their agreement.

Aug 9 Qld adopts an optional preferential (contingent) voting system.
17 Henry Dobson becomes Premier of Tas. following the resignation of the Fysh government.
– First Labour-in-Politics convention held in Brisbane. (Labour party issues its first manifesto, 9 Sept.)

Sep 10 Rioting in Broken Hill over the arrival of non-union labour to work in mines; strike leaders arrested by police with fixed bayonets (15th); further arrests made in Sydney (19th).
17 Arthur Bayley and William Ford report their discovery of gold at Coolgardie, WA.

Oct 10 Jacky Howe shears a record 321 sheep in a standard working day of 8 hours 40 mins using hand shears.
15 Sir John Downer becomes Premier of SA for a second time, following Holder's resignation.
30 Six Broken Hill union leaders gaoled for conspiring to prevent non-union labour working in the mines. (Amnesty granted 3 July 1893.)

Nov 6 Strike at Broken Hill collapses; miners return to work (11th).

Dec 24 Hurricane strikes WA coast between Roebourne and Busselton (to 27th); at Onslow 15 luggers wrecked and 20 men drown.

* William Lane founds the New Australia Co-operative Settlement Association.

A Architecture, Building
W. G. Watson, Law Courts, Bendigo (–1896).
Construction of Fremantle Harbour begins (16 Nov.) to a plan by C. Y. O'Connor.

B Science, Technology, Discovery, etc.
Western Australian Museum opens in Perth.
First milking machines in Australia installed at Bodalla, NSW.

C Arts and Entertainment
G. W. L. Marshall-Hall forms a symphony orchestra in Melbourne.
Lyceum Theatre opens in Sydney (26 Dec.). (Destroyed by fire in 1964.)

D Books and Writing
"John Miller" (William Lane), *The Working Man's Paradise.*
Price Warung, *Tales of the Convict System.*

1892

E Sport and Recreation

Sheffield Shield cricket competition inaugurated.

NSW Amateur Swimming Association formed in Sydney.

Glenloth wins the Melbourne Cup.

F Statistics, Social Change, the Environment

Estimated population of Australia: 3,305,753 (NSW, 1,183,157; Tas., 150,212; WA, 58,569; SA, 335,392; Vic., 1,168,747; Qld., 409,676).

In the 12 months to 30 June, 133 limited companies in Vic. go into liquidation.

Baby farming outlawed in NSW with the passing of the Children's Protection Act, after discovery of the bodies of several babies in Sydney in Oct.

Primary education made free in SA.

G Births and Deaths

Apr 13   Gladys Moncrieff b. (–1976).

Apr 16   Florence Austral b. (–1968).

Apr 20   Grace Cossington Smith b. (–1984).

May 2   Barcroft Boake d. (26).

Dec   8   Bert Hinkler b. (–1933).

1893

Jan 23   J. B. Patterson replaces William Shiels as Premier of Vic.

28   Federal Bank of Australia in Melbourne fails.

Feb 2   Disastrous record floods in south-east Qld (to 21st); Brisbane inundated (6th); Indooroopilly railway bridge and Victoria Bridge swept away.

Mar 27   Sir Thomas McIlwraith becomes Premier of Qld following Sir Samuel Griffith's retirement.

–   Mount Lyell Mining and Railway Co. formed.

Apr 5   Commercial Bank of Australia in Melbourne suspends payment, setting off a panic. (Reopens 6 May after "reconstruction".)

13   English, Scottish and Australian Chartered Bank closes for reconstruction. (Reopens 19 Aug.)

15   United Labour Party candidates win eight seats in the SA election.

20   Australian Joint Stock Bank suspends payment, followed by the London Chartered Bank of Australia (25th), the Standard Bank of Australia (28th), and the National Bank of Australasia (1 May).

–   Labour candidates win 16 seats in the Qld Legislative Assembly election.

–   Smallpox epidemic in WA (to 1894).

May 1   Government of Vic. proclaims a five-day moratorium in the form of a bank holiday to give banks time to consider their position and allow public excitement to cool down. Some banks stay open.

3   NSW legislates to make bank notes a first charge on assets (as in Vic. and SA) and declares all bank notes legal tender (16th).

5   Colonial Bank of Australasia in Melbourne suspends payment, followed by the Bank of Victoria (9th), the Queensland National Bank and the Bank of North Queensland (15th), the Commercial Banking Co. of Sydney (16th), and the City of Melbourne Bank and the Royal Bank of Queensland (17th). All eventually reopen after reconstruction.

26   NSW authorizes payment in Treasury notes to people with deposits locked up in suspended banks.

1893

29 Sir Robert Duff becomes Governor of NSW.

Jun 14 Patrick Hannan discovers gold at Kalgoorlie, WA.
16 C. C. Kingston replaces Sir John Downer as Premier of SA.
22 Australasian Federation League established in Sydney.

Jul 4 Seamen strike unsuccessfully over an enforced reduction of wages.
16 *Royal Tar*, carrying 220 passengers—members of William Lane's New Australia Co-operative Settlement Association and their children—sails from Sydney for South America.
31 Federation conference held at Corowa, NSW (to 1 Aug.), called by the Australasian Federation League.

Aug 8 Viscount Gormanston becomes Governor of Tas.
25 Coolgardie, WA, proclaimed a town site.

Sep 20 Sydney's first regular electric tramway service begins, from North Sydney to Spit Junction.
21 Electric tramway begins operating in Hobart.

Oct 13 Homestead Act passed in WA allowing free selection of 160-acre (65-hectare) homestead farms.
16 Submarine cable between New Caledonia and Bundaberg, Qld, opened.
27 Hugh Nelson becomes Premier of Qld on McIlwraith's retirement.

Dec 5 Electoral Act abolishes plural voting in NSW.
15 Esperance, WA, gazetted as a town site.
28 SS *Alert* sinks off Cape Schanck, Vic; 14 lives lost.
31 *Royal Tar* sails from Adelaide with another 199 settlers for the New Australia settlement in Paraguay (81 of the first settlers having already been lost to the community through expulsion or disaffection).

* Farmers and Settlers' Association of NSW founded.

A Architecture, Building
George McRae, Queen Victoria Building, Sydney (–1898; remodelled 1918, 1935, 1983–86).
John Sulman, Thomas Walker Convalescent Hospital, Concord, Sydney.
George Adams's new Tattersall's Hotel opens in Sydney (since demolished).

B Science, Technology, Discovery, etc.
Technological Museum opens in Ultimo, Sydney (4 Aug.).
NSW's first public telephone installed at Sydney GPO (8 Mar.).
Thargomindah, Qld, lit by electric power generated from artesian water (first hydro-electric plant in Australia).

C Arts and Entertainment
Arthur Streeton, *The Railway Station, Redfern* (painting).
Bertram Mackennal, *Circe* (sculpture).
Julian Ashton's murals decorate the Marble Bar of Adams's Hotel.
Harry Rickards acquires the Garrick Theatre in Sydney and renames it the Tivoli (opens 18 Feb.).
J. C. Williamson buys out Arthur Garner and assumes full control of "the Firm".

D Books and Writing
Simpson Newland, *Paving the Way*.

E Sport and Recreation
(Royal) Sydney and (Royal) Adelaide golf clubs formed.
John Wren sets up an illegal tote in Collingwood, Melbourne.

1893

Tarcoola wins the Melbourne Cup.

F Statistics, Social Change, the Environment

Estimated population of Australia: 3,361,895 (NSW, 1,206,497; Tas., 150,396; WA, 64,923; SA, 344,916; Vic., 1,176,170; Qld, 418,993).

"Larrikin pushes now terrorise Sydney" (Melbourne *Argus*, 1 July).

G Births and Deaths

Jan 31   Roy Cazaly b. (–1963).
May 26   Eugene Goossens b. (–1962).
Jun 10   Martin Boyd b. (–1972).
Jun 23   Frank Dalby Davison b. (–1970).
Sep   3   Harold Williams b. (–1976).
Sep 18   Arthur Benjamin b. (–1960).
Nov   1   John Anderson b. (–1962).
Nov 27   Frank Clune b. (–1971).
Dec   2   Raphael Cilento b. (–1985).

1894

Jan 4   Two severe hurricanes (the second on 9th) hit the north-west coast of WA; 12 pearling luggers and a steamer lost and about 50 men drown.
     15   Australia's first steel rolling mill opens at the Eskbank ironworks, near Lithgow, NSW.
           Baby-farmer Frances Knorr, convicted of murdering her charges, is hanged at the old Melbourne Gaol.

Feb 19   Steam trams begin operating to Bondi, Sydney. (Able to reach 65 km/h, they give rise to the phrase "shoot through like a Bondi tram".)
      –   Shearers' and shed hands' unions of Qld, NSW, Vic., and SA amalgamate to form the Australian Workers' Union, with W. G. Spence as secretary.

Mar 8   Central business area of Melbourne lit by electric street lighting generated by the City Council.
      –   Widespread and serious floods in NSW (to Apr.).

Apr 14   Sir Edward Braddon replaces Henry Dobson as Premier of Tas.
      24   Nineteen NSW Labour MPs refuse to sign the Electoral League pledge to vote as a bloc according to caucus decisions. (Joseph Cook becomes leader of the independent Labour faction.)

Jun 17   Qld shearers' strike begins in Longreach over a new agreement imposed by pastoralists and a reduction in wages.

Jul 2   Unionists fight with strike-breakers on Oondooroo station, Qld, and during the month a number of woolsheds are burnt and violent incidents occur.
      16   Election in NSW results in the Protectionists and the two Labour groupings losing ground to the Free Traders. George Reid replaces Sir George Dibbs as Premier (3 Aug.).

Aug 10   New Sydney Hospital opens.
      21   Tas. introduces a flat-rate personal income tax.
      26   Unionists force strike-breakers off the river steamer *Rodney* near Pooncarie, NSW, and burn and sink the vessel.

Sep 2   Dagworth station, Qld, woolshed burnt down; shots fired by both sides.

5　Bill for the Better Preservation of Peace in Queensland passes through the Qld Legislative Assembly after bitter debate.

10　Shearers call off their strike, having been unable to prevent strike- breakers from working.

27　George Turner becomes Premier of Vic. following the Liberals' success in the elections.

Oct 28　SS *Wairarapa*, en route from Sydney to Auckland, is wrecked off the coast of NZ with the loss of 112 lives.

31　Suburban train and country train collide at Redfern, Sydney; 11 people killed and 27 injured.

Nov 24　Railway from Perth (Midland Junction) to Geraldton completed.

Dec 21　SA enacts legislation to establish a statutory authority to conciliate in disputes between employers and employees.

　＊　Monthly magazine *Australian Home Journal* founded in Sydney.

　＊　(Royal) Life Saving Society formed in Sydney.

A Architecture, Building

Perth railway station completed (25 March.).

B Science, Technology, Discovery, etc.

Horn Scientific Expedition to Central Australia (May–Aug.).

Lawrence Hargrave, experimenting with boxkites, is lifted six metres off the ground at Stanwell Park, NSW (12 Nov.).

David Shearer of Mannum, SA, develops a steam car, the first car built in Australia.

C Arts and Entertainment

Sydney Long, *By Tranquil Waters* (painting).

Tom Roberts, *The Golden Fleece* (painting).

Percy Grainger, aged 12, gives his first piano recital in Melbourne (10 Sept.).

D Books and Writing

Louis Becke, *By Reef and Palm.*

Henry Lawson, *Short Stories in Prose and Verse.*

Ethel Turner, *Seven Little Australians.*

The term *fair dinkum*, meaning genuine, first appears in print in the *Bulletin* (5 May).

E Sport and Recreation

Popular jockey Tom Corrigan is fatally injured in the Caulfield Grand National.

Patron wins the Melbourne Cup.

F Statistics, Social Change, the Environment

Estimated population of Australia: 3,426,760 (NSW, 1,231,755; Tas., 152,506; WA, 81,579; SA, 348,774; Vic., 1,182,155; Qld, 429,991).

SA becomes the first Australian colony to grant women the right to vote and to stand for parliament (act passed 21 Dec; assented to 21 Mar. 1895).

Street collections for charities begin in Sydney with the first annual Hospital Saturday collection (28 Apr.).

Rabbits reach Eucla on the WA border.

G Births and Deaths

Feb　24　Douglas Copland b. (–1971).

Apr　13　Arthur Fadden b. (–1973).

Apr　30　Herbert Vere Evatt b. (–1965).

Jul　　1　Bernard Heinze b. (–1982).

1894

Sep 9 Bert Oldfield b. (–1976).
Nov 27 George Rayner Hoff b. (–1937).
Dec 20 Robert Gordon Menzies b. (–1978).

1895

Jan 1 Qld standardizes its time at ten hours ahead of Greenwich Mean Time (Eastern Standard Time).
   24 C. E. Borchgrevink, a Qld surveyor, and H. J. Bull of Melbourne, travelling with a Norwegian expedition in the whaler *Antarctic*, land at Cape Adare, the first men to land on the Antarctic continent.
   29 Income tax introduced in Vic.
      Premiers' Conference held in Hobart to discuss federation calls for a convention of ten representatives from each colony to frame a federal constitution, which would then be put to a plebiscite.

Feb 1 NSW, Vic., and SA standardize their times, NSW and Vic. on EST, SA nine hours ahead of GMT (changed to 9½ hours ahead of GMT—Central Standard Time—in 1899).
   15 Municipality proclaimed at Hannan's Find, WA, and named Kalgoorlie.

May 24 Labour Electoral Leagues and the Australian Labour Federation in NSW merge to form the Political Labour League, with J. S. T. McGowen as leader.

Jun 28 Sydney ferry-master George Dean, condemned to death for poisoning his wife, is released after an inquiry by royal commission. (His lawyer, R. D. Meagher, MP, is subsequently struck off the rolls as a solicitor when it is revealed that he knew Dean to be guilty, and Dean is sentenced to 14 years' gaol for perjury.)

Jul 18 Nine men killed and many injured in a rock fall in Broken Hill South mine, NSW.

Aug 8 SS *Catterthun*, bound for China from Sydney, is wrecked off Seal Rocks, NSW, with the loss of 55 lives.

Sep 1 Tas. standardizes its time on EST.
   14 *Kalgoorlie Miner* begins publication as a daily newspaper.

Oct 2 State aid to religion abolished in WA.
   15 Suppression of Gambling Act passed in Qld, forcing Tattersall's Sweeps (already forced out of NSW by similar legislation) to move to Hobart.
   25 Baron Brassey becomes Governor of Vic.
   29 Sir Thomas Buxton becomes Governor of SA.

Nov 17 Visiting English actors Arthur Dacre and his wife, Amy Roselle, commit suicide in Sydney the day before they are to open in *The Silence of Dean Maitland*.
   22 Viscount Hampden becomes Governor of NSW.

Dec 1 WA standardizes its time at eight hours ahead of GMT (Western Standard Time).
   10 Launceston lit by electricity.
   12 Land and income taxes introduced in NSW.
   20 SA enacts federal enabling legislation, as does NSW (23rd).
   23 Sir Gerard Smith becomes Governor of WA.

   * Sydney Church of England Grammar School for Girls (SCEGGS) founded.

* Drought experienced in NSW, Qld, and SA—the beginning of an extensive and severe drought lasting in some areas until 1903.

A Architecture, Building

Reinforced concrete first used in Australia in two arches spanning creeks in Forest Lodge, Sydney.

The cavity wall, an Australian development of the previous decade, now standard building practice.

B Science, Technology, Discovery, etc.

Tasmania's first hydro-electric station, at Duck Reach on the South Esk River, comes into service.

C Arts and Entertainment

E. Phillips Fox, *Art Students* (painting).

Tom Roberts, *Bailed Up* (painting).

Walter Withers, *The Yarra below Eaglemont* (painting).

Qld and WA Art Galleries open (29 Mar. and 31 July).

G. W. L. Marshall-Hall founds a conservatorium of music as part of the University of Melbourne (opens 28 Feb.).

"Waltzing Matilda" (words by A. B. Paterson) first sung in public at the North Gregory Hotel in Winton, Qld (6 Apr.).

Edison Electric Parlour, with Kinetoscopes (moving picture peep-shows) and gramophones, opens in Pitt Street, Sydney (Mar.).

D Books and Writing

A. B. Paterson, *The Man from Snowy River and Other Verses.*

The word *cobber* first appears in print in the *Bulletin* (9 Feb.).

Mark Twain makes a lecture tour of Australia (arrives Sydney 16 Sept.).

E Sport and Recreation

Warrnambool road race (between Warrnambool and Melbourne), the world's oldest cycling event, held for the first time.

Auraria wins the Melbourne Cup.

F Statistics, Social Change, the Environment

Estimated population of Australia: 3,491,621 (NSW, 1,255,503; Tas., 154,895; WA, 100,515; SA, 351,968; Vic., 1,185,676; Qld, 443,064).

G Births and Deaths

Jan   7   Hudson Fysh b. (–1974).

Mar 17   Lloyd Rees b. (–1988).

Jun   4   George Wallace b. (–1960).

Oct 31   Les Darcy b. (–1917).

1896

Jan   7   Tattersall's first lottery in Tas. conducted by George Adams to dispose of the assets of the liquidated Van Diemen's Land Bank.

    10   Federation enabling legislation passed in Tas.

    12   Heat wave in Bourke, NSW (to 25th), during which 47 people die; daily top temperatures average 116.6°F (47°C).

    26   Cyclone causes severe damage in Townsville and Bowen; 18 people killed in Townsville.

    –   Brisbane Public Library (now the State Library of Qld) instituted. (Officially opened to the public on 29 Apr. 1902.)

1896

Feb 13 Steam ferry *Pearl* sinks while conveying passengers across the flooded Brisbane River; number drowned uncertain, but 28 bodies are subsequently recovered.

Mar 4 Premiers' Conference agrees that colonies should amend anti-Chinese legislation to restrict immigration of all coloured races.
7 Federation enabling act passed in Vic.
First Japanese consulate in Australia opens in Townsville, because of the large number of Japanese working in CSR canefields.
24 Railway from Perth to Coolgardie opened. (Reaches Kalgoorlie 8 Sept.)

Apr 9 Baron Lamington becomes Governor of Qld.
25 Women vote for the first time in an Australian parliamentary election—for the SA Legislative Assembly. (New members include King O'Malley.)
26 Newcastle coalminers begin an 11-week strike over reduction in wages. (Return to work on company terms, 14 July.)

Jun 25 Smelting begins at Mount Lyell, Tas.

Jul 28 Vic.'s Factories and Shops Act amended to provide for the setting up of minimum wage boards.

Sep 29 American lone sailor Joshua Slocum, the first person to sail single-handed round the world, arrives at Newcastle from Boston in his yawl *Spray*. (Leaves Australian coast 24 June 1897.)

Oct 23 Port Hedland, WA, declared a town site.
27 Federation enabling act passed in WA.

Nov 17 People's Federal Convention held in Bathurst, NSW (to 21st).

Dec 4 Boulder, WA, declared a town site.
6 Eleven miners die from the effects of gas in the Stockton Mine, Newcastle.

* National Council of Women of Australia founded.

A Architecture, Building
A. B. Brady, Victoria Bridge, Brisbane (first half opened in Oct; completed bridge officially opened 22 June 1897; replaced in 1969).

B Science, Technology, Discovery, etc.
Charles Henry Packham breeds the Packham's Triumph pear on his property "Clifton", near Molong, NSW.

C Arts and Entertainment
Paintings: G. W. Lambert, *A Bush Idyll*; Frederick McCubbin, *On the Wallaby Track*; Arthur Streeton, "*The Purple Noon's Transparent Might*".
Julian Ashton establishes the Sydney Art School.
First national brass band contest held in Sydney.
Motion pictures shown for the first time in Australia by an American, Carl Hertz, at Harry Rickards's Opera House (Tivoli) in Melbourne (22 Aug.). (Subsequently shown at Sydney's Tivoli, 19 Sept., and in Brisbane in Oct.)
Frenchman Marius Sestier exhibits films at Australia's first "cinema", the Salon Lumière in Sydney (28 Sept.) and shoots the first moving film in Australia.
George Adams's Palace Theatre opens in Sydney (19 Dec.).

D Books and Writing
W. H. Fitchett, *Deeds that Won the Empire*.
Henry Lawson, *In the Days When the World Was Wide* and *While the Billy Boils*.
Mrs K. Langloh Parker, *Australian Legendary Tales*.

Bulletin's "Red Page", edited by A. G. Stephens, first appears under that title (29 Aug.).

E Sport and Recreation

E. H. Flack of Vic., sole Australian representative at the first modern Olympic Games in Athens, wins the 800 metres and 1,500 metres track events.

William Virgin cycles from Perth to Brisbane in 60 days (1 Sept. to 31 Oct.).

Newhaven wins the Melbourne Cup. (Part of the race is filmed by Marius Sestier with his Lumière Cinematographe.)

Victorian Football League formed by a breakaway group from the VFA. (First round played on 8 May 1897.)

F Statistics, Social Change, the Environment

Estimated population of Australia: 3,553,093 (NSW, 1,272,364; Tas., 159,296; WA, 136,816; SA, 352,067; Vic., 1,179,850; Qld, 452,705).

Child adoption by law approved in WA, the first of the colonies to legislate for this.

Queen Victoria Memorial Hospital for Women and Children (managed and professionally staffed by women) established in Melbourne. (Officially opened in July 1899.)

G Births and Deaths

Jan   2   Lawrence Wackett b. (–1982).
Jan 22   Norman Gilroy b. (–1977).
Apr 27   Sir Henry Parkes d. (80).
Jul   5   Thomas Playford b. (–1981).
Aug 28   Arthur Calwell b. (–1973).
Oct 10   Baron Sir Ferdinand von Mueller d. (71).
Oct 21   P. G. Taylor b. (–1966).

1897

Jan   7   Cyclone devastates Palmerston (Darwin); 28 lives lost, 15 of them at sea.
     15   Order in council transfers the government of Norfolk Is. to NSW (from 19 Mar.).
     20   Hare-Clark proportional-representation voting system used for the first time in the Tas. election (for only the multi-member electorates of Hobart and Launceston). Braddon Liberal government retains office.

Feb   8   Scotch College opens in Perth.

Mar   4   Election of representatives for the Federal Convention held in NSW, Vic., SA, and Tas. (WA representatives chosen by parliament.)
     22   Federal Convention meets in Adelaide (to 23 Apr.), attended by representatives of all colonies except Qld.

Apr 22   Draft constitution bill accepted by the Federal Convention.

May   4   First ship enters the newly opened Fremantle Harbour.
      –   Mining engineer (and future US President) Herbert Hoover arrives in Coolgardie as a representative of a mining consultation firm.

Jun   4   Narrogin, WA, declared a town site.
     21   Electric trams begin running in Brisbane.

Jul   7   Gatton Agricultural College, Qld, officially opened.

1897

24 Premiers of the Australian colonies in London for Queen Victoria's Diamond Jubilee celebrations attend the Colonial Conference.

27 William Saumarez Smith becomes the first Anglican Archbishop of Sydney.

Sep 2 Federal Convention reassembles in Sydney (to 24th) to consider amendments to the draft constitution bill.

Oct 2 *Tocsin* (later *Labor Call*), a radical weekly founded by Bernard O'Dowd and others, begins publication in Melbourne.

27 St Patrick's Cathedral, Melbourne, consecrated and (31st) formally opened.

Nov 21 Fire sweeps through the two-hectare Melbourne city block between Swanston and Elizabeth streets and Flinders Street and Flinders Lane.

Dec 3 Collie, WA, declared a town site. (Coal mining begins during the month.)

19 *Sunday Times* begins publication in Perth.

31 Bushfires raging in southern Tas. reach their peak; at least six people die.

* Seventh Day Adventist missionary training college built at Cooranbong, NSW.

A Architecture, Building

B Science, Technology, Discovery, etc.

Mueller Botanic Society (later Royal Society) of WA founded.

Prof. William Bragg demonstrates wireless at a public lecture in Adelaide University (21 Sept.).

Henry Austin of Melbourne builds Australia's first internal-combustion-engine car, the Pioneer.

C Arts and Entertainment

Rupert Bunny, *A Summer Morning* (painting).

Wynne Prize awarded for the first time (to Walter Withers for his painting *The Storm*).

Achille Simonetti's sculpture of Governor Phillip in Sydney's Botanic Gardens unveiled (22 June).

Bequest by Sir Thomas Elder endows a chair of music at Adelaide University and finances establishment of the Elder Conservatorium.

Theatre Royal opens in Perth (19 Apr.).

Salvation Army in Melbourne begins film production.

D Books and Writing

Barcroft Boake, *Where the Dead Men Lie* (ed. A. G. Stephens).

Christopher Brennan, *XXI Poems: Towards the Source*.

A. C. Rowlandson acquires the NSW Bookstall Co.

E Sport and Recreation

Percy Cavill, holder of Australian swimming records from 440 yards to a mile, wins the world 440 yards and five-mile championships.

Gaulus wins the Melbourne Cup.

F Statistics, Social Change, the Environment

Estimated population of Australia: 3,617,783 (NSW, 1,295,589; Tas., 163,962; WA, 160,495; SA, 352,337; Vic., 1,182,106; QLD, 463,294).

Qld imports 10,800 kg of opium (per year).

Qld's Aboriginal Protection and Restriction of the Sale of Opium Act (15 Dec.) provides for the setting up of closed reserves for Aborigines and prescribes penalties for supplying them with opium or liquor.

Employers' Liability Act in NSW (7 Dec.) provides for payment to employees injured at work.

NT completely quarantined following the increasing prevalence of tick fever in cattle.

G Births and Deaths

Feb 9 Charles Kingsford Smith b. (–1935).
Mar 6 Thomas Elder d. (78?).
Jul 9 Enid Lyons b. (–1981).
Aug 16 Marjorie Barnard b. (–1987).
Oct 5 Percy Spender b. (–1985).
Oct 7 Charles Chauvel b. (–1959).
Oct 22 Jessie Couvreur ("Tasma") d. (48).
Nov 3 Doris Fitton b. (–1985).
Nov 13 Ernest Giles d. (62).
Nov 20 Margaret Sutherland b. (–1984).

1898

Jan 20 Federal Convention meets in Melbourne for the third and final session (to 17 Mar.); draft constitution approved.
– Bushfires sweep through the Otway Range and south and west Gippsland districts of Vic., flaring up again in Feb; townships destroyed and several settlers burnt to death.

Feb 4 Cyclone severely damages Mackay, Qld.
5 Melbourne officially connected to the Melbourne and Metropolitan Board of Works sewerage system.
9 Barque *Atacama* founders on its way from Sydney to San Francisco; 13 lives lost, and 5 rescued after several days in a boat.

Mar 21 Mine explosion at the Dudley Colliery, near Newcastle, causes 15 deaths.

Apr 13 T. J. Byrnes becomes Premier of Qld following the resignation of Sir Hugh Nelson to become president of the Legislative Council.
27 Sanitarium Health Food Agency (later Company) registered.

May 5 Paddle-steamer *Maitland* wrecked near Broken Bay, NSW; 26 lives lost.
7 SS *Merksworth* founders in Stockton Bight; nine of the crew drown.
29 Greeks and Syrians begin building Australia's first Greek Orthodox church in Surry Hills, Sydney.

Jun 3 Referendums held in NSW, Vic., and Tas. (and SA on 4th) to decide on the draft federal constitution. All the colonies vote in favour of acceptance, but NSW's vote falls short of the statutory minimum required.

Jul 21 Sydney's Queen Victoria Markets open.
27 Federation dominates the NSW election; George Reid remains Premier but with reduced support.
Death duties introduced in NSW.

Aug 16 NSW's new parliament meets for the first time and suggests amendments to the draft federal constitution.

Sep 8 Sidney and Beatrice Webb arrive in Sydney at the beginning of a visit to Australia. (Leave Adelaide in Nov.)

Oct 1 J. R. Dickson becomes Premier of Qld on the death of Thomas Byrnes.

1898

17 David Scott Mitchell makes known his intention to bequeath his collection of Australiana to the Sydney Public Library on condition that suitable accommodation is provided for the Public Library and his collection is preserved in a separate wing called the Mitchell Library.

28 Early Closing Act in WA provides for shops to be closed at 6 p.m. on five days a week and at 10 p.m. on Sat. (or Wed.).

Nov 18 Hobart lit by electricity.

* First Christian Science services held in Australia and a reading room opened in Melbourne.

A Architecture, Building
A. B. Brady, Customs House, Rockhampton, Qld.
Swan Barracks, Perth, completed.

B Science, Technology, Discovery, etc.
Edgeworth David confirms Darwin's theory about the growth of coral reefs.
Zoological gardens opened in South Perth (17 Oct.).

C Arts and Entertainment
Sydney Long, *Pan* (painting).
Dattilo Rubbo opens an art school in Sydney.

D Books and Writing
Victor Daley, *At Dawn and Dusk.*
Edward E. Morris, *Austral English: A Dictionary of Australasian Words, Phrases, and Usages.*
Will H. Ogilvie, *Fair Girls and Gray Horses.*
Wide World Magazine begins serializing *The Adventures of Louis de Rougemont* (June). On 7 Oct. the London *Daily Chronicle* exposes "Louis de Rougemont" as the hoaxer Henri Grin.

E Sport and Recreation
Dick Cavill, aged 15, wins the NSW swimming championship (31 Dec.) using the crawl stroke (probably introduced into Australia by Alick Wickham from the Solomon Is.).
The Grafter wins the Melbourne Cup.

F Statistics, Social Change, the Environment
Estimated population of Australia: 3,664,715 (NSW, 1,317,445; Tas., 168,437; WA, 166,878; SA, 354,813; Vic., 1,182,281; Qld, 474,861).
First referendums held in Australia (3, 4 June; see chronological list); voting not compulsory and women allowed to vote only in SA.

G Births and Deaths
Feb 10   Judith Anderson b. (–1992).
Feb 12   Sali Herman b. (–1993).
May 26   Laurence Hartnett b. (–1986).
Jun 26   W. K. Hancock b. (–1988).
Aug 29   Walter Lindrum b. (–1960).
Sep 19   Sir George Grey d. (86).
Sep 24   Howard Florey b. (–1968).
Oct 18   C. T. P. Ulm b. (–1934).
Nov 2   George Goyder d. (72).

1899

Jan 29   Premiers of all six colonies meet (to 3 Feb.) to discuss amendments to the Constitution Bill to make it acceptable to NSW and Qld.

Mar 5   Cyclone devastates the far north coast of Qld; 55 pearling luggers in the Bathurst Bay area sink, with the loss of some 300 lives.

Apr 10   Baron Tennyson (son of the poet Alfred, Lord Tennyson) becomes Governor of SA.

    11   NSW Legislative Council enlarged by 12 new members favourable to federation (including the first Labour members), in order to gain approval for a further referendum on federation.

    24   Iron clipper *Loch Sloy* wrecked on Kangaroo Is., SA; 30 lives lost.

    29   SA begins the second round of referendums on federation (held in all colonies except WA): 65,900 vote in favour; 17,053 against.

May 11   NSW Army Nursing Service Reserve founded. (Australian Army Nursing Service formed in 1902.)

    18   Earl Beauchamp becomes Governor of NSW.

Jun 10   Qld passes enabling legislation for a referendum on federation.

    20   NSW holds its second referendum and gains the required number of votes: 107,420 in favour; 82,741 against.
Branch of the Royal Mint opens in Perth, mainly to convert the colony's gold into sovereigns and half-sovereigns (to 1931).

Jul 11   Qld offers volunteers for South Africa in the event of hostilities breaking out. (NSW and Vic. make similar offers within a few days.)

    12   During a heavy gale off the coast of WA, the *City of York* is wrecked on Rottnest Is. and the *Carlisle Castle* near Rockingham; 22 lives lost.

    27   Referendums on federation held in Vic. (152,653 in favour; 9,805 against) and Tas. (13,437 in favour; 791 against).

Aug 30   Plural voting abolished in Vic.

    –   William Lane and his family withdraw from the New Australia settlement at Cosme, Paraguay, and go to New Zealand.

Sep 2   Qld holds its first and only referendum on federation: 38,488 vote in favour; 30,996 against.

    12   Fire burns out Sydney's Tivoli Theatre. (Reopens in six months.)

    14   W. J. Lyne replaces George Reid as Premier of NSW.

    24   Electric tramway begins operating in Hay Street, Perth.

Oct 5   Education made free and compulsory in WA.

    11   Outbreak of the Boer War sparks off enthusiastic volunteering throughout Australia.

    12   N. E. Lewis replaces Sir Edward Braddon as Premier of Tas.

    28   Vic.'s first contingent of volunteers for the Boer War leaves Melbourne in the *Medic* (which picks up contingents from Tas., SA, and WA). In Sydney, the first NSW contingent marches through city streets to board the *Kent* (which embarks the Qld contingent in Brisbane).

Nov 14   NSW government appoints a royal commission to investigate sites for a national capital.

    28   Anderson Dawson forms a Labour government in Qld—the first Labour

government in the world. (Sworn in on 1 Dec., the ministry is forced to resign four days later.)

Dec 1 V. L. Solomon becomes Premier of SA following the fall of the Kingston government but is himself replaced by F. W. Holder a week later.

5 Allan McLean replaces Sir George Turner as Premier of Vic.

7 Robert Philp forms a ministry in Qld.

8 Electric tramway begins running in George Street, Sydney.

16 WA legislates for triennial parliaments and votes for women.

22 Early Closing Act in NSW; shops in Sydney and Newcastle to close on four days at 6 p.m., one at 10 p.m., and one at 1 p.m.

* WA introduces a company tax.

A Architecture, Building
John Sulman, Yaralla, in Concord, Sydney.

B Science, Technology, Discovery, etc.
W. Baldwin Spencer and F. J. Gillen publish their study *The Native Tribes of Central Australia.*

C. E. Borchgrevink and a scientific party arrive at Cape Adair, Antarctica (17 Feb.) and become the first to spend a winter on the Antarctic continent.

Prof. W. H. Bragg of Adelaide University and SA Postmaster-General Sir Charles Todd carry out the first successful transmission of a wireless message in Australia (10 May).

National Museum opens in the Public Library Building, Melbourne.

Herbert Thomson of Armadale, Vic., builds a successful steam-driven motor car, the Thomson Motor Phaeton (demonstrated in July).

Rosella Preserving and Manufacturing Co. makes its first tomato sauce.

C Arts and Entertainment
G. W. Lambert, *Across the Blacksoil Plains* (awarded the Wynne Prize).

Lambert, Max Meldrum, and Hans Heysen leave Australia to study in Europe.

First gramophones arrive in Australia.

D Books and Writing
E. J. Brady, *The Ways of Many Waters.*

Arthur W. Jose, *A Short History of Australasia.*

Ethel C. Pedley, *Dot and the Kangaroo.*

Roderic Quinn, *The Hidden Tide.*

Steele Rudd, *On Our Selection.*

A. G. Stephens launches the *Bookfellow.* (Ceases publication in 1925.)

E Sport and Recreation
F. C. V. Lane wins the English 220 yards swimming championship and establishes other records.

First Australia–England Rugby Union test match played, at Sydney (1 July), Australia winning 13–3.

Fred and Bert James cycle 4,170 km from Mt Magnet, WA, to Melbourne in 48 days.

Merriwee wins the Melbourne Cup.

F Statistics, Social Change, the Environment
Estimated population of Australia: 3,715,988 (NSW, 1,339,214; Tas., 172,362; WA, 170,258; SA, 359,298; Vic. 1,188,541; Qld, 486,315).

Phylloxera attacks vines at Rutherglen, Vic., and the SA Phylloxera Board is created to protect SA against the introduction of the insect to SA vineyards.

G Births and Deaths

Jan 17 Nevil Shute b. (–1960).
Jan 21 Ernestine Hill b. (–1972).
Feb 21 Sir George Bowen d. (77).
Feb 22 Ian Clunies Ross b. (–1959).
Sep   3 Macfarlane Burnet b. (–1985).
Sep 24 William Dobell b. (–1970).

1900

Jan   4 Adelaide streets lit by electricity.
    15 Suspected cases of bubonic plague reported in Adelaide—the beginning of an epidemic affecting all mainland states over the next ten years.
    19 Sydney's first case of plague discovered. (103 deaths occur in Sydney over the following eight months.)
    24 Intercolonial conference held at the Sydney Trades Hall (to 25th) to consider forming a federal Labour party.

Feb 22 Whaling operations out of Hobart cease.
    28 Detachments of Citizen's Bushmen's Corps from NSW and SA leave for South Africa. (Detachments from Tas., Vic., and WA leave during March.)

Mar 25 SS *Glenelg* wrecked off Vic. coast; 31 lives lost.

Apr 23 Contingents of Imperial Bushmen begin leaving for South Africa.
    25 William Sandford blows in Australia's first open-hearth steel-making furnace at his Eskbank works in Lithgow, NSW.

May 10 *Sierra Nevada* wrecked at Back Beach, Portsea, Vic; 23 drown.

Jun 13 WA passes federal referendum enabling legislation.

Jul   2 Naval contingent leaves Sydney in the *Wallaroo* to help the British suppress the Boxer Rebellion in China.
     9 Commonwealth of Australia Constitution Act, passed by the British parliament, receives royal assent.
    20 Jimmy Governor, with his brother Joe and another Aboriginal named Jacky Underwood, murder five whites at Breelong, NSW. (Kill another four during a 14-week rampage.)
    24 Capt. N. R. Howse wins the Victoria Cross at Vredefort, South Africa (first member of Australian forces awarded the VC).
    31 Referendum on federation held in WA: 44,800 vote in favour; 19,691 against. Women vote for the first time in WA.

Aug 4 Australian Bushmen hold out for 13 days under siege at Elands River, South Africa.
     6 SA gunboat *Protector* leaves Port Adelaide for service in the Boxer war.
     8 NSW and Vic. naval contingents leave Sydney for China.

Sep   9 Brisbane *Truth* (later renamed the *Sunday Sun*) begins publication.
    14 Tas. enacts legislation to introduce adult male suffrage, abolishing plural voting and property qualification.
    17 Queen Victoria proclaims that on and after 1 Jan. 1901 the six colonies "shall be united in a Federal Commonwealth under the name of the Commonwealth of Australia".
    21 Earl of Hopetoun officially appointed first Governor-General of Australia.

1900

Oct 27 Jimmy Governor captured. (Tried and convicted, 22–23 Nov; hanged at Darlinghurst Gaol on 18 Jan. 1901.)

31 Joe Governor shot dead.

Nov 19 Sir George Turner again becomes Premier of Vic.

Dec 5 Conciliation and Arbitration Act passed in WA. Legislation also passed providing for the payment of MPs.

SA Factories Act amended to introduce wages boards and early closing.

15 Lord Hopetoun arrives in Sydney and (19th) invites NSW Premier Sir William Lyne to form a federal ministry, but Lyne, an anti-federalist, is unable to gain support and (24th) Edmund Barton is commissioned.

28 Qld enacts early closing legislation (Sat. to be half day).

30 Barton announces his ministers for the first federal government.

A Architecture, Building

Art Gallery of South Australia (extended in 1936, 1962, 1996).

B Science, Technology, Discovery, etc.

Dr J. Ashburton Thompson establishes that bubonic plague is transmitted to humans by fleas from infected rats.

Bore in Roma, Qld, yields Australia's first natural gas.

C Arts and Entertainment

John Longstaff, *Henry Lawson* (painting).

G. W. L. Marshall-Hall is removed as Ormond Professor of Music in Melbourne because of criticism of his views; he continues with his music school, which later becomes the Melba Memorial Conservatorium.

Her Majesty's Theatre opens in Melbourne (19 May).

Joseph Perry's film, *Soldiers of the Cross*, produced for the Salvation Army, has its first public showing at the Melbourne Town Hall (13 Sept.).

D Books and Writing

Henry Lawson, *On the Track*; *Over the Sliprails*; and *Verses, Popular and Humorous*.

E Sport and Recreation

At the Paris Olympics, F. C. V. Lane wins the 200 m freestyle swimming event, Donald Mackintosh wins the game-shooting event, and Stanley Rowley participates as a co-opted fifth man in the winning British 5,000 m cross-country team.

Donald Mackay completes a 240-day bicycle ride around Australia.

Herbert Thomson drives his Thomson steam car from Bathurst to Melbourne (30 Apr. to 9 May).

Clean Sweep wins the Melbourne Cup.

F Statistics, Social Change, the Environment

Estimated population of Australia: 3,765,300 (NSW, 1,360,305; Tas., 172,900; WA, 179,967; SA, 357,250; Vic., 1,196,213; Qld, 493,847; NT, 4,857).

Cases of bubonic plague in Australia: NSW, 303; Vic., 10; Qld, 136; SA, 3; WA, 6; Tas., nil.

G Births and Deaths

Jan 21 Charles Moses b. (–1988).

Mar 29 John McEwen b. (–1980).

Jul 17 Sir Thomas McIlwraith d. (65).

Oct 20 Jack Lindsay b. (–1990).

1901

Jan 1 Commonwealth of Australia proclaimed at a ceremony in Centennial Park, Sydney. Lord Hopetoun assumes office as Governor-General, and Prime Minister Edmund Barton and his cabinet ministers (Executive Council) are sworn in.

    – Whyalla (then known as Hummock Hill), SA, comes into existence as the terminal for the BHP tramway from Iron Knob.

Feb 12 Alexander Peacock becomes Premier of Vic. following Sir George Turner's resignation to become federal Treasurer.

    15 George Throssell becomes Premier of WA, Sir John Forrest having resigned to become a Commonwealth minister.

Mar 1 Naval and military forces and establishments of the states are transferred to the Commonwealth, which also assumes control of all postal and telegraphic services.

    21 SS *Federal* sinks in Bass Strait with the loss of 21 lives.

    28 John See becomes Premier of NSW following the transfer of Lyne, Reid, and others to federal politics.

    29 First federal elections held (to 30th). Supporters of Barton's Protectionist government win most seats in the House of Representatives; Free Traders dominate in the Senate. Labour wins enough seats in both houses to hold the balance of power.

Apr 7 Missionary James Chalmers and ten others killed by natives of Goaribari Is. in the Gulf of Papua.

    25 Australian naval contingent returns to Sydney from China.

May 8 Federal parliamentary Labour party formed, with J. C. Watson as leader.

    9 Duke of Cornwall and York (later King George V) opens the first Commonwealth parliament in the Exhibition Building, Melbourne. Parliament then meets in the Vic. Legislative Assembly building (and continues to do so until 1927).

    15 J. G. Jenkins becomes Premier of SA, F. W. Holder having resigned to become Speaker in the Commonwealth parliament.

    27 George Leake replaces Throssell as Premier of WA.

Jun 12 At Wilmansrust, South Africa, 18 Vic. troops are killed and more than 40 wounded in a guerrilla attack by the Boers.

Jul 10 Anthony Hordern's department store in Sydney almost destroyed by fire; five shop assistants die.

    24 Presbyterian Church of Australia formed out of the federal union of state churches.

Sep 3 Australian flag chosen by competition from 30,000 designs displayed at the Exhibition Building in Melbourne. (Gazetted officially in 1903; status and dimensions officially established by act of parliament on 20 Nov. 1953.)

Oct – Tasmanian Workers' Political League (forerunner of the Tasmanian Labor Party) formed in Hobart.

Nov 19 Commonwealth parliament resolves to accept responsibility for British New Guinea. (Legislation not passed until 1905.)
Lying-in Hospital (later Royal Hospital for Women) opens in Paddington, Sydney. (Relocated within Prince of Wales Hospital in 1997.)

1901

21 A. E. Morgans replaces Leake as Premier of WA until 23 Dec., when Leake returns to office.

Dec 10 NSW's Industrial Arbitration Act introduces compulsory arbitration.
17 Federal parliament legislates to end recruitment of kanakas by 31 Mar. 1904 and to deport any found in Australia after 1906.
23 Immigration Restriction Act introduces a dictation test as a way of keeping out those regarded as undesirable. (Repealed 1958.)

A Architecture, Building

John Pearson, St John's Cathedral, Brisbane (–1910).
Hobart GPO (–1905).
Rocks Resumption Board set up in Sydney to replan the area.

B Science, Technology, Discovery, etc.

Baldwin Spencer and F. J. Gillen make a year-long investigation of the Aborigines of northern central Australia.
William Farrer releases his early-maturing, drought-resistant "Federation" wheat.
First wireless message between ship and shore in Australia exchanged between H. W. Jenvey in Queenscliff, Vic., and the Royal Yacht carrying the Duke and Duchess of York when it enters Port Phillip (5 May).
Tarrant Motor and Engineering Co., of Melbourne, manufactures the first successful Australian petrol-driven car.

C Arts and Entertainment

W. C. Piguenit, *Thunderstorm on the Darling* (awarded Wynne Prize).
Sydney Conservatorium founded by W. H. Wale.
Marie Lloyd appears at Harry Rickards's new Opera House, Melbourne.
J. C. Williamson presents *Floradora*, with Grace Palotta and Carrie Moore.

D Books and Writing

Miles Franklin, *My Brilliant Career.*
Henry Lawson, *Joe Wilson and His Mates.*
John Quick and Robert Garran, *Annotated Constitution of the Australian Commonwealth.*
George Essex Evans wins the prize for an ode to celebrate the inauguration of the Commonwealth.
Alfred Deakin begins writing an anonymous weekly article on Australian public affairs for the London *Morning Post* (to 1914).

E Sport and Recreation

George Towns wins the world sculling championship in Canada (7 Sept.).
Revenue wins the Melbourne Cup.
Ping-pong becomes "the game of the moment".

F Statistics, Social Change, the Environment

Estimated population of Australia 3,824,913 (simultaneous census, 31 Mar: 3,773,801).
National debt: £200 million.
Tuberculosis causes 3,557 deaths during the year.
Old-age pension schemes introduced in Vic. and NSW.

G Births and Deaths

Feb 22 Ken G. Hall b. (–1994).
Mar 27 Kenneth Slessor b. (–1971).
Apr 17 Eugen von Guerard d. (89).
May 15 Xavier Herbert b. (–1984).
Jun 6 Andrew Garran d. (75).

1901

Aug 26 Eleanor Dark b. (–1985).
Oct 8 Marcus Oliphant b.
Nov 30 Edward John Eyre d. (86).

1902

Jan 1 Australian Methodist sects unite.

Feb 19 First battalion of Commonwealth troops (wearing the forerunner of the "rising sun" badge) embark for South Africa.

27 Lt Harry ("Breaker") Morant and Lt P. J. Handcock executed by firing squad outside Pretoria, in the Transvaal, for shooting Boer prisoners.

Mar 9 British New Guinea (Papua) formally transferred to Australian control (but responsibility not accepted by Australia until Sept. 1906).

10 C. Y. O'Connor, engineer-in-chief of WA, commits suicide as a result of criticism of his goldfields water supply scheme.

23 Her Majesty's Theatre, Sydney, destroyed by fire.

– Post Office refuses to deliver mail addressed to Tattersall's Sweep. (Ban not lifted until 1930.)

May 5 Commonwealth Public Service Act establishes Australia's civil service.

31 Boer War ends with a peace treaty signed in Pretoria.

Jun 10 W. H. Irvine becomes Premier of Vic. following the defeat of the Peacock government.

12 Commonwealth Franchise Act grants the vote to all British subjects of six months' residence aged 21 and over (Asians, Africans, and Australian Aborigines excluded).

24 Frederick Illingworth becomes Premier of WA on the death of George Leake.

30 Imperial Conference in London (to 11 Aug.); Naval Agreement negotiated, providing for a RN squadron to be stationed in Australia, its cost subsidized by Australia. (Ratified 28 Aug. 1903.)

– Mundaring Weir, on the Helena River near Perth, completed.

Jul 1 W. H. James replaces Illingworth as Premier of WA.

17 Lord Tennyson becomes acting Governor-General following the resignation of Lord Hopetoun. (Appointment confirmed 9 Jan. 1903.)

31 Disastrous explosion at Mount Kembla colliery, NSW; 94 miners and two rescuers killed.

Aug 1 Women's magazine *New Idea* begins publication in Melbourne.

27 Women's Franchise Act (NSW) gives women the right to vote in state elections in keeping with their right to vote in federal elections.

Sep 16 Customs Tariff Act introduces the Commonwealth's first uniform tariff, a compromise between policies of Protectionists and Free Traders (retrospective to 8 Oct. 1901).

Oct 2 W. H. Gocher, proprietor and editor of a Manly (NSW) newspaper, defies the law forbidding sea bathing between 6 a.m. and 8 p.m. by entering the water at noon.

Nov 3 Submarine cable between Southport, Qld, and Vancouver, Canada, officially opened. (First message sent 31 Oct.)

Dec 2 Qld imposes a personal income tax.

18 Title of Lord Mayor conferred in Sydney and Melbourne.

1902

26 Brisbane, Rockhampton, and Townsville, Qld, declared cities.

* After eight successive dry years, the worst drought since settlement reaches its peak.

A Architecture, Building
J. H. Grainger, Parliament House, Perth (first portion completed 1904).
Supreme Court building, Perth (–1903).
Sydney's second Pyrmont Bridge opened.

B Science, Technology, Discovery, etc.
T. L. Bancroft establishes how the young hookworm enters the body through the skin.
R. C. Sticht carries out the world's first successful pyritic smelting at Mount Lyell, Tas.

C Arts and Entertainment
W. C. Piguenit, *Mount Kosciusko* (painting).
Bertram Mackennal, statues of Queen Victoria in Ballarat and T. J. Byrnes in Centenary Park, Brisbane.
Nellie Melba makes her first return visit to Australia.
Nellie Stewart appears for the first time in *Sweet Nell of Old Drury* at Melbourne's Princess Theatre (15 Feb.).

D Books and Writing
Barbara Baynton, *Bush Studies*.
Mrs Campbell Praed, *My Australian Girlhood*.
A. G. Stephens, *Oblation* (illustrated by Norman Lindsay).

E Sport and Recreation
Dick Cavill swims 100 yards in 58.6 sec. (becoming the first to break 1 min.) using the "Australian crawl" stroke (23 Sept.).
Victor Trumper scores 100 before lunch at Manchester, UK.
NSW Trotting Club formed (June).
The Victory wins the Melbourne Cup.

F Statistics, Social Change, the Environment
Estimated population of Australia: 3,875,318.
Australian casualties in the Boer War: 251 killed in action, 267 dead from disease, and 882 wounded, out of a total of 16,175 sent to South Africa.
Women granted the right to be elected to federal parliament together with the right to vote.
Ada Evans, the first woman to qualify in law in Australia, graduates from Sydney University but is not allowed to practise.
Workers' compensation legislation passed in WA (Qld in 1905, NSW and Tas. in 1910, SA in 1911, Vic. in 1914; Commonwealth legislation in 1912).
Rabbit-proof fence begun from Starvation Harbour, near Esperance, WA, to the north-west coast near Port Hedland. (Second fence later built to the west of No. 1 to contain rabbits found to be already established. Completed 1907.)
Cattle tick fever reaches the NSW border.

G Births and Deaths
Feb 22   Robert D. FitzGerald b. (–1987).
Mar 15   Nicholas Chevalier d. (73).
May 2   Alan Marshall b. (–1984).
Jun 29   James Brunton Stephens d. (67).
Jul 17   Christina Stead b. (–1983).
Jul 28   Albert Namatjira b. (–1959).
Sep 22   Dymphna Cusack b. (–1981).

1903

Jan 24 WA goldfields water supply scheme opened, water flowing through a steel pipeline from Mundaring Weir, near Perth, to Kalgoorlie.

Mar 9 Cyclone Leonta demolishes a swathe of buildings in Townsville; ten killed.
20 Automobile Club of Australia formed in Sydney. (Granted "Royal" prefix in 1919.)
– Lightning Ridge, NSW, opal field opened up.

Apr 5 Sydney's *Sunday Sun* begins publication (to 1953).
9 Liberal Democrat W. B. Propsting forms a ministry in Tas. following an election in which Premier Lewis and four ministers lose their seats and three Labour candidates are elected.
15 Electric trams begin running in Bendigo (to 1972).

May 8 Railway engine-drivers and firemen in Vic. go on strike, causing the first large-scale disruption of a public utility. (Called off on 15th after Coercion Act introduced into parliament.)
26 SS *Oakland* wrecked near Port Stephens, NSW, with the loss of 11 lives.

Jul 30 Bounty provided for sugar growers.

Aug 3 Vida Goldstein stands as a candidate for the Senate, becoming the first woman in the British Empire to contest an election to a national parliament.
25 Commonwealth Judiciary Act assented to, providing for the establishment of the High Court of Australia.

Sep 17 Arthur Morgan becomes Premier of Qld, in coalition with Labour's W. H. Browne, following the resignation of Robert Philp.
24 Alfred Deakin becomes Prime Minister on the resignation of Sir Edmund Barton to become a judge of the High Court.
30 Automobile and Motor Cycle Club of South Australia formed. (Becomes the Automobile Association of SA in 1911; "Royal" prefix added in 1929.)

Oct 3 Brisbane *Daily Mail*, edited by C. H. Buzacott, begins publication (to 1933).
5 Sir Samuel Griffith appointed first Chief Justice of the High Court (Barton and R. E. O'Connor the other two judges).
6 High Court of Australia formally opened in Melbourne.
22 Commonwealth Defence Act assented to. (Comes into force on 1 Mar. 1904.)

Nov – NSW Legislative Assembly reduced from 125 to 90 members.

Dec 9 Automobile Club of Victoria formed. (Granted "Royal" prefix in 1916.)
10 Women gain the vote in Tas. state elections.
16 Election for House of Representatives and half Senate, women voting for the first time. Deakin retains office with the support of the 25 Labour members elected. (Vida Goldstein and the other three women candidates for parliament fail to win seats.)

* Australia's first crematorium established, at West Terrace Cemetery, Adelaide.
* Seventh Day Adventist Sanitarium and medical training centre opens at Wahroonga, Sydney.
* Jehovah's Witnesses established in Melbourne.
* Great Drought breaks in most states after eight years.

A Architecture, Building
Sydney (Central) Station (foundation stone laid 26 Sept; completed in 1906).

1903

B Science, Technology, Discovery, etc.

C Arts and Entertainment

Arundel Orchard arrives in Sydney to conduct the Sydney Liedertafel.

Contralto Ada Crossley returns to Australia for a concert tour with Percy Grainger as accompanist.

J. C. W.'s new Her Majesty's Theatre opens in Sydney.

D Books and Writing

"Tom Collins" (Joseph Furphy), *Such Is Life*.

Bernard O'Dowd, *Dawnward?*.

E Sport and Recreation

First Australia–New Zealand Rugby Union Test match played (15 Aug.), NZ winning 22–3.

World's first fully enclosed artificial ice rink opens in Adelaide.

Lord Cardigan wins the Melbourne Cup.

F Statistics, Social Change, the Environment

Estimated population of Australia: 3,916,592.

Gold production in Australia peaks at 3,836,095 oz for the year.

Women admitted to the practice of law in Vic.

The sheep blowfly (probably established in Australia from South Africa or India in the previous decade) becomes a serious pest.

G Births and Deaths

Feb 9 Sir Charles Gavan Duffy d. (86).

Jun 22 Garfield Barwick b. (–1997).

Jul 26 Quong Tart d. (53?).

Aug 5 Phil May d. (39).

Oct 15 Pixie O'Harris b. (–1991).

1904

Jan 21 Baron Northcote becomes Governor-General.

Feb 16 Thomas Bent succeeds W. H. Irvine as Premier of Vic.

Mar 1 Commonwealth Defence Act (1903) comes into force, providing for conscription of men between 18 and 60 in time of war for service within the Commonwealth or territory controlled by the Commonwealth.

Capt. W. R. Creswell appointed director of Commonwealth naval forces.

31 Recruiting of Pacific Island labour ceases.

Apr 21 Deakin government defeated in the House of Representatives on an amendment to the Arbitration Bill; Deakin resigns (22nd).

27 J. C. Watson forms a minority Labour government (the first federal Labour ministry).

May 25 Five miners die in a mine-shaft fall at the Great Boulder gold mine, East Coolgardie, WA.

Jun 15 Thomas Waddell becomes Premier of NSW on the retirement of John See to the Legislative Council.

20 C. S. Robinson, Chief Judicial Officer and Acting Administrator of British New Guinea, shoots himself following criticism of his punitive expedition to Goaribari.

1904

Jul 8 Sydney streets lit by electricity when Pyrmont power station officially switched on.

10 SS *Nemesis* founders off the coast of NSW during a storm, with the loss of all 21 aboard.

12 J. W. Evans forms a government in Tas. following the resignation of W. B. Propsting.

20 P & O liner *Australia* runs aground on a reef at the entrance to Port Phillip; no lives lost but ship a total loss.

Aug 10 Henry Daglish forms WA's first Labour ministry.

12 Watson government defeated on the Arbitration Bill; Watson resigns.

17 George Reid becomes Prime Minister, forming a composite ministry in coalition with Protectionist Allan McLean.

30 J. H. Carruthers becomes Premier of NSW following the defeat of the Waddell government in the election on 6 Aug.

– Hubert Murray appointed Chief Judicial Officer of British New Guinea.

Sep 30 French barque *Adolphe* wrecked on the northern breakwater at Newcastle. (Ship eventually built into the breakwater.)

Oct 14 Fire at the Brilliant gold mine, Charters Towers, Qld, causes the death of seven miners.

20 Toowoomba, Qld, proclaimed a city.

Nov 5 Iron barque *Brier Holme* wrecked on the south-west coast of Tas; one survivor out of the crew of 20 (not rescued until Feb. 1905).

Dec 3 Ipswich, Qld, proclaimed a city.

15 Commonwealth Conciliation and Arbitration Act finally passed, setting up the Commonwealth Court of Conciliation and Arbitration.

* First Australian Rhodes Scholars selected.

A Architecture, Building

His (Her) Majesty's Hotel and Theatre, Perth.

B Science, Technology, Discovery, etc.

Auguste de Bavay patents a flotation process for the separation of zinc.

C Arts and Entertainment

Hugh Ramsay, *The Sisters* (painting).

Hans Heysen's *Mystic Morn* awarded the Wynne Prize.

Norman Lindsay's drawing *Pollice Verso* in the Royal Art Society of NSW's exhibition causes a public outcry.

Melbourne businessman Alfred Felton leaves a large bequest to the Art Gallery of Vic.

Alfred Hill, *Tapu* (opera).

Polish pianist Ignace Paderewski tours Australia.

Leon Brodsky founds the Australian Theatre Society in Melbourne.

D Books and Writing

Tom Petrie's Reminiscences of Early Queensland.

Steele Rudd, *Sandy's Selection* (first book published by A. C. Rowlandson in the NSW Bookstall Co.'s shilling paperback series).

A. G. Stephens, *The Red Pagan.*

E Sport and Recreation

First Australian Open golf championship held (2 Sept; won by Hon. Michael Scott).

Lawn Tennis Association of Australasia (later Australia) formed.

1904

Henley-on-Yarra regatta first held (19 Mar; won by Ballarat).

First motor car race in Australia held at Sandown Park, Melbourne (12 Mar; won by Harley Tarrant in a twin-cylinder, 8 hp car he built).

Acrasia wins the Melbourne Cup.

F Statistics, Social Change, the Environment

Estimated population of Australia: 3,974,150.

Motor Car Act in SA specifies a speed limit of 15 mph (24 km/h).

Legislation passed to allow Melbourne Gallery and Library to open on Sundays (last city in British Empire to do so).

Royal commission investigating the decline in the birthrate in NSW condemns contraception.

G Births and Deaths

Jan 25 Sir Graham Berry d. (81).

Apr 7 Roland Wilson b. (–1996).

Apr 8 John Antill b. (–1986).

May 2 Wilfrid Thomas b. (–1991).

May 29 Hubert Opperman b. (–1996).

Jun 24 Alfred Felton d. (72).

Aug 4 Brian Penton b. (–1951).

Aug 5 Sir George Dibbs d. (69).

Sep 23 George Adams d. (65).

1905

Jan 12 Board of Administration of Naval Forces (Naval Board) established, with Capt. W. R. Creswell as director. (Also set up under the Defence Act are a Council of Defence and a Military Board.)

17 Peter Board appointed first Director of Education in NSW. (New Syllabus subsequently introduced.)

25 Full adult franchise (subject to racial exclusions) granted in Qld, and plural voting abolished.

Feb 10 Justice R. E. O'Connor appointed first president of the Commonwealth Court of Conciliation and Arbitration.

15 First state secondary school in Vic., the Continuation School (later Melbourne High School), opens in Melbourne.

Mar 1 Richard Butler succeeds J. G. Jenkins as Premier of SA.

May 24 Empire Day inaugurated (on the late Queen Victoria's birthday).

31 (Royal) Automobile Club of Queensland formed in Brisbane.

Jul 4 George Reid resigns as Prime Minister after a defeat in the House and the refusal of his request for a dissolution of parliament.

5 Alfred Deakin forms a government with Labour support.

26 Labour leader Thomas Price replaces Jenkins as Premier of SA, leading a coalition government with a Labour majority.

Aug 25 C. H. Rason forms a Liberal ministry in WA following the resignation of Henry Daglish.

Sep 1 Vic. Socialist Party founded in Melbourne by English trade union leader Tom Mann.

2 Hobart GPO opened.

5 Australian National Defence League formed in NSW to press for compulsory military training.

– Iron clipper *Loch Vennachar* lost off Kangaroo Is., SA, with the loss of all 26 hands.

Oct 18 Wireless Telegraphy Act gives the Postmaster-General control of the operation of wireless stations.

Nov 30 Electric tramway service begins in Fremantle, WA. (Closed Nov. 1952.)

Dec 1 Steam bus begins operating in Melbourne between Prahran and Malvern.

21 Immigration Registration Act amended to allow for the dictation test to be applied in "any prescribed language" rather than in a European language.

– Motor bus service begins in Sydney.

A Architecture, Building
Flinders Street Station, Melbourne (–1910).

B Science, Technology, Discovery, etc.
T. L. Bancroft demonstrates that mosquitoes carry the dengue fever pathogen.

A. G. Michell of Vic. patents his thrust bearing, which eliminates metallic contact of moving surfaces by oil lubrication.

C Arts and Entertainment
Cosens Spencer arrives in Sydney and begins exhibiting films at the Lyceum Theatre.

D Books and Writing
Mrs Aeneas Gunn, *The Little Black Princess.*

Henry Lawson, *When I Was King and Other Verses.*

A. B. Paterson, ed., *The Old Bush Songs.*

Joseph Furphy's *Rigby's Romance* begins serialization in the *Barrier Truth.* (Published as a book in 1921.)

E Sport and Recreation
Barney Kieran establishes eight world swimming records in England over distances from 200 yards to 1 mile.

Harley Tarrant in an Argyll car wins the first reliability trial in Australia, between Sydney and Melbourne (Feb.–Mar.).

Blue Spec wins the Melbourne Cup.

F Statistics, Social Change, the Environment
Population of Australia reaches four million.

Typhoid fever causes 630 deaths in Australia.

Women given the vote and admitted to the practice of law in Qld.

Wilsons Promontory National Park officially reserved. (Coastal strip added in 1908.)

G Births and Deaths
Apr 1 Paul Hasluck b. (–1993).

Jun 25 Sir Augustus Charles Gregory d. (85).

Dec 18 Roy Grounds b. (–1981).

Dec 29 Victor Daley d. (47).

1906

Jan 19 William Kidston succeeds Arthur Morgan as Premier of Qld.

1906

28 Cyclone severely damages Cairns and Innisfail.

– Mater Misericordiae Hospital founded at Crows Nest, Sydney.

– Flooding of northern NSW inland rivers (to March).

Feb 6 Bondi Surf Bathers Life Saving Club—Australia's (and the world's) first surf lifesaving club—founded in Sydney.

Apr 2 First issue of the *Socialist*, edited by Tom Mann, published in Melbourne.

May 5 Electric trams begin operating in Melbourne between St Kilda and Brighton.

7 N. J. Moore replaces C. H. Rason as Premier of WA.

29 A. W. Canning leaves Wiluna, WA, to explore towards Halls Creek (arrives Jan. 1907), with a view to establishing a stock route from the Kimberleys to the markets in the south of the state.

Jul 12 Wireless telegraphy between Queenscliff, Vic., and Devonport, Tas., operated by the Marconi Co., officially opened.

14 Unregistered bookmaker Donald McLeod, unable to meet his financial commitments, is killed by an angry mob at Flemington.

25 Methodist minister Henry Worrall is summoned before the bar of the Vic. Legislative Assembly for impeaching the Chief Secretary (accusing him of being responsible for McLeod's death by not legislating to stop gambling).

– Murray River in high flood at Albury.

Aug 4 Sydney (Central) railway station formally opened for traffic.

30 First driver's licence issued, to W. A. Hargreaves of Adelaide.

Sep 1 Australia assumes responsibility for the administration of British New Guinea, renaming it Papua (by the Papua Act of 1905).

24 Australian Industries Preservation Act provides protection against the dumping of foreign goods on the Australian market.

26 WA parliament proposes holding a referendum to withdraw from the Commonwealth. (No action taken until 1933.)

– Rivers in southern NSW and northern Vic. in flood (to Oct.).

Oct 1 South African Preference Act introduces the first Commonwealth preferential tariff.

8 Free Education Act assented to in NSW, making primary education free in the state.

15 Isaac Isaacs and H. B. Higgins sworn in as justices of the High Court.

Dec 12 Election for House of Representatives and half Senate; Deakin government retains office with Labour support. Referendum proposing minor changes concerning Senate elections carried.

Royal Alexandra Hospital for Children opens in Camperdown, Sydney.

19 Legislation enacted authorizing the construction of the Barren Jack (now Burrinjuck) Dam and the Murrumbidgee irrigation scheme.

* NSW resumes assisted migration.

* Sydney Teachers' College established at Blackfriars.

* Anthony Hordern's emporium, the biggest department store in the Southern Hemisphere, opens on Brickfield Hill, Sydney. (Building demolished in 1987.)

* Phosphate mining begins on Nauru under a concession granted by the German government.

* Kiwi boot polish put on the market by McKellow & Ramsay.

A Architecture, Building

Mitchell Library, Sydney (–1910).

WA Art Gallery (–1908).

B Science, Technology, Discovery, etc.
Natural gas used to light the streets of Roma, Qld (June). (Supply runs out after ten days.)
Lyster Ormsby devises the surf lifesaving reel (demonstrated 23 Dec.).

C Arts and Entertainment
Frederick McCubbin, *The Pioneer* triptych.
Statue of Colonel Light unveiled in Victoria Square, Adelaide (27 Nov.). (Moved to Montefiore Hill in May 1938.)
Alberto Zelman forms the Melbourne Symphony Orchestra.
Lyceum Theatre, Sydney, converts to moving pictures.
Charles Tait's full-length film *The Story of the Kelly Gang* first shown at the Athenaeum Hall, Melbourne (26 Dec.).

D Books and Writing
Edward Dyson, *Fact'ry 'Ands.*
Bernard O'Dowd, *The Silent Land.*
Johns's Notable Australians (later *Who's Who in Australia*) first published.

E Sport and Recreation
Qld professional runner Arthur Postle beats Irish world champion Bernard Day over 75 and 300 yards at Kalgoorlie (5 Dec.).
Black American cyclist Major Taylor draws 50,000 people to the Sydney Cricket Ground.
Poseidon wins the AJC Derby, Caulfield Cup, Victoria Derby, and Melbourne Cup.

F Statistics, Social Change, the Environment
Estimated population of Australia: 4,091,485.
Population of Sydney (est. 559,800) overtakes that of Melbourne (est. 530,660).
More than 4 million Australian possum skins marketed in London and New York.
Surf bathing in the daytime on Sydney's beaches made legal.
Lake Eyre partially fills with water (according to geological records).

G Births and Deaths
Feb   6   James Bonwick d. (88).
Feb 24   H. C. Coombs b. (–1997).
Mar 14   George Coppin d. (86).
Apr 16   William Farrer d. (61).
Aug 12   Harry Hopman b. (–1985).
Dec   3   Frank Packer b. (–1974).

1907

Jan 1 Excise Tariff (Agricultural Machinery) Act of 1906 comes into force, requiring manufacturers to pay their employees a "fair and reasonable" wage in order to avoid paying excise duty. (Act declared invalid by High Court in June 1908.)

3 First rescue by Bondi Surf Bathers Life Saving Club—of two schoolboys, one of them Charles Kingsford Smith.

19 Cooktown, Qld, severely damaged by cyclone; government ketch *Pilot* sinks with the loss of eight lives.

Mar 19 Floodwaters trap miner Modesto Vareschetti in a mine at Bonnievale, WA,

1907

for nine days. (Rescued by fellow miner Frank Hughes after being repeatedly brought food by Hughes in a diving suit.)

Apr 8 Wireless telegraphy first used between ships in Australian waters: German mail steamer *Bremen* to HMS *Encounter* in Port Jackson notifying arrival time in Sydney.

9 Hubert Murray becomes Acting Administrator of Papua. (Appointed Lt-Governor on 27 Nov. 1908.)

May 8 Carlton and United Breweries Ltd established in Melbourne by the amalgamation of six breweries.

Jul 10 Telephone trunk line opens between Sydney and Melbourne.

16 Broken Hill proclaimed a city.

Aug 14 Italian barque *Ingeborg* sinks after a collision with SS *Arawatta* off Port Stephens, NSW; seven lives lost.

15 Members of federal parliament vote themselves their first pay increase (of 50%).

27 Frederick Peters establishes Peters' American Delicacy Co. Ltd in Sydney to make ice-cream.

Sep 4 H. B. Higgins succeeds R. E. O'Connor as the High Court judge presiding over the Arbitration Court.

15 Disastrous night fire in Murwillumbah, NSW, destroys 59 buildings in the business section.

– Amalgamated Workers' Association formed in Irvinebank, Qld, by E. G. Theodore and William McCormack.

Oct 2 C. G. Wade becomes Premier of NSW on the retirement of J. H. Carruthers.

18 Surf Bathing Association of NSW formed at a meeting of seven surf lifesaving clubs in Sydney.

30 J. C. Watson resigns the leadership of the federal Labour party and is succeeded by Andrew Fisher.

– Branches of the Industrial Workers of the World (IWW) established in Australia.

Nov 1 Hare-Clark system of voting extended to the whole of Tas.

8 Justice Higgins in the Arbitration Court, hearing H. V. McKay's application for exemption from duty on his Sunshine Harvesters, finds that wages paid by McKay are not "fair and reasonable" and subsequently sets a minimum wage adequate for "the normal needs of the average employee" (with a wife and three children)—thereby establishing the principle of the basic wage.

19 Robert Philp replaces William Kidston as Premier of Qld.

Dec 19 Invalid Pensions Act passed in NSW, introducing the world's first non-contributory invalid pension (payable on 1 Jan. 1908).

20 Plural voting abolished and adult suffrage introduced for Legislative Assembly elections in WA.

Land tax and income tax introduced in WA.

– Railway from Townsville reaches Cloncurry.

* Cataract Dam, NSW, completed.

A Architecture, Building

Florence Parsons (later Taylor) establishes herself as the first woman architect in Australia (later as structural and civil engineer).

B Science, Technology, Discovery, etc.

Frank Bottrill patents his "pedorail", a caterpillar-type road wheel used on many tractors in Australia.

C Arts and Entertainment

Arthur Streeton, *Sydney Harbour* (painting).

Cathedral organist George Sampson forms an orchestra in Brisbane.

Nellie Melba makes her second Australian tour.

Bert Bailey and Edmund Duggan, *The Squatter's Daughter* (play).

T. J. West opens the Glaciarium in Sydney as a film theatre.

George and Arthur Cornwell, *Eureka Stockade* (film).

Charles MacMahon, *Robbery Under Arms* (film).

D Books and Writing

Barbara Baynton, *Human Toll.*

Monthly journal the *Lone Hand*, published by the *Bulletin* and edited by Frank Fox, first appears (1 May). (Ceases publication in 1921.)

E Sport and Recreation

Norman Brookes (Aust.) and Anthony Wilding (NZ), playing as the Australasian team, win the Davis Cup. Brookes also wins the Wimbledon singles, doubles (with Wilding), and mixed doubles.

NSW Rugby Football League formed as a breakaway professional code.

Francis Birtles, having cycled from Fremantle to Sydney, leaves Sydney (21 Aug.) and cycles to Darwin via Brisbane, Bowen and Normanton and returns via Alice Springs, Adelaide and Melbourne (arr. Sydney 23 Sept. 1908).

Apologue wins the Melbourne Cup.

F Statistics, Social Change, the Environment

Estimated population of Australia: 4,161,722.

Commonwealth basic wage (set by Harvester judgement): £2 2s per six-day week.

G Births and Deaths

Feb   8   Jack Davey b. (–1952).

Feb 17   Marjorie Lawrence b. (–1979).

Jul 21   A. D. Hope b.

Jul 24   David Scott Mitchell d. (71).

Aug 12   Andrew ("Boy") Charlton b. (–1975).

Aug 21   Betty Archdale b. (–2000).

1908

Jan 16   Outer Harbour, Port Adelaide, declared officially open.

Feb 18   William Kidston resumes the premiership of Qld following an election on 5 Feb.

Mar 10   Australians T. W. Edgeworth David and Douglas Mawson, of Sir Ernest Shackleton's British Antarctic expedition, ascend Mt Erebus in Antarctica.

17   A. W. Canning sets out to equip a stock route between Hall's Creek and Wiluna, WA. (Puts down 52 wells; route completed Dec. 1909.)

Apr 20   Two trains filled with holidaymakers collide at Sunshine, Vic; 44 killed and more than 400 injured.

27   Cyclone hits a pearling fleet at Eighty Mile Beach, WA, causing the loss of more than 50 lives.

1908

May 7 Coat of arms granted to the Commonwealth. (Design amended in 1912.)

16 Commonwealth Literary Fund established to assist needy authors.

– Ship *Orion* disappears between Smithton and Melbourne; 27 lives lost.

Jun 3 Tariff Act increases the duty on imported goods and the number of items liable for duty, but allows a 5% rebate on goods from the UK.

30 H. H. Dutton and Murray Aunger leave Adelaide in a Talbot car to drive to Darwin (arr. 20 Aug.), the first crossing of Australia by car.

Jul 1 Old-age pension scheme comes into force in Qld.

– Federal Labour conference adopts the title Australian Labor Party.

Aug 20 US fleet of 16 battleships and 5 auxiliaries—the Great White Fleet—under the command of Rear-Admiral Charles Sperry, arrives in Sydney at the beginning of a goodwill visit to Australia.

Sep 5 Rock fall at Mt Morgan, Qld, mine kills seven men. (Another fall on 4 Nov. kills five more miners.)

9 Earl of Dudley succeeds Lord Northcote as Governor-General.

20 Women granted the vote in Vic. state elections. (Act not proclaimed until 31 Mar. 1909, after the Dec. election.)

Nov 10 Deakin government defeated in the House of Representatives when Labor withdraws its support; Deakin resigns (11th), and Labor leader Andrew Fisher becomes Prime Minister (13th).

– Yass–Canberra chosen by federal parliament as the site for the federal capital.

Dec 3 Tas. Education Act provides for free primary education.

7 BHP notifies its employees that wages will be cut by 12½% from 1 Jan. 1909; miners refuse to accept this and a strike/lockout begins (to 24 May 1909).

– Cyclone strikes north-west coast of WA; 50 lives lost.

* Dockyard established on Cockatoo Is., Sydney, by the NSW government. (Transferred to Commonwealth in 1913.)

A Architecture, Building

Cantilevered awnings first appear on buildings in Australia.

B Science, Technology, Discovery, etc.

Commonwealth Bureau of Meteorology opens in Melbourne (1 Jan.).

Riverview College Observatory, Sydney, proclaimed a seismological station.

C Arts and Entertainment

WA Art Gallery opens in Perth (25 June).

Chloe (painting) goes on display in Young and Jackson's Hotel in Melbourne.

Sydney Symphony Orchestra founded, with Arundel Orchard as conductor.

Bryceson Treharne forms the Adelaide Literary Theatre (later the Adelaide Repertory Theatre).

Charles MacMahon, *For the Term of His Natural Life* (film).

D Books and Writing

E. J. Banfield, *The Confessions of a Beachcomber.*

Mrs Aeneas Gunn, *We of the Never Never.*

Henry Handel Richardson, *Maurice Guest.*

Official Year Book of the Commonwealth of Australia first issued.

Dorothea Mackellar's poem "My Country" appears in the London *Spectator* (5 Sept.).

E Sport and Recreation

Wallabies Rugby Union and Kangaroos Rugby League teams both make their first tours of Britain, the Wallabies winning gold medals at the London Olympic Games.

First surf carnival held, at Manly, Sydney (Jan.).

Hugh D. McIntosh opens the Sydney Stadium (21 Aug.) and stages the first world title bout in Australia (24 Aug.) between Canadian Tommy Burns and local boxer Bill Squires (Burns winning on a KO in the 13th round). McIntosh then arranges a bout between Burns and American Negro Jack Johnson for the world heavyweight championship (26 Dec.); Johnson is declared the winner after police stop the fight in the 14th round.

Lord Nolan wins the Melbourne Cup.

Australasia (Norman Brookes and A. F. Wilding) retains the Davis Cup, played in Melbourne (27–29 Nov.).

F Statistics, Social Change, the Environment

Estimated population of Australia: 4,232,278.

Boy Scout movement begins in Australia; groups formed in all states.

National park established at Mt Tamborine, Qld.

G Births and Deaths

Feb 14   David Syme d. (80).

Feb 23   William McMahon b. (–1988).

May 20   Henry Bolte b. (–1990).

Aug 5   Harold Holt b. (–1967).

Aug 27   Donald Bradman b.

1909

Jan 5   Pinnace of HMS *Encounter* sinks in Sydney Harbour after being struck by the collier *Dunmore*; 15 sailors drown.

8   John Murray replaces Sir Thomas Bent as Premier of Vic.

9   Police clash with striking miners in Broken Hill; 27 miners and leader Tom Mann arrested. (Henry Holland, another leader, arrested on 20 Feb., charged with sedition and later sentenced to two years' gaol; Mann freed.)

16   T. W. Edgeworth David, Douglas Mawson, and A. F. McKay of the Shackleton expedition reach the South Magnetic Pole.

31   SS *Clan Ranald* founders in Gulf St Vincent, SA; 40 lives lost.

Feb 5   Fisher government orders the building of three destroyers in Britain for an Australian naval squadron.

11   Eastern Suburbs Technical College (now Swinburne Institute of Technology) opens in Melbourne.

Mar 9   Electric tram service begins in Adelaide.

12   Arbitration Court awards striking Broken Hill miners their former wages. (Miners return to work on 24 May.)

Apr 5   Cyclone at Onslow, WA; four luggers and 24 lives lost.

May 24   Alfred Deakin's Liberal Protectionists and Joseph Cook's Free Traders, with the corner group led by Sir John Forrest, combine to form "the Fusion", or Liberal Party.

Jun 2   Deakin becomes Prime Minister (with Cook his deputy), Andrew Fisher having been forced to resign on the resumption of parliament.

1909

5 A. H. Peake forms an all-Liberal ministry in SA following the death of Premier Tom Price on 31 May.

19 Sir Neil Lewis becomes Premier of Tas., leading a "Liberal Fusion" group.

30 Children's Hospital opens in Perth.

Jul 1 Commonwealth old-age pensions—for men over 65 and women over 60, subject to means test—come into operation.
Commonwealth quarantine service begins, for the purposes of preventing the introduction of human, animal, and plant diseases.

23 Sir Frederick Holder, Speaker of the House of Representatives, collapses and dies after an unruly all-night sitting.

27 SS *Waratah*, bound for London from Adelaide with 211 passengers (mostly Australians), disappears mysteriously between Durban and Cape Town, leaving no trace.

28 Creation of an independent Australian fleet unit agreed upon at an Imperial Conference on defence in London.

– Motor taxis first used in Sydney.

Aug 23 Deakin makes a financial agreement with the states under which the Commonwealth would pay 25 shillings per capita per year to the states.

– Long Bay Gaol opens in Sydney, at first as a women's reformatory. (Men transferred from Darlinghurst Gaol in 1912.)

Oct 18 NSW agrees to surrender approx. 2,400 sq. km of the state to the Commonwealth as a seat for the federal government.

20 John Earle forms the first Labor ministry in Tas., following the resignation of the Lewis government.

27 Lewis resumes the premiership of Tas. on the defeat of the week-old Earle government.

Nov 6 NSW coalminers strike on the Newcastle coalfields (to 11 Mar. 1910).

11 Vic. government establishes a state coalmine at Wonthaggi.

Dec 4 Miners' leader Peter Bowling and other strikers arrested and gaoled.

5 First flight in a heavier-than-air machine (unpowered) in Australia made by G. A. Taylor at Narrabeen beach in Sydney. (Four days later, Colin Defries makes the first powered flight in Australia at Victoria Park Racecourse, Sydney.)

8 Deakin orders the building of the battle-cruiser *Australia.*
Lady Dudley calls a meeting at Government House, Melbourne, which leads to the formation of the Bush Nursing Service.

10 University of Queensland founded. (Opens in the former Government House on 14 Mar. 1911.)

13 Defence Act provides for the introduction of compulsory military training.

16 Legislation passed in NSW providing harsh penalties for instigating or aiding a strike.

21 Lord Kitchener visits Australia (to 12 Feb. 1910) to advise on Australia's military defence.

A Architecture, Building

N. G. Peebles, State Library of Vic. reading room (–1913); reinforced concrete dome designed by John Monash.
Hotel Kosciuszko.

B Science, Technology, Discovery, etc.

Australian Institute of Tropical Medicine established in Townsville.

C Arts and Entertainment

Harold Cazneaux holds a one-man show of "pictorial" photography.

Amy Castles and Peter Dawson tour Australia jointly, and Nellie Melba makes her third concert tour.

Dr Arthur Russell begins exhibiting films in Melbourne, using the name Hoyts.

D Books and Writing

Hugh McCrae, *Satyrs and Sunlight.*

Bernard O'Dowd, *Poetry Militant.*

B. R. Wise, *The Commonwealth of Australia.*

E. A. Petherick's collection of Australiana becomes the basis of the National Library of Australia.

E Sport and Recreation

Norman Brookes and A. F. Wilding win the Davis Cup for Australasia for the third time.

Exhibition matches held between the Kangaroos (Rugby League) and the Wallabies (Rugby Union) touring teams; Wallabies defect to League.

Prince Foote wins the Melbourne Cup.

F Statistics, Social Change, the Environment

Estimated population of Australia: 4,323,960.

Vic. parliament grants a Saturday half-holiday for Melbourne (1 May); shops close at 1 p.m. but with Friday night opening as alternative.

Wyperfield National Park, Vic., proclaimed.

G Births and Deaths

Feb   9   Charles Conder d. (40).

Feb 13   R. M. Ansett b. (–1981).

Mar 26   Chips Rafferty b. (–1971).

Apr   4   R. W. Askin b. (–1981).

Apr   9   Robert Helpman(n) b. (–1986).

Apr 18   Archbishop William Saumarez Smith d. (73).

May 22   Bob Dyer b. (–1984).

Jun 10   Lang Hancock b. (–1992).

Jun 20   Errol Flynn b. (–1959).

Aug   8   Mother Mary MacKillop d. (67).

1910

Jan 22   Sir George Reid becomes Australia's first High Commissioner in London.

Feb 12   Lord Kitchener makes his report on Australia's defences.

Mar 8   Mitchell Library, Sydney, officially opened.

    17   F. C. Custance flies a Bleriot monoplane for five minutes at Bolivar, SA; next day, American escape artist Harry Houdini makes the first certified successful series of flights in a powered aircraft in Australia, in a French Voisin at Digger's Rest, Vic.

Apr 2   Labor wins a majority in SA elections. (When parliament resumes, John Verran forces A. H. Peake's resignation and forms SA's first Labor government on 3 June.)

    13   Election for House of Representatives and half Senate; Labor obtains a clear-cut majority in both houses; Andrew Fisher again becomes Prime Minister (29th).

1910

Referendum on a proposal for the Commonwealth to take over state debts carried; another, to incorporate the financial agreement into the Constitution, rejected.

Jul 1 Sydney *Sun*, Australia's first newspaper with front-page news, begins publication (to 1988).

16 John Duigan makes the first flight in an Australian designed and built aircraft, at Mia Mia, Vic.

18 Train collision at Richmond, Vic; nine killed and nearly 500 injured.

– Commonwealth legislates to make an annual per capita payment to the states instead of a percentage of customs and excise revenue.

Sep 16 Australian Bank Notes Act gives the Commonwealth Treasury power to issue Australian paper currency. (A 10% tax is subsequently imposed on private bank notes and sterling to force them out of circulation.)
Frank Wilson succeeds N. J. Moore as Premier of WA.

19 Liberal Union formed in SA by the formal amalgamation of the Australasian Nationalist League, the Farmers' and Producers' Political Union, and the Liberal and Democratic Union.

Oct 21 J. S. T. McGowen becomes the first Labor Premier of NSW.

Nov 3 Berri, SA, irrigation area proclaimed. (Town proclaimed 9 Feb. 1911.)

16 Commonwealth government imposes a land tax on all estates with an unimproved value of more than £5,000 (first direct federal tax; abandoned in 1952).

20 Cyclone causes extensive damage to Broome, WA; 26 pearling vessels wrecked and 40 lives lost.

23 Torpedo-boat destroyers *Parramatta* and *Yarra*, the first ships to be built for the Australian navy, arrive in Fremantle from Britain.

25 Naval Defence Act assented to, creating the Commonwealth Naval Forces. (Title changed to Royal Australian Navy on 5 Oct. 1911.)

– Australian Wireless Co. in Sydney establishes a shore station for communicating with ships at sea.

Dec 8 Geelong proclaimed a city.

15 Commonwealth invalid pension comes into operation.

23 Education Act passed in Vic., initiating a state scheme of technical, preparatory trade, higher elementary, and high schools.

28 Murrumbidgee Irrigation Trust established.

* First Australian Commonwealth silver coins issued.
* Perth Modern School established.

A Architecture, Building

G. D. Payne, St Andrew's Presbyterian Church, Brisbane, completed.

L. S. Robertson, Nelson House, Clarence Street, Sydney—the first selfsupporting steel-framed building in Australia.

Chalet built at Mount Buffalo, Vic.

B Science, Technology, Discovery, etc.

NSW Government Astronomer W. E. Raymond photographs Halley's Comet on its transit of the sun (19 May).

Wireless Institute of Australia founded in Sydney by G. A. Taylor.

J. S. Dethridge invents a water meter to measure the amount of water delivered in irrigation channels.

C Arts and Entertainment

E. Phillips Fox, *The Ferry* (painting).

Louis Esson, *The Woman Tamer* (play).
Bert Bailey, *The Squatter's Daughter* (film).
S. A. Fitzgerald, *The Life and Adventures of John Vane, Bushranger* (film).

D Books and Writing
C. E. W. Bean, *On the Wool Track.*
Mary Grant Bruce, *A Little Bush Maid.*
John Flynn, *The Bushman's Companion.*
Mary Gilmore, *Marri'd and Other Verses.*
Henry Lawson, *The Rising of the Court.*
Henry Handel Richardson, *The Getting of Wisdom.*

E Sport and Recreation
Vic. professional runner Jack Donaldson, competing in South Africa, establishes a world record of 9⅜ sec. for 100 yards (unbroken for 38 years).
Surfboat with five-man crew demonstrated at Manly (Syd.) surf carnival (19 Mar.).
Comedy King wins the Melbourne Cup.

F Statistics, Social Change, the Environment
Estimated population of Australia: 4,425,083.

G Births and Deaths
Apr   3   Catherine Helen Spence d. (84).
Jul   16   Stan McCabe b. (–1968).
Sep   1   Peggy Van Praagh b. (–1990).

1911

Jan   1   Federal Capital Territory (now ACT) vested in Commonwealth.
Commonwealth formally takes over from South Australia administration of the Northern Territory. (Palmerston renamed Darwin, 3 Mar.)
Legislation proclaimed introducing compulsory military training for males aged from 12 to 25. (Training begins 1 July.)
   –   *Land* newspaper launched by the NSW Farmers and Settlers' Association.

Feb   2   Western Australia adopts a compulsory preferential voting system (optional preferential having been in force since 1907).
   7   Digby Denham replaces William Kidston as Premier of Qld.
   16   University of Western Australia established by act of parliament. (Senate appointed 13 Feb. 1912; lectures begin 31 Mar. 1913.)

Mar   11   Reconstituted Naval Board gazetted, with Rear-Admiral Sir William Creswell as First Naval Member.
   16   Cyclone severely damages Cairns, Innisfail, and Port Douglas; two people killed.
   24   Passenger steamer *Yongala* founders in a cyclone off Cape Bowling Green, Qld, with the loss of 120 lives. (Wreck discovered in 1958.)

Apr   3   First Commonwealth census held.
   4   HMAS *Warrego* launched in Sydney, having been assembled at Cockatoo Island Dockyard from parts prefabricated in Britain.
   26   Referendums on extending Commonwealth powers over trade and commerce and the control of monopolies rejected.

May   1   Uniform penny postage comes into operation.

1911

Jun 11 Sidney Myer opens a drapery business in Bourke Street, Melbourne.
27 Royal Military College, Duntroon, opens, with Col. W. T. Bridges as commandant.

Jul 31 Baron Denman succeeds Lord Dudley as Governor-General.

Aug 4 Electric trams begin operating in Launceston. (Replaced by trolley buses in 1952.)

Sep 11 SS *Rosedale* founders between Smoky Cape, NSW, and Sydney; 26 drown.
30 Victoria adopts a preferential voting system.

Oct 3 Labor wins office in WA; John Scaddan becomes Premier (7th).
6 Enrolment for federal elections made compulsory.
11 SS *Macleay* founders near Port Stephens, NSW; 15 lives lost, 2 saved.
25 HMAS *Australia* launched in Britain. (Commissioned in 1913.)

Dec 2 Douglas Mawson's Australasian Antarctic Expedition leaves Hobart in the *Aurora*.
5 W. E. Hart becomes the first Australian to qualify as an air pilot.
15 Queensland Farmers' Union formed as a country political party.
22 Legislation enacted to establish the Commonwealth Bank.

* Australian bronze coins (pennies and halfpennies) first issued.

A Architecture, Building
World-wide competition held for a design for the federal capital.

B Science, Technology, Discovery, etc.
First permanent building erected at Mount Stromlo Observatory, ACT.
Meteorological station established on Macquarie Is. by Mawson's Antarctic expedition.

C Arts and Entertainment
Commonwealth Art Advisory Board established.
Melba–Williamson opera company tours Australia.
Adelphi Theatre opens in Sydney (5 Apr.). (Becomes the Grand Opera House in 1916, later the Tivoli.)
Gregan McMahon founds the Melbourne Repertory Theatre.
Hugh D. McIntosh acquires Harry Rickards's theatrical interests.
Raymond Longford's films *Sweet Nell of Old Drury* (with Nellie Stewart) and *The Fatal Wedding* (with Longford and Lottie Lyell) released.

D Books and Writing
Victor Daley, *Wine and Roses.*
Louis Stone, *Jonah.*

E Sport and Recreation
Dally Messenger scores a record 270 points in the Rugby League season.
Australasia retains the Davis Cup, beating the US at Christchurch, NZ.
The Parisian wins the Melbourne Cup.

F Statistics, Social Change, the Environment
Population of Australia (census, 3 Apr.): 4,455,005
NSW 1,646,734 (Sydney 629,503)
Vic. 1,315,551 (Melbourne 593,237)
Qld 605,813 (Brisbane 139,480)
SA 408,558 (Adelaide 199,760 [est.])
WA 282,114 (Perth 111,400 [est.])
Tas. 191,211 (Hobart 39,937)

NT 3,310
ACT 1,714
Women admitted to the practice of law in SA.
SA legislates to "protect and control" Aborigines.
Vaucluse House and gardens in Sydney proclaimed a public park (24 Apr.).

G Births and Deaths
Jan 11 Nora Heysen b.
Jan 13 Johannes Bjelke-Petersen b.
Feb 16 Hal Porter b. (–1984).
Jun 21 Chester Wilmot b. (–1954).
Aug 16 Cardinal P. F. Moran d. (80).
Sep 9 John Gorton b.
Oct 5 William Astley (Price Warung) d. (56).
Oct 13 Harry Rickards d. (67).

1912

Jan 8 Douglas Mawson sets up base at Commonwealth Bay, King George V Land.
31 General strike begins in Brisbane following the suspension of tramway employees for wearing union badges (to 6 Mar.).

Feb 10 Election in SA results in a defeat for Labor; John Verran resigns (16th), and A. H. Peake becomes Premier again (17th).
– Queensland's first state high schools open, in Bundaberg, Charters Towers, Gympie, Mackay, Mount Morgan, and Warwick.

Mar 7 Norwegian explorer Roald Amundsen arrives in Hobart in his ship *Fram*, bringing the news that he had reached the South Pole on 14 Dec. 1911.
14 Electric trams begin operating in Geelong.
21 Adelaide SS Co. liner *Koombana* founders between Port Hedland and Broome, WA, during a cyclone, with the loss of some 150 lives.
– S. R. Ferguson and Francis Birtles drive a Brush motor car from Fremantle to Sydney in 28 days (first latitudinal crossing of the continent by car).

Apr 25 HMAS *Tingira* (formerly the clipper and reformatory ship *Sobraon*) commissioned as a training ship for boys in Sydney.
– J. A. Gilruth arrives in Darwin to take up his post as Administrator of the NT.

May 18 W. A. Watt replaces John Murray as Premier of Vic.
30 HMAS *Melbourne*, the RAN's first cruiser, launched in Britain.

Jun 1 Denison Miller takes up his appointment as first governor of the Commonwealth Bank.
14 Albert Solomon becomes Premier of Tas. on the retirement of Sir Neil Lewis.
29 W. E. Hart wins (by default) Australia's first air race, from Botany to Parramatta and return, against "Wizard" Stone of the USA.

Jul 6 First automatic public telephone exchange in Australia installed in Geelong.
13 Official opening of the Murrumbidgee Irrigation Area at Yanco.
15 Commonwealth Bank of Australia opens for business as a savings bank. (Trading bank opens on 20 Jan. 1913.)

Aug 7 Kingsley Fairbridge opens a farm school for underprivileged British migrant children at Pinjarra, WA.

1912

Sep 14 Construction begins on the transcontinental railway from Port Augusta, SA, to Kalgoorlie, WA.

20 Ministry of Defence approves the formation of the Australian Flying Corps. (Recruiting begins 1 Jan. 1913.)

26 Rev. John Flynn's report to the Presbyterian Church of Australian leads to the founding of the Australian Inland Mission.

Oct 12 Fire in the underground pumping house at the North Lyell tin mine, Tas; 42 trapped miners die.

24 Harry Hawker establishes a British endurance flying record (8 hours 23 min.).

Nov 9 Mawson sets out with two companions (Ninnis and Mertz) to examine King George V Land.

– Daisy Bates becomes honorary Protector of Aborigines at Eucla, SA.

Dec 14 One of Mawson's party (Ninnis) disappears into a crevasse with a sledge containing nearly all their provisions; Mawson and Mertz set off on the return journey to base camp.

* Commonwealth Small Arms Factory opens in Lithgow, NSW.

A Architecture, Building

Walter Burley Griffin wins the competition for a design for Canberra.

High-rise era begins in Australia with the erection by Spain and Cosh of the 14-storey, 52 m high Culwulla Chambers in Sydney (–1913).

Fibrous plaster sheets first imported into Melbourne from New Zealand.

B Science, Technology, Discovery, etc.

Construction of a new zoological gardens in Sydney begun at Taronga Park. (Animals from the old Moore Park zoo moved in 1915–16.)

L. E. de Mole invents a tracked, armoured vehicle that anticipates the war tank.

C Arts and Entertainment

Norman Lindsay's pen drawing *The Crucified Venus* exhibited at the Society of Artists' exhibition in Sydney (Nov.).

Irish promoter Thomas Quinlan brings an opera company of 200 people, 300 tons of scenery, and 3,000 costumes to Australia.

Bert Bailey appears in the stage adaptation of *On Our Selection*.

Cosens Spencer's film studio at White City, Rushcutters Bay, Sydney, opened by the NSW Premier (Aug.).

Australia's first luxury cinema, the Majestic, opens in Melbourne.

D Books and Writing

Bernard O'Dowd, *The Bush*.

E Sport and Recreation

C. P. Paterson brings the first surfboard to Sydney from Hawaii.

At the Stockholm Olympics, Fanny Durack wins the 100 m freestyle swimming event and the Australasian men's team wins the 800 m relay swim.

William Longworth, a member of the Olympic team, wins all Australian and NSW swimming championships from 100 yards to 1 mile.

Jimmy Sharman forms his travelling boxing troupe.

Piastre wins the Melbourne Cup.

F Statistics, Social Change, the Environment

Estimated population of Australia: 4,746,589.

46,712 migrants arrive in Australia during the year.

Cost-of-living index ("A" series) first compiled (with 1911 as base year), and subsequently used in making adjustments to the basic wage.

Commonwealth maternity allowance—the "baby bonus"—of £5 a child introduced. (Abolished 1978.)

School leaving age raised from 12 to 14 in Qld.

G Births and Deaths

Feb   7   Russell Drysdale b. (–1981).
Mar 12   Kylie Tennant b. (–1988).
May 24   Joan Hammond b. (–1996).
May 28   Patrick White b. (–1990).
Jun   4   William Dargie b.
Jun 13   Ivor Hele b. (–1993).
Jul 20   George Johnston b. (–1970).
Sep 13   Joseph Furphy d. (68).
Nov 21   Eileen Joyce b. (–1991).
Dec 16   George Rignold d. (73).
Dec 29   Peggy Glanville-Hicks b. (–1990).

1913

Jan 2   First Commonwealth postage stamp issued (one penny, showing a kangaroo on an outline map of Australia).

     8   Douglas Mawson's companion, Mertz, dies in Antarctica; Mawson makes an epic lone struggle back to base at Commonwealth Bay. (Arrives 8 Feb; *Aurora* had left that day, leaving six men to stay for the winter.)

   29   Cyclone strikes Qld's north coast (to 4 Feb.); Cairns, Innisfail, and surrounding areas flooded, Cooktown damaged, SS *Innamincka* wrecked.

   30   Passenger train and breakdown train collide at Murphy's Creek, Qld; six people killed.

    –   Tasmania's first state high schools open in Hobart and Launceston.

Mar 1   Royal Australian Naval College officially opened in temporary premises at Geelong.

   12   Lady Denman, wife of the Governor-General, names the federal capital Canberra at the official ceremony to mark the start of building.

   19   Farmers and Settlers' Association in Western Australia resolves to form a political party to be known as the Country Party.

   23   Daniel Mannix arrives in Melbourne as Catholic Coadjutor Archbishop of Melbourne.

Apr 2   First sale of town sites at Leeton, NSW.

May 1   First Commonwealth Treasury banknotes issued.

   31   Election for House of Representatives and half Senate; Labor loses its majority in the lower house; results; 38 Liberals (including six country members endorsed by the NSW Farmers and Settlers' Assoc.), 37 Labor.
Referendums on proposals to give the Commonwealth power to legislate on trade and commerce, corporations, industrial matters, trusts, nationalization of monopolies, and railway disputes all rejected.

Jun 24   Joseph Cook replaces Andrew Fisher as Prime Minister.

   29   W. A. Holman becomes Premier of NSW on the retirement of James McGowen.

Jul 1   All Royal Navy establishments in Australia transferred to the Commonwealth.

    –   Melbourne Hospital's new building opens.

1913

- Frensham girls' school founded at Mittagong, NSW, by Winifred West and Phyllis Clubbe.

Sep – Workers' Educational Association of NSW founded, with David Stewart as secretary.

Oct 4 Royal Australian Navy squadron—battle-cruiser and flagship *Australia*, light cruisers *Melbourne*, *Sydney*, and *Encounter*, and destroyers *Parramatta*, *Warrego*, and *Yarra*—ceremonially enters Port Jackson.

Nov 14 Melbourne Public Library's new domed reading room officially opened.
20 Bundaberg, Qld, declared a city.

Dec 9 G. A. Elmslie forms Vic.'s first Labor ministry, after W. A. Watt loses support of country members. (Watt resumes the premiership on 22nd.)
12 *Aurora* picks up Mawson and his party from Commonwealth Bay. (Expedition returns to Adelaide, 26 Feb. 1914.)
29 Norfolk Island Act authorizes the transfer of Norfolk Island to the Commonwealth. (Transfer takes effect on 1 July 1914.)

* Amalgamated Wireless (Australasia) Ltd—AWA—founded, with Ernest Fisk as managing director.
* H. C. Sleigh begins to market Californian oil under the name Golden Fleece.

A Architecture, Building
Australia House, London (–1918).
Construction begins on the federal capital (King O'Malley drives the first survey peg, 20 Feb.).
Yarralumla (built 1891) purchased by the Commonwealth as the Governor-General's official residence in Canberra (5 May).

B Science, Technology, Discovery, etc.
H. S. Taylor patents a new type of header-harvester.
G. A. Julius's invention, the automatic totalizator, first operates (on Ellerslie Racecourse in Auckland, NZ).

C Arts and Entertainment
Max Meldrum, *Portrait of the Artist's Mother* (painting).
Thomas Quinlan's visiting opera company presents the first complete cycle of *The Ring of the Niebelung* in Australia.
Adeline Genée and company of dancers from the Imperial Russian Ballet tour Australia.
Raymond Longford, *Australia Calls*, with airman W. E. Hart (film).
Frank Hurley, *Home of the Blizzard* (documentary film of the Mawson expedition to Antarctica).

D Books and Writing
Ada Cambridge, *The Hand in the Dark.*
C. J. Dennis, *Backblock Ballads.*
Henry Lawson, *Triangles of Life.*
Norman Lindsay, *A Curate in Bohemia.*

E Sport and Recreation
Posinatus wins the Melbourne Cup.

F Statistics, Social Change, the Environment
Estimated population of Australia: 4,893,741.
Commonwealth basic wage increased to 8 shillings a day.

G Births and Deaths

Jan 15 Miriam Hyde b.
Jan 23 Adrian Quist b. (–1991).
Feb 18 Louis Becke d. (57).
Mar 19 Henry Herbert ("Smoky") Dawson b.
May 6 Douglas Stewart b. (–1985).
Jul 6 J. C. Williamson d. (67).
Aug 3 Sir William Lyne d. (69).
Sep 25 Kenneth (Seaforth) Mackenzie b. (–1955).

1914

Feb 10 Geelong Grammar School opens at Corio.
16 Court of Industrial Arbitration determines the first NSW basic wage.

Mar 16 Trains collide at Exeter, NSW; 14 killed and 32 injured.
27 SS *Saint Paul* wrecked at Cape Moreton, Qld, with the loss of 18 lives.

Apr 6 John Earle becomes Premier of Tas. for the second time.
11 G. J. Coles opens a "nothing over a shilling" store in Collingwood, Melbourne.
18 Victorian Farmers' Union formed. (Later becomes the Country Party.)

May 18 Sir Ronald Munro Ferguson succeeds Lord Denman as Governor-General.

Jun 5 Prime Minister Joseph Cook asks the Governor-General for a double dissolution. (Parliament prorogued 27 June, dissolved 30 July.)
18 Sir Alexander Peacock becomes Premier of Vic. again following W. A. Watt's resignation to enter federal politics.

Jul 16 French airman Maurice Guillaux leaves Melbourne in a Bleriot monoplane with Australia's first air mail. (Arrives Sydney 18th.)
25 Telephone line established between Melbourne and Adelaide.
30 Warning of impending war reaches Australia by cable from London.
31 Leaders of both political parties, electioneering, pledge Australian support of the Empire in the event of war—in Andrew Fisher's words, "to our last man and our last shilling".

Aug 3 Cook offers an expeditionary force of 20,000 troops to the Imperial government. (Accepted on 6th.)
5 News of the declaration of war between Britain and Germany reaches Australia. The first Allied shot in the war is fired at midday by Australian artillery at Fort Nepean, Port Phillip, when the German ship *Pfalz* attempts to leave.
10 Recruiting begins for the Australian Imperial Force (AIF).
17 Training of military pilots begins at Point Cook, Vic.
19 Australian Naval and Military Expeditionary Force, under Col. William Holmes, leaves Sydney in the *Berrima* for training at Palm Island before being sent to New Britain.
– Australian Red Cross Society established.

Sep 5 Election for federal parliament; Labor gains a clear majority in both houses; Fisher becomes Prime Minister for the third time (17th).
11 Expeditionary force captures the German wireless station on New Britain with the loss of six lives and four wounded, the first Australian casualties of the war.

1914

12 Australian forces capture Rabaul and (15th) accept the surrender of the government of German New Guinea.

14 Australia loses its first naval vessel, the submarine *AE1*, off the coast of New Britain.

Oct 29 Commonwealth Crimes Act and War Precautions Act assented to.

Nov 1 First convoy of AIF and NZ forces leaves Albany, WA, for Europe, escorted by HMAS *Sydney* and HMAS *Melbourne*, HMS *Minotaur*, and the Japanese cruiser *Ibuki*.

6 Australian forces occupy Nauru.

9 HMAS *Sydney* disables the German cruiser *Emden* at Cocos Island and (10th) takes the crew prisoner.

Dec 3 Australian and New Zealand troops disembark at Alexandria to undergo war training in Egypt, where the Australian and New Zealand Army Corps (ANZAC) is formed.

Commonwealth fisheries research ship *Endeavour* leaves Macquarie Island with Director of Fisheries H. K. Dannevig and his staff and is not heard of again.

21 Lt-Gen. Sir William Birdwood arrives in Egypt to take up his appointment as commander of ANZAC.

23 Enrolment and voting made compulsory in Qld.

* Severe and protracted drought affects most of Australia.

A Architecture, Building

A. B. Brady, Administration Building, Brisbane (–1922).

B Science, Technology, Discovery, etc.

W. Baldwin Spencer publishes his study *The Native Tribes of the Northern Territory*.

C Arts and Entertainment

NSW State Conservatorium of Music founded. (Opens in May 1915.)

W. W. Francis first publicly sings his song "Australia Will Be There" at the Gaiety Theatre, Melbourne (15 Aug.).

Raymond Longford, *The Silence of Dean Maitland* (film).

D Books and Writing

Christopher Brennan, *Poems*.

E Sport and Recreation

Norman Brookes wins the men's singles at Wimbledon for the second time.

Australasia (headed by Brookes and Anthony Wilding) beats the US at Forest Hills, NY, to win the Davis Cup.

Kingsburgh wins the Melbourne Cup.

F Statistics, Social Change, the Environment

Estimated population of Australia: 4,971,778.

NSW basic wage: £2 8s a week.

Paid annual leave awarded to printers in Western Australia.

G Births and Deaths

Jul 17 W. C. Piguenit d. (77).

Sep 7 Graeme Bell b.

Sep 9 John Passmore (philosopher) b.

Sep 24 John Kerr b. (–1991).

Oct 4 J. F. (Jim) Cairns b.

Oct 13 Walter Withers d. (59).

Dec 29 Albert Tucker b. (–1999).

1915

Jan 1 "Battle of Broken Hill": two men flying the Turkish flag fire on a train carrying picnickers from Broken Hill to Silverton; six killed (including the two attackers), and seven wounded.

Feb 1 Coober Pedy, SA, opal field discovered.
  10 Royal Australian Naval College transferred to Jervis Bay.

Apr 3 Crawford Vaughan replaces A. H. Peake as Premier of SA.
  20 First Australian Flying Corps unit leaves for Mesopotamia.
  25 Anzacs and other Allied forces land at Gallipoli.
  30 Submarine *AE2* lost in the Sea of Marmara; crew captured. (Wreck discovered in 1998.)

May 2 Anzacs attack Baby 700 and Gaba Tepe.
  19 Anzacs beat off a determined Turkish attack, in which some 3,000 Turks are killed. Truce arranged to bury the dead. (Another on 24th.)
    John Simpson (Kirkpatrick), "the man with the donkey", killed.
    Lance-corporal Albert Jacka wins the first VC awarded to an Australian in World War I.
  22 Labor gains a clear majority in the Qld election; T. J. Ryan becomes Premier (1 June).

Jun 2 BHP's steelworks at Newcastle officially opened.
  30 Attack by the Turks at the Nek repulsed by Anzacs.

Jul 23 War Census Act passed. (Census of males 18 to 60 taken, 6–15 Sept.)

Aug 6 Australians attack Lone Pine; Battle of Sari Bair begins (to 9th).
  7 Australian Light Horsemen (unmounted) go to their deaths in successive charges against Turkish machine-guns at the Nek.

Sep 4 Area of 73 square kilometres at Jervis Bay transferred from NSW to the Commonwealth for use as a port.
  13 Income tax imposed by the Commonwealth to pay for the war.
    Voting in federal referendums made compulsory.
  14 Tom Barker, editor of the IWW journal *Direct Action*, gaoled for publishing material likely to prejudice recruiting.
  23 Journalist Keith Murdoch, after visiting Gallipoli, writes to Prime Minister Andrew Fisher criticizing the conduct and prospects of the Dardanelles operation.
  30 HMAS *Brisbane*, the first cruiser built in Australia, launched in Port Jackson.

Oct 27 Fisher resigns because of ill health (becomes High Commissioner in London, Jan. 1916); W. M. Hughes succeeds him as Prime Minister.

Nov 15 River Murray Waters Agreement ratified by NSW, Vic., SA, and Commonwealth governments. (Comes into force 31 Jan. 1917.)

Dec 1 Australian Wheat Board begins operations.
  8 Evacuation of Anzacs from Gallipoli begins. (Completed 20th.)
  14 Farmers and Settlers' Association formed in Adelaide. (Becomes the Country Party Association in 1923.)
  29 Land tax imposed in Qld.

A Architecture, Building

1915

B Science, Technology, Discovery, etc.

W. H. and W. L. Bragg share the Nobel Prize for their work in X-ray crystallography.

Melbourne chemists George Nicholas and H. W. Shmith discover how to make aspirin, a German-patented product cut off by the war, and begin manufacture. (Trade name Aspro registered by G. R. and A. M. Nicholas in 1917.)

C Arts and Entertainment

Henri Verbrugghen becomes first director of the NSW State Conservatorium of Music and re-forms the Sydney Symphony Orchestra.

Actor-manager Allan Wilkie arrives in Australia. (Tours Australia with his Shakespearean company from 1916 to the 1930s.)

Alfred Rolfe, *The Hero of the Dardanelles* (film).

Francis Birtles, *In the Track of Burke and Wills* (documentary film).

D Books and Writing

C. J. Dennis, *The Songs of a Sentimental Bloke*.

Douglas Mawson, *The Home of the Blizzard*.

Literary journal the *Triad* (first published in NZ), begins publication in Sydney. (Ceases in 1942, after reverting to NZ.)

E Sport and Recreation

Les Darcy knocks out American Eddie McGoorty, contender for the world middleweight championship (27 Dec.).

Duke Kahanamoku visits Australia from Hawaii and popularizes surfboard riding.

First state surf lifesaving championships held at Bondi (20 Mar.).

Patrobus wins the Melbourne Cup.

F Statistics, Social Change, the Environment

Estimated population of Australia: 4,959,457.

Australian casualties on Gallipoli: approx. 7,600 killed, 19,000 wounded.

Women given the right to sit in parliament in Qld.

Lamington National Park proclaimed (31 July).

G Births and Deaths

Feb   6   Donald Friend b. (–1989).

Mar   3   Manning Clark b. (–1991).

Mar 11   T. A. Browne (Rolf Boldrewood) d. (88).

Apr 19   Dorian le Gallienne b. (–1963).

May 31   Judith Wright b. (–2000)

Jun 28   Victor Trumper d. (37).

Jul 14   Lawrence Hargrave d. (65).

Jul 16   David Campbell b. (–1979).

Jul 18   G. W. L. Marshall-Hall d. (53).

Aug 14   B. A. Santamaria b. (–1998).

Oct   8   E. Phillips Fox d. (50).

1916

Jan 16   Prime Minister Hughes leaves Sydney to visit England and the European war zone.

Feb   8   Presbyterian Ladies' College opens in Pymble, Sydney.

   14   Troops from Casula and Liverpool army camps in NSW mutiny; one man shot dead and six wounded in a riot at Sydney's Central Station.

1916

15 Launceston–Hobart express train crashes at Campania, Tas; four killed and 39 injured.

Mar 24 Wartime price control regulations introduced.

Apr 15 Sir Walter Lee replaces John Earle as Premier of Tas.
25 Anzac Day first celebrated.

May – News of the Easter Rebellion in Dublin reaches Australia, leading to a wave of anti-British and anti-war feeling among Irish Australians and Catholics.

Jun 2 Electrolytic Zinc Co. of Australasia established in Tas.
6 Returned Sailors' and Soldiers' Imperial League of Australia founded (now the Returned and Services League of Australia, or RSL).
15 Hughes arranges for the purchase of 15 merchant ships in London to begin a Commonwealth shipping line.

Jul 19 Australian troops attack Fromelles in the Battle of the Somme.
23 Australian troops capture Pozières, winning four VCs.
27 Frank Wilson again becomes Premier of WA following the defeat of the Scaddan government.
31 Hughes returns to Australia from Britain and France concerned about the decline in enlistments for the AIF.

Aug 4 Anzac Mounted Division engages in the Battle of Romani in Sinai.
24 War office cables a request to Australia for reinforcements.
30 Hughes announces that a referendum would be held on compulsory overseas military service.

Sep 3 Australian troops capture Mouquet Farm (but later relinquish it).
4 Hughes expelled from the NSW Labor executive.
8 First of twelve incendiary acts, thought to be the work of the IWW, attempted in Sydney (to 12th).
9 Daniel Mannix, Catholic Coadjutor Archbishop of Melbourne, begins publicly expressing his opposition to conscription and the war.
14 Minister for Trade and Customs Frank Tudor resigns from the government over conscription. (Three other ministers resign on 27 Oct.)
30 Australian Farmers' Federal Organization formed in Melbourne.
– Premier Holman of NSW loses Labor Party endorsement for campaigning in favour of conscription.

Oct 17 Miners in NSW demand increased wages and reduced hours. (Locked out 1 Nov; all mines in Australia idle by 3 Nov; work resumes on 5 Dec. after demands met.)
28 Referendum on conscription results in a "no" vote by a narrow margin.
– Full-time correspondence school begins in NSW.

Nov 14 Hughes walks out of federal Labor caucus, taking 23 supporters with him. (Expelled from ALP leadership, he forms the National Labor Party and a new ministry with support of the Liberal Party.)
15 Holman forms a coalition ministry in NSW with five expelled Labor members, six Liberals, and a Progressive.
25 British government agrees to buy the entire Australian wool clip for the duration of the war.

Dec 1 Trial of 12 IWW members charged with arson and sedition; 10 sentenced to between 5 and 15 years' gaol.
21 Australian Light Horsemen capture El Arish and (on 23rd) Magdhaba in the Sinai.

1916

28 Most of Clermont, Qld, washed away and 62 people drown in floods following a cyclone.

– Two members of the IWW hanged at Bathurst after being found guilty of murdering a policeman at Tottenham, NSW.

A Architecture, Building
J. C. Hawes, Cathedral of St Francis Xavier, Geraldton, WA (–1938).

B Science, Technology, Discovery, etc.
Commonwealth Serum Laboratories established in Melbourne.
Walter and Eliza Hall Institute of Medical Research founded in Melbourne.

C Arts and Entertainment
Elioth Gruner, *Morning Light* (awarded the Wynne Art Prize).
Sydney Ure Smith, Bertram Stevens, and Charles Lloyd Jones found *Art in Australia* (–1942).
Oscar Asche writes and produces the play *Chu-Chin-Chow*. (Runs to 1921.)
Stiffy and Mo (Nat Phillips and Roy Rene) first perform as a comedy team.
Raymond Longford, *The Mutiny of the Bounty* (film).
Hippodrome (later the Capitol Theatre) opens in Sydney (Apr.)

D Books and Writing
C. J. Dennis, *The Moods of Ginger Mick*.
Ernest Scott, *A Short History of Australia*.

E Sport and Recreation
Les Darcy stows away on a freighter to America (27 Oct.), against war regulations preventing able-bodied men leaving the country.
John Wren gains control of Stadiums Ltd and thus virtual control of boxing and wrestling in Sydney, Melbourne, and Brisbane.
Sasanof wins the Melbourne Cup.

F Statistics, Social Change, the Environment
Estimated population of Australia: 4,917,949.
Six o'clock closing of hotels introduced in NSW, Vic., SA, and Tas. as a wartime measure.
Mount Field and Freycinet national parks established in Tas.
Mediterranean mustard first noted near Merredin, WA. (Becomes chief plant pest of WA and spreads east.)

G Births and Deaths
Jan 21 George Musgrove d. (62).
Apr 9 John Norton d. (58).
Apr 10 J. J. Hilder d. (34).
Apr 26 Morris West b. (–1999).
May 24 Arthur Roden Cutler b.
Jun 6 Tom Bass b.
Jul 11 Gough Whitlam b.
Sep 28 Peter Finch b. (–1977).

1917

Jan 1 Daylight saving introduced throughout Australia (to Mar.). (Unpopular, not reintroduced till World War II.)

9 Anzac mounted forces capture Rafa in Palestine.

31 River Murray Commission begins operating.

Feb 7 W. M. Hughes's National Labor group merges with the Liberal Party to form the Nationalist (or National) Party.

15 Qld enacts Australia's first soldier settlement legislation.

17 Hughes forms his first Nationalist ministry (Labor having refused to join an all-party government).

Mar 17 Australian troops in France enter Bapaume and continue their advance towards the Hindenburg Line.

26 First Battle of Gaza in Palestine.

Apr 11 First Battle of Bullecourt, on the Hindenberg Line; 3,000 Australian casualties.

19 Second Battle of Gaza.

– Vestey's meatworks opens in Darwin. (Closes 1919.)

May 3 Second Battle of Bullecourt begins (7,000 Australian casualties).

5 Election for House of Representatives and half Senate; Hughes's Nationalists win 53 of the 75 lower house seats and all 18 vacant seats in the Senate. Referendum held in Qld on the abolition of the Legislative Council: 116,196 for; 179,105 against.

6 Daniel Mannix becomes Catholic Archbishop of Melbourne on the death of Archbishop Carr and subsequently makes several anti-conscription speeches.

12 Australian and British troops capture Bullecourt and (15th) repulse a German counter-attack.

13 Commonwealth railway line extended from Pine Creek, NT, to Katherine.

Jun 7 Messines ridge, Flanders, captured by II Anzac Corps after Australian tunnellers blow up Hill 60.

14 First drawing of Qld's Golden Casket lottery (opened in Dec. 1916 in aid of patriotic war funds).

28 H. B. Lefroy forms a National Coalition ministry in WA.

30 All Lutheran day schools in SA closed by act of parliament.

Jul 6 SS *Cumberland* strikes a mine laid by the German raider *Wolf* off Gabo Island and sinks while under tow. (Explosion attributed in Australia to a bomb placed by the IWW.)

14 A. H. Peake again becomes Premier of SA.

Aug 2 Sydney tramwaymen strike over a new work-record system, initiating a general strike involving railwaymen, miners, wharf labourers, seamen, and other unionists.

14 "Loyal labour" camps of strike-breakers set up in the Sydney Cricket Ground.

18 Three strike leaders arrested. (Railway union deregistered 24th.)

23 NSW government takes over all coalmines in the state.

30 Strikers attack two "loyalist" lorry drivers in Sydney; one striker shot dead and another wounded.

Crowd of 10,000 assemble in front of federal Parliament House in Melbourne to protest against the cost of living; 12 arrested.

– IWW declared illegal under the Unlawful Associations Act of Dec. 1916.

Sep 19 Rail strike officially ends (with a trial period for new system).

20 Australian troops fight in the Battle of Menin Road, during the Third Battle of Ypres, and (26th) capture Polygon Wood.

22 Legislation assented to introducing a wartime profits tax (to 1919).

Oct 3 Coalfields strike ends.

1917

4 Anzac forces take part in the assault on Broodseinde ridge and (12th) on Passchendaele.

17 Transcontinental railway completed. (First train runs 22 Oct; official opening 12 Nov.)

24 Collapse of strike by seamen and wharf labourers.

31 Australian Light Horsemen, commanded by General Harry Chauvel, attack and capture Beersheba.

Nov 7 Hughes announces that another conscription referendum is to be held.

8 German place names in SA changed by act of parliament.

19 Qld Premier T. J. Ryan speaks at an anti-conscription rally; his speech is censored in the press. (He repeats his speech in parliament three days later; censors seize *Hansard* copies next day. He repeats his speech outside parliament following a challenge from Hughes to do so; he and his deputy, E. G. Theodore, are charged with breaches of the War Precautions Act. Charges dropped at trial, 6 Dec.)

29 Hughes is hit by an egg while addressing a conscription rally at Warwick, Qld. (Angered by the lack of response from the Queensland police, he forms the Commonwealth Police Force on 12 Dec; disbanded in 1921.)
John Bowser replaces Sir Alexander Peacock as Premier of Vic.

Dec 20 Second conscription referendum held; conscription again rejected.

* Holden's Motor Body Builders establishes a factory in Adelaide.

* Star of the West pearl (of more than 100 grains) found at Broome, WA.

A Architecture, Building

First national town-planning and housing conference held in Adelaide.
Eadith Walker establishes a convalescent home for soldiers in the grounds of her home, Yaralla, in Sydney.

B Science, Technology, Discovery, etc.

Anzac forces in Gaza find the Shellal Mosaic, formerly the floor of a Byzantine church of AD 561–62 (now in the War Memorial, Canberra).

C Arts and Entertainment

Sidney Long, *Fantasy* (painting).
Max Meldrum founds a school of painting in Melbourne.
Pat Sullivan creates the animated cartoon "Felix the Cat".
Beaumont Smith, *Our Friends the Hayseeds* (film).

D Books and Writing

C. J. Dennis, *The Glugs of Gosh.*
Leon Gellert, *Songs of a Campaign.*
A. B. Paterson, *Saltbush Bill, J.P.* and *Three Elephant Power and Other Stories.*
Henry Handel Richardson, *Australia Felix* (vol. 1 of *The Fortunes of Richard Mahony*).

E Sport and Recreation

Les Darcy dies of pneumonia in Memphis, Tennessee (24 May).
Automatic totalizator first used in Australia at Randwick (8 Sept.).
Federal government restricts the number of sporting fixtures as a wartime measure.
Westcourt wins the Melbourne Cup.

F Statistics, Social Change, the Environment

Estimated population of Australia: 4,982,063.
The word *digger* comes into use among the AIF.
Lake Eyre partially fills with water (according to geological records).

G Births and Deaths
Feb 7 Harry Gibbs b.
Mar 21 Frank Hardy b. (–1994).
Apr 22 Sidney Nolan b. (–1992).
May 24 Les Darcy d. (21).
Jul 12 Larry Foley d. (70).
Aug 26 William Lane d. (55).
Oct 12 James McAuley b. (–1976).
Dec 20 Frederick McCubbin d. (62).

1918

Jan 1 Australian Corps formed from all five Australian divisions in France.
8 Prime Minister W. M. Hughes tenders his resignation after failing to carry the conscription referendum; ALP leader F. G. Tudor is unable to command a majority in either house, and Hughes is recommissioned (10th).
20 Cyclone devastates Mackay, Qld (to 22nd); 30 lives lost.

Feb 2 Sir John Forrest becomes the first native-born Australian to be raised to the peerage (as Baron Forrest of Bunbury).
21 Anzac Mounted Division captures Jericho.

Mar 9 Cyclone in north Queensland (to 10th) almost completely demolishes Innisfail and Babinda and severely damages Cairns, Ingham, and Cardwell; 17 people killed.
21 H. S. W. Lawson replaces John Bowser as Premier of Vic.
28 Australian forces in France stop the German advance at Dernancourt.

Apr 8 Warrnambool, Vic., proclaimed a city.
24 Hughes and Navy Minister Joseph Cook leave Australia to attend the Imperial Conference in London; W. A. Watt becomes Acting Prime Minister.
25 Australian troops in France recapture Villers-Bretonneux.
– Repatriation Commission set up.

May 31 Lt-Gen. John Monash takes command of the Australian Corps in France, with Brig.-Gen. T. A. Blamey as chief of staff.

Jun 11 Hughes attends the second session of the Imperial War Cabinet in London.

Jul 5 Australian (and American) troops under Monash capture Hamel.
22 Cranbrook School opens in Sydney.

Aug 3 Australia House in London officially opened by King George V.
8 Australian and Canadian troops break through on the Somme.

Sep 1 Australian troops capture and hold Mont St Quentin and (2nd) Pèronne.
18 Australian troops spearhead the attack on the Hindenburg Line.
19 Desert Mounted Corps, led by Gen. Harry Chauvel, begins its great ride round the enemy's rear to Nablus in Palestine.
20 SS *Undola* sinks with all hands off Wollongong, NSW, after apparently striking one of the mines laid by the German raider *Wolf.*
22 First direct wireless message transmitted from Britain to Australia (from Marconi's station in Carnarvon, Wales) received by Ernest Fisk of AWA at his home in Wahroonga, Sydney.
25 Anzac Mounted Division captures Amman.

1918

Oct 1 Australian Light Horsemen enter Damascus, having cut off the enemy's retreat and taken 4,000 prisoners.

5 In their last engagement on the Western Front, Australian troops capture Montbrehain.

16 House of Representatives permits the use of the "guillotine".

30 Turkish Armistice ends fighting in Palestine.

Nov 11 Armistice concluded between Allies and Germany. (News received in Australia at 6 p.m.)

21 Preferential voting introduced in elections for House of Representatives. In the Corangamite by-election (14 Dec.) Victorian Farmers' Union candidate W. G. Gibson wins on the distribution of preferences and becomes the first country party member of federal parliament.

Dec 18 Proportional representation in multi-member electorates introduced in NSW (to 1926).

21 Mass meeting in Darwin demands an inquiry into the Northern Territory Administration and the removal of Administrator J. A. Gilruth; Government House picketed. (Gilruth leaves 20 Feb. 1919.)

* State Labour organizations adopt the name Australian Labor Party.

* Influenza pandemic reaches Australia.

A Architecture, Building

Leslie Wilkinson takes up the first chair of architecture at an Australian university, at the University of Sydney.

B Science, Technology, Discovery, etc.

John McGarvie Smith discloses the formula of his safe, one-shot-dose vaccine for anthrax in sheep and cattle, developed in the 1890s.

C Arts and Entertainment

The Enemy Within, with Snowy Baker (film).
The Lure of the Bush, with Snowy Baker and Rita Tress (film).

D Books and Writing

May Gibbs, *Snugglepot and Cuddlepie*.
Mary Gilmore, *The Passionate Heart*.
Norman Lindsay, *The Magic Pudding*.

E Sport and Recreation

Nightwatch wins the Melbourne Cup.

F Statistics, Social Change, the Environment

Australia's population reaches five million.
Total number of troops raised in Australia for World War I: 416,809, of whom 331,781 were sent overseas; 59,342 were killed, and 166,819 were wounded.
Women in NSW admitted to the practice of law and allowed to be elected to parliament.

G Births and Deaths

Mar 14 John McCallum b.
Sep 3 Sir John Forrest d. (71).
Sep 12 Sir George Reid d. (73).
Dec 16 E. W. Cole d. (86).

1919

Jan 13 Peace Conference begins in Versailles, with W. M. Hughes and Sir Joseph Cook as Australia's delegates.

29 Compromise on Pacific mandates reached at the Peace Conference after wrangling between Hughes and US President Wilson.

Feb – Influenza pandemic causes the closure of theatres, libraries, churches, and schools in NSW; wearing of masks made compulsory.

Mar 1 *Smith's Weekly,* founded by Joynton Smith, Claude McKay, and R. C. Packer, begins publication in Sydney (to 1950).

6 War Service Homes Act becomes operative.

10 Commonwealth government offers a prize of £10,000 to the first Australian crew to fly a British-made aircraft from Britain to Australia in 30 days before the end of the year.

24 Several thousand "anti-Bolsheviks" led by returned soldiers clash with police in Brisbane; shots fired and 19 wounded.

Apr 17 Hal Colebatch, MLC, replaces H. B. Lefroy as Premier of WA.

May 4 "Battle of the Barricades" on Fremantle waterfront (to 8th) between striking wharf labourers, non-unionist strike-breakers, and police; one killed and 33 injured.

7 Australia granted a "C" class League of Nations mandate over former German Territories in the Pacific.

17 James Mitchell replaces Colebatch as WA Premier.

19 Broken Hill mines closed by strike (to Nov. 1920).
Seamen's strike (to 26 Aug.) halts most shipping around Australia.

28 Electric trains begin running in Melbourne (Sandringham–Essendon).

Jun 28 Hughes and Cook sign the Peace Treaty in Versailles.

29 Striking meatworkers in Townsville clash with police; nine wounded in an exchange of gunshots.

Jul 19 Peace Day processions held throughout Australia, followed in Melbourne by riots and clashes between returned soldiers and police.

Aug 18 Hudson Fysh and P. J. McGinness leave Longreach, Qld, in a T model Ford to survey an air route to Darwin.

24 Hughes arrives back in Australia.

Sep – F. H. Gordon and Co. of Sydney begins producing the Australian Six car.

Oct 17 Sir Samuel Griffith retires as Chief Justice of the High Court; Sir Adrian Knox is appointed in his place (18th).

22 E. G. Theodore succeeds T. J. Ryan as Premier of Qld.

28 Preferential voting system introduced for Senate elections (to 1948).

– Daisy Bates sets up a tent camp in Ooldea, SA, and begins caring for the Aborigines there (to 1935).

– WA becomes the first state to legislate for Anzac Day (25 April) to be gazetted as a public holiday.

Nov 12 Ross and Keith Smith, with Sergeants J. M. Bennett and W. H. Shiers, leave England in a Vickers Vimy aircraft to fly to Australia.

16 H. N. Wrigley and A. W. Murphy make the first transcontinental flight from Point Cook, Vic., to Darwin (arrive 12 Dec.).

1919

26 Victoria's State Electricity Commission decides to establish a powerhouse on the Morwell brown coal field in the Latrobe Valley.

Dec 10 Ross and Keith Smith land at Darwin, winning the race to be first to fly from England to Australia and carrying the first overseas airmail between the two countries.

13 Election for House of Representatives and half Senate; Nationalists, with the support of 11 country members, are returned with a reduced majority. Two referendums on proposals to extend the Commonwealth's wartime powers fail to receive sufficient support.

16 A. L. Long makes the first crossing of Bass Strait by plane.

* Mascot chosen as the site for Sydney's airport.

* Severe and widespread drought throughout Australia.

A Architecture, Building

First reinforced concrete building erected in Sydney (Angus and Coote building in George Street).

B Science, Technology, Discovery, etc.

Australian National Research Council founded.

Polwarth sheep breed (bred in the 1880s near Colac, Vic.) officially named as a distinctive Australian breed.

Ernest Fisk demonstrates radio broadcasting in Sydney (13 Aug.).

C Arts and Entertainment

Elioth Gruner, *Spring Frost* (awarded the Wynne Art Prize).

Roland Wakelin and Roy de Maistre hold an influential exhibition of "synchromies" in Sydney (Aug.).

J. F. Archibald leaves part of his estate to found an annual prize for portraiture.

Raymond Longford, *The Sentimental Bloke* (silent film), with Arthur Tauchert and Lottie Lyell.

D Books and Writing

William Gosse Hay, *The Escape of the Notorious Sir William Heans.*

John Shaw Neilson, *Heart of Spring.*

E Sport and Recreation

AIF cricket team tours England and South Africa.

AIF rowing eight wins the first King's Cup at Henley-on-Thames.

Gerald Patterson wins the men's singles at Wimbledon.

A. D. Felton wins the world sculling championship in England.

Alick Wickham dives into the Yarra River at Dight's Falls from a height of 62.5 metres, a world high-dive record still (1999) unbroken.

Artilleryman wins the Melbourne Cup.

F Statistics, Social Change, the Environment

Estimated population of Australia: 5,303,574.

Influenza pandemic causes nearly 12,000 deaths in Australia.

Average weekly wage: men, £3 14s 11d ($7.49); women, £1 17s 1d.

Kikuyu grass introduced into NSW from the Belgian Congo.

G Births and Deaths

Jan 3 Robin Boyd b. (–1971).

Jul 25 Nat Gould d. (61).

Sep 10 J. F. Archibald d. (63).

Oct 7 Alfred Deakin d. (63) and Zelman Cowen b.

1920

Jan 8 Ray Parer and J. C. McIntosh in a DH9 biplane make the first single-engined aircraft flight from England to Australia (arrive 2 Aug.).

10 League of Nations comes into force, with Australia an original member.

22 Australian Country Party founded at a meeting of country MPs in Melbourne.

Feb 19 During the Governor's absence, Lt-Governor William Lennon appoints 14 new members to Qld's Legislative Council, allowing the government to pass legislation increasing rents paid by pastoral companies.

Mar 20 Holman government defeated at the NSW election; John Storey forms a Labor ministry (13 Apr.).

– David Fletcher Jones establishes his tailoring company. (Sets up shop in Warrnambool, Vic, in 1924.)

Apr 8 Sir Henry Barwell becomes Premier of SA following the death of A. H. Peake.

May 27 Prince of Wales (later King Edward VIII) arrives in Melbourne in HMS *Renown* to begin a tour of all states (to 18 Aug.).

31 Bert Hinkler flies from London to Turin non-stop, setting a long-distance record.

– Qld Premier E. G. Theodore fails to negotiate a much-needed loan in London because of a financial boycott organized by pastoral companies. He subsequently borrows in New York and calls an election.

Jul 10 Civil servants and teachers in WA strike over wages (to 31st).

Aug 3 Trains collide at Hurstville, Sydney; five people killed, 50 injured.

21 Collier *Amelia J* leaves Newcastle for Hobart and disappears, with the loss of 12 crew.

Sep 1 Flinders Naval Base (Depot from 1921) officially opened.

– Brigantine *Southern Cross* disappears in Bass Strait; 11 lives lost.

Oct 1 Sir John Monash becomes general manager of the State Electricity Commission of Vic. (chairman from 10 Jan. 1921).

2 C. J. De Garis launches the *Sunraysia Daily* in Mildura.

6 Baron Forster succeeds Sir Ronald Munro Ferguson as Governor-General.

9 Theodore government re-elected in Qld but with its majority reduced to four.

30 Communist Party of Australia founded at a meeting in Sydney.

Nov 11 Federal Labor MP Hugh Mahon is expelled from Parliament for making "seditious and disloyal utterances" at a demonstration in Melbourne (on 7th) organized by the Irish Ireland League.

16 Queensland and Northern Territory Aerial Services Ltd (Qantas) formed by Hudson Fysh, P. J. McGinness, and Fergus McMaster.

23 Royal commission chaired by A. B. Piddington recommends a 25% increase in the basic wage; Justice Powers of the Commonwealth Arbitration Court subsequently awards only three shillings, on the ground that industry could not afford to pay more.

Dec 14 Commonwealth Bank takes over the issuing of banknotes from the Treasury.

17 League of Nations confirms Australia's mandates to control Nauru and German New Guinea (20th).

* Baha'i faith established in Australia.

1920

A Architecture, Building

Hall and Prentice, Brisbane City Hall (–1930).

Sydney Central Station's clock tower erected. (Clock started 10 Mar. 1921.)

Walter Burley Griffin's appointment as designer of Canberra is not renewed.

B Science, Technology, Discovery, etc.

Commonwealth Institute of Science and Industry (predecessor of the CSIRO) established by act of parliament.

A. C. Howard first patents a rotary hoe.

C Arts and Entertainment

Australia's longest-running comic strip, "The Potts" (original title "You and Me"), created by Stan Cross, begins in *Smith's Weekly* (7 Aug.). (Taken over by Jim Russell in 1940.)

J. and N. Tait amalgamate with J. C. Williamson.

Gregan McMahon founds the Sydney Repertory Theatre Society.

Eric Edgley and Clem Dawe are brought to Australia by the Taits for pantomime.

Films: Franklyn Barrett's *The Breaking of the Drought*; Kenneth Brampton's *Robbery Under Arms*; Raymond Longford's *On Our Selection*; Harry Southwell's *The Kelly Gang*; Frank Hurley's documentary *In the Grip of Polar Ice*.

D Books and Writing

Hugh McCrae, *Colombine*.

Competition run by C. J. De Garis for the "great Australian novel" is won by F. A. Russell with *The Ashes of Achievement*.

E Sport and Recreation

Cyclist Bob Spears wins the world professional sprint title in Antwerp.

Poitrel wins the Melbourne Cup.

F Statistics, Social Change, the Environment

Estimated population of Australia: 5,411,297.

Women gain the right to be elected to parliament in WA.

Spiritualism in Australia is stimulated by the visit of Sir Arthur Conan Doyle.

One million koalas and $5\frac{1}{4}$ million possums killed in Qld in the 1919–20 trapping season.

Commonwealth Prickly Pear Board established to combat the pest covering 9.3 million hectares of land in Qld and northern NSW.

G Births and Deaths

Jan   7   Sir Edmond Barton d. (70).

May 30 G. E. ("Chinese") Morrison d. (58).

Jun   2   Vic Patrick b.

Jul 24   Arthur Boyd b. (–1999).

Aug 9   Sir Samuel Griffith d. (75).

Aug 12 Louisa Lawson d. (72).

Aug 15 Judy Cassab b.

Nov 11 Florence Young d. (50).

1921

Feb 5 Work begins on the Yallourn, Vic., power station site.

    28 Essington Lewis succeeds G. D. Delprat as general manager of BHP.

Mar 12 Mitchell government re-elected in WA; among the successful candidates for the Legislative Assembly is Mrs Edith Cowan, the first woman to become a member of any parliament in Australia.

31 Australian Air Force formed (*Royal* added on 13 Aug.).

Apr 4 John Lysaght begins producing galvanized sheet steel at Newcastle.
5 Earle Page elected permanent leader of the Country Party.
11 Bert Hinkler flies from Sydney to Bundaberg, Qld, non-stop in 8½ hours, breaking his own long-distance flying record.
21 Australia's first Rotary Club founded in Melbourne.

May 1 Legislation enacted to set up peacetime military forces.
9 New Guinea Act comes into force; military administration in the Mandated Territory is replaced by a civil government.
29 Bulk wheat first shipped from a terminal in Sydney.

Jun 25 SS *Our Jack* sinks in a gale off Cape Hawke, NSW, with the loss of five lives. Next day, SS *Fitzroy* goes down in the same area; 31 drowned.

Jul 12 Harry Hawker dies in a test-flight accident in England.

Aug 11 Essendon airport opens in Melbourne.
23 Bubonic plague breaks out in Brisbane (to Apr. 1922; 64 deaths).
31 Keith Murdoch becomes editor-in-chief of the Melbourne *Herald*.

Sep 19 Explosion at Mt Mulligan colliery, Qld, kills 75 miners.
24 Rockhampton and Mackay linked by rail.

Oct 10 James Dooley becomes Premier of NSW on the death of John Storey.
11 At the federal conference of the ALP in Brisbane, the party adopts a socialization objective.
27 Act to abolish the Qld upper house passed. (Not proclaimed until 23 Mar. 1922.)

Nov 11 Sir Joseph Cook resigns from federal parliament to become High Commissioner in London.
12 Senator G. F. Pearce represents Australia at the Washington conference on disarmament (to 6 Feb. 1922).

Dec 5 Australia's first official airmail service begins, between Geraldton and Derby, WA. (Service disrupted by the crash of one of the three planes on the inaugural flight, killing the crew of two.)
6 Six miners die when a cage falls down the shaft of the Golden Horseshoe mine, Kalgoorlie, WA.
7 SS *Moreton Bay*, first of the "Bay" ships built for the Commonwealth Government Line, leaves Britain on its maiden voyage.
13 Fire guts a wool store in Kirribilli, Sydney, threatening adjacent Admiralty House.
15 Legislation enacted providing for the establishment of the Tariff Board and increasing tariff duties.
20 Sir George Fuller becomes Premier of NSW for one day when the Dooley Labor government is temporarily unseated over tax proposals.

* Underprivileged British children begin coming to Australia under the Barnardo's Homes scheme.
* Miena Dam, in central Tas., completed.

1921

A Architecture, Building

B Science, Technology, Discovery, etc.
R. S. Falkiner patents a sugarcane harvester that cuts and tops the stalks in a continuous operation.

C Arts and Entertainment
Archibald Prize awarded for the first time; won by W. B. McInnes for his portrait of Desbrowe Annear.

Elioth Gruner, *The Valley of the Tweed* (awarded the Wynne Art Prize).

"Ginger Meggs" comic strip, created by Jimmy Bancks, appears for the first time (13 Nov.).

Gladys Moncrieff makes her first appearance as Teresa in *The Maid of the Mountains*, at the Theatre Royal, Melbourne (21 Jan.).

Violinist Jascha Heifetz tours Australia.

Beaumont Smith, *While the Billy Boils* (film).

Raymond Longford, *The Blue Mountains Mystery* (film).

AWA begins broadcasting radio concerts in Melbourne (Oct.).

D Books and Writing
C. E. W. Bean, *The Story of Anzac* (vol. 1 of *The Official History of Australia in the War of 1914–1918*; last vol. published in 1943).

C. J. Dennis, *A Book for Kids*.

Mary E. Fullerton, *Bark House Days*.

John O'Brien, *Around the Boree Log*.

Katharine Susannah Prichard, *Black Opal*.

E Sport and Recreation
Roy Cazaly, after 12 years with St Kilda Australian Rules football team, begins playing for South Melbourne and gives rise to the cry "Up there, Cazaly".

Sister Olive wins the Melbourne Cup.

F Statistics, Social Change, the Environment
Estimated population of Australia: 5,510,944; second Commonwealth census, 4 Apr: non-Aboriginal population: 5,435,734; Aboriginal population: 70,403.

Automatic quarterly cost-of-living adjustments to the basic wage introduced.

Women gain the right to be elected to parliament in Tas.

G Births and Deaths
Jan 25   Russell Braddon b. (–1995).
Apr 13   Max Harris b. (–1995).
Jul 12   Harry Hawker d. (33).
Nov 6   Robert Logan Jack d. (76).
Nov 21   Shirley Smith, "Mum Shirl" b. (–1998).
Dec 26   Donald Horne b.

1922

Jan 6   *Daily Mail* begins publication in Sydney. (Becomes the *Labor Daily* in 1924, *Daily News* in 1937; incorporated in the *Daily Telegraph* in 1940.)
–   Rachel Forster Hospital opens in Sydney as "The New Hospital for Women and Children".

Feb 4   A shark fatally attacks Milton Coughlan at Coogee Beach, Sydney. (Olympic swimmer Frank Beaurepaire goes to the young man's aid.)

Mar 23   Act proclaimed abolishing the Qld Legislative Council (from 4 July).

Apr 11 Australia and New Zealand sign an agreement for reciprocal preferential tariffs.

13 Sir George Fuller forms a coalition ministry in NSW, following Labor's defeat at the election on 25 Mar.

Sir Ross Smith and Lt J. M. Bennett killed on a trial flight in England.

21 Country Women's Association formed in Sydney on the initiative of the *Stock and Station Journal*.

– BHP closes its Newcastle steelworks because of falling prices and rising costs (to May 1923).

May 31 Empire Settlement Act comes into force, with the object of establishing British settlers on the land in Australia.

Jul 3 All-Australia "New States" convention held in Albury.

Aug 12 J. B. Hayes replaces Sir Walter Lee as Premier of Tas., leading a National-ist–Country Party government.

Sep 11 Hugh Denison launches the morning tabloid *Sun News-Pictorial* in Melbourne.

Oct 15 Northern Territory granted one member in the House of Representatives, but without voting rights.

Nov 2 Qantas begins its first regular air service, between Charleville and Cloncurry, Qld.

Dec 16 Election for House of Representatives and half Senate; Nationalists lose ground (28 lower house seats to Labor's 30); Country Party, with 14 seats, holds the balance of power.

* Vic. parliament reintroduces payment for members of the Legislative Council.

* Smith Family welfare organization founded in Sydney.

* Maj.-Gen. Sir John Gellibrand founds the first Legacy Club (called at first the Remembrance Club) in Hobart, Tas.

A Architecture, Building

B Science, Technology, Discovery, etc.

Australian Commonwealth Engineering Standards Association formed. (Reconstituted as the Standards Association of Australia in 1929.)

Crossley gravity davit patented.

C Arts and Entertainment

W. B. McInnes, *Professor Harrison Moore*, wins the Archibald Prize.

Lionel Lindsay's *Book of Woodcuts* published.

Henri Verbrugghen resigns as director of the NSW Conservatorium of Music, and his orchestra is subsequently disbanded.

Jack O'Hagan composes the song "Along the Road to Gundagai", which sells 97,000 copies of the sheet music within two years.

D Books and Writing

Hugh McCrae, *Idyllia*.

Who's Who in Australia first published under that title (formerly *Johns' Notable Australians*).

Melbourne University Press founded.

D. H. Lawrence arrives in Fremantle (4 May), Sydney (27 May); leaves Sydney for America (11 Aug.).

E Sport and Recreation

Gerald Patterson wins the men's singles at Wimbledon for the second time.

King Ingoda wins the Melbourne Cup.

1922

F Statistics, Social Change, the Environment
Estimated population of Australia: 5,637,286.
Commonwealth basic wage: £3 16s.
Qld abolishes the death penalty.
Sick leave of six days a year awarded by the Commonwealth Arbitration· Court.

G Births and Deaths
Mar 28   Neville Bonner b. (–1999)
Jun 17   Sir Robert Philp d. (70).
Aug 2   Geoffrey Dutton b. (–1998)
Aug 31   Lionel Murphy b. (–1986).
Sep   2   Henry Lawson d. (55).

1923

Jan 17   Country Party refuses to support or co-operate with a ministry led by or including W. M. Hughes.
    29   Trains collide at Clapham in Adelaide; 2 killed and 22 injured.

Feb 2   Hughes resigns the prime ministership in favour of S. M. Bruce, who forms a Nationalist–Country Party coalition government with Earle Page (9th).
    –   Silver-lead deposits found at Mt Isa, Qld, by John Campbell Miles.
    –   Agreement signed between UK and WA governments for the settlement of groups of British migrants in the south-west of the state.

Mar 23   Hurricane in the Gulf of Carpentaria (to 9 Apr.); SS *Douglas Mawson* leaves Normanton (26 Mar.) for Darwin and is lost with all aboard.
    –   Barrier Industrial Council formed in Broken Hill, with E. P. (Paddy) O'Neill as president.

May 24   Postmaster-General approves a sealed-set broadcasting system, under which radio receivers would be tuned to only the station to which the listener paid a subscription.

Jun 9   Premiers' Conference agrees to the establishment of a voluntary loan council to co-ordinate borrowing.
    26   SS *Sumatra* founders in a storm off Port Macquarie, NSW; 46 lives lost.
    –   Commonwealth financial aid for main roads introduced.
    –   *Sunday Mail* first published in Brisbane.

Jul 2   *Daily Guardian* begins publication in Sydney (to 1931).
    24   Adelaide evening newspaper the *News* first published.

Aug 4   James Cavill opens the Surfers Paradise Hotel at a site known as Elston on the Qld south coast, which eventually takes the name of the hotel.
    14   Sir Walter Lee again becomes Premier of Tas., replacing John Hayes.

Sep 1   Explosion at Bellbird coalmine, near Cessnock, NSW; 21 miners killed.

Oct 1   Imperial Conference held in London (to 8 Nov.); Australia votes in favour of the planned naval base in Singapore.
    10   Sydney and Brisbane linked by trunk telephone.
    12   Cairns proclaimed a city.
    25   J. A. Lyons forms a Labor government in Tas. after the fall of Lee ministry.

Nov 1   Vic. police strike over the use of plain-clothes supervisors; rioting and looting occur in Melbourne over the next two days; the government dismisses the strikers and (4th) swears in volunteers as special police until a new regular force is recruited.

23 Regular radio broadcasting begins in Australia, from station 2SB (later 2BL) in Sydney.

Dec 5 Radio station 2FC, established by the department store Farmer & Co., begins broadcasting in Sydney.

10 General Motors signs an agreement with Holden's for the manufacture of car bodies at Woodville, SA.

– National Roads and Motorists' Association (NRMA) of NSW founded (begun in 1920 as NSW branch of the National Roads Association).

* Pacific telephone cable extended from Southport, Qld, to Sydney.

* First house connected to the sewerage system in Brisbane.

A Architecture, Building

Work begins on Sydney Harbour Bridge (28 Apr; completed 1932).

Work begins on the temporary Parliament House at the foot of Camp Hill in Canberra (28 Aug; completed 1927).

Forrest Place, Perth, officially opened (26 Sept.).

First electric lifts in Australia installed in the railway building at Spencer Street, Melbourne.

B Science, Technology, Discovery, etc.

Qld meteorologist Inigo Jones begins his long-range forecasting of the weather.

C. P. Callister of the Melbourne firm Fred Walker & Co. creates Vegemite, and Hoadley's Chocolates first produces the Violet Crumble Bar.

C Arts and Entertainment

W. B. McInnes, *Portrait of a Lady*, wins the Archibald Prize.

Arundel Orchard, the new director of the NSW Conservatorium, begins building up a new symphony orchestra in Sydney.

Hobart Symphony Orchestra gives its first concert (19 Mar.).

D Books and Writing

V. Gordon Childe, *How Labour Governs*.

D. H. Lawrence, *Kangaroo*.

John Shaw Neilson, *Ballad and Lyrical Poems*.

Vision, a literary quarterly produced by Jack Lindsay, Kenneth Slessor, and Frank Johnson, first published (1 May; ceases after four issues).

E Sport and Recreation

W. H. Ponsford scores 429 runs in a match between Vic. and Tas. at the MCG.

Bitalli wins the Melbourne Cup.

F Statistics, Social Change, the Environment

Estimated population of Australia: 5,755,986.

Women gain the right to stand for parliament in Vic. and are admitted to the practice of law in WA.

Unemployment insurance scheme introduced in Qld.

G Births and Deaths

Feb 1 John Perceval b.

May 27 Jon Molvig b. (–1970).

Jun 2 E. J. Banfield d. (70).

Jun 15 Ninian Stephen b.

Jun 25 Harry Seidler b.

Aug 22 Sir James Burns d. (77).

Oct 25 Don Banks b. (–1980).

1924

Jan 23 *Daily Mail* (Sydney) becomes the *Labor Daily*.
26 Radio station 3AR begins broadcasting in Melbourne.

Feb 1 Australian Loan Council meets for the first time.
27 HMS *Hood*, the biggest battleship afloat, arrives at Fremantle with five light cruisers at the beginning of a visit to Australian ports. (Sails from Sydney on 20 Apr.)

Mar 7 Greek Orthodox Holy Metropolis of Australia and New Zealand established, with Christopher Knites as first Metropolitan.

Apr 6 S. J. Goble and I. E. McIntyre leave Point Cook, Vic., in a Fairey 111D seaplane to make the first round-Australia flight (to 19 May).
7 Longest recorded period in Australia of above-century temperatures (over 37.8°C)—161 days (from 30 Oct. 1923), at Marble Bar, WA—comes to an end.
12 HMAS *Australia* is sunk with naval honours off Sydney Heads in agreement with the terms of the Washington disarmament treaty.
16 John Gunn becomes Premier of SA and Phillip Collier Premier of WA following Labor victories in both state elections.
26 SS *City of Singapore*, carrying petrol, catches fire at Port Adelaide; three firemen killed and ten others injured.
28 Sir Alexander Peacock replaces H. S. W. Lawson as Premier of Vic.

Jun 2 Airmail service begins between Adelaide and Sydney.
4 Radio station 6WF begins broadcasting in Perth.
15 Morwell power station in the Latrobe Valley begins generating electricity for Melbourne.

Jul 17 Dual classification for radio stations adopted—"A" class to be financed by listeners' fees, "B" class by advertising revenue.
18 G. M. Prendergast forms a Labor ministry in Vic. following the election of 26 June.
25 Traces of oil found in an exploratory bore at Lakes Entrance, Vic.
31 Voting in federal elections made compulsory.

Aug 14 Cobb & Co. make their last coach run, from Surat to Yuleba, Qld.
21 Open-cut mining of brown coal begins at Yallourn, Vic.

Sep 23 Big Brother movement, under which British migrant youths are sponsored by Australians, officially launched in Melbourne by Richard Linton.

Oct 3 City of Brisbane Act creates "Greater Brisbane".
13 Radio station 3LO begins broadcasting in Melbourne.

Nov 18 John Allan becomes Premier of Vic. (the first Country Party Premier in Australia) following the fall of the Prendergast government.
20 Radio station 5CL begins broadcasting in Adelaide.

Dec 5 H. P. Christmas opens Australia's first Woolworths store, in the Imperial Arcade, Sydney.
8 Completion of gaps on Qld's coastal railway gives an unbroken rail link between Brisbane and Cairns.
17 Radio station 7ZL begins broadcasting in Hobart.
– Pilot briquette plant completed at Yallourn. (Commercial production begins in 1925.)

- R. G. Casey becomes Australian Liaison Officer to the UK Foreign Office in London.
* Far West Children's Health Scheme in NSW started by Methodist minister Stanley Drummond.
* King Gee Clothing Co. founded in Sydney.

A Architecture, Building
Walter Burley Griffin, Capitol Theatre, Melbourne.
Amphitheatre at Balmoral, Sydney, built by the Order of the Star in the East.

B Science, Technology, Discovery, etc.
Mt Stromlo Observatory, Canberra, opened (1 Jan.), with Prof. W. G. Duffield as director.
National Museum of Australian Zoology (later the Australian Institute of Anatomy) established to house Sir Colin Mackenzie's collection of preserved Australian fauna.

C Arts and Entertainment
W. B. McInnes wins the Archibald Prize for the fourth consecutive time.
Dame Nellie Melba gives her first "farewell performance" in Australia in *La Bohème* at His Majesty's Theatre in Melbourne (13 Oct.), broadcast over the new station 3LO.
Bernard Heinze begins presenting orchestral concerts for children in Melbourne.
Palatial cinemas open in Brisbane (the Wintergarden), Sydney (Prince Edward), and Melbourne (Capitol).

D Books and Writing
D. H. Lawrence and M. L. Skinner, *The Boy in the Bush*.
Vance Palmer, *Cronulla*.
Kenneth Slessor, *Thief of the Moon*.
William Dixson offers his collection of Australiana to the Public Library of NSW.

E Sport and Recreation
At the Olympic Games in Paris, "Boy" Charlton wins the 1,500 m freestyle swimming event, R. C. Eve the plain high-tower dive, and Nick Winter the hop, step, and jump.
Hubert Opperman becomes Australian road cycling champion and wins a series of road events in Europe.
Melbourne Motordrome opens at Olympic Park. (Demolished in 1932.)
Brownlow Medal, for fairest and best VFL footballer, first awarded: to Edward ("Carji") Greeves of Geelong club.
Blackwood wins the Melbourne Cup.

F Statistics, Social Change, the Environment
Estimated population of Australia: 5,882,002.
About two million koala pelts exported from eastern Australia, almost exterminating koalas in NSW and Vic.

G Births and Deaths
Sep 13 Harold Blair b. (–1976).
Oct 1 Leonie Kramer b.
Dec 17 Clifton Pugh b. (–1990).

1925

Jan 1 Federal Capital Commission constituted in place of the Canberra Advisory Committee.

Main Roads Board set up in NSW.

26 Radio station 2UE, Australia's oldest "B" class (commercial) station, begins broadcasting in Sydney.

Feb 1 Melbourne Town Hall gutted by fire.

21 First election held for the Greater Brisbane Council.

24 Adelaide's first commercial radio station, 5DN, begins broadcasting.

26 W. N. Gillies becomes Premier of Qld after the resignation of E. G. Theodore to contest a seat in federal parliament.

Mar 8 Radio 3UZ, Melbourne's first commercial station, begins broadcasting.

Apr 3 May Holman wins a by-election for the state seat of Forrest, WA, and becomes the first Labor woman to sit in an Australian parliament.

25 Australian War Memorial founded in Canberra. (Building not completed and open to the public until 1941.)

May 30 Labor wins government at the NSW state election. (J. T. Lang sworn in as Premier on 17 June.) New MLAs include H. V. Evatt and Millicent Preston-Stanley (Nationalist), the first woman to be elected to NSW parliament.

Jun 4 Seamen's Union deregistered following a series of disputes; a strike follows.

9 Train derailment on a bridge at Traveston, near Gympie, Qld; 10 killed and 28 injured in a falling carriage.

Jul 6 Lang withdraws NSW from the Loan Council.

13 Lang orders the NSW Railway Commissioner to reinstate men dismissed in the 1917 strike.

17 Federal government suspends the Navigation Act to allow overseas ships to operate in coastal waters and (20th) amends the Immigration Act to provide for the deportation of "alien agitators".

22 Regular airmail service begins between Sydney and Melbourne.

23 Two squadrons of US Navy ships (56 vessels in all) visit Melbourne and Sydney simultaneously.

27 "A" class (government) station 4QG begins broadcasting in Brisbane.

Aug 4 N. R. Westwood and G. L. Davies set out from Perth in a two-seater Citroën and become the first to drive round Australia (to 30 Dec.).

14 Country Party of NSW formed out of a split in the Progressive Party.

30 Peace Officers Bill rushed through federal parliament to establish a federal police force (because NSW police would not serve Commonwealth summonses on union leaders).

Sep 1 Thomas Blamey becomes Chief Commissioner of Police in Vic.

Oct 8 Baron Stonehaven succeeds Lord Forster as Governor-General.

22 William McCormack replaces Gillies as Premier of Qld.

31 Radio station 2KY begins broadcasting in Sydney. (Taken over by J. T. Lang, it becomes the world's first Labor-owned radio station.)

Nov 14 Election for House of Representatives and half Senate (the first federal election under compulsory voting). Bruce–Page government re-elected with a large majority.

Dec – Melbourne *Punch* incorporated in *Table Talk*.

    * Melbourne *Herald* acquires the *Sun News-Pictorial*.
    * Eagle Farm officially chosen as an airport in Brisbane.
    * A. H. Appleroth and Albert Lenertz found the Clarence Manufacturing Co. (later Traders Ltd) in Sydney to make Aeroplane Jelly.

A Architecture, Building

B Science, Technology, Discovery, etc.
Waite Agricultural Research Institute founded by the University of Adelaide.
Ancient Aboriginal skull discovered at Cohuna, Vic.

C Arts and Entertainment
John Longstaff, *Maurice Moscovitch*, wins the Archibald Prize.
C. Web Gilbert's bronze memorial to Matthew Flinders unveiled outside St Paul's Cathedral, Melbourne (8 Nov.).
Bertram Mackennal's bronze of T. J. Ryan unveiled in Queen's Park, Brisbane.
Percy Grainger, violinist Fritz Kreisler, and soprano Amelita Galli-Curci make concert tours of Australia.
Arthur Shirley, *The Mystery of the Hansom Cab* (film).

D Books and Writing
A. W. Jose, ed., *Australian Encyclopaedia*, 2 vols (–1926).
Henry Handel Richardson, *The Way Home* (vol. 2 of *The Fortunes of Richard Mahony*).
J. T. Kirtley and Jack Lindsay found the Fanfrolico Press.

E Sport and Recreation
Banked concrete motor speedway opens at Maroubra, Sydney (5 Dec.). (Demolished in 1934.)
Windbag wins the Melbourne Cup, which is broadcast for the first time.

F Statistics, Social Change, the Environment
Population of Australia reaches six million.
Qld introduces a 44-hour working week.

G Births and Deaths
Apr 20 Rose Scott d. (77).
Aug 21 Don Chipp b.
Sep 23 John Coburn b.
Oct 3 Charles Web Gilbert d. (58).
Nov 17 Charles Mackerras b.

1926

Jan 21 Five miners killed in an explosion at the Redhead colliery, NSW.

Feb 15 Radio station 2GB begins broadcasting in Sydney.
    –   Bushfires sweep through west Gippsland, Vic., causing 31 deaths and extensive damage to forests.

Mar 1 NSW's first electric train service begins—between Sydney's Central Station and Oatley.
    16 Commonwealth Crimes Act amended to give the government power to deal with Communists and political agitators.

1926

17 Proportional representation abolished for NSW Legislative Assembly elections, and marking of preferences allowed.

Apr 2 SS *Dorrigo* sinks off Double Island Point, Qld; 22 lives lost; captain and his son rescued after 34 hours on a raft.

May 16 Federal Aid Roads Agreement regulates Commonwealth assistance to the states for building and maintaining roads.

26 Three killed and 153 injured in a train collision at Caulfield, Vic.

Jun 4 Northern Australia Act divides the Northern Territory into North Australia and Central Australia, each with a separate administration. (Takes effect 1 Mar. 1927; NT reverts to a single entity in 1931.)

10 Sydney–Brisbane express train falls through a timber bridge near Aberdeen, NSW; five killed and 50 injured.

25 Beryl Mills of WA wins the first "Miss Australia" competition.

Jul 21 Development and Migration Commission established.

Aug 23 Cotton Bounty Act introduces a bounty on seed grown and yarn made in Australia.

28 L. L. Hill succeeds John Gunn as Premier of SA.

Sep 3 *Canberra Times* begins publication as a bi-weekly. (Becomes a morning daily in 1928.)

4 Referendums to allow the Commonwealth to regulate commerce and industry and to protect the public against interruption of essential services both rejected.

13 Runaway goods trucks collide with a passenger train at Murulla, NSW, killing 27 people and injuring 42.

Oct 19 Imperial Conference in London (to 23 Nov.); Balfour formula defines relations between the UK and the self-governing dominions as autonomous communities, equal in status.

Nov 1 General Motors (A/asia) Pty Ltd begins operations in Australia, with assembly plants in Sydney, Melbourne, Adelaide, and Perth; bodies supplied by Holden's in Adelaide.

– Special NSW Labor conference confers almost dictatorial powers on Premier J. T. Lang.

Dec 20 Sydney's underground railway begins operating on its first section— Central to St James Station.

23 Compulsory voting introduced for Vic. Legislative Assembly elections.

* Oxley Memorial Library, Brisbane, established. (Officially opened in 1934.)

* Twofold Bay whaling station closes down.

A Architecture, Building

Yarralumla, Canberra, renovated as the official residence of the Governor-General.

B Science, Technology, Discovery, etc.

Council for Scientific and Industrial Research (CSIR) formed, to replace the Institute of Science and Industry. (David Rivett appointed chief executive officer in 1927.)

Pedal radio transceiver developed by A. H. Traeger. (Introduced in Qld in 1929.)

C Arts and Entertainment

W. B. McInnes, *Silk and Lace*, wins the Archibald Prize.

Hans Heysen, *Farmyard, Frosty Morning* (awarded the Wynne Art Prize).

Bertram Mackennal's Shakespeare Memorial sculpture erected near the State Library of NSW.

Feodor Chaliapin, Clara Butt, Toti dal Monte, the Don Cossack Choir, and Wilhelm Backhaus make concert tours of Australia.

Anna Pavlova tours Australia with a company of dancers.

St James Theatre opens in Sydney (26 Mar.). (Later becomes a cinema; demolished in 1971.)

Hoyts Theatres cinema chain formed, with F. W. Thring as managing director.

Frank Hurley, *The Jungle Woman* (film).

D Books and Writing

Jack McLaren, *My Crowded Solitude.*

Katharine Susannah Prichard, *Working Bullocks.*

Kenneth Slessor, *Earth-Visitors.*

E Sport and Recreation

Clarrie Grimmett takes 11 wickets for 82 in a test match against England.

Dirt-track motorcycle racing begins at Sydney Showground.

Spearfelt wins the Melbourne Cup.

F Statistics, Social Change, the Environment

Estimated population of Australia: 6,124,020.

Working hours reduced from 48 to 44 and widows' pensions introduced by the Lang Labor government in NSW.

Eggs of caterpillar *Cactoblastis cactorum* released in Qld and NSW to control prickly pear.

G Births and Deaths

Apr 2 Jack Brabham b.
Jun 4 Fred Spofforth d. (72).
Jul 19 Ada Cambridge d. (81).
Sep 21 Don Dunstan b. (–1999).
Oct 11 Neville Wran b.
Nov 7 Joan Sutherland b.
Dec 31 Billy Snedden b. (–1987).

1927

Jan 1 Newspaper tax of ½d a copy imposed by the Lang government in NSW. (Declared invalid by the High Court on 3 Mar.)
Sydney Mint closes.

Feb 9 Collier *Galava* sinks off Terrigal, NSW, with the loss of seven lives.
21 Radio station 3DB begins broadcasting in Melbourne.

Mar 17 Heavy cruiser HMAS *Australia* launched in Scotland.
25 Radio 5KA Adelaide begins broadcasting.
26 Duke and Duchess of York (later King George VI and Queen Elizabeth) arrive in Sydney on a visit to all states (to 23 May).

Apr 8 R. L. Butler forms a Liberal–Country Party coalition ministry in SA.

May 3 All-Australian Trade Union Congress in Melbourne forms the Australasian (later Australian) Council of Trade Unions (ACTU), to act as a federal executive for the trade union movement; state Labor Councils are reorganized as branches of the ACTU.

1927

9   Duke of York opens Parliament House in Canberra, which becomes the official seat of government of the Commonwealth of Australia.

20   E. J. Hogan replaces John Allan as Premier of Vic.

26   NSW Premier J. T. Lang resigns in order to secure an early dissolution of parliament; recommissioned, he selects a new ministry without the assistance of caucus.

Aug 8   Cenotaph in Martin Place, Sydney, dedicated by Premier Lang. (Statues added in 1929.)

Sep 27   ACT Police Force established.

28   Commonwealth parliament begins sitting in Canberra.

Oct 8   Labor loses its slim majority in the NSW election; T. R. Bavin replaces Lang as Premier (18th), leading a coalition government.

27   Melbourne criminals Squizzy Taylor and Snowy Cutmore die in a gun duel in Carlton.

Nov 3   Ferry *Greycliffe* sinks with the loss of more than 40 lives after being cut in two by the liner *Tahiti* in Sydney Harbour.

Dec 14   Financial agreement entered into by Commonwealth and states: Commonwealth to take over all state debts and make an annual contribution toward interest and sinking-fund payments; Loan Council to be put on a statutory and constitutional (instead of voluntary) basis.

–   Bruce–Page government amends the Commonwealth Arbitration Act to provide severe penalties for union leaders involved in strikes. (Amending act comes into force in 1928.)

*   John Anderson becomes Challis Professor of Philosophy at the University of Sydney.

*   Burrinjuck Dam completed.

*   Severe drought throughout mainland Australia.

A Architecture, Building

P. B. Hudson and J. H. Wardrop, Melbourne's Shrine of Remembrance (–1934).
Civic Centre in Canberra opened by Prime Minister S. M. Bruce.

B Science, Technology, Discovery, etc.

W. B. Spencer and F. J. Gillen publish their study of the Aborigines in the MacDonnell Ranges area, *The Arunta*.

C Arts and Entertainment

George W. Lambert, *Mrs Murdoch*, wins the Archibald Prize.
Tom Roberts finishes his painting *Bailed Up* (begun 1895).
Margaret Preston draws attention to Aboriginal art in an article in *Art in Australia* (Mar.).
May Brahe publishes her song "Bless This House".
Jascha Heifetz and Ignace Paderewski make return visits to Australia.
Empire Theatre opens in Sydney (27 Feb.).
Norman Dawn, *For the Term of His Natural Life* (film).
Tal Ordell, *The Kid Stakes* (film).

D Books and Writing

R. D. FitzGerald, *The Greater Apollo: Seven Metaphysical Songs*.
Ion L. Idriess, *Madman's Island*.

E Sport and Recreation

First greyhound track meeting in Australia held at Epping Racecourse (now Harold Park) in Forest Lodge, Sydney (28 May).

W. H. Ponsford scores 437 runs for Vic. against Qld in Melbourne (Dec.).
Trivalve wins the Melbourne Cup.

F Statistics, Social Change, the Environment
Estimated population of Australia: 6,251,016.
Child-endowment scheme introduced in NSW.
584,738 koalas and 1,014,632 possums slain in Queensland in one month (Aug.).

G Births and Deaths
Jan 23 Fred Williams b. (–1982).
Jun 6 Alan Seymour b.
Jun 13 David Kirkpatrick (Slim Dusty) b.
Aug 21 Livingston Hopkins ("Hop") d. (81).
Aug 24 David Ireland b.
Dec 7 Albert Griffiths ("Young Griffo") d. (58).

1928

Jan 10 J. R. Moncrieff and G. Hood leave Sydney in an attempt to make the first flight from Australia to New Zealand and are not seen again.

Feb 22 Bert Hinkler lands at Darwin in his Avro Avian after a record-breaking (15½ days) solo flight from London (first solo flight from the UK to Australia).

May 15 Australian Inland Mission's Flying Doctor Service begins operating from Cloncurry, Qld.
31 Charles Kingsford Smith and C. T. P. Ulm, with Americans Harry Lyon and James Warner, leave Oakland, California, in the *Southern Cross* to make the first flight across the Pacific (arrive Brisbane 9 June).
– Cadbury's Dairy Milk chocolate first produced at Claremont, Tas.

Jun 9 Commonwealth Savings Bank of Australia established as a separate entity.
15 J. C. McPhee replaces J. A. Lyons as Premier of Tas. following Labor's defeat at the polls on 30 May. (Lyons resigns from state parliament.)

Jul 25 Francis Birtles arrives in Melbourne after driving a 25 h.p. Bean motor car from London (only failing by a small section in Burma to complete the overland link).

Aug 8 Kingsford Smith, Ulm, H. A. Litchfield and T. H. McWilliams fly from Point Cook, Vic., to Perth in the *Southern Cross* on the first non-stop trans-Australian flight.
29 Australian Iron and Steel Ltd's blast furnace at Port Kembla, NSW, begins production.

Sep 1 Liquor referendum in NSW and the ACT results in a vote against prohibition.
10 Kingsford Smith, Ulm, Litchfield, and McWilliams fly from Sydney to Christchurch in the *Southern Cross*, making the first flight across the Tasman (arrive 11th).
12 Waterside workers repudiate a new award handed down by Justice Beeby of the Commonwealth Arbitration Court, beginning months of industrial trouble on the waterfront, mainly in Melbourne.
25 British Economic Mission arrives in Australia to report on the Australian economy for the British government.

Nov 2 Union demonstrators are fired on as they attack volunteer labourers on Melbourne wharves; one wharf labourer killed and four wounded.

1928

16 Hubert Wilkins makes the first Antarctic flight, from Deception Island in the South Shetlands.

17 Election for House of Representatives and half Senate; Bruce–Page government returned with a reduced majority; new members include John Curtin and J. B. Chifley.

Referendum to endorse the Financial Agreement between the Commonwealth and states and to set up a permanent Loan Council carried.

22 Sir William McPherson forms a Nationalist ministry in Vic. following the defeat of the Hogan government over its handling of the waterfront dispute.

Dec 12 Australian National Airways Ltd formed in Sydney by Kingsford Smith and Ulm. (Goes into liquidation in June 1931.)

* Commonwealth Government Line disbanded and most of the ships sold to British interests.

* Voting made compulsory in NSW and Tas.

* Speedo swimsuits first produced.

A Architecture, Building

Adelaide railway station.

Double-deck (road and rail) steel bascule bridge over the Clarence River at Grafton, NSW (–1932).

B Science, Technology, Discovery, etc.

First traffic lights in Australia installed in Melbourne, at the corner of Collins and Swanston streets.

C Arts and Entertainment

John Longstaff, *Dr Alexander Leeper*, wins the Archibald Prize.

Arthur Streeton, *Afternoon Light, Goulburn Valley* (awarded the Wynne Art Prize).

Melba makes her last appearance in opera in Australia at a matinee in Melbourne (27 Sept.) and her final Australian appearance at a concert in Geelong, Vic., in November.

Comedy Theatre opens in Melbourne (28 Apr.).

Two Sydney cinemas—the Regent and the Lyceum—begin showing talking films (Dec.).

Royal commission into the film industry calls for a Censorship Board and a quota for Empire films.

D Books and Writing

"Brent of Bin Bin" (Miles Franklin), *Up the Country.*

Martin Mills (Martin Boyd), *The Montforts.*

Fellowship of Australian Writers formed by Mary Gilmore and John Le Gay Brereton.

E Sport and Recreation

H. R. (Bobby) Pearce wins the single sculls at the Amsterdam Olympics.

Hubert Opperman wins the French Bol d'Or 24-hour cycle event, covering a record 909 km, and cycles on to break the 1,000 km record.

Australian Grand Prix motor race first held (31 Mar.), on Phillip Island, Vic.

Statesman wins the Melbourne Cup.

F Statistics, Social Change, the Environment

Estimated population of Australia: 6,355,770.

Liquor first sold in the ACT (22 Dec.); territory previously "dry".

G Births and Deaths

Jan 21 John Olsen b.

May 30 Pro Hart b.

1928

Jul 22 George Dreyfus b.
Aug 8 Don Burrows b.
Aug 12 Charles Blackman b.
Oct 8 Leonard French b.
Oct 22 Andrew Fisher d. (66).

1929

Jan – Riots in Adelaide over loading of ships by non-union labour.
– British Economic Mission recommends a policy of deflation by reducing government developmental work.

Feb 1 Timber workers go on strike (to Oct.) over a new award increasing their working hours from 44 to 48.
5 Miners' Federation rejects a government proposal for a cut in wages as part of a plan to reduce coal prices.
15 Mine owners in northern NSW announce their intention to reduce wages by 12½%; miners refuse to accept this and are locked out (1 Mar.—to 3 June 1930).

Mar 31 Charles Kingsford Smith, C. T. P. Ulm, H. A. Litchfield, and T. H. McWilliams leave Sydney in the *Southern Cross* to fly to England but are forced down 400 km from Wyndham, WA. (Found 13 Apr.)
– *Australian Quarterly* begins publication.

Apr 4 Dam on the Cascade River, Tas., bursts after heavy rain, flooding Derby town and tin mines and causing the deaths of 14 people.
27 *Kookaburra*, an aircraft that had gone searching for the *Southern Cross*, is found with its crew, Keith Anderson and H. S. Hitchcock, dead from thirst.

May 11 McCormack government defeated in the Qld election; A. E. Moore becomes Premier (21 May); Irene Longman, the first woman elected to the Qld parliament, wins the seat of Bulimba.
Tom Ugly's Bridge, across the Georges River south of Sydney, opened.

Jun 3 Fremantle proclaimed a city.
25 Kingsford Smith, Ulm, Litchfield, and McWilliams set out again for England in the *Southern Cross*. (Reach London on 10 July in the record time of 12 days 18 hours.)
– Mount Morgan Ltd formed to work the derelict mine by open-cut methods.

Aug 2 Railway line from Alice Springs to Adelaide completed.
22 Prime Minister Bruce introduces the Maritime Industries Bill with the object of repealing the Commonwealth Arbitration Act and passing arbitration over to the states.

Sep 10 W. M. Hughes, expelled from the Nationalist Party for voting with Labor in a no-confidence motion, successfully moves an amendment to the Maritime Industries Bill that the bill should be submitted to a referendum, thereby bringing about the defeat of the government.
29 *Sunday Guardian* first published in Sydney (to 1931).
– Railway from Darwin reaches Birdum. (Service runs to 1976.)

Oct 12 Election for House of Representatives; Labor has a sweeping victory; new members include J. A. Lyons; Bruce loses his seat; J. H. Scullin becomes Prime Minister (on 22nd).
21 Dixson wing of the State Library of NSW opened.

1929

Nov 1 Compulsory military training replaced by a voluntary system.
    24 War Memorial in King's Park, Perth, unveiled.
    28 Export of merino rams banned.

Dec 12 E. J. Hogan becomes Premier of Vic. for the second time.
    14 Electric trams (and buses) replace trains between Adelaide city and Glenelg.
    16 Miners demonstrating at Rothbury colliery, NSW, against the use of non-union labour to open the mines clash with police; one miner killed and at least nine wounded by police bullets.
    17 Scullin government takes Australia off the gold standard.

    * Tas. Hydro-Electric Commission established.

A Architecture, Building
Henry White, State Theatre building, Sydney.

B Science, Technology, Discovery, etc.
Jervois Skull found in Central Australia.

C Arts and Entertainment
John Longstaff, *W. A. Holman, KC*, wins the Archibald Prize.
Sir Bertram Mackennal's bronze statues on Sydney's Martin Place Cenotaph unveiled (21 Feb.).
Australian-born pianist and composer Arthur Benjamin returns for a concert tour.
Anna Pavlova makes her second tour of Australia.
Fox Movietone News records the first talking film in Australia, an interview (8 Aug.).
Sydney's Empire Theatre converts to a cinema.
State Theatre (cinema) opens in Sydney (7 June).
State and Regent Theatres (cinemas) open in Melbourne (23 Feb., 15 Mar.).

D Books and Writing
M. Barnard Eldershaw, *A House Is Built*.
Robert D. FitzGerald, *To Meet the Sun*.
Katharine Susannah Prichard, *Coonardoo*.
Henry Handel Richardson, *Ultima Thule* (vol. 3 of *The Fortunes of Richard Mahony*).
David Unaipon, *Native Legends*.
Arthur W. Upfield, *The Barrackee Mystery* (introduces Inspector Napoleon Bonaparte).

E Sport and Recreation
Jockey W. Thomas rides the winner of all seven races at a meeting in Townsville, Qld, on 29 July.
Nightmarch wins the Melbourne Cup.

F Statistics, Social Change, the Environment
Estimated population of Australia: 6,436,213.
Commonwealth basic wage: £4 10s 6d.

G Births and Deaths
Jan 13 Henry Bournes Higgins d. (77).
Apr 29 Peter Sculthorpe b.
Jun 10 Ian Sinclair b.
Jul 14 Sir Walter Baldwin Spencer d. (69).
Oct 17 Ada Crossley d. (55).
Dec   9 R. J. L. (Bob) Hawke b.
Dec 31 J. D. Anthony b.

1930

Jan 1 Australian National Airways begins a Sydney–Brisbane air service (Sydney–Melbourne service begins 1 June).

5 Sir Douglas Mawson, in a plane from the British–Australian–New Zealand Antarctic Research Expedition, discovers MacRobertson Land.

31 Francis Chichester arrives in Sydney in his Gypsy Moth plane after a solo flight from London.

Feb 10 Australian Council for Educational Research (ACER) established in Melbourne.

12 Spencer Street Bridge, Melbourne, opened.

Mar 31 Lectures begin at Canberra University College.

– Prime Minister James Scullin asks the Bank of England to fund Australia's interest payments due to the UK; the bank offers to send out a representative to investigate Australia's economic problems.

Apr 2 Sir Isaac Isaacs succeeds Sir Adrian Knox as Chief Justice of the High Court.

5 Labor wins office in SA; L. L. Hill becomes Premier for the second time (17th).

8 Brisbane City Hall officially opened.

24 Sir James Mitchell forms a coalition ministry in WA.

30 Radio telephone service between Australia and the UK inaugurated.

– Mass meeting of unemployed in Melbourne establishes the Anti-Starvation Crusade.

May 24 Amy Johnson, the first woman to fly solo from Britain to Australia, arrives at Darwin.

Jun 24 Kingsford Smith flies from Ireland to New York (arr. 26th) and thence to Oakland, California (arr. 4 July), thereby completing his circumnavigation of the world in the *Southern Cross*.

26 Royal Australian Naval College transfers from Jervis Bay, NSW, to Flinders Naval Depot at Westernport, Vic.

Jul 4 Royal commission into the sale of Mungana Mines to the Qld government finds former Premiers E. G. Theodore and William McCormack guilty of fraud and dishonesty.

5 Theodore resigns as federal Treasurer and (9th) Scullin takes over.

21 L. H. B. Lasseter leaves Alice Springs with an expedition to a rich gold reef he claims to have found years before. (Dissension occurs, and Lasseter goes on alone into the Petermann Range and does not return; his remains and diaries are found in May 1931.)

Aug 18 Sales tax imposed for the first time by the federal government.

21 Sir Otto Niemeyer, the Bank of England's representative, addresses the Premiers' Conference and advises a heavy deflationary program. Commonwealth and state governments agree to balance their budgets, raise no more overseas loans, and undertake only productive works.

Oct 25 Election in NSW; Bavin government defeated; J. T. Lang again becomes Premier (4 Nov.).

– Douglas Social Credit Association founded in Perth. (Established in Sydney, Melbourne, and Brisbane in Dec.)

Nov 29 Scullin, in London for the Imperial Conference, obtains King George V's

1930

reluctant agreement to the appointment of Sir Isaac Isaacs as Governor-General.
- Apex Club founded in Geelong.

Dec 18 Perth connected by telephone to Adelaide (and thus to the rest of Australia).
19 H. V. Evatt and E. A. McTiernan (on 20th) appointed to the High Court.
- NSW government legislates to introduce a state lottery to finance public hospitals.

A Architecture, Building
Queensland National Anzac Memorial, Brisbane (dedicated 11 Nov.).

B Science, Technology, Discovery, etc.
Australorp declared an Australian breed of poultry.

C Arts and Entertainment
W. B. McInnes, *Drum Major Harry McClelland*, wins the Archibald Prize.
Doris Fitton founds the Independent Theatre in Sydney (30 May). (Opens the North Sydney theatre on 3 Sept. 1939.)
Sydney's Palace Theatre becomes a mini-golf course.
F. W. Thring forms Efftee Film Productions in Melbourne.

D Books and Writing
"Brent of Bin Bin" (Miles Franklin), *Ten Creeks Run.*
W. K. Hancock, *Australia.*
Norman Lindsay, *Redheap* (banned in Australia until 1959).
L. W. Lower, *Here's Luck.*
Frederic Manning, *Her Privates We.*
Vance Palmer, *The Passage.*
F. J. Thwaites, *The Broken Melody.*

E Sport and Recreation
Don Bradman scores a record 452 not out for NSW against Queensland (6 Jan.) and 334 in a test match against England at Leeds.
Bobby Pearce wins the single sculls, and Noel Ryan wins the 440 and 1,500 yards freestyle swimming events at the first Empire Games, held at Hamilton, Canada.
First visit to Australia by a West Indian cricket team.
Phar Lap wins the Melbourne Cup.

F Statistics, Social Change, the Environment
Estimated population of Australia: 6,500,751.
State governments pay a "dole" to the deserving poor and issue sustenance rations free of charge.
Unemployed camp in tents and bag humpies in Sydney Domain.
First milk bar in Australia opens in Sydney.

G Births and Deaths
Mar 11 Geoffrey Blainey b.
Mar 30 Rolf Harris b.
May 21 Malcolm Fraser b.
May 28 George W. Lambert d. (56).
Sep 29 Richard Bonynge b.
Oct 6 Richie Benaud b.

1931

Jan 22 Sir Isaac Isaacs, the first Australian-born Governor-General, sworn in; Sir Frank Gavan Duffy succeeds him as Chief Justice.

28 All for Australia League launched at a meeting in Sydney.

29 E. G. Theodore reinstated as Federal Treasurer.

Feb 1 All wages controlled by the Commonwealth Arbitration Court reduced by 10%.

Cyclones (to 8th) cause flooding from Innisfail to Brisbane, where more than a thousand houses are inundated and two men drown.

4 J. A. Lyons and J. E. Fenton resign from cabinet in protest against the reinstatement of Theodore.

6 Premiers' Conference (to 26th); Treasurer Theodore and NSW Premier J. T. Lang put forward differing financial plans.

7 Royal Military College moved from Duntroon to Victoria Barracks in Sydney as an economy measure. (Returns to Duntroon Feb. 1937.)

16 *Daily Guardian* (Sydney) incorporated into the *Daily Telegraph*.

Eric Campbell forms the New Guard in Sydney.

18 Sir Douglas Mawson takes possession of MacRobertson Land, Antarctica.

Mar 2 Prime Minister James Scullin re-forms his cabinet, dropping J. A. Beasley and other NSW members, who withdraw from caucus (12th) to form the "Lang Labour" group.

5 Adelaide Bridge (across the Torrens at King William Road) opened.

13 Lyons, Fenton, and three other Labor members vote against the government in a no-confidence motion, thereby placing themselves outside the party.

17 Theodore introduces a measure to create "fiduciary notes" to the extent of £18 million. (Senate blocks the legislation.)

21 Sydney's *Evening News* ceases publication.

ANA airliner *Southern Cloud* disappears on a flight between Sydney and Melbourne. (Wreckage found in the Snowy Mountains in 1958.)

26 Lang informs Scullin that NSW will not meet payment of interest to overseas bondholders on 1 Apr.

28 Special federal conference of the ALP expels the Lang Labour group and the NSW branch executive.

– Holden's Motor Body Builders merges with the US firm General Motors to form General Motors–Holden's Ltd.

Apr 2 Burns Philp ship *Malabar* wrecked at Long Bay, Sydney.

23 Government Savings Bank of NSW ceases operations following heavy withdrawals by depositors fearing reduction of interest or repudiation. (Absorbed by the Commonwealth Savings Bank in Dec.)

First experimental Australia-England airmail leaves Melbourne.

– Federal government begins legal action in the High Court to recover money due from NSW for interest payments paid by the Loan Council on NSW's behalf.

May 5 Nationalist Party merges with the Lyons group to form the United Australia Party; Lyons becomes opposition leader (7th).

25 Premiers' Conference (to 10 June) adopts a plan involving increased taxation and cuts in wages, pensions, and interest rates.

Jun 19 Pitched battle between police and anti-evictionists in Newtown, Sydney.

1931

Jul 22 Queensland government brings Theodore and three others to trial over the Mungana Mines affair. (Jury rules in favour of defendants, 25 Aug.)

Aug 20 First NSW State Lottery drawn.

Nov 25 Scullin government defeated on a motion by the Lang Labour group; parliament dissolved (27th).

Dec 3 Exchange rate of the Australian pound is fixed at £A125 = £stg100.
11 Statute of Westminister gives effect to resolutions passed at Imperial Conferences of 1926 and 1930; the UK parliament would not enact legislation for the dominions without their request or consent.
19 Election for House of Representatives and half Senate; UAP wins an absolute majority in both houses; Theodore loses his seat; S. M. Bruce is re-elected; Lyons becomes Prime Minister (6 Jan. 1932).

* Coinage of sovereigns ceases.
* Brisbane airport moved from Eagle Farm to Archerfield.
* Flooding occurs in all states during the year.

A Architecture, Building
National War Memorial, Adelaide (sculptures by Rayner Hoff), unveiled (25 Apr.).

B Science, Technology, Discovery, etc.
Arthur Carrington Smith develops a system of recording sound on film subsequently used by Cinesound Productions.

C Arts and Entertainment
Sir John Longstaff, *Sir John Sulman*, wins the Archibald Prize.
Hans Heysen, *Red Gums of the Far North* (awarded the Wynne Art Prize).
George Lambert's memorial sculpture of Henry Lawson unveiled in the Sydney Domain (28 July).
Mischa Burlakov (from the Pavlova company) and Louise Lightfoot form the First Australian Ballet in Sydney.
F. W. Thring's *Diggers* (Australia's first commercially successful talking film).

D Books and Writing
"Brent of Bin Bin" (Miles Franklin), *Back to Bool Bool.*
Neville W. Cayley, *What Bird Is That?*
Frank Dalby Davison, *Man-Shy.*
Ion L. Idriess, *Lasseter's Last Ride.*
Arthur W. Upfield, *The Sands of Windee.*

E Sport and Recreation
Hubert Opperman wins the Paris–Brest–Paris cycle race.
Jimmy Carlton equals the world record of 9.4 sec. for the 100 yards sprint. (Record disallowed because only two timekeepers present.)
White Nose wins the Melbourne Cup.

F Statistics, Social Change, the Environment
Estimated population of Australia: 6,552,606.
Commonwealth Financial Emergency Act reduces the maternity allowance and invalid and old-age pensions.

G Births and Deaths
Jan 21 Malcolm Williamson b.
Feb 23 Dame Nellie Melba d. (69).
Feb 24 Barry Oakley b.
Mar 11 Rupert Murdoch b.
Apr 26 John Cain b.

Jun 20 Nellie Stewart d. (72).
Sep 14 Tom Roberts d. (75).
Oct 8 Sir John Monash d. (66).
Oct 10 Sir Bertram Mackennal d. (68).

1932

Jan 29 Premier J. T. Lang says NSW will again default if the Loan Council fails to approve his application to the Commonwealth Bank for money to meet interest debts.

Feb 4 Severe bushfires in Vic., especially in Gippsland; nine lives lost.
28 Central-to-Wynyard section of Sydney's underground railway opened.

Mar 12 Commonwealth passes legislation to take over the liability for the debts of the states and to recoup itself by appropriating state funds. Lang withdraws £1,150,000 in notes from banks and holds them in the Treasury.
19 Sydney Harbour Bridge officially opened by Lang (but New Guard member F. E. De Groot cuts the ribbon before him).
30 William Jolly Bridge, Brisbane, opened.

Apr 5 Phar Lap dies in California.
6 High Court upholds the validity of the Commonwealth legislation (challenged by Lang) to recover money not paid by NSW.
12 Lang directs NSW government departments to pay revenue directly to the Treasury in cash.

May 6 Commonwealth issues a proclamation requiring state officials to pay specific revenues into the Commonwealth Bank by 11 May.
8 Bridge over the Clarence River at Grafton completed, allowing unbroken passage of trains between Sydney and Brisbane on standard-gauge line.
10 Lang issues confidential circular instructing government departments not to pay money to the Commonwealth.
13 NSW Governor Sir Philip Game dismisses Lang from office and asks B. S. B. Stevens, leader of the newly formed UAP, to form a provisional government.
19 Sir Stanley Argyle becomes Premier of Vic., leading to a coalition ministry.

Jun 9 Liberal and Country League formed in SA.
11 Labor defeated overwhelmingly at NSW election (UAP 41 seats, CP 25, Lab. 25); Stevens continues as Premier.
Labor government elected in Queensland; William Forgan Smith becomes Premier (on 17th).

Jul 1 Australian Broadcasting Commission established (takes over all "A" class stations).
10 SS *Casino* founders in Apollo Bay, Vic., with the loss of ten lives.
21 Imperial Economic Conference in Ottawa, Canada (to 20 Aug.), introduces Empire trade preference.

Aug 26 NSW basic wage reduced from £4 2s 6d to £3 10s.

Sep – S. M. Bruce becomes Resident Commissioner in London. (Resigns from parliament to become High Commissioner on 7 Oct. 1933.)
– Ivan and Victor Holyman begin an air service between Launceston and Flinders Island (later extended to Melbourne).

1932

Nov 23 "Dog on the Tuckerbox" pioneer memorial unveiled by Prime Minister J. A. Lyons.
    – E. G. Theodore and Frank Packer form Sydney Newspapers Ltd (to take over the Sydney evening daily the *World*).
    29 Ottawa Agreement ratified by parliament. (Assented to, 2 Dec.)

A Architecture, Building
C. Bruce Dellit, Anzac Memorial, Hyde Park, Sydney, with sculptural decorations by Rayner Hoff (–1934).

B Science, Technology, Discovery, etc.

C Arts and Entertainment
William Dobell, *Boy at the Basin* (painting).
Ernest Buckmaster, *Sir William Irvine*, wins the Archibald Prize.
Paul Montford's statue of Adam Lindsay Gordon erected in Spring Street, Melbourne.
Mike Connors and Queenie Paul reopen Sydney's Grand Opera House, renaming it the New Tivoli.
New Theatre founded in Sydney.
Ken G. Hall remakes *On Our Selection* as a talking film, with Bert Bailey.
Cinesound Productions Ltd formed.

D Books and Writing
Ion L. Idriess, *Flynn of the Inland.*
Leonard Mann, *Flesh in Armour.*
Kenneth Slessor, *Cuckooz Contrey.*
Helen Simpson, *Boomerang.*
Endeavour Press founded, with P. R. Stephenson as manager.

E Sport and Recreation
Walter Lindrum makes a world-record billiards break of 4,137 in his match against Joe Davis (19–20 Jan.).
At the Los Angeles Olympics, Clare Dennis wins the 200 m breaststroke (world record), Bobby Pearce the single sculls (for the second time), and E. L. (Dunc) Gray the 1,000 m cycling time trial.
Peter Pan wins the Melbourne Cup.
Stan McCabe scores 187 not out in the first test of the "bodyline" series.

F Statistics, Social Change, the Environment
Estimated population of Australia: 6,603,785.
Commonwealth basic wage: £3 3s 11d.
Over 30% of the Australian workforce unemployed.

G Births and Deaths
Mar 1 George Chaffey d. (84)
Apr 27 Sir Adrian Knox d. (68)
Jun 17 Sir John Quick d. (80)
Aug 24 Richard Meale b.
Oct 5 Christopher Brennan d. (61)

1933

Jan 7 Bert Hinkler dies in a plane crash in Italy on a flight from England to Australia.
   18 Australian Cricket Board of Control cables the MCC protesting against

"unsportsmanlike" bodyline bowling "likely to upset friendly relations existing between Australia and England".

23 MCC replies deploring the Australian cable and expressing full confidence in the English team and captain Douglas Jardine.

Feb 7 Britain's Antarctic claims between 45° and 160° east longitude ceded to Australia. (Formally becomes Australian Antarctic Territory in 1936.)

13 R. S. Richards replaces Lionel Hill as Premier of SA.

Mar 14 SS *Kinsen Maru* founders in a cyclone off Sandy Cape, Qld; 25 lives lost; 13 saved from a raft.

Apr 8 Elections held in SA and WA; Liberal and Country League wins office in SA, R. L. Butler becoming Premier for the second time (18th); Labor wins in WA, Phillip Collier again becoming Premier (24th).
In a compulsory referendum, WA votes heavily in favour of seceding from the Commonwealth. (House of Commons rejects a submission, and the issue eventually lapses.)

May 13 Referendum carried in NSW for reform of the Legislative Council—to be reduced to 60 members, chosen by joint sittings of both houses, 15 retiring every three years. (Takes effect on 23 Apr. 1934.)

30 Commonwealth Grants Commission established to deal with applications from the less populous states for special grants of funds.

Jun 10 E. G. Theodore and Frank Packer (Sydney Newspapers Ltd), having agreed not to publish a Sydney evening daily, launch the *Australian Women's Weekly*.

24 Collier *Christina Fraser* disappears off Gabo Is; all 17 hands lost.

Jul 1 Rural Bank of NSW (later State Bank) begins operations in Sydney.

Aug 22 Legislation introduced to extend the life of the SA parliament to five years. (Three-year term restored in 1939.)

28 Brisbane *Courier-Mail* first issued (formed by the amalgamation of the *Brisbane Courier* and the *Daily Mail*).

Sep 5 Trade pact signed between Australia and NZ under Ottawa Agreement.

Oct 13 First traffic lights installed in Sydney.

Nov 11 Lady Millie Peacock becomes the first woman elected to the Vic. parliament on winning her late husband's seat in the Legislative Assembly.

* Sister Elizabeth Kenny opens her first infantile paralysis (poliomyelitis) clinic, in Townsville, Qld.

A Architecture, Building

B Science, Technology, Discovery, etc.

C Arts and Entertainment

François Sicard's Archibald Memorial fountain in Sydney's Hyde Park handed over to the citizens of Sydney (14 Mar.).

Charles Wheeler, *Ambrose Pratt*, wins the Archibald Prize.

Alex Gurney's comic strip "Ben Bowyang" begins in the Melbourne *Herald* (7 Oct.).

F. W. Thring presents Varney Monk's *Collits' Inn* (musical) at the Princess Theatre, Melbourne.

First City of Sydney Eisteddfod held (19 Aug.).

Her Majesty's Theatre in Sydney and the Theatre Royal in Melbourne close and are demolished.

1933

Films: Charles Chauvel's *In the Wake of the Bounty*, with Errol Flynn; Ken G. Hall's *The Squatter's Daughter*.

D Books and Writing

Frank Clune, *Try Anything Once*.
Frank Dalby Davison, *The Wells of Beersheba*.
A. B. Paterson, *The Animals Noah Forgot*.
Dorothy Wall, *Blinky Bill*.

E Sport and Recreation

Bodyline controversy comes to a head in the third test in Adelaide (Jan.); MCC team wins the series.
Jack Crawford beats American Ellsworth Vines to win the men's singles at Wimbledon.
Bobby Pearce turns professional and wins the world sculling championship.
Hall Mark wins the Melbourne Cup.

F Statistics, Social Change, the Environment

Estimated population of Australia 6,656,695 (Commonwealth census, 30 June: 6,629,839).
Aboriginal population at its lowest—an estimated 67,000.

G Births and Deaths

Jan 23   Bill Hayden b.
Apr 15   A. G. Stephens d. (67).

1934

Jan 18   Qantas Empire Airways (QEA) formed in association with Imperial Airways of Britain to operate the Singapore–Brisbane section of the England–Australia air trunk route.

29   Mob violence breaks out in Kalgoorlie and Boulder, WA (to 30th) against Italian and Yugoslav communities after the death of a man in a fight with an Italian barman; two killed and many buildings looted and burnt.

Mar 11   Cyclone sweeps north Qld from Thursday Is. to Townsville (to 13th), causing the sinking of several pearling luggers and the loss of 75 lives.

15   Sir Walter Lee becomes Premier of Tas. for the third time following the retirement of John McPhee.

Apr 11   Charles Ulm in the aircraft *Faith in Australia* carries the first airmail from Australia to NZ.

17   Commonwealth Arbitration Court rescinds the 10% wage cut of 1931 but abolishes the "Powers three shillings" and adopts the "C" series index to set a new "needs" basic wage.

Jun 9   Labor wins Tas. election; A. G. Ogilvie becomes Premier (on 22nd).

Aug 13   Towns on Gulf St Vincent, SA, flooded (to 14th) by a combination of heavy rains, gales, and high tides; 2 drown.

24   Mildura, Vic., proclaimed a city.

Sep 1   Body of the "pyjama girl" found in a culvert near Albury, NSW.

15   Election for House of Representatives and half Senate; Lyons government retains office but loses its absolute majority (32 UAP, 15 CP, 8 ALP, 9 Lang Labour); new members include R. G. Menzies and John McEwen.

Oct 4 Prince Henry, Duke of Gloucester, arrives at Fremantle to begin a tour of all states (to 11 Dec.).

18 Duke of Gloucester opens Victoria's centenary celebrations in Melbourne.

19 Holyman's Airways DH86 *Miss Hobart* disappears over Bass Strait; 12 killed, including proprietor Victor Holyman.

21 Charles Kingsford Smith and P. G. Taylor leave Brisbane in the *Lady Southern Cross* on the first west–east crossing of the Pacific (arr. Oakland, Cal., 4 Nov.).

23 C. W. A. Scott and T. Campbell Black win the Centenary Air Race from England to Melbourne in 2 days 23 hours.

Nov 9 J. A. Lyons and Earle Page form a joint UAP–CP federal cabinet.

11 Melbourne's Shrine of Remembrance dedicated by the Duke of Gloucester.

12 Czech journalist Egon Kisch jumps off the *Strathaird* in Melbourne after being refused admission. (Taken back on board with broken leg.)

16 Kisch is given a dictation test in Gaelic and gaoled as a prohibited immigrant. (Conviction quashed on ground that Gaelic is not a European language; Kisch stays in Australia until Mar. 1935.)

24 Anzac Memorial in Hyde Park, Sydney, unveiled by Duke of Gloucester.

Dec 1 Record floods on the Yarra and eastern Port Phillip streams, and in central and south Gippsland; 35 lives lost.

2 SS *Coramba* wrecked on Seal Rocks, NSW; all 17 hands lost.

4 Aircraft *Stella Australis* lost off Hawaii on a flight from USA to Australia; Charles Ulm one of three crew killed.

10 Inaugural flight of QEA–Imperial Airways airmail service between Australia and England leaves Brisbane.

A Architecture, Building

Captain Cook's cottage in Melbourne's Fitzroy Gardens formally handed over to Vic. by philanthropist Russell Grimwade (Oct.).

B Science, Technology, Discovery, etc.

Long-range weather forecaster Inigo Jones builds an observatory at Crohamhurst, Qld.

Ford and GM-H independently produce the coupé utility.

T. M. B. Elliott and Val McDowall transmit Australia's first successful experimental television transmissions from the Old Windmill to Redhill in Brisbane.

C Arts and Entertainment

Albert Namatjira comes under the influence of artist Rex Battarbee.

Henry Hanke, *Self Portrait*, wins the Archibald Prize.

Edgar Bainton succeeds Arundel Orchard as director of the NSW State Conservatorium of Music.

Olga Spessiva tours Australia with the Dandré-Levitoff Russian Ballet.

Melbourne's new His Majesty's Theatre opens (28 July).

Ken G. Hall, *Strike Me Lucky* (film), with Roy Rene ("Mo").

D Books and Writing

Mary Gilmore, *Old Days Old Ways.*

William Moore, *The Story of Australian Art.*

A. B. Paterson, *Happy Dispatches.*

Brian Penton, *Landtakers.*

Christina Stead, *The Salzburg Tales* and *Seven Poor Men of Sydney.*

P. L. Travers, *Mary Poppins.*

1934

E Sport and Recreation

English women's cricket team captained by Betty Archdale visits Australia for a series of matches in which it is unbeaten.

Peter Pan wins the Melbourne Cup for the second time.

Hollow plywood surfboards begin to displace solid wooden boards.

F Statistics, Social Change, the Environment

Estimated population of Australia: 6,707,247.

G Births and Deaths

Jan 22 Arthur W. Jose d. (70).
Feb 15 Graham Kennedy b.
Feb 17 Barry Humphries b.
Jun 5 W. A. Holman d. (62).
Aug 28 Sir T. W. Edgeworth David d. (76).
Sep 5 Sidney Myer d. (55).
Nov 2 Ken Rosewall b.
Nov 23 Lew Hoad b. (–1994).
Dec 4 C. T. P. Ulm d. (36).

1935

Jan 14 Tasmania legislates for triennial parliaments.

Feb 26 QEA begins its first scheduled flight to an overseas airport (Darwin hitherto being its terminus), carrying mail to Singapore to be taken on to London by Imperial Airways.

Mar 25 Severe cyclone on the north-west coast of WA (to 27th); 20 pearling luggers sink and 140 lives lost.

Apr 2 A. A. Dunstan forms Vic.'s first Country Party government, with Labor support.

25 A recently captured shark on exhibition at Coogee Aquarium in Sydney disgorges the arm of a man identified by tattoos as missing ex-boxer James Smith. (A criminal associate suspected of murdering Smith implicates Smith's former employer, Reginald Holmes. Holmes is shot dead the day before Smith's inquest. Neither murder is ever solved.)

May 15 On an airmail flight to NZ, *Southern Cross*, piloted by Kingsford Smith, develops engine trouble, and P. G. Taylor climbs out under the wing to transfer oil from one engine to the other, for which he is awarded the Empire Gallantry Medal (later the George Cross).

Jul 1 Australian Associated Press (AAP) established by newspaper proprietors as a co-operative body to collect world news.

Sep 25 Goldsbrough Mort's nine-storey wool store in Pyrmont, Sydney, burnt out with the loss of 30,000 bales of wool.

– Nepean Dam, NSW, completed.

Oct 1 J. H. Scullin resigns as federal Labor leader and is succeeded by John Curtin.

2 Holyman's Airways' DH86 *Loina* crashes into the sea off Flinders Is., Bass Strait; five killed.

4 Hornibrook Highway, between Sandgate and Redcliffe, Qld, opened.

11 Sir John Latham succeeds Sir Frank Gavan Duffy as Chief Justice of the High Court.

1935

- BHP and Australian Iron and Steel merge to become an industrial monopoly.

Nov 5 Charles Moses becomes general manager of the ABC (to 1965).
8 Sir Charles Kingsford Smith, on a flight from England to Australia in the *Lady Southern Cross*, disappears in the Bay of Bengal.
15 Australia imposes trade sanctions against Italy in response to Italy's invasion of Abyssinia (Ethiopia).

* Australian Consolidated Press Ltd formed (registered in Jan. 1936), bringing together the *Daily Telegraph* and the *Australian Women's Weekly*.
* Grafton Jacaranda Festival first held.

A Architecture, Building
St Stephen's Presbyterian Church, Macquarie Street, Sydney.
Story Bridge, Brisbane (–1940).

B Science, Technology, Discovery, etc.
E. H. Derrick investigates a febrile illness which he names Q fever, its pathogen being subsequently identified by Macfarlane Burnet.
Herbert Sachse of the Esplanade Hotel in Perth creates the pavlova.
R. G. Whitehead develops Tarzan's Grip glue.

C Arts and Entertainment
Sir John Longstaff, *A. B. ("Banjo") Paterson*, wins the Archibald Prize.
Gertrude Johnson begins the National Theatre Movement, directed principally towards opera performance.
Sydney's Criterion Theatre closes and is demolished, half the site surrendered to widen Park Street, half becoming the Criterion Hotel.
Luna Park opens in Sydney (4 Oct.).
Charles Chauvel, *Heritage* (film).

D Books and Writing
Kylie Tennant, *Tiburon* (winner of the S. H. Prior Memorial Prize).
Patrick White, *The Ploughman and Other Poems*.

E Sport and Recreation
J. P. Metcalfe sets the world triple-jump record.
Marabou wins the Melbourne Cup.

F Statistics, Social Change, the Environment
Estimated population of Australia: 6,755,662.
Swimming costumes—for both men and women—in NSW required by regulation to have legs at least 76 mm long and cover the front of the body to the armpits and the back to the waist.
Giant cane toad introduced into north Qld to control a sugar-cane pest (the grey-backed beetle).

G Births and Deaths
Jan 19 Johnny O'Keefe b. (–1978).
Apr 11 Rosa Campbell Praed d. (84).
May 13 Nigel Butterley b.
Sep 2 Sir Sidney Kidman d. (78).
Sep 26 Louis Stone d. (63).
Oct 7 Thomas Keneally b.
Oct 11 Arthur Hoey Davis (Steele Rudd) d. (66).
Nov 8 Sir Charles Kingsford Smith d. (38).

1936

Jan 1 SS *Paringa* sinks in Bass Strait while towing a tanker to Japan; 31 lives lost.

Service pension introduced for ex-servicemen at age 60 or if permanently unemployable.

23 Baron Gowrie succeeds Sir Isaac Issacs as Governor-General.

Feb 1 *Catholic Worker*, edited by B. A. Santamaria, begins publication in Melbourne.

17 R. M. Ansett begins Ansett Airways with a service between Melbourne and Hamilton, Vic.

24 Special unity conference of the Labor Party rescinds the 1931 expulsion of J. T. Lang and his followers; NSW state party again becomes a branch of the federal ALP.

Mar 23 Ampol Petroleum Ltd established.

25 Submarine telephone cable between Vic. and Tas., via King Is., begins operating.

– Voting made compulsory in WA state elections.

May 6 Australian Council for Civil Liberties founded in Melbourne.

22 Federal government announces its trade diversion policy, prohibiting or restricting certain imports from countries outside the Empire.

Jun 25 Japan bans imports of Australian wool, wheat, and flour in retaliation to Australia's trade diversion policy.

Jul 1 Australian National Airways (ANA), incorporating Holyman's Airways, Adelaide Airways, and West Australian Airways, registered as a company (no connection with the earlier company of the same name).

9 Sir Thomas Blamey forced to resign as Chief Commissioner of Police in Vic. for suppressing facts at a royal commission into the shooting of a police superintendent.

22 New Theatre in Sydney defies the ban by the NSW Chief Secretary on Clifford Odets's anti-Nazi play *Till the Day I Die.*

Aug 1 America withdraws Australia's most-favoured-nation concessions in response to Australia's trade diversion policy. (Restored Feb. 1938.)

13 SA abandons multiple electorates in favour of 39 single-member electorates with a 2:1 ratio of country to metropolitan seats.

20 J. C. Willcock succeeds Phillip Collier as Premier of WA.

24 Australian Antarctic Territory Acceptance Act comes into force, formally passing responsibility for the territory to Australia.

Oct 30 Mrs Mary Freer, a British subject travelling to Australia, is given a dictation test in Italian to prevent her admission. (The case attracts much public attention, and after an unsuccessful High Court challenge Mrs Freer is allowed to enter the country in June 1937.)

– Commonwealth Aircraft Corporation formed in Melbourne to make mili–tary aircraft; L. J. Wackett manager.

Nov 21 Hume Reservoir on the Murray River officially opened.

Dec 4 Ernabella station in SA bought by the Presbyterian Church for an Aboriginal mission. (Opens Nov. 1937.)

– *Man* magazine begins publication (–1974).

* Tasmania's first two Area Schools (renamed District Schools in 1973) opened at Hagley and Sheffield.

A Architecture, Building

B Science, Technology, Discovery, etc.
National Health and Medical Research Council established.

C Arts and Entertainment
William Dobell, The Dead Landlord and *The Sleeping Greek* (paintings).
W. B. McInnes, *Dr Julian Smith,* wins the Archibald Prize.
Leslie Bowles, *Diana* (sculpture in Melbourne's Fitzroy Gardens).
Sir John Sulman Prize awarded for the first time (to Henry Hanke).
ABC sets up orchestras in each state capital city.
Tex Morton makes his first country music records.
Sydney's Trocadero dance restaurant opens (3 Apr.).

D Books and Writing
Eleanor Dark, *Return to Coolami.*
M. Barnard Eldershaw, *The Glasshouse.*
Miles Franklin, *All That Swagger.*
Brian Penton, *Inheritors.*
P. R. Stephensen, *The Foundations of Culture in Australia.*

E Sport and Recreation
First Inter-Dominion Pacing Championship held, at Perth, WA (won by Logan Derby, from Tas.).
Wotan wins the Melbourne Cup.

F Statistics, Social Change, the Environment
Estimated population of Australia: 6,810,413.
Paid annual leave first included in a federal award—for commercial printers (31 Dec.).

G Births and Deaths
Feb 27   Ron Barassi b.
Mar 23   Oscar Asche d. (65).
Jun 16   Charles Perkins b.

1937

Feb 15   Explosion at the State Coal Mine, Wonthaggi, Vic; 13 miners killed.
19   Stinson airliner crashes in Lamington National Park, near the Qld–NSW border; five killed. (Plane and two survivors found a week later by bushman Bernard O'Reilly.)

Mar 6   Referendums held on proposals to increase the powers of federal parliament to make laws with respect to aviation and marketing; both rejected.
23   Tas. reverts to a five-year parliamentary term.

Apr 1   First Police-Citizens Boys' Club opens in Woolloomooloo, Sydney.
11   Darwin Town Council disbanded. (Re-established in 1951.)
15   Harold Nossiter and his two sons, the first Australians to sail a yacht round the world, arrive back in Sydney in their yacht Sirius (having set out on 14 July 1935).
20   Regular airmail service begins between Australia and America.

1937

May 29 Volcanic eruptions at Rabaul, New Britain (to 3 June), largely destroy the town and cause some 500 casualties.

– Australia's first diplomatic representative in a foreign country, F. K. Officer, takes up duty as Australian counsellor at the British Embassy in Washington.

Jun 23 Commonwealth Arbitration Court adds "prosperity loadings" to the basic wage.

– Infantile paralysis (poliomyelitis) epidemic begins, most severely in Vic. (to Mar. 1938).

Jul 16 Royal commission into the monetary and banking system presents its report.

26 Standard-gauge railway line opened from Port Augusta to Port Pirie; also a broad-gauge line from Port Pirie to Redhill (and thus to Adelaide).

Sep – National Secretariat of Catholic Action in Australia established, with B. A. Santamaria as deputy director.

Oct 23 Election for House of Representatives and half Senate; Lyons government retains office; new members include Percy Spender.

Nov 23 Spirit of Progress train begins running from Melbourne to Albury.

Dec – *Labor Daily* (Sydney) becomes the *Daily News*.

* Open-cut mining of black coal begins at Blair Athol, Qld.

A Architecture, Building

Foundation stone laid of new University of Queensland buildings at St Lucia, Brisbane (6 Mar.).

B Science, Technology, Discovery, etc.

CSIR establishes a Fisheries Investigation Section at Cronulla, Sydney (later CSIRO Division of Fisheries and Oceanography).

Geologist and explorer C. T. Madigan discovers the kernel of a meteorite weighing nearly 1.5 tonnes at Huckitta station, NT.

C Arts and Entertainment

William Dobell, Mrs South Kensington (painting).

Elioth Gruner, *Weetangera* (awarded the Wynne Art Prize).

Normand Baker, *Self-Portrait*, wins the Archibald Prize.

"Dad and Dave" radio serial begins (–1953).

Films:

Ken G. Hall's *Tall Timbers*, with Shirley Ann Richards.

Frank Hurley's documentary *A Nation Is Built.*

D Books and Writing

Eleanor Dark, *Sun Across the Sky.*

Ernestine Hill, *The Great Australian Loneliness.*

Kenneth (Seaforth) Mackenzie, *The Young Desire It.*

Katharine Susannah Prichard, *Intimate Strangers.*

Helen Simpson, *Under Capricorn.*

Literature Censorship Board established.

E Sport and Recreation

The Trump wins the Melbourne Cup and the Caulfield Cup.

F Statistics, Social Change, the Environment

Estimated population of Australia: 6,871,492.

Commonwealth basic wage: £3 15s.

Assimilation of some Aborigines into the white community adopted as official federal policy.

Ten o'clock closing of hotels reintroduced in Tas.

G Births and Deaths
Feb 14 Walter Burley Griffin d. (60).
Jun   1 Colleen McCullough b.
Jul 27 Robert Holmes à Court b. (–1990).
Sep   4 Dawn Fraser b.
Nov 19 George Rayner Hoff d. (42).
Dec 17 Kerry Packer b.

1938

Jan 5 Royal commission into the treatment of poliomyelitis reports adversely on Sister Kenny's method.
26 Aboriginies meet in the Australian Hall, Sydney, in a Day of Mourning and call for land rights, citizenship rights, and self-determination.

Feb 6 Nearly 200 bathers swept out to sea at Bondi, Sydney, by the backwash of three huge waves; five drown, and 180 have to be rescued by lifesavers.
13 Double-deck ferry *Rodney* capsizes and sinks in Sydney Harbour while farewelling USS *Louisville*; 19 drown.

Mar 4 Assisted immigration from Britain resumes (after being in abeyance since 1930).

Apr – New England University College established at Armidale by the University of Sydney. (Becomes the University of New England in Feb. 1954.)

Jul 1 All exports of iron ore from Australia suspended (ostensibly to conserve supplies; actually to prevent export to Japan).
5 Flying-boat *Cooee* leaves Rose Bay, Sydney, on the first flight of the QEA–Imperial Airways flying-boat service to London.
– At a meeting of 31 nations at Evian, France, Australia agrees to accept 15,000 political refugees from Europe.

Oct 24 Attorney-General R. G. Menzies makes an oblique attack on the leadership of J. A. Lyons in a speech calling for "inspiring leadership" in case of war in Europe.
25 ANA aircraft *Kyeema* crashes at Mount Dandenong, Vic; 18 killed.
27 Parramatta becomes a city within the metropolitan area of Sydney.

Nov 5 Thomas Playford, jun., becomes Premier of SA on the resignation of Richard Butler.
7 Federal cabinet resigns following public criticism of the government's defence policy; Lyons forms a reconstructed ministry.
16 Waterside workers in Port Kembla refuse to load pig-iron for Japan. (Menzies threatens them with the "Dog Collar" [Transport Workers] Act if they continue to refuse.)
23 Tasman Empire Airways Ltd (TEAL) formed by the governments of Australia, NZ, and the UK.

Dec 1 Federal government announces that it would welcome refugees from Nazi Germany.
21 Direct radio-telephone link established between Canberra and Washington.
28 *Sydney Mail* ceases publication.

* Australian Red Cross Society starts its Blood Transfusion Service.

1938

A Architecture, Building

Work begins on the floating bridge across the Derwent estuary at Hobart (–1943).

B Science, Technology, Discovery, etc.

National Standards Laboratory founded by the CSIR.

Australian Pulp and Paper Mills Ltd at Burnie, Tas., begins using Australian hardwood to produce paper.

C Arts and Entertainment

Albert Namatjira's first exhibition held in Melbourne (5 Dec.).

Nora Heysen, *Mme Elink Schuurman*, wins the Archibald Prize.

Contemporary Art Society formed in Melbourne.

Covent Garden Russian Ballet tours Australia.

Five-year-old Joy King records the "Aeroplane Jelly Song" (composed *c.* 1930; registered with APRA by Albert Lenertz in 1937).

Ken G. Hall, *Let George Do It* (film), with George Wallace.

D Books and Writing

Daisy Bates, *The Passing of the Aborigines.*

H. V. Evatt, *Rum Rebellion.*

Robert D. FitzGerald, *Moonlight Acre.*

Xavier Herbert, *Capricornia* (winner of the Commonwealth government's sesqui-centenary prize).

Norman Lindsay, *Age of Consent.*

Christina Stead, *House of All Nations.*

Rex Ingamells founds the Jindyworobak movement.

E Sport and Recreation

Empire Games held in Sydney; Decima Norman wins the 100 and 220 yards track events and the broad jump, setting Empire Games records in each.

Australian Grand Prix held at Mount Panorama, Bathurst, NSW, for the first time.

Catalogue wins the Melbourne Cup.

F Statistics, Social Change, the environment

Estimated population of Australia: 6,935,909.

Some 2,000 cases of polio reported in Vic. in the nine months to March.

Men officially allowed to wear swimming trunks on Melbourne beaches.

G Births and Deaths

Jan 21 Will Dyson d. (57).
Feb 25 Herb Elliott b.
Apr 20 Betty Cuthbert b.
Apr 22 Alan Bond b.
Jun 22 C. J. Dennis d. (61).
Aug 9   Rod Laver b.
Oct 17 Les A. Murray b.
Dec 4   Yvonne Minton b.
Dec 21 Frank Moorhouse b.

1939

Jan 12 Temperature in Adelaide reaches 117.7°F (47.6°C), the highest recorded in an Australian capital city.

13 "Black Friday" in Vic.—the culmination of days of disastrous bushfires; 71

1939

lives lost and more than a thousand houses and millions of hectares of forest destroyed; temperature in Melbourne reaches 114.1°F (45.6°C).

14   Bushfires in many parts of NSW; eight lives lost; temperature in Sydney reaches 113.6°F (45.3°C).

22   Waterside workers at Port Kembla, under government pressure, agree to load pig-iron for Japan.

Mar 14   R. G. Menzies resigns his ministerial portfolios (effective on 20th) and the deputy leadership of the UAP because of cabinet's failure to implement the National Insurance scheme (legislation passed in July 1938).

27   Australia's first locally built military aircraft, the Wirraway (built by the Commonwealth Aircraft Corporation), test flown in Melbourne.

Apr 7   J. A. Lyons dies suddenly; Sir Earle Page becomes caretaker Prime Minister.

18   Menzies elected leader of the UAP; Page (having failed to obtain the return of S. M. Bruce to federal politics) announces that the Country Party would not participate in a government led by Menzies.

26   Menzies becomes Prime Minister and forms a new ministry.

Jun 11   Edmund Dwyer-Gray becomes Premier of Tas. following the death of Albert Ogilvie.

Jul 6   Defence Act extended to cover Papua and New Guinea as territories to which conscripts could be sent.

–   National register of manpower taken.

Aug 5   Alexander Mair replaces B. S. B. Stevens as Premier of NSW.

Sep 3   Australia declares war on Germany immediately following Britain's declaration of war. (Next day, the first Allied shot fired in the war, as in World War I, is fired from Fort Nepean, Port Phillip, at an escaping German ship.)

5   W. J. McKell replaces J. T. Lang as leader of the NSW parliamentary Labor Party following a struggle between opposing factions at the state conference in Aug.

9   National Security Act assented to (granting the executive of the federal government authority to govern by regulation).

13   Page resigns from Country Party leadership; A. G. Cameron replaces him.

15   Menzies forms a war cabinet (first meeting 27 Sept.) and announces that a volunteer division (i.e., the 6th Division) would be formed for service at home or abroad.

28   Price control introduced under a commissioner, Prof. D. B. Copland.

Oct 11   Empire Air Training Scheme inaugurated.

20   Reintroduction of compulsory service in the militia announced (to begin 1 Jan. 1940); unmarried men aged 21 to undergo three months' training.

Nov 19   *Sunday Telegraph* begins publication in Sydney.

Dec 1   Import licensing imposed on goods from non-sterling countries.

18   Robert Cosgrove replaces Dwyer-Gray as Premier of Tas.

20   Short-wave radio service "Australia Calling" (later Radio Australia) begins broadcasting in English, French, Dutch, and Spanish.

*   Yarrawonga weir on the Murray River completed.

*   Youth Hostels Association movement in Australia founded in Vic.

*   National Fitness movement inaugurated by the Commonwealth Dept of Health.

A Architecture, Building

Arthur Stephenson, Royal Melbourne Hospital (–1943).

1939

Central section of the State Library of NSW (–1942).

Ready Mixed Concrete Co.—the first of its kind in the world—formed in Sydney (July).

B Science, Technology, Discovery, etc.

Sliced bread introduced by Sunshine Bakeries, of Newtown, Sydney.

C Arts and Entertainment

Contemporary Art Society holds its first exhibition (includes early works of Nolan, Drysdale, Tucker).

Melbourne *Herald* exhibition of post-impressionist art creates great public interest.

Max Meldrum, *G. J. Bell, Speaker*, wins the Archibald Prize.

David N. Martin opens the Minerva Theatre in Sydney (18 May).

Edouard Borovansky and his wife, Xania, open the Borovansky Ballet Academy in Melbourne.

Lux Radio Theatre launched.

Outbreak of war with Germany traps the touring groups the Vienna Mozart Boys' Choir and the Bodenwieser Ballet in Australia for the duration of the war.

D Books and Writing

Kenneth Slessor, *Five Bells*.

Kylie Tennant, *Foveaux*.

Patrick White, *Happy Valley*.

Literary quarterly *Southerly* begins publication (Sept.).

E Sport and Recreation

Australia (John Bromwich and Adrian Quist) wins the Davis Cup for the first time (previously won by Australasia).

Jim Ferrier wins both the Australian Open and Amateur golf championships for the second year running.

Rivette wins the Melbourne Cup and the Caulfield Cup.

F Statistics, Social Change, the Environment

Population of Australia reaches seven million.

Commonwealth basic wage: £3 18s.

Argentine ants first recorded in Australia, near Melbourne.

G Births and Deaths

Jan 29 Germaine Greer b.

Feb 13 Andrew Peacock b.

Apr 7 J. A. Lyons d. (59) and Brett Whiteley b. (–1992).

Jul 12 Phillip Adams b.

Jul 26 John Howard b.

Oct 17 Elioth Gruner d. (56).

Oct 22 Sir John Langdon Bonython d. (91).

Dec 6 Sir Ernest Scott d. (72).

Dec 26 Fred Schepisi b.

1940

Jan 10 First contingent of the AIF (6th Division) sails from Sydney for the Middle East.

26 R. G. Casey resigns from federal parliament to become Australia's Minister to the United States.

1940

Mar 8 N. T. Gilroy becomes Catholic Archbishop of Sydney.

11 Coalminers strike for higher wages and shorter hours (to 16 May).

14 Country Party members once again included in federal cabinet.

18 War Savings Certificates go on sale.

Apr 17 *Queen Mary* arrives at Sydney as a troop carrier.

18 Six federal MPs, led by J. A. Beasley, break away from the ALP and form the Non-Communist Labor Party.

30 TEAL begins a flying-boat service between Sydney and Auckland.

May 21 Essington Lewis appointed Director-General of Munitions.

– Nine newspapers banned for refusing to abide by censorship regulations.

Jun 8 Sir Keith Murdoch appointed Director-General of the newly formed Department of Information.

11 Australia declares war on Italy (following Italy's declaration of war against Britain and France).

15 Communist and Fascist parties in Australia declared illegal under the National Security Act.

21 Commonwealth government given increased powers to control Australia's resources, production, manpower, and people.

Jul 6 Story Bridge, Brisbane, opened by the Qld Governor.

17 Call-up extended to 24-year-olds.
Press, broadcasting, and film industry placed under the control of the Director-General of Information.

19 HMAS *Sydney* sinks the Italian cruiser *Bartolomeo Colleoni* off Crete.

26 *Daily News* (Sydney) incorporated in the *Daily Telegraph*.

Aug 13 Three federal cabinet ministers—G. A. Street, Sir Henry Gullett, and J. V. Fairbairn—and Lt-Gen. Sir Brudenell White killed in an aircraft crash near Canberra.

18 Sir John Latham appointed Minister to Japan (to 1941).

Sep 6 Prison ship *Dunera* arrives at Sydney with over 2,000 German and Austrian internees from Britain.

21 Election for House of Representatives and half Senate; Menzies government remains in office with the support of two independents; new members include A. A. Calwell and H. V. Evatt.

Oct 1 Petrol rationing begins.

16 A. G. Cameron resigns as Country Party leader; A. W. Fadden becomes acting leader.

26 Last cable tram runs in Melbourne.

28 Advisory War Council formed, with Labor Party participation.

– German raiders *Atlantis* and *Pinguin* lay mines off Newcastle, Wilsons Promontory, Cape Otway, Hobart, and Adelaide (–Nov.).

Nov 7 British steamer *Cambridge* strikes a mine and sinks off Wilsons Promontory; next day, American steamer *City of Rayville* sinks after striking a mine off Cape Otway.

20 Minesweeper HMAS *Goorangai* sinks after a collision with MV *Duntroon* in Port Phillip; 24 lives lost.

Dec 5 Australian coaster *Nimbin* strikes a mine and sinks off Newcastle; seven lives lost.

7 German raiders *Komet* and *Orion* sink five phosphate ships (including three Australian vessels) off Nauru (to 8th).

13 Call-up extended to age 33 for single men.

1940

* Severe drought conditions over most of the country.

A Architecture, Building
AWA Tower, Sydney.
Captain Cook Graving Dock at Garden Is., Sydney (–1945).

B Science, Technology, Discovery, etc.
Radiophysics laboratory set up in Sydney for research into the design and use of radar equipment (Mar.).
Ancient Aboriginal skull found at Keilor, Vic. (Oct.).

C Arts and Entertainment
William Dobell, *The Cypriot* (painting).
Max Meldrum, *Dr J. Forbes McKenzie*, wins the Archibald Prize.
Alex Gurney's comic strip "Bluey and Curley" begins regular publication.
Hélène Kirsova opens a school of ballet in Sydney. (Forms a professional ballet company in 1941.)
Colonel de Basil's Ballets Russes de Monte Carlo gives the world première of Lichine's *Graduation Ball* in Sydney (1 Mar.).
Charles Chauvel, *Forty Thousand Horsemen* (film), with Grant Taylor and Chips Rafferty.

D Books and Writing
E. Morris Miller, Australian Literature (extended by Frederick T. Macartney in 1956).
Christina Stead, *The Man Who Loved Children*.
Literary magazines *Meanjin Papers* (Brisbane) and *Angry Penguins* (Adelaide) begin publication.

E Sport and Recreation
Old Rowley wins the Melbourne Cup.

F Statistics, Social Change, the Environment
Estimated population of Australia: 7,077,586.
ABC appoints its first female announcer (Margaret Doyle).

G Births and Deaths
Jan 15 Keith Looby b.
Feb 17 Marilyn Jones b.
Feb 27 Sir Hubert Murray d. (78).

1941

Jan 1 Income tax payment by instalments introduced.
5 Australian forces (6th Division) capture Bardia, Libya.
17 Jehovah's Witnesses organization declared illegal under National Security regulations.
22 Australian forces capture Tobruk and (30th) enter Derna.

Feb 5 Women's Auxiliary Australian Air Force (WAAAF) authorized.
6 Australian forces take Benghazi.
20 Training period for the militia doubled.
22 Australian Newsprint Mills at Boyer, Tas., begin producing newsprint.

Mar 11 Breakaway Labor MPs readmitted to the ALP.
14 Heidelberg Repatriation Hospital, Vic., officially opened.

20 Seven US warships arrive at Sydney on a goodwill visit.
Trawler *Millimumul* strikes a mine off Newcastle and sinks; 7 killed.
21 Australian forces capture Giarabub, Libya.
28 HMA Ships *Perth*, *Stuart*, and *Vendetta* take part in the Battle of Matapan, in which the Italian fleet suffers a crushing defeat.
– AIF 9th Division relieves the 6th Division in Cyrenaica to enable the 6th Division to be sent to Greece.

Apr 1 *Queen Elizabeth*, the world's biggest passenger ship, arrives in Sydney on a troop-carrying mission.
7 Women's Royal Australian Naval Service (WRANS) formed.
Work begins on a military road from Mount Isa to Tennant Creek. (Completed May 1943.)
10 Siege of Tobruk begins, pinning down the 9th Division—the "Rats of Tobruk". (Relieved, Aug.–Nov.)
25 Australian troops withdraw from Greece to Crete (to 2nd May).

May 10 Labor swept into office in NSW election; W. J. McKell becomes Premier (on 16th).
12 *Daily Mirror* begins publication in Sydney.
HMAS *Whyalla* (corvette), the first ship built at BHP's Whyalla shipyard, launched.
31 British and Australian troops evacuated from Crete, but three battalions of 6th Division are left behind and taken prisoner.

Jun 8 Allied forces (including AIF 7th Division) invade Syria.
21 Damascus taken by Allied forces.
30 Destroyer HMAS *Waterhen* sunk off the Libyan coast.

Jul 1 Payroll tax introduced by the Commonwealth.
12 Armistice arranged in Syria as Australian forces approach Beirut.
28 Some militia units in Australia called up for full-time duty.
– Sir Frederic Eggleston appointed Minister to China at the newly established legation in Chungking.

Aug 13 Australian Women's Army Service (AWAS) formed.
14 Catholic Social Studies Movement ("The Movement"), founded by B. A. Santamaria, holds its first meeting.
22 Prime Minister Menzies makes an offer to Labor to serve in an all-party government led by John Curtin; offer rejected (26th).
28 Menzies resigns as Prime Minister; Arthur Fadden, leader of the Country Party, succeeds him. (W. M. Hughes replaces Menzies as UAP leader.)

Oct 3 Fadden government defeated in a no-confidence motion when independent MPs A. W. Coles and Alexander Wilson withdraw their support; Curtin commissioned to form a Labor government (sworn in on 7th).
20 Australia First movement founded in Sydney, with P. R. Stephensen as president.
– Woronora Dam, NSW, completed.

Nov 19 HMAS *Sydney* sinks with the loss of 645 lives after a gunnery duel with the German raider *Kormoran* (which also sinks) off the WA coast.
25 Legislation enacted to establish the NSW Housing Commission.
27 HMAS *Parramatta* (sloop) sunk off Tobruk; 136 lives lost.
– Import licensing extended to goods from sterling countries.

Dec 8 Prime Minister Curtin announces that Australia is at war with Japan following Japanese attacks on Kota Bharu (Malaya), Thailand, Pearl Harbor (Hawaii),

1941

Singapore, and Guam earlier in the day (Australian time). RAAF bombers based in Malaya attack Japanese landing at Kota Bharu.

Australia declares war on Finland, Hungary, and Romania.

11 Single men 18 to 45 and married men 18 to 35 called up for full-time duty.

22 First American servicemen arrive in Australia, disembarking at Brisbane.

27 Curtin, in a New Year message to the Australian people, states, "Australia looks to America, free of any pangs as to our traditional links or kinship with the United Kingdom."

– Air-raid precautions instituted in Sydney; construction of shelters begins; many people move to the Blue Mountains.

A Architecture, Building

Emil Sodersten and J. Crust, Australian War Memorial, Canberra, opened to the public (11 Nov.).

B Science, Technology, Discovery, etc.

Norman Gregg links defects in new-born babies with rubella infection in their mothers during pregnancy.

E. E. Owen of Wollongong, NSW, patents the Owen gun.

C Arts and Entertainment

William Dobell, *The Strapper* (painting).

William Dargie, *Sir James Elder*, wins the Archibald Prize.

Ola Cohn's *Pioneer Woman* memorial statue unveiled in Adelaide (19 Apr.).

Douglas Stewart's drama for radio *Fire on the Snow* first broadcast (6 June).

"Argonauts' Club" children's program begins on ABC radio.

D Books and Writing

Eleanor Dark, *The Timeless Land*.

J. A. Ferguson, *Bibliography of Australia* (–1969).

Ernestine Hill, *My Love Must Wait*.

Kylie Tennant, *The Battlers*.

Patrick White, *The Living and the Dead*.

E Sport and Recreation

Skipton wins the Melbourne Cup.

F Statistics, Social Change, the Environment

Estimated population of Australia: 7,143,598.

Child endowment introduced by the Commonwealth—ten shillings a fortnight for each child after the first (begins 1 July).

G Births and Deaths

Feb 5 A. B. ("Banjo") Paterson d. (76).

Jul 7 Randolph Bedford d. (72).

Jul 31 Heather Blundell (McKay) b.

Aug 30 Gregan McMahon d. (67).

Oct 1 Sir John Longstaff d. (80).

Nov 18 J. C. Watson d. (74).

1942

Jan 1 Daylight saving begins in all states as a wartime measure (to 29 Mar.). (Reintroduced each year between Oct. and Mar. until 1944.)

4 Rabaul bombed by the Japanese.

14 Australian troops engage the Japanese for the first time in Malaya.

21 Japanese bomb Salamaua, Lae, Madang, and Bulolo.

23 Rabaul falls to the Japanese.

31 Manpower Directorate set up.

Feb 3 Australian forces on Ambon surrender to the Japanese. Aerial bombardment of Port Moresby begins.

15 Singapore falls to the Japanese; more than 15,000 Australians, mainly of the 8th Division, imprisoned; Gen. Gordon Bennett escapes.

17 Curtin cables London demanding the return of the AIF 6th and 7th Divisions from the Middle East to Australia. Federal cabinet orders complete mobilization of Australia's human and material resources.

19 Darwin bombed (the first of more than 60 air attacks); eight ships sunk in the harbour and 243 people killed.

23 Main Australian force on Timor surrenders to the Japanese.

26 Allied Works Council established.

Mar 1 Cruiser HMAS *Perth* sunk in the Sunda Strait; 357 lives lost (and 106 survivors later die in prison camps).

2 Australia declares war on Thailand.

3 Japanese aircraft attack Broome, WA, destroying several flying-boats and other aircraft and causing 73 deaths, then attack Wyndham.

4 Sloop HMAS *Yarra* sunk south of Java.

8 Japanese occupy Lae and Salamaua. Australian forces in Java surrender to the Japanese.

10 Sixteen members of the Australia First movement arrested in Sydney and imprisoned without trial. (P. R. Stephensen held until Sept. 1945.)

11 Registration of all persons over 16 required; the carrying of identity cards to be compulsory.

17 Gen. Douglas MacArthur arrives in Australia from the Philippines.

28 Sydney receives its first shipload of US servicemen (8,398).

– Northern part of the NT placed under military control.

Apr 10 Destroyer HMAS *Vampire* sunk off Ceylon.

18 MacArthur takes up his post as Supreme Commander, South-West Pacific Area, with headquarters in Melbourne; Gen. Sir Thomas Blamey in command of Allied land forces.

– Civil Constructional Corps formed.

May 7 Battle of the Coral Sea (to 8th) forces a Japanese invasion fleet to turn back and abandon its attempt to capture Port Moresby.

31 Three Japanese midget submarines enter Sydney Harbour; one is sunk by depth charges; one tangles in boom nets and is blown up by its crew; the third apparently escapes after torpedoing a naval depot ship (the ferry *Kuttabul*), which sinks with the loss of 19 lives.

Jun 3 SS *Iron Chieftain* torpedoed and sunk by a Japanese submarine off Sydney, with the loss of 12 lives. Next day, SS *Iron Crown* torpedoed and sunk near Gabo Is; 37 lives lost.

7 Japanese submarines shell Sydney and Newcastle.

13 Ration books issued. (Clothes rationing begins on 15 June, tea on 6 July, sugar on 31 Aug.)

16 Destroyer HMAS *Nestor* sunk in the Mediterranean.

Jul 1 Uniform income tax introduced, with the Commonwealth the sole collector (state income taxes abolished).

Montevideo Maru, a Japanese ship carrying an estimated 1,053 Australians

1942

captured in New Guinea, is sunk by a US submarine off Luzon; none of the Australians survive.
21 Japanese troops land at Gona, on the Papuan coast, and advance towards Kokoda (which they occupy on 29th).
25 Townsville experiences the first of three Japanese air raids.
27 Australian Women's Land Army established.
30 Port Hedland, WA, sustains a Japanese air raid.

Aug 9 Cruiser HMAS *Canberra* lost in the Battle of Savo Is.
26 Japanese forces occupy Nauru.
Japanese land at Milne Bay but are defeated by Australian forces and forced to withdraw (6 Sept.).
29 Destroyer HMAS *Arunta* sinks the Japanese submarine *RO 33* off the coast of Papua.

Sep 16 F. A. Cooper becomes Premier of Qld following the retirement of William Forgan Smith.
21 Mass breakout attempted at Tatura PoW camp, Vic; eight wounded; all recaptured.
23 Destroyer HMAS *Voyager* runs aground on a reef near Timor. (Abandoned and destroyed on 25th.)

Oct 9 Australia adopts the Statute of Westminster (retrospective to 1939).
19 Labor MP E. J. Ward accuses the previous Menzies and Fadden governments of responsibility for a "Brisbane Line" plan of defence.
23 AIF 9th Division plays a major part in the Battle of El Alamein (to 4 Nov.).
28 Williamstown Dockyard taken over by the RAN.

Nov 2 Australian troops recapture Kokoda.
9 US serviceman Edward Leonski executed at Pentridge Gaol, Melbourne, for the "brown-out murders" of three Melbourne women in May.
26 "Battle of Brisbane" between Australian and American servicemen; one Australian shot and killed by an American MP and many seriously injured.

Dec 1 Corvette HMAS *Armidale* sunk by a Japanese air attack in the Arafura Sea.
3 Women aged 18 to 30 called up for war work.
9 Optional preferential voting abolished in Qld in favour of a first-past-the-post system. (Preferential voting restored in 1962.)
Australian troops recapture Gona.
16 Voting (preferential) made compulsory in SA lower-house elections.
18 Ban on the Communist Party of Australia lifted.
22 Dept of Post-War Reconstruction created, with J. B. Chifley as minister.

A Architecture, Building

Sydney GPO tower and clock removed as a safety measure (restored 1964).

B Science, Technology, Discovery, etc.

Commonwealth Aircraft Corporation produces the Boomerang, the only fighter aircraft designed and built in Australia during World War II (test flown 29 May).

C Arts and Entertainment

William Dargie, *Corporal Jim Gordon, VC*, wins the Archibald Prize.
Art in Australia ceases publication.
Douglas Stewart's verse drama *Ned Kelly* first broadcast by the ABC (21 June).
ABC radio's "The Village Glee Club" launched (to March 1971).
Kokoda Front Line, a Cinesound Review documentary with cinematography by Damien Parer, wins Australia's first Academy Award.

Federal entertainments tax imposed. (Abolished 1953.)

D Books and Writing

Gavin Casey, *It's Harder for Girls*.

Eve Langley, *The Pea Pickers*.

E Sport and Recreation

Horse racing banned in SA as a wartime measure (28 Feb.). (Ban lifted 30 Oct. 1943.)

Colonus wins the Melbourne Cup.

F Statistics, Social Change, the Environment

Estimated population of Australia: 7,201,096.

More than 12,000 vehicles in NSW equipped with charcoal gas-producer units.

Commonwealth widows' pensions begin (30 June).

"Victory suits" and other simplified styles of clothing enforced by regulation to save materials, and "austerity" meals served in cafes and restaurants. Restriction imposed on interstate rail travel; priority permits required by civilians.

G Births and Deaths

Jan 17 Ita Buttrose b.

Feb 2 Hugh D. McIntosh d. (65).

Feb 24 David Williamson b.

Apr 27 Julian Ashton d. (91).

May 12 John Shaw Neilson d. (70).

Jul 16 Margaret Smith (Court) b.

Sep 3 Sir Mungo MacCallum d. (88).

Dec 20 Roger Woodward b.

1943

Jan 2 Allied troops recapture Buna in Papua.

22 Sanananda recaptured.

Feb 3 Commonwealth government establishes the Universities Commission and a scheme of scholarships for needy students.

5 Australian troops repulse the Japanese attack on Wau after reinforcements are flown in under fire.

8 SS *Iron Knight* torpedoed by a Japanese submarine off Twofold Bay; 33 lives lost.

19 Legislation passed enabling conscripts to be sent outside Australian territories as far north as the Equator in the South-West Pacific Area.

Japanese aircraft flies over Sydney, causing an alert and anti-aircraft fire.

– AIF 9th Division returns to Australia from the Middle East.

Mar 3 Battle of the Bismarck Sea foils Japanese attempts to reinforce their New Guinea bases.

15 J. T. Lang expelled from the Labor Party. (Readmitted in 1971.)

17 Gen. Douglas MacArthur, reviewing his year in Australia, refers to the "Brisbane Line", claiming that Australia's plans before his arrival envisaged northern Australia in the hands of the Japanese.

30 National Welfare Scheme established to increase the number and variety of social services.

31 Australian and American servicemen unload ships in Sydney during a strike by wharf labourers.

1943

Apr – Pay-as-you-earn taxation introduced with deductions spread over the year.
– Prices of all goods and services pegged at current levels.

May 8 Bus carrying soldiers and servicewomen collides with a train at a level crossing near Wodonga, Vic; 25 killed.
14 Hospital ship *Centaur* sinks after being torpedoed off Cape Moreton, Qld, on its way to the war zone; 268 lives lost.
20 Naval installations at Exmouth Gulf, WA—the most southerly point attacked by Japanese aircraft—suffer an air raid (again on 21st).

Jun 7 Butter and household drapery rationed.
11 Minesweeper HMAS *Wallaroo* sinks after colliding with a US liberty ship off Fremantle.
– Sealed road completed between Darwin and Alice Springs.

Jul 5 Royal commission held (to 7th) on E. J. Ward's "Brisbane Line" allegations; Ward does not appear, owing to parliamentary privilege.
20 Cruiser HMAS *Hobart* torpedoed in the Solomons area and badly damaged.

Aug 2 John Woolcott Forbes extradited from the USA for trial on 31 counts of fraud. (Given five years' gaol on 22 Mar. 1944.)
21 Election for House of Representatives and half Senate; Curtin government returned with a majority in both houses; new members include the first women elected to federal parliament—Enid Lyons and Senator Dorothy Tangney.

Sep 3 Agreement between governments of Australia and NZ for reciprocal provision of social services comes into operation.
11 Allied forces recapture Salamaua.
14 John Cain forms a brief Labor government in Vic. before being replaced (on 18th) by A. A. Dunstan's UAP–CP coalition government.
16 Lae recaptured by Australian forces.
22 Menzies resumes leadership of the UAP and the opposition.
26 Task force in the disguised fishing boat *Krait* blows up seven ships in Singapore Harbour (and returns to Exmouth Gulf without loss).
– Eleanor Roosevelt visits Australia during a Pacific tour.

Oct 2 Australian forces recapture Finschhafen.

Nov 25 Australian forces capture Sattelberg.

Dec 22 Floating bridge across the Derwent at Hobart officially opened.

A Architecture, Building

B Science, Technology, Discovery, etc.
Commonwealth Serum Laboratories begins producing penicillin in commercial quantities for civilian use.

C Arts and Entertainment
William Dobell, *Joshua Smith*, wins the Archibald Prize. (Award challenged in the NSW Supreme Court in Oct.–Nov. 1944 by two artists claiming the picture to be not a portrait but a caricature; verdict given in gallery trustees' favour.)
J. J. W. Power leaves a £1 million art bequest to Sydney University (made public in 1962, following the death of his widow).

D Books and Writing
Kylie Tennant, *Ride on Stranger*.

E Sport and Recreation
 Sydney Turf Club formed. (First meeting held at Randwick on 15 Jan. 1944.)
 Dark Felt wins the Melbourne Cup.

F Statistics, Social Change, the Environment
 Estimated population of Australia: 7,269,658.
 School leaving age raised to 15 in NSW.
 Funeral benefits for age and invalid pensioners introduced.
 Means test removed from maternity allowance.
 Zoot suits make their appearance in defiance of austerity regulations.

G Births and Deaths
 Sep 1 Sir Arthur Streeton d. (76).
 Sep 26 Ian Chappell b.
 Oct 10 Sir Joynton Smith d. (85).
 Nov 6 William Lister Lister d. (83).

1944

Jan 17 Meat rationing begins.
  20 Kempsey mail train strikes a bus at a level crossing near the Hawkesbury River, NSW; 17 killed.
  21 Australia–New Zealand Agreement (Anzac Pact) signed in Canberra.
  26 Australian forces occupy Shaggy Ridge in the Finisterre Ranges.

Feb 1 Commonwealth Reconstruction Training Scheme begins operating.
  14 Strike by southern coalminers in NSW (to 15 Mar.).
  – Bushfires burning since Dec. 1943 in the Western District, Gippsland, and Yallourn areas of Vic. cause 51 deaths.

Mar 6 Sydney waiter Antonio Agostini charged with the murder in 1934 of his wife, Linda, the "pyjama girl". (Tried in June and sentenced to six years' gaol for manslaughter; deported to Italy in 1949.)
  31 Pipeline bringing water from the Murray River at Morgan, SA, to Whyalla, on the Spencer Gulf, via Port Augusta, completed.

Apr 15 Fred Paterson, the only Communist to be elected to an Australian parliament, wins the seat of Bowen in the Qld state election. (Cooper government re-elected.)
    News appears on the front page of the *Sydney Morning Herald* for the first time (in place of advertisements).
  17 All Sydney daily newspapers (and the Melbourne *Herald* and Adelaide *News*) suppressed by the censor for defying censorship regulations. (Censorship relaxed on 19 May after a High Court injunction and a conference of the parties.)
  24 Australian forces reoccupy Madang.
  29 Playford government re-elected in SA in the first election under compulsory voting.

May 3 Labor returned to office in NSW with an increased majority.

Aug 5 Japanese prisoners of war at Cowra, NSW, stage a mass escape attempt; 234 killed and 108 wounded; all 378 who escape from the camp precincts accounted for within nine days; 4 guards killed and 108 wounded.
  19 "Fourteen powers" referendum on post-war reconstruction and democratic rights defeated.

1944

Sep 11 Aerogrammes first issued in Australia.
    – Brown-out restrictions removed.
    – Kiewa, Vic., hydro-electric scheme's first power station begins operating.

Oct 7 Strike at Sydney's *Sun* newspaper over a 40-hour-week campaign leads to a complete newspaper stoppage (to 19th); during the strike, the proprietors issue a composite paper and the strikers produce their own paper, the *News*.
    13 Liberal Party of Australia founded at a conference (to 16th) of 18 anti-Labor organisations convened in Canberra by R. G. Menzies. (Party formally constituted at another conference in Albury in Dec.)
    18 Minesweeper HMAS *Geelong* lost in a collision off New Guinea.
    21 Cruiser HMAS *Australia* severely damaged by a Japanese kamikaze aircraft; 20 killed and 54 wounded, including Commodore J. A. Collins.

Nov 4 Australian forces land at Jacquinot Bay, New Britain.
    23 Australian forces replace Americans at Torokina, Bougainville.

A Architecture, Building

B Science, Technology, Discovery, etc.
Russell Grimwade donates £50,000 to the University of Melbourne to establish a school of biochemistry.

C Arts and Entertainment
Noel Counihan, *At the Start of the March* (painting).
Sali Herman, *McElhone Steps* (awarded the Wynne Art Prize).
Joshua Smith, *S. Rosevear, MHR, Speaker*, wins the Archibald Prize.
Albert Tucker paints his "Images of Modern Evil" series.
ABC's Concerto and Vocal Competition held for the first time.
Borovansky Ballet makes its first tour.
Arts Council of Australia founded by Dorothy Helmrich.
"The Lawsons" (later "Blue Hills") radio serial, by Gwen Meredith, begins on the ABC (–1976).
Charles Chauvel, *The Rats of Tobruk* (film), with Grant Taylor, Peter Finch, and Chips Rafferty.

D Books and Writing
Rosemary Dobson, *In a Convex Mirror*.
Lawson Glassop, *We Were the Rats*. (Banned as obscene in 1946.)
Christina Stead, *For Love Alone*.
Angry Penguins publishes the Ern Malley hoax poems. (James McAuley and Harold Stewart reveal their responsibility, 25 June.)

E Sport and Recreation
Cruising Yacht Club of Australia formed in Sydney.
Sirius wins the Melbourne Cup.

F Statistics, Social Change, the Environment
Estimated population of Australia: 7,347,024.
97 merchant ships sunk or damaged in Australian and New Guinea waters.
Commonwealth basic wage: £4 16s.
Reginald Saunders becomes the first Aboriginal officer in the Australian army.
Free public hospital service begins in Qld.
Kosciuszko State (later National) Park established.

G Births and Deaths
Jan 18 Paul Keating b.
Mar 18 Dick Smith b.

May 23   John Newcombe b.
Aug 27   Barry Conyngham b.

1945

Jan 30   Duke of Gloucester replaces Lord Gowrie as Governor-General.

Feb 21   R. G. Menzies formally notifies parliament of his party's change of name from United Australia Party to Liberal Party of Australia.

Mar 24   Captain Cook Graving Dock in Sydney officially opened.

Apr 25   H. V. Evatt and F. M. Forde represent Australia at the 50-nation United Nations Conference on International Organization in San Francisco (to 26 June).

May 1   Australian forces land at Tarakan Is., Borneo.
       9   VE Day (8th) celebrated in Australian cities.
      11   Australian forces capture Wewak, New Guinea.
      30   White Paper on post-war plans for full employment presented to parliament.

Jun 10   Australian forces land at Brunei and Labuan Is.
      20   Australian forces land at Sarawak.
      26   Australia signs the United Nations Charter in San Francisco.

Jul 3   Australian forces capture Balikpapan, Borneo.
       5   John Curtin dies suddenly; F. M. Forde sworn in next day as temporary Prime Minister.
      13   J. B. Chifley, elected leader of the Labor Party, replaces Forde as Prime Minister.
           Department of Immigration created, with A. A. Calwell as minister.
       –   Federal government introduces legislation to nationalize interstate airlines. (Ruled invalid by the High Court.)

Aug 1   F. J. S. Wise succeeds John Willcock as Premier of WA.
       6   Atom bomb dropped on Hiroshima and (9th) on Nagasaki.
      15   VJ Day—Japan surrenders, ending the war in the Pacific.
      16   Legislation passed to provide for the establishment of a government interstate airline (named Trans-Australia Airlines—TAA—in Aug. 1946).
      21   Banking Act and Commonwealth Bank Act come into operation, extending federal government control over private trading banks and financial policy.
      28   Liberal Party of Australia formally inaugurated at the first meeting of its federal council in Sydney.
       –   Taxes increased to pay for increased social services.

Sep 2   General MacArthur accepts the Japanese surrender on board USS *Missouri* in Tokyo Bay, with Australian representatives in attendance.
      24   Waterside workers, in support of Indonesian independence, ban the loading of Dutch ships bound for the Netherlands East Indies.

Oct 1   General demobilization begins.
       2   Ian Macfarlan replaces A. A. Dunstan as Premier of Vic.
      30   Military court of inquiry finds Gen. Gordon Bennett not justified in leaving Singapore in 1942. (Royal commission held 26 Nov. to 13 Dec. finds that he was legally justified in escaping but had shown an error of judgement in doing so.)

Nov 8   Commonwealth Office of Education established.

1945

Strikes by steelworkers, coalminers, and printers break out in NSW.

21 John Cain becomes Premier of Vic. following Labor's election win.
– Commonwealth–States Housing Agreement signed.

Dec 1 Sir Thomas Blamey removed as Commander-in-Chief of Australian Forces.
7 Maitland, NSW, proclaimed a city.
12 Lithgow, NSW, proclaimed a city.

* ALP Industrial Groups formed in NSW to counter Communist influence in trade unions.
* Alcoholics Anonymous established in Australia.

A Architecture, Building
Hawkesbury River road bridge at Peat's Ferry completed (May).

B Science, Technology, Discovery, etc.
Howard Florey shares the Nobel Prize for Medicine for this work in developing penicillin.

C Arts and Entertainment
Russell Drysdale, *The Drover's Wife* (painting).
Albert Namatjira's first Sydney exhibition sells out within minutes.
William Dargie, *Lt-Gen. the Hon. Edmund Herring*, wins the Archibald Prize.
Musica Viva founded.
Richard Boyer becomes chairman of the ABC.
Australian National Film Board established (26 Apr.).

D Books and Writing
Sidney J. Baker, *The Australian Language*.
Robert Close, *Love Me Sailor*. (Banned as obscene in 1948; author sentenced to three months' gaol; publisher fined £300.)
Eleanor Dark, *The Little Company*.

E Sport and Recreation
Rainbird wins the Melbourne Cup.
"Magic eye" camera first tested at Canterbury Racecourse, Sydney (15 Dec.).
Bernborough wins the Villiers Stakes (21 Dec.), the first of 15 successive race wins.
Sydney–Hobart yacht race held for the first time (winner *Rani*).

F Statistics, Social Change, the Environment
Estimated population of Australia: 7,430,197.
Australian casualties in World War II: 33,826 killed; 180,864 wounded.
Commonwealth unemployment and sickness benefits introduced (1 July).
National Trust of Australia formed in NSW.

G Births and Deaths
Mar   4   Gen. Sir Harry Chauvel d. (79).
Mar 27   Johnny Famechon b.
Jul   5   John Curtin d. (60).

1946

Jan – Commonwealth acquires Darwin and its environs to a distance of 16 km to allow for replanning.

Feb 13 British Commonwealth Occupation Force (BCOF), under an Australian commander-in-chief (the first being Lt-Gen. John Northcott), begins duty in Japan.

18 Archbishop Gilroy of Sydney becomes the first Australian-born cardinal.

– Australian Council of the World Council of Churches constituted.

Mar 7 E. M. Hanlon succeeds Frank Cooper as Premier of Qld.

10 ANA DC3 airliner crashes at Hobart, Tas; 25 killed.

Apr 11 Weekly magazine the *Australasian* becomes the *Australasian Post*.

17 Wagga Wagga, NSW, proclaimed a city.

May 1 Wartime manpower controls end.
Aboriginal stockmen throughout the Pilbara, WA, walk off the job in protest against their slave-like working conditions.

2 Commonwealth Employment Service begins.

31 Ansett Transport Industries established.

Jun 7 Australia and the US sign an agreement terminating Lend-Lease.

24 British Commonwealth Pacific Airlines Ltd (BCPA) registered in Sydney. (Begins service between Sydney and Vancouver on 15 Sept.)

Jul 1 Hawkesbury River railway bridge opened.

10 Broadcasts of the proceedings of federal parliament begin.

18 Tamworth, NSW, proclaimed a city.

19 Orange, NSW, proclaimed a city.

Aug 1 Legislation enacted to establish the Australian National University in Canberra, primarily for research and post-graduate studies.

4 Second Women's Charter Conference opens in Sydney.

7 Overseas Telecommunications Commission (OTC) established as a statutory body to take over services previously conducted by AWA and Cable and Wireless Ltd. (Begins operations 1 Feb. 1947.)

22 Six-storey wool store in Ultimo, Sydney, gutted by fire.

30 Lismore, NSW, proclaimed a city.

Sep 2 Wool auctions resume in Sydney (after seven years of government purchase of the whole clip); prices rise significantly.

9 Trans-Australia Airlines (TAA) begins operations with a daily service between Melbourne and Sydney.

28 Election for House of Representatives and half Senate; Chifley government returned to office. Referendum to give the Commonwealth power to legislate on social services approved; proposals concerned with marketing and industrial employment rejected.

Oct 16 Strike of ironworkers in Vic. begins a metal trades strike which lasts to 7 May 1947.

30 Commonwealth Arbitration Court declares itself in favour of the 40-hour week (but sets no time for its introduction).

Nov 19 Federal government approves a proposal to set up a guided-missile range in Australia as a joint venture with the UK.

Dec 13 Australian trusteeship over the former Mandated Territory of New Guinea approved by the UN.

14 National Security regulations extended for a further year.

18 Albury, NSW, proclaimed a city.

A Architecture, Building

1946

B Science, Technology, Discovery, etc.
Lance Hill of Adelaide begins producing the Hills Hoist rotary clothes line.

C Arts and Entertainment
Sidney Nolan begins his first Ned Kelly series of paintings.
William Dargie, *L. C. Robson*, wins the Archibald Prize.
Sydney Symphony Orchestra established by the ABC as a full-time body.
John Antill's *Corroboree* ballet music given its first performance.
Australian Jazz Convention held for the first time, in Melbourne.
Cyril Ritchard and Madge Elliott tour Australia in *Tonight at 8.30*.
Films:
> Ken G. Hall's *Smithy*, with Ron Randell.
> Harry Watt's *The Overlanders*, with Chips Rafferty.

D Books and Writing
Martin Boyd, *Lucinda Brayford*.
Frank Dalby Davison, *Dusty*.
Miles Franklin, *My Career Goes Bung*.
James McAuley, *Under Aldebaran*.
Rohan Rivett, *Behind Bamboo*.
Douglas Stewart, *The Dosser in Springtime*.
Judith Wright, *The Moving Image*.

E Sport and Recreation
Russia wins the Melbourne Cup.

F Statistics, Social Change, the Environment
Estimated population of Australia: 7,517,981.
Commonwealth basic wage: £4 18s.
School leaving age raised to 16 years in Tas.

G Births and Deaths
Mar 20   Henry Handel Richardson d. (76).

1947

Feb 6   South Pacific Commission established at a meeting in Canberra of representatives from Australia, France, the Netherlands, New Zealand, the UK, and USA. (Agreement ratified on 29 July 1948.)
James McGirr succeeds W. J. McKell as Premier of NSW.

15   Referendum held in NSW on hotel closing hours; majority in favour of 6 p.m.

Mar 11   W. J. (later Sir William) McKell succeeds the Duke of Gloucester as Governor-General.

31   Assisted migration scheme reintroduced for British migrants to Australia (with free passages for ex-servicemen).

–   Joint Coal Board, set up to regulate and assist the coal industry in NSW, begins operations.

Apr 1   D. R. McLarty forms a coalition government in WA following Labor's defeat in the election on 15 Mar. Florence Cardell-Oliver, appointed minister without portfolio, becomes the first woman to hold cabinet rank in Australia.

May 5   Sixteen people killed and 38 injured when a speeding train derails at Camp Mountain, Qld.

1947

25 Australia joins the International Monetary Fund and the International Bank for Reconstruction and Development (World Bank).

Jun 1 ABC begins an independent radio news service.

12 NT granted a Legislative Council, comprising the Administrator, seven official members, and six elected members.

30 Qantas Empire Airways taken over by the Commonwealth.

Jul 1 NSW introduces the 40-hour working week for workers under state awards.

3 Sugar rationing ends.

21 Immigration Minister A. A. Calwell signs an agreement with the International Refugee Organization for Australia to accept displaced persons from Europe. (First batch—843 Latvians, Lithuanians, and Estonians—arrives in the *General Heintzelman* in Nov.)

Aug 1 RAAF College established at Point Cook, Vic.

7 Freighter *Mahia* burnt out at Victoria Dock, Melbourne; ten painters and dockers killed.

13 High Court declares parts of the 1945 Banking Act invalid.

16 Prime Minister Chifley announces his intention to nationalize private banks.

Sep 8 Commonwealth Arbitration Court grants a 40-hour week (to take effect on 1 Jan. 1948).

24 City of Greater Wollongong created.

Oct 15 Bill to nationalize banking introduced into federal parliament.

18 Two mail trains collide head-on at Tamaree, Qld; eight people killed.

Nov 1 Nauru becomes a United Nations Trusteeship Territory administered jointly by Australia, the UK, and NZ.

8 Cain government voted out of office in Vic; T. T. Hollway (Lib.) forms a coalition government (20 Nov.).

18 Australia conforms to the General Agreement on Tariffs and Trade (GATT).

30 Australian Regular Army formed.

Dec 1 Inaugural flight of QEA's regular air service to Britain.

13 First election for the NT Legislative Council held.

18 Edward Brooker becomes Premier of Tas. on Robert Cosgrove's resignation to face bribery and corruption charges.

26 Heard Is. and the McDonald Islands transferred from British to Australian administration.

31 Wartime Commonwealth control over the production and marketing of eggs ends, and State Egg Boards take over.

* Long Range Weapons Establishment (later Weapons Research Establishment) set up at Salisbury, SA, with a rocket range at Woomera.

* Barossa Valley wine festival first held.

* Golden Circle factory set up in Brisbane by a co-operative of pineapple growers.

A Architecture, Building

B Science, Technology, Discovery etc.

Cloud-seeding experiments by the CSIR near Bathurst, NSW, cause the first man-made rain to fall (5 Feb.).

Australian National Antarctic Research Expeditions (ANARE) establishes a scientific station on Heard Is. (Closes 1955.)

C Arts and Entertainment

Russell Drysdale, *Sofala* (awarded the Wynne Art Prize).

1947

William Dargie, *Sir Marcus Clark*, wins the Archibald Prize.
Eugene Goossens appointed director of the NSW State Conservatorium and conductor of the Sydney Symphony Orchestra.
Queensland Symphony Orchestra formed.
Graeme Bell's jazz band makes a European tour, initiating an international resurgence of traditional jazz.
Evie Hayes stars in *Annie Get Your Gun*.
"McCackie Mansion", with Roy Rene ("Mo"), begins on radio.
Bush Christmas (film).

D Books and Writing

Jon Cleary, *You Can't See Round Corners*.
M. Barnard Eldershaw, *Tomorrow and Tomorrow*.

E Sport and Recreation

First visit to Australia of an Indian cricket team.
Jim Ferrier wins the US Professional Golf Association championship.
Hiraji wins the Melbourne Cup.

F Statistics, Social Change, the Environment

Estimated population of Australia 7,637,963 (census, 30 June: 7,579,358).
Aerial crop spraying first used in Australia (near Narrabri, NSW).

G Births and Deaths

May 25   Rupert Bunny d. (82).
Jul   30   Sir Joseph Cook d. (86).

1948

Jan   1   Employees under federal awards begin working a 40-hour week.
4   Melbourne tramway employees strike over 40-hour-week rosters, prompting the state government to pass an Essential Services Act (15th).
22   J. S. (Jock) Garden, former secretary to E. J. Ward, charged with forgery concerning timber leases in New Guinea. (Later sentenced to gaol term.)
28   Immigration Minister A. A. Calwell announces that all coloured people who found refuge in Australia during the war must leave the country.

Feb   3   Qld railway workers strike (to 2 Apr.) for increased pay; state government responds by legislating to give the government and police power to deal with emergencies. (State of emergency declared on 27th.)
16   NT Legislative Council sits for the first time.
25   Robert Cosgrove resumes the premiership of Tas., having been acquitted of bribery, conspiracy, and corruption charges.

Mar   2   Department store of Charles Moore & Co. in Adelaide gutted by fire.

Apr   2   Customs Dept bond store in Waterloo, Sydney, burnt out.

May 11   Inaugural session of the South Pacific Commission held in Sydney.
18   Legislation enacted for proportional representation in Senate elections.
29   Referendum seeking permanent Commonwealth power to control rents and prices defeated.

Jun   1   Commonwealth pharmaceutical benefits become available.
24   Rationing of meat and clothing ends.
30   Mail train derailed near Rocky Ponds, NSW; 4 killed and 19 injured.

Jul   1   Citizen Military Forces (CMF) re-established.

Aug 11 High Court declares much of the Bank Nationalization Act invalid.
   16 Rent control transferred from Commonwealth to states.
   31 RAN commissions its first air station, HMAS *Albatross* at Nowra, NSW.

Sep 2 ANA DC3 *Lutana* crashes near Quirindi, NSW; 13 killed, including Margaret McIntyre, the first woman member of Tas. parliament (elected to the Legislative Council on 8 May).
   20 Price control transferred from Commonwealth to states.
   24 H. V. Evatt elected president of the UN General Assembly.

Oct 1 Australia and NZ acquire full rights to mine phosphate on Christmas Is. (Buy out Christmas Island Phosphate Co.'s interests on 31 Dec.)
    First Holden motor car comes off the assembly line. (Publicly displayed and named on 29 Nov.)
   6 NSW coalminers strike (to 8 Nov.).
   27 Covent Gardens Restaurant in Adelaide destroyed by fire; five killed.

Nov 25 Wheat Industry Stabilization Act provides for a five-year stabilization plan with a guaranteed price to growers.

Dec 6 Legislation enacted granting the ACT a non-voting member of the House of Representatives.
   10 Commonwealth Rehabilitation Service comes into operation.
   16 RAN's first aircraft carrier, HMAS *Sydney*, commissioned.
   – Town of South Coast (later City of Gold Coast), Qld, established.

   * Senate enlarged to 60 members (10 per state instead of 6), House of Representatives to 121.
   * Nuffield Foundation travelling scholarships first made to Australians.
   * Dyason Foundation established to finance an annual lecture tour by an overseas scholar.

A Architecture, Building

B Science, Technology, Discovery, etc.
   ANARE sets up a permanent research station on Macquarie Is.

C Arts and Entertainment
   William Dobell wins both the Archibald Prize (with *Margaret Olley*) and the Wynne Prize (with *Storm Approaching, Wangi*).
   Russell Drysdale, *The Cricketers* (painting).
   Sidney Nolan, *Pretty Polly Mine* (painting).
   Tasmanian Symphony Orchestra established.
   Raymond Hanson composes his Trumpet Concerto.
   Eileen Joyce, the Williamson Italian Grand Opera Company, the Ballet Rambert, and the Old Vic Company, led by Laurence Olivier and Vivien Leigh, make tours of Australia.
   Sumner Locke Elliott's play *Rusty Bugles* banned in NSW (until language subdued).
   Bob Dyer's quiz show "Pick a Box" begins on radio.
   Importation of horror films banned.

D Books and Writing
   Ruth Park, *The Harp in the South*.
   Francis Webb, *A Drum for Ben Boyd*.
   Patrick White, *The Aunt's Story*.

E Sport and Recreation
   At the London Olympic Games, John Winter wins the high jump and Merv Wood the single sculls.

1948

Ossie Pickworth wins the Australian Open golf championship for the third time running.

Rimfire wins the Melbourne Cup.

F Statistics, Social Change, the Environment

Estimated population of Australia: 7,792,465.

Commonwealth basic wage: £5 19s.

Cost of Holden sedan: £760.

Migrant intake reaches 20,000 a year.

National anti-tuberculosis campaign begins (Sept.).

Charges for patients in mental hospitals abolished.

G Births and Deaths

Feb 12 Sir Isaac Isaacs d. (92).

Jun 18 Robyn Archer b.

Jun 19 George Sorlie d. (63).

Jun 21 Lionel Rose b.

Aug 7 Greg Chappell b.

1949

Jan 21 Royal commission held (to 18 Apr.) to consider whether E. J. Ward had any part in the granting of timber leases in New Guinea. (Ward exonerated 24 June.)

23 *Sunday Herald* begins publication in Sydney.

26 Nationality and Citizenship Act comes into force, creating the status of "Australian citizen".

Feb 26 Severe cyclone damages Rockhampton, Gladstone, and Bundaberg (Qld); 4 lives lost.

– Commonwealth government legislates to establish an Australian shipping line.

Mar 10 Queensland Airlines Lockheed Lodestar crashes at Coolangatta; 21 killed.

15 Australian Broadcasting Control Board comes into being.

16 Shepparton, Vic., created a city.

18 High Court rules that Mrs O'Keefe, an Indonesian married to an Australian, and her eight children should not be deported.

25 Federal franchise extended to certain Aborigines: (a) those entitled to vote in their own state; (b) members or former members of the armed services.

– Australian Security Intelligence Organization (ASIO) established.

Apr – Ten thousand people attend a meeting of the Australian Peace Congress in Melbourne addressed by the Dean of Canterbury, Dr Hewlett Johnson.

May 19 Royal commission appointed in Vic. to investigate the activities of the Communist Party (sits from 20 June to 6 Mar. 1950).

25 Horsham, Vic., proclaimed a city.

Jun 6 Petrol rationing lifted when the High Court declares the regulations invalid. (Reimposed temporarily in all mainland states on 15 Nov.)

27 Nation-wide coalminers' strike (to 15 Aug.), which causes severe gas and electricity restrictions.

29 National Emergency (Coal Strike) Act passed, freezing union funds and forbidding support for strikers. (Eight union leaders subsequently gaoled.)

Jul 1 Papua and New Guinea Act comes into force, formally merging the two territories into an administrative union.
New South Wales University of Technology incorporated by act of parliament. (Renamed the University of New South Wales in 1958.)

2 MacRobertson-Miller Airlines DC3 *Fitzroy* crashes near Guildford, WA; 18 killed.

7 Snowy Mountains Hydro-Electric Authority established by act of parliament. (Work begins on the Snowy Mountains scheme on 17 Oct.)

26 Privy Council upholds the High Court decision that bank nationalization was beyond the Commonwealth government's powers.

Aug 1 Federal government orders troops to begin operating open-cut mines.

15 Coal strike collapses and miners resume work.

– J. M. White finds uranium ore at Rum Jungle, NT.

Sep 19 Australia, in line with Britain, devalues the pound against the US dollar (£A=$US2.24).
A. E. Monk becomes the first full-time president of the ACTU.

Oct 17 L. L. Sharkey, chairman of the Communist Party, sentenced to three years' gaol for uttering seditious words.

Nov 22 Hamilton, Vic. proclaimed a city.

26 Australia and America sign an agreement in Canberra for educational and cultural exchanges under the Fulbright Scheme.

Dec 1 Unions lift their four-year ban on Dutch shipping to Indonesia.

10 Election for House of Representatives (increased to 121 members) and half Senate (increased from 36 to 60 members); Chifley government defeated; new members include Paul Hasluck, William McMahon, and Sen. John Gorton; R. G. Menzies becomes Prime Minister.

19 Menzies government sworn in; A. W. Fadden Deputy Prime Minister; Enid Lyons, the first woman to serve in a Commonwealth ministry, Vice-President of the Executive Council.

* Poliomyelitis epidemic in most states.

A Architecture, Building

B Science, Technology, Discovery, etc.
CSIR becomes the Commonwealth Scientific and Industrial Research Organization (CSIRO).

C Arts and Entertainment
Arthur Murch, *Bonar Dunlop*, wins the Archibald Prize.
Joan Sutherland wins the Sydney Sun Aria competition.
ABC establishes permanent symphony orchestras in Vic. and SA.
Shakespeare Memorial Theatre Co., with Anthony Quayle and Diana Wynyard, tours Australia, as does Robert Morley in his own play, *Edward My Son*.
Films:
Charles Chauvel's *Sons of Matthew*.
Harry Watt's *Eureka Stockade*.

D Books and Writing
David Campbell, *Speak with the Sun*.
Ruth Park, *Poor Man's Orange*.
Percival Serle, *Dictionary of Australian Biography*.
Judith Wright, *Woman to Man*.

1949

E Sport and Recreation
Cyclist Sid Patterson wins the world amateur sprint championship.
Dave Sands wins the Empire middleweight boxing championship.
Foxzami wins the Melbourne Cup.

F Statistics, Social Change, the Environment
Population of Australia reaches eight million.
During the year the 100,000th British migrant and the 50,000th European displaced person since the end of the war arrive in Australia.
A. A. Calwell calls for the use of the term *New Australian*.

G Births and Deaths
Jul 18 Dennis Lillee b.
Aug 15 Roderic Quinn d. (81).
Oct 11 Sydney Ure Smith d. (62).

1950

Jan 9 British Commonwealth foreign ministers meet in Colombo (to 14th), where Australia's Percy Spender initiates the Colombo Plan for economic aid to South-East Asia.

18 Cyclone moving from Qld to Sydney causes seven deaths and widespread damage (to 19th).

25 Explosion on HMAS *Tarakan* at Garden Is. dockyard in Sydney; eight killed.

Feb 8 Petrol rationing finally ends.

Apr 27 Communist Party Dissolution Bill introduced into federal parliament. (Passed by both houses; receives royal assent 20 Oct.)

May 16 Electricity Commission of NSW established to take over the generation of electricity in the state.

31 Sale, Vic, proclaimed a city.

Jun 8 Sir Thomas Blamey becomes the first Australian to attain the rank of field marshal.

16 Butter rationing ends.

26 ANA DC4 *Amana* crashes near York, WA; 29 killed.

27 J. G. B. McDonald forms a Country Party ministry in Vic. with Labor support following the election on 13 May.

29 Prime Minister Menzies announces that two RAN ships—the frigate *Shoalhaven* and the destroyer *Bataan*—would be placed at the disposal of the UN in Korea (North Korea having invaded South Korea on 25 June).

– Severe gales, flood rains, and high seas cause 26 deaths in NSW.

Jul 2 RAAF Mustangs of 77th Fighter Squadron, based in Japan, begin operational duties in Korea.

3 Rationing of tea ends.

17 Aircraft of No. 1 Squadron RAAF fly to Tengah, Singapore, for duty during the Malayan Emergency.

26 Australian government announces that ground troops would be sent to Korea.

Sep 17 Advance party of Australian troops from Japan land in Korea. (Main body of the 3rd Battalion, RAR, arrive on 28th.)

22 Menzies announces that, in future, personnel recruited for army and citizen military units would be liable for service anywhere.

1950

Oct 16 Railwaymen in Vic. begin a 54-day strike.

17 Australian ground forces in Korea go into action at Sariwon and (22nd) have their first hard fight near Yongyu, north of Pyongyang.

23 Rail strike in SA (to 19 Nov.).

27 Australian forces in Korea win the Battle of the Broken Bridge.

28 *Smith's Weekly* (Sydney) ceases publication.

Nov 11 Adult suffrage introduced in elections for the Vic. Legislative Council.

14 High Court hears a challenge to the validity of the Communist Party Dissolution Act made by the party and ten unions (to 20 Dec.); H. V. Evatt, ALP deputy leader, appears for the Waterside Workers' Federation.

Dec 9 Liquor prohibition rejected in WA referendum.

– Australian troops withdraw from North Korea to the south, and RAN ships *Warramunga* and *Bataan* take part in the evacuation of UN forces and refugees from Chinnampo.

* Bauxite deposits discovered on Marchinbar Is., off the Gove Peninsula, NT.

A Architecture, Building

Work begins on the overhead railway at Circular Quay, Sydney (–1956).

B Science, Technology, Discovery, etc.

CSIRO successfully releases the rabbit virus disease myxomatosis in the Murray Valley.

C Arts and Entertainment

William Dargie, *Sir Leslie McConnan*, wins the Archibald Prize.

Lloyd Rees, *The Harbour from McMahons Point* (awarded Wynne Prize).

June Bronhill wins the Sydney Sun Aria competition.

ABC establishes a permanent symphony orchestra in WA.

Eddie Samuels's musical *The Highwayman* and the ballet *Corroboree* (music by John Antill, choreography by Rex Reid) first performed.

Bitter Springs (film).

D Books and Writing

"Brent of Bin Bin" (Miles Franklin), *Prelude to Waking*.

Frank Hardy, *Power Without Glory* (subject of a criminal libel action brought by Mrs John Wren; author eventually found not guilty).

Brian James, *The Advancement of Spencer Button*.

Nevil Shute, *A Town Like Alice*.

E Sport and Recreation

Australia (Frank Sedgman, Ken McGregor, and John Bromwich) beats the US to win the Davis Cup.

Sid Patterson wins the world amateur 4,000 m pursuit cycling title in Belgium.

Keith Barry sets a world speed record in his hydroplane *Firefly*.

Comic Court wins the Melbourne Cup.

F Statistics, Social Change, the Environment

Estimated population of Australia: 8,307,481.

Female basic wage set at 75% of the male wage.

Child endowment extended to cover the first child.

Commonwealth introduces a free milk scheme for schoolchildren.

"Bodgies" and "widgies" first noted in newspapers.

Sydney has a record-breaking 2,193 mm of rain during the year.

Lake Eyre fills with water—the first time to be observed by Europeans.

1950

Feb 9 E. G. Theodore d. (65).

1951

Feb 19 Melbourne prostitute Jean Lee and her two pimps are hanged in Melbourne for the torture and murder of a 73-year-old bookmaker.
 21 Pensioner Medical Service begins, providing all pensioners with free medical care.
 24 Train and bus collide at a level crossing at Horsham, Vic; 11 killed.

Mar 9 High Court declares the Communist Party Dissolution Act invalid.
 11 Australian forces in Korea capture Chisan.
 17 National Service Act requires males aged 19 to register for compulsory training in the armed services.
 19 Prime Minister Menzies obtains a double dissolution of parliament following the failure of the Labor-dominated Senate to pass banking legislation.

Apr 24 Australian forces in Korea halt the Chinese advance at Kapyong.
 26 R. G. Casey replaces Percy Spender as Minister for External Affairs; Spender becomes ambassador in Washington.
 28 Election for federal parliament; Menzies government returned to office with a reduced majority in the lower house but with control of the Senate.

Jun 8 School of the Air begins, broadcasting from the Flying Doctor base at Alice Springs.
 13 J. B. Chifley dies. (H. V. Evatt replaces him as leader of the opposition on 20 June.)

Jul – Pensioner pharmaceutical benefits introduced.

Aug 16 *Australian Financial Review* begins publication in Sydney, as a weekly.

Sep 1 Security treaty between Australia, NZ, and the US—the ANZUS Treaty—signed at San Francisco. (Ratified on 29 Apr. 1952.)
 8 Treaty of Peace between Allied Powers and Japan signed in San Francisco (comes into force on 28 Apr. 1952); Australia's occupation force in Japan ceases operations.
 22 Referendum to give the Commonwealth government power to ban the Communist Party defeated by a narrow margin (2,317,927 in favour; 2,370,009 against).
 26 Federal government introduces a "horror Budget", greatly increasing sales taxes.

Oct 1 Australian and New Zealand Bank Ltd formed by the amalgamation of the Union Bank of Australia and the Bank of Australasia.
 8 Australian forces in Korea advance to the Jamestown Line in the British Commonwealth Division's "Operation Commando".

Nov – Aborigines holding certificates of citizenship are given the vote in WA.

Dec – Newcastle University College established as a college of the NSW University of Technology. (Becomes the University of Newcastle in 1965.)

 * Division of the NSW University of Technology established in Wollongong, NSW. (Becomes the University of Wollongong in 1975.)
 * Commonwealth Scholarship scheme for university students begins operating.
 * Justice A. V. Maxwell heads a royal commission into liquor laws in NSW.

A Architecture, Building

County of Cumberland Scheme, controlling town planning for the City of Sydney and 68 adjacent local government areas, becomes law (27 June).

Foundation stone laid of the La Trobe wing of the State Library of Vic. (2 July).

B Science, Technology, Discovery, etc.

F. G. McEncroe of Bendigo, Vic., creates the Chiko Roll.

C Arts and Entertainment

Blake Prize for religious art, awarded for the first time, goes to Justin O'Brien.

Ivor Hele, *Laurie Thomas, Esq.*, wins the Archibald Prize.

Borovansky ballet company re-formed.

Aboriginal tenor Harold Blair makes an Australian tour for the ABC.

NSW National Opera Co. presents its first season.

D Books and Writing

Dymphna Cusack and Florence James, *Come In Spinner*.

Eric Lambert, *Twenty Thousand Thieves*.

Seaforth (Kenneth) Mackenzie, *Dead Men Rising*.

Colin Simpson, *Adam in Ochre*.

Dal Stivens, *Jimmy Brockett*.

Alan Yates begins publication of his Carter Brown crime stories.

E Sport and Recreation

Australia (Frank Sedgman, Mervyn Rose, Ken McGregor) beats the US (Seixas and Schroeder) to win the Davis Cup.

Delta wins the Melbourne Cup.

F Statistics, Social Change, the Environment

Estimated population of Australia: 8,527,907.

Price of wool reaches a record 375 pence per pound (average 144 pence), compared with 10 pence in 1939.

More than 1,500 cases and 121 deaths from poliomyelitis reported in NSW.

Commonwealth and state governments agree to implement a policy of assimilation of Aborigines.

Paid sick leave and paid long-service leave introduced in NSW.

Waverley Council in Sydney bans the bikini swimsuit on its beaches.

G Births and Deaths

Apr 18   Daisy Bates d. (91).

May 5   John Flynn ("Flynn of the Inland") d. (70).

May 27   Sir Thomas Blamey d. (67).

Jun 13   J. B. Chifley d. (65).

Jul 31   Evonne Goolagong (Cawley) b.

Aug 24   Brian Penton d. (47).

Dec 22   Jan Stephenson b.

1952

Jan 11   Frederick McDermott, imprisoned for life in 1946 for the murder of a Grenfell, NSW, storekeeper, is released after a royal commission finds him innocent.

   17   V. C. Gair becomes Premier of Qld following the death of E. M. Hanlon.

   –   Bushfires in NSW (which started in Dec. 1951) and Vic. (to Mar.) claim 16 lives and cause great destruction to land and property.

1952

Feb 8 *Northern Territory News* begins publication in Darwin.

Mar 7 Severe import restrictions imposed on all commodities; tourists' travelling allowances reduced.

Apr 1 Agreement between Commonwealth and SA governments and the Combined Development Agency of the UK and USA on development of uranium deposits at Radium Hill, SA.

    3 J. J. Cahill becomes Premier of NSW following the resignation of James McGirr.

   18 Sir Owen Dixon succeeds Sir John Latham as Chief Justice of the High Court.

May 7 Ten people killed and 81 injured in a train crash at Berala, Sydney.

    – Sixty-year-old artist Ian Fairweather sails a home-made raft from Darwin to the island of Roti, south-west of Timor.

Jun 1 Train and bus collision at a level crossing at Boronia, Vic; nine people killed.

    – Serious flooding of the Lachlan, Murrumbidgee, and Macquarie systems in NSW (to Aug.); in Gippsland and south-west Vic. (to July; two deaths); and in Tas. (most destructive in the state's history to date).

Aug 4 ANZUS Council opens its first session at Honolulu.

    – Floods on the Hunter, Macleay, Macquarie, Clarence, and Nepean rivers in NSW.

Sep 10 MV *Awahou* disappears between Sydney and Lord Howe Is; all 12 hands lost.

Oct 3 Britain explodes its first atomic bomb in the Monte Bello Islands, WA (Operation Hurricane).

   25 Buddhist Society of NSW holds its first meeting in Sydney.

   27 T. T. Hollway forms a brief ministry in Vic. following refusal of supply by the upper house; John McDonald resumes office on 31st.

Nov 18 Two-airlines policy legislation enacted to maintain competition between ANA and TAA while ensuring the existence of ANA.

   29 Gough Whitlam enters parliament, winning a by-election for the seat of Werriwa, NSW.

    – Australian Army Observer Unit sent to Malaya during emergency.

Dec 6 Labor wins Vic. election; John Cain again becomes Premier (17 Dec.).

   25 Body of Shirley Butler found in Waverton, Sydney; murderer never found.

    * Severe drought continues in Qld, NT, and WA.

    * Lang Hancock discovers the Hamersley, WA, iron-ore deposits.

A Architecture, Building
Perth Causeway Bridge completed.

B Science, Technology, Discovery, etc.
Australian Academy of Science founded. (Constituted on 16 Feb 1954.)
Jindivik pilotless jet target aircraft makes its first controlled flight.
Alan Walsh of the CSIRO develops the atomic absorption spectrophotometer.
Mervyn Victor Richardson begins producing the Victa rotary lawnmower.

C Arts and Entertainment
William Dargie, *Mr Essington Lewis*, wins the Archibald Prize.
Joan Sutherland makes her debut at Covent Garden in *The Magic Flute*.
Kira Bousloff founds the West Australian Ballet Company.

Kangaroo (film).

D   Books and Writing

Martin Boyd, *The Cardboard Crown*.
Russell Braddon, *The Naked Island*.
Jon Cleary, *The Sundowners*.
Robert D. FitzGerald, *Between Two Tides*.
T. A. G. Hungerford, *The Ridge and the River*.
Judah Waten, *Alien Son*.
Chester Wilmot, *The Struggle for Europe*.

E   Sport and Recreation

At the Helsinki Olympics, Marjorie Jackson wins the 100 m and 200 m track events, Shirley Strickland wins the 80 m hurdles, John Davies wins the 200 m breaststroke swimming, and Russell Mockridge wins the 1,000 m cycling time trial and (with L. Cox) the 2,000 m tandem race.
Frank Sedgman wins the men's singles at Wimbledon.
Australia (Sedgman, McGregor) wins the Davis Cup.
Jimmy Carruthers beats Vic Toweel in Johannesburg to take the world bantamweight boxing title (15 Nov.).
Horace Lindrum becomes world professional snooker champion.
Dalray wins the Melbourne Cup.

F   Statistics, Social Change, the Environment

Estimated population of Australia: 8,739,569.
Inflation rate rises to 21%.
Commonwealth basic wage: £11 11s.

G   Births and Deaths

Mar 10   Sir Benjamin Fuller d. (76).
Aug 17   Sir William Dixson d. (82).
Aug 22   E. J. Brady d. (83).
Oct   4   Sir Keith Murdoch d. (67).
Oct 28   W. M. Hughes d. (88).
Nov 30   Elizabeth Kenny d. (72).

1953

Jan 7   Japan's first post-war ambassador to Australia arrives in Sydney.

22   NT Legislative Council passes legislation to give full citizenship rights to NT Aborigines other than those committed to state care.

Feb 14   Labor wins office in WA election; A. R. G. Hawke becomes Premier (sworn in on 23 Feb.).

Apr 29   Commonwealth Trading Bank of Australia established as separate body.

May 8   Sir William Slim succeeds Sir William McKell as Governor-General.

9   Election for half Senate. (Subsequent party affiliations: 29 ALP, 31 Lib.–CP.)

Jun 8   Britain and Australia sign an agreement for reciprocity in social service benefits. (Comes into operation on 7 Jan. 1954.)

Jul 1   Commonwealth medical benefits scheme begins operating. (Benefits paid only to contributors to a voluntary health insurance fund.)

27   Armistice signed at Panmunjom ends fighting in Korea.

1953

Sep 12 Automatic quarterly cost-of-living adjustments to the basic wage discontinued.

Oct 11 Sydney's *Sunday Herald* and *Sunday Sun* merge to form the *Sun-Herald*, following the purchase by the Fairfax organization of a controlling interest in Associated Newspapers.

15 Britain explodes the first of two nuclear devices at Emu Field, Woomera, SA (Operation Totem; second explosion on 27th).

Nov – West Australian Petroleum Ltd (WAPET) strikes oil at Rough Range, near North-West Cape, WA. (Announcement made on 4 Dec.)

Dec 2 Trial in Sydney of "Mr One-By-One" (Edward Charles Windeyer), who forged £10 notes and used them one at a time at race meetings; sentenced to seven years' gaol.

19 Two trains collide at Sydenham, Sydney; five killed and 748 injured.

A Architecture, Building

B Science, Technology, Discovery, etc.
B. Y. Mills develops the Mills Cross radio-telescope.
Australian Atomic Energy Commission established (15 Apr.).
CSIRO discovers an anti-shrink process for wool.

C Arts and Entertainment
Ivor Hele, *Sir Henry Simpson Newland*, wins the Archibald Prize.
Lance Solomon, *The River Bend* (awarded the Wynne Art Prize).
John Sumner forms the Union Theatre Repertory Company in Melbourne (becomes the Melbourne Theatre Company in 1968).
Dick Diamond's musical play *Reedy River* first produced at Sydney's New Theatre.
Festival of Perth first held.
Lee Robinson, *The Phantom Stockman* (film).
Royal commission appointed to inquire into the establishment of television.

D Books and Writing
Nevil Shute, *In the Wet*.

E Sport and Recreation
Lew Hoad, Ken Rosewall, and Rex Hartwig beat Tony Trabert and Vic Seixas of the US to win the Davis Cup.
Hoad and Rosewall win the Wimbledon doubles.
Cyclist Sid Patterson wins the world professional pursuit title for the second year in a row.
Redex round-Australia car trial first held.
Wodalla wins the Melbourne Cup.

F Statistics, Social Change, the Environment
Estimated population of Australia: 8,902,686.
Total Australian army casualties in Korean War: 1,538, including 281 killed.
Compulsory unionism legislation passed in NSW (though never enforced).
Australia proclaims sovereignty over the resources of its continental shelf.
Fluoridation of water supply first introduced in Australia at Beaconsfield, Tas. (Sydney's water supply fluoridated in 1968, Melbourne's in 1977.)

G Births and Deaths
Jan 28 J. H. Scullin d. (76).
Mar 30 Bert Bailey d. (84).
Sep 1 Bernard O'Dowd d. (87).

Oct 26 John Wren d. (82).
Dec 2 R. L. ("Snowy") Baker d. (69).
Dec 20 King O'Malley d. (95?).

Feb 3 Queen Elizabeth II, the first reigning monarch to visit Australia, arrives in Sydney with Prince Philip for a visit to all states (to 1 Apr.).

20 NSW experiences its worst cyclone (to 22nd), which causes disastrous flooding of northern rivers and the deaths of 26 people; sustained and widespread flooding also occurs in Qld, where at least 10 lives are lost and Rockhampton is cut off.

Mar 1 Earthquake (5.4 on Richter scale) causes extensive damage in the Adelaide area.

Apr 3 Vladimir Petrov defects from the Soviet Embassy in Canberra and seeks political asylum in Australia.

13 Prime Minister Menzies informs parliament of Petrov's defection and announces that a royal commission will be held into Soviet espionage in Australia.

20 Mrs Evdokia Petrov leaves the aircraft taking her back to the Soviet Union at Darwin and seeks political asylum in Australia with her husband.

29 Australia and Russia break off diplomatic relations.

May 7 British interests in TEAL taken over by Australia.

17 Petrov royal commission begins its inquiry.

29 Election for House of Representatives; Menzies–Fadden government re-elected with a reduced but safe majority.

Jun 6 Severe flooding in eastern and southern Tas. (to 7th).

Jul 5 Tattersall's lotteries transfer from Hobart to Melbourne.

12 Heavy rain and gales (to 13th) cause floods in river districts of south-east Qld and northern NSW.

– Large deposit of uranium discovered at Mary Kathleen, Qld.

Aug 16 Federal opposition leader H. V. Evatt appears for two witnesses (members of his secretariat) in the Petrov royal commission. (His leave to appear is withdrawn on 7 Sept. after he makes charges of political conspiracy.)

Sep 1 Telex (teleprinter exchange) service introduced in Sydney and Melbourne.

8 South-East Asia Collective Defence Treaty and Pacific Charter signed at Manila, leading to the creation of the South-East Asia Treaty Organization (SEATO).

17 Treatment plant opened at Rum Jungle uranium mine, NT.

Oct 5 Evatt publicly attacks Vic. right-wing members of the ALP, accusing them of disloyal and subversive actions directed from outside the party (i.e., by the Industrial Groups, organized by the Catholic Social Studies Movement).

13 Seven miners killed by gas in a coalmine at Collinsville, Qld.

Nov 11 Legislation introduced in WA to legalize off-course betting.

13 Australia's first automatic telephone time service begins operating in Sydney. Referendum in NSW on hotel closing hours; majority in favour of 10 p.m.

Dec 9 Mt Gambier, SA, becomes a city.

1954

A Architecture, Building

Australian–American War Memorial in Canberra unveiled by the Queen (16 Feb.).

B Science, Technology, Discovery, etc.

ANARE establishes a scientific research station at Mawson, on the coast of MacRobertson Land, Australian Antarctic Territory (13 Feb.).

Nuclear Research Foundation established in Sydney (12 May).

Stromatolites, "living fossils" built by marine micro-organisms representing the most primitive life on earth, discovered in Hamelin Pool, Shark Bay, WA. (Identified and described in 1961.)

David Warren of the Aeronautical Research Laboratories develops the black box flight recorder.

C Arts and Entertainment

Ivor Hele, *Rt Hon. R. G. Menzies*, wins the Archibald Prize.

Australian Elizabethan Theatre Trust founded (Sept.).

William Orr's revues begin at the Phillip Street Theatre, Sydney.

Films: John Heyer's documentary *The Back of Beyond*; Lee Robinson's *King of the Coral Sea*.

Australia's first drive-in cinema opens in Burwood, Melbourne (Feb.).

D Books and Writing

Vance Palmer, *The Legend of the Nineties*.

Literary quarterly *Overland* launched by Stephen Murray-Smith.

E Sport and Recreation

John Landy breaks two world records, running a mile in 3 min. 58 sec. and 1,500 metres in 3 min. 41.8 sec.

Hector Hogan runs 100 yards in 9.3 sec., equalling the world record.

Peter Thomson wins the British Open golf championship.

"Gelignite" Jack Murray wins the second Redex round-Australia car trial.

Film star Peter Lawford introduces the Malibu surfboard to Australia.

Rising Fast wins the Melbourne Cup and the Caulfield Cup.

F Statistics, Social Change, the Environment

Estimated population of Australia reaches nine million (Commonwealth census, 30 June: 8,986,530).

Proportion of Australia's workforce unionized peaks at 62%.

G Births and Deaths

Jan 10 Chester Wilmot d. (42).
Sep 19 Miles Franklin d. (74).
Nov 14 Inigo Jones d. (81).
Nov 22 Roy Rene ("Mo") d. (63).

1955

Jan   2 "Black Sunday" in Adelaide, with bushfires, gale-force winds, and a temperature of 40°C; two firefighters die and the vice-regal residence at Marble Hill is destroyed.

  11 Harbour at Cockburn Sound, WA, opened to provide shipping facilities for Kwinana.

Feb   1 Six o'clock closing of hotels in NSW ends; bars allowed to open till 10 p.m. (with, for some time, a break from 6.30 to 7.30).

   7 Australia's first aluminium plant, at Bell Bay, Tas., begins production.

1955

19 Labor retains office in a tied election in Tas., in which the first women (Liberals Mabel Miller and Amelia Best) are elected to the House of Assembly.

22 First power generated by the Snowy Mountains scheme—from the Guthega power station—is fed into the NSW electricity system.

23 First meeting of SEATO council held in Bangkok.

25 Disastrous floods in northern NSW; more than 2,000 homes flooded in Maitland and about 100 swept away; at least 22 people drown.

– Adelaide's new airport at West Beach opens.

– British Petroleum's refinery at Kwinana, WA, comes into operation.

Mar 15 Split in the Labor Party over activities of the Industrial Groups comes to a head at the ALP federal conference in Hobart.

31 Federal cabinet agrees to send ground troops to Malaya.

Apr 7 ALP Vic. executive expels 104 Industrial Group members of the party, including 18 members of the Vic. parliament and six members of the House of Representatives, who subsequently form the Australian Labor Party (Anti-Communist), later the Democratic Labor Party.

29 Catholic bishops and archbishops issue a joint pastoral attacking communism in unions and criticizing the withdrawal by the ALP of official recognition of the Industrial Groups.

May 28 Cain Labor government defeated in Vic. election; Henry Bolte becomes Premier (8 June).

Jun 10 Frank Browne and Raymond Fitzpatrick charged before the bar of the House of Representatives with a breach of parliamentary privilege and sentenced to three months' imprisonment.

24 Strike by Sydney newspaper printers (to 15 July); proprietors bring out a composite paper, and journalists and printers produce their own daily, the *Clarion*.

Jul – Huge deposits of bauxite discovered at Weipa, Cape York, by geologist Henry J. Evans.

Aug 30 Pilotless Auster aircraft takes off from Bankstown and flies over Sydney for three hours before being shot down by navy planes.

Australian Iron and Steel Ltd's new hot-strip steel mill opened at Port Kembla.

Sep 1 Advance party of Australian troops leave for Malaya to become part of the British Commonwealth Strategic Defence Force in South-East Asia.

14 Petrov royal commission final report tabled in federal parliament. (No new spies uncovered and no prosecutions begun.)

17 Referendum in the ACT on hotel closing hours results in a majority for 10 p.m.

27 Severe import restrictions imposed.

Oct 19 Opposition leader H. V. Evatt reveals that he wrote to Soviet Foreign Minister Molotov to ascertain the truth of evidence given before the Petrov commission.

27 Aircraft-carrier HMAS *Melbourne* (formerly HMS *Majestic*) commissioned in Britain.

Nov 16 New satellite town of Elizabeth, SA, named.

23 Cocos (Keeling) Islands become Australian territory.

Dec 10 Election for House of Representatives and half Senate; Menzies government returned with an increased majority; Anti-Communist Labor members lose their seats in the House of Representatives (but have two seats in the Senate); new members include J. F. Cairns, Malcolm Fraser, and B. M. Snedden.

18 Adelaide's *Sunday Advertiser* merges with the *Mail* to become the *Sunday Mail*.

A Architecture, Building

B Science, Technology, Discovery, etc.

C Arts and Entertainment

John Brack, *Collins Street 5 p.m.* (painting).

Ivor Hele, *Robert Campbell, Esq.*, wins the Archibald Prize.

Ray Lawler's play *The Summer of the Seventeenth Doll* first produced in Melbourne by the Union Theatre Repertory Co. (28 Nov.).

Barry Humphries' character Edna Everage makes her stage debut (19 Dec.).

Elizabethan Theatre opens in Newtown, Sydney (27 July; destroyed by fire in 1980).

Melbourne's Moomba Festival inaugurated.

Charles Chauvel, *Jedda* (film).

D Books and Writing

Martin Boyd, *A Difficult Young Man*.

A. D. Hope, *The Wandering Islands*.

Alan Marshall, *I Can Jump Puddles*.

D'Arcy Niland, *The Shiralee*.

Patrick White, *The Tree of Man*.

E Sport and Recreation

Australia (Hoad, Rosewall, Hartwig) beats the US to win the Davis Cup.

Laurie Whitehead in a Volkswagen wins the third and last (and longest) Redex round-Australia car trial.

Toparoa wins the Melbourne Cup.

F Statistics, Social Change, the Environment

Estimated population of Australia: 9,311,825.

Millionth post-war migrant arrives (Nov.).

Death penalty for murder and rape abolished in NSW.

G Births and Deaths

Jan 19 Kenneth Mackenzie d. (41).

Jan 23 Sydney Long d. (83).

Feb 10 Greg Norman b.

Jun 6 Max Meldrum d. (79).

Jul 27 Allan Border b.

1956

Jan 1 Australian troops take part in their first action in Malaya against Communist terrorists in Kedah state.

17 Waterside workers begin a month-long strike for pay increases.

19 Two new savings banks opened (the Bank of NSW and ANZ Bank), ending the virtual monopoly of the Commonwealth Savings Bank.

22 Sydney underground railway's Circular Quay loop comes into use.

23 Floods in south-west Qld wipe out the tobacco crop.

Feb 9 Floods in NSW central districts, and in Vic. and north-east Tas. (to Mar.).

1956

23 Shearers begin a four-month strike over a reduction in wage rates.

Mar 3 Cahill government re-elected in NSW, and the Playford government re-elected in SA.

6 Cyclone Agnes batters Cairns and Townsville; four people drown.

14 Federal government in its "little Budget" greatly increases company tax and sales tax on cars, petrol, cigarettes, beer, and spirits.

16 Prof. Sydney Sparkes Orr is summarily dismissed by the University of Tas; grounds for dismissal include misconduct with one of his female students. (Orr sues university for wrongful dismissal; claim dismissed, 19 Nov.).

Apr 7 Hawke government re-elected in WA.

May 16 Britain explodes the first of two nuclear tests (Operation Mosaic) at the Monte Bello Islands. (Second, on 19 June, raises a radioactive cloud that drifts over the mainland.)

19 Labor wins its eighth successive election in Qld.

Jun 12 ALP Federal executive dismisses the NSW executive, replacing it with a "balanced" group of members.

30 Conciliation and Arbitration Act amended to replace the Federal Court of Conciliation and Arbitration with the Commonwealth (later, Australian) Industrial Court (to deal with judicial matters) and the Commonwealth (later, Australian) Conciliation and Arbitration Commission (for the arbitral function).

Jul 9 Federal government announces its decision to subsidize Church schools in the ACT by paying interest on loans for new school buildings.

31 Poker machines legalized in NSW clubs.

– Immunization campaign against poliomyelitis using Salk vaccine begins.

Sep 3 Prime Minister Menzies leads a five-nation delegation to Cairo to try to settle the Suez Canal nationalization dispute (to 6th).

16 Channel TCN-9 in Sydney launches Australia's first regular television service. (GTV-9 in Melbourne begins transmission on 27 Sept., ABC on 5 Nov.)

27 Britain conducts the first of a series of four atomic weapons tests (Operation Buffalo) at Maralinga, WA (other tests on 4, 11, and 12 Oct.).

29 NSW Democratic Labor Party formed in Sydney by expelled ALP executive members and Industrial Group supporters.

Oct 1 Australian Coastal Shipping Commission established to operate government ships, to be known as the Australian National Line.

13 Labor retains government in Tas. in a second tied election.

Nov 1 Menzies announces his government's support of Anglo-French military action against Egypt in the Suez crisis.

8 Diplomatic relations between Egypt and Australia broken off.

10 Prince Philip arrives at Port Moresby on his way to open the Olympic Games in Melbourne (on 22nd).

Dec 1 Train collision at Wallumbilla, Qld; five people killed.

24 *Woman's Day*, formed by the amalgamation of *Woman* and *Woman's Day and Home*, begins publication.

– Australia agrees to provide sanctuary for up to 10,000 refugees from Hungary following the Soviet invasion to quell uprisings.

* Subscriber Trunk Dialling (STD) services first introduced (in Sydney and Melbourne).

* Church of the New Faith (Scientology) introduced from the US.

1956

A Architecture, Building

B Science, Technology, Discovery, etc.

C Arts and Entertainment

William Dargie, *Mr Albert Namatjira*, wins the Archibald Prize.

Elizabethan Theatre Trust Opera Co. presents its first season.

Qld Conservatorium of Music founded.

Sir Eugene Goossens resigns as director of the NSW Conservatorium and conductor of the Sydney Symphony Orchestra (11 Apr.) following the discovery by Customs officers of prohibited imports in his baggage (9 Mar.).

Richard Beynon, *The Shifting Heart* (play).

Smiley and *Walk into Paradise* (films).

Sydney's first drive-in cinemas open at Frenchs Forest and Chullora.

D Books and Writing

Ethel Anderson, *At Parramatta*.

David Campbell, *The Miracle of Mullion Hill*.

Alan Moorehead, *Gallipoli*.

Randolph Stow, *A Haunted Land*.

Westerly and *Quadrant* begin publication.

E Sport and Recreation

Australian winners at Melbourne's Olympic Games: *athletics*, Betty Cuthbert (100 m and 200 m), Shirley Strickland (80 m hurdles), women's team (4 × 100 m relay); *swimming*, Dawn Fraser (100 m freestyle), Lorraine Crapp (400 m freestyle), women's team (4 × 100 m relay), Jon Hendricks (100 m freestyle), Murray Rose (400 m and 1,500 m freestyle), David Theile (100 m backstroke), men's team (4 × 200 m relay); *cycling*, I. Browne and A. Marchant (200 m tandem).

Lorraine Crapp breaks 18 world records while training for the Olympics.

Dave Stephens runs six miles in a world record time of 27 min. 54 sec.

Lew Hoad wins the men's singles at Wimbledon.

Hoad and Rosewall retain the Davis Cup for Australia.

Peter Thomson wins the British Open golf championship for the third year in a row.

Evening Peal wins the Melbourne Cup.

F Statistics, Social Change, the Environment

Estimated population of Australia: 9,530,871.

Australia's first motel opened, in Canberra (2 May).

G Births and Deaths

May 19   Sir Frank Beaurepaire d. (65).

Sep 23   Shane Gould b.

1957

Jan 26   Melbourne *Argus* ceases publication.

Mar 18   "Meals on Wheels" service introduced in Sydney.

Apr 24   Qld central executive of the ALP expels Premier V. C. Gair from the party.

26   Gair and his supporters form the Queensland Labor Party.

29 Commonwealth Arbitration Commission increases the basic wage by ten shillings a week and decides to institute an annual review.

May 1 Federal government announces amendments to the National Service system: number of trainees to be reduced; training in the navy and air force to be discontinued; registration to remain compulsory, but intake to be determined by a ballot based on the date of birth.

Jun 12 Qld government falls when ALP members vote with the opposition to block supply.

22 Closing of the Adaminaby Dam outlet gates completes the second major phase of the Snowy Mountains scheme.

26 Melbourne *Leader* ceases publication.

Jul 6 Australia and Japan sign a trade agreement on most-favoured-nation terms.

13 Australia and the US conclude an agreement concerning atomic information for mutual defence purposes.

– Asian flu epidemic breaks out.

Aug 3 Labor loses office in Qld after 25 years in power; G. F. R. Nicklin becomes Premier (12 Aug.).

27 State anti-Communist Labor breakaway groups form the national Democratic Labor Party, with Senator George Cole as parliamentary leader.

Sep 14 Britain conducts the first of three Operation Antler nuclear weapons tests at Maralinga, WA (other tests on 25 Sept. and 9 Oct.).

Oct 4 Ansett Transport Industries takes over Australian National Airways, becoming Ansett–ANA.

21 Australia's first automatic telephone weather service begins in Melbourne.

Nov 6 Special Christmas postage stamps issued for the first time.

– Wyndham committee reports on secondary education in NSW. (Wyndham Scheme not introduced until 1962.)

Dec 2 Bushfires in the Blue Mountains, NSW, destroy 158 houses and cause the deaths of five people.

– National executive of "The Movement" leave that organization and subsequently form the National Civic Council, with B. A. Santamaria as president.

* Mount Whaleback iron ore deposits discovered by prospector Stan Hilditch.

A Architecture, Building

Joern Utzon of Denmark wins the competition for a design for Sydney's Opera House.

National Capital Development Commission established to carry out the planning, development, and construction of Canberra.

B Science, Technology, Discovery, etc.

Davis scientific research station established on the coast of Princess Elizabeth Land, Antarctica, by ANARE (13 Jan.).

International Geophysical Year begins (1 July), over 250 Australian scientists taking part.

C Arts and Entertainment

William Dobell, *Dame Mary Gilmore* (painting).

Arthur Boyd begins his "Love, Marriage and Death of a Half-Caste" series of paintings (–1959).

Ivor Hele, *Self Portrait*, wins the Archibald Prize.

Slim Dusty's "A Pub With No Beer" awarded Australia's first gold record.

1957

Peter Scriven's *Tintookies* puppets and the musical *Lola Montez* first presented.
Bob Dyer's quiz show "Pick a Box" begins on television.
The Shiralee (film), with Peter Finch.

D Books and Writing

Martin Boyd, *Outbreak of Love*.
"Nino Culotta" (John O'Grady), *They're a Weird Mob*.
John Passmore, *A Hundred Years of Philosophy*.
Vance Palmer, *Seedtime*.
Nevil Shute, *On the Beach*.
Patrick White, *Voss* (winner of the inaugural Miles Franklin Award).
Australian Letters begins publication.

E Sport and Recreation

Lew Hoad wins the men's singles at Wimbledon for the second year running.
Australia (Mal Anderson, Ashley Cooper, Mervyn Rose) wins the Davis Cup.
Australian Soccer Federation formed.
Straight Draw wins the Melbourne Cup.
The hula hoop, developed by Australian toy manufacturer Alex Tolmer, begins a ten-year international craze.

F Statistics, Social Change, the Environment

Estimated population of Australia: 9,744,087.
Commonwealth basic wage: £12 16s.
Aboriginal artist Albert Namatjira granted full Australian citizenship.

G Births and Deaths

Jan 11 Sir Robert Garran d. (89).
Feb 27 Robert de Castella b.

1958

Jan 10 First Opera House lottery drawn in NSW.
14 Qantas inaugurates a round-the-world air service.
20 Royal Australian Naval College transferred from Flinders Naval Depot back to Jervis Bay.
28 British Prime Minister Harold Macmillan arrives in Sydney for a two-week visit to Australia, the first by a British PM in office.

Feb 14 Queen Elizabeth the Queen Mother arrives in Canberra to begin a visit to all states (to 7 Mar.).
22 Fortnightly journal the *Observer* begins publication in Sydney (–1961).

Mar 21 John McEwen succeeds Sir Arthur Fadden as federal Country Party leader.
24 Sydney's Cahill Expressway opened. (Completed to Woolloomooloo in 1962.)

Apr 3 Cyclone damages or destroys nearly every building in Bowen, Qld.
5 Bushfire near Glencoe, SA; eight fire-fighters die.
15 Monash University, Melbourne, established by act of parliament.

May 11 Work finishes on Adaminaby Dam, completing Lake Eucumbene (4,807 mil. kilolitres capacity).
31 Bolte government re-elected in Vic.

Jul 19 Trams cease running in Perth.

Aug 26 Eric Reece succeeds Robert Cosgrove as Premier of Tas.

Sep 26 Fortnightly independent journal *Nation*, founded by T. M. Fitzgerald, begins publication in Sydney (–1972).

Oct 1 Administration of Christmas Is. in the Indian Ocean transferred from British-ruled Singapore to Australia.

7 Albert Namatjira sentenced to six months' gaol (reduced on appeal to three months) for supplying liquor to another Aboriginal.

26 Wreckage of the airliner *Southern Cloud*, lost in 1931, found in the Snowy Mountains.

Nov 20 Australia linked with Britain, Canada, the USA, and Japan by telex.
Australian Association of Airline Pilots strike over wages (to 27th).

22 Election for House of Representatives and half Senate; Menzies government returned with a substantial majority helped by DLP preferences.
Trams cease running in Adelaide (except on the line from city to Glenelg).

Dec 10 Agreement reached in Canberra between Australia and the Netherlands on administrative problems of New Guinea.
Legislation enacted in NSW to prevent the defamation of dead as well as living persons.

20 Aboriginal itinerant worker Rupert Max Stuart murders nine-year-old Mary Hattam at Ceduna, SA. (Stuart is subsequently sentenced to death, but after a series of appeals, a royal commission, and much public controversy, his sentence is commuted to life imprisonment.)

A Architecture, Building

B Science, Technology, Discovery, etc.
Australia's first nuclear reactor, at Lucas Heights, NSW, becomes operational (18 Apr.).

C Arts and Entertainment
W. E. Pidgeon, *Mr Ray Walker*, wins the Archibald Prize.
National Institute of Dramatic Art (NIDA) established at the University of NSW.
"Bandstand", hosted by Brian Henderson, begins on television.

D Books and Writing
Australian Encyclopaedia (10 vols.).
Christopher Koch, *The Boys in the Island*.
Jack Lindsay, *Life Rarely Tells*.
Cyril Pearl, *Wild Men of Sydney*.
A. A. Phillips, *The Australian Tradition*.
J. M. D. Pringle, *Australian Accent*.
Randolph Stow, *To the Islands* (Miles Franklin Award winner).
Russel Ward, *The Australian Legend*.

E Sport and Recreation
Herb Elliott runs a world record 3 min. 54.5 sec. for the mile.
Marlene Mathews wins the Australian 100 and 220 yards championships in world record times.
Ashley Cooper wins the men's singles at Wimbledon.
Baystone wins the Melbourne Cup.

F Statistics, Social Change, the Environment
Estimated population of Australia: 9,947,358.
Three weeks' annual leave granted to all employees under NSW awards (effective from 1 Jan. 1959).
Legislation enacted in NSW to provide for equal pay for "work of the same or

1958

like nature and of equal value" performed by men and women (female wage to be increased progressively).

Clean Air Act passed in Vic., the first state to legislate to control air pollution.

Uluru National Park (Ayers Rock–Mt Olga), NT, proclaimed.

G Births and Deaths

Feb 17 Hugh McCrae d. (81).
Apr 8 Ethel Turner d. (88).
Jul 2 Mary Grant Bruce d. (80).
Oct 14 Sir Douglas Mawson d. (76).
Nov 30 Sir Hubert Wilkins d. (70).

1959

Jan 26 Darwin attains city status.

Feb 12 Evangelist Billy Graham arrives in Sydney to begin his first crusade in Australia (to 31 May).
16 Cyclone Connie, the most powerful cyclone for forty years, causes severe damage and the death of one man at Bowen, Qld.
23 National Heart Foundation formed at a conference in Canberra.

Mar 7 Playford government re-elected in SA; new MPs include Joyce Steele and Jessie Cooper, the first women elected to the SA parliament.
21 Labor loses office in WA election; David Brand becomes Premier of a coalition government.
Cahill government re-elected in NSW by a narrow majority.

May 2 Reece Labor government re-elected in Tas.
4 First major power station of the Snowy Mountains scheme (T1 underground station) begins operating.
7 Legislation enacted establishing a permanent Australian Universities Commission.
– Town of South Coast, Qld, reconstituted as the City of Gold Coast.

Jun 1 Migration Act comes into force, abolishing the dictation test as means of excluding ineligible persons entering Australia and substituting an entry permit.
4 Australia and the Soviet Union resume diplomatic relations.

Jul 2 Qantas receives its first 707 jet aircraft (which makes its initial flight, to San Francisco, on the 29th).

Aug 14 Princess Alexandra arrives in Australia for the Qld centenary celebrations (leaves 26 Sept.).

Oct 2 ANL's vehicular ferry *Princess of Tasmania* begins operations between Melbourne and Devonport, inaugurating the roll-on/roll-off concept.
19 Australia and the United Arab Republic (Egypt) agree to resume diplomatic relations.
22 R. J. Heffron becomes Premier of NSW on the death of J. J. Cahill (sworn in on 28th).

Nov 26 National Service training scheme suspended.
27 Commonwealth Conciliation and Arbitration Commission increases margins for skill in the metal trades by 28%.

Dec 1 Australia and eleven other nations sign a thirty-year treaty in Washington to preserve Antarctica for peaceful scientific research and to retain the status quo of sovereignty.

A Architecture, Building

Work begins on the Sydney Opera House (plaque laid by J. J. Cahill, 2 Mar.).
Roy Grounds, Academy of Science building, Canberra, completed (official opening, 7 May).
Narrows Bridge, Perth, completed.

B Science, Technology, Discovery, etc.

Australia takes over custody of Wilkes Antarctic research station from the USA (Feb.).

C Arts and Entertainment

William Dobell, *Dr Edward McMahon*, wins the Archibald Prize.
Myer Music Bowl, Melbourne, opened (Feb.).
Peter Kenna, *The Slaughter of Saint Teresa's Day* (play).
Theatre Royal, Brisbane, closes down.
Summer of the Seventeenth Doll and *On the Beach* (films).

D Books and Writing

Mary Durack, *Kings in Grass Castles.*
Vance Palmer, *The Big Fellow* (winner Miles Franklin Award).
Morris West, *The Devil's Advocate.*
Judith Wright, *The Generations of Men.*

E Sport and Recreation

Jack Brabham wins the world motor-racing championship.
Australia (Neale Fraser, Roy Emerson, Rod Laver) wins the Davis Cup.
Macdougal wins the Melbourne Cup.

F Statistics, Social Change, the Environment

Population of Australia reaches ten million.
Australia receives its 1,500,000th migrant since 1945.
Working hours in state-owned coalmines in NSW reduced to 37½ a week.
Legislation introduced into federal parliament to provide for a uniform code of divorce law throughout Australia (grounds for divorce reduced to 14).

G Births and Deaths

Apr 2 Raymond Longford d. (80?).
Jun 20 Sir Ian Clunies Ross d. (60).
Jul 15 Vance Palmer d. (73).
Aug 8 Albert Namatjira d. (57).
Sep 11 Percy Leason d. (70).
Oct 14 Jack Davey d. (52) and Errol Flynn d. (50).
Oct 22 J. J. Cahill d. (68).
Nov 11 Charles Chauvel d. (62).
Nov 24 Dally Messenger d. (76).
Dec 18 Edouard Borovansky d. (57).

1960

Jan 14 Three federal banking bodies established in 1959—the Reserve Bank of Australia, the Commonwealth Development Bank, and the Commonwealth Banking Corporation—begin operations.

1960

Feb 1   Australian Council of Churches holds its first national conference.
      2   Viscount Dunrossil succeeds Lord Slim as Governor-General.
    10   H. V. Evatt resigns as leader of the federal opposition and (15th) becomes Chief Justice of the NSW Supreme Court.
    23   Import licensing removed from 90% of all imported goods.
    26   Seven people die when a bridge collapses under a train at Bogantungan, Qld.

Mar 1   Charge for Pharmaceutical Benefits Scheme prescriptions introduced.
      7   Arthur Calwell elected federal ALP leader to replace Evatt.
    26   Cyclone strikes Carnarvon, WA; houses blown away; town flooded.

Apr 21   New Commonwealth Police Force, incorporating the Peace Officers and the Commonwealth Investigation Service, begins operations.
    22   Severe floods in the Derwent Valley, Tas. (to 23rd); Hobart business basements under water and houses swept away.

May 11   Futures trading begins in Australia with the establishment of Sydney's Greasy Wool Futures Exchange.
    19   Legislation passed prohibiting telephone tapping except in the interests of national security.
    28   Nicklin coalition government re-elected in Qld.

Jun 3   First of the "Mutilator" murders discovered in Sydney.
    10   TAA Fokker Friendship *Abel Tasman* crashes into the sea off Mackay, Qld; 29 killed.
    30   National Service training officially ends; remaining trainees discharged.

Jul 7   Eight-year-old Graeme Thorne, son of an Opera House lottery winner, is kidnapped on his way home from school in Sydney; kidnapper demands £25,000 ransom.

Aug 16   Body of Graeme Thorne found at Seaforth. (Police arrest killer Stephen Bradley at Colombo on his way to England on 10 Oct.)
    –   Consumer Price Index (CPI) compiled for the first time (retrospectively to the Sept. quarter 1948), to replace the "C" series index.
    –   NSW Humanist Society founded (as the Sydney Humanist Group).

Oct 14   Warragamba Dam, NSW, officially opened (begun in 1948).

Nov 15   Treasurer Harold Holt introduces a credit squeeze, raising interest rates and heavily increasing sales tax on motor vehicles.

Dec 3   Commonwealth relaxes its 22-year-old embargo on the export of iron ore.
      7   National Library of Australia, Canberra, formerly part of the Commonwealth Parliamentary Library, established as an independent institution.
    20   Australia's first commercial heliport opens in Melbourne on the Yarra.

A Architecture, Building
    Harry Seidler, Australia Square, Sydney (–1967).

B Science, Technology, Discovery, etc.
    Sir Macfarlane Burnet shares the Nobel Prize for medicine with Sir Peter Medawar for their work on acquired immunological tolerance.

C Arts and Entertainment
    Judy Cassab, *Stanislaus Rapotec*, wins the Archibald Prize.
    Rolf Harris composes and records "Tie Me Kangaroo Down, Sport".
    Adelaide Festival of the Arts first held.
    Albert Arlen's musical *The Sentimental Bloke* first produced.
    The Sundowners (film).

D Books and Writing

Thea Astley, *A Descant for Gossips.*
Robin Boyd, *The Australian Ugliness.*
Jack Lindsay, *The Roaring Twenties.*
Elizabeth O'Conner, *The Irishman* (Miles Franklin Award winner).
Bernard Smith, *European Vision and the South Pacific 1767–1850.*

E Sport and Recreation

Australian winners at the Rome Olympic Games: *athletics*, Herb Elliott
(1,500 m); *swimming*, Dawn Fraser (100 m freestyle), John Devitt (100 m
freestyle), Murray Rose (400 m freestyle), John Konrads (1,500 m freestyle),
David Theile (100 m backstroke); *equestrian*, Laurie Morgan (indiv. event),
Australian team (3-day trial).

Dawn Fraser sets five world records at the Australian swimming championships.

Neale Fraser wins the men's singles at Wimbledon.

Australia (Fraser, Emerson, Laver) retains the Davis Cup.

First cricket test between Australia and the West Indies ends in a tie after a throw
out on the second-last delivery with both teams twice dismissed and the scores
level.

James Hardie 1,000 motor race first held (as the Armstrong 500; later the Hardie
Ferodo 500) at Phillip Is., Vic.

Jack Brabham wins the world motor-racing championship for the second year in
a row.

Hi Jinx wins the centenary Melbourne Cup (NZ horses taking first three places).

F Statistics, Social Change, the Environment

Estimated population of Australia: 10,391,920.
Provision made for Social Service Benefits to be paid to Aborigines.

G Births and Deaths

Jan 12   Nevil Shute d. (60).
Apr 10   Arthur Benjamin d. (66).
Jul 30   Walter Lindrum d. (61).
Oct 30   Alfred Hill d. (89).

1961

Jan 9   Myer Emporium Ltd takes over Farmer & Co. of Sydney.

Feb 1   Commonwealth Matrimonial Causes Act of 1959 comes into operation
unifying state divorce laws.
25   Last trams run in Sydney.

Mar 2   Three timber towns in south-west WA—Karridale, Pemberton, and Augusta—
destroyed by bushfires (to 5th).
16   Monash University opens in Melbourne.
29   Stephen Bradley, kidnapper of Graeme Thorne, found guilty of murder and
sentenced to life imprisonment.
31   Maryborough, Vic., declared a city.

Apr 20   "C" series retail price index discontinued.
29   NSW votes at referendum to retain the Legislative Council.

Jun 21   First aircraft to fly non-stop from UK to Australia (RAF Vulcan jet bomber)
arrives at Richmond, NSW, after refuelling in mid-air three times during the
20-hour flight.

1961

29 Australia and the US announce a joint guided missile research project to be carried out at Woomera, SA.

Jul 15 Bolte government re-elected in Vic. with the help of a solid DLP vote; government majority slightly reduced.

26 Australia sells its interests in Tasman Empire Airways to NZ.

Aug 1 International trade fair opens in Sydney (to 12th).

3 Viscount De L'Isle becomes Governor-General following the death of Lord Dunrossil on 3 Feb.

9 Australia's last coastal passenger liner, the *Manoora* (sold to Indonesia on 3 July), arrives in Sydney at the end of its last interstate voyage.

Oct 19 Whyalla, SA, becomes a city.

24 *Australian Financial Review* changes from weekly to twice-weekly publication.

Nov 6 Artist Leonard Lawson, released in May after serving seven years of a 14-year sentence for the rape of two models at Terrey Hills (Syd.), rapes and kills a 16-year-old girl at Collaroy and then attempts to take several students hostage at Moss Vale where one girl is shot dead.

12 Discovery of vast iron-ore deposits in the Pilbara, WA, announced.

30 Viscount aircraft crashes into Botany Bay soon after take-off from Sydney Airport; all 15 on board killed.

Dec 3 Australia's first commercially proved oilfield discovered at Moonie, some 300 km west of Brisbane.

9 Election for House of Representatives and half Senate; Menzies government returned (as a result of DLP preferences), but with a majority in the House of Representatives of one after electing a Speaker; new members include Bill Hayden and Sen. Lionel Murphy.

30 Australian government expresses its concern over the controversy between the Netherlands and Indonesia in West New Guinea.

* College of the University of Qld established in Townsville. (Becomes the independent James Cook University of North Queensland in 1970.)

A Architecture, Building

Peddle, Thorp and Walker, AMP Building, Sydney (–1962).
Woodward and Taranto, El Alamein Fountain in Kings Cross, Sydney.
Baha'i house of worship at Ingleside, Sydney, completed (dedicated 16 Sept.).

B Science, Technology, Discovery, etc.

William McBride confirms the link between birth abnormalities and the drug thalidomide taken during pregnancy.
CSIRO's 64 m radio-telescope at Parkes commissioned (Oct.).
Moving footway from Sydney's Domain parking station to College Street opens (9 June).
Malley's registers the trade name Esky for its insulated metal food container.

C Arts and Entertainment

Ian Fairweather, *Monastery* (painting).
John Olsen, *Journey into You Beaut Country* (painting).
William Pidgeon, *Rabbi Dr I. Porush*, wins the Archibald Prize.
Alan Seymour's play *The One Day of the Year* and Patrick White's *The Ham Funeral* first produced.
ABC's current affairs television program "Four Corners" launched.

D Books and Writing

H. M. Green, *A History of Australian Literature*.

Elizabeth Kata, *A Patch of Blue*.

Hal Porter, *The Tilted Cross*.

Patrick White, *Riders in the Chariot* (Miles Franklin Award winner).

Australian National Bibliography begins publication (Jan.).

E Sport and Recreation

Rod Laver wins the men's singles at Wimbledon.

Australia (Laver, Roy Emerson, Neale Fraser) wins the Davis Cup.

Lord Fury wins the Melbourne Cup.

Totalizator Agency Boards established in Vic. and WA. (NSW in 1964.)

F Statistics, Social Change, the Environment

Estimated population of Australia 10,642,654 (Commonwealth census, 30 June: 10,508,186).

China buys more than a million tonnes of wheat from Australia.

Contraceptive pill introduced in Australia.

Population outbreaks of the crown-of-thorns starfish observed in the Cairns region of the Great Barrier Reef.

G Births and Deaths

Feb 20 Percy Grainger d. (78).

Apr 1 Sir David Rivett d. (75).

May 22 Sir Lionel Lindsay d. (86).

Jun 5 Sir Richard Boyer d. (69).

Jun 9 Mrs Aeneas Gunn d. (91).

Sep 27 Peter Dawson d. (79).

Oct 2 Essington Lewis d. (80).

Dec 20 Sir Earle Page d. (81).

1962

Jan 2 Standard-gauge railway line opened between NSW and Melbourne; first express freight through train leaves Sydney.

12 Australia accepts Indonesian sovereignty over West New Guinea.

13 Banks in all states except Vic. open on Saturday morning for the last time. (Vic. banks adopt the five-day week on 5 Jan. 1963.)

Bushfires within 20 km of central Melbourne cause eight deaths and the destruction of 300 houses.

Mar 3 Labor wins its seventh successive election in NSW, with an increased majority, and the Playford government retains office in SA with the support of two independents.

31 Brand government re-elected in WA.

Apr 9 Co-axial cable telephone link opened between Melbourne, Canberra, and Sydney.

10 Tax clearances no longer required by people travelling overseas.

12 *Southern Aurora* leaves Sydney on its first run to Melbourne, inaugurating the through-train passenger service between the two capitals.

May 8 US Secretary of State Dean Rusk arrives in Canberra for a two-day session of the ANZUS Council.

9 External Affairs Minister Sir Garfield Barwick announces that Australia, if invited, would send "a handful" of military instructors to South Vietnam. (Up to 30 instructors committed on 24th.)

1962

10 Prime Minister Menzies foreshadows the establishment of a US naval communications centre at North-West Cape, WA.

28 Australia commits a squadron of RAAF Sabre jets to Thailand.

Jul 27 Minister for Air Leslie Bury is asked to resign for differing publicly with cabinet on the impact of British membership of the EEC.

29 Australian army advisers (29 men of the Australian Army Training Team Vietnam) leave for Vietnam. (Arrive Saigon 3 Aug.)

Sep 11 Huge iron-ore deposits discovered at Mount Tom Price, WA.

Nov 4 Qld Labor Party agrees to become the state branch of the DLP. (Retains QLP title for state elections.)

5 Death sentence on Robert Peter Tait, murderer of Ada Hall at Hawthorn vicarage on 8 Aug 1961, commuted to life imprisonment.

20 Prince Philip arrives in Australia to open the Commonwealth Games in Perth (on 22nd).

Dec 1 Country Party re-established in Tas.

* Secondary school course in NSW extended to six years under the Wyndham Scheme.

* STD telephone service introduced between Sydney and Canberra.

* Branches of Amnesty International established in NSW and Vic.

A Architecture, Building

Roy Grounds, Victorian Art Centre (National Gallery completed in 1968, Melbourne Concert Hall in 1982, Theatres in 1984).

B Science, Technology, Discovery, etc.

Snake antivenene developed capable of counteracting poison from most common Australian snakes.

C Arts and Entertainment

Ian Fairweather, *Epiphany* (painting).

Jeffrey Smart, *The Cahill Expressway* (painting).

Louis Kahan, *Patrick White*, wins the Archibald Prize.

Australian Ballet established, with Peggy Van Praagh artistic director.

Patrick White's play *The Season at Sarsaparilla* first produced.

Barry Humphries presents *A Nice Night's Entertainment*.

Frank Ifield's record of "I Remember You" becomes the first Australian record to appear in US charts.

D Books and Writing

John Anderson, *Studies in Empirical Philosophy*.

Thea Astley, *The Well-Dressed Explorer* (co-winner of the Miles Franklin Award with George Turner, *The Cupboard under the Stairs*).

Martin Boyd, *When Blackbirds Sing*.

C. M. H. Clark, *A History of Australia*, vol. 1 (–1987).

Jack Lindsay, *Fanfrolico and After*.

Hal Porter, *A Bachelor's Children*.

First chair of Australian literature established, at the University of Sydney.

E Sport and Recreation

Rod Laver becomes the first Australian to win the tennis Grand Slam (Australian, French, Wimbledon, and US singles).

Australia (Laver, Neale Fraser, Roy Emerson) wins the Davis Cup.

Margaret Smith (Court) wins the US Open tennis championship (the first of five times).

Heather Blundell (McKay) wins the British Open squash championship (the first of 16 consecutive times).

Gretel makes Australia's first challenge for the America's Cup. (Defeated by *Weatherly*.)

Sculler Stuart Mackenzie wins the Diamond Sculls at Henley for the sixth year in succession.

Even Stevens wins the Melbourne Cup and the Caulfield Cup.

Commonweath Games held in Perth.

F Statistics, Social Change, the Environment

Estimated population of Australia: 10,846,059.

Aborigines in Qld, WA, and NT given the right to vote in federal elections if enrolled (though enrolment not compulsory).

Roma Mitchell becomes Australia's first female QC.

Crown-of-thorns starfish infest Green Is. on the Great Barrier Reef.

G Births and Deaths

Jan 16 Frank Hurley d. (76).
Jun 13 Sir Eugene Goossens d. (69).
Jul   6 John Anderson d. (68).
Dec   3 Dame Mary Gilmore d. (97).

1963

Jan 1 CSIRO physicist Gilbert Bogle and Mrs Margaret Chandler found dead in bushland beside the Lane Cove River near Fullers Bridge, Sydney; circumstances of their deaths remain unexplained.

28 Shark fatally attacks actress Marcia Hathaway in shallow water at Sugarloaf Bay in Sydney's Middle Harbour.

Feb 18 Queen Elizabeth and Prince Philip arrive in Australia for a visit to all states (–27 Mar.) and to attend Canberra's jubilee celebrations.

Mar 16 Lifeline, Australia's first telephone counselling service, founded in Sydney by the Central Methodist Mission.

Apr 1 Satirical monthly magazine *Oz* begins publication in Sydney.

28 Wreckage of the Dutch ship *Vergulde Draeck*, lost in 1656, found by skindivers about 95 km north of Perth.

– Comalco begins full-scale mining of bauxite at Weipa on Cape York Peninsula.

May 9 Australia and the US sign an agreement allowing the US to establish and operate a naval communications station at North-West Cape, WA.

Townsville's bulk sugar terminal, containing 78,000 tonnes of raw sugar, catches fire and burns for five days.

14 "The Mutilator"—William McDonald—arrested for the murder and sexual mutilation of derelict men in Sydney over the previous two years.

Jun 1 Nicklin coalition government re-elected in Qld.

Jul – First stage of the Ord River irrigation scheme in WA opened.

Aug 5 Australia and Japan conclude a new trade agreement extending full rights and privileges accorded to members of GATT.

15 External Affairs Minister Garfield Barwick announces Australia's signing of the Nuclear Test Ban Treaty.

1963

Sep 1 Commonwealth Marriage Act of 1961 comes into operation, placing the marriage laws of the states and territories on a uniform basis.

2 Serial killer Eric Cooke is arrested by Perth police. (Hanged 27 Oct. 1964.)

20 Floodgates closed on the Molonglo River at Canberra, beginning the filling of Lake Burley Griffin.

25 Australia pledges military assistance to the new nation of Malaysia against direct or indirect aggression.

Oct 10 Moura open-cut coalfield in Qld begins large-scale production.

21 *Australian Financial Review* changes from twice-weekly to daily publication.

24 Australia agrees to buy 24 American F-111 aircraft for the RAAF.

Nov 15 Police evict Aborigines of the Mapoon community on Cape York Peninsula and raze community buildings to allow for the mining of bauxite.

30 Election for House of Representatives; Menzies government returned with an additional 10 seats; new members include Ian Sinclair.

Dec 3 Commonwealth Pacific Cable (Compac) officially opened, connecting Australia by direct telephone link to NZ, Fiji, Hawaii, and Canada.

* Dutch ship *Batavia*, wrecked in 1629, located in Houtman Abrolhos, WA.

* Vic. board of inquiry investigates the activities of Scientology.

A Architecture, Building

Royal Australian Mint, Canberra (–1965).

NSW State Planning Authority established.

B Science, Technology, Discovery, etc.

Sir John Eccles shares the Nobel Prize for his research on transmission of nerve impulses.

C Arts and Entertainment

Leonard French designs the stained-glass ceiling for the Great Hall of the Melbourne Arts Centre.

J. Carington Smith, *Prof. James McAuley*, wins the Archibald Prize.

Barry McKenzie, a comic-strip (later, film) character created by Barry Humphries and artist Nicholas Garland, first appears in the English magazine *Private Eye*.

Richard Meale composes *Las Alboradas* and *Homage to Garcia Lorca*.

Patrick White's play *A Cheery Soul* first produced.

Old Tote Theatre opens on the campus of the University of NSW (2 Feb.).

D Books and Writing

Sumner Locke Elliott, *Careful, He Might Hear You* (Miles Franklin Award winner).

Alan Moorehead, *Cooper's Creek*.

Hal Porter, *The Watcher on the Cast-Iron Balcony*.

Randolph Stow, *Tourmaline*.

Morris West, *The Shoes of the Fisherman*.

Australian Society of Authors founded (26 June).

E Sport and Recreation

Margaret Smith (Court) wins the Wimbledon singles tennis championship.

Bernard ("Midget") Farrelly wins the Makaha (Hawaii) international surfboard-riding competition (2 Jan.).

Gatum Gatum wins the Melbourne Cup.

F Statistics, Social Change, the Environment

Population of Australia reaches eleven million.

School leaving age raised to 15 in SA.

1963

Three weeks paid annual leave granted by the Commonwealth Arbitration Commission.

Children born out of wedlock become legitimate by the subsequent marriage of their parents.

G Births and Deaths

Jan 13 Will Ogilvie d. (93).
May 28 Margaret Preston d. (88).
Jul 29 Dorian Le Gallienne d. (48).
Sep 20 Sir David Low d. (72).
Oct 10 Roy Cazaly d. (70).
Nov 6 Archbishop Daniel Mannix d. (99).

1964

Jan 29 RAAF receives its first two Mirage jet fighters.

Feb 3 Double-deck carriages begin trial runs on Sydney's suburban railway.
10 Destroyer HMAS *Voyager* sinks after being cut in two by the aircraft carrier HMAS *Melbourne* in a collision off Jervis Bay; 82 lives lost.
25 Fire destroys Sydney's Lyceum Theatre.

Mar 10 Sir Percy Spender becomes president of the International Court of Justice (–1967).
– Split in the Communist Party of Australia results in the founding of the pro-Chinese Communist Party of Australia (Marxist–Leninist).

Apr 8 Opening of the Moonie-to-Brisbane oil pipeline marks the beginning of production on Australia's first commercial oilfield.
12 Rev. Ted Noffs opens the Wayside Chapel in Kings Cross, Sydney.
27 Sir Garfield Barwick resigns from parliament to become Chief Justice of the High Court. (Paul Hasluck replaces him as Foreign Minister.)
29 J. B. Renshaw becomes Premier of NSW following the retirement of R. J. Heffron.

May 2 Reece Labor government re-elected in Tas.
28 Legislation enacted authorizing Commonwealth financial aid to public and private schools for science education (from 1 July), thereby reviving state aid to Church schools.
– Australian army engineers sent to Sabah, Malaysia.

Jun 8 Australian army advisers in Vietnam increased to 80 and committed to active service.
12 Macquarie University (Syd.) founded. (First undergraduates accepted in 1967.)
27 Bolte government re-elected in Vic. with a majority in both houses.

Jul 15 Australia's first national daily newspaper, the *Australian*, begins publication in Canberra.
19 Thirty-four RAAF personnel leave Sydney for South Vietnam to fly and maintain Caribou transport aircraft.

Aug 24 AWU members begin industrial action at Mount Isa over dissatisfaction with a wage increase.

Sep 23 *Oz* magazine judged to be obscene by a Sydney magistrate; publishers Richard Walsh, Richard Neville, and Martin Sharp sentenced to terms of imprisonment. (Convictions quashed in Feb. 1965 after an appeal.)

1964

26 Princess Marina, Duchess of Kent, visits Australia (to 8 Oct.) for the British Exhibition and the opening of Sydney's Gladesville Bridge.

Oct 2 Gladesville Bridge, Sydney, officially opened.
23 Pat Mackie, leader of a rival union faction in the Mt Isa Mines dispute, is sacked on the eve of a vital mass meeting.
27 NSW's biggest oil fire at Mobil storage depot, Hunters Hill, Sydney.
30 Australian troops capture Indonesian guerrillas in Malacca during their first action in the Indonesia–Malaysia Confrontation.

Nov 10 Prime Minister Menzies announces the re-introduction of National Service from July 1965; 20-year-olds to be selected on a birthday lottery for two years' full-time service; conscripts liable for service anywhere.
14 Mount Isa Mines shuts down its copper smelter because of dispute.

Dec 5 Election for half Senate; government retains its majority; V. C. Gair wins a Qld seat and becomes DLP leader, replacing a defeated George Cole.
10 Qld government declares a state of emergency in an attempt to end the Mt Isa dispute.
16 La Trobe University established in Melbourne. (First students admitted in Mar. 1967.)
27 Australia's first offshore oil well spudded in in the Gippsland Basin of Bass Strait.

A Architecture, Building

Tasman Bridge, Hobart, opened (Aug.).
Bridge over Pumicestone Passage to Bribie Is., Qld, completed.
Sydney GPO clock tower re-erected.

B Science, Technology, Discovery, etc.

Australia and 17 other countries agree to set up a communications satellite system. (Group becomes the management body of the International Telecommunications Satellite Organization, or Intelsat.)
Space tracking station opens at Carnarvon, WA.
World's first purpose-built container ship, the Australian-built MV *Koorinya*, begins service between Fremantle and Melbourne.

C Arts and Entertainment

Sidney Nolan, *Riverbend* (painting).
No award made for the Archibald Prize.
Tas. Conservatorium established.
The Beatles make an Australian concert tour.
Robert Helpmann's ballet *The Display* (music by Malcolm Williamson) has its world première at the Adelaide Festival.
Margot Fonteyn and Rudolf Nureyev appear with the Australian Ballet.
Patrick White's play *Night on Bald Mountain* first produced.
"The Mavis Bramston Show" begins on television.

D Books and Writing

Patsy Adam-Smith, *Hear the Train Blow*.
Donald Horne, *The Lucky Country*.
George Johnston, *My Brother Jack* (Miles Franklin Award winner).
James McAuley, *Captain Quiros*.
Kath Walker, *We Are Going*.

E Sport and Recreation

Australian winners at the Tokyo Olympic Games: *athletics*, Betty Cuthbert

(400 m); *swimming,* Dawn Fraser (100 m freestyle—for the third time), Bob Windle (1,500 m freestyle), Kevin Berry (200 m butterfly), Ian O'Brien (200 m breaststroke); *yachting,* 5.5 m race (Bill Northam becomes the oldest competitor to win an Olympic gold medal).

Englishman Donald Campbell breaks the world wheel-driven land speed record on Lake Eyre in the *Bluebird* (17 July) and the world water speed record at Lake Dumbleyung, WA, in the hydroplane *Bluebird* (Dec.).

Roy Emerson wins the tennis singles at Wimbledon.

Australia (Emerson, Fred Stolle) wins the Davis Cup.

Polo Prince wins the Melbourne Cup.

Bernard Farrelly wins the first organized world surfboard-riding championship at Manly, NSW.

F Statistics, Social Change, the Environment

Estimated population of Australia: 11,280,429.

NSW government employees granted four weeks' annual leave.

Child endowment extended to children 16–21 in full-time education; rates increased for third and subsequent children.

NT Legislative Council passes legislation removing much discrimination against Aborigines.

G Births and Deaths

Feb 12 Arthur W. Upfield d. (73).

Jul   25 Sir John Latham d. (86).

Oct 19 Nettie Palmer d. (79).

Oct 20 Sir Adolph Basser d. (77).

1965

Jan   7 Australia's first hydrofoil ferry begins service to Manly, in Sydney.

12 Bodies of two 15-year-olds, Christine Sharrock and Marianne Schmidt, found at Wanda Beach, Sydney; case remains unsolved.

16 Passenger and car ferry *Empress of Australia* begins operating between Sydney and Hobart.

27 Police at Mt Isa given the power to arrest without warrant and ban any person aiding the strike there; Pat Mackie banned.

Feb 11 Mt Isa Mines suspends all operations.

18 Gas (later, oil) struck in Bass Strait from Esso–BHP's Barracouta well.

20 Brand government re-elected in WA.

    Duke of Edinburgh visits Australia (to 26th).

22 Royal Australian Mint opened in Canberra by Prince Philip. (Begins producing the first Australian-made decimal coins.)

– Charles Perkins leads a "freedom ride" through NSW in an attempt to end Aboriginal segregation.

Mar   1 Echuca, Vic., gazetted as a city.

 6 Labor wins government in SA for the first time in 32 years; Frank Walsh becomes Premier, replacing Sir Thomas Playford, who had been in office for 26 years and four months, a record term in Australia.

10 First drawing of the birthday lottery to determine those eligible for National Service training.

12 Swan Hill, Vic., becomes a city.

1965

17 Legislation introduced outlawing picketing and restricting pamphlets and banners at Mt Isa. (Strikers begin returning to work later in month.)

20 Duke and Duchess of Gloucester visit Australia (to 26 Apr.).

24 Prime Minister Menzies announces a new concept in tertiary education as recommended by the Martin Committee on the Future of Tertiary Education in Australia.

Apr 29 Menzies announces the government's decision to send a combat force to Vietnam following a request from Saigon for more military aid.

May 1 Labor defeated in NSW after 24 years in office; R. W. Askin becomes Premier.

27 First Battalion, Royal Australian Regiment, leaves Sydney in the aircraft-carrier *Sydney* for active duty in Vietnam.

29 Captain Cook Bridge, Sydney, opened.

Jul 2 Secondary school teachers in Vic. stage a strike, the first teachers' strike in Australia since 1920.

Aug 13 Limited free-trade agreement negotiated between Australia and NZ.

21 Report of the Vernon Committee of Economic Inquiry tabled in federal parliament. (Principal recommendations rejected by government.)

22 Baron Casey succeeds Lord De L'Isle as Governor-General.

Sep 23 Roma Mitchell appointed judge of the Supreme Court of SA—the first woman to become a judge in Australia.

Oct 7 Sir Robert Menzies appointed Lord Warden of the Cinque Ports.

Nov 7 Underground fire at the Bulli colliery, NSW; four miners killed.

16 Economic sanctions imposed on Rhodesia following that country's unilateral declaration of independence.

– Churchill Fellowships awarded for the first time.

Dec 15 Harry Chan becomes the first elected president of the NT Legislative Council.

– First section of the Sydney–Newcastle expressway opened.

A Architecture, Building

B Science, Technology, Discovery, etc.
Siding Spring Observatory established in the Warrumbungle Ranges, NSW.
Mills Cross radio-telescope opened near Hoskinstown, NSW (Nov.).
Collapsible-bag-in-a-box wine cask patented by C. H. Malpas.

C Arts and Entertainment
Ian Fairweather, *The Drunken Buddha* paintings.
Clifton Pugh, *R. A. Henderson*, wins the Archibald Prize.
Larry Sitsky, *The Fall of the House of Usher* (opera).
Peter Sculthorpe, *Sun Music I*, presented at the Commonwealth Festival of Arts in London.
Joan Sutherland returns to Australia after 14 years abroad for the Sutherland–Williamson International Grand Opera season.
The Seekers' record "I'll Never Find Another You" becomes the first Australian record to sell a million copies.
Canberra School of Music established.
Sydney Dance Company founded (as Ballet in a Nutshell) and the Australian Dance Theatre formed in Adelaide.
South Australian Theatre Company formed.

D Books and Writing

Thea Astley, *The Slow Natives* (Miles Franklin Award winner).
"Prof. Afferbeck Lauder" (Alistair Morrison), *Let Stalk Strine*.
Hal Porter, *The Cats of Venice*.
Randolph Stow, *The Merry-Go-Round in the Sea*.
Morris West, *The Ambassador*.

E Sport and Recreation

Roy Emerson wins the Wimbledon singles for the second year in a row.
Australia (Emerson, Fred Stolle, John Newcombe, and Tony Roche) wins the
    Davis Cup.
Margaret Smith (Court) wins the Wimbledon singles for the second time.
Linda McGill becomes the first Australian to swim the English Channel.
Dawn Fraser is suspended for ten years by the Amateur Swimming Union.
Ron Clarke becomes the first person to run 3 miles in less than 13 minutes and
    sets 6 world records in 17 races.
Peter Thomson wins the British Open golf championship for the fifth time.
Light Fingers wins the Melbourne Cup.

F Statistics, Social Change, the Environment

Estimated population of Australia: 11,505,408.
Kevin Sarre machine-shears a record 346 full-grown merino sheep in 7 hours 48
    minutes at Batesworth station, Penshurst, Vic.
£737 million ($1,474 million) spent by Australians on gambling in year.
ALP removes the White Australia policy from its platform.
Provisional drivers' licences introduced in Tas.
Males begin to adopt unorthodox long hairstyles.
Australian Conservation Foundation established in Melbourne.
Australian Council of National Trusts set up in Canberra.

G Births and Deaths

Apr   1 Helena Rubinstein d. (93).
Apr 10 Archbishop Sir James Duhig d. (93).
May 27 Pat Cash b.
Jul   8 Sir Ernest Fisk d. (78).
Nov 2 H. V. Evatt d. (71).

1966

Jan 20 Sir Robert Menzies retires after a record 16 successive years as Prime
        Minister; Harold Holt replaces him.
     26 Dame Annabelle Rankin, appointed to Holt's new ministry, becomes the first
        woman to hold a federal portfolio.
        Three Beaumont children disappear on their way to Glenelg beach, Adelaide,
        and are never seen again.
     28 Rich nickel-ore deposits found at Kambalda, WA, by Western Mining Corp.
     30 Prince Charles arrives in Australia to attend Geelong Grammar's Timbertop
        school (to 1 Aug.).

Feb   1 Hotel trading hours in Vic. extended from 6 p.m. to 10 p.m., and driving
        with a blood-alcohol level of 0.05% becomes a criminal offence.
     14 Decimal currency introduced.

Mar   8 Prime Minister Holt announces a trebling of Australian forces in Vietnam,
        including 1,500 National Servicemen.

1966

22 Queen Elizabeth the Queen Mother visits Australia (to 7 Apr.).
25 Flinders University of South Australia officially opened.
30 Legislation enacted granting the ACT member of the House of Representatives full voting rights (from 21 Feb. 1967).

Apr 24 Andrew Peacock wins the by-election for Menzies' vacated seat of Kooyong.

May 26 Australia's third commercial oilfield declared at Barrow Is., WA.
28 Nicklin coalition government re-elected in Qld.
29 Harry Chan, MLC, becomes mayor of Darwin, the first of Asian ancestry to hold such a position.

Jun 16 Australia and eight other countries form the Asian and Pacific Council.
21 Opposition leader Arthur Calwell is injured when shot at after attending a political meeting in Mosman (Syd.).
30 Holt, on a visit to Washington, promises complete support for the US escalation of the Vietnam War ("all the way with LBJ").

Jul 11 Arbitration Commission introduces a minimum wage for adult male employees under federal awards.

Aug 13 Fire guts a Salvation Army hostel for men in Little Lonsdale Street, Melbourne; 29 die.
18 Australian forces in Vietnam inflict heavy losses on a large enemy force in the Battle of Long Tan.
26 Some 200 Gurindji people (including 80 station hands), led by Vincent Lingiari, walk off Wave Hill station, NT, in protest against low wages and poor conditions and begin a fight to obtain title to their tribal territory.

Sep 12 Dubbo, NSW, becomes a city.
22 Ansett–ANA Viscount crashes near Winton, Qld; 24 killed.

Oct 20 President Lyndon Johnson's visit to eastern Australian cities (to 23rd) sparks off rowdy political demonstrations.
21 Five miners killed in a cave-in at Wyee (NSW) state coalmine.

Nov 3 Liberal Reform Group (later Australian Reform Movement) established as a result of businessman Gordon Barton's publicized opposition to the Vietnam War.
24 Qantas pilots begin a worldwide strike (to 22 Dec.).
26 Election for the House of Representatives; Holt government returned with an increased majority; new members include Phillip Lynch.

Dec 9 Agreement for an American satellite base at Pine Gap, NT, negotiated.
12 Lone round-the-world sailor Francis Chichester arrives at Sydney in his yacht *Gypsy Moth IV.*
22 Australian commitment in Vietnam increased to 6,300 men, with an additional 12 tanks, two minesweepers, and eight bombers.

* Severe and widespread drought which began in 1957 and affected the whole country, especially NSW and Qld, finally eases.

A Architecture, Building
Joern Utzon resigns as architect of the Sydney Opera House (28 Feb.).

B Science, Technology, Discovery, etc.
World's largest solar still set up at Coober Pedy, SA, to supply town water (June).
OTC opens its first satellite communications earth station at Carnarvon, WA (29 Oct.).

First TV programs transmitted between UK and Australia by way of satellite (25 Nov.).

C Arts and Entertainment

Jon Molvig, *Charles Blackman*, wins the Archibald Prize.

Fred Williams, *Upwey Landscape* (awarded Wynne Art Prize).

Nigel Butterley's musical collage for radio *In the Head the Fire* wins the Italia Prize.

Don Banks, *Horn Concerto*, composed for Barry Tuckwell.

John Cargher's "Singers of Renown" program begins on ABC radio.

Melbourne and Sydney Tivoli theatres close.

Marian Street Theatre opens in Sydney.

Thomas Keneally, *Halloran's Little Boat* (play).

They're a Weird Mob (film).

"Play School" begins on ABC television (18 July).

D Books and Writing

Australian Dictionary of Biography, vol. 1.

Geoffrey Blainey, *The Tyranny of Distance*.

Elizabeth Harrower, *The Watch Tower*.

Peter Mathers, *Trap* (Miles Franklin Award winner).

Patrick White, *The Solid Mandala*.

E Sport and Recreation

Jack Brabham wins the world motor-racing championship for the third time.

Australia (Emerson, Stolle, Newcombe, Roche) wins the Davis Cup.

Galilee wins the Melbourne Cup and the Caulfield Cup.

F Statistics, Social Change, the Environment

Population of Australia (Commonwealth census, 30 June): 11,550,462—NSW 4,233,822 (Syd. 2,447,219); Vic., 3,219,526 (Melb. 2,110,336); Qld, 1,663,685 (Bris. 719,278); SA, 1,091,875 (Adel. 728,279); WA, 836,673 (Perth 500,246); Tas., 371,435 (Hob. 119,469); NT, 37,433 (Darwin 21,205); ACT, 96,013 (Canb. 93,314).

Japan replaces Britain as Australia's best customer.

Restrictions on the entry of persons of non-European descent relaxed.

Margaret Valadian (Qld) and Charles Perkins (Syd.) become Australia's first Aboriginal university graduates.

SA legislates to ban race and colour discrimination.

Sunday Observance Act repealed in NSW, allowing theatres and cinemas to open, sporting fixtures to charge admission, and clubs to sell liquor on Sundays.

Miniskirts and pantyhose come into fashion.

G Births and Deaths

Dec 16 Sir Gordon Taylor d. (70).

1967

Jan 18 Marshal Ky, Premier of South Vietnam, visits Australia (to 23rd), setting off protest demonstrations by opponents of the Vietnam War.

    26 AWU agrees to affiliate with the ACTU.

Feb 3 Ronald Ryan, the last person executed in Australia, is hanged in Melbourne for killing a warder while escaping from Pentridge Gaol on 9 Dec. 1965.

    7 Bushfires ravage south-east Tas., penetrating suburban Hobart; more than 50 people killed and more than 3,000 made homeless.

1967

8 E. G. Whitlam replaces Arthur Calwell as leader of the federal ALP.
24 Princess Alexandra visits Australia (to 26 Mar.).

Mar 1 Prince Philip visits Australia (to 10th).
13 Record floods in northern Qld.
30 South-East Asia Commonwealth telephone cable (Seacom) officially opened.
– Gurindji people occupy part of Wave Hill station, NT.

Apr 29 Referendum held in northern NSW on a proposal to create a new state; majority opposed.
Bolte government re-elected in Vic. with a 44-seat majority.

May 1 National campaign of immunization against poliomyelitis with Sabin oral vaccine begins.
16 Liberal members of parliament, including Edward St John in his maiden speech, call for a new inquiry into the *Voyager* sinking in 1964.
27 Two Commonwealth referendums held—proposal to end the nexus between numbers in both houses of parliament defeated; proposal to end constitutional discrimination against Aborigines approved.
29 Five-dollar note goes into circulation.
31 Oil strike in Kingfish well in Bass Strait.

Jun 1 D. A. Dunstan becomes Premier of SA on the retirement of Frank Walsh.
5 Total wage concept introduced by the Commonwealth Arbitration Commission to replace the basic wage plus margins. (Operates from 1 July.)

Jul – Postcode system introduced.

Sep 1 Commonwealth Trade Practices Act comes into force.
6 Commonwealth government announces its intention to limit appeals from the High Court to the Privy Council. (Act assented to 6 Aug. 1968.)
8 Police arrest 114 demonstrators in Brisbane protesting against changes in the law governing street marches.
16 North-West Cape naval communications station officially commissioned.
17 Prime Minister Holt announces that Australia would increase its military aid to South Vietnam by another battalion and support groups.

Nov 20 Fixed rate of exchange between the Australian dollar and the pound sterling ends when Australia decides not to devalue in line with sterling.
25 Election for half Senate; DLP wins two more seats, giving it the balance of power in the Senate (27 ALP, 28 L–CP, 4 DLP, 1 ind.).

Dec 17 Prime Minister Harold Holt disappears in the surf at Cheviot Beach, Portsea, Vic. (Body never found.)
19 Country Party leader John McEwen sworn in as Prime Minister.
22 Representatives of 26 nations, including President Johnson and Prince Charles, attend the Holt memorial service in Melbourne.

A Architecture, Building
State Office Block, Sydney, completed.

B Science, Technology, Discovery, etc.
Honeysuckle Creek space tracking station, near Canberra, opened (17 Mar.).
Australia's first satellite, WRESAT 1, successfully launched from Woomera Rocket Range (29 Nov.).
Joint Defence Space Research Facility established at Pine Gap, near Alice Springs. (Becomes operational in 1969.)

C Arts and Entertainment

Judy Cassab, *Margo Lewers*, wins the Archibald Prize.

Australian Elizabeth Theatre Trust forms a permanent orchestra in Sydney for opera and ballet performances.

National Training Orchestra (later the ABC Sinfonia) established by the ABC. (Disbanded 1986.)

Richard Meale composes *Nocturnes*.

Dorothy Hewett's play *This Old Man Comes Rolling Home* and Jack Hibberd's *White with Wire Wheels* first produced.

Melbourne's La Mama theatre opens.

Current affairs program "This Day Tonight" begins on ABC TV (10 Apr.).

Talkback radio begins.

D Books and Writing

Donald Horne, *The Education of Young Donald*.

Thomas Keneally, *Bring Larks and Heroes* (Miles Franklin Award winner).

Joan Lindsay, *Picnic at Hanging Rock*.

R. G. Menzies, *Afternoon Light*.

Barry Oakley, *A Wild Ass of a Man*.

Kylie Tennant, *Tell Morning This*.

E Sport and Recreation

John Newcombe wins the men's singles at Wimbledon.

Australia (Newcombe and Roy Emerson) wins the Davis Cup.

Australia challenges for the America's Cup (*Dame Pattie* beaten by *Intrepid*).

Red Handed wins the Melbourne Cup.

F Statistics, Social Change, the Environment

Estimated population of Australia: 11,912,253.

Commonwealth subsidizes sheltered workshops and introduces the Sheltered Employment Allowance.

SA's Simpson Desert Conservation Park and Qld's Simpson Desert National Park proclaimed.

National Parks and Wildlife Service set up in NSW.

G Births and Deaths

Feb   7   David Unaipon d. (94).

Aug 25   Viscount (S. M.) Bruce d. (84).

Dec 17   Harold Holt d. (59).

Dec 31   Arthur Mailey d. (81).

1968

Jan 10   Senator John Gorton sworn in as Prime Minister after defeating Paul Hasluck for the leadership of the Liberal Party (William McMahon having declined to stand because of CP opposition).

17   J. C. A. Pizzey becomes Premier of Qld on the retirement of Frank Nicklin.

31   Nauru becomes an independent republic.

Feb 24   Gorton, having resigned from the Senate, wins the by-election for Harold Holt's vacant seat.

Askin government re-elected in NSW.

25   Report of the second *Voyager* royal commission clears *Melbourne*'s commanding officer (Capt. R. J. Robertson) of any blame and places responsibility for the disaster on the *Voyager*.

1968

– Twenty Australian soldiers killed and 80 wounded in Operation Coburg following the Tet offensive in Vietnam.

Mar 2 Labor and LCL win 19 seats each in the SA election; Raymond Steele Hall becomes Premier (17 Apr.) when the independent Speaker gives his support to the LCL, forcing Don Dunstan to resign the premiership.

22 Helicopter crashes on the Barracouta natural gas platform in Bass Strait, killing two journalists and an oil company officer.

23 Brand government re-elected in WA.

29 Australian Resources Development Bank opens for business.

Apr 1 Evangelist Billy Graham makes his second visit to Australia (to 28th).

23 Australia's first liver transplant performed at Sydney Hospital by a medical team headed by A. G. R. Sheil.

May 10 Prince Philip visits Australia (to 5 June) for the third Duke of Edinburgh Study Conference.

14 Haile Selassie, Emperor of Ethiopia, begins a five-day visit to Australia.

15 NT member in the House of Representatives granted full voting rights.

21 Indira Gandhi, Prime Minister of India, visits Australia (to 27th).

28 Sydney vice king Joe Borg dies when a bomb explodes in his car at Bondi. (Leaves $250,000 to RSPCA.)

– Mineral boom begins on Australian stock exchanges.

Jun 18 Warringah Expressway opens in Sydney.

24 National Service Act increases penalties for evasion of National Service. British comedian Tony Hancock suicides in Sydney.

Jul 2 Students demonstrating against conscription clash with police in Sydney; 30 arrested.

4 Mounted police charge a crowd of about 1,500 anti-Vietnam War demonstrators outside the US Consulate in Melbourne; more than 45 arrested.

– Major epidemic of Hong Kong flu breaks out in Melbourne and spreads to other states.

Aug 1 Following the death of Qld Premier Jack Pizzey, Liberal leader Gordon Chalk temporarily takes over the premiership.

8 Johannes Bjelke-Petersen, elected unopposed as Country Party leader in Qld (2 Aug.), replaces Chalk as Premier.

Oct 14 Earthquake in south-west WA devastates the town of Meckering.

23 Australia's first heart-transplant operation performed by Dr Harry Windsor at St Vincent's Hospital, Sydney.

28 Postal deliveries in suburbs reduced from two to one a day. Disastrous bushfires in NSW around Wollongong and in the Blue Mountains (29th), where three firefighters die and over 100 houses are destroyed.

Dec 14 Referendum in Tas. approves a proposal for the Wrest Point Casino.

19 Breathalizer introduced in NSW.

31 MacRobertson-Miller Airlines Viscount crashes at Port Hedland, WA; all 26 on board killed.

A Architecture, Building

Bunning and Madden, National Library, Canberra, completed (opens 15 Aug.). Work begins on the West Gate Bridge, Melbourne (–1978).

B Science, Technology, Discovery, etc.

Earl Owen restores the amputated finger of a two-year-old Sydney girl, the world's first successful microsurgery operation.

Melbourne becomes one of the three vital links in World Weather Watch.

Partial skeleton of a young woman found at Lake Mungo in western NSW dated 25,000 years old. At Kow Swamp in northern Vic., excavations reveal skeletal remains dated to between 9,000 and 15,000 years ago.

C Arts and Entertainment

Australian Council for the Arts (later Australia Council) established.

New National Gallery of Vic. opens (20 Aug.).

William Pidgeon, *Lloyd Rees*, wins the Archibald Prize.

Alexander Buzo, *Norm and Ahmed* (play).

Robert Helpmann's ballet *Sun Music* (music by Peter Sculthorpe) first performed.

D Books and Writing

Frank Dalby Davison, *The White Thorntree*.

David Ireland, *The Chantic Bird*.

Thomas Keneally, *Three Cheers for the Paraclete* (Miles Franklin Award winner).

National Literature Board of Review Established, and uniform Commonwealth–state censorship laws come into force.

E Sport and Recreation

Lionel Rose beats Masahiko ("Fighting") Harada in Japan to win the world bantamweight boxing title (27 Feb.).

Bill Emmerton of Tas. becomes the first man to run through Death Valley, Cal. (200 km in 3 days 3 hrs 23 mins).

Bill Moyes flies a hang-glider in the Snowy Mountains to a height of 518 m and a distance of 2.4 km (world's longest unassisted flight).

Rod Laver wins the first Wimbledon Open men's singles.

Rain Lover wins the Melbourne Cup.

Australian winners at the Mexico City Olympic Games: *athletics*, Maureen Caird (80 m hurdles), Ralph Doubell (800 m); *swimming*, Lynn McClements (100 m butterfly), Michael Wenden (100 m and 200 m freestyle).

F Statistics, Social Change, the Environment

Population of Australia reaches 12 million.

Shops in Tas. allowed to open 24 hours a day seven days a week.

Twelve-mile fishing limit around Australia comes into force (30 Jan.).

Woodchip industry begins with a clear-felling project at Eden. NSW.

G Births and Deaths

Feb 14 Dorothea Mackellar d. (82).

Feb 21 Lord (Howard) Florey d. (69).

May 15 Florence Austral d. (76).

May 28 Kylie Minogue b.

Jul   2 Sir Hans Heysen d. (90).

Aug 25 Stan McCabe d. (58).

Aug 30 C. E. W. Bean d. (88).

Sep 28 Sir Norman Brookes d. (90).

1969

Jan   8 Bushfires in Vic. (to 9th) cause 23 deaths—15 at Lara, near Geelong—and the loss of more than 200 houses and large numbers of livestock.

       13 Cannons from Captain Cook's ship *Endeavour* recovered from Endeavour Reef, off Cooktown, north Qld.

1969

Feb   7   Sydney–Melbourne express train *Southern Aurora* collides head-on with a goods train at Violet Town, Vic; nine killed.

Mar 13   Natural gas piped from Bass Strait into Vic. (Enters Melbourne's metropolitan system later in the month.)

     17   With the opening of the pipeline from Roma, Brisbane becomes the first Australian capital to receive a natural gas supply.

     20   Liberal MP Edward St John accuses Prime Minister Gorton of impropriety in his personal conduct.

     25   Nimmo Committee report strongly criticises aspects of health insurance.

Apr   1   First shipment of iron ore from Mount Newman, WA, leaves for Japan.

      3   Arrival of the container ship *Encounter Bay* in Sydney inaugurates the containerization of sea cargo between Britain and Australia.

     13   Trams cease running in Brisbane.

     30   Sir Paul Hasluck succeeds Lord Casey as Governor-General.

May   1   Australia becomes party to the Universal Copyright Convention.

     10   Labor Party defeated in Tas. after 35 years in office; W. A. Bethune, leader of the Liberal–Centre Party coalition, becomes Premier. (For the first time since 1910, no Labor government holds office in Australia.)

     15   Clarrie O'Shea, secretary of the Vic. tram and bus employees' union, is gaoled following his union's refusal to pay fines imposed by the Commonwealth Industrial Court. (National strikes protesting against the penal clauses follow; O'Shea is released on 21 May after the union's fines are paid anonymously.)

     17   Bjelke-Petersen government re-elected in Qld.

     29   Coral Sea Islands Territory, off the Qld coast between the Barrier Reef and 157° east, comes under Commonwealth control.

     30   Launceston experiences its worst floods for forty years.

Jun   3   HMAS *Melbourne* collides with USS *Frank E. Evans* during SEATO naval exercises in the south China Sea, cutting the American ship in two; 73 American lives lost.

     19   Commonwealth Arbitration Commission adopts the principle of equal pay for women doing the same work as men (increases to be introduced over three years).

Jul   4   Thousands demonstrate in Sydney, Melbourne, Brisbane, Canberra, and Adelaide against America and the war in Vietnam.

     20   Australian Reform Movement becomes the Australia Party; Sen. R. J. D. Turnbull, formerly an independent, becomes the party's sole parliamentary representative. (Resigns from party on 3 Mar. 1970.)

Aug   9   Duke and Duchess of Kent visit Australia (to 3 Sept.) to open the third Pacific Conference Games in Port Moresby.

     25   ANL freighter *Noongah* founders off Smokey Cape, NSW, with the loss of 21 crew members; five rescued.

     –   Twelve-sided cupro-nickel 50-cent piece replaces the round silver coin.

Sep 29   Poseidon mining company announces the discovery of a massive lode of nickel at Windarra, WA, setting off a share boom. ($1 shares peak at $280 in Feb. 1970; company in receivership in 1977.)

Oct   1   *Oz* magazine ceases publication in Australia.

     11   Australia's steam train era ends with the last journey of loco 3801 between Sydney and Goulburn.

     25   Election for the House of Representatives; Gorton government returned with

its majority reduced to seven (DLP preferences keeping Labor out of office); new members include Lionel Bowen and Paul Keating.

- Bass Strait oil piped to shore.

Nov 7 Gorton re-elected Liberal Party leader after challenges from McMahon and Fairbairn.

29 Standard-gauge railway line between Sydney and Perth completed. (Inaugural freight train leaves Sydney on 12 Jan. 1970.)

- Sydney publisher Francis James detained by the authorities in China on a charge of espionage.

* Natural gas from the Moomba–Gidgealpa field reaches Adelaide through an 832 km pipeline.

* Remains of the English ship *Tryal*, wrecked on the WA coast in 1622, found near the Monte Bello Islands.

A Architecture, Building
Qantas building, Sydney (–1983).

B Science, Technology, Discovery, etc.
Casey Antarctic base established by ANARE.

C Arts and Entertainment
Ray Crooke, *George Johnston*, wins the Archibald Prize.
John Olsen, *The Chasing Bird Landscape* (awarded the Wynne Prize).
Christo Javacheff wraps up Little Bay (Syd.) in plastic sheeting.
Alexander Buzo's play *Rooted* and Jack Hibberd's *Dimboola* first produced.
Rock musical *Hair* presented in Sydney.
Age of Consent and Tim Burstall's *Two Thousand Weeks* (films).
"Australia All Over" (originally called "All Ways on Sunday") begins on ABC radio (July).

D Books and Writing
Bruce Beaver, *Letters to Live Poets*.
George Johnston, *Clean Straw for Nothing* (Miles Franklin Award winner).
Frank Moorhouse, *Futility and Other Animals*.
Commonwealth government introduces a protective bounty on the manufacture of books.

E Sport and Recreation
Johnny Famechon wins the world featherweight boxing title in London from Jose Legra (21 Jan.).
Victor Browne cycles from Perth to Sydney in 11 days 6 hrs 47 mins, breaking Hubert Opperman's 32-year-old record.
Rod Laver wins the tennis Grand Slam for the second time.
Rain Lover wins the Melbourne Cup for the second year in a row.

F Statistics, Social Change, the Environment
Estimated population of Australia: 12,407,217.
First women's liberation groups formed in Sydney and Adelaide.
Abortion law liberalized in SA, allowing abortion under certain conditions.
Tapered means test for pensions introduced.
High Court rules that the states have no rights or jurisdiction over territorial waters or the sea bed adjacent to their coastline.

G Births and Deaths
May 7 Sir John Ferguson d. (87).

1969

Oct   2   Katharine Susannah Prichard d. (85).
Nov 21   Norman Lindsay d. (90).
Nov 27   May Gibbs d. (93).

1970

Jan   1   R. J. Hawke succeeds Albert Monk as president of the ACTU.
         18   Cyclone Ada devastates Daydream and Hayman island holiday resorts off the central Qld coast (to 19th); 13 lives lost.
         27   Reports that Tasminex mining company had discovered a large nickel field raise share prices from $3.35 to $85.60. (Prices fall back to $7.50 on 3 Mar. when company reveals only traces of nickel were found.)

Feb 23   *Indian Pacific* train makes its inaugural transcontinental journey (–26th).
         28   Nine Australians killed and 29 wounded in three incidents in the Long Hai mountains of Phuoc Tuy Province, Vietnam.

Mar 30   Queen Elizabeth, Prince Philip, Princess Anne, and Prince Charles visit Australia (to 3 May) for the Captain Cook Bicentenary.
          –   Rural Bank secretary Peter Huxley sentenced to 20 years' gaol for fraudulently manipulating more than $5 million. (Released in 1978.)

Apr 21   WA wheat farmer L. G. Casley declares his independence from the Commonwealth, naming his property the Hutt River Province and himself the Administrator (later Prince Leonard).

May   3   International terminal at Sydney's Kingsford Smith Airport officially opened by the Queen.
          8   More than 70,000 people, led by federal MP Jim Cairns, march through Melbourne in protest against Australian participation in the Vietnam War; similar "moratorium" rallies held in other capital cities.
         30   Labor wins SA election; Don Dunstan again becomes Premier.
                Bolte government re-elected in Vic.

Jun 16   Newington College (Syd.) headmaster D. A. Trathen calls on Australian youth to defy the National Service Act. (Forced to resign in Sept.)

Jul   1   Melbourne's Tullamarine Airport opened. (Freeway opened in Feb.)
         26   Hans Tholstrup completes a circumnavigation of Australia in a 5.2 m runabout.
         31   Her Majesty's Theatre, Sydney, destroyed by fire.

Sep   1   Queensland Mines Ltd announces the discovery of a rich uranium field at Nabarlek, NT.
                Federal government bans a visit by US comedian and pacifist Dick Gregory.
         14   Vic. branch of the ALP dissolved by the federal executive.
         18   Further Vietnam moratorium rallies held in capital cities throughout Australia; 200 marchers arrested in Sydney, 100 in Adelaide.

Oct 11   *Sunday Review* (later *The Review*) begins publication in Melbourne.
         15   Melbourne's West Gate Bridge collapses, killing 35 bridge workers.
          –   Black ban imposed by unions on the redevelopment of Carlton (Melb.).

Nov   2   Legislation passed establishing the Australian Wool Commission, to operate a flexible reserve price scheme.
          5   *La Balsa* raft, with a crew of four men, reaches Mooloolaba, Qld, from Ecuador.

12 Australia's withdrawal of troops from Vietnam begins with the return of the 8th Battalion, which is not replaced.

21 Election for half Senate (resulting party affiliation: 26 ALP, 26 Lib.–CP, 5 DLP, 3 other).

30 Pope Paul VI, the first Pope to visit Australia, arrives in Sydney.

A Architecture, Building

John Andrews, King George Tower (American Express Building), Sydney (– 1976).

Collins Place, Melbourne (–1981).

Martin Plaza, Sydney (opened 1 Sept.).

Carillon on Aspen Is. and Capt. Cook Memorial Water Jet in Lake Burley Griffin, Canberra.

B Science, Technology, Discovery, etc.

National Botanic Gardens officially opened in Canberra.

Ralph Sarich of Perth begins developing his orbital combustion engine.

C Arts and Entertainment

Eric Smith, *Gruzman—architect*, wins the Archibald Prize.

Elizabethan Theatre Trust Opera Co. becomes the Australian Opera.

Nimrod Theatre opens in Sydney, and the Palace Theatre is demolished to make way for the Hilton Hotel.

Australian Performing Group begins performing at the Pram Factory in Melbourne.

Michael Boddy and Bob Ellis, *The Legend of King O'Malley* (play).

Ned Kelly (film), with Mick Jagger.

Australian Film Development Corporation set up (17 Aug.).

D Books and Writing

Germaine Greer, *The Female Eunuch*.

Shirley Hazzard, *The Bay of Noon*.

Humphrey McQueen, *A New Britannia*.

Barry Oakley, *A Salute to the Great McCarthy*.

Dal Stivens, *A Horse of Air* (Miles Franklin Award winner).

Patrick White, *The Vivisector*.

Penguin Books defy censorship laws by publishing *Portnoy's Complaint*.

E Sport and Recreation

Margaret Court wins the tennis Grand Slam (Australian, French, Wimbledon, and US singles).

John Newcombe wins the Wimbledon singles and doubles.

Shane Gould breaks world swimming records for the 200 m, 800 m, and 1,500 m.

VFL Park opens at Mulgrave in Melbourne (18 Apr.).

Record crowd of 121,696 see Carlton recover from 44 points behind at half time to beat Collingwood in the VFL grand final.

Cyclist Gordon Johnson wins the world professional sprint championship.

Baghdad Note wins the Melbourne Cup.

Sir Frank Packer's *Gretel II* challenges for the America's Cup and loses to *Intrepid*.

Sydney Stadium closes.

F Statistics, Social Change, the Environment

Estimated population of Australia: 12,663,469.

A record 185,325 migrants arrive in Australia.

Sheep numbers in Australia peak at 180 million.

Margaret Sleeman becomes Australia's first female magistrate.

1970

Eighteen-year-olds get the vote in WA (SA and NSW in 1971, Qld and Vic. in 1973).

Right to Life movement formed in Qld (spreads to other states).

Campaign Against Moral Persecution (CAMP) founded to press for homosexual law reform.

G Births and Deaths

Feb 27 Sir Edward Hallstrom d. (83).
May 13 Sir William Dobell d. (70).
May 15 Jon Molvig d. (46).
May 24 Frank Dalby Davison d. (76).
Jul   2 Jessie Street d. (81).
Jul 22 George Johnston d. (58).
Jul 30 Sir Walter Murdoch d. (95).

1971

Jan 1 Wearing of seat belts in cars made compulsory in Vic. (Made compulsory in NSW on 1 Aug; throughout Australia in 1972.)

Feb 1 Australian Industry Development Corporation begins operations.

2 J. D. Anthony succeeds Sir John McEwen as federal Country Party leader.

5 Mining investment group Mineral Securities (Aust.) Ltd crashes.

7 *National Times* begins publication in Sydney. (Becomes the broadsheet [*National*] *Times on Sunday* in 1986.)

13 Askin government re-elected in NSW with a reduced majority.

20 Labor wins office in WA election; John Tonkin becomes Premier.

Mar 8 Malcolm Fraser resigns as Defence Minister, accusing Prime Minister Gorton of disloyalty.

10 William McMahon replaces Gorton as Prime Minister (Gorton having resigned after his supporters moved a vote of confidence in him without having the numbers to carry it.)

Apr 27 Yirrkala Aborigines lose their two-year legal battle for land rights at Gove, NT, site of Nabalco's bauxite mining project.

– Five Power Defence Arrangements concluded by Australia, New Zealand, Singapore, Malaysia, and Britain.

– Relics from the 1629 wreck *Batavia* recovered from Houtman Abrolhos, WA.

May 24 Neville Bonner, chosen by the Liberal Party to fill a casual Senate vacancy, becomes the first Aboriginal member of any Australian parliament.

26 Qantas pays $500,000 to bomb hoaxer-extortionist "Mr Brown" (Peter Macari). (Arrested three months later.)

– Seabed agreement between Australia and Indonesia signed in Canberra.

Jun 7 Australia becomes a full member of the OECD.

27 ALP delegation led by Gough Whitlam visits the People's Republic of China (to 14 July).

– Work begins on Melbourne's underground railway.

Jul 3 Police at Melbourne's Olympic Park oval attack demonstrators protesting against the visit of the South African Springboks football team. (In Sydney on 6 July demonstrators interrupt play and, on 10th, clash with 1,000 police; 140 arrested.)

1971

14 State of emergency declared in Qld for the Springboks' visit (terminated on 2 Aug.).

Aug 9 Retail price maintenance becomes illegal.

12 McMahon dismisses Gorton from the Defence Ministry. (Gorton resigns the deputy leadership of the Liberal Party soon after.)

Sep 1 Payroll tax transferred from the Commonwealth to the states.

19 Trams stop running in Ballarat.

Oct 31 Daylight saving introduced on a trial basis throughout Australia except in WA and NT. (Qld decides in Aug. 1972 not to reintroduce daylight saving.)

Nov 25 Late-night shopping introduced in Vic. (and in NSW on 14 Dec.).

– Operational role of the Australian task force in Vietnam ends.

Dec 5 Socialist Party of Australia formed by Moscow-sympathetic former members of the CPA.

7 Det.-Sgt Philip Arantz suspended from the NSW Police Force for leaking confidential material on crime statistics to the press. (Given $250,000 in compensation in 1985; dismissal revoked in 1989.)

24 Cyclone Althea damages hundreds of buildings in Townsville and causes the deaths of three people.

* Griffith University established in Brisbane. (Teaching begins in 1975.)

* Mass immunization of girls against rubella (German measles) begins.

A Architecture, Building

Jeffrey Howlett, Perth Concert Hall (–1973).

Harry Seidler, MLC Centre, Sydney (–1977).

B Science, Technology, Discovery, etc.

Large deposits of natural gas discovered on the North-West Shelf, off the WA coast 1,200 km north of Perth.

C Arts and Entertainment

Clifton Pugh, *Sir John McEwen*, wins the Archibald Prize.

David Williamson, *The Removalists* and *Don's Party* (plays).

Tim Burstall, *Stork* (film), with Bruce Spence.

"The Village Glee Club" and "The Argonauts' Club" end after 29 and 30 years on ABC radio (Mar. and Apr.), and quiz show "Pick a Box" finishes after 23 years with Bob Dyer's retirement (28 July).

Sydney's Trocadero dance restaurant closes down (14 Apr.).

"R" certificate introduced for categorizing films.

D Books and Writing

George Johnston, *A Cartload of Clay*.

David Ireland, *The Unknown Industrial Prisoner* (Miles Franklin Award winner).

E Sport and Recreation

Inaugural one-day international cricket match held in Melbourne (5 Jan.).

Evonne Goolagong and John Newcombe win Wimbledon singles titles.

Sydney's City to Surf race held for the first time.

Springbok Rugby tour sparks off anti-apartheid demonstrations.

Jimmy Sharman's boxing troupe makes its last appearance, at the Shepparton (Vic.) show.

Silver Knight wins the Melbourne Cup.

1971

F Statistics, Social Change, the Environment

Estimated population of Australia reaches 13 million (Commonwealth census 30 June: 12,755,638).

Albany (WA) whaling station takes a record 823 male sperm whales.

Australia's first sex shop opens in Sydney (Oct.).

World's first green bans (a term applied by Jack Mundey of the Builders' Labourers Federation) imposed on building development in Sydney: Kelly's Bush (18 June) and the Rocks (Nov.).

Environmental Protection Authority set up in Vic.

Fraser Island Defence Organization formed by John Sinclair to oppose sand mining on the island.

G Births and Deaths

Mar 11   Frank Clune d. (77).
May 27   Chips Rafferty d. (62).
May 28   Roland Wakelin d. (84).
Jun 30   Kenneth Slessor d. (70).
Sep 27   Sir Douglas Copland d. (77).
Oct 16   Robin Boyd d. (52).

1972

Jan 27   "Aboriginal Tent Embassy" set up outside Parliament House, Canberra, in a demonstration for land rights. (Removed by police in July.)
   28   General Motors-Holden's dismisses 1,240 employees in NSW, Vic., and SA.

Feb –   Women's Electoral Lobby formed.

Mar 15   Steele Hall resigns as leader of the Liberal and Country League opposition in SA and (28th) forms the Liberal Movement within the party.

Apr 16   Trams cease running in Bendigo.
   22   Labor sweeps back into office in Tas; Eric Reece again becomes Premier.
   24   WA appoints Australia's first ombudsman by legislation enacted in 1971 (Ombudsmen appointed by SA in 1972, Vic. 1973, Qld 1974, NSW 1975, NT and Commonwealth 1977, Tas. 1979).

May 10   Adelaide University lecturer George Duncan drowns in the Torrens River after being thrown in by a group of men. (Special investigation winds up in 1990 without casting light on allegations against police officers.)
   27   Bjelke-Petersen government re-elected in Qld with a reduced majority.
   –   ACTU places a black ban on all French ships and aircraft as a protest against continuation of French nuclear tests in the Pacific.

Jun 30   Ord River Dam (Lake Argyle) officially opened as the second stage of the Ord River scheme.

Jul 22   *Nation* mergers with the *Sunday Review* to become *Nation Review.*
   31   Underground explosion at the Box Flat colliery, near Ipswich, Qld, kills 17 miners.

Aug 23   R. J. Hamer becomes Premier of Vic. following the retirement of Sir Henry Bolte.
   30   Three metal trades unions merge to form Australia's largest union, the Amalgamated Metal Workers' Union.
       Prof. R. F. Henderson appointed by the federal government to head a national inquiry into poverty.

Sep 16 Terrorists explode two bombs inside Yugoslav travel agencies in Sydney.

Oct 6 Six schoolchildren and their teacher, Mary Gibbs, are kidnapped from Faraday state school, Vic., but escape next day while their captors go to arrange the ransom. (Kidnappers captured on 9th.)

7 Princess Margaret and Lord Snowden visit Australia (to 17th) for the opening of the Princess Margaret Hospital for Children in Perth.

21 Snowy Mountains Hydro-Electric Scheme officially completed.

Nov 15 Hijacker of a Fokker Friendship aircraft at Alice Springs is fatally wounded in an exchange of gunfire.

– Monthly magazine *Cleo* begins publication.

Dec 2 Election for the House of Representatives: Labor Party wins office after 23 years in opposition.

5 Interim two-man ministry of Prime Minister Gough Whitlam and deputy Lance Barnard sworn in. Barnard announces the immediate end of National Service call-up. (Gaoled draft resisters released next day.)

11 Federal government announces the withdrawal of the remaining troops in Vietnam. (Last Australian servicemen leave on 19th.)

12 Australian Schools Commission interim committee set up.

19 Full Whitlam ministry sworn in.

20 B. M. Snedden replaces William McMahon as leader of the federal parliamentary Liberal Party.

22 Diplomatic relations established with the People's Republic of China and the German Democratic Republic.

23 Australian dollar revalued upwards by 7.05%.

A Architecture, Building
Bates, Smart, and McCutcheon, AMP Tower and Square, Melbourne.

B Science, Technology, Discovery, etc.
Production of the Nomad aircraft approved by the federal government (23 May).
Celsius temperature scale adopted in place of Fahrenheit (1 Sept.).
Interscan aviation guidance system developed by the CSIRO.

C Arts and Entertainment
Clifton Pugh, *The Hon. E. G. Whitlam*, wins the Archibald Prize.
George Dreyfus's opera *Garni Sands* first presented.
La Boite Theatre opens in Brisbane.
National Black Theatre presents *Basically Black*.
Jack Hibberd, *A Stretch of the Imagination* (play).
Bruce Beresford, *The Adventures of Barry McKenzie* (film), with Barry Crocker.

D Books and Writing
Thea Astley, *The Acolyte* (Miles Franklin Award winner).
Thomas Keneally, *The Chant of Jimmie Blacksmith*.
Peter Mathers, *The Wort Papers*.
Frank Moorhouse, *The Americans, Baby*.
Dennis Altman, *Homosexual: Oppression and Liberation*.

E Sport and Recreation
Australian winners at the Munich Olympic Games: *swimming*, Shane Gould (200 m and 400 m freestyle, 200 m indiv. medley), Gail Neall (400 m indiv. medley), Beverley Whitfield (200 m breaststroke), Brad Cooper (400 m freestyle); *yachting*, Dragon and Star class crews.
Tony Mundine wins the Commonwealth middleweight boxing championship.

1972

Bill Moyes sets a hang-gliding altitude record of 1,447.8 m over Lake Ellesmere, NZ.

Piping Lane wins the Melbourne Cup.

Federal government excludes all racially selected sporting teams from Australia.

F Statistics, Social Change, the Environment

Estimated resident population of Australia: 13,409,288.

Australian servicemen involved in the Vietnam War (1962–72); 49,211, including 19,450 National Servicemen. Casualties: 499 killed; 2 missing presumed dead; 2,069 injured in action.

Australian Conservation Foundation loses its 16-month battle to stop the flooding of Lake Pedder, Tas., as part of a hydro-electric scheme.

G Births and Deaths

Jun 3   Martin Boyd d. (78).

Jul   7   Sir Owen Dixon d. (86).

Aug 22 Ernestine Hill d. (73).

1973

Jan 1   Australian Wool Corporation takes over the functions of the Australian Wool Commission and the Australian Wool Board.

16   Francis James released from detention in China.

Feb 10   Australia's first legal casino opens at Wrest Point, Hobart.

18   International Eucharistic Congress held in Melbourne (to 25th).

28   Bill introduced into federal parliament reducing the voting age in federal elections from 21 to 18.

Mar 8   Whiskey Au Go Go nightclub in Brisbane deliberately set on fire; 15 people killed.

10   Dunstan government re-elected in SA.

16   Attorney-General Lionel Murphy and Commonwealth police raid ASIO headquarters in Melbourne to demand information on Croatian terrorists.

31   Liberal Movement in SA formally separates from the LCL.

May 19   Hamer government re-elected in Vic.

–   Karmel report for the Australian Schools Commission recommends a big increase in spending on education.

Jun 1   RAAF receives the first six of its 24 F-111C strike aircraft.

25   HMAS *Supply* leaves Sydney to rendezvous with NZ frigate *Otago* at the French nuclear test zone in protest against nuclear testing in the Pacific.

Jul 6   ACTU president R. J. Hawke elected president of the ALP.

18   All tariffs reduced by 25%.

25   Murdoch University of Western Australia, Perth, formally established. (First undergraduates enrolled in 1975.)

Aug 1   Prices Justification Tribunal established.

Sep 9   Australian dollar revalued upward by 5%.

26   Bus carrying elderly tourists plunges 100 metres into the Tumut Pond Dam near Cabramurra in the Snowy Mountains; 18 people killed.

Oct 9   Fifty-dollar note goes into circulation.

13   Coastal freighter *Blythe Star* capsizes and sinks off South West Cape, Tas.

1973

(Seven survivors of the crew of ten rescued on 24th after drifting in an open life raft.)

- 17 Queen Elizabeth joins Prince Philip in Australia for the opening of the Sydney Opera House (leaves on 22nd).
- 23 Albury–Wodonga declared a growth centre.
- 24 Police arrest 77 green-ban demonstrators preventing the demolition of a building in the Rocks, Sydney. (Another 21 arrested next day.)

Nov 17 Askin government re-elected in NSW with an increased majority.
- 24 Aborigines throughout Australia vote to elect a National Aboriginal Consultative Committee of 41 members to advise the government on Aboriginal needs.

Dec 1 Papua New Guinea achieves self-government.
- 8 Referendums to give government control of prices and incomes defeated.

- * Widespread flooding affects much of Australia during the second half of the year, continuing to mid-1974.

A Architecture, Building
Adelaide's Festival Centre opens (2 June; complex completed in 1977).
Sydney Opera House completed (officially opened 20 Oct.).

B Science, Technology, Discovery, etc.

C Arts and Entertainment
John Olsen, *Salute to Five Bells* mural in the Sydney Opera House.
Tapestry curtains designed by John Coburn in the Sydney Opera House.
Janet Dawson, *Michael Boddy*, wins the Archibald Prize.
Australian government buys Jackson Pollock's *Blue Poles* for $1.3 million.
Competition for an Australian national anthem results in the rejection of all 1,300 entries for the music.
Perth Concert Hall opens (26 Jan.).
Inaugural Country Music Festival held in Tamworth, NSW.
Sunbury (Vic.) pop festival held (27–29 Jan.).
Sydney's new Her Majesty's Theatre opens (30 Nov.).
Australian Film and Television School established.
Peter Kenna, *A Hard God* (play).
Tim Burstall, *Alvin Purple* (film), with Graeme Blundell and Abigail.

D Books and Writing
Patrick White, *The Eye of the Storm*. White wins the Nobel Prize for Literature; with the prize money, he sets up the Patrick White Award (first winner Christina Stead).
No Miles Franklin Award made.
Literature Board (of the Australian Council for the Arts) replaces the Commonwealth Literary Fund.

E Sport and Recreation
Jenny Turrall breaks the world record for 1,500 m freestyle swimming and at 13 becomes the youngest world record holder.
Stephen Holland sets a world record for the men's 1,500 m freestyle.
Australia (John Newcombe, Rod Laver) wins the Davis Cup.
Tony Rafferty runs from Fremantle to Surfers Paradise.
Gala Supreme wins the Melbourne Cup.

F Statistics, Social Change, the Environment
Estimated resident population of Australia: 13,614,344.
Inflation rate 13.2%.

1973

Supporting mother's benefit comes into operation (3 July).

Means test abolished on old-age pensions for persons aged 75 or over.

Age of majority reduced to 18.

Maternity leave granted to Commonwealth Public Service employees.

Federal government appoints an adviser on women's affairs (Elizabeth Reid).

Export ban placed on kangaroo products.

Environmental impact statement required for all federal developmental projects having significant environmental consequences.

G Births and Deaths

Apr 21 Sir Arthur Fadden d. (79).

Jul   8 Arthur Calwell d. (76).

Aug 14 Kieren Perkins b.

Dec   3 Bee Miles d. (71).

1974

Jan 1 Federal government takes over financial responsibility for tertiary education from the states; fees abolished.

Industries Assistance Commission replaces the Tariff Board.

27 Brisbane suffers its worst floods of the century following Cyclone Wanda (to 30th); 7,000 houses inundated; 12 people drown.

Feb 3 Prisoners riot in Bathurst Gaol (NSW); much of the gaol destroyed by fire; 12 prisoners wounded by gunshots.

23 Saturday mail deliveries cease.

Mar 9 Australian Country Party (federal) changes its name to the National Country Party of Australia.

26 Ruth Dobson, the first female career diplomat to be appointed an Australian ambassador, becomes ambassador to Denmark.

30 Labor loses office in WA election; Sir Charles Court becomes Premier.

Apr 2 Prime Minister Whitlam announces the appointment of DLP senator V. C. Gair as ambassador to Eire in a move to replace him with a Labor senator in the forthcoming half Senate election; Qld Premier Bjelke-Petersen counters by issuing writs for the return of five instead of six senators.

6 Country Party in Qld becomes the National Party of Australia (Qld).

8 Whitlam announces that "Advance Australia Fair" (chosen by 51.4% of respondents to a public opinion poll) would supersede "God Save the Queen" as Australia's national anthem.

10 Whitlam obtains a double dissolution after the opposition moves to defer appropriation bills in the Senate.

May 18 Election for federal parliament; Labor government re-elected with a reduced majority in the House of Representatives and still without control of the Senate (29 ALP, 29 Lib.–NCP, 2 ind.). Referendums on democratic elections, simultaneous elections, mode of altering the Constitution, and local government defeated.

Jun – Builders' Labourers Federation deregistered. (Federal office takes over NSW branch on 7 Oct., expelling Jack Mundey and other officials.)

Jul 11 Sir John Kerr succeeds Sir Paul Hasluck as Governor-General.

22 Liberal and Country League in SA changes its name to the Liberal Party of Australia (SA Division).

1974

Aug 6 Federal parliament sits for the first time as a single legislature (–7th) to pass six bills previously blocked by the Senate (first parliamentary debate to be telecast).

14 Report of the Moffitt royal commission into organized crime in clubs tabled in NSW parliament.

Sep 1 Radio and television licences abolished.

25 Australian dollar devalued by 12% and no longer linked to the US dollar but to an average of foreign currencies.

28 Election for the ACT Legislative Assembly (an advisory body replacing the ACT Advisory Council).

30 Finance company Cambridge Credit Corp. collapses and is placed in receivership with debts of about $100 million.

Oct 1 Restrictive trade practices legislation comes into force.

– Bankcard introduced.

Nov 20 First meeting of NT's new 19-member Legislative Assembly (replacing the Legislative Council).

Dec 7 Bjelke-Petersen government re-elected in Qld with an increased majority.

14 Minerals and Energy Minister R. F. X. Connor is given Executive Council authority to raise an overseas loan of $US4,000 million.

15 Regular FM broadcasting in Australia begins, from 2MBS in Sydney.

25 Cyclone Tracy devastates Darwin; 62 people killed, some 1,000 seriously injured, and 45,000 rendered homeless (nine out of ten homes destroyed).

A Architecture, Building
Colin Madigan, Australian National Gallery (–1982; extended 1997–98).

B Science, Technology, Discovery, etc.
Adult male skeleton found at Lake Mungo in western NSW (26 Feb.) dated over 56,000 years old.

Anglo-Australian 3.9 m optical telescope at Siding Spring, NSW, opened by Prince Charles (16 Oct.). (Becomes fully operational in 1975.)

C Arts and Entertainment
Sam Fullbrook, *Jockey Norman Stephens*, wins the Archibald Prize.

Peter Sculthorpe, *Rites of Passage* (opera).

Sister Janet Mead's record of "The Lord's Prayer" sells over two million copies.

Ron Blair's play *The Christian Brothers* first produced.

"Countdown", hosted by Ian ("Molly") Meldrum, begins on television (–1987).

Village Theatres open a three-screen cinema in George Street, Sydney.

D Books and Writing
Ronald McKie, *The Mango Tree* (Miles Franklin Award winner).

Frank Moorhouse, *The Electrical Experience*.

Public Lending Right scheme introduced.

E Sport and Recreation
Eddie Charlton wins the World's Masters snooker championship.

Think Big wins the Melbourne Cup.

Trifecta first introduced in Melbourne.

F Statistics, Social Change, the Environment
Estimated resident population of Australia: 13,831,978.

Beer consumption peaks at 140.3 litres per head before beginning to fall as wine consumption increases.

1974

Arbitration Commission grants four weeks' paid annual leave to Metal Industry Award, subsequently extended to other federal awards.

Lake Eyre fills with water to possibly the highest level since European settlement.

G Births and Deaths

Apr 6 Sir Hudson Fysh d. (79).
May 1 Sir Frank Packer d. (67).
May 20 Ian Fairweather d. (82).

1975

Jan 1 University of Wollongong established.
  3 Sir Robert Askin retires as Premier of NSW; T. L. Lewis succeeds him.
  5 Tasman Bridge in Hobart collapses when the bulk carrier *Lake Illawarra* strikes two supporting piers; ship sinks and four cars crash off the bridge, with the loss of 12 lives.
  7 Mineral and Energy Minister Rex Connor's authority to raise an overseas loan of $US4,000 million withdrawn. (Given authority by Executive Council on 28th to raise $US2,000 million.)
 19 ABC rock radio station 2JJ (later 2 JJJ-FM) opens in Sydney, broadcasting 24 hours a day.

Feb 9 Attorney-General Lionel Murphy resigns to become a High Court judge.
 26 Legislation passed abolishing appeals to the Privy Council on High Court decisions having no federal context.
 27 NSW Premier Lewis breaks convention by replacing Murphy in the Senate with a non-Labor nominee (Cleaver Bunton).

Mar 1 Colour television officially introduced.
 21 Malcolm Fraser replaces B. M. Snedden as federal Liberal Party leader.
 31 W. A. Neilson replaces Eric Reece as Premier of Tas.

Apr 23 Princess Anne and Capt. Mark Phillips visit Australia (to 6 May).
 30 Arbitration Commission introduces wage indexation, providing quarterly (later half-yearly) adjustments to award wages in line with movements of the CPI.

May 20 Connor's authority to raise an overseas loan revoked.
 29 Family Law Bill passed. (No-fault divorce laws come into effect on 5 Jan. 1976.)

Jun 2 Lance Barnard announces his resignation from federal parliament to become ambassador to Sweden. (J. F. Cairns replaces him as deputy Prime Minister on 12th.)
  5 Whitlam reshuffles his cabinet; W. G. Hayden replaces Cairns as Treasurer.
  9 Order of Australia awarded for the first time.
 16 Ethnic radio begins experimental broadcasting from 2EA in Sydney. (3EA begins in Melbourne on 23rd.)
 28 Liberal candidate (Kevin Newman) wins the by-election for Barnard's seat of Bass.
 30 Qld Labor senator Bert Milliner dies, and Premier Bjelke-Petersen appoints an anti-Whitlam nominee, Albert Field, as a replacement (3 Sept.).

Jul 1 Medibank health insurance scheme begins. Australian Postal Commission (Australia Post) and the Australian Telecommunications Commission (Telecom) take over former functions of the Postmaster-General's Dept.

Commonwealth Railways become Australian National Railways (taking over SA non-metropolitan and Tas. railway systems).

2 Cairns is dismissed from the ministry for misleading parliament over the existence of a letter to a loans broker.

4 Sydney newspaper publisher Juanita Neilsen disappears, presumed murdered.

12 Dunstan government re-elected in SA.

14 Frank Crean becomes deputy Prime Minister in place of Cairns.

Aug 2 ALP federal executive expels Tas. TLC secretary Brian Harradine from the Labor Party.

16 Gurindji people of NT given title to some of their traditional land. (Receive inalienable freehold title to almost all of Wave Hill station—now called Daguragu—on 11 May 1986.)

28 Report of the Henderson Commission of Inquiry into Poverty tabled in federal parliament.

Sep 16 Papua New Guinea becomes an independent nation, ending Australia's 69-year rule.

21 Thirteen miners killed by an explosion during a fire in the Kianga coalmine at Moura, central Qld.

Oct 14 Connor resigns as minister following revelations of his continued loan-raising activities.

15 Fraser announces the opposition's intentions to block appropriation bills in the Senate until the government agrees to an election.

16 Five Australian newsmen die at Balibo, East Timor, during the capture of the town by pro-Indonesian forces.

23 Eleven killed when a DH114 Heron aircraft crashes near Cairns, Qld.

31 Commonwealth Racial Discrimination Act proclaimed; A. J. Grassby becomes Commissioner for Community Relations.

Nov 11 Governor-General Sir John Kerr dismisses the Whitlam government and asks Fraser to form a caretaker government; double dissolution of parliament proclaimed.

19 Letter-bomb addressed to the Qld Premier injures two staff members.

Dec 13 Election for federal parliament; Liberal–NCP coalition wins majorities in both houses (91 of the 127 House seats and 35 Senate seats).

25 Fifteen people die in a fire at the Savoy private hotel in Kings Cross, Sydney.

A Architecture, Building

Goodsir, Baker, and Wilde, Conservatorium of Music, Brisbane.

B Science, Technology, Discovery, etc.

John Cornforth shares the Nobel Prize for chemistry with Vladimir Prelog for their work on the structure of living matter.

C Arts and Entertainment

Kevin Connor, *The Hon. Sir Frank Kitto, KBE*, wins the Archibald Prize. (Original winning portrait—John Bloomfield's *Tim Burstall*—is disqualified on the grounds of being painted from photographs.)

Malcolm Williamson appointed Master of the Queen's Musick.

Australian Council for the Arts becomes the Australia Council.

Seymour Centre opens in Sydney (Sept.).

Jack Hibberd's play *A Toast to Melba* and Robert Merritt's *The Cake Man* first produced.

Reg Livermore presents his *Betty Blokk Buster Follies*.

ABC radio's "Hospital Hour" ends after 37 years.

1975

Peter Weir's *Picnic at Hanging Rock* and Ken Hannam's *Sunday Too Far Away* (films).

Australian Film Commission established.

D Books and Writing

Murray Bail, *Contemporary Portraits and Other Stories.*
Geoffrey Blainey, *Triumph of the Nomads.*
Frank Hardy, *But the Dead Are Many.*
Xavier Herbert, *Poor Fellow My Country* (Miles Franklin Award winner).
Thomas Keneally, *Gossip from the Forest.*
David Malouf, *Johnno.*
Peter Singer, *Animal Liberation.*
Anne Summers, *Damned Whores and God's Police.*

E Sport and Recreation

Think Big wins the Melbourne Cup for the second year in succession.
Bruce Hunt cycles from Perth to Sydney in 11 days and 29 mins, breaking previous inter-capital and coast-to-coast records.
George Perdon wins the Transcontinental Run (Fremantle to Sydney via Adelaide and Melbourne) in 47 days 1 hr 54 mins.
Skateboard craze arrives in Australia.

F Statistics, Social Change, the Environment

Estimated resident population of Australia: 13,968,881.
Inflation rate for 1974/75: 16.9%.
Means test on old-age pensions abolished for persons aged 70 and over. (Reintroduced in 1983.)
Capital punishment abolished in Vic. (23 Apr.).
"Irretrievable breakdown" after 12 months' separation becomes the sole ground for divorce.
Australia's first legal nude-bathing beach declared in SA (Feb.).
Australian Heritage Commission established. (Begins operating in July 1976.)
High Court rules that the Commonwealth has sovereign rights over territorial sea and continental shelf (17 Dec.).
SA becomes the first state to decriminalize homosexuality.

G Births and Deaths

Sep 27 J. T. (Jack) Lang d. (98).
Dec 10 Andrew ("Boy") Charlton d. (68).

1976

Jan 5 Family Law Act comes into operation; Elizabeth Evatt is sworn in as Chief Justice of the Family Court of Australia.
22 Prime Minister Fraser reinstates "God Save the Queen" as Australia's official anthem.
23 Sir Eric Willis replaces T. L. Lewis as Premier of NSW.
24 ABC's FM stereo radio service, with stations in Adelaide (network centre), Sydney, Melbourne, and Canberra, begins transmission.
30 Restrictions removed on the ownership and trading of gold.

Mar 20 Hamer government re-elected in Vic.

Apr 1 ISD telephone service introduced in Sydney, with direct dialling to 13 countries.

21 Bandits steal $1.4 million in bookmakers' settlements from the Victorian Club in Melbourne.

28 First of the Vietnamese "boat people" refugees arrive in Darwin seeking asylum.

30 Skeleton of Truganini cremated and (1 May) her ashes scattered on the waters of D'Entrecasteaux Channel, Tas.

May 1 Labor government elected in NSW; Neville Wran becomes Premier. Referendum on proposal to continue with daylight saving approved.
Steele Hall and a majority of the Liberal Movement in SA rejoin the Liberal Party.

Jun 16 Australia and Japan sign the Basic Treaty of Friendship and Co-operation.

Jul 12 ACTU calls a nationwide 24-hour strike as a protest against the Fraser government's proposed changes to Medibank.

– Press Council established to consider complaints about the conduct of the press.

Sep 1 Cigarette and tobacco advertising banned on radio and television.

20 Large "Kerr and the Consequences" rally in the Sydney Town Hall calls for Australia to become a republic.

Oct 1 First of several major changes to Medibank comes into effect.

23 Total eclipse of the sun in south-eastern Australia.

Nov 28 Report of the Ranger Uranium Environmental Inquiry (Fox Commission) gives qualified approval to development of Australia's uranium reserves.

29 Australian dollar devalued by 17.5%.

Dec 1 Aboriginal pastor Sir Douglas Nicholls becomes Governor of SA—the first Aboriginal to fill a vice-regal position.

4 Fire, deliberately lit, at HMAS *Albatross* naval base at Nowra, NSW, destroys 12 of the navy's 13 Grumman Tracker aircraft (half the navy's anti-submarine strength).

9 Federal Court of Australia created to take over jurisdiction of the Industrial Court and the Bankruptcy Court. (Begins exercising its jurisdiction on 1 Feb. 1977.)

11 Neilson government re-elected in Tas.

16 Aboriginal Land Rights (Northern Territory) Act gives Aborigines freehold title to former reserve land in the NT and provides a procedure for them to claim other Crown land.

23 First of seven young women abducted in Adelaide over a six-week period disappears. (Bodies of all seven found in 1978–79 near Truro.)

* Random breath testing introduced in Vic.

A Architecture, Building
Sydney Square opened (23 Sept.).

B Science, Technology, Discovery, etc.

C Arts and Entertainment
Brett Whiteley, *Self Portrait in the Studio*, wins the Archibald Prize.
Australian Chamber Orchestra established.
Sydney's new Theatre Royal opens, replacing the old theatre demolished to make way for the MLC Centre.
Steve J. Spears, *The Elocution of Benjamin Franklin* (play), starring Gordon Chater.
Radio serial "Blue Hills" ends its 32-year run (13 Sept.).
Festival of Sydney first held (from New Year's Eve through Jan. 1977).

1976

NSW Film Corporation established (18 Aug.).
Films:
Bruce Beresford's *Don's Party*.
Donald Crombie's *Caddie*.
Henry Safran's *Storm Boy*.
Fred Schepisi's *The Devil's Playground*.

D Books and Writing

David Ireland, *The Glass Canoe* (Miles Franklin Award winner).
Frank Moorhouse, *Conference-ville*.
Gavin Souter, *Lion and Kangaroo*.

E Sport and Recreation

At the inaugural World Open squash championships, Heather McKay wins the women's title and Geoff Hunt the men's.
Tom Hayllar completes a 12,000 km walk around Australia (Mar. 1975 to 25 Jan. 1976).
Van Der Hum wins the Melbourne Cup.
Sailboarding takes off in Australia.

F Statistics, Social Change, the Environment

Population of Australia reaches 14 million. (Commonwealth census, 30 June: 13,548,467, including 160,915 Aborigines and Torres Strait Islanders.)
Cattle numbers in Australia peak at 33.4 million.
During the first year of the Family Law Act's operation, 63,267 petitions for divorce are granted.
Henderson Inquiry into Poverty reports that 10.2% of households in Australia are "very poor" and a further 7.7% "rather poor"—amounting to about two million people.
Family allowance scheme introduced (superseding child endowment).
Patricia O'Shane becomes Australia's first Aboriginal barrister (6 Feb.).
Nude bathing allowed on two Sydney beaches.
Sand mining on Fraser Is. stops (31 Dec.) after the federal government refuses export licences for its mineral sands.

G Births and Deaths

Feb 8 Gladys Moncrieff d. (83).
May 21 Harold Blair d. (51).
Jun 5 Harold Williams d. (82).
Jun 17 Lord Casey d. (85).
Aug 10 Bert Oldfield d. (81).
Oct 15 James McAuley d. (59).
Dec 25 Sir Daryl Lindsay d. (86).

1977

Jan 1 Death duties abolished in Qld.
Australian Broadcasting Tribunal replaces the Australian Broadcasting Control Board.
5 Sacked Connair pilot Colin Forman flies a stolen plane into the Connair building in Alice Springs, killing himself and three others.
18 Australia's worst railway disaster occurs when a commuter train from the Blue Mountains crashes into a concrete bridge at Granville, Sydney; 83 people killed and many injured by the falling bridge.

1977

Feb 14   Escaped convict Edwin Eastwood, gaoled for the Faraday school kidnapping in 1972, kidnaps nine schoolchildren and their teacher at Woreen, Vic. (Arrested after a high-speed chase in an escape attempt with the hostages in a van.)

19   Court government re-elected in WA.

Mar 7   Queen Elizabeth and Prince Philip visit all states and territories (to 30th) during the Queen's Silver Jubilee year.

18   Moomba–Sydney natural gas pipeline officially commissioned.

Apr 27   Five nickel miners die at Agnew, WA, after falling 35 metres down the mine shaft in an ore bucket.

–   Robyn Davidson sets out from Alice Springs with four camels to travel overland to the west coast. (Arrives at Hamelin Pool, south of Carnarvon, WA, eight months later.)

May 15   Australian Democrats party launched by former Liberal MP Don Chipp.

21   Referendums on proposals to fill casual Senate vacancies with members of the same party, to allow territorial electors to vote in referendums, and to set a retiring age for judges carried; proposal to hold simultaneous House of Representatives and Senate elections rejected. National poll held to determine the public choice of a national song; results: "Advance Australia Fair" 2,940,854, "Waltzing Matilda" 1,918,206; "God Save the Queen" 1,257,341, and "Song of Australia" 652,858.

25   Second report of the Fox Commission makes no firm recommendation that uranium mining go ahead and recommends more stringent controls for the Ranger mine's development.

Jun 22   Uniting Church in Australia formed by the merger of the Methodist Church with major elements of the Presbyterian and Congregational churches.

30   SEATO disbanded.

Jul 1   Office of the Commonwealth Ombudsman established.

Licensing regulations introduced for Citizen Band radio.

7   ALP adopts a policy to defer uranium mining development until nuclear waste safeguards are developed and other problems resolved.

15   Griffith (NSW) anti-drug campaigner Donald Mackay disappears, presumed murdered.

Aug 10   Royal commission headed by Justice P. M. Woodward begins its inquiries into drug trafficking in NSW.

25   Commonwealth government announces its intention to allow uranium mining to proceed. (Legislation passed 31 May 1978.)

Sep 4   Qld government bans street protest marches.

17   Dunstan government re-elected in SA with an increased majority.

Oct 8   Tasman Bridge, Hobart, reopens.

Nov 1   Prince Charles visits all states (to 11th).

12   Bjelke-Petersen government re-elected in Qld.

National Aboriginal Conference of 36 members elected, replacing the NACC.

17   Wreck of the *Pandora*, lost near Torres Strait in 1791, located.

Dec 1   D. A. Lowe replaces W. A. Neilson as Premier of Tas.

3   Police in Brisbane make more than 200 arrests in clashes with civil liberties demonstrators protesting against street-march restrictions.

8   Sir Zelman Cowen becomes Governor-General, following Sir John Kerr's resignation.

10   Election for House of Representatives and half Senate; Fraser government

1977

re-elected; Democrats win two Senate seats; new members include Neal Blewett and Barry Jones; Gough Whitlam announces he will step down as leader of the Labor Party.

22 W. G. Hayden elected ALP leader.

A Architecture, Building

Robin Gibson, Queensland Cultural Centre, Brisbane (Queensland Art Gallery completed in 1982, Performing Arts Centre in 1985).

B Science, Technology, Discovery, etc.

Geostationary meteorological satellite—GMS 1—launched by Japan (14 July), provides cloud pictures of Australia for the Bureau of Meteorology.

Western Plains Zoo, Australia's first open-range zoo, opens at Dubbo, NSW.

Australia's first automated teller machine (ATM) begins operating in Qld.

C Arts and Entertainment

Kevin Connor, *Robert Klippel*, wins the Archibald Prize.

David Williamson's play *The Club* and Patrick White's *Big Toys* first produced.

Independent Theatre, Sydney, closes down.

Films:

Bruce Beresford's *The Getting of Wisdom*.

Peter Weir's *The Last Wave*.

Bruce Petty's animated cartoon *Leisure* wins an Academy Award.

D Books and Writing

Australian Encyclopaedia, 3rd edition (6 vols.).

Sumner Locke Elliott, *Water under the Bridge*.

Helen Garner, *Monkey Grip*.

Colleen McCullough, *The Thorn Birds*.

Paul Hasluck, *Mucking About*.

Ruth Park, *Swords and Crowns and Rings* (Miles Franklin Award winner).

E Sport and Recreation

Kerry Packer launches World Series Cricket.

Australia (Tony Roche, John Alexander, Phil Dent) beats Italy to win the Davis Cup.

Ken Warby sets a world water speed record of 464.44 km/h in a boat of his own design and construction.

National Soccer League of Australia formed.

Gold and Black wins the Melbourne Cup.

F Statistics, Social Change, the Environment

Estimated resident population of Australia: 14,281,533.

Supporting parent's benefit introduced to replace the supporting mother's benefit.

Smoking banned on public transport in Sydney.

G Births and Deaths

Jan 14 Peter Finch d. (60).

Oct 21 Cardinal Sir Norman Gilroy d. (81).

Dec 4 Sir George Coles d. (92).

Dec 18 Cyril Ritchard d. (80).

1978

Jan 1 Special Broadcasting Service established to provide multilingual radio and television services.

17 SA Police Commissioner Harold Salisbury dismissed for misleading the government over dossiers kept by the Special Branch.

Feb 9 Sir John Kerr appointed ambassador to Unesco. (Resigns before taking up the position, following public opposition.)

10 Unions involved in the uranium industry allow existing contracts to be honoured but ban any new mining until safeguards established.

13 Bomb explodes outside the Hilton Hotel in Sydney, where Commonwealth Heads of Government are meeting; two council workers and a policeman killed.

Mar 30 Commonwealth police raid five Sydney doctors' clinics and begin arresting some 180 Greek–Australians said to be involved in a conspiracy to defraud the Dept of Social Security.

Apr 7 Qld government abolishes Aurukun and Mornington Is. Aboriginal reserves to circumvent the federal government's plan to allow the communities to manage themselves.

May 11 Australia's first open university, Deakin, at Geelong, Vic., officially opened.

18 Prince Charles in Melbourne (to 19th) for the funeral of Sir Robert Menzies.

28 *Canberra Times* begins Sunday publication.

Jun 16 Three Ananda Marga members—Ross Dunn, Timothy Anderson, and Paul Alister—are arrested in Sydney and charged with conspiring to murder National Front leader Robert Cameron. (Found guilty in Aug. 1979 and sentenced to 16 years' imprisonment.)

17 Referendum carried in NSW to change the method of choosing members of the Legislative Council from a vote by sitting members of both houses to a popular vote.

Jul 1 NT achieves self-government; Paul Everingham becomes Chief Minister.

10 Light aircraft crashes into a house in Essendon, Vic., killing six members of the one family.

28 Passenger train services discontinued in Tas.

31 Gough Whitlam resigns from federal parliament to take up a position as visiting fellow at the ANU.

Aug 24 Legislation enacted establishing fishing rights over a 200-mile zone around Australia and its external territories (from 1 Nov. 1979).

Sep 1 Australian government buys the Clunies Ross holdings on the Cocos Islands except for the family home and grounds.

14 Commonwealth Arbitration Commission decides to hold half-yearly rather than quarterly wage-indexation hearings in future.

Oct 7 Wran government re-elected in NSW with an increased majority; opposition leader Peter Coleman loses his seat.

11 Sydney Rugby League footballer Paul Hayward, Warren Fellows, and William Sinclair are arrested in Thailand for attempted heroin smuggling.

Nov 1 Medibank health scheme undergoes further modifications.

15 West Gate Bridge opened in Melbourne.

1978

A Architecture, Building

Sri Venkateswari Temple at Helensburgh, NSW, the first Hindu temple in Australia (–1986).

B Science, Technology, Discovery, etc.

Anglo-Australian telescope at Siding Spring identifies the star SS433 and makes the first optical viewing of a neutron star.

Rich diamond deposit (the Argyle Deposit) discovered in the Kimberley region, WA. (First diamonds mined, cut, and polished in Australia go on sale in Aug. 1985.)

C Arts and Entertainment

Brett Whiteley wins the Archibald Prize (with *Art, Life and the Other Thing*), the Wynne Prize (with *Summer at Carcoar*), and the Sulman Prize (with *Yellow Nude*).

Gay Mardi Gras first held in Sydney.

Films:

Fred Schepisi's *The Chant of Jimmie Blacksmith*.

Phil Noyce's *Newsfront*.

D Books and Writing

Jessia Anderson, *Tirra Lirra by the River* (Miles Franklin Award winner).

Nancy Cato, *All the Rivers Run* (combining three earlier novels).

C. J. Koch, *The Year of Living Dangerously*.

Geoffrey Lehmann, *Ross's Poems*.

Morris Lurie, *Flying Home*.

David Malouf, *An Imaginary Life*.

E Sport and Recreation

Ken Warby becomes the first person to break the 500 km/h and 300 mph barrier on water (reaching 511.11 km/h) in his jet hydroplane *Spirit of Australia* on Blowering Dam, NSW.

Tracey Wickham sets a 400 m freestyle world record and wins two gold medals at the World Swimming Championships (24 Aug.) and sets an 800 m freestyle world record at the Commonwealth Games.

Arwon wins the Melbourne Cup.

F Statistics, Social Change, the Environment

Estimated resident population of Australia: 14,430,830.

Road deaths during year: 3,671.

Number of Vietnamese refugee boats to have arrived in Australia (Apr. 1975 to Sept. 1978): 45, carrying 1,634 people.

China buys 4.6 million tonnes of wheat from Australia.

Maternity allowance abolished.

Equal Opportunity Act comes into force in Vic. (3 Apr.).

Whaling from Australia ends with the closing of the Cheynes Beach station near Albany, WA.

G Births and Deaths

May 15   Sir Robert Menzies d. (83).

Jul   27   R. J. Heffron d. (87).

Oct   6   Johnny O'Keefe d. (43).

1979

Jan 9 Federal government signs an agreement to allow the Ranger consortium to start mining uranium in the NT.

Feb 8 Finance company Associated Securities Ltd goes into receivership.
12 Harry M. Miller's Computicket organization collapses.
15 Don Dunstan resigns as Premier of SA because of ill health; Des Corcoran replaces him as Premier.

Mar 8 Prince Charles visits Australia (to 1 Apr.) for WA's 150th anniversary celebrations.

Apr 3 Truck drivers blockade major NSW highways (to 12th) in protest against road taxes and cartage rates.
29 Evangelist Billy Graham makes his third crusade in Australia (to 21 May).

May 5 Hamer government re-elected in Vic.
30 Norfolk Island Act assented to, providing for a Legislative Assembly of nine members and an Executive Council of three Assembly members.
– Remains of the last of the seven young women who disappeared in Adelaide in 1976–77 found in bushland near Truro, SA. (James William Miller arrested on 24th and charged with their murder.)

Jun 2 Election held for the ACT House of Assembly (replacing the Legislative Assembly).
5 Royal commission into the Vic. Housing Commission land deals announced.
8 Hijacker of a TAA plane between Coolangatta and Brisbane overpowered by the crew.
9 Seven die in a fire in the Ghost Train at Luna Park, Sydney.
21 One-day general strike called by the ACTU to protest against the use of a controversial public assembly law to arrest union officials in WA during strike meetings.
23 Sydney's Eastern Suburbs Railway begins operating.

Jul 1 Commonwealth estate duty and gift duty abolished.
12 Pieces of the disintegrating US space station Skylab fall on WA.
24 Fourteen coalminers die at Appin, NSW, when methane gas ignites in a mine tunnel.
28 Lowe government re-elected in Tas.
29 Fire, deliberately lit, extensively damages the Morphettville (SA) racecourse.

Aug – Conservationists and police clash over logging at Terania Creek, NSW.

Sep 15 Liberals led by David Tonkin win the SA election.
27 Ian Sinclair resigns as federal Minister for Primary Industry following the Finnane Commission's report that he forged his father's name on company annual returns. (Reinstated in Aug. 1980 after being acquitted of all charges.)
– Ban on protest marches in Brisbane eased.

Oct 8 Bunbury, WA, proclaimed a city.
14 ACTU president Bob Hawke wins preselection for the safe federal seat of Wills.
19 Australian Federal Police formed, incorporating the Commonwealth and ACT police forces.
22 Lotto tickets go on sale in NSW. (First draw held 5 Nov.)
– Report of the Woodward royal commission into drug trafficking in NSW tabled in parliament.

1979

- *Nation Review* ceases publication. (Revived Feb. 1980 to Dec. 1981.)

Nov 21 ABC reporter Tony Joyce shot while on assignment in Zambia. (Dies in Feb. 1980.)

Dec 14 Hotels in NSW allowed to trade on Sundays.

A Architecture, Building
Lionel Glendenning, Powerhouse Museum, Sydney (–1988).
Historic Bellevue Hotel in Brisbane demolished (21 Apr.).
Japanese millionaire Yohachiro Iwasaki starts a $100 million tourist development at Yeppoon, Qld (opened in May 1986).
Centrepoint Tower (designed by Donald Crone in 1969) begins rising over Sydney (opened in Sept. 1981).
Birkenhead Point complex completed in Sydney.
Melbourne City Square completed.
Art Gallery of WA completed.

B Science, Technology, Discovery, etc.
Skull of a diprotodon (largest marsupial) found near Coonabarabran, NSW (Sept.).

C Arts and Entertainment
Wes Walters, *Portrait of Phillip Adams*, wins the Archibald Prize.
Robyn Archer presents her *Tonight: Lola Blau*.
Films:
  Gillian Armstrong's *My Brilliant Career*.
  George Miller's *Mad Max*.

D Books and Writing
David Ireland, *A Woman of the Future* (Miles Franklin Award winner).
Thomas Keneally, *Confederates*.
Roger McDonald, *1915*.
Patrick White, *The Twyborn Affair*.

E Sport and Recreation
Australia wins the Admiral's Cup. (During the last event, the Fastnet race, 17 yachtsmen of other countries die in a storm.)
Des Renford swims the English Channel three times during the year, taking his total crossings to 16.
Tracey Wickham breaks the world 1,500 m freestyle swimming record.
Robyn Burley becomes the first Australian to win an individual world ice skating championship.
Hyperno wins the Melbourne Cup.

F Statistics, Social Change, the Environment
Estimated resident population of Australia: 14,602,481.
Highest recorded daily rainfall in Australia—1,140 mm—registered at Bellenden Ker station, Qld (4 Jan.).
Unpaid maternity leave awarded by the federal Arbitration Commission to women in private industry.
Kakadu National Park (NT), Nullarbor National Park (SA), and the first section—Capricornia—of the Great Barrier Reef Marine Park proclaimed.

G Births and Deaths
Jan 14 Marjorie Lawrence d. (71).
Jun   6 Ion L. Idriess d. (89).
Jul   9 A. P. Elkin d. (88).
Jul 29 David Campbell d. (64).

1980

Jan 24 First section of Melbourne's underground rail loop opens.

27 Merchant banker Frank Nugan found dead in his car at Bowenfels, near Lithgow, NSW.

Feb 21 Thirteen people die when a Beechcraft plane crashes at Sydney Airport attempting an emergency landing after take-off.

23 Court government re-elected in WA.

Mar 1 ALP federal executive votes for intervention in the Qld branch, replacing most of the key office-holders.

Apr 30 Japanese company Mitsubishi takes over Chrysler Australia Ltd.

May 23 Australian Olympic Federation votes to send a team to the Olympic Games in Moscow despite a call by the federal government for a boycott because of Russia's intervention in Afghanistan. (Individual athletes subsequently withdraw.)

24 Queen Elizabeth and Prince Philip visit Australia for the opening of the High Court building in Canberra (26th).

29 Convicted bank robber Darcy Dugan released from Maitland Gaol, NSW, after spending more than 30 of his 59 years in prison. (Re-arrested and charged on 2 July 1981 with armed hold-up of a service station.)

Jun 23 Unknown gunman shoots dead Justice David Opas of the Family Court in Sydney on the doorstep of his Woollahra home.

Australia's first "test tube" baby (Candice Reed) born at the Royal Melbourne Women's Hospital.

Jul 4 *Newcastle Sun* (founded 1918) ceases publication.

17 NSW MLC Peter Baldwin is beaten up by an intruder in his Marrickville home following attempts to clean up Sydney inner city Labor Party branches.

Aug 17 Baby Azaria Chamberlain disappears from a campsite at Ayers Rock, reportedly taken by a dingo.

Sep 30 Bob Hawke retires as president of the ACTU to contest the forthcoming federal election. (Replaced as ACTU president by Cliff Dolan.)

Oct 1 Royal commission into the activities of the Federated Ship Painters and Dockers Union, under F. X. Costigan, begins sitting in Melbourne.

9 Standard-gauge line from Tarcoola (SA), on the Trans-Australian Railway, to Alice Springs opened by Princess Alexandra.

15 Violet Roberts and her son Bruce, convicted of killing their husband and father, are freed from prison in NSW after a public campaign for their release.

18 Election for House of Representatives and half Senate; Fraser government re-elected with a reduced majority; Democrats win three more Senate seats; new members include Bob Hawke and Senator Florence Bjelke-Petersen, wife of the Qld Premier.

24 Multicultural television begins in Sydney and Melbourne.

Nov 3 Five volunteer firemen die fighting a bushfire at Waterfall, NSW.

29 Bjelke-Petersen government re-elected in Qld.

Dec 2 Federal government lifts controls on interest rates offered by banks on customer deposits.

15 Inquest into the death of Azaria Chamberlain begins in Alice Springs.

1980

17 Turkish Consul-General Sarik Ariyak and his bodyguard are shot dead in Dover Heights, Sydney; assassins escape on a motorcycle.

24 Bomb explodes in Woolworths' Town Hall store in Sydney, the third bombing of a Woolworths store in a $1 million extortion attempt.

A Architecture, Building

Andrew Andersons, NSW Parliament House offices (–1985).

World-wide competition for a design for the new Parliament House in Canberra won by the US-based Romaldo Giurgola.

B Science, Technology, Discovery, etc.

Museum of Australia, Canberra, established by act of parliament.

Telecommunications tower on Black Mountain, Canberra, officially opened (15 May).

Australia's Landsat data-acquisition station at Alice Springs begins receiving direct information from US remote-sensing satellites.

Automatic teller machines introduced in Sydney.

Oil and gas discovered in the Cooper Basin, SA.

C Arts and Entertainment

Ron Robertson-Swann's plate-steel sculpture *The Vault* erected in Melbourne's City Square. (Removed to Batman Park after public controversy.)

No award made for the Archibald Prize.

"Wilfrid Thomas Show" ends after 39 years on ABC radio.

Bruce Beresford, *Breaker Morant* (film).

AC/DC, *Back in Black* (rock album).

D Books and Writing

Jessica Anderson, *The Impersonators* (Miles Franklin Award winner).

Murray Bail, *Homesickness*.

Geoffrey Blainey, *A Land Half Won*.

Shirley Hazzard, *The Transit of Venus*.

Clive James, *Unreliable Memoirs*.

Les A. Murray, *The Boys Who Stole the Funeral*.

E Sport and Recreation

Michelle Ford wins the 800 m freestyle swimming event at the Moscow Olympic Games, and the men's team wins the 4 × 100 m medley relay.

Evonne Cawley wins the women's singles at Wimbledon.

Grant Kenny wins the National Open Iron Man and Junior Iron Man titles in consecutive events at the Australian surf championships.

Des Renford swims the English Channel for a record 19th time.

Alan Jones wins the world Formula One driver's championship.

Beldale Ball wins the Melbourne Cup.

F Statistics, Social Change, the Environment

Estimated resident population of Australia: 14,807,370.

Women allowed to become full members of surf lifesaving clubs.

Deborah Wardley becomes the first woman in Australia to be appointed a pilot for a major commercial airline.

G Births and Deaths

May 2 Clarrie Grimmett d. (88).

Sep 5 Don Banks d. (56).

Nov 20 Sir John McEwen d. (80).

1981

Jan 13   Sydney police trap Gregory McHardy attempting to collect the Woolworths ransom in the water at Taronga Park wharf. (McHardy and accomplice Larry Danielson sentenced on 27 Apr. to 20 years' imprisonment.)

Feb 8   Headless and fingerless body of Kim Barry found on a cliff ledge at Jamberoo, NSW. (Graham Gene Potter subsequently arrested and sentenced to life imprisonment for her murder.)

     10   International airport opened at Townsville.

     11   Sir Garfield Barwick retires as Chief Justice of the High Court and is succeeded by Sir Harry Gibbs.

     14   Australia withdraws diplomatic recognition of the Pol Pot regime in Kampuchea.

     20   Alice Springs coroner Denis Barritt finds that a dingo killed Azaria Chamberlain.

Apr 12   Prince Charles visits Australia (to 28th).

     15   Andrew Peacock resigns from federal cabinet, accusing Prime Minister Fraser of "gross disloyalty".

     29   Sixteen patients die in a fire in a nursing home at Sylvania, Sydney.

     30   Federal government "Razor Gang" institutes cuts in spending on public services and instrumentalities.

     –   Public funding of election campaigns becomes law in NSW.

May 7   Alleged crime boss Robert Trimbole flees Australia.

     28   R. J. Hamer resigns as Premier of Vic. and is replaced by Lindsay Thompson (2 June).

     –   Grant of assisted passage restricted to refugees.

Jun 16   Jack ("Puttynose") Nicholls, due to give evidence to the Costigan royal commission, found shot dead in a car at Wangaratta, Vic.

     25   Royal commission into drug trafficking (Justice Donald Stewart) established.

Jul 31   Wage indexation abandoned.

Aug 18   Senate reconvenes with government members in the minority, Democrats and independent Brian Harradine holding the balance of power.

     20   Federal and Vic. governments set up a royal commission to investigate allegations of corruption and impropriety in the Builders' Labourers Federation.

     24   Church of England in Australia becomes the Anglican Church in Australia.

     25   Nine people die in a fire at the Rembrandt Apartments in Kings Cross, Sydney.

Sep 1   Medibank health scheme undergoes further changes: free treatment for uninsured in hospital standard wards ends.

     5   First death from AIDS in Australia: a 72-year-old man in Sydney's Royal Prince Alfred Hospital (established in Nov. 1993 by biopsy analysis).

     19   NT Chief Minister Paul Everingham orders the police to reopen investigation into the disappearance of Azaria Chamberlain.

         Wran government re-elected in NSW with an increased majority; opposition leader Bruce McDonald loses his seat. Referendums to extend the term of the Legislative Assembly from three years to four and to require MPs to disclose certain pecuniary interests both carried.

1981

26 Queen Elizabeth and Prince Philip visit Australia (to 12 Oct.) to open the Commonwealth Heads of Government Meeting in Melbourne.

Oct 1 National Bank of Australasia and Commercial Banking Company of Sydney merge to form the National Australia Bank.

Nov 2 Bank of New South Wales and the Commercial Bank of Australasia merge. (Begin trading under the name Westpac on 1 Oct. 1982.)
Rural Bank of New South Wales becomes the State Bank.

4 Pitjantjatjara people in SA granted land rights.

11 Tas. Premier Doug Lowe resigns and leaves the ALP following a caucus vote of no confidence in him; Harry Holgate replaces him as Premier.

20 Justice Toohey of the NT Supreme Court quashes coroner Barritt's findings in the Azaria Chamberlain inquest. (Second inquest opens on 30th.)

Dec 12 Referendum held in Tas. to decide the site of the dam on the Franklin River (44.89% vote "No dams" or informal.)

31 Death duties abolished in NSW.

A Architecture, Building
Work begins on Parliament House, Canberra (foundation stone laid by Prime Minister Hawke on 4 Oct. 1983).
AMP Building, Brisbane, wins the BOMA Award.

B Science, Technology, Discovery, etc.
Antivenene for funnel-web spider bites, developed by Struan Sutherland of the Commonwealth Serum Laboratories over 22 years, first used (Feb.).
National genetic engineering centre established at the Research School of Biological Sciences at the ANU, Canberra.
Powerhouse Museum, stage 1, opens in Sydney. (Fully opened in 1988.)
Radio-astronomers at the CSIRO's Parkes station discover pulsars in the Magellanic Clouds.

C Arts and Entertainment
Eric Smith, *Rudy Komon*, wins the Archibald Prize.
Olivia Newton-John's record "Physical" tops the charts in the US.
Melbourne's Pram Factory theatre closes down.
Peter Weir, *Gallipoli* (film).

D Books and Writing
Peter Carey, *Bliss* (Miles Franklin Award winner).
Blanche d'Alpuget, *Turtle Beach*.
A. B. Facey, *A Fortunate Life*.
The Macquarie Dictionary.
Eric Rolls, *A Million Wild Acres*.
Gavin Souter, *Company of Heralds*.
Patrick White, *Flaws in the Glass*.

E Sport and Recreation
Australian Institute of Sport opens at the National Sports Centre in Canberra (Jan.).
Dennis Lillee takes his 310th test wicket, setting a new world record.
Trevor Chappell bowls the last ball underarm in a World Series Cricket match against NZ in Melbourne to prevent NZ scoring the six runs it needed to draw.
Brothers Glen, Mark, and Gary Ella play in Australia's Rugby Union test team.
Jan Stephenson wins the women's world golf championship in Japan.
Ron Grant runs across the Simpson Desert.
Just a Dash wins the Melbourne Cup.

1981

F Statistics, Social Change, the Environment

Estimated resident population of Australia reaches 15 million (Commonwealth census, 30 June: 14,926,800, including 160,915 Aborigines and Torres Strait Islanders).

Four-millionth Holden vehicle comes off the assembly line (June).

Metal trades gain a 38-hour week.

Pat O'Shane, appointed permanent head of the NSW Dept of Aboriginal Affairs on 25 Nov., becomes the first woman to head a government department in Australia.

Cairns section of the Great Barrier Reef Marine Park proclaimed.

G Births and Deaths

May   2   Sir Roy Grounds d. (75).
Jun 16   Sir Thomas Playford d. (84).
Jun 29   Sir Russell Drysdale d. (69).
Sep   2   Dame Enid Lyons d. (84).
Sep   9   Sir Robert Askin d. (72).
Oct 19   Dymphna Cusack d. (79).
Dec 23   Sir Reginald Ansett d. (72).

1982

Jan 25   Sir Charles Court steps down as Premier of WA and is succeeded by Ray O'Connor.

Feb 2   Lindy Chamberlain committed for trial for the murder of her baby daughter, Azaria. (Found guilty and sentenced to life imprisonment, 29 Oct.)

 6   Fairlea Women's Prison at Fairfield, Vic., extensively damaged by fire; three killed.

Apr 3   Labor elected to government in Vic., ending 27 years of Liberal rule; John Cain (son of former Premier John Cain) becomes Premier.

 8   XPT (Express Passenger Train) begins operation in NSW.

 16   Archbishop John Grindrod appointed Anglican Primate of Australia, to succeed Sir Marcus Loane.

 19   Health Minister Michael McKellar and Minister for Customs John Moore resign from the ministry following McKellar's failure to declare and pay duty on a colour television set.

May 15   Liberal government elected in Tas; Robin Gray becomes Premier.

Jun 7   Allegation of a mass conspiracy among doctors, patients, and prominent members of the Greek community dismissed by magistrate Bruce Brown on the 386th day of the hearing.

 18   Legislation passed in SA authorizing the development of the Roxby Downs copper-uranium deposit, despite controversy.

Jul 7   ALP reverses its policy on uranium mining to allow for the continuation of existing mining projects.

 21   Aboriginal Northern Land Council agrees to the mining of uranium at Jabiluka, NT.

 29   Sir Ninian Stephen succeeds Sir Zelman Cowen as Governor-General. Australian dollar falls below parity with the American dollar for the first time.

Aug 2   Brisbane's *Daily Sun* begins publication.

1982

8 Dalai Lama arrives in Australia for the 30th anniversary of the establishment of Buddhism in Australia.

24 Fourth interim report of the royal commission into the activities of the Federated Ship Painters and Dockers Union highlights the "bottom of the harbour" tax-avoidance schemes.

Sep – Uranium mining ceases at Mary Kathleen. (Everything in the town auctioned in 1983.)

Oct 5 Queen Elizabeth visits Australia (to 13th) to open the Australian National Gallery (Prince Phillip having arrived on 27th Sept. for the opening of the Commonwealth Games in Brisbane).

13 Inquest into the Hilton Hotel bombing finds a prima facie case of murder against Ross Dunn and Paul Alister.

16 National Country Party, at the federal level, changes its name to the National Party of Australia.

Nov 6 Labor wins office in SA election; John Bannon becomes Premier.

15 Instant lotteries introduced in NSW.

– First case of AIDS (Acquired Immune Deficiency Syndrome) in Australia diagnosed in Sydney. (But see 1981 **9**.)

Dec 1 Commonwealth Freedom of Information Act comes into operation.

17 Random breath testing introduced in NSW.

31 *Australian Women's Weekly* first published as a monthly.

* Much of Australia in the fourth year of drought.

A Architecture, Building

Gerard de Preu, Rialto building, Melbourne (–1985)—Australia's tallest building to date (56 storeys; 242 metres).

B Science, Technology, Discovery, etc.

Bionic ear developed by Prof. Graeme Clark at Melbourne University in the 1970s is successfully implanted.

Omega maritime navigational station at Darriman, in Gippsland, Vic., becomes operational (16 Aug.).

First electronic funds transfer at point of sale (EFTPOS) terminal in Australia begins operating in WA.

C Arts and Entertainment

Australian National Gallery, Canberra, opened (12 Oct.).

Queensland Art Gallery (first stage of the Qld Cultural Centre, Brisbane) opened (21 June).

Eric Smith, *Peter Sculthorpe*, wins the Archibald Prize.

Melbourne Concert Hall of the Victorian Arts Centre opened (6 Nov.).

Opera in the Park (Joan Sutherland in *La Traviata*) first held in Sydney's Domain during the Festival of Sydney (16 Jan.).

Records of the pop group Men at Work top the Australian, British and American charts.

The Man from Snowy River (film).

Peter Weir, *The Year of Living Dangerously* (film).

D Books and Writing

Rodney Hall, *Just Relations* (Miles Franklin Award winner).

Elizabeth Jolley, *Mr Scobie's Riddle*.

Thomas Keneally, *Schindler's Ark* (British Booker Prize winner; film, titled *Schindler's List*, 1994).

Geoffrey Serle, *John Monash*.

E Sport and Recreation

Commonwealth Games held in Brisbane (1–9 Oct.).

Mark Richards wins the world professional surf-riding championship for the fourth year in succession.

Gurner's Lane wins the Melbourne Cup and the Caulfield Cup.

F Statistics, Social Change, the Environment

Estimated resident population of Australia: 15,276,805.

Tasmania's south-west wilderness area placed on the World Heritage Commission list; conservationists blockade work on the Gordon Dam.

Cane toads reach Coffs Harbour, NSW, in the south and the Qld–NT border in the west.

G Births and Deaths

Mar 18   Sir Lawrence Wackett d. (86).

Apr 22   Fred Williams d. (55).

Jun   9   Sir Bernard Heinze d. (87).

1983

Jan 9   Bushfires kill four fire-fighters in NSW and Vic.

Feb 3   Prime Minister Malcolm Fraser obtains a double dissolution of parliament; Bob Hawke replaces Bill Hayden as leader of the Labor Party.

8   Severe dust storm envelops Melbourne in darkness and deposits 11,000 tonnes of topsoil on the city.

16   "Ash Wednesday" bushfires in Vic. and SA result in the loss of 72 lives and the destruction of more than 2,000 houses.

19   Labor wins election in WA; Brian Burke becomes Premier.

21   ACTU endorses the prices and incomes accord.

Mar 5   Election for federal parliament; Labor wins office. Malcolm Fraser resigns from the Liberal leadership.

8   Dollar devalued by 10%.

11   Hawke ministry sworn in. Andrew Peacock elected Liberal Party leader.

20   Prince Charles and Princess Diana with baby Prince William visit Australia (to 20 Apr.).

–   Australian Catholic priest Brian Gore gaoled in the Philippines on charges of murder and inciting rebellion. (Released on 3 July 1984 after being exonerated; returns to Australia 22 July.)

Apr 11   National Economic Summit held in Canberra (to 14th).

22   Soviet Embassy first secretary Valeriy Ivanov expelled for alleged spying.

27   Archbishop Edward Clancy succeeds Cardinal Sir James Freeman as Catholic Archbishop of Sydney.

May 10   Canberra lobbyist and former ALP federal secretary David Combe declared persona non grata by the federal government for his association with expelled Soviet diplomat Valeriy Ivanov.

16   NSW Premier Neville Wran steps aside while a royal commission investigates allegations made on the TV program "Four Corners" that he attempted to influence the magistracy.

17   Royal commission under Justice R. M. Hope set up to inquire into Australia's security and intelligence agencies.

31   Final report of the royal commission into drug trafficking tabled in federal parliament.

1983

- Floods in northern NSW and southern Qld (to June) end four years of drought.

Jul 1 Australian Broadcasting Commission reconstituted as the Australian Broadcasting Corporation.

22 Dick Smith completes the first solo flight around the world in a helicopter (begun on 5 Aug. 1982).

28 Neville Wran exonerated by the royal commission and resumes post as NSW Premier. (Chief magistrate Murray Farquhar charged with perverting the course of justice, 1 Aug.).

Aug 2 Paul Sharp becomes the first white person to cross the Simpson Desert alone and on foot.

14 Roslyn Kelly becomes the first sitting member of parliament to give birth.

17 Seven Liberal ministers resign from Qld government. (National–Liberal Party coalition formally ends at midnight on 18th.)

18 Five people killed and 20 injured when a road train is deliberately driven into a motel at Ayers Rock, NT. (Driver Douglas Edwin Crabbe found guilty of murder in Mar. 1984.)

Sep 23 Australian Conciliation and Arbitration Commission sets out guidelines for a centralized system of wage-fixing (full indexation).

Oct 22 Qld state election: increased support for the National Party and the subsequent defection of two Liberals allows the National Party to govern in its own right.

- WA introduces daylight saving on a trial basis. (People vote against continuation at a referendum in Apr. 1984.)

Nov 30 Australian Secret Intelligence Service (ASIS) agents raid the Sheraton Hotel in Melbourne in a training exercise.

Dec 9 Australian dollar allowed to float.

A Architecture, Building

Foundations of Sydney's first Government House uncovered by Heritage Council archaeologists (May).

Second building for the State Library of NSW, Sydney (–1988).

B Science, Technology, Discovery, etc.

Fossil of a mammal that lived between 110 million and 120 million years ago found at Lightning Ridge, NSW.

C Arts and Entertainment

Nigel Thomson, *Chandler Coventry*, wins the Archibald Prize.

Sydney Entertainment Centre opens (1 May).

Careful, He Might Hear You (film).

D Books and Writing

Australian Encyclopaedia, 4th edition (12 vols.).

Nancy Cato, *Forefathers*.

Bruce Dawe, *Sometimes Gladness: Collected poems 1954–78*.

Clive James, *Brilliant Creatures*.

No Miles Franklin Award made.

E Sport and Recreation

Grant Kenny wins the national ironman surf title for the fourth consecutive year.

Cliff Young, aged 61, wins the inaugural Sydney–Melbourne foot race.

Jan Stephenson wins the US Women's Open golf championship.

1983

Robert de Castella wins the marathon at Rotterdam and at the world athletic championships in Helsinki.

Australia II wins the America's Cup (the first time in 132 years a nonAmerican yacht has won).

Ron Grant completes a 217-day run around Australia (31 Oct.).

Kiwi wins the Melbourne Cup.

Australia (Pat Cash, Mark Edmondson, Paul McNamee, John Fitzgerald) beats Sweden to win the Davis Cup.

F Statistics, Social Change, the Environment

Estimated resident population of Australia: 15,464,235.

Melbourne Cricket Club votes to allow women members.

High Court decision (1 July) blocks construction of the Gordon-below-Franklin dam in Tas.

G Births and Deaths

Jan 28 F. M. Forde d. (92).

Mar 31 Christina Stead d. (80).

Sep 29 Alan Moorehead d. (73).

1984

Jan 17 Ian Sinclair succeeds J. D. Anthony as federal National Party leader.

31 Bank robber Hakki Bahadi Atahan takes ten hostages from the Commonwealth Bank in George St, Sydney, but is shot dead by police on the Spit Bridge after a car chase through the suburbs.

Feb 1 Medicare scheme begins operation.

2 Melbourne *Age* publishes extracts from tapes of phone taps, made by members of the NSW Police Department, incriminating an unnamed judge.

22 High Court dismisses Lindy Chamberlain's appeal against her conviction and life sentence for the murder of her baby daughter Azaria.

Mar 6 Bomb blast wrecks the Belrose (Sydney) home of Family Court judge Richard Gee, injuring him.

Justice Lionel Murphy of the High Court named in parliament as the judge referred to in the "*Age* tapes".

14 Neighbourhood Watch introduced in Vic. to help cut home burglaries.

24 Wran government re-elected in NSW with a reduced majority.

26 $100 note goes into circulation.

Apr 1 Stockbroking industry deregulated.

6 Cocos Islands vote for integration with Australia.

15 Family Court in Parramatta extensively damaged by a bomb explosion.

19 "Advance Australia Fair" proclaimed as Australia's official national anthem and green and gold as Australia's national colours.

May 14 One-dollar coin goes into circulation. (Note gradually withdrawn.)

Jun 3 Electrification of railway from Sydney to Newcastle inaugurated.

– Surgical specialists resign from NSW public hospitals in a dispute over Medicare. (Return in March 1989.)

Jul 4 Justice Ray Watson of the Family Court in Sydney narrowly escapes death and his wife is killed when an explosion devastates their Greenwich home. Heavy snowfalls block roads and railways in eastern Australia; Sydney has its coldest July day since 1896.

1984

18　National Crime Authority, chaired by Justice Donald Stewart, takes over investigations of the Costigan royal commission.

Aug 1　Banks deregulated.

8　Friday night and Saturday afternoon shopping allowed in NSW. (Begins 10, 11 Aug.).

12　First stage of the North-West Shelf natural gas project begins operations, gas being piped to Perth and industrial areas of WA.

Sep 2　Seven shot dead and 15 wounded in a clash between rival bikie gangs the Comancheros and the Bandidos at the Viking Tavern, Milperra, Sydney.

10　Federal government invites foreign banks to set up in Australia.

–　Regular air service begins between Australia and China.

Oct 2　Royal commission into British nuclear tests in Australia between 1952 and 1963 begins hearings in Sydney. (Sittings in London begin 4 Jan. 1985.) Newcastle City Council dismissed by the NSW government.

3　Tim Macartney-Snape and Greg Mortimer become the first Australians to climb Mt Everest and the first to ascend the north face without oxygen.

17　Ian Tuxworth becomes Chief Minister of NT following the resignation of Paul Everingham to enter federal politics.

25　Crime boss Robert Trimbole arrested in Dublin. (Released 6 Feb. 1985.)

31　Senate select committee finds that Justice Murphy could have been guilty of behaviour serious enough to warrant his removal from the High Court.

Nov 1　Costigan Report, tabled in Vic. parliament, links media magnate Kerry Packer with crime and urges prosecution. (Packer exonerated of all allegations in Mar. 1987.)

18　Federal task force set up to co-ordinate the campaign against AIDS.

26　Former NSW Minister for Corrective Services Rex Jackson appears in court to face conspiracy charges over the early release of prisoners.

Dec 1　Election for House of Representatives and half Senate. Hawke government returned with a reduced majority. Democrat numbers in the Senate increased to seven. Recently formed Nuclear Disarmament Party wins one Senate seat. Referendums on simultaneous elections for Senate and House and to allow interchange of powers between Commonwealth and states defeated.

13　Director of Public Prosecutions, Ian Temby, decides that Justice Murphy should be charged with having attempted to pervert the course of justice.

17　More than 76,000 square kilometres of land at Maralinga returned to traditional Aboriginal owners.

A Architecture, Building

Hyde Park Barracks, Sydney, restored and converted to a museum of social history.

Australia's first Mormon temple built in Carlingford, Sydney (dedicated 20 Sept.).

B Science, Technology, Discovery, etc.

World's first frozen-embryo baby born in Melbourne (Mar.).

Rich area of 15-million-year-old fossils discovered on Riversleigh cattle station, about 200 km north of Mt Isa, Qld.

C Arts and Entertainment

Keith Looby, *Max Gillies*, wins the Archibald Prize.

Victorian Arts Centre Theatres in Melbourne officially opened (29 Oct.).

National Film and Sound Archives (later ScreenSound Australia) opens in Canberra (3 Nov.).

Compulsory classification of all video films introduced (June).

D Books and Writing

Nicholas Hasluck, *The Bellarmine Jug* (*Age* Book of the Year).
David Malouf, *Harland's Half Acre.*
Les A. Murray, *The People's Otherworld.*
Bernard Smith, *The Boy Adeodatus.*
Tim Winton, *Shallows* (Miles Franklin Award winner).

E Sport and Recreation

At the Los Angeles Olympics, Glynis Nunn wins the women's heptathlon, John Sieben wins the 200 m butterfly swimming, the Australian men's cycling team wins the 4,000 m team pursuit, and Dean Lukin wins the super heavyweight weight-lifting.

AJC "warns off" Bill and Robbie Waterhouse following the substitution of the racehorse Bold Personality for Fine Cotton at Brisbane on 18 Aug.

Sunday VFL football games begin in Vic. (9 Sept.).

State Sports Centre opens in Homebush, Sydney (22 Nov.).

Black Knight wins the Melbourne Cup.

Wallabies Rugby Union team achieve the grand slam, beating England, Ireland Wales, and Scotland, and also the Barbarians.

Tom Carroll wins the world surfing championship for the second year in succession.

F Statistics, Social Change, the Environment

Estimated resident population of Australia: 15,648,861.

Migrants from Asia increase by 17%, while those from Europe fall by 37%.

More than a hundred of the thousand companies listed on the stock exchange are taken over during the year.

Commonwealth and state anti-discrimination legislation becomes operative (1 Aug.).

Homosexual acts between consenting adults decriminalized in NSW.

Brothels legalized in Vic.

Video-cassette boom cuts attendance at cinemas and forces the closure of some drive-in cinemas.

Mice plague sweeps NSW, Vic., and SA country districts.

More than 220,000 red and grey kangaroos culled from an estimated population of 4¼ million in NSW.

G Births and Deaths

Jan   9   Bob Dyer d. (74).
Jan 21   Alan Marshall d. (82).
Sep 29   Hal Porter d. (73).
Nov 10   Xavier Herbert d. (83)
Dec 20   Grace Cossington Smith d. (92).

1985

Jan 1   Australia begins a two-year term on the UN Security Council. (Australia's ambassador takes over as president for the month of Nov.)
       14   More than 140 bushfires flare through Vic. and SA (to 17th); five people killed.

Feb 1   AM stereo radio broadcasting begins.
        5   US withdraws from a planned ANZUS naval exercise after NZ refuses to allow nuclear-capable US warships to call at its ports.

1985

Australia cancels its involvement in American MX missile tests.

7 State of emergency declared in Qld (to 7 Mar.) after Electricity Board workers go on strike. (Some 900 strikers subsequently sacked; new employment contract includes a no-strike clause.)

Mar 1 Uniform credit legislation comes into effect in NSW, Vic., and WA.

2 Cain government re-elected in Vic. with a reduced majority, the first time a Labor government in Vic. has been elected for a successive term.

4 Annual meeting of the ANZUS Council cancelled by the Australian government at the request of the US.

8 Former NSW Chief Stipendiary Magistrate Murray Farquhar found guilty of attempting to pervert the course of justice and (15th) sentenced to four years' gaol.

13 ALP gains control of the Vic. Legislative Council for the first time when the returning officer draws the winner's name out of a hat following a tied recount. (Loses control on 17 Aug. with the loss of the Nunawading by-election.)

21 Qld enacts harsh anti-strike legislation.

31 More than 300,000 people across Australia march in Palm Sunday anti-nuclear rallies.

Apr 1 Mary Beasley becomes SA's Ombudsman (the first female ombudsman in Australia). (Resigns in Oct.)

18 Duke and Duchess of Kent visit Australia (to 25th).

26 High Court judge Lionel Murphy is committed for trial on two charges of attempting to pervert the course of justice. (Found guilty, 5 July; sentenced to 18 months' gaol, 3 Sept., sentence not to be enforced until appeal heard; granted new trial by NSW Court of Appeal and previous conviction set aside, 28 Nov.)

28 Nuclear Disarmament Party splits when 35 members, including the NDP's only parliamentary representative, walk out of the national conference.

– Australian dollar collapses, falling to a low of 63 cents US (and 77.56 on the Reserve Bank's trade-weighted index).

May 15 Ananda Marga members Ross Dunn, Timothy Anderson, and Paul Alister are pardoned and released from gaol after serving seven years of a sixteen-year sentence.

Jun 2 *Empress of Australia* makes its last voyage between Tas. and the mainland.

13 BLF federal secretary Norm Gallagher found guilty of 20 charges of receiving secret commissions and (21st) sentenced to four years and three months' gaol. (Released on 7 Oct; convictions quashed.)

Jul 7 Opening of a desalination plant at Coober Pedy, SA, inaugurates the town's piped water supply.

21 Bomb blast tears apart the Jehovah's Witnesses hall at Casula, Sydney, killing one man and injuring 48 other churchgoers.

Aug 6 G. J. Coles takes over the Myer Emporium to become Coles Myer Ltd.

22 Agent Orange royal commission finds no link between chemical defoliants sprayed in Vietnam and health problems of veterans.

23 Bond Corporation takes over Castlemaine Tooheys in the biggest takeover operation yet in Australia.

Sep 5 John Howard replaces Andrew Peacock as leader of the federal opposition.

10 Simon Crean succeeds Cliff Dolan as president of the ACTU.

Oct 12 Canon Arthur Malcolm becomes Australia's first Aboriginal bishop.

26 Freehold title to Ayers Rock and the Uluru National Park handed over to the Mutijulu Aboriginal community.

27 Prince Charles and Princess Diana visit Australia (to 8 Nov.) for Vic.'s 150th anniversary celebrations.

Dec 2 Australia Act passed by federal parliament, abolishing the right of Australians to appeal to the Privy Council and cutting Australia's last remaining constitutional ties with Britain. (Comes into force 3 Mar. 1986.)

5 Royal commission into British atomic tests in Australia, tabled in the Senate, criticizes Britain for breaching safety standards and recommends compensation and a British clean-up of contaminated areas.

7 Labor government of John Bannon re-elected in SA.

A Architecture, Building

Construction begins on the redevelopment of Darling Harbour, Sydney.

B Science, Technology, Discovery, etc.

Telecom Australia's national videotex information-retrieval service, Viatel, begins operation (28 Feb.).

Commission for the Future established (July).

Aussat, Australia's first domestic communications satellite, launched from Cape Canaveral, USA (27 Aug.).

A living Huon pine estimated to be more than 10,500 years old is discovered on a Tasmanian mountain top by a Forestry Tasmania forester.

C Arts and Entertainment

Guy Warren, *Flugelman with Wingman*, wins the Archibald Prize.

NSW Supreme Court rules that the Archibald Prize should be retained in perpetuity (having been reassessed, under the terms of the will).

Performing Arts Centre, Brisbane (second stage of Qld Cultural Centre), officially opened (20 Apr.).

Long-running ABC television program "Weekend Magazine" comes to an end (3 Mar.), and "Neighbours" begins (13 Mar.).

D Books and Writing

Peter Carey, *Illywhacker.*

Kate Grenville, *Lilian's Story.*

C. J. Koch, *The Doubleman* (Miles Franklin Award winner).

E Sport and Recreation

Jeff Fenech wins the IBF world bantamweight boxing championship against Satoshi Shingaki in Sydney (26 Apr.).

Dr Geoffrey Edelsten buys the Sydney Swans VFL football team for $6.3 mil.

Adair Ferguson wins lightweight single sculls women's world championship.

Formula One Australian Grand Prix first held in Adelaide.

What a Nuisance wins the Melbourne Cup.

F Statistics, Social Change, the Environment

Estimated resident population of Australia: 15,858,700.

$2.28 billion outstanding on Bankcard.

Annual per capita consumption of alcoholic beverages: beer, 115 litres; wine, 22 litres; spirits, 1.1 litre.

Assets test for pensioners comes into effect (Mar.).

De Facto Relationships Act gives couples living in de facto relationships rights and obligations similar to those of married couples.

Women begin training alongside men in the Australian Army.

Washpool rainforest, NSW, declared a wilderness area.

1985

G Births and Deaths

Jan 11 Sir William McKell d. (93).
Feb 14 Douglas Stewart d. (71).
Apr 2 Dame Doris Fitton d. (87).
Apr 15 Sir Raphael Cilento d. (91).
May 3 Sir Percy Spender d. (87).
Aug 31 Sir Macfarlane Burnet d. (85).
Sep 15 Eleanor Dark d. (84).
Dec 28 Harry Hopman d. (79).

1986

Jan – Australian Defence Force Academy, Canberra, enrols its first cadets.
– *Australian Geographic* magazine launched by Dick Smith.

Feb 1 Cyclone Winifred devastates a 200 km stretch of coast between Cairns and Ingham, Qld; one man killed, scores injured, hundreds of houses destroyed.
2 Nurse Anita Cobby is abducted, robbed, raped, and murdered by John Travers, Michael Murdoch, and Leslie, Gary, and Michael Murphy at Prospect, Sydney. (All five men sentenced on 16 June 1987 to life imprisonment with the recommendation never to be released.)
7 Lindy Chamberlain released from gaol on licence after serving 39 months of a life sentence for the murder of her daughter Azaria. (Commission of inquiry into the Chamberlains' convictions begins in Darwin 8 May.)
8 Liberal government of Robin Gray re-elected in Tas; Labor government of Brian Burke re-elected in WA.
9 First women (eight) ordained as deacons of the Anglican Church in Australia, at Melbourne's St Paul's Cathedral.
11 Joan Child becomes first woman Speaker of House of Representatives.
12 Ernie Bridge becomes the first Aboriginal cabinet minister on being elected to the Burke ministry in WA.
– Halley's Comet visible in the night sky (to late Apr.).

Mar 2 Queen Elizabeth and Prince Philip visit ACT, NSW, Vic., and SA (to 13th).
9 First stage of Adelaide's O-Bahn guided busway begins operating.
27 Car bomb explodes outside the Russell Street police headquarters in Melbourne; 21 people injured (one policewoman subsequently dies).
– Loggers and conservationists clash at Farmhouse Creek wilderness, Tas.

Apr 11 Builders' Labourers Federation deregistered following an Arbitration Commission findings of serious industrial misconduct by the BLF.
14 Second trial of High Court judge Lionel Murphy begins in Sydney. (Jury acquits Murphy, 28th.)
16 James Bazley convicted of conspiring to murder Griffith anti-drugs campaigner Donald Mackay and sentenced to life imprisonment.
20 *Queenslander* train begins running between Brisbane and Cairns.

May 10 NT Chief Minister Ian Tuxworth resigns following pressure from his party. (Steve Hatton elected to replace him, 14th.)

Jul 1 Fringe benefits tax comes into effect.
4 NSW Premier Neville Wran retires from politics and is succeeded as Premier by Barrie Unsworth.
16 Twelve miners die when an explosion and cave-in traps them in a coalmine at Moura, Qld.

24 Patricia O'Shane becomes NSW's first Aboriginal magistrate.

28 Australian dollar falls to an all-time low of 57.3 cents US and (on 31st) 49.3 on the Reserve Bank's trade-weighted index.

– Australian Nugget gold coins first struck in WA. (Issued in Oct; officially launched on 23 Apr. 1987.)

Aug 3 *Southern Aurora* and *Spirit of Progress* trains combine to become the Melbourne/Sydney Express.

4 Trans-Australia Airlines becomes Australian Airlines.

5 Sydney has its wettest 24 hours on record, with more than 327 mm of rain falling; six people killed, 1,500 evacuated; transport in chaos.

18 Australian Democrats leader Don Chipp retires from federal parliament and is succeeded as party leader by Senator Janine Haines, the first woman and the first South Australian to become a parliamentary party leader.

19 Federal government introduces a $250 administration charge for all tertiary students, to take effect in the 1987 academic year.

Sep 7 Sealed road around Australia completed with the opening of the section between Fitzroy Crossing and Halls Creek in the far north-west of WA.

10 Australia's credit rating reduced from AAA to AA1 in the US.

Oct 8 ACTU approves a two-tier wage-fixing system, to end three years of wage indexation. (Endorsed by Arbitration Commission, 23 Dec.)

21 Justice Murphy dies of cancer (a special inquiry into his conduct having been dropped in Aug.).

24 Last link of Australia's microwave telephone system completed at Kununurra, WA.

26 Perth's new international airport opens.

Nov 1 Bjelke-Petersen government re-elected in Qld, the National Party winning an outright majority of seats.

11 David and Catherine Birnie charged with the murder of four women found in shallow graves near Perth, WA.

23 Bomb destroys the Turkish consulate in South Yarra, Melbourne; bomber killed in explosion.

24 Pope John Paul II arrives in Canberra to begin a 6½-day tour of Australia, visiting each capital city and Alice Springs.

Dec 1 Two youths, James Annetts and Simon Amos, vanish mysteriously from isolated cattle stations in East Kimberley, WA. (Skeletal remains found in the Great Sandy Desert in April 1987.)

7 Adelaide hit by two fierce storms, which cause extensive damage.

8 Mary Gaudron becomes the first woman appointed to the High Court.

* Severe downturn in rural sector threatens survival of many farmers.

* Five currency futures trading companies collapse during the year.

A Architecture, Building

Gateway Bridge, Brisbane, the world's longest cantilevered box girder bridge (1,027 metres), opens (11 Jan.).

B Science, Technology, Discovery, etc.

Edgeworth David research base established in Queen Mary Land, Antarctica.

Supernova science and technology centre opens in Newcastle (20 June).

C Arts and Entertainment

Davida Allen, *Dr John Arthur McKelvie Shera*, wins the Archibald Prize.

Richard Meale's opera *Voss* (libretto by David Malouf) has its world premiere at the Adelaide Festival (1 Mar.).

1986

Films: Peter Faiman's *Crocodile Dundee*, with Paul Hogan, and Nadia Tass's *Malcolm*.

D Books and Writing

Sir Edward Dunlop, *The War Diaries of Weary Dunlop*.
Elizabeth Jolley, *The Well* (Miles Franklin Award winner).

E Sport and Entertainment

Marathon runners Ron Grant and Tony Rafferty race on foot across the Simpson Desert in midsummer. (Grant wins.)

Greg Norman wins the British Open and the European Open golf championships.

Peter Antonie wins the single sculls and the Australian eight also wins a gold medal at the world rowing championships at Nottingham, UK.

Kerry Saxby sets a world record time (45 min. 8 sec.) in winning the women's 10,000 metre walk at the Moscow Goodwill Games.

At Talaq wins the Melbourne Cup.

Australia (Pat Cash, Paul McNamee, John Fitzgerald) wins the Davis Cup.

NSW celebrates "cracker night" for the last time (7 June).

F Statistics, Social Change, the Environment

Population of Australia reaches 16 million, including 3.3 million born overseas. (Commonwealth census, 30 June: 16,020,000, including 227,644 Aborigines and Torres Strait Islanders.)

Australia's gross foreign debt reaches a record $101.37 billion (about 34 per cent of GDP) in the September quarter.

Number of millionaires grows by 3,000 to an estimated total of 31,829.

Fifty-seven thousand Australians lose their jobs in July.

Roman Catholic Church becomes Australia's largest religious denomination (26.25% of pop.).

All new cars must be designed to run on unleaded petrol.

G Births and Deaths

Apr 4   Sir Laurence Hartnett d. (87).
Sep 28   Sir Robert Helpmann d. (77).
Oct 4   Desiderius Orban d. (101).
Oct 21   Lionel Murphy d. (64).
Dec 29   John Antill d. (82).

1987

Feb 1   Princess Anne visits WA (to 8th) during the America's Cup races.
     6   News Ltd takes over the Herald and Weekly Times.
        Sir Anthony Mason succeeds Sir Harry Gibbs as Chief Justice of the High Court.
   15   All-weather road between Adelaide and Darwin completed with the sealing of the last section near Marla Bore, 230 km north of Coober Pedy, SA.

Mar 26   NSW government dismisses the Sydney City Council. (Three-man commission subsequently appointed to run the city.)
   29   Crocodile kills an American woman at the Prince Regent River, north-west WA—the eighth person in two years to be killed by crocodiles.

Apr 1   Capital city stock exchanges amalgamate to form the Australian Stock Exchange.

1987

28 Dick Smith becomes the first person to reach the North Pole by a solo helicopter flight.

– Legionnaires' disease breaks out in the Wollongong district. (Forty-five confirmed cases and nine deaths by July.)

May 12 Robert Trimbole, wanted in Australia on numerous charges involving murder, drugs, race fixing and corruption, dies in Spain.

27 Prime Minister Bob Hawke is granted a double dissolution of parliament; election called for 11 July.

Jun 2 Morling Report tabled in NT parliament results in a pardon for Lindy and Michael Chamberlain.

12 After a trial lasting 332 days, 30 members of rival motorcycle gangs are found guilty (nine of murder, 21 of manslaughter) of the "Fathers Day massacre" at Milperra, Sydney, in Sept. 1984.

19 Police shoot dead West German tourist Joseph Schwab, believed to have shot and killed five people in northern Australia in the past 11 days.

Jul 11 Election for federal parliament. Hawke government returned with a slightly increased majority.

27 Commission of inquiry into corruption in the Qld police force, headed by G. E. Fitzgerald, begins sitting in Brisbane.

Aug 9 Five people shot dead and 11 others injured when 19-year-old Julian Knight opens fire at random in Hoddle Street, Clifton Hill, Melbourne.

12 Federal government announces the setting up of a royal commission to investigate the deaths in custody of 44 Aborigines since 1980. (Headed by Justice James Muirhead, the commission begins sitting on 12 Nov.; Report tabled in May 1991.)

28 Former NSW Minister for Corrective Services Rex Jackson found guilty of conspiring to accept bribes for the release of prisoners.

Oct 19 Share prices on Australian stock exchanges suffer a record fall, in line with the world-wide stockmarket crash.

Nov 1 First transcontinental race by solar-powered cars begins from Darwin. (Winner, General Motors' *Sunraycer*, arrives in Adelaide on 6 Nov.)

6 Oldest Australian, Caroline Mockridge, dies in Geelong at the age of 112 years and 330 days.

Dec 1 Sir Joh Bjelke-Petersen resigns as Premier of Qld and retires from parliament; Mike Ahern is sworn in as the new Premier.

8 Gunman Frank Vitkovic shoots dead nine people and wounds five others in a Melbourne office building before plunging 11 storeys to his death.

10 Federal government announces its intention of acknowledging, in the preamble to legislation, that Aborigines were the first owners of Australia.

17 Federal Minister for Tourism, John Brown, resigns from the ministry after admitting he misled parliament over tenders for an Expo contract.

A Architecture, Building

Perth's Superdrome sports complex completed.

B Science, Technology, Discovery, etc.

Carbon dating of ancient artefacts found near Penrith, NSW, indicates that humans occupied Australia 47,000 years ago.

Telecom switches on MobileNet, inaugurating the mobile phone in Australia.

C Arts and Entertainment

William Robinson, *Equestrian Self-Portrait*, wins the Archibald Prize.

1987

Musical *Rasputin* premières in Sydney.

David Williamson's play *Emerald City* first produced.

John Duigan, *The Year My Voice Broke* (film).

D Books and Writing

Glenda Adams, *Dancing on Coral* (Miles Franklin Award Winner).

Murray Bail, *Holden's Performance*.

C. M. H. Clark, final volume (vol. 6) of *A History of Australia*.

Robert Hughes, *The Fatal Shore*.

E Sport and Recreation

American yacht *Stars and Stripes* beats Australia's *Kookaburra III* in a series of races off Fremantle to win back the America's Cup.

Jeff Fenech knocks out Samart Payakarun in Sydney to win the WBC super-bantamweight boxing championship (8 May) and becomes the first Australian to have held two world boxing titles.

Pat Cash wins the Wimbledon men's singles tennis championship.

Martin Vinnicombe of Sydney wins the amateur 1,000-metre time trial at the world cycling championships in Vienna.

Wayne Gardner wins the world 500-cc motorcycle championship.

Kensei wins the Melbourne Cup, in which a female jockey (Maree Lyndon) rides for the first time.

Allan Border overtakes Greg Chappell to become Australia's greatest run-scorer in test cricket.

F Statistics, Social Change, the Environment

Estimated resident population of Australia: 16,263,300.

Hole in the earth's ozone layer moves over southern Australia for about a month (Dec.).

Possession of small amounts of cannabis for personal use legalized in SA.

G Births and Deaths

May 8 Marjorie Barnard d. (89).

May 25 Robert D. FitzGerald d. (85).

Jun 26 Sir Billy Snedden d. (60).

Jul 26 Lady Cilento d. (93).

1988

Jan 15 Aboriginal television station Imparja begins transmission in Alice Springs.

18 First Fleet Re-enactment vessels arrive at Botany Bay.

22 Two earthquakes, one registering 7 on the Richter scale, strike the Tennant Creek area of the NT, generating a 20-km fault scarp.

25 Prince and Princess of Wales arrive in Sydney for the Bicentennial celebrations.

26 Australia Day Bicentennial celebrations on Sydney Harbour draw the biggest crowd yet (est. 2.5 million) to attend a single Australian event.

Feb 5 Brisbane *Telegraph* ceases publication.

15 Afternoon newspaper the *Sun* begins publication in Brisbane, the morning paper the *Daily Sun* having closed on 13 Feb. (ceases publication 10 Dec. 1991).

25 Peter Dowding replaces Brian Burke as Premier of WA (Burke having been appointed ambassador to Ireland).

Mar 13 Yachtsman John Sanders completes the first non-stop solo triple circumnavigation of the world.
Times on Sunday published for the last time.

14 Sydney *Sun* ceases publication.

19 Unsworth Labor government defeated in NSW election. (Lib.–Nat. coalition government led by N. F. H. Greiner sworn in on 25th.)

– Prolonged heavy rain causes flooding in southern Qld and northern NSW and across the centre of Australia from Port Hedland to Alice Springs.

Apr 19 Queen Elizabeth and Prince Philip arrive at Perth to begin a three-week visit to five states.

29 Stockman's Hall of Fame, at Longreach, Qld, opened by the Queen.

30 World Expo 88 opens in Brisbane (to 30 Oct.).

May 4 Darling Harbour (Syd.) redevelopment officially opened by the Queen.

9 Parliament House on Capital Hill, Canberra, officially opened by the Queen.

Jun 5 Kay Cottee in her yacht *First Lady* arrives back at Port Jackson to become the first woman to sail single-handed non-stop round the world.

20 Two-dollar coin goes into circulation to replace the note.

Jul 13 Marshall Perron replaces Steve Hatton as Chief Minister of the NT.

21 Sydney's monorail begins operating.

Aug 14 Stage one of Qld's Burdekin Dam and irrigation scheme officially opened.

Sep 1 *Acacia pycnantha* proclaimed Australia's official floral emblem.

3 Federal referendums on four-year parliamentary terms; fair and democratic elections; recognition of local government; and trial by jury, freedom of religion, and fair terms for persons whose property is acquired by governments are all defeated.

15 NT Court of Criminal Appeal quashes the convictions of Michael and Lindy Chamberlain and enters verdicts of acquittal.

Oct 1 Cain Labor government returned to office in Vic. with a reduced majority.
John Flynn memorial complex in Cloncurry, Qld, officially opened.

Nov 3 WA merchant bank Rothwells Ltd goes into provisional liquidation.

29 ACT granted self-government (to take effect on 4 March 1989).

A Architecture, Building
Construction work begins on the Sydney Harbour Tunnel (completed 1992).

B Science, Technology, Discovery, etc.
Australia Telescope—eight linked radio-telescope dishes at three dispersed sites in north-western NSW—formally opened (2 Sept.).
Fragment of human skull estimated to be up to 60,000 years old found in an ancient river bed north of Lake Eyre.
First plastic laminated banknote issued—the Bicentennial $10.

C Arts and Entertainment
Fred Cress, *John Beard*, wins the Archibald Prize.
Canberra Institute of the Arts established, incorporating the Canberra School of Music and the Canberra School of Art.
Fred Schepisi, *Evil Angels* (film).
Luna Park (Syd.) closes down (10 Apr.). (Reopens, rebuilt, in January 1995.)
Rock groups INXS and Midnight Oil achieve international success with their respective albums *Kick* and *Diesel and Dust*.

1988

D Books and Writing

Australian Encyclopaedia, 5th edition (9 vols.).

Australian National Dictionary, ed. W. S. Ramson.

Peter Carey, *Oscar and Lucinda* (Booker Prize and 1989 Miles Franklin Award winner).

No Miles Franklin Award made for 1988; rules changed so that books published in one year will be judged for the next year's award.

E Sport and Recreation

National Tennis Centre, Flinders Park, Melbourne, opens (11 Jan.).

Kerry Saxby twice breaks the world record for the 5,000 metres walk.

Aboriginal cricket team tours England.

Sydney Football Stadium opens (4 Mar.).

Jeff Fenech beats Puerto Rican Victor Callejas to win the World Boxing Council featherweight title and his third world championship.

Damien Hardman becomes the 1987–88 world surfing champion.

Corinne Dibnah becomes the first Australian to win the British Women's Open golf championship.

At the Olympic Games in Seoul, Korea, Duncan Armstrong wins the 200 metres freestyle; Sue Williams wins the women's judo; Debbie Flintoff-King wins the 400 metres hurdles; and the women's team wins at hockey.

Empire Rose wins the Melbourne Cup.

F Statistics, Social Change, the Environment

Estimated resident population of Australia: 16,538,200.

Number of motor vehicles on Australia's roads: more than 9.3 million.

RAAF's first female pilots graduate.

Bicentennial Park in Homebush (Syd.) officially opened (1 Jan.).

Australia signs the Ozone Layer Treaty.

G Births and Deaths

Feb 9 Sir Charles Moses d. (88).

Feb 28 Kylie Tennant d. (75).

Mar 31 Sir William McMahon d. (80).

Jun 4 Sir Douglas Nicholls d. (81).

Aug 13 Sir Keith Hancock d. (90).

Dec 1 Lloyd Rees d. (93).

1989

Jan 1 Hawkesbury Agricultural College and the Nepean College of Advanced Education combine to form the University of Western Sydney.

10 Asst Commissioner Colin Winchester of the Australian Federal Police shot dead in the driveway of his home in Canberra.

Feb 4 Dowding Labor government re-elected in WA with reduced majority.

16 W. G. Hayden succeeds Sir Ninian Stephen as Governor-General.

Mar 1 Australian Conciliation and Arbitration Commission abolished and replaced by the Industrial Relations Commission.

4 First election for ACT Legislative Assembly under self-government. (After a complicated series of deals over 69 days, the ALP forms a minority government with Rosemary Follett as Chief Minister.)

23 Vic. division of the National Safety Council found to have debts amounting to $180 million. (Chief executive John Friedrick found dead July 1991.)

1989

- Central Australia experiences worst flooding since white settlement.

Apr 4 Cyclone Aivu causes extensive damage, one death and dozens of injuries in the Burdekin area of north Qld.

May 11 ACT Legislative Assembly sits for the first time.
13 Election in Tas. Results: Liberal 17, Labor 13, independents 5. (Robin Gray's minority Liberal government sworn in 1 June.)
15 Australia's first private tertiary institution, Bond University, opens at Burleigh Heads, Qld.
28 Dick Smith completes a round-the-world flight via both poles.
30 Timothy Anderson arrested on charges related to the Hilton Hotel bombing in Sydney on 13 Feb. 1978. (Found guilty, 25 Oct. 1990; sentenced to 14 years' gaol. Acquitted 6 June 1991 following appeal.)

Jun 29 Tas. Premier Robin Gray resigns after losing a no-confidence vote. Labor's Michael Field becomes Premier, leading an alliance of Labor and (Green) independents led by Bob Brown.

Jul 3 Report of the Fitzgerald inquiry into possible illegal activities and associated police misconduct released in Qld.
- Charles Sturt University established, incorporating campuses at Albury, Bathurst and Wagga, NSW.

Aug 13 Thirteen people die in a hot-air balloon accident near Alice Springs, NT. (Six die in another accident near Melbourne, 7 Oct.)
20 Three Sunday newspapers—*Sunday Herald*, *Sunday Age*, and *Sunday Sun*—begin publication in Melbourne.
24 All 1,645 pilots from Australia's domestic airlines resign in face of the airlines' move to sack and sue them over a dispute.

Sep 10 Katherine Gorge (Nitmiluk), NT, handed over to the Jawoyn people, the traditional owners. (Leased back to NT government for continued use as a national park.)
14 Former Ananda Marga member Evan Pederick convicted of Hilton Hotel bombing murders. (Sentenced to 20 years' gaol; released in Nov. 1997.)
22 Russell Cooper replaces Mike Ahern as Premier of Qld.

Oct 20 Brisbane-bound tourist coach collides with a semi-trailer north of Grafton, NSW; twenty killed.

Nov 7 Asia–Pacific Economic Co-operation forum holds its first meeting, in Canberra.
10 Gaby Kennard, the first Australian woman to fly single-handed round the world, arrives back at Bankstown airport.
25 Election in SA. Bannon Labor government retains office with the support of two independents.

Dec 2 Labor government elected in Qld after 32 years in opposition. (Wayne Goss sworn in as Premier on 7 Dec.)
5 ACT Labor government defeated on a no-confidence motion; coalition government led by Trevor Kaine takes over.
22 Two tourist coaches collide on the Pacific Highway north of Kempsey, NSW; 35 killed and 39 injured.
28 Earthquake strikes Newcastle, NSW, killing 13 people, injuring more than 120, and damaging many city buildings.
- Communist Party of Australia decides to disband.

* Several large corporations, including Equiticorp, Hooker Corporation, Spedley Securities and Qintex, collapse during year.

1989

* Opal rock weighing more than 5 kg and a gem-quality opal of 765 carats found by a mining syndicate at Coober Pedy, SA.

A Architecture, Building
Adelaide Plaza completed, with the opening of Exhibition Hall.

B Science, Technology, Discovery, etc.
Adelaide Botanic Gardens conservatory officially opened (Nov.).

C Arts and Entertainment
Bryan Westwood, *Elwyn Lynn*, wins the Archibald Prize.
Kylie Minogue's debut LP "Kylie" and its associated singles sell more than 12 million copies and top the charts in 20 countries.

D Books and Writing
Bryce Courtenay, *The Power of One*.
Tom Flood, *Oceana Fine* (1990 Miles Franklin Award winner).
Jill Ker Conway, *The Road from Coorain*.

E Sport and Recreation
Kerry Saxby breaks her own 3,000 m and 5,000 m walk world records.
Wayne Gardner wins the inaugural Australian 500 cc Motorcycle Grand Prix on Phillip Is., Vic. (9 Apr.).
Jeff Harding wins the world light heavyweight boxing title (24 June).
Australian cricket team captained by Allan Border wins the Ashes in England for the first time in 55 years (2 Aug.).
Victorian Football League (VFL) becomes Australian Football League.
Tawriffic wins the Melbourne Cup.

F Statistics, Social Change, the Environment
Estimated resident population of Australia: 16,957,100.
Lakes Eyre and Torrens, SA, fill with water, Lake Torrens for the first time this century.
Sydney has 94 rainy days out of 151 in the first five months of the year—the highest on record to date.
Ian Kiernan organizes Clean Up Sydney Harbour. (Clean Up Australia day begins in 1990.)

G Births and Deaths
Aug 17   Donald Friend d. (74).

1990

Jan – Fierce bushfires around Cootamundra, Tocumwal and Albury and in the Riverina; 40 homes destroyed, 70,000 sheep lost.

Feb 12   Carmen Lawrence replaces Peter Dowding as Premier of WA, becoming Australia's first female Premier.

23   Report released that the State Bank of Victoria incurred a loss of $1.345 billion, the largest in Australia's corporate history.

Mar 20   Serial murderer John Glover arrested after having killed six elderly women in Sydney's northern suburbs since March 1989. (Found guilty 29 Nov. 1991 and sentenced to prison for the rest of his life.)

24   Election for House of Representatives and half Senate: Hawke Labor gov-

ernment re-elected with a reduced majority. New members include Ted Mack, the first independent elected to the House for 35 years.

- Aboriginal and Torres Strait Islander Commission (ATSIC) established, with Lois (Lowitja) O'Donoghue as chair.

Apr 18 Martin Ferguson succeeds Simon Crean as president of the ACTU.

19 Canberra CAE becomes the University of Canberra.

22 All 4,000 residents of Charleville, Qld, evacuated as floods cover vast tracts of eastern Australia. (Nyngan, NSW, inundated on 23rd.)

May 6 InterCity train crashes into the rear of a stationary chartered steam train (3801) near Cowan, NSW; six killed and many injured.

7 Tas. businessman Edmund Rouse gaoled for three years for offering a bribe to a state Labor MP to cross floor in no-confidence vote. (Royal commission in Nov. 1991 finds that Liberal leader Robin Gray was involved.)

11 Tim Macartney-Snape becomes the first person to climb Mount Everest from sea level (having begun at the Bay of Bengal on 5 Feb.).

Business jet aircraft crashes near Atherton, north Qld, killing all 11 people on board, including the mayor of Cairns.

Jun 24 Vic.'s largest building society, Pyramid, collapses.

Jul – Property trusts in Vic. and NSW freeze funds as financial crisis of confidence develops.

Aug 5 Flooding in and around Forbes and Warren in western NSW.

7 Vic. Premier John Cain resigns; Joan Kirner succeeds him (10th).

13 (and 14th) Three navy warships leave Sydney for the Persian Gulf as part of a multinational force to enforce the UN embargo of Iraq following its annexation of Kuwait.

22 Direct broadcasting of Senate question time begins on television.

Sep 11 Perth's *Daily News* ceases publication.

25 Tour coach crashes in Qld's Gold Coast hinterland; 11 killed.

28 Floor trading ends at the Australian Stock Exchange.

Oct 8 Sydney's *Daily Telegraph* and *Daily Mirror* and Melbourne's *Herald* and *Sun News-Pictorial* merge to become the 24-hour tabloids the *Daily Telegraph Mirror* (reverts to *Daily Telegraph* in Jan. 1996) and the *Herald-Sun*.

27 Marshall Perron's CLP government re-elected in NT with an increased majority.

28 Qld adopts daylight saving permanently. (Legislation repealed June 1992, after referendum.)

31 Domestic aviation market deregulated; two-airline policy ends.

Nov 19 WA Premier Carmen Lawrence announces a royal commission into the state government's commercial activities ("WA Inc.").

29 Treasurer Paul Keating announces that Australia is experiencing an economic recession.

Dec 6 George Herscu, former head of Hooker Corporation, found guilty of corruptly paying $100,000 to former Qld minister Russ Hinze; Alan Bond arrested in Perth on criminal charges related to his role in the 1987 operation to rescue Rothwells; Brian Yuill charged in Sydney with fraud as director of Spedley Securities.

10 John Fairfax group placed in receivership.

22 *SeaCat Tasmania* begins operating across Bass Strait.

23 Bushfires destroy more than 20 houses around Sydney and burn at 500 locations in NSW.

1990

31 Rockhampton district declared a disaster area as residents prepare for major flooding in the aftermath of Cyclone Joy. (Floodbound in early Jan. 1991; more than 1,000 residents evacuated.)

A Architecture, Building

B Science, Technology, Discovery etc.

Prof. Allen Kerr of the Waite Agricultural Research Institute, Adelaide, shares the inaugural Australia Prize for work on developing a bacterium to transfer genes in plants.

Sydney Tropical Centre, incorporating the Arc Glasshouse, officially opened (16 Sept.).

Telecom introduces Phonecard.

Wave-piercing catamaran *Hoverspeed Great Britain*, designed in Sydney and built in Hobart, breaks New York–London passenger vessel record.

Dead specimen of the night parrot, last sighted in 1912, found near Boulia, Qld.

C Arts and Entertainment

Geoffrey Proud, *Dorothy Hewett*, wins the Archibald Prize.

Jimmy Chi's Aboriginal musical *Bran Nue Dae* premières at the Festival of Perth (Feb.).

Joan Sutherland gives her final performance, in *Les Huguenots* at the Sydney Opera House (2 Oct.).

D Books and Writing

Thea Astley, *Reaching Tin River*.

David Malouf, *The Great World* (1991 Miles Franklin Award winner).

E Sport and Recreation

Susie Maroney, 15, swims the English Channel (1 Aug.) and wins the Manhattan Island marathon (20 Aug.).

Kingston Rule wins the Melbourne Cup.

Twin brothers Mark and Steve Waugh compile a record fifth-wicket partnership score of 464 for NSW against WA at the WACA in Perth.

Surfboard-rider Pam Burridge wins the Association of Surf Professionals world title at Hawaii.

F Statistics, Social Change, the Environment

Population of Australia reaches 17 million.

Women in Australia's defence forces are allowed to do combat-related duties (though excluded from direct combat).

London Bridge arch on Vic.'s south-west coastline collapses (15 Jan.).

Sydney has the wettest February and the driest December on record.

G Births and Deaths

Jan   4   Sir Henry Bolte d. (81).
Jan 15   Dame Peggy Van Praagh (79).
Mar   8   Jack Lindsay d. (89).
Jun 25   Peggy Glanville-Hicks d. (77).
Sep   2   Robert Holmes à Court d. (53).
Sep 30   Patrick White d. (78).
Oct 14   Clifton Pugh d. (65).

1991

Jan 1 Australian Catholic University opens, with eight campuses in Sydney, Melbourne, Ballarat, Canberra, and Brisbane.
Western Australian College of Advanced Education, Perth, becomes the Edith Cowan University.

21 Violent storm in Sydney causes widespread damage; many homes left without power for a week.

31 Perth experiences its highest recorded temperature (45.8°C).

– Floods in north Queensland (to Feb.) isolate more than ten towns and cause at least seven deaths; floodwaters cover about 50,000 square kilometres in Gulf Country.

Feb 6 Dame Roma Mitchell becomes Governor of SA and the first woman to hold vice-regal office in Australia.

10 SA government forced to bail out State Bank of South Australia, facing losses of up to $3 billion.

25 Reserve price scheme for wool suspended. (Price of wool subsequently drops to lowest on record in Oct.)

27 Pemulwuy Koori College opens in Newtown, Sydney.

Mar 3 Seven killed in a helicopter crash on the Gold Coast.

12 WA Inc. royal commission public hearings begin.

28 Adelaide Steamship group reports a loss of $3.7 billion.

Apr 3 Communist newspaper *Tribune* (first published in 1932) published for the last time.

7 *Sunday Herald-Sun* replaces *Sunday Herald* and *Sunday Sun* in Melbourne.

18 Bell Group, corporate flagship of Robert Holmes à Court until bought by Bond Corp. in 1988, collapses with debts of $910 million.

19 ACTU dumps centralized wage fixing in favour of wage increase plus superannuation and freedom to negotiate additional pay rises under enterprise bargaining.

29 Former WA Premier Brian Burke resigns as ambassador to Ireland after revealing to the WA Inc. royal commission that he was controlling donations to the ALP while in Dublin.

May 25 Election in NSW. Results: Liberal–National coalition 49, Labor 46, independents 4. Nick Greiner forms a minority government, agreeing to a charter of reform to obtain support of independents.

Jun 6 Rosemary Follett's Labor government resumes office in ACT following the coalition government's defeat in a no-confidence vote.

13 Entrepreneur Christopher Skase declared bankrupt with personal debts of $170 million. (Subsequently flees to Spain.)

Jul 1 Telecom's phone monopoly ends.

4 Sydney heart surgeon Victor Chang shot dead in a Mosman street.

7 Australian Republican Movement launched in Sydney, with Thomas Keneally as chairman.

17 Shares in the Commonwealth Bank go on sale to the public in a partial privatization. (Government's remaining holding sold off in June–July 1996.)

Aug 5 Sir Terence Lewis, former Qld Police Commissioner, sentenced to 14 years' gaol after being found guilty on 15 corruption charges.

1991

17 A 33-year-old taxi-driver kills seven people and wounds six others in Strathfield Mall, Sydney, before shooting himself.

21 Fire engulfs six tanks at Australia's biggest chemical storage plant, at Coode Island in Melbourne, following a series of explosions caused by an electrical weather occurrence known as St Elmo's Fire.

Oct 19 After deliberating for 61 hours over five days, a jury fails to reach a verdict on whether Sir Joh Bjelke-Petersen had lied to the Fitzgerald inquiry, and the charge is dropped.

Nov 17 WA introduces daylight saving on a trial basis. (Abandons it after a referendum on 4 Mar. 1992.)

Dec 20 Paul Keating replaces Bob Hawke as Prime Minister. (Hawke resigns from Parliament on 20 Feb. 1992.)

Compass Airlines, in operation since 1 Dec. 1990, collapses, leaving thousands of passengers stranded. (After resuming operation on 31 August 1992, the company collapses again on 11 Mar. 1993.)

A Architecture, Building

B Science, Technology, Discovery, etc.
National Food Authority established (Aug.).
Australian National Maritime Museum, at Darling Harbour, Sydney, officially opened (30 Nov.).

C Arts and Entertainment
Sydney's Museum of Contemporary Art opens (12 Nov.).
No Archibald Prize awarded owing to rescheduling of the competition (1991/92 prize awarded in Feb. 1992).
Rock group Yothu Yindi's "Treaty" becomes an international hit and their album *Tribal Voice* a double-platinum seller.
Children's entertainers, The Wiggles, begin performing.

D Books and Writing
David Marr, *Patrick White: A Life.*
Tim Winton, *Cloudstreet* (1992 Miles Franklin Award winner).

E Sport and Recreation
At the world swimming championships in Perth, Hayley Lewis wins the 200 m freestyle, Linley Frame the 100 m breaststroke, and Shelley Taylor-Smith the women's section of the 25 km marathon event.
Kerry Saxby sets her 30th world record (the 3,000 m walk, in Melbourne), becoming the most prolific breaker of world records (7 Feb.).
Susie Maroney completes a double crossing of the English Channel in a record 17 hours 14 minutes (23 July).
Australia beats New Zealand to win the world netball championship.
Let's Elope wins the Melbourne Cup and the Caulfield Cup.

F Statistics, Social Change, the Environment
Estimated resident population of Australia: 17,384,500. National census, 6 Aug: 16,850,540 (11.3% aged 65 and over; 22.3% under 15; 22.3% born overseas).
Darwin's 1990–91 wet season rainfall is the highest on record. (Calculated from 1 Sept. it passes the previous record of 1,790 mm on 26 Feb.)
Blue-green algae infests 1,000 km of the Darling River system (Nov.–Dec.).

G Births and Deaths
Mar 24 Sir John Kerr d. (76).
Mar 25 Eileen Joyce d. (78).

Apr 6 Bill Ponsford d. (90).
May 23 Manning Clark d. (76).

1992

Jan 16   Thirty-four men and women claiming to be teachers and students from Beijing reach Doongan cattle station, west of Wyndham, WA, after walking for about ten days from their wrecked boat at Swift Bay. (Last of the 56 found alive on 25th, about 150 km from Swift Bay.)

      24   Rev. Dawn Kenyon (ordained in New Zealand) becomes Australia's first female Anglican priest when commissioned at Southern Cross, WA.

Feb 1   One-cent and two-cent coins no longer currency.
Election in Tas. Results: Liberal 19; Labor 11; Green Independents 5. Ray Groom becomes Premier.

      15   Follett Labor government re-elected in ACT. Electors choose Hare-Clark voting system in referendum.

      18   Queen Elizabeth and Prince Philip begin an eight-day visit to celebrate the sesquicentenary of local government in Sydney.

Mar 2   Open Learning university begins broadcasting on ABC television.

       3   Bomb blast damages Blue Mountains City Council chambers in Katoomba, NSW, during discussion of a controversial building development.

       7   Ten women ordained as priests at St George's Cathedral in Perth, the first Anglican women to be ordained in Australia. (The Anglican Church agrees to the ordination of women on 23 Nov., and the first five are officially ordained in Adelaide on 5 Dec.)

      27   Australia's last afternoon newspaper, *The News* of Adelaide, ceases publication.

Apr 12   Brisbane's *Sunday Sun* published for the last time.

May 29   Businessman Alan Bond is sentenced to 2½ years' gaol for acting illegally during the 1987 rescue of Rothwells merchant bank. (Released in August and acquitted in November after a retrial.)

Jun 2   John Elliott's holding company controlling the Foster's brewing group goes into receivership.

       3   High Court judgment in the "Mabo case" (that the Murray Islands in Torres Strait belong to the Meriam people) recognizes a new class of ownership right, native title, and ends the notion of *terra nullius*.

      16   Former WA Premier Brian Burke is charged with defrauding parliamentary travel expenses. (Found guilty in July 1994 of four charges of false pretences and sentenced to two years' gaol.)

      24   NSW Premier Nick Greiner resigns in response to a threat by the three non-aligned independents to bring down his government following an ICAC report that he had acted in a corrupt manner (finding subsequently rejected by Supreme Court). John Fahey replaces him as Premier.

Jul 7   Plastic five-dollar note goes into circulation.

Aug 29   Sydney Harbour Tunnel officially opened. (Opens for traffic on 31st.)

Sep 1   John Bannon steps down as SA Premier and Labor Party leader. Lynn Arnold takes his place.

      15   Qantas acquires Australian Airlines in preparation for privatization.

1992

19 Election in Qld. Wayne Goss's Labor government returned with a comfortable majority.

30 In its judgment invalidating the federal government's legislation banning political advertising on radio and TV, the High Court acknowledges the existence of an implied freedom of speech guarantee in the Constitution.

Oct 1 Command of the joint naval communications station at Exmouth, WA, is handed over to Australia.

3 Election in Vic. Coalition has a landslide victory. Liberal Party's Jeff Kennett replaces Labor's Joan Kirner as Premier.

5 Prime Minister Paul Keating announces that the Queen would not accept any further recommendations for Australians to be made knights or dames.

Nov 19 Westpac Banking Corporation reveals a 1991–92 loss of $1.56 billion.

Dec 3 NSW announces that no more Queen's Counsel will be appointed.

A Architecture, Building

Glen Murcutt is awarded the Alvar Aalto Medal for his "ecologically responsive and socially responsible buildings".

Sydney's new Glebe Island (later Anzac) Bridge (–1995).

B Science, Technology, Discovery, etc.

Most of Sydney, Melbourne, and Canberra get access to the Optus telecommunications network (official launch on 1 Jan. 1993).

C Arts and Entertainment

Bryan Westwood's portrait of Paul Keating, *The Prime Minister*, wins the 1991/92 Archibald Prize.

Baz Luhrmann, *Strictly Ballroom* (film).

D Books and Writing

Alex Miller, *The Ancestor Game* (winner of 1993 Miles Franklin Award and Commonwealth Writers' Prize).

E Sport and Recreation

Kieren Perkins breaks the world freestyle swimming records for the 800 metres (16 Feb.), 400 metres (3 Apr.), and 1,500 metres (5 Apr.)

At the Olympic Games in Barcelona, cyclist Kathryn Watt wins the women's individual road race; swimmer Kieren Perkins wins the 1,500 metres freestyle; equestrian Matt Ryan wins the individual three-day show jumping, and the Australian team wins the team event; rowers Peter Antonie and Stephen Hawkins win the double sculls, and the Australian crew win the coxless fours; canoeist Clint Robinson wins the KI 1,000 metres.

Subzero wins the Melbourne Cup.

F Statistics, Social Change, the Environment

Estimated resident population of Australia: 17,494,700.

Unemployment reaches 11.4 per cent of the workforce (Nov.), the highest rate since the Great Depression.

Women in the Defence Forces permitted to fly fighter aircraft and serve on submarines.

Proclamation ordains that National Wattle Day be held on 1 September "throughout Australia and in the national territories" (to take effect from 1993).

G Births and Deaths

Jan 4 Dame Judith Anderson d. (93).

Jan 21 Eddie Mabo d. (55).

Jun 16 Brett Whiteley d. (53).

Aug 24   Francis James d. (74).
Nov 29   Sir Sidney Nolan d. (75).

1993

Feb   6   Labor government of Carmen Lawrence is defeated in WA election. Richard Court becomes Premier of Liberal–National Party coalition government.

Mar 13   Election for House of Representatives and half Senate. Paul Keating's Labor government re-elected with an increased majority.

    30   Gunman who led a five-murder rampage through two states suicides after a 26-hour siege at Cangai, NSW.

    –   Perth's new metropolitan railway line to the northern suburbs opened.

Jun 11   Monarch Air commuter jet crashes near Young, NSW; seven killed.

    18   Businessman–adventurer Dick Smith and co-pilot John Wallington become the first to cross Australia by balloon (Carnarvon, WA, to Tabulam on the NSW north coast).

Sep 24   International Olympic Committee announces that Sydney has been chosen as host of the 2000 Olympic Games.

    30   Legislation passed to introduce a new citizenship oath in which new Australians no longer swear allegiance to the Queen and her heirs. ("From this time forward [under God] I pledge my loyalty to Australia and its people whose democratic beliefs I share, whose rights and liberties I respect, and whose laws I will uphold and obey.")

Oct   5   Republic Advisory Committee of ten eminent Australians, appointed in May to spearhead the federal government's push for a republic by 2001, reports that "a republic is achievable without threatening Australia's cherished democratic traditions".
Skeletal remains of two people are found in Belanglo State Forest, NSW, not far from where the bodies of two backpackers were found in Sept. 1992. (Remains of three more bodies are subsequently found nearby.)

Nov   1   Plastic ten-dollar note (featuring Banjo Paterson and Mary Gilmore) goes into circulation.
Federal government announces that 29,000 Chinese nationals, mostly students who were given temporary sanctuary in June 1989 following the violent suppression of pro-democracy demonstrators in Beijing, will be given permanent residency, with spouses and children.
Former WA Premier Ray O'Connor is charged with stealing a $25,000 political donation to the Liberal Party. (Found guilty on 17 Feb. 1995 and sentenced to 18 months' imprisonment.)

    2   Tour coach carrying 44 passengers collides with a truck on the Hume Highway north of Wangaratta, Vic; 9 killed and 36 injured.

    11   Remains of Australia's unknown soldier of World War I, retrieved from a grave site near Villers-Bretonneux, is entombed in the Australian War Memorial, Canberra.

Dec 11   Labor government defeated in SA election. Liberal Party's Dean Brown replaces Lynn Arnold as Premier.

    22   Native title legislation passed by federal parliament. (Comes into operation on 1 Jan. 1994.)

    23   John Elliott, former Liberal Party president and head of Elders IXL, is charged over the theft of $66.5 million in a conspiracy related to the

1993

A Architecture, Building

B Science, Technology, Discovery, etc.
First Australian patent for an animal granted to an Adelaide company which produced a genetically engineered pig.
Rock art and stone tools, first thought to predate Homo sapiens but later dated at 6,000 to 10,000 years old, discovered at Jinmium, NT.
Fossilised stromatolites thought to be 3.5 billion years old discovered in rocks about 60 km from Marble Bar, WA.

C Arts and Entertainment
Garry Shead, *Tom Thompson*, wins the Archibald Prize.
Jane Campion's film *The Piano* wins two Cannes Film Festival awards and three Academy Awards.

D Books and Writing
Rodney Hall, *The Grisly Wife* (1994 Miles Franklin Award winner).
Frank Moorhouse, *Grand Days*.

E Sport and Recreation
Allan Border, in a match against New Zealand on 26 Feb., becomes Test cricket's greatest run-scorer. (Retires from international cricket on 11 May 1994, having scored 11,174 runs in 156 Test matches and taken 156 catches in Tests.)
Irish horse Vintage Crop wins the Melbourne Cup. (First time the race won by a horse not from Australia or NZ.)

F Statistics, Social Change, the Environment
Estimated resident population of Australia: 17,667,100.
Australia joins an élite group of nations with more than 50 per cent of students proceeding to tertiary education.

G Births and Deaths
Jan   9 Sir Paul Hasluck d. (87).
Feb 10 Fred Hollows d. (63).
Apr   3 Sali Herman d. (95).
Jul   2 Sir Edward ("Weary") Dunlop d. (85).
Sep 16 Oodgeroo Noonuccal (Kath Walker) d. (81).

1994

Jan 2 (to 14th). Hot, windy weather fans bushfires in eastern NSW from Qld border to south coast, several around Sydney (at Marsfield, Turramurra, Menai, Bundeena, etc.). About 450 square kilometres burnt on Central Coast; more than 100 homes destroyed in Sutherland shire; Royal National Park almost completely burnt out.

26 Prince Charles, on a 12-day visit to Australia, is attacked by a man who fires two shots from a starting pistol during an open-air function at Darling Harbour, Sydney.

Feb 1 Christopher Skase, wanted in Australia to face charges relating to the collapse of his Qintex media company, gives himself up to authorities in Spain. (Spends 11 months in gaol hospital; released in December after Australia's extradition attempts fail on medical grounds.)

22 Oz Lotto drawn for the first time.

Mar 2 Letter bomb kills a policeman and injures five other people at the National Crime Authority's Adelaide headquarters.

11 Former Spedley Securities managing director Brian Yuill sentenced to eight years' gaol for dishonesty as a director. (Conviction quashed in July and retrial ordered; sentenced to two years and ten months on 14 Sept.)

30 Federal government's Industrial Relations Reform Act comes into operation: provides for certified agreements between employers and unions and flexibility in enterprise agreements between employers and their employees, and bans employers sacking workers for taking industrial action.

May 7 Residents of Christmas Island vote at a referendum for greater self-rule but reject secession.

9 Entrepreneur Laurie Connell found guilty of conspiring to pervert the course of justice; sentenced to five years' gaol.

24 Two drivers and two officials die as one of the cars competing in the Cannonball Run from Darwin to Uluru and back crashes near Alice Springs. Massive wind storm blows millions of tonnes of dust across south-eastern Australia (to 27th).

31 Ten days after his arrest, 49-year-old road worker Ivan Milat is charged with the murder of the seven backpackers whose bodies were found in Belanglo State Forest, NSW. (Found guilty and sentenced to life imprisonment 27 July 1996.)

Jun 4 Marshall Perron's CLP government re-elected in NT with an increased majority.

Jul 25 Phone numbers throughout Australia begin converting to eight digits (Mona Vale, Sydney, first to change).

Aug 6 Earthquake measuring 5.3 on the Richter scale rocks Cessnock, NSW, but causes only minor damage.

7 Underground mine explosion at Moura, Qld, traps 11 miners, whose bodies are left entombed after further explosions make their recovery impossible.

15 News Radio, the ABC's 24-hour news service, begins operating.

16 Ten-tonne tropical Bryde's whale crosses the bar at the mouth of the Manning River, NSW, and swims upstream to the outskirts of Taree. (Helped back to sea on 24 Nov. after 100 days in the river.)

Sep 5 NSW state MP for Cabramatta, John Newman, shot dead outside his house. (A former Fairfield councillor and three others are later charged with the murder.)

Oct 2 Seaview Air twin-jet aircraft with nine people aboard disappears on a scheduled flight from Williamtown to Lord Howe Island.

12 High Court finds that the Constitution guarantees a right to free political speech and that "in future defendants need only prove that they did not knowingly publish false material, did not act in reckless disregard for the truth, and took reasonable steps to substantiate their claims".

24 Tour coach overturns in the Brisbane suburb of Boondall, killing 11 women and a child.

31 Plastic twenty-dollar note, featuring Mary Reibey and John Flynn, goes into circulation.

Nov 4 Sydney Airport's third runway opens, prompting sustained protest about increased aircraft noise.

15 Australia and other APEC members sign a free-trade agreement pledging to remove regional trade barriers by the year 2020.

1994

* More boat people arrive during the year than at any time since the Vietnam War (at least 930, mostly Chinese, and mainly from refugee camps in Indonesia).
* Queensland and New South Wales in the fourth year of severe drought. (Breaks in many areas, accompanied in some places by floods, in early 1995.)

A Architecture, Building
NT's Parliament House completed (officially opened 18 Aug.).

B Science, Technology, Discovery, etc.
Remains of more than 10,000 people dating back at least 6,000 years discovered in Lake Victoria, south-western NSW, when lake drained for repair work.

Living specimen of a tree thought to have been extinct for 150 million years discovered in Wollemi National Park, NSW (Aug.).

C Arts and Entertainment
Francis Giacco, *Homage to John Reichard*, wins the Archibald Prize.

Stephan Elliott, *Priscilla, Queen of the Desert* (film).

P. J. Hogan, *Muriel's Wedding* (film).

Les Girls all-male revue in Kings Cross, Sydney, closes after 31 years.

D Books and Writing
Helen Demidenko, *The Hand That Signed the Paper* (1995 Miles Franklin Award Winner).

Tim Flannery, *The Future Eaters*.

E Sport and Recreation
Rebecca Brown breaks the world record for the 200 m breaststroke.

Shelley Taylor-Smith breaks her own 42 km world marathon swimming record at Lake Magog, Canada, setting her 11th world record.

Australian women's hockey team wins the World Cup in Dublin.

Swimmer Kieren Perkins breaks the 800 m and 1,500 m world freestyle records in the one race at the Commonwealth Games.

Jeune wins the Melbourne Cup.

F Statistics, Social Change, the Environment
Estimated resident population of Australia: 17,854,700.

Lowest temperature ever recorded in Australia; –23°C (–9°F), at Charlotte's Pass, Mt Kosciuszko, on 29 June.

G Births and Deaths
Jan 28 Frank Hardy d. (76).
Feb   8 Ken G. Hall d. (92).
Jul   3 Lew Hoad d. (59).
Dec 16 Dame Mary Durack Miller d. (81).

1995

Jan 19 Pope John Paul II conducts a mass at Randwick Racecourse to celebrate the beatification of Mary MacKillop.

26 John Howard becomes leader of the federal Liberal Party (and the Opposition) following Alexander Downer's resignation.

Feb 17 Former WA Premier Ray O'Connor is found guilty of stealing a Bond Corporation cheque in 1984. (Sentenced to 18 months' gaol.)

18 Election in ACT results in a hung parliament. Kate Carnell forms a minority Liberal government on 9 Mar.

25 Cyclone sinks two fishing vessels near Onslow, WA, with the loss of seven lives.

Mar 25 Election for NSW parliament. Labor wins narrowly. Bob Carr replaces John Fahey as Premier.

Apr 21 Sir Gerard Brennan succeeds Sir Anthony Mason as Chief Justice of the High Court.

May 1 Gold bullion worth more than $5.4 million is discovered missing from the Sydney headquarters of Kerry Packer's Consolidated Press Holdings.

9 Senate elects its first woman presiding officer, Margaret Reid (Lib.), who replaces the disgraced senator Noel Crichton-Browne as deputy president. (Becomes president in 1996.)

25 NT parliament passes the Rights of the Terminally Ill Act, which allows voluntary euthanasia. Chief Minister Marshall Perron, proposer of the legislation, resigns and is replaced by Shane Stone.

Jun 4 Standard-gauge railway line between Melbourne and Adelaide officially opened. (Freight train makes the first journey from Brisbane to Perth on standard gauge 1–7 June.)

Jul 1 Telecom officially becomes Telstra.

15 Election in Qld. Goss Labor government re-elected, gaining a one-seat majority by just 16 votes 11 days after the poll.

31 Official listing of stock of Qantas; sale of 75%, the remaining shares being owned by British Airways.

Sep 27 Jennie George selected to succeed Martin Ferguson as president of the ACTU. (Takes over in March 1996. Resigns in Dec. 1999.)

Oct 18 Tas. government legislates to return twelve cultural sites, including Risdon Cove, Oyster Cove, and five Bass Strait islands, to those who still identify as Tas. Aborigines.

24 Sydney's Royal Alexandra Hospital for Children begins moving patients from Camperdown to the New Children's Hospital at Westmead. (Move completed 6 Nov.)

Nov 3 Former public servant David Eastman is found guilty of killing Federal Police assistant commissioner Colin Winchester in 1989. (Sentenced to life imprisonment without parole.)

14 Royal commission finds that former WA Premier Carmen Lawrence, now a minister in the federal government, acted improperly over the tabling of a misleading petition in Nov. 1992.

15 Owning or working in a brothel decriminalized in NSW.

Dec 4 Sydney's new Glebe Island Bridge opens to traffic. (Renamed the Anzac Bridge on 11 Nov. 1998.)

13 NT coroner brings down an open verdict in the third and final inquest into the disappearance of Azaria Chamberlain.

18 Prime Minister Paul Keating and Indonesian President Soeharto sign a mutual security agreement for their countries.

A Architecture, Building

Construction begins on the underground train line from Sydney's Central station to Sydney Airport and on to the East Hills line. (Opens 21 May 2000.)

1995

B Science, Technology, Discovery, etc.

Mathematical physicist Paul Davies wins the international Templeton Prize for Progress in Religion.

C Arts and Entertainment

William Robinson, *Self Portrait with Stunned Mullet*, wins the Archibald Prize.

Chris Noonan, *Babe* (film).

Cable television (pay TV) launched.

Frogstomp, the debut album of teenage Newcastle rock group silverchair, released.

D Books and Writing

Helen Garner, *The First Stone*.

Peter Goldsworthy, *Wish*.

Christopher Koch, *Highways to a War* (1996 Miles Franklin Award winner).

E Sport and Recreation

Australia's entry for the America's Cup breaks apart and sinks off San Diego during a race against New Zealand's entry.

News Ltd attempts to start a new Rugby League competition called Super League. (A Federal Court judgment in Feb. 1996 disallowing the competition is later overturned, and Super League begins in 1997.)

Mark Woodforde and Todd Woodbridge win the Wimbledon doubles for the third successive year.

Squash player Michelle Martin wins the World Open for the third successive year.

Doriemus wins the Melbourne Cup and the Caulfield Cup.

F Statistics, Social Change, the Environment

Estimated resident population of Australia: 18,071,800.

Same-sex partners recognized as a "family" in NSW and granted equal entitlements by federal public service.

Rabbit calicivirus escapes from field testing on SA's Wardang Is. (Oct.) and quickly spreads across Australia. (Appears in all mainland states and territories by May 1996.)

Darling River flows again after its driest year since 1940, having been dried out at Wilcannia for 125 days during the year.

G Births and Deaths

Mar 20 Russell Braddon d. (74).

Apr 1 Ted Noffs d. (69).

1996

Jan 23 Inaugural meeting in Canberra of the Canberra Commission on the Elimination of Nuclear Weapons.

Feb 16 Qld Premier Wayne Goss resigns after a by-election loss leaves Labor without a majority in Parliament. (Coalition government led by Rob Borbidge sworn in on 19th.)

High Court Judge Sir William Deane succeeds Bill Hayden as Governor-General.

24 Election in Tas. results in a hung parliament, the independents holding the balance of power. Ray Groom remains Premier, leading a minority Liberal government.

Mar 1 NSW Government House no longer to be occupied by the Governor; henceforth to be used for public purposes and the grounds incorporated in the Botanic Gardens.

2 Sweeping victory to Liberal–National Party coalition in federal election. John Howard replaces Paul Keating as Prime Minister. New members include independent Pauline Hanson, who wins the seat of Oxley with a policy of opposition to Asian immigration and Aboriginal welfare.

15 Tas. Premier Ray Groom resigns Lib. leadership and is succeeded as Premier by Tony Rundle.

30 Election in Vic. Kennett government returned with a loss of two seats but still with a 30-seat majority.

Apr 28 Gunman Martin Bryant massacres 35 people at Port Arthur, Tas. (At his trial in Nov., Bryant pleads guilty to all charges and is sentenced to imprisonment for the rest of his life.)

Jun 12 Two SAS helicopters collide and crash during a night training exercise near Townsville; 18 killed and 12 injured.

Jul 1 Law allowing voluntary euthanasia in NT comes into force.

Aug 16 Former business tycoon Alan Bond is convicted of fraud. (Sentenced to three years' gaol. In Dec. he pleads guilty to other charges of fraud and is subsequently sentenced to four year's gaol, increased to seven years after an appeal by the DPP.)

Sep 20 Former WA Labor deputy Premier David Parker is sentenced to 18 months' gaol after being convicted of lying to the WA Inc. royal commission.

22 Darwin resident Bob Dent, assisted by pro-euthanasia doctor Philip Nitschke, becomes the first person in the world to die using euthanasia legislation.

27 A cliff face collapses on spectators at a primary school surf carnival at Gracetown, WA, killing five adults and four children.

Oct 9 NSW recognizes native title over 12.4 ha of land at Crescent Head—the first native title claim to succeed on mainland Australia (registered Feb. 1997).

10 Legality of abortion in NSW is confirmed when a High Court test case on abortion lapses after the parties sign a confidential settlement agreement.

Nov 4 Former Supreme Court judge David Yeldham commits suicide after being named in Parliament in relation to the paedophile hearings of the royal commission into the NSW police.

17 Perth teenager David Dicks becomes the youngest person to sail solo non-stop round the world (turned 18 during voyage).

19 US President Bill Clinton makes a visit to Australia (to 23rd), during which he addresses the joint houses of parliament in Canberra.

27 John Olsen replaces Dean Brown as Premier of SA after disenchanted backbenchers vote to declare the leadership open.

Dec 6 Gatjil Djerrkura succeeds Lowitja O'Donoghue as chairman of the Aboriginal and Torres Strait Islander Commission.

14 Election in WA. Coalition government of Richard Court returned.

21 Deacon Gloria Shipp ordained as Australia's first Aboriginal priest, to preside over the Koori Anglican fellowship in Dubbo, NSW.

23 In a judgment on a claim by the Wik and Thayorre peoples lodged in 1993, the High Court rules that native title and pastoral leases can co-exist and that the granting of a pastoral lease does not necessarily extinguish native title.

1996

A Architecture, Building
Art Gallery of SA's restored and augmented Elder and Melrose wings and its new West Wing opened to the public (2 Mar.).

Work begins on Melbourne's City Link freeway connection.

B Science, Technology, Discovery, etc.
Prof. Peter Doherty shares the Nobel Prize for Medicine for discovering how the immune system recognizes virus-infected cells.

C Arts and Entertainment
Wendy Sharpe, *Self-Portrait as Diana of Erskineville*, wins the Archibald Prize.

Scott Hicks, *Shine* (film), with Geoffrey Rush.

NSW government gives Rupert Murdoch's Fox Studios permission to develop Sydney Showground into an entertainment complex and film studios. (Fox Studios Australia opens 7 Nov. 1999.)

D Books and Writing
David Foster, *The Glade within the Grove* (1997 Miles Franklin Award winner).

Peter Robb, *Midnight in Sicily*.

E Sport and Recreation
Tammy van Wisse becomes the first person to swim across Bass Strait, crossing from King Island to Apollo Bay in 17 hr 46 min.

Professional Rugby Union begins with the first matches of the international Rugby Super 12 competition (1 March).

Australian Grand Prix Formula One motor race transferred from Adelaide to Melbourne's Albert Park.

At the Olympic Games in Atlanta, USA, gold medals are won by Kieren Perkins (1,500 metres freestyle swimming), Susie O'Neill (200 metres butterfly), Mark Woodforde and Todd Woodbridge (men's tennis doubles), Michael Diamond (trap shooting), Russell Mark (double trap shooting), the men's coxless four and the women's coxless pair (rowing), and the women's hockey team.

Saintly wins the Melbourne Cup.

Pole vaulter Emma George sets an indoor world record, adding to the outdoor record she set a year previously and had broken five times since.

F Statistics, Social Change, the Environment
Estimated resident population of Australia: 18,310,700.

Marriage rates fall to their lowest level this century, and divorces rise to their highest level since the Family Law Act took effect in 1976.

Bob Bellear is appointed as a judge of the NSW District Court, the highest legal rank yet attained by an Aboriginal.

G Births and Deaths
Sep 3 Emily Kame Kngwarreye d. (*c.* 86)

Nov 26 Dame Joan Hammond d. (84)

1997

Jan 1 Workplace Relations Act, enforcing voluntary unionism, comes into operation. (Second phase, launching non-union individual contracts [Australian Workplace Agreements], begins operating on 12 Mar.)

9 HMAS *Adelaide* rescues British yachtsman Tony Bullimore, trapped in his upturned yacht for 89 hours deep in the Southern Ocean. Two other competitors in the single-handed round-the-world race are also rescued.

21 Bushfires on Melbourne's eastern outskirts destroy at least 44 homes and cause three deaths.

Feb 28 Former WA Premier Brian Burke is found guilty of stealing from ALP campaign funds and is sentenced to imprisonment. (Conviction quashed by Court of Appeal in July.)

Mar 13 Royal Commission into the NSW Police Service has its last sitting, after 370 hearing days and 640 witnesses and the exposing of police corruption and paedophile rings. (Final report of commissioner James Wood handed down on 26 Aug.)

14 A third young woman disappears from the nightlife precinct in the Perth suburb of Claremont. (Body found on 3 Apr. Previous two disappearances in Jan. and June 1996.)

25 Federal parliament overturns NT's voluntary euthanasia legislation.

Apr 9 Report of the Wallis Inquiry into the financial system released.

11 One Nation Party formed in support of federal independent MP Pauline Hanson.

18 Brian Quinn, former CEO of Coles Myer, is found guilty of conspiring to defraud the firm of $4.46 million. (Sentenced to four years' imprisonment.)

21 Former WA Premier Carmen Lawrence is charged with three counts of perjury over her evidence to the Marks royal commission. Now a federal MP, she subsequently steps down from the Labor front bench. (Acquitted by jury in July 1999.)

May 6 Kerry Whelan, wife of a Sydney company director, is kidnapped in Parramatta, held for ransom, and never seen again. (Bruce Burrell, a former employee of her husband, charged with murder on 1 April 1999.)

26 Australian Reconciliation Convention held in Melbourne (to 28th). Prime Minister John Howard refuses to make a formal apology for past injustices to indigenous Australians.

Human Rights and Equal Opportunities Commission's report into the government policy of forcibly removing Aboriginal children from their parents is tabled in federal parliament. (Govt rejects central recommendations of report.)

Jul 1 Telecommunications industry deregulated.

13 Demolition by implosion of the Royal Canberra Hospital causes the death of a 12-year-old girl and injury to many of the 100,000 spectators.

15 About a hundred Australian athletes at the Maccabiah Games in Tel Aviv, Israel, plunge into a polluted river when a temporary bridge collapses beneath them. Two drown and two more die later; others suffer long-term effects from the polluted water.

30 Landslide at Thredbo in the Snowy Mountains destroys two lodges and causes 18 deaths. Sole survivor Stuart Diver is rescued after 65 hours under a concrete slab in wet and freezing conditions.

Aug 30 Election in NT. Shane Stone's Country–Liberal Party government is re-elected with an increased majority.

31 Trams begin operating again in Sydney on a 3.6 km light-rail loop between Central station and Wentworth Park.

Sep 2 Head of Aboriginal warrior Yagan, sent to Britain in 1833, is brought back to WA.

Oct 11 Election in SA. Olsen Liberal government retains office but without a lower house majority.

1997

15 Australian Democrats leader Cheryl Kernot resigns from the party and the Senate to stand as an ALP candidate at the next election.

Nov 3 Shares in one-third of Telstra floated. (Second tranche of shares, equal to 16.6% of capital, listed on stock exchange in Oct 1999.)

20 AMP Society policy holders vote in favour of demutualization. (Shares listed on stock exchange 15 June 1998.)

First contingent of Australian troops arrive at Bougainville, PNG, as part of an international peace-keeping force.

22 Lead singer of the rock group INXS, Michael Hutchence, suicides in his hotel room in Sydney.

Dec – More than 200 bushfires, many out of control, burn across NSW; two bush firefighters die at Lithgow. (Another firefighter dies and seven others are injured at Wingelo on 1 Jan. 1998.)

A Architecture, Building
Crown Entertainment Complex at Southbank, Melbourne.

B Science, Technology, Discovery, etc.
Fossil of a 220-million-year-old amphibian found on the Central Coast of NSW.

C Arts and Entertainment
Nigel Thomson's portrait of Barbara Blackman wins the Archibald Prize.

Geoffrey Rush wins an Academy Award for best actor (in the Australian film *Shine*), and cinematographer John Seale wins an Academy Award for his work on *The English Patient*.

D Books and Writing
Peter Carey, *Jack Maggs* (1998 Commonwealth Writers' Prize and Miles Franklin Award winner).

Sir Ronald Wilson, *Bringing Them Home* (report on the "lost generations" of Aboriginal children).

Bob Ellis's political memoir *Goodbye Jerusalem* is withdrawn and pulped within days of publication because it defamed federal ministers Peter Costello and Tony Abbott and their wives, who successfully sue the publishers for damages.

E Sport and Recreation
Marathon swimmer Susie Maroney becomes the first person to swim across the Straits of Florida (from Havana, Cuba, to Key West, Florida, in 24 hr 31 min.).

Cathy Freeman wins the 400 m final at the World Athletics Championships in Athens.

Golfer Karrie Webb wins the British Open for the second time, scoring a course record nine-under-par 63 in her third round.

Patrick Rafter wins the US Open tennis tournament.

Michael Klim sets a word record of 52.15 s for the 100 m butterfly 15 minutes after a false start during which all competitors swim 65 m.

Might and Power wins the Melbourne Cup and the Caulfield Cup.

Michelle Martin wins the British Open squash championship for the fifth time in succession.

After the failure of Super League in its inaugural season, News Ltd and the Australian Rugby League agree to the joint conduct of a 20-team competition starting in 1998 (scaled down to 14 teams by 2000) run by a new National Rugby League.

F Statistics, Social Change, the Environment
Estimated resident population of Australia: 18,532,200.

1997

Two century-old Tasmanian laws criminalizing homosexuality are repealed, bringing Tas. into line with the rest of Australia.

G Births and Deaths

Jul   13   Sir Garfield Barwick d. (94)

Aug 18   Burnum Burnum (Harry Penrith) d. (61)

Oct   29   H.C. Coombs d. (91)

Nov 18   Stanislaus Rapotec d. (86)

1998

Jan 26   Katherine, NT, inundated by flood; three killed, 1,100 homes damaged; more than 2,000 people evacuated.

Feb 2   Constitutional Convention meeting in Old Government House, Canberra (to 13th), supports, in principle, Australia becoming a republic.

17   Australian troops and aircraft fly to the Persian Gulf in support of the US in the event of a military attack on Iraq.

21   Election for ACT Assembly. Liberal Chief Minister Kate Carnell continues to lead a minority government, the balance of power held by independents and Greens.

Apr 1   High Court upholds the validity of Hindmarsh Island Bridge Act, the subject of an Aboriginal challenge, and rules that the federal government may make laws for the detriment as well as the benefit of particular races.

7   Patrick Stevedores sacks its entire workforce across the nation to purge its operations of the Maritime Union of Australia. (High Court on 4 May orders the reinstatement of all the workers.)

30   Commonwealth Employment Service ceases operations after 52 years.

May 5   Fire engulfs the engine room of HMAS *Westralia* during training exercises off Perth; four crew killed.

22   NSW Chief Justice Murray Gleeson replaces Sir Gerard Brennan as Chief Justice of the High Court.

26   Sorry Day, to commemorate the forced removal of Aboriginal children from their families, is held throughout Australia.

Jun 13   Election in Qld. Pauline Hanson's One Nation Party draws 23% of the vote and wins 11 seats. Labor leader Peter Beattie forms a government with the support of an independent and replaces Rob Borbidge as Premier on 25 June. (When a One Nation member resigns on 4 Nov., Labor wins the by-election, giving Beattie enough seats to govern in his own right.)

Jul 8   Senate passes the government's Wik legislation (Native Title Act Amendment Bill) after a debate lasting 105 hours. (New act comes into operation on 1 Oct.)

22   Tas. Liberal and Labor parties combine to pass legislation curtailing the Hare-Clark electoral system and reducing the number of seats in parliament in order to subdue the Greens as a political force.

30   Residents of Sydney are warned to boil all tap water because of contamination by giardia and cryptosporidium. (Water declared fit to drink on 4 Aug. Warning reimposed 25 Aug.–19 Sept.)

Aug 8   Worst flooding of the Macquarie River at Bathurst in 175 years.

17   Torrential rain and mudslides in Wollongong area wreck homes, trap car travellers, and strand rail commuters.

1998

29 Election in Tas. Labor wins 14 seats in the new 25-seat House of Assembly. Jim Bacon replaces Tony Rundle as Premier. Only one Green elected.

Sep 25 Explosions at Vic.'s main gas plant, at Longford near Sale in Gippsland, cut gas supplies to most of the state. Two die and eight injured in blasts. Industries shut down (workers begin returning to work on 6 Oct.); household gas supplies cut till 8 Oct.

Oct 3 Federal election. Howard government returned with a reduced majority. One Nation Party wins only one Senate seat and Pauline Hanson loses her seat in the lower house. New members include Democrats senator Aden Ridgeway, the second Aboriginal to be elected to federal Parliament.
In a referendum in the NT, the majority vote against the proposal for the territory to become a state.

19 Australian Stock Exchange ceases to be a mutual owned by stockbroker members and becomes a company listed on its own sharemarket.

Dec – Storm-force winds and mountainous seas cause havoc in the Sydney-to-Hobart yacht race. Five yachts sink, six sailors die and 55 have to be rescued; 71 of the 115 yachts fail to finish.

A Architecture, Building
Work begins on the erection of spires on St Mary's Cathedral in Sydney.

B Science, Technology, Discovery, etc.

C Arts and Entertainment
Lewis Miller's portrait of artist Allan Mitelman wins the Archibald Prize.
Channel 9's "Midday Show" ceases after 25 years on the air.

D Books and Writing
Murray Bail, *Eucalyptus* (1999 Miles Franklin Award and Commonwealth Writers' Prize winner).
Roger McDonald, *Mr Darwin's Shooter*.

E Sport and Recreation
Emma George sets her fourteenth pole vault world record (4.59 m).
Michelle Martin wins her sixth successive British Open squash title.
Tas. axeman David Foster takes out five championships at the Sydney RAS Show, winning his one-thousandth championship and becoming the most ribboned contestant in Australian sporting history.
Susie Maroney becomes the first person to swim from Mexico to Cuba, setting a new world distance ocean swimming record.
Marathon swimmer Shelley Taylor-Smith wins her fifth round-Manhattan race.
Racing at Phillip Is., Michael Doohan wins his fifth successive 500-cc motorcycle world championship.
In the second cricket test against Pakistan, captain Mark Taylor scores 334 not out, equalling Don Bradman's highest test score by an Australian.
Australian women's hockey team win their second World Cup.
NZ mare Jezabeel wins the Melbourne Cup.

F Statistics, Social Change, the Environment
Estimated resident population of Australia: 18,730,359.
The largest recorded ozone hole over the Southern Hemisphere leaves more than 26 million kilometres of the planet temporarily unprotected (Sept.).
Australia experiences its hottest year since records began in 1910, with a mean temperature of 22.54°C.

G Births and Deaths
    Feb 25   B. A. Santamaria d. (82)
    Apr 28   Shirley Smith (Mum Shirl) d. (76)
    Sep 17   Geoffrey Dutton d. (76)

1999

Jan 23   Inquiries into corruption among International Olympic Committee officials reveals that Australian Olympic Committee president, John Coates, offered inducements to African IOC members.

Feb 8   NT Chief Minister Shane Stone resigns after losing the confidence of his party and is replaced by Denis Burke.
      10   AOC official Phil Coles stands down after allegations that he and his family received lavish trips and entertainment in the lead-up to the Winter Olympics.
      11   Convicted paedophile and former millionaire Philip Bell is sentenced to 10½ years' imprisonment.
       –   Floods in south-east Qld; six die and about 70 families evacuated from their homes in Gympie.

Mar 22   Cyclone Vance destroys 112 homes and damages 200 other buildings in Exmouth, WA.
      27   Election in NSW. Bob Carr's Labor government returned with an increased majority.
      30   Two CARE Australia workers, Steve Pratt and Peter Wallace, are detained by authorities in Yugoslavia and later charged with spying. (Convicted by closed military court and gaoled on 29 May; granted clemency and released on 1 Sept.)

Apr 14   Severe hailstorm in southern and eastern suburbs of Sydney damages about 20,000 homes and buildings, the most expensive disaster in Australia's history.

May 7   The first of about 4,000 ethnic Albanian refugees from Kosovo arrive in Australia for temporary sanctuary.
      20   Remains of eight people are discovered by police in a disused bank vault in Snowtown, SA. (Two other bodies later found in a backyard in North Salisbury and remains found on a farm in 1994 are also linked with the Snowtown killings.)

Jul 8   Legislation for the introduction of a goods and services tax (GST) given royal assent (to be introduced on 1 July 2000).
      28   Fourteen Australians die in a flash flood that sweeps away a group of adventure travellers in a canyon near Interlaken, Switzerland.

Aug 7   Four snowboarders from Sydney leave on a three-day overland adventure in Kosciuszko National Park and fail to return. (Bodies found in a snow cave on 16 Nov.)
      14   Melbourne's City Link freeway connection officially opened.
      26   Following Senator Aden Ridgeway's maiden speech and the government's negotiations with the Democrats, federal parliament passes a declaration of "deep and sincere regret" for past injustices to Aborigines.

Sep 7   President Jiang Zemin of China begins a four-day visit to Australia, the first by a Chinese president.
      10   RAAF begins airlifting UN staff and East Timorese refugees from UN

headquarters in Dili to Darwin following the campaign of killing and destruction waged by pro-Indonesian militia after East Timor's vote for independence.

16 Indonesia abrogates the 1995 mutual security agreement with Australia.

18 Election in Vic. A state-wide swing against the Kennett government leaves the Coalition without a parliamentary majority. (Kennett resigns on 19 Oct., and Labor leader Steve Bracks forms a minority government with support of the three independents.)

20 Australian troops enter East Timor as the major part of a UN peace-keeping force, led by Australia.

30 BHP ceases its steelmaking operations in Newcastle.

Oct 12 US–Australian joint defence communications facility Nurrungar, near Woomera, SA, is officially shut down after 29 years.

19 Australian Broadcasting Authority begins an inquiry into allegations of "cash for comment" in the commercial arrangements of talkback radio broadcasters John Laws and Alan Jones.

Nov 6 Referendums on proposals: (a) to establish the Commonwealth of Australia as a republic with a President appointed by a two-thirds majority of the members of the Commonwealth Parliament; and (b) to alter the Constitution to insert a preamble both defeated.

Dec 2 Seven people die and 51 are injured when an inter-urban train crashes into the rear of the Indian Pacific near Glenbrook in the Blue Mountains, NSW.

16 Geoff Clark succeeds Gatjil Djerrkura as chairman of the Aboriginal and Torres Strait Islander Commission, becoming the first elected chairman.

* More than 2,000 illegal immigrants, mainly Pakistanis, Afghans, Iraqis, and other Middle Eastern nationals, arrive in Australia as boat people in the second half of the year.

A Architecture, Building

Stadium Australia, at Sydney's Olympic Park, officially opened (6 Mar.).

Sydney's refurbished GPO building reopens as a hotel with other functions including ballrooms, food hall, meeting rooms, and post office (1 Sept.).

B Science, Technology, Discovery, etc.

Archaeologists on Beacon Is., off Geraldton, WA, unearth what appears to be a mass grave of victims of the *Batavia* mutiny in 1629.

C Arts and Entertainment

Euan Macleod's *Self-Portrait/Hole Like a Head* wins the Archibald Prize.

Long-running television program "Hey Hey It's Saturday" has its final performance (20 Nov.).

D Books and Writing

Peter Alexander's biography of poet Les Murray is withdrawn before publication and pulped because of threats of prosecution for defamation.

Thea Astley, *Drylands*, and Kim Scott, *Benang* (joint winners of the Miles Franklin Award for 2000).

E Sport and Recreation

Karrie Webb wins the Australian Ladies Master golf tournament with a world record score for a women's 72-hole tournament: 26 under par.

Grant Hackett breaks the world records for 200 m freestyle and 400 m shortcourse freestyle.

Sydney Swans full-forward Tony Lockett breaks Gordon Coventry's 62-year-old record of 1,299 career goals, kicking nine goals in a match against Collingwood to finish the day with 1,306 goals from 265 games.

Cathy Freeman wins the 400 m at the World Athletics Championships in Seville, Spain, becoming the first Australian athlete to win a gold medal at two world championships.

Over three days during the Pan Pacific Championships, Ian Thorpe sets world records for 400 m freestyle, 200 m freestyle (twice, in the semi-final and then in the final), and swims in the record-breaking 4 × 200 m team.

Susie Maroney swims from Jamaica to Cuba—197 km in 34 hr 50 min.

Australia's netball team win their third successive world championship (and eighth out of the ten played since the event's inception).

Rogan Josh wins the Melbourne Cup.

Wallabies beat France to win the Rugby World Cup in Cardiff, Wales.

Eighteen-year-old amateur golfer Aaron Baddeley wins the Australian Open, the youngest winner and the first amateur to win since 1960.

Australia (Mark Woodforde, Todd Woodbridge, Mark Philippoussis, Lleyton Hewitt) wins the Davis Cup against France.

F Statistics, Social Change, the Environment

Population of Australia reaches 19 million.

G Births and Deaths

Feb   6   Don Dunstan d. (72).
Apr 24   Arthur Boyd d. (78).
Sep   1   Bobby Limb d. (74)
Oct   9   Morris West d. (83).
Oct 23   Albert Tucker d. (84).

INDEX

EACH INDEX ENTRY is followed by a year number, then a number from 1 to 12, or a letter from A to G, or an asterisk. A number following the year denotes the month in which an event occurred. An asterisk signifies that the event cannot be assigned to a particular month; text entries for such events are located immediately following calendar entries for the year. A letter indicates that the entry is located under the subject heading for one of the categories from A to G which appear for each year. For example, the following entry appears:

Antarctic exploration: Borchgrevink, 1895 **1**, 1899 B . . .

Text entries referring to Borchgrevink's exploration will appear in January 1895, and in 1899 under the heading **B Science, Technology, Discovery etc**.

An explanation of the principles upon which the index is organized appears in the Introduction.

INDEX

A

Abbey, The (Annandale, Syd.), 1882 A
Abbott, Anthony John, Liberal politician (1957–), 1997 D
Abbott, Edward, NSW Corps officer (1766–1832), 1807 **3**
à Beckett, Sir William, Chief Justice of Vic. (1806–69), 1852 **2**
Aboriginal Protection (Act) WA, 1886 **9**
Aboriginal Protection and Restriction of the Sale of Opium Act (Qld), 1897 F
Aboriginal Tent Embassy, 1972 **1**
Aboriginal and Torres Strait Islander Commission (ATSIC), 1990 **3**, 1996 **12**, 1999 **12**
Aborigines, mainland. *See also names of individual Aborigines*
anthropological studies of, 1899 B, 1901 B
archaeological remains of: at Talgai station, Qld, 1886 B; at Cohuna, Vic., 1925 B; Jervois skull, 1929 B; at Keilor, Vic., 1940 B; at Lake Mungo, NSW, 1968 B, 1974 B; near Lake Eyre, SA, 1988 B; in Lake Victoria, NSW, 1994 B; at Jinmium, NT, 1996 B
art of, 1838 C, 1927 C. *See also* Namatjira, Albert
assimilation of, 1937 F, 1951 F
Bates, Daisy, and, 1912 **11**
Batman and, 1835 **5 8**
blacktrackers used for first time, 1834 **12**
citizenship rights, 1938 **1**, 1953 **1**, 1957 F, 1967 **5**
conflict with whites:
in NSW, 1788 **5**, 1790 **12**, 1801 **5**, 1824 **8**, 1827 **5**; at Hawkesbury/Nepean, 1797 **7**, 1799 **10**, 1816 **3**; at Parramatta/ Toongabbie, 1802 **6**, 1805 **4**; T. L. Mitchell ambushes and kills, 1836 **5**; Faithfull massacre, 1838 **4**; Myall Creek massare, 1838 **6**; Rufus River massacre, 1841 **8**; Dora Dora murder, 1891 **5**; Governor brothers' rampage, 1900 **7 10**
in NT: attack Leichhardt's party, 1845 **6**
in Qld: at Blaxland's Gin Gin station, 1849 **6**; Stapylton and assistant killed, 1840 **5**; at Hornet Bank station, 1857 **10**; at Cullin-la-ringo station, 1861 **10**; Kalkadoons, near Cloncurry, 1883 **1**, 1884 **9**
in SA: *Maria* castaways killed, 1840 **6**
in WA, 1831 **8**, 1832 **6**, 1833 **5 7**; "Battle of Pinjarra", 1834 **10**
cricketers, 1868 E, 1988 E
discrimination against, removed, 1964 F, 1967 **5**
and disease, 1789 **4**

education, 1815 **1**
first: army officer, 1944 F; university graduates, 1966 F; member of parliament, 1971 **5**; vice-regal appointee, 1976 **12**; barrister, 1976 F, bishop, 1985 **10**; cabinet minister, 1986 **2**; magistrate in NSW, 1986 **7**; priest, 1996 **12**; judge, 1996 F
forcible removal of children, 1997 **5**, 1998 **5**
freedom rides, 1965 **2**
land rights: meeting calls for, 1938 **1**; Gurindji people at Wave Hill, 1966 **8**, 1976 **3**, 1975 **8**; Yirrkala at Gove, 1971 **4**; granted in NT, 1976 **12**; Aurukun and Mornington Is. reserves abolished, 1978 **4**; Pitjantjatjara granted rights, 1981 **11**; Maralinga land returned to traditional owners, 1984 **12**; Mutijulu granted freehold to Ayers Rock, 1985 **10**; Katherine Gorge handed over to Jawoyn people, 1989 **9**; High Court's Mabo judgment, 1992 **6**; native title legislation, 1993 **12**, 1996 **11**, 1998 **7**; first successful native title claim, 1996 **10**; High Court's Wik judgment, 1996 **12**
language studies, 1827 D, 1834 D, 1839 D
and legal system, 1805 **7**, 1836 F, 1841 F, 1998 **4**
Macquarie and, 1814 **12**
and mining operations, 1963 **11**, 1982 **7**
missions: Lake Macquarie (NSW), 1826 *; Hermannsburg (NT), 1877 **6**; Ernabella (SA), 1936 **12**
native police, 1842 **2**, 1883 **1**
occupation of Australia, 1968 B, 1987 **12** B, 1992 **6**
Phillip's relations with, 1788 **12**, 1789 **11**, 1792 **12**. *See also* Arabanoo; Bennelong; Yemmerrawannie
population: at white settlement, 1788 F; declines in Vic., 1879 F; at its lowest, 1933 F; at censuses, 1976 F, 1981 F, 1986 F
protection, 1838 **1**, 1886 **9**, 1897 F, 1911 F
reconciliation, 1997 **5**, 1999 **8**
royal commission into deaths in custody, 1987 **8**
Social Service benefits paid to, 1960 F
Sorry Day, 1998 **5**
television station, 1988 **1**
voting rights, 1949 **3**, 1951 **11**, 1962 F
whites live with: absconders at Port Stephens, 1790 **9**; John Wilson, 1798 **1 3**; William Buckley, 1803 **12**, 1835 **7**; John Graham, 1833 **11**; John Ireland and William D'Oyley, 1834 **8**; John Storry Baker, 1840 **8**; David Bracewell and James Davis, 1842 **5**; James Murrell, 1846 **3**, 1863 **1**; Barbara Thompson, 1845 **4**, 1849 **10**; "Normanby woman", 1886 **9**

INDEX

working conditions, protests against, 1946 **5**, 1966 **8**

Aborigines, Tasmanian: estimated population at time of white settlement, 1803 F; "Black War" begins, 1804 **5**; killed at Port Dalrymple, 1804 **11**; Musquito and Black Jack, 1823 **11**, 1824 **8**, 1825 **2**; excluded from settled areas, 1828 **4**; hunted by roving parties, 1828 **11**; at Bruny Is., 1829 **3**; and the Black Line, 1830 **10**; captured by Robinson, 1831 **1**, 1835 **1**; kill whalers, 1841 **10**, 1842 **1**; last full-blood male dies, 1869 **3**; Truganini dies, 1876 **5**; cultural sites returned to, 1995 **10**

Abortion law, liberalized in SA, 1969 F; legalized in NSW, 1996 **10**

Abrahams, Charles J., sculptor (1816–85), 1843 C

Abrahams, Louis, artist (1852–1903), 1885 C, 1886 C

Absorption spectrophotometer, 1952 B

Academy of Music Theatre (Adel.), 1886 **12**

Academy of Science, 1959 A

Acclimatization societies, 1861 F, 1862 F, 1863 F

Account of a Voyage to . . . Port Phillip (J. Tuckey), 1805 D

Account of the English Colony in New South Wales, An (D. Collins), 1798 D

AC/DC (rock group), 1980 C

Acolyte, The (T. Astley), 1972 D

Acquired Immune Deficiency Syndrome (AIDS), 1981 **9**, 1982 **11**, 1984 **11**

Active (convict transport), 1791 **9**

ACTU. *See* Australian Council of Trade Unions

Adam in Ochre (C. Simpson), 1951 D

Adam-Smith, Patricia Jean (Patsy), author (1924–), 1964 D

Adamante (ship), 1816 **9**

Adaminaby Dam, 1957 **6**, 1958 **5**

Adams, George, Tattersall's founder (1839–1904), 1829 G, 1881 **4**, 1896 **1**, 1904 G; builds new Tattersall's Hotel, 1893 A; opens Palace Theatre, 1896 C

Adams, Glenda, author (1940–), 1987 D

Adams, John (alias Alexander Smith), *Bounty* mutineer (*c.* 1766–1829), 1808 **2**, 1829 G

Adams, Phillip Andrew, journalist and film-maker (1939–), 1939 G, 1979 C

Adare, Cape (Antarctica), 1895 **1**

Addison, George Henry Male, architect, (1858–1922), 1891 A

Address to the Inhabitants of the Colonies Established in New South Wales and Norfolk Island (R. Johnson), 1794 D

Adelaide (SA): site of, chosen, 1836 **12**; Col. Light surveys and lays out, 1837 **1**; first land sales, 1837 **3**; first newspaper published, 1837 **6**; Government House built, 1839 A; Australia's first

municipality, 1840 **8 10**; water supply, 1860 **12**; lit by gas, 1863 **6**; Town Hall opened, 1866 **6**; St Peter's Cathedral built, 1869 A; new GPO opened, 1872 **5**; University established, 1874 **11**; Parliament House built, 1881 A; telephone exchange opened, 1883 **5**; St Francis Xavier Cathedral built, 1886 A; lit by electricity, 1900 **1**; electric tram service begins, 1909 **3**; railway station built, 1928 A; highest temperature recorded, 1939 **1**; airport opens, 1955 **2**; Festival first held, 1960 C; Festival Centre opens, 1973 A; Formula One Grand Prix first held, 1985 E; O-Bahn guided busway inaugurated, 1986 **3**; hit by storms, 1986 **12**; Adelaide Plaza completed, 1989 A

Adelaide (ship), 1849 **12**

Adelaide Botanic Gardens conservatory, 1989 B

Adelaide Cup, first run, 1864 E

Adelaide Liedertafel, 1857 C

Adelaide Observer (newspaper), 1843 **7**

Adelaide Repertory Theatre, 1908 C

Adelaide River (NT), discovered, 1839 **7**

Adelaide sovereigns, 1852 **12**

Adelaide Steamship Co., founded, 1875 **10**; group collapses, 1991 **3**

Adelphi Theatre (Syd.). *See* Tivoli Theatre

Admiral Barrington (convict transport), 1791 **10**

Admiral Gambier (convict transport), 1809 **3**, 1811 **12**

"Advance Australia Fair" (song), 1878 C, 1974 **4**, 1977 **5**, 1984 **4**

Advancement of Spencer Button, The (B. James), 1950 D

Adventure disasters: canyoners at Interlaken, 1999 **7**; snowboarders in Kosciuszko National Park, 1999 **8**

Adventures of Barry McKenzie, The (film), 1972 C

Advertiser (newspaper, Adel.), 1858 **7**

Advertiser (newspaper, Melb.), 1838 **1**

Advisory War Council, 1940 **10**

AE1 (submarine), 1914 **9**

AE2 (submarine), 1915 **4**

Aeolus (convict transport), 1809 **1**

Aerial crop spraying, 1947 F

Aeroplane Jelly, 1925 *; song, 1938 C

Afternoon Light (R. G. Menzies), 1967 D

Agar, Alex, pugilist, 1884 E

Age (newspaper, Melb.), 1854 **10**, 1956 **6**; sued for libel, 1892 **3**; publishes tapes of phone taps, 1984 **2 3**

Age of Consent (N. Lindsay), 1938 D; film of, 1969 C

Age at death, greatest, 1987 **11**

Age of majority, 1973 F

Agents-general, first: SA, 1858 **5**; Qld, 1860 **10**; NSW, 1863 **1**; Vic., 1868 **12**, 1892 **2**; Tas., 1886 **3**; WA, 1892 **4**

Agnew (WA), 1977 **4**

INDEX

Agnew, Sir James Willson, Premier of Tas. (1815–1901), 1886 **3**

Agostini, Antonio, "pyjama girl" killer (1903–69), 1944 **3**

Agricultural colleges
Dookie (Vic.), 1886 **10**
Gatton (Qld), 1897 **7**
Hawkesbury (NSW), 1891 **3**
Longerenong (Vic.), 1889 **3**
Roseworthy (SA), 1885 **2**

Agricultural machinery: Ridley's wheat stripper, 1843 B; steam cultivator imported, 1864 B; stumpjump plough, 1876 B; stripper-harvester, 1884 B; header-harvester, 1913 B; rotary hoe, 1920 B

Agricultural societies: Tas., 1822 **1**; NSW, 1822 **7**, 1869 **5**, 1882 **4**; WA, 1831 **5**; SA, 1839 **11**; Vic. 1848 *, 1871 **11**

Ahern, Michael John, National Party Premier of Qld (1942–), 1987 **12**, 1989 **9**

AIDS. *See* Acquired Immune Deficiency Syndrome

Air accidents and disasters: Harry Hawker killed, 1921 **7**; crash of first airmail plane, 1921 **12**; Sir Ross Smith killed, 1922 **4**; Moncrieff and Hood lost, 1928 **1**; *Southern Cloud* lost, 1931 **3**; Bert Hinkler killed, 1933 **1**; airliners crash, 1934 **10**, 1935 **10**; *Stella Australis* lost, 1934 **12**; Kingsford Smith disappears, 1935 **11**; Stinson on Lamington Plateau, 1937 **2**; *Kyeema*, 1938 **10**; cabinet ministers killed, 1940 **8**; ANA airliner at Hobart, 1946 **3**; ANA airliner near Quirindi, 1948 **9**; Queensland Airlines at Coolangatta, 1949 **3**; near Guildford (WA), 1949 **7**; near York (WA), 1950 **6**; pilotless plane over Sydney, 1955 **8**; TAA airliner off Mackay, 1960 **6**; Viscount crashes into Botany Bay, 1961 **11**; Ansett-ANA Viscount near Winton, 1966 **9**; helicopter on Bass Strait platform, 1968 **3**; at Port Hedland, 1968 **12**; Heron near Cairns, 1975 **10**; Connair suicide crash, 1977 **1**; at Essendon, 1978 **7**; Beechcraft at Sydney Airport, 1980 **2**; hot-air balloon, 1989 **8**; business jet in north Qld, 1990 **5**; helicopter on Gold Coast, 1991 **3**; commuter jet near Young, 1993 **6**; Seaview Air flight to Lord Howe Is., 1994 **10**; SAS helicopters collide, 1996 **6**. *See also* Aviation

Air pollution, 1958 F

Air services. *See* Aviation

Aircraft industry, 1936 **10**, 1939 **3**, 1972 B

Airmail: first, 1914 **7**; first official service, 1921 **12**; intercapital, 1924 **6**, 1925 **7**; Australia–UK, 1931 **4**; Australia–NZ, 1934 **4**; Australia–US, 1937 **4**

Albany (WA), 1826 **12**, 1834 **4**; Eyre reaches, 1841 **7**; whaling station, 1971 F, 1978 F. *See also* King George Sound

Albatross, HMAS (shore station), 1948 **8**; fire at, 1976 **12**

Alberga River (SA), 1873 **8**

Albermarle (convict transport), 1791 **10**

Albert, Prince, son of Edward VII, 1881 **5**

Albert River (north Qld), 1841 **7**

Albion (storeship/whaler), 1799 **6** F, 1801 **8**, 1803 **9**, 1804 **9**

Albury (NSW), 1839 **4**, 1946 **12**, 1973 **10**; Murray navigated to, 1855 **10**; bridge across Murray at, 1861 **9**, 1883 **6**; railway reaches, 1881 **2**; flood at, 1906 **7**

Albury (riverboat), 1855 **10**, 1858 **8**, 1859 **1**

Alcohol consumption, 1985 F

Alcoholics Anonymous, 1945 *

Alexander, John, tennis player (1951–), 1977 E

Alexander, Peter Fraser, academic and author, 1999 D

Alexander (convict transport), 1806 **8**

Alexander (First Fleet transport), 1788 **1 7**

Alexandra, Princess, 1959 **8**, 1967 **2**, 1980 **10**

Alexandrina, Lake (SA); Sturt at, 1830 **2**; Barker killed at, 1831 **4**

Alfred, Prince, Duke of Edinburgh, 1867 **10 11**; shot at Clontarf, 1868 **3**

Alfred Hospital (Melbourne), 1869 A, 1871 **5**

Alice Springs (NT), site of, discovered, 1871 **3**; township surveyed, 1888 **10**; railway to Adelaide, 1929 **8**

Alien Son (J. Waten), 1952 D

Alister, Paul Shaun, Ananda Marga member, 1978 **6**, 1982 **10**, 1985 **5**

All for Australia League, 1938 **1**

All Saints Church (Bathurst, NSW), 1845 A

All Saints Church (Upper Swan, WA), 1839 A

All That Swagger (M. Franklin), 1936 D

All the Rivers Run (N. Cato), 1978 D

Allan, John, Premier of Vic. (1866–1936), 1924 **11**, 1927 **5**

Allan's Music Warehouse (Melb.), 1850 C, 1877 A; destroyed by fire, 1889 **9**

Allen, Davida, artist (1951–), 1986 C

Allied Works Council, 1942 **2**

Alligator River (NT), 1818 **4**

Allman, Francis, soldier (1780–1860), founds settlement at Port Macquarie, 1821 **3**

Almorah (ship), 1825 **2**

"Along the Road to Gundagai" (song), 1922 C

Alt, Augustus Theodore Henry, surveyor (1731–1815), 1788 A, 1815 G

Alt, M. B., ship's master, 1793 **7**

Altman, Dennis Patkin, author (1943–), 1972 D

Aluminium industry, 1955 **2**. *See also* Bauxite

Alvin Purple (film), 1973 C

Amalgamated Metal Workers' Union, 1972 **8**

INDEX

Anzac Mounted Division, 1916 **8**

Anzac Pact, 1944 **1**

ANZUS Treaty, 1951 **9**; Council, 1952 **8**, 1962 **5**, 1985 **3**; US withdraws from naval exercise, 1985 **2**

APEC. *See* Asia-Pacific Economic Co-operation

Apex Club, 1930 **11**

Appin (NSW), mine disaster, 1979 **7**

Appleroth, Adolphus Herbert, jelly maker (d. 1952), 1925 *

Apples, exported from Tas., 1849 *

Arabanoo, Aboriginal captive, 1788 **12**, 1789 **4**

Araluen (NSW), 1851 **8**

Arantz, Philip, policeman (d. 1998), 1971 **12**

Ararat (Vic.), 1858 **9**; goldfield, 1845 **6**, 1857 **5**

Arbitration. *See* Conciliation and Arbitration

Archdale, Helen Elizabeth (Betty), cricketer and educationist (1907–2000), 1907 G, 1934 E

Archer, John Lee, architect (1791–1852), 1791 G, 1827 A, 1834 A, 1835 A, 1837 A, 1852 G

Archer, Robyn (*née* Smith), singer, actress, and writer (1948–), 1948 G, 1979 C

Archerfield Airport (Bris.), 1931 *

Archibald, John Feltham (Jules François), journalist and magazine proprietor (1856–1919), 1856 G, 1919 G; founds *Bulletin,* 1880 **1**; goes to gaol, 1882 **3**; edits *Bulletin,* 1886 D; establishes Archibald Prize, 1919 C

Archibald Memorial (Syd.), 1933 C

Archibald Prize: founded, 1919 C; first awarded, 1921 C; no award made, 1964 C, 1980 C, 1991 C; retained in perpetuity, 1985 C. *For winners, see section C from 1921*

Argentine ant, 1939 F

Argo (ship), 1805 **6**, 1814 **6**

"Argonauts' Club", 1941 C, 1971 C

Argus (newspaper, Melb.), 1846 **6**, 1856 **11**, 1862 **4**, 1866 **3**, 1957 **1**

Argyle, Sir Stanley Seymour, Premier of Vic. (1867–1940), 1932 **5**

Argyle, Lake (WA), 1972 **6**

Argyle Cut (Syd.), 1843 A

Ariel (ship), 1848 **12**

Arlen, Albert, composer (1905–93), 1960 C

Armidale (NSW), 1849 **3**, 1885 **3**; St Peter's Cathedral, 1875 A

Armidale, HMAS, 1942 **12**

Armstrong, Duncan, swimmer (1968–), 1988 E

Armstrong, Gillian May, film maker (1950–), 1979 C

Armstrong, Helen Porter. *See* Melba, Dame Nellie

Army. *See* Military forces

Arnhem Land (NT): Flinders at, 1803 **2 3**; Lindsay explores, 1883 **6**

Arnold, Lynn Maurice Ferguson, Labor Premier of SA (1949–), 1992 **9**, 1993 **12**

Arnott, William, biscuit manufacturer (1827–1901), 1865 *

Around the Boree Log (J. O'Brien), 1921 D

Art exhibition, first, 1845 C

Art galleries and museums
Adelaide
Art Gallery of South Australia, 1881 C, 1900 A, 1996 A
South Australian Museum, 1856 B
Brisbane
Brisbane Museum, 1855 B
Queensland Art Gallery, 1895 C, 1982 C
Queensland Museum, 1855 B, 1871 B, 1891 A
Canberra
Australian National Gallery, 1974 A, 1982 **10** C
Australian War Memorial, 1925 **4**
Museum of Australia, 1980 B
Hobart
Tasmanian Museum and Art Gallery, 1863 A
Launceston
Queen Victoria Museum and Art Gallery, 1887 A, 1891 B
Melbourne
Museum of Applied Science 1870 B
Museum of Art, 1861 C, 1864 C
National Gallery of Victoria, 1864 C, 1869 **12**, 1883 C, 1904 C F, 1962 A, 1968 C; School, 1870 C
National Museum, 1854 B, 1869 **12**, 1899 B
Perth
Art Gallery of Western Australia, 1895 C, 1906 A, 1908 C, 1979 A
Western Australian Museum, 1892 B
Sydney
Art Gallery of New South Wales, 1875 C, 1885 A
Australian Museum, 1827 B, 1836 B, 1846 A, 1853 B
Museum of Applied Arts and Sciences, 1880 B, 1893 B
Museum of Contemporary Art, 1991 C
Powerhouse Museum, 1979 A, 1981 B
Technological Museum. *See* Museum of Applied Arts and Sciences

Art in Australia (periodical, Syd.), 1916 C, 1942 C

Artesian water: first discovered, 1878 B; used for generating electric power, 1893 B

Arthur, Sir George, Governor of Tas. (1784–1854), 1854 G; replaces Sorell as Lt-Gov., 1824 **5**; assumes governorship of separate colony, 1825 **12**; suspends Gellibrand, 1826 **2**; curtails press, 1827 **9**; excludes Aborigines from settled areas,

INDEX

INDEX

INDEX

Australian National Gallery (Canb.), 1974 A, 1982 **10** C

Australian National Line, 1956 **10**, 1959 **10**, 1969 **8**

Australian National Maritime Museum (Syd.), 1991 B

Australian National Research Council, 1919 B

Australian National University, 1946 **8**

Australian Natives' Association, 1871 **5**

Australian Naval and Military Expeditionary Force, 1914 **8 9**

Australian Newsprint Mills Ltd, 1941 **2**

Australian Nuggets (gold coins), 1986 **7**

Australian Olympic Committee, 1999 **1**

Australian Olympic Federation, votes to send a team to Moscow, 1980 **5**

Australian Opera, 1970 C

Australian Patriotic Association, 1835 **5**

Australian Peace Congress, 1949 **4**

Australian Performing Group, 1970 C

Australian Postal Commission (Australia Post), 1975 **7**

Australian Pulp and Paper Mills Ltd, 1938 B

Australian Quarterly (periodical), 1929 **3**

Australian Racing and Jockey Club, 1828 E

Australian Reconciliation Convention, 1997 **5**

Australian Red Cross Society, 1914 **8**; starts Blood Transfusion Service, 1938 *

Australian Reform Movement. *See* Australia Party

Australian Religious Tract Society, 1823 **9**

Australian Republican Movement, 1991 **7**

Australian Resources Development Bank, 1968 **3**

Australian Schools Commission, 1972 **12**, 1973 **5**

Australian Secret Intelligence Service (ASIS), raids Sheraton Hotel, 1983 **11**

Australian Security Intelligence Organization (ASIO), 1949 **3**; raided by Murphy and Commonwealth Police, 1973 **3**

Australian Sketch Book, The (J. Martin), 1838 D

Australian Sketchbook, The (S. T. Gill), 1865 C

Australian Soccer Federation, 1957 E

Australian Social Lodge (Syd.), 1820 **8**

Australian Socialist League, 1887 **5**

Australian Society of Authors, 1963 D

Australian Steam Navigation Co., 1833 **4**

Australian Subscription Library, 1826 **3**, 1843 **2**, 1869 **9**. *See also* State Library of New South Wales

Australian Telecommunications Commission (Telecom), 1975 **7**; introduces Viatel, 1985 B, mobile phones, 1987 B; phone monopoly ends, 1991 **7**; becomes Telstra, 1995 **7**

Australian Theatre Society, 1904 C

Australian Town and Country Journal (magazine, Syd.), 1870 **1**

Australian Tradition, The (A. A. Phillips), 1958 D

Australian Ugliness, The (R. Boyd), 1960 D

Australian Union Benefit Society, 1834 **4**

Australian Universities Commission, 1943 **2**, 1959 **5**

Australian War Memorial (Canberra), 1925 **4**, 1993 **11**

Australian Wheat Board, 1915 **12**

Australian Wireless Co., 1910 **11**

Australian Women's Army Service, 1941 **8**

Australian Women's Land Army, 1942 **7**

Australian Women's Weekly (magazine, Syd.), 1933 **6**, 1982 **12**

Australian Wool Commission, 1970 **11**, 1973 **1**

Australian Wool Corporation, 1973 **1**

Australian Worker (newspaper, Syd.), 1891 **10**

Australian Workers' Union, 1894 **2**; and Mount Isa strike, 1964 **8 10**; affiliates with ACTU, 1967 **1**

Australind colony, 1841 **3**, 1843 **12**

Australorp (poultry), 1930 B

Aviation: Hargrave's experiments, 1894 B; first flights in Australia, 1909 **12**, 1910 **3 7**; first qualified pilot, 1911 **12**; first air race, 1912 **6**; Hawker sets endurance record, 1912 **10**; first airmail, 1914 **7**; UK–Australia air race, 1919 **3 11 12**; first transcontinental flight, 1919 **11**; first Bass Strait crossing, 1919 **12**; first single-engined UK–Australia flight, 1920 **1**; Hinkler sets long-distance records, 1920 **5**, 1921 **4**; Qantas founded, 1920 **11**; first round-Australia flight, 1924 **4**; first flight across Tasman, 1928 **1**; UK–Australia solo flights, 1928 **2**, 1930 **1 5**; Flying Doctor service founded, 1928 **5**; first trans-Pacific flights, 1928 **5**, 1934 **10**; first non-stop trans-Australia flight, 1928 **8**; QEA services, 1934 **1 12**; Melbourne Centenary Air Race, 1934 **10**; flying-boat services, 1938 **7**, 1940 **4**; attempt to nationalize interstate airlines, 1945 **7**; federal government establishes TAA, 1945 **8**; two-airline policy, 1952 **11**, 1990 **10**; first UK–Australia non-stop flight, 1961 **6**; Australia–China service begins, 1984 **9**; all domestic pilots resign, 1989 **8**; domestic market deregulated, 1990 **10**. *See also* Air accidents and disasters; Airmail; *and under names of aviators and airlines*

Avon River (Vic.), 1840 **1**

Avon River (WA), 1830 **7**

AWA. *See* Amalgamated Wireless (Australasia) Ltd

Awnings, cantilevered, 1908 A

AWU. *See* Australian Workers' Union

Ayers, Sir Henry, Premier of SA (1821–97), 1863 **7**, 1865 **9**, 1867 **5**, 1868 **9**, 1872 **1**, 1873 **7**

INDEX

Bank of New South Wales: first bank in Australia, 1817 **4**; opens savings bank, 1956 **1**; merges with CBA to form Westpac, 1981 **11**

Bank of North Queensland, 1893 **5**

Bank of Van Diemen's Land, 1824 **3**, 1891 **8**; assets disposed of by lottery, 1896 **1**

Bank of Victoria, 1853 **1**, 1893 **5**

Bank of Western Australia, 1837 **6**

Bank robberies: Bank of Australia, Sydney, 1828 **9**; Kelly Gang, 1879 **2**; Hakki Bahadi Atahan, 1984 **1**

Bankcard: introduced, 1974 **10**; outstanding debt on, 1985 F

Banking: first bank in Australia, 1816 **11**, 1817 **11**; first savings banks, 1819 **6 7**, 1832 **8**, 1841 **9**; Commonwealth Bank established, 1911 **12**; royal commission, 1937 **7**; government control of, 1945 **3**; Banking Act and Commonwealth Bank Act, 1945 **8**, 1947 **8**; nationalization attempt, 1947 **8 10**, 1948 **8**; legislation held up in Senate, 1951 **3**; new savings banks, 1956 **1**; Saturday closing, 1962 **1**; interest-rate controls lifted, 1980 **12**; automated teller machines introduced, 1977 B, 1980 B; banks deregulated, 1984 **8**; foreign banks invited, 1984 **9**. *See also* Economic crises and depressions

Banknotes: declared legal tender in NSW, 1893 **5**; Commonwealth Treasury given power to issue, 1910 **9**; first Treasury issue, 1913 **5**; Commonwealth Bank begins issuing, 1920 **12**; five-dollar note issued, 1967 **5**; fifty-dollar note issued, 1973 **10**; hundred-dollar note issued, 1984 **3**; plastic notes, 1988 B, 1992 **7**, 1993 **11**, 1994 **10**

Bankruptcy Court, 1976 **12**

Banks, Donald Oscar, composer (1923–80), 1923 G, 1966 C, 1980 G

Banks, Sir Joseph, botanist (1743–1820), 1820 G

Banks, Cape (SA), 1800 **12**

Banks, Mount (NSW), 1804 **11**

Bannister, Saxe, first Attorney-General of NSW and writer (1790–1877), 1790 G, 1824 **5**, 1877 G; fights duel with Wardell, 1826 **10**

Bannister, Thomas, soldier and explorer, 1830 **12**

Bannon, John Charles, Labor Premier of SA, 1982 **11**, 1985 **12**, 1989 **11**, 1992 **9**

Baptist Church, 1831 **4**, 1835 **11**

Barassi, Ronald Dale, footballer (1936–), 1936 G

Barcaldine (Qld), strikers arrested at, 1891 **3 5**

Barcoo River (Qld), 1846 **9**, 1847 **8**

Bark House Days (M. E. Fullerton), 1921 D

Barker, Collet, soldier and explorer (1784–1831), 1828 **9**, 1829 **12**, 1831 **3 4**

Barker, Tom, IWW official (1887–1970), 1915 **9**

Barkly, Sir Henry, Governor of Vic. (1815–98), 1856 **12**

Barkly Tableland (NT–Qld), 1861 **12**

Barlee, Lake (WA), 1869 **4**

Barnard, Lance Herbert, Labor politician (1919–97), 1972 **12**, 1975 **6**

Barnard, Marjorie Faith, author and historian (1897–1987), 1897 G, 1987 G. *See also* Eldershaw, M. Barnard

Barnardo's Homes, 1921 *

Barnes, Frederick, architect (d. 1884), 1863 A, 1867 A, 1868 A

Barnes, Stephen, schoolteacher, 1793 **2**

Barnet, James Johnstone, architect (1827–1904), 1866 A, 1869 A, 1876 A, 1878 A, 1879 A, 1885 A

Barney, George, engineer (1792–1862), 1841 A, 1847 **1**, 1855 A

Barney, Mount (Qld), 1828 **8**

Barossa Valley (SA): first vineyard established, 1847 *; wine festival first held, 1947 *

Barrackee Mystery, The (A. W. Upfield), 1929 D

Barrallier, Francis Luis, explorer (1773–1853), 1800 **4**, 1802 **11**, 1853 G

Barramundi (fish), 1845 B

Barrett, Franklyn (Walter Franklyn Brown), film director (1874–1961), 1920 C

Barrett, Thomas, first person executed in NSW, 1788 **2**

Barrier Industrial Council, 1923 **3**

Barrier Miner (newspaper, Broken Hill), 1888 **2**

Barritt, Denis, coroner (1926–97), 1981 **2 11**

Barron River (Qld), 1875 **4**, 1879 **3**

Barrow Island (WA), 1818 **6**, 1966 **5**

Barry, Edmond, policeman, 1864 **11**

Barry, Keith, speedboat driver, 1950 E

Barry, Kim Narelle, murder victim, 1981 **2**

Barry, Sir Redmond, judge (1813–80), 1813 G, 1880 G

Barton, Charlotte, author (1797–1862), 1841 D

Barton, Sir Edmund, Australia's first Prime Minister (1849–1920), 1849 G, 1900 **12**, 1901 **1**, 1920 G; on High Court, 1903 **9 10**

Barton, Gordon Page, businessman (1929–), forms Australia Party, 1966 **11**

Barwell, Sir Henry Newman, Liberal Premier of SA (1877–1959), 1920 **4**

Barwell (convict transport), 1798 **5**

Barwick, Sir Garfield Edward John, lawyer and Liberal politician (1903–97), 1903 G, 1997 G; Foreign Minister, 1962 **5**, 1963 **8**; Chief Justice of the High Court, 1964 **4**, 1981 **2**

Basic wage, Commonwealth: Harvester

INDEX

judgment sets, 1907 **11**; "A" series index, 1912 F; Powers award, 1920 **11**, 1934 **4**; automatic quarterly adjustments to, 1921 F; cut by 10%, 1931 **2**, 1934 **4**; "C" series index, 1934 **4**, 1961 **4**; "prosperity loadings", 1937 **6**; female rate set, 1950 F; automatic quarterly adjustments discontinued, 1953 **9**; annual review instituted, 1957 **4**; Consumer Price Index compiled, 1960 **8**; superseded by total wage, 1967 **6**. *See also* Wages.
    rates: 1907 F, 1913 F, 1922 F, 1929 F, 1937 F, 1939 F, 1944 F, 1946 F, 1948 F, 1952 F, 1957 F

Basically Black (theatrical production), 1972 C

Basilisk, HMS, 1872 **2**, 1873 **2**

Bass, George, naval surgeon and explorer (1771–*c*. 1803), 1795 **2 9**, 1803 **2** G; explores with Flinders, 1795 **10**, 1796 **3**, 1798 **10 11 12**, 1799 **1**; attempts to cross Blue Mountains, 1796 **6**; discovers coal, 1797 **8**; explores south coast, 1797 **12**, 1798 **1 2**; returns to England, 1799 **5**; and *Venus*, 1801 **8 11**, 1803 **2**

Bass, Thomas Dwyer, sculptor (1916–), 1916 G

Bass Strait: existence of, suspected 1797 **5**; established, 1798 **11**; named, 1798 **2**; Grant passes through, 1800 **12**; Baudin's expedition in, 1802 **11 12**; submarine cables across, 1859 **9**, 1869 **5**, 1936 **3**; ferries across, 1959 **10**, 1990 **12**; oil and gas wells, 1964 **12**, 1965 **2**, 1967 **5**, 1968 **3**; gas piped from, 1969 **3**; oil piped from, 1969 **10**; islands returned to Aborigines, 1995 **10**; swum across, 1996 E

Basser, Sir Adolph, businessman and philanthropist (1887–1964), 1887 G, 1964 G

Bataan, HMAS, 1950 **6 12**

Batavia (Dutch ship), 1963 *, 1971 **4**

Bates, Daisy May (*née* O'Dwyer), social worker and writer on Aborigines (1859–1951), 1859 G, 1938 D, 1951 G; becomes Protector of Aborigines at Eucla, 1912 **11**; settles at Ooldea, 1919 **10**

Bates, Smart, and McCutcheon, architects, 1972 A

Bathing machines, 1857 E

Bathing regulations, 1833 F; Gocher defies law, 1902 **10**; daytime bathing legalized, 1906 F; swimsuit regulations, 1935 F, 1938 F; nude bathing allowed, 1975 F, 1976 F

Bathurst (NSW): named and laid out, 1815 **5**; martial law at, 1824 **8**; gazetted as town, 1833 **1**; cathedral built, 1845 A; railway reaches, 1876 **4**; courthouse built, 1878 A; proclaimed a city, 1885 **3**; flooded, 1998 **8**

Bathurst (brig), 1821 **5 12**, 1822 **9**

Bathurst Bay (Qld), 1819 *, 1899 **3**

Bathurst burr, introduced, 1840 F

Bathurst Gaol, riot at, 1974 **2**

Bathurst Island (NT), 1818 **5**

Bathurst Plains (NSW), 1813 **11**

Batman, John, pioneer (1801–39), 1801 G, 1839 G; captures Matthew Brady, 1826 **3**; and Port Phillip settlement, 1835 **5 7 8 11**, 1836 **4**

Battarbee, Reginald Ernest (Rex), artist (1893–1973), 1934 C

"Battle of Brisbane", 1942 **11**

"Battle of Broken Hill", 1915 **1**

"Battle of Pinjarra", 1834 **10**

"Battle of the Barricades", 1919 **5**

Battlers, The (K. Tennant), 1941 D

Baudin, Nicolas Thomas, French navigator and explorer (1754–1803), 1803 G; explores WA coast, 1801 **5 7**; on Tas. coast, 1802 **1 3**; meets Flinders, 1802 **4**; in Bass Strait, 1802 **11 12**; at Kangaroo Is., 1803 **1**; at King George Sound, 1803 **2 4**

Baughan, John, carpenter, (1754?–97), 1796 **2**

Bauxite: discoveries, 1950 *, 1955 **7**; mining of, 1963 **4 11**, 1971 **4**

Bavay, Auguste Joseph François de, scientist (1856–1944), 1904 B

Bavin, Sir Thomas Rainsford, Premier of NSW (1874–1941), 1927 **10**, 1930 **10**

Baxter, John, explorer, 1841 **2 4**

Bay of Noon, The (S. Hazzard), 1970 D

Bayley, Arthur Wellesley, prospector (1865–96), 1892 **9**

Bayly, Nicholas, soldier (1770–1823), 1803 **1**

Baynton, Barbara Janet Ainsleigh, author (1857–1929), 1902 D, 1907 D

Bazley, James Frederick, murderer, 1986 **4**

BCOF (British Commonwealth Occupation Force), 1946 **2**

Beach, William, sculler (1850–1935), 1884 E, 1887 E

Beagle, HMS, 1836 **1**, 1837 **11**, 1838 **2**, 1839 **7**, 1841 **3 7**

Beamont, John, explorer (1789–1872), 1817 **12**

Bean, Annette, suffragist, 1884 **6**

Bean, Charles Edwin Woodrow, journalist and historian (1879–1968), 1879 G, 1910 D, 1921 D, 1968 G

Beasley, John Albert, Labor politician (1895–1949), 1931 **3**, 1940 **4**

Beasley, Mary Constance, SA Ombudsman (1937–), 1985 **4**

Beatles (pop group), tour Australia, 1964 C

Beattie, Peter Douglas, Labor Premier of Qld (1952–), 1998 **6**

Beauchamp, Earl (Sir William Lygon), Governor of NSW (1872–1938), 1899 **5**

Beaumont, William, hotelier, 1850 C

Beaumont children, disappearance of, 1966 **1**

INDEX

Beaurepaire, Sir Frank (Francis Joseph Edmund), swimmer and businessman (1891–1956), 1922 **2**, 1956 G
Beaver, Bruce, poet (1928–), 1969 C
Becke, George Lewis (Louis), author (1855–1913), 1855 G, 1894 D, 1913 G
Bedford, George Randolph, author and Labor politician (1868–1941), 1868 G, 1941 G
Beeby, Sir George Stephenson, judge (1869–1942), 1928 **9**
Beechworth (Vic.), 1852 **2**, 1853 **7**
Beer. *See* Brewing
Bees, successfully introduced, 1822 F, 1831 F
Bega (NSW), 1851 **12**
Behind Bamboo (R. Rivett), 1946 D
Belair Recreation Park (SA), 1891 F
Belfast (Vic.). *See* Port Fairy
Belisario, John, dental surgeon (1820–1900), 1847 B
Bell, Archibald, soldier and pioneer (1773–1837), 1823 **8**
Bell, Graeme Emerson, jazz musician (1914–), 1914 G, 1947 C
Bell, Philip Harold, paedophile, 1999 **2**
Bell Bay (Tas.), aluminium plant, 1955 **2**
Bell Group, 1991 **4**
Bellarmine Jug, The (N. Hasluck), 1984 D
Bellbird (NSW), mine disaster, 1923 **9**
Bellear, Robert William, judge (1944–), 1996 F
Bellenden Ker (Qld), 1979 F
Bellevue Hotel (Bris.), 1979 A
Bellingshausen, Faddei Faddeevich, commander of Russian expedition (1778–1852), 1820 **4**
Bellona (ship), 1793 **1**
Bell's Life in Sydney (newspaper), 1845 **1**
Bell's Life in Victoria (newspaper, Melb.), 1857 **1**
Bell's Line (of Road), 1823 **8**
Belmore, Earl of (Somerset Richard Lowry-Corry), Governor of NSW (1835–1913), 1868 **1**
Belvoir (Vic.). *See* Wodonga
Belyando River (Qld), 1846 **6**
"Ben Bowyang" (comic strip), 1933 C
Benalla (Vic.), 1848 **4**
Benang (K. Scott), 1999 D
Benaud, Richard, cricketer (1930–), 1930 G
Bendigo (Vic.), 1855 **4**, 1871 **7**; gold at, 1851 **8**, 1853 **6**; first land sales, 1854 **8**; tramways, 1890 **6**, 1903 **4**, 1972 **4**; Public Offices and Post Office, 1883 A; Law Courts, 1892 A
Bendigo Advertiser (newspaper), 1853 **12**
Bendigo Independent (newspaper), 1862 **1**
Benevolent Asylum (Syd.), 1820 *
Benevolent Society of NSW, 1813 **5**, 1820 *
Benjamin, Arthur Leslie, composer and conductor (1893–1960), 1893 G, 1929 C, 1960 G
Bennelong, Aboriginal (*c.* 1763–1813),

1789 **11**, 1790 **5 7** A, 1813 G; goes to England, 1792 **12**; returns to NSW, 1795 **2**
Bennelong Point (Syd.); battery at, 1788 A, 1791 A; hut for Bennelong at, 1790 A
Bennett, George, naturalist (1804–93), 1833 B
Bennett, Henry Gordon, soldier (1887–1962), 1887 G; escapes from Singapore, 1942 **2**; inquiries into, 1945 **10**
Bennett, James M., aviator, 1919 **10**, 1922 **4**
Bennett, Samuel, journalist (1815–78), 1867 **7**, 1870 **1**
Bent, Andrew, pioneer printer (1790–1851), 1812 **1**, 1818 D, 1825 **5**; publishes *Hobart Town Gazette*, 1816 **6**
Bent, Ellis, Judge-Advocate of NSW (1783–1815), 1809 **5**, 1815 **11** G; conflict with Macquarie, 1814 **12**, 1815 **7**
Bent, Jeffery Hart, judge (1781–1852), 1814 **7**; rejects emancipist attorneys, 1815 **5**; conflict with Macquarie, 1815 **7**, 1816 **10 12**; returns to UK, 1817 **5**
Bent, Sir Thomas, Premier of Vic. (1838–1909), 1904 **2**, 1909 **1**
Berala (Syd.), rail accident at, 1952 **5**
Beresford, Bruce, film director (1940–), 1972 C, 1976 C, 1977 C, 1980 C
Beresford, Marcus de la Poer, native police officer, 1883 **1**
Bermagui (NSW), men disappear at, 1880 **10**
Bernborough (racehorse), 1945 E
Berne, Dagmar, first female medical student (1866–1900), 1885 F
Bernhardt, Sarah, French actress (1844–1923), 1891 C
Berri (SA), 1910 **11**
Berrima (NSW), 1831 **5**; Courthouse, 1835 A; Gaol, 1839 A
Berringer, John, prize fighter, 1814 E
Berry, Alexander, pioneer merchant (1781–1873), 1808 **1**, 1846 **8**
Berry, Sir Graham, Premier of Vic. (1822–1904), 1822 G, 1875 **8 10**, 1877 **5**, 1880 **3 7**, 1881 **7**, 1904 G; stonewalls in Leg. Ass., 1876 **2**; sacks civil servants, 1878 **1**; seeks reform of Leg. Co., 1878 **1**
Berry, Kevin John, swimmer (1945–), 1964 E
Best, Amelia Martha, Liberal politician, 1955 **2**
Bethune, Walter Angus, Liberal Premier of Tas. (1908–), 1969 **5**
Between Two Tides (R. D. FitzGerald), 1952 D
Beynon, Richard, playwright (1925–), 1956 C
Bibb, John, architect (1810–62), 1841 A
Bible Society of NSW, 1817 **3**
Bicentennial celebrations, 1970 **3**, 1988 **1**
Bicentennial Park (Syd.), 1988 F
Bicycles. *See* Cycling
Big Brother movement, 1924 **9**

INDEX

Big Fellow, The (V. Palmer), 1959 D
Big River tribe (Tas.), 1832 **1**
Big Toys (play), 1977 C
Bigge, John Thomas, judge and king's
  commissioner (1780–1843), 1819 **1 9** A,
  1821 **2**; reports, 1822 **5 8**, 1823 **1**
Biggs, Jack, axeman, 1874 E
Bijou Theatre (Melb.), 1876 C, destroyed by
  fire, 1889 **4**
Bikie gang shootings, 1984 **9**; trial, 1987 **6**
Bikini (swimsuit), banned, 1951 F
Billiards, 1851 E, 1932 E
Bionic ear, 1982 B
Birds of Australia (J. Gould), 1840 D
*Birds of New Holland with Their Natural
  History* (J. W. Lewin), 1808 D
Birds of New South Wales (J. W. Lewin),
  1813 D
Birdwood, Sir William Riddell, commander
  of ANZAC (1865–1951), 1914 **12**
Birkenhead Point (Syd.), 1979 A
Birnie, David John and Catherine Margaret,
  charged with murder, 1986 **11**
Birthrate, royal commission into decline of,
  1904 F
Births, deaths, and marriages, registration of,
  1826 F, 1839 F
Birtles, Francis Edwin, overlander
  (1881–1941): bicycle ride, 1907 E; car
  drives, 1912 **3**, 1928 **7**; documentary film,
  1915 C
Bischoff, Mount (Tas.), 1871 **12**
Bishop, Anna, English soprano, 1855 C
Bishop, Charles, master mariner
  (1765?–1810), 1798 **5 10 12**, 1799 **5**, 1801 **8**
Bismarck Archipelago, 1884 **11**
Bismarck Sea, Battle of, 1943 **3**
Bitter Springs (film), 1950 C
Bjelke-Petersen, Florence Isabel (*née*
  Gilmour), senator (1920–), 1980 **10**
Bjelke-Petersen, Sir Johannes, National Party
  Premier of Qld (1911–), 1911 G,
  1975 **11**; becomes Premier, 1968 **8**;
  government re-elected, 1969 **5**, 1972 **5**,
  1974 **12**, 1977 **11**, 1980 **11**, 1983 **10**,
  1986 **11**; and Gair affair, 1974 **4**; appoints
  anti-Whitlam Senate nominee, 1975 **6**;
  resigns and retires from parliament,
  1987 **12**; and perjury charges, 1991 **10**
Black, John, naval officer, 1801 **1**
Black, John, theatre owner, 1855 C
Black, T. Campbell, aviator, 1934 **10**
Black Ball Line, 1852 **9**
Black box flight recorder, 1954 B
Black Caesar. *See* Caesar, John
"Black Friday", 1939 **1**
Black Jack, Aboriginal guerrilla, 1823 **11**,
  1824 **8**, 1825 **2**
Black Line, 1830 **10**
Black Mountain (ACT) telecommunications
  tower, 1980 B
Black Opal (K. S. Prichard), 1921 D

"Black Sunday", 1955 **1**
"Black Thursday", 1851 **2**; painting, 1864 C
"Black War", 1804 **5**
"Black Wednesday", 1878 **1**
Blackall, Samuel Wensley, Governor of Qld
  (1809–71), 1868 **8**
Blackberries introduced: in Tas. 1843 F; in
  NSW, 1863 F
Blackbirding: Lewin recruits for Towns,
  1863 **8**; *Syren* outcry, 1868 **1**; legislation
  to control, 1868 **3**; *Carl* massacre, 1871 **9**;
  Morrison's account of, 1882 D; *Hopeful*
  affair, 1884 **7**; royal commission
  condemns recruiting methods, 1885 **5**. *See
  also* Pacific Islanders
Blacket, Cyril, architect (1857–1937), 1889 A
Blacket, Edmund Thomas, architect
  1817–83), 1817 G, 1883 G; arrives in
  Sydney, 1842 A; works, 1848 A, 1854 A,
  1878 A
Blackman, Charles Raymond, artist (1928–),
  1928 G
Blackman, James, explorer (1792?–1868),
  1821 *
Blacktrackers, 1834 **12**
Blackwood, Francis Price, naval officer
  (1809–54), 1842 **10**
Blainey, Geoffrey Norman, historian and
  author (1930–), 1930 G, 1966 D, 1975 D,
  1980 D
Blair, Harold, singer and teacher (1924–76),
  1924 G, 1951 C, 1976 G
Blair, Ronald Hugh, playwright (1942–),
  1974 C
Blair Athol (Qld), 1937 *
Blake Prize, first awarded, 1951 C
Blamey, Sir Thomas Albert, soldier
  (1884–1951), 1884 G, 1951 G; Monash's
  chief of staff, 1918 **5**; Chief
  Commissioner of Police in Vic., 1925 **9**,
  1936 **7**; in World War II, 1942 **4**; removed
  as commander-in-chief of forces, 1945 **12**;
  promoted to field marshal, 1950 **6**
Bland, William, physician and politician
  (1789–1868), 1789 G, 1815 **10**, 1843 **6**,
  1851 B, 1868 G
Blaxcell, Garnham, merchant and trader
  (1778–1817), 1802 **10**, 1807 **6**, 1810 **11**,
  1814 **12**
Blaxland, Gregory, pioneer farmer and
  explorer (1778–1853), 1806 **4**, 1849 **6**,
  1853 G; and crossing of Blue Mountains,
  1813 **5**, 1823 D
Blaxland, John, landowner and merchant
  (1769–1845), 1807 **4**
Blaxland, Mount (NSW), 1813 **5**
Blaxland's River (NSW), 1823 **4**
"Bless This House" (song), 1927 C
Blewett, Neal, Labor politician (1933–),
  1977 **12**
Bligh, William, naval officer and Governor
  of NSW (1754–1817), 1817 G; and

INDEX

INDEX

Bookfellow (periodical), 1899 D
Boomerang (fighter aircraft), 1942 B
Boomerang (H. Simpson), 1932 D
Boomerang, HMS, 1891 **9**
Boomerang (newspaper, Bris.), 1887 **11**, 1888 F
Boothby, Benjamin, judge (1803–68), 1867 **7**
Borbidge, Robert Edward, National Party Premier of Qld (1954–), 1996 **2**, 1998 **6**
Borchgrevink, Carsten Egeberg, Antarctic explorer (1864–1934), 1895 **1**, 1899 B
Border, Allan Robert, cricketer (1955–), 1955 G, 1987 E, 1989 E, 1993 E
Bordertown (SA), railway reaches, 1886 **5**
Borg, Joseph, vice king, 1968 **5**
Boronia (Vic.), level-crossing accident, 1952 **6**
Borovansky, Edouard, ballet company director (1902–59), 1939 C, 1944 C, 1951 C, 1959 G
Borrowdale (First Fleet storeship), 1788 **1 7**
Bosisto, Joseph, research chemist (1824–98), 1852 B
Boston, John, early brewer (d. 1804), 1796 *
Botanic Gardens
  Brisbane, 1828 B, 1862 B
  Canberra (National), 1970 B
  Melbourne, 1857 B
  Parramatta (Cayley's), 1800 B
  Sydney, 1816 B, 1838 B, 1897 C, 1996 **3**
Botany (Syd.), 1813 **9**, 1842 C
Botany Bay (NSW), First Fleet arrives at, 1788 **1**; explored, 1789 **9**, 1795 **10**; woollen mill at, 1815 B
Botany Bay (J. Lang), 1859 D
Bottom-of-the-harbour tax avoidance scheme, 1982 **8**
Bottrill, Frank, inventor (1871–1953), 1907 B
Boucaut, Sir James Penn, Premier of SA (1831–1916), 1866 **3**, 1867 **5**, 1875 **6**, 1876 **6**, 1877 **10**, 1878 **9**
Boucicault, Dionysius George, actor and director (1859–1929), 1885 C, 1886 C
Bougainville (PNG), 1997 **11**
Boulder (WA), 1896 **12**
Boundaries, state, 1825 **7**, 1839 **6**, 1861 **12**, 1862 **6**
Bounty, HMS, 1788 **10**, 1789 **4**, 1790 **1**
Bounty mutineers: seize ship, 1789 **4**; group go to Pitcairn Is., 1790 **1**; those at Tahiti arrested by *Pandora*, 1791 **3 8**, 1792 **3**; survivor and descendants found at Pitcairn, 1808 **2**; descendants move to Norfolk Is., 1856 **6**
Bourke, Sir Richard, Governor of NSW (1777–1855), 1831 **12**, 1836 **4 10**, 1855 G; and settlement at Port Phillip, 1835 **8**, 1837 **3**; and education system, 1836 **8**; resigns, 1837 **7**; leaves Australia, 1837 **12**; statue of, 1842 C
Bourke (NSW), 1835 **5**; railway reaches, 1885 **9**; heat wave at, 1896 **1**

Bousloff, Kira, ballet company director, 1952 C
Boussole (French ship), 1788 **1 3**
Bowen, George Ferguson, Governor of Qld and Vic. (1821–99), 1821 G, 1859 **12**, 1873 **3**, 1899 G; and financial crisis, 1866 **7**
Bowen, J., mate of *Lady Nelson*, 1802 **1**
Bowen, John, naval officer and founder of Hobart (1780–1827), 1803 **3 9**, 1804 **5 8**
Bowen, Lionel Frost, Labor politician (1922–), 1969 **10**
Bowen, Richard, naval officer (1761–97), 1791 **8**
Bowen (Qld), damaged by cyclones, 1867 **3**, 1870 **1**, 1876 **2**, 1884 **1**, 1896 **1**, 1958 **4**, 1959 **2**
Bowen Downs station (Qld), 1870 **3**
Bowen River (Qld), 1859 **8**
Bowles, William Leslie, sculptor (1855–1954), 1936 C
Bowling, Peter, miners' leader (1864–1942), 1909 **12**
Bowls: first green, 1844 E; Melbourne Bowling Club founded, 1864 E
Bowman, James, surgeon and pioneer (1784–1846), 1819 **9 10**
Bowser, Sir John, Premier of Vic. (1856–1936), 1917 **11**, 1918 **3**
Box Hill (Vic.), artists' camp at, 1885 C
Boxer Rebellion, 1900 **7 8**, 1901 **4**
Boxing: first recorded prize fight in Australia, 1814 E; "Young" Kable v. Sam Clark, 1824 E; Ned Chalker v. Kable, 1832 E; longest fight on record, 1855 E; Tom Curran v. Harry Sellars, 1860 E; Larry Foley v. Abe Hicken, 1879 E; Jem Mace introduces Queensberry Rules, 1877 E; "Professor" Miller v. Foley, 1883 E; bare fist, banned, 1884 E; "Young Griffo" v. "Torpedo" Bill Murphy, 1890 E; Australian world champions: Jimmy Carruthers, 1952 E; Lionel Rose, 1968 E; Johnny Famechon, 1969 E; Jeff Fenech, 1985 E, 1987 E, 1988 E; Jeff Harding, 1989 E
Boy Adeodatus, The (B. Smith), 1984 D
Boy at the Basin (painting), 1932 C
Boy in the Bush, The (D. H. Lawrence and M. L. Skinner), 1924 D
Boy Scouts, 1908 F
Boyd, Arthur Merric Bloomfield, painter, sculptor, and potter (1920–99), 1920 G, 1957 C, 1999 G
Boyd, Benjamin, pioneer (1801–51), 1801 G, 1842 **7**, 1851 G; and Twofold Bay, 1843 * A, 1844 *; employs indentured labour, 1846 **3**, 1847 **4**; schemes collapse, 1849 **8**; disappears, 1851 **10**
Boyd, Martin à Beckett, novelist (1893–1972), 1893 G, 1928 D, 1946 D, 1952 D, 1955 D, 1957 D, 1962 D, 1972 G

INDEX

Boyd, Robin Gerard Penleigh, architect and author (1919–71), 1919 G, 1960 D, 1971 G
Boyd (convict transport), 1809 **7 12**
Boydtown (NSW), 1843 A
Boyer, Sir Richard James Fildes, ABC chairman (1891–1961), 1891 G, 1945 C, 1961 G
Boyle, Henry Frederick, cricketer (1847–1907), 1878 E
Boys in the Island, The (C. J. Koch), 1958 D
Boys Who Stole the Funeral, The (L. A. Murray), 1980 D
Brabham, Sir Jack (John Arthur), racing-car driver and designer (1926–), 1926 G, 1959 E, 1960 E, 1966 E
Bracewell, David, wild white man (1803?–44), 1842 **5**
Brack, Cecil John, artist (1920–99) 1955 C
Bracks, Stephen Phillip, Labor Premier of Vic. (1954–), 1999 **9**
Braddon, Sir Edward Nicholas Coventry, Premier of Tas. (1829–1904), 1894 **4**, 1897 **1**, 1899 **10**
Braddon, Russell Reading, author (1921–95), 1921 G, 1952 D, 1995 G
Bradley, Stephen Leslie (1926–68), murderer, 1960 **8**, 1961 **3**
Bradman, Sir Donald George, cricketer (1908–), 1908 G, 1930 E
Brady, Alfred Barton, architect (1856–1932), 1896 A, 1898 A, 1914 A
Brady, Edwin James, poet and author (1869–1952), 1869 G, 1899 D, 1952 G
Brady, Matthew, bushranger (1799–1826), 1824 **6**, 1826 **3**
Bragg, Sir William Henry, physicist (1862–1942), 1897 B, 1899 B, 1915 B
Bragg, Sir William Lawrence, physicist (1890–1971), 1915 B
Brahe, Mary Hannah (May), song composer (1884–1956), 1927 C
Braidwood (NSW), 1839 **4**
Bramble (cutter), 1842 **10**
Brampton, Kenneth, film director, 1920 C
Bran Nue Dae (musical), 1990 C
Brand, Sir David, Liberal Premier of WA (1912–79), 1959 **3**, 1962 **3**, 1965 **2**, 1968 **3**
Brass bands, 1845 C, 1896 C
Brassey, Thomas, 1st Earl Brassey, Governor of Vic. (1836–1918), 1895 **10**
Bray, Sir John Cox, Premier of SA (1842–94), 1881 **6**, 1884 **6**
Bread, sliced, 1939 B
Breaker Morant (film), 1980 C
Breaking of the Drought, The (film), 1920 C
Breathalizer, 1968 **12**
Breelong (NSW), murders at, 1900 **7**
Bremer, Sir James John Gordon, naval officer (1786–1850), 1824 **8 9**, 1838 **10**
Bremer, Lady, 1841 D
Brennan, Christopher John, poet

(1870–1932), 1870 G, 1897 D, 1941 D, 1932 G
Brennan, Sir Francis Gerard, Chief Justice of the High Court (1928–), 1995 **4**, 1998 **5**
Brennan, Louis, inventor (1852–1932), 1877 B
Brennan, Thomas, soldier, 1832 **4**
Brent of Bin Bin. *See* Franklin, Stella Maria Sarah Miles
Brereton, John Le Gay, author (1871–1933), 1928 D
Brewarrina (NSW), 1859 **2**
Brewing, 1795 **7**, 1804 **9**, 1849 F; first beer brewed in Australia, 1796 *; consumption of beer, 1974 F, 1985 F
breweries:
    Carlton and United, 1858 *, 1907 **5**
    Cascade, 1832 *
    Castlemaine, 1879 *
    Fosters' 1888 *, 1992 **6**
    Swan, 1874 *
    Tooheys, 1870 *
    Tooth's 1835 **10**
Bribie Island (Qld), bridge to, 1964 A
Bridge, Ernest Francis, Labor politician (1936–), 1986 **2**
Bridge disasters: West Gate (Melb.), 1970 **10**; Tasman (Hobart), 1975 **1**; at Maccabiah Games, 1997 **7**
Bridges, Sir William Throsby, soldier (1861–1915), 1911 **6**
Bridges
    Adelaide, 1931 **3**
    Anzac (Syd.), 1992 A, 1995 **12**
    across Brisbane River, 1865 **6**
    Captain Cook (Syd.), 1965 **5**
    across Clarence River (Grafton), 1928 A, 1932 **5**
    floating (Hobart), 1939 A, 1943 **12**
    Gateway (Bris.), 1986 A
    Gladesville (Syd.), 1884 A, 1964 **9** A
    Glebe Island (Syd.), 1992 A
    Hawkesbury River, 1889 **5**, 1945, A, 1946 A
    Hindmarsh Island (SA), 1998 **2**
    Lennox (Lapstone), 1833 A; (Parramatta), 1836 A
    across Murray River: at Albury–Wodonga, 1861 **9**; 1883 **6**; at Murray Bridge (SA), 1873 A, 1879 **3**; at Echuca, 1878 **12**
    Narrows (Perth), 1959 A
    Perth Causeway, 1952 A
    Princes (Melb.), 1886 A, 1888 **10**
    Pyrmont (Syd.), 1858 A
    Queen's (Melb.), 1890 A
    Richmond (Tas.), 1825 A
    Ross (Tas.), 1831 A
    Spencer Street (Melb.), 1930 **2**
    Stony Creek (Qld), 1890 A
    Story (Bris.), 1935 A, 1940 **7**
    Sydney Harbour, 1923 A, 1932 **3**

INDEX

Broughton, William Robert, naval officer, 1791 **9**, 1795 **8**

Brown, Carter. *See* Yates, Alan

Brown, Dean Craig, Liberal Premier of SA (1943–), 1993 **12**, 1996 **11**

Brown, John Joseph, Labor politician (1931–), 1987 **12**

Brown, Rebecca Kate, swimmer (1977–), 1994 E

Brown, Robert, pioneer botanist (1773–1858), 1810 B

Brown, Robert James, environmentalist and politician, 1989 **6**

Browne, Frank Courtney, journalist, 1955 **6**

Browne, Thomas Alexander ("Rolf Boldrewood"), author (1826–1915), 1826 G, 1882 D, 1884 D, 1888 D, 1890 D, 1915 G

Browne, Sir Thomas Gore, Governor of Tas. (1807–87), 1862 **6**

Browne, Victor, cyclist, 1969 E

Browne, William Henry, Labor politician (1846–1904), 1903 **9**

Brownlow Medal, 1924 E

Broxbornebury (convict transport), 1814 **7**

Bruce, Mary (Minnie) Grant, writer (1878–1958), 1878 G, 1910 D, 1958 G

Bruce, Stanley Melbourne (1st Viscount Bruce), Nationalist Prime Minister (1883–1967), 1883 G, 1967 G; becomes Prime Minister, 1923 **2**; government defeated, 1929 **8 9**; loses seat, 1929 **10**; re-elected to parliament, 1931 **12**; becomes Commissioner in London, 1932 **9**

Brunei, fighting at, 1945 **6**

Brunswick Bay (WA), 1820 **6**

Bruny d'Entrecasteaux, Joseph-Antoine Raymond, French navigator (1739–93), 1792 **4 12**, 1793 **1 2 7**

Bruny Island (Tas.), Aboriginal station, 1829 **3**

Bryant, Martin, killer, 1996 **4**

Bryant, Mary (*née* Broad), convict (1765–?), 1788 **2**, 1791 **3 4 6 10**, 1792 **3 6**, 1793 **5**

Bryant, William, convict (d. 1791), 1788 **2**, 1791 **3 4 6 10**

Bubonic plague, 1900 **1** B F, 1921 **8**

Buckland River (Vic.), 1853 **7**

Buckley, William, wild white man (1780–1856), 1803 **12**, 1835 **7**

Buckmaster, Ernest, artist (1897–1968), 1932 C

Buddhism, 1952 **10**, 1982 **8**

Buffalo (storeship), 1799 **5**, 1800 **10**, 1802 **10**; and Port Dalrymple settlement, 1804 **10 11**; conveys King to UK, 1806 **8**, 1807 **2**

Buffalo, HMS, 1840 **2**

Buffalo, Mount (Vic.), Chalet at, 1910 A

Buffaloes introduced, 1825 F

Buhot, John, sugar manufacturer (1831–81), 1862 B

Builders' Labourers Federation,1971 F; deregistered, 1974 **6**, 1986 **4**; royal commission into, 1981 **8**

Bull, Henryk Johan, businessman and Antarctic adventurer (1844–1930), 1895 **1**

Bulletin (newspaper, Syd.), 1880 **1**; sued for libel, 1882 **3**; Archibald edits, 1886 D; Red Page inaugurated, 1896 D

Bulli (NSW), mining disaster, 1887 **3**

Buna (Papua), 1943 **1**

Bunbury (WA), 1841 **2**, 1979 **10**

Bundaberg (Qld), 1872 **8**, 1893 **10**, 1913 **11**, 1949 **2**

Buninyong Range (Vic.), 1851 **8**

Bunker, Eber, whaler (1761–1836), 1791 **8**, 1799 **6**

Bunn, Anna Maria (*née* Murray), novelist (1808–89), 1838 D

Bunning and Madden, architects, 1968 A

Bunny, Rupert Charles Wulsten, artist (1864–1947), 1864 G, 1897 C, 1947 G

Bunton, Cleaver Ernest, senator (d. 1999), 1975 **2**

"Bunyip aristocracy", 1853 **8**

Burdekin Dam (Qld), 1988 **8**

Burdekin River (Qld), 1845 **4**

Burke, Brian Thomas, Labor Premier of WA (1947–), 1983 **2**, 1986 **2**, 1988 **2**; and WA Royal Commission, 1991 **4**; charged with corruption offences, 1992 **6**, 1997 **2**

Burke, Denis Gabriel, Country Liberal Chief Minister of NT (1948–), 1999 **2**

Burke, Michael, bushranger, 1863 **10**

Burke, Robert O'Hara, explorer (1821–61), 1821 G, 1861 G; sets out on expedition, 1860 **8**; reaches Cooper's Creek, 1860 **11**; makes dash for Gulf, 1860 **12**, 1861 **2**; return journey, 1861 **4 9**; funeral, 1863 **1**; memorial, 1865 C

Burlakov, Mischa, ballet dancer, 1931 C

Burley, Robyn, ice skater (1957–), 1979 E

Burley Griffin, Lake (ACT), 1963 **9**, 1970 A

Burn, David, playwright (1799?–1875), 1829 C, 1842 D

Burnet, Sir Frank Macfarlane, medical scientist (1899–1985), 1899 G, 1935 B, 1960 B, 1985 G

Burnley (Vic.), rail collision, 1882 **12**

Burns, Sir James, founder of Burns Philp (1846–1923), 1846 G, 1883 **4**, 1923 G

Burns, Tommy, Canadian boxer, 1908 E

Burns Philp and Co. Ltd, 1883 **4**

Burnum Burnum (Harry Penrith), Aboriginal rights campaigner (1936–97), 1997 G

Burra Burra (SA), 1845 **5**

Burridge Pam, surfboard rider (1964–), 1990 E

Burrinjuck Dam (NSW), 1906 **12**, 1927 *

Burrows, Donald Vernon, musician (1928–), 1928 G

Burstall, Tim, film director (1929–),

INDEX

INDEX

INDEX

Cattle dog, 1890 B
Caulfield Cup, 1879 E
Caulfield Racecourse (Vic.), 1859 E
Cavanagh, Jeremy, schoolmaster, 1806 *
Cavill, James F., hotelier, 1923 **8**
Cavill, Percy, swimmer (1875–1840), 1897 E
Cavill, Richmond Theophilus (Dick),
  swimmer (1884–1938), 1898 E, 1902 E
Cavity wall, 1895 A
Cawley, Evonne Fay (*née* Goolagong), tennis
  player (1951–), 1951 G, 1971 E, 1980 E
Cayley, Neville William, ornithological artist
  (1886–1950), 1931 D
Cazaly, Roy, footballer (1893–1963),
  1893 G, 1921 E, 1963 G
Cazneaux, Harold Pierce, photographer
  (1878–1953), 1909 C
Cedar, first exported, 1795 **11**
Ceilings, pressed-metal, 1888 A
Celsius temperature scale, 1972 B
Cemeteries, 1820 **1**, 1826 F, 1867 **12**, 1903 *
Censorship
  book, 1930 D, 1945 D, 1968 D, 1970 D
  film, 1948 C
  press, 1824 **10**, 1940 **5**, 1944 **4**
  theatre, 1936 **7**, 1948 C
  videotape, 1984 C
Censuses: NSW, 1828 F, 1846 F, 1851 F,
  1856 F, 1861 F; Tas., 1841 F, 1847 F,
  1851 F, 1857 F, 1861 F; SA, 1844 F,
  1846 F, 1851 F, 1855 F, 1861 F; WA,
  1848 F, 1854 F, 1859 F; Vic., 1854 F,
  1857 F, 1861 F; Qld, 1861 F, 1864 F,
  1868 F; simultaneous, 1881 **4** F, 1891 F,
  1901 F; Commonwealth, 1911 **4**, 1921 F,
  1933 F, 1947 F, 1954 F, 1961 F, 1966 F,
  1971 F, 1976 F, 1981 F, 1986 F, 1991 F
Centaur (hospital ship), 1943 **5**
Centennial International Exhibition,
  Melbourne, 1888 **8**
Centennial Park (Syd.): water supply from,
  1827 **9**; reserved, 1888 F; Commonwealth
  proclaimed at, 1901 **1**
Central Australia, 1926 **6**
Central Mount Stuart (NT), 1860 **4**
Centrepoint Tower (Syd.), 1979 A
Cerberus, HMVS, 1871 **4**
Cessnock (NSW), 1994 **8**
Chaffey, George, irrigation pioneer
  (1848–1932), 1848 G, 1886 **10**, 1887 **2**,
  1932 G
Chaffey, William Benjamin, irrigation
  pioneer (1856–1926), 1887 **2**
Chaliapin, Feodor, Russian bass, 1926 C
Chalk, Sir Gordon William, Liberal Premier
  of Qld (1913–), 1968 **8**
Chalker, Ned, prizefighter, 1832 E
Chalmers, James, missionary (1841–1901),
  1901 **4**
Chamberlain, Alice Lynne (Lindy), 1982 **2**,
  1984 **2**, 1986 **2**; pardoned, 1987 **6**;
  conviction quashed, 1988 **9**

Chamberlain, Azaria Chantal Loren,
  disappearance of, 1980 **8**; first inquest,
  1980 **12**, 1981 **2 11**; investigation
  reopened, 1981 **9**, 1982 **2**, 1986 **2**, 1987 **6**;
  open verdict found, 1995 **12**
Chamber of Manufactures, NSW, 1885 **7**
Chambers of Commerce: Sydney, 1826 **6**,
  1851 **3**; Melbourne, 1851 **4**
Champ, William Thomas Napier, Premier of
  Tas. (1808–92), 1856 **11**
Champion Bay (WA), 1848 **12**
Chan, Harry, president of the NT Legislative
  Council and mayor of Darwin (1918–69),
  1965 **12**, 1966 **5**
Chandler, Margaret Olive (1934–63),
  mysterious death of, 1963 **1**
Chang, Victor Peter, heart surgeon
  (1937–91), 1991 **7**
Chant of Jimmie Blacksmith, The (T.
  Keneally), 1972 D; film of, 1978 C
Chantic Bird, The (D. Ireland), 1968 D
Chapman, Thomas Daniel, Premier of Tas.
  (1815–84), 1861 **8**
Chapman (convict transport), 1817 **7**
Chappell, Gregory Stephen, cricketer
  (1948–), 1948 G
Chappell, Ian Michael, cricketer (1943–),
  1943 G
Chappell, Trevor Martin, cricketer (1952–),
  1981 E
Charles, Prince of Wales (1948–): attends
  Timbertop school, 1966 **1**; visits of,
  1967 **12**, 1970 **3**, 1974 B, 1977 **11**, 1978 **5**,
  1979 **3**, 1981 **4**, 1983 **3**, 1985 **10**, 1988 **1**;
  attacked, 1994 **1**
Charles Sturt University, 1989 **7**
Charleville (Qld), 1865 **1**, 1922 **11**, 1990 **4**
Charlotte (First Fleet transport), 1788 **1 5**
Charlton, Andrew Murray ("Boy"),
  swimmer (1907–75), 1907 G, 1924 E,
  1975 G
Charlton, Edward Francis, snooker player
  (1929–), 1974 E
Charter of Justice: second, 1814 **2 7**; third,
  1823 **10**, 1824 **5**
Charterisville (Vic.), artists' colony at,
  1890 C
Charters Towers (Qld): goldfield at,
  1871 **12**; mine disaster at, 1904 **10**
Chater, Gordon, actor (1922–99), 1976 C
Chatham (brig), 1791 **9**
Chauvel, Charles Edward, film producer and
  director (1897–1959), 1897 G, 1959 G;
  films, 1933 C, 1935 C, 1940 C, 1944 C,
  1949 C, 1955 C
Chauvel, Sir Harry (Henry George), soldier
  (1865–1945), 1865 G, 1917 **10**, 1918 **9**,
  1945 G
Cheery Soul, A (play), 1963 C
Chester, Henry Marjoribanks, police
  magistrate (1832–1914), 1883 **4**
Chesterfield (whaler), 1793 **7**

INDEX

Chevalier, Nicholas, artist (1828–1902), 1828 G, 1854 C, 1864 C, 1902 G

Chevert (barque), 1875 B

Chi, Jimmy, composer (1948–), 1990 C

Chichester, Sir Francis, British airman and yachtsman, 1930 **1**, 1966 **12**

Chifley, Joseph Benedict, Labor Prime Minister (1885–1951), 1885 G, 1928 **11**, 1942 **12**, 1951 **6** G; becomes Prime Minister, 1945 **7**; and bank nationalization, 1947 **8**; government defeated, 1949 **12**

Chiko Roll, 1951 B

Child, Joan (*née* Olle), Labor politician, 1986 **2**

Child endowment. *See* Family allowance

Childe, Vere Gordon, archaeologist (1892–1957), 1923 D

Children: adoption of, 1896 F; illegitimate, 1963 F

Children's Hospital (Melb.), 1870 **9**

Children's Protection Act (NSW), 1892 F

Childs, Joseph, commandant at Norfolk Is. (1787–1870), 1844 **2**, 1846 **8**

China: diplomatic contacts with, 1941 **7**, 1972 **12**; buys Australian wheat, 1961 F; air service to, 1984 **9**; President visits Australia, 1999 **9**

Chinese in Australia: indentured labourers, 1848 **7**; Vic. imposes tax on immigrants, 1855 **6**; walk from SA to Vic. to avoid tax, 1856 *; driven off Vic. goldfields, 1857 **5 7**, 1872 **6**; SA imposes tax on arrivals, 1857 **11**; number on Vic. goldfields, 1859 F; attacked at Lambing Flat, 1860 **12**, 1861 **6**; NSW restricts immigration, 1861 **11**; number on Palmer River (Qld), 1875 F, 1877 F; Qld imposes tax on arrivals, 1877 **8**; seamen strike in protest against, 1878 **11**; find gold in NT, 1880 **5**; colonies plan uniform restrictive legislation 1881 **1**; visit of investigative commission, 1887 **5**; anti-Chinese demonstrations, 1887 **7**, 1888 **5**; unions demand restrictive legislation, 1888 **3**; NSW passes Chinese Exclusion Bill, 1888 **5**; intercolonial conference calls for restrictive legislation, 1888 **6**; peak population, 1888 F; boat people, 1992 **1**, 1994 *; 29,000 given permanent residency, 1993 **11**

Chipp, Donald Leslie, Liberal politician and Australian Democrats leader (1925–), 1925 G, 1977 **5**, 1986 **8**

Chisholm, Caroline (*née* Jones), pioneer social worker (1808–77), 1808 G, 1841 **12**, 1849 *, 1850 **9**, 1877 G

Chloe (painting), 1908 C

Chloroform, first used, 1848 B

Christ Church St Laurence (Syd.), 1840 A

Christian, Fletcher, *Bounty* mutineer (1763–92), 1789 **4**, 1790 **1**, 1792 G

Christian Brothers, 1868 **11**

Christian Brothers, The (play), 1974 C

Christian Science, first services and reading room, 1898 *

Christmas, Harold Percival, retailer (1884–1947), 1924 **12**

Christmas Island, 1888 **6**, 1948 **10**, 1958 **10**, 1994 **5**

Christo. *See* Javacheff, Christo

Christ's College (Longford, Tas.), 1846 **10**

Chu-Chin-Chow (play), 1916 C

Church Act (NSW), 1836 **7**

Church and School Corporation, 1826 **3**, 1833 **2**

Church of England. *See* Anglican Church

Church of Jesus Christ of Latter-day Saints (Mormons), 1851 **10**, 1984 A

Church of the New Faith (Scientology), 1956 *, 1963 *

Churchill Fellowships, 1965 **11**

Chusan (mail steamer), 1852 **7**

Cigarette advertising, 1976 **9**. *See also* Smoking; Tobacco

Cilento, Lady Phyllis Dorothy (*née* McGlew), nutritionist, doctor, and writer (1894–1987), 1987 G

Cilento, Sir Raphael West, medical administrator (1893–1985), 1893 G, 1985 G

Cinema. *See* Film industry

Cinesound Productions, 1931 B, 1932 C

Circular Head (Tas.), 1826 **10**

Circular Quay (Syd.), 1837 A, 1843 A; railway, 1950 A, 1956 **1**

Citizen military forces. *See* Military forces

Citizenship: "Australian citizen" status, 1949 **1**; new oath, 1993 **9**

City of Edinburgh (ship), 1808 **1**

City of Melbourne (clipper), 1868 **1**

City of Melbourne Bank, 1893 **5**

City to Surf race, 1971 E

Civil Constructional Corps, 1942 **4**

Clancy, Edward Bede, Catholic Archbishop of Sydney (1923–), 1983 **4**

"Clancy of the Overflow" (A. B. Paterson), 1889 D

Clara Morison: A Tale of South Australia during the Gold Fever (C. H. Spence), 1854 D

Clarence River (NSW), railway bridge over, 1932 **5**

Claremont (Perth), 1997 **3**

Clarion (strikers' newspaper, Syd.), 1955 **6**

Clark, Charles Manning Hope, historian (1915–91), 1915 G, 1962 D, 1987 D, 1991 G

Clark, Geoffrey Wayne, ATSIC chairman (1952–), 1999 **12**

Clark, Graeme Milbourne, scientist (1935–), 1982 B

Clark, J.H., writer, 1813 D

Clark, John James, architect (1838–1915), 1857 A, 1885 A

INDEX

Clarke, Andrew, Governor of WA
(1793–1847), 1846 **1**, 1847 **2**

Clarke, John and Thomas, bushrangers,
1867 **4**

Clarke, Marcus Andrew Hislop, author
(1846–81), 1846 G, 1870 D, 1874 D,
1881 G

Clarke, Ronald William, athlete (1937–),
1965 E

Clarke, William Branwhite, geologist and
clergyman (1798–1878), 1841 **4**

Clean Straw for Nothing (G. Johnston),
1969 D

Clean Up Australia, 1989 F

Cleary, Jon, novelist (1917–), 1947D,
1952 D

Cleo (magazine), 1972 **11**

Clermont (Qld), 1916 **12**

Cleveland Bay (Qld), 1864 **7**

Clinton, Bill, US President, 1996 **11**

Cloncurry (Qld), 1877 **3**, 1883 **1**, 1884 **9**,
1988 **10**; copper found at, 1867 **5**; air
service to, 1922 **11**; Flying Doctor Service
based at, 1928 **5**

Clontarf (Syd.), 1868 **3**, 1882 **3**

Close, Robert Shaw, novelist (1903–95),
1945 D

Cloudstreet (T. Winton), 1991 D

Club, The (play), 1977 C

Clubbe, Phyllis, educator (d. 1973), 1913 **7**

Clubs, licensed (NSW): poker machines in,
1956 **3**; royal commission into crime in,
1974 **8**

Clune, Francis Patrick, author (1893–1971),
1893 G, 1933 D, 1971 G

Clunes (Vic.), gold discovered at, 1851 **7**;
Chinese driven from, 1872 **6**, 1873 **12**

Clyde River (NSW), 1821 **12**

Clyde River (Tas.), 1807 **2**

Coaches and coaching: between Sydney and
Richmond/Windsor, 1814 **10**, 1821 **3**; first
hackney coach in Sydney, 1830 **11**;
between Launceston and Hobart, 1831 **6**;
Sydney–Bathurst service, 1834 **8**. *See also*
Cobb & Co.

Coal: discovered at Newcastle, 1791 **3**,
1797 **9**, 1801 **7**; discovered near Port
Stephens, 1796 **6**; discovered on Illawarra
Coast, 1797 **5 8**; exported to Bengal,
1801 **10**; discovered at Ipswich (Qld),
1827 **6**; Australian Agricultural Co.'s
activities, 1825 **7**, 1831 **10**; working
conditions in industry, 1862 F, 1873 **2**,
1876 F; Newcastle companies form "the
vend", 1873 **1**; mined at Collie (WA),
1897 **12**; state mine at Wonthaggi (Vic.),
1909 **11**, 1937 **2**; in Latrobe Valley,
1919 **11**, 1924 **8 12**; open cut at Blair
Athol (Qld), 1937 ***; Joint Coal Board set
up in NSW, 1947 **3**; troops ordered into
mines, 1949 **8**; open cut at Moura (Qld),

1963 **10**. *See also* Mining disasters;
Strikes and lockouts

Coalcliff (NSW), 1797 **8**

Coast Hospital. *See* Prince Henry Hospital

Coates, John Dowling, Australian Olympic
Committee president (1950–), 1999 **1**

Cobar (NSW), 1869 ***

Cobb, Freeman, coach service proprietor
(1830–78), 1853 ***

Cobb and Co., 1853 ***, 1854 **1**, 1862 **6**,
1924 **8**

"Cobber", word first appears in print,
1895 D

Cobby, Anita Lorraine, murder victim
(1959–86), 1986 **2**

Coburn, John, artist (1925–), 1925 G,
1973 C

Cockatoo Island (Syd.), 1857 **12**, 1908 ***,
1911 **4**

Cockburn, Sir John Alexander, Premier of
SA (1850–1929), 1889 **6**

Cockburn (SA), railway line reaches, 1887 **6**

Cockburn Sound (WA), 1955 **1**

Cockle Bay (Balmain, Syd.), 1800 **4**, 1815 B

Cocos (Keeling) Islands: settled by John
Clunies Ross, 1827 ***; proclaimed a
British possession, 1857 ***; granted to
George Clunies Ross, 1886 **7**; *Emden*
disabled at, 1914 **11**; become
Commonwealth territory, 1955 **11**;
Australia buys Clunies Ross holdings,
1978 **9**; vote for integration with
Australia, 1984 **4**

Coercion Act (Vic.), 1903 **5**

Cohn, Carola (Ola), sculptor (1892–1964),
1941 C

Cohuna (Vic.), 1836 **6**; Aboriginal skull
found at, 1925 B

Coins: silver dollars imported, 1791 **11**,
1812 **11**; copper coins imported, 1800 **11**;
value of coinage regulated, 1800 **11**; holey
dollar, 1813 **7**, 1814 **1**, 1828 **9**; foreign
coins no longer accepted, 1829 **8**; tokens
first issued, 1849 ***; bullion as legal
tender, 1852 **1**; Adelaide sovereigns
1852 **12**; minted in Sydney, 1855 **5**;
Australian sovereigns legal tender in UK,
1866 **2**; sovereigns minted in Perth,
1899 **6**; Commonwealth, first issued,
1910 ***, 1911 ***; coinage of sovereigns
ceases, 1931 ***; minting of decimal coins
begins, 1965 **2**; decimal currency
introduced, 1966 **2**; 50-cent coin, 1969 **8**;
one-dollar coin, 1984 **5**; Australian
Nuggets, 1986 **7**; two-dollar coin, 1988 **6**;
one- and two-cent coins withdrawn from
currency 1992 **2**

Colac (Vic.), 1848 **11**

Colbee, Aboriginal, 1789 **11**, 1790 **9**

Cole, Edward William, bookseller
(1832–1918), 1832 G, 1865 D, 1879 D,
1883 D, 1918 G

INDEX

INDEX

1841 **7**; establishment in NSW closes, 1847 **5**; murder Inspector-General Price, 1857 **3**; establishment in WA closes, 1886 **3**. *See also* Emancipists; Penal settlements; Transportation

absconders, 1791 **11**, 1794 **11**, 1795 **8**, 1797 **10**; Black Caesar, 1789 **12**, 1795 **12**; live with Aborigines, 1790 **9**, 1803 **12**, 1833 **11**, 1840 **8**; Bryant party, 1791 **3 4 6 10**, 1792 **3 6**; escape on visiting ships, 1794 **7**, 1805 **3**, 1807 **6**; Thomas Muir, 1796 **2**; steal *Cumberland* from Hawkesbury, 1797 **9**; from Newcastle, become first overlanders to Sydney, 1805 **12**; seize *Venus* at Port Dalrymple, 1806 **6**; seize *Harrington* at Farm Cove, 1808 **5**; seize *Unity* at Derwent, 1813 **4**; seize *Argo* at Derwent, 1814 **6**; from Hobart, 1814 **8**; seize *Trial* at Port Jackson, 1816 **9**; seize *Young Lachlan* at Derwent, 1819 **2**; Alexander Pearce eats companions, 1824 **8**; seize *Wellington* en route to Norfolk Is., 1826 **12**; seize *Cyprus* at Recherche Bay, 1829 **8**; seize *Frederick* at Macquarie Harbour, 1834 **1**; kill Wardell, 1834 **9**

assigned: entitlements of, 1800 F, 1804 F, 1838 F; punishment for misbehaviour, 1822 F, 1828 F

"exiles", 1844 **11 12**, 1849 **12**, 1850 **4**

female: first landed, 1788 **2**; make blankets at Parramatta, 1801 **12**; Female Factory at Parramatta, 1818 A, 1821 **2**; at Cascades, Tas., 1828 **12**; conflict with employers, 1822 **8**, 1834 **1**

punishment of, 1822 F, 1823 F, 1833 F 1837 F

revolts: at Castle Hill, 1804 **3**; on Norfolk Is., 1789 **1**, 1800 **12**, 1826 **9**, 1834 **1**; at Parramatta, 1791 **12**; on transports, 1796 **2**, 1802 **6**, 1817 **7**, 1831 **8**

statistics, 1790 F; population, 1791 F, 1820 F, 1836 F; total number transported, 1840 F, 1842 F

Conyngham, Barry Ernest, composer (1944–), 1944 G

Coober Pedy (SA), 1915 **2**, 1966 B, 1985 **7**, 1989 *

Coode Island (Melb.), 1991 **8**

Cook, James, navigator (1728–79); statue of, in Hyde Park, 1879 C; cottage of, 1934 A; *Endeavour*'s cannons recovered, 1969 **1**; Bicentenary celebrations, 1970 **3**

Cook, Sir Joseph, Prime Minister (1860–1947), 1860 G, 1894 **4**, 1947 G; and "the Fusion", 1909 **5**; becomes Prime Minister, 1913 **9**; granted double dissolution, 1914 **6**; offers expeditionary force, 1914 **8**; goes to London, 1918 **4**; at Peace Conference, 1919 **1 6**; becomes High Commissioner, 1921 **11**

Cooke, Edgar Eric, murderer (1931–64), 1963 **9**

Cooksland, 1849 **1**

Cooktown (Qld), 1873 **10**, 1875 **8**, 1907 **1**

Coolangatta (Qld), 1846 **8**, 1949 **3**

Coolangatta (ship), 1846 **8**

Coolgardie (WA), 1893 **8**, 1897 **5**; gold discovered at, 1892 **9**; railway reaches, 1896 **3**; mining disaster at, 1904 **5**

Coolies, importation of, 1842 **9**, 1846 **3**. *See also* Chinese in Australia

Cooma (NSW), 1849 **8**

Coombs, Herbert Cole, economist and administrator (1906–97), 1906 G, 1997 G

Coonardoo (K. S. Prichard), 1929 D

Cooper, Ashley, tennis player (1936–), 1957 E, 1958 E

Cooper, Bradford Paul, swimmer (1954–), 1972 E

Cooper, Frank Arthur, Labor Premier of Qld (1872–1949), 1942 **9**, 1946 **3**

Cooper, Frederick de Brébant, writer, 1857 D

Cooper, Jessie Mary (*née* McAndrew), Liberal politician, 1959 **3**

Cooper, Theo Russell, National Party Premier of Qld (1941–), 1989 **9**

Cooper Basin (SA), 1980 B

Cooper's Creek (SA), 1845 **8**, 1847 **8**; Burke and Wills at, 1860 **11 12**, 1861 **4**

Cooper's Creek (A. Moorehead), 1963 D

Cooranbong (NSW), 1897 *

Coorong, The (SA), 1840 **6**

Cootamundra (NSW), 1861 **8**, 1885 **1**

Copland, Sir Douglas Berry, economist (1894–1971), 1894 G, 1939 **9**, 1971 G

Copper discoveries: at Kapunda (SA), 1842 *; at Burra (SA), 1845 **5**; on Yorke Peninsula (SA), 1859 **12**, 1861 **5**; at Cloncurry (Qld), 1867 **5**; at Cobar (NSW), 1869 *; at Mt Lyell (Tas.), 1886 *; in Chillagoe area (Qld), 1888 *

Copper smelting, 1844 **8**

Coppin, George Selth, theatrical entrepreneur (1819–1906), 1819 G, 1843 C, 1845 C, 1855 C, 1862 C, 1906 G

Copyright, 1969 **5**

Coral Sea, Battle of, 1942 **5**

Coral Sea Islands Territory, 1969 **5**

Corbett, Henry, sheep breeder, 1882 F

Corcoran, James Desmond, Labor Premier of SA (1928–), 1979 **2**

Corio Bay (Port Phillip, Vic.), 1824 **12**

Corio Villa (Geelong, Vic.), 1855 A

Corner Inlet (Vic.), 1841 **1**

Cornforth, Sir John Warcup, scientist (1917–), 1975 B

Cornwall and York, Duke of. *See* George V

Cornwall Turf Club (Launceston, Tas.), 1830 E

Cornwell, George and Arthur, film makers, 1907 C

INDEX

INDEX

INDEX

Cycling: Kernot builds boneshaker, 1868 E;
first race held, 1869 E; penny farthings
imported, 1875 E; Melbourne Bicycle
Club formed, 1878 E; first six-day race,
1881 E; Sydney–Melbourne on penny
farthing, 1884 E; Austral Wheel Race first
held, 1886 E; safety bicycles introduced,
1886 E; long-distance rides, 1896 E,
1899 E, 1900 E, 1907 E, 1969 E. *See also
under names of cyclists*
Cyclone Tracy, 1974 **12**. *See* Storms
Cyprus (brig), 1829 **8**

D

Dacre, Arthur (Arthur Culver James), actor,
1895 **11**
"Dad and Dave" (radio serial), 1937 C
Daedalus (storeship), 1793 **4**, 1794 **1 2**
Daglish, Henry, Premier of WA (1866–1920),
1904 **8**, 1905 **8**
Daily Guardian (newspaper, Syd.), 1923 **7**,
1931 **2**
Daily Mail (newspaper, Bris.), 1903 **10**,
1933 **8**
Daily Mail (newspaper, Syd.), 1922 **1**, 1924 **1**
Daily Mirror (newspaper, Syd.), 1941 **5**,
1990 **10**
Daily News (newspaper, Melb.), 1848 **10**
Daily News (newspaper, Perth), 1882 **7**,
1990 **9**
Daily News (newspaper, Syd.), 1922 **1**,
1937 **12**, 1940 **7**
Daily Sun (newspaper, Bris.), 1982 **8**, 1988 **2**
Daily Telegraph (newspaper, Syd.), 1879 **7**,
1922 **1**, 1940 **7**, 1990 **10**
Daily Telegraph Mirror (newspaper, Syd.),
1990 **10**
Daintree, Richard, geologist (1832–78),
1869 **3**
Dal Monte, Toti, Italian soprano, 1926 C
Dalai Lama, visits Australia, 1982 **8**
D'Albertis, Luigi Maria, Italian explorer
(1841–1901), 1876 **5**
Dalby (Qld), 1854 **3**, 1868 **4**
Dale, Robert, surveyor and explorer
(1810–56), 1830 **7**
Daley, Victor James William Patrick, poet´
(1858–1905), 1858 G, 1898 D, 1905 G,
1911 D
Dalley, William Bede, orator and politician
(1831–88), 1831 G, 1887 *, 1888 G
D'Alpuget, Josephine Blanche, author
(1944–), 1981 D
Dalrymple, George Augustus Frederick
Elphinstone, explorer (1826–76), 1826 G,
1859 **8**, 1876 G; founds Bowen, 1861 **2**;
founds Cardwell, 1864 **1**; explores north

coast of Qld, 1873 **9**; founds Cooktown,
1873 **10**
Daly, Sir Dominick, Governor of SA
(1798–1868), 1862 **3**
Damned Whores and God's Police
(A. Summers), 1975 D
Dampier, Alfred, actor and dramatist
(1848?–1908), 1877 C, 1890 C
Dana, Henry Edward Pulteney, native police
superintendent (1820–52), 1842 **2**
Dancing on Coral (G. Adams), 1987 D
Dangar, Henry, surveyor and pastoralist
(1796–1861), 1822 **8**, 1838 **6**, 1847 *
Danielson, Larry Burton, criminal, 1981 **1**
Dannevig, Harald Kristian, Director of
Fisheries (1871–1914), 1914 **12**
Darcy, James Leslie, boxer (1895–1917),
1895 G, 1917 G; knocks out Eddie
McGoorty, 1915 E; goes to America,
1916 E; death of, 1917 E
Dargie, Sir William Alexander, artist
(1912–), 1912 G; wins Archibald Prize,
1941 C, 1942 C, 1945 C, 1946 C, 1947 C,
1950 C, 1952 C, 1956 C
Dark, Eleanor (*née* O'Reilly), novelist
(1901–85), 1901 G, 1936 D, 1937 D,
1941 D, 1945 D, 1985 G
Darling, Sir Charles Henry, Governor of Vic.
(1809–70), 1863 **9**, 1866 **1 2**
Darling, Sir Ralph, Governor of NSW
(1772?–1858), 1825 **7 11**, 1828 **3**, 1831 **4**,
1858 G; proclaims independence of Van
Diemen's Land and takes over as governor
of NSW, 1825 **1 2**; cancels tickets of
occupation, 1826 **8**; and Sudds-Thompson
affair, 1826 **11**; conflict with newspapers,
1827 **3 4 9**, 1829 **4**; impeached, 1829 **3**;
proclaims Nineteen Counties, 1829 **10**;
recalled, 1831 **3 10**
Darling Downs (Qld), 1827 **6**, 1828 **7 8**,
1840 **3**
Darling Harbour (Syd.), 1873 B, 1880 **11**,
1985 A, 1988 **5**, 1994 **1**
Darling Range (WA), 1829 **9**
Darling River (Qld–NSW): discovered,
1829 **2**; Mitchell's expedition on,
1835 **3 5 6**; paddle-steamers navigate,
1859 **1 2**, floods, 1890 *, blue-green algae
infests, 1991 F; dries out, then flows
again, 1995 F
Darlinghurst (Syd.): courthouse, 1836 A;
gaol, 1822 A, 1909 **8**
Darnley Island (Torres Strait), 1793 **7**
Darrell, George Frederick Price, actor and
dramatist (1851?–1921), 1883 C
Darr (ship), 1807 **3 10**
Darwin (NT): port named, 1839 **9**;
settlement established, 1869 **2**; cyclones
damage, 1878 **1**, 1882 **1**, 1897 **1**; gaol
built, 1883 A; meatworks opens in,
1917 **4**; Town Council disbanded; 1937 **4**;
bombed by Japanese, 1942 **2**; acquired by

404

INDEX

Commonwealth, 1946 **1**; attains city status, 1959 **1**; devastated by Cyclone Tracy, 1974 **12**; highest wet season rainfall, 1991 F; receives East Timorese refugees, 1999 **9**

Darwin, Charles, British scientist (1809–82), 1836 **1** B

Davey, John Andrew (Jack), radio and television entertainer (1907–59), 1907 G, 1959 G

Davey, Thomas, Lt-Governor of Tas. (1758–1823), 1811 **9**, 1823 G; arrives in Sydney, 1812 **10**; takes up position, 1813 **2**; proclaims martial law, 1815 **4**; replaced by Sorell, 1817 **4**

David, Margaret Edgeworth. *See* McIntyre, Margaret Edgeworth

David, Sir Tannatt William Edgeworth, geologist (1858–1934), 1858 G, 1898 B, 1934 G; ascends Mt Erebus, 1908 **3**; reaches South Magnetic Pole, 1909 **1**

David Clark (migrant ship), 1839 **10**

David Jones, retailing establishment, 1838 *

Davidson, Robyn, overlander (1950–), 1977 **4**

Davies, G.L., long-distance motorist, 1925 **8**

Davies, John, newspaper proprietor (1813–72), 1854 **7**

Davies, John J., swimmer (1929–), 1952 E

Davies, Paul Charles William, scientist and writer (1946–), 1995 B

Davis, Arthur Hoey (pseud. Steele Rudd), author (1868–1935), 1868 G, 1899 D, 1904 D, 1935 G

Davis, Edward, bushranger, 1840 **12**

Davis, James, wild white man, 1842 **5**

Davis Antarctic station, 1957 B

Davison, Frank Dalby, author (1893–1970), 1893 G, 1931 D, 1933 D, 1946 D, 1968 D, 1970 G

Dawe, Bruce, poet (1930–), 1983 D

Dawe, Clem (Clement Edward White), entertainer (d. 1955), 1920 C

Dawes, William, soldier and scientist (1762–1836), 1836 G; builds observatory, 1788 B; builds battery, 1788 A, 1791 A; makes explorations, 1789 **12**, 1791 **5**; lays out Rose Hill, 1790 **6**; returns to England, 1791 **12**

Dawes Point (Syd.), 1788 B, 1790 **7**, 1791 A, 1798 **6**, 1842 **8**

Dawn, Norman, film director (1887–1975), 1927 C

Dawn (periodical), 1888 **5**

Dawnward? (B. O'Dowd), 1903 D

Dawson, Alexander, architect, 1857 A

Dawson, Anderson (Andrew), Labor Premier of Qld (1863–1910), 1899 **11**

Dawson, Herbert Henry ("Smoky"), entertainer (1913–), 1913 G

Dawson, Janet, artist (1935–), 1973 C

Dawson, Peter Smith, singer (1882–1961), 1882 G, 1909 C, 1961 G

Dawson River (Qld), 1844 **11**

Daydream Island (Qld), 1970 **1**

Daylesford (Vic.), 1851 **8**

Daylight saving: as wartime measure, 1917 **1**, 1942 **1**; introduced on trial basis, 1971 **10**; referendum in NSW, 1976 **5**; in WA, 1983 **10**, 1991 **11**; in Qld, 1990 **10**

De Castella, François Robert, athlete (1957–), 1957 G, 1983 E

De Facto Relationships Act, 1985 F

De Garis, Clement John, financier (1884–1926), 1920 **10** D

De Grey River (WA), 1861 **5**, 1863 **4**

De Groot, Francis Edward, New Guard member (1888–1969), 1932 **3**

De L'Isle, Viscount (William Philip Sidney), Governor-General (1909–91), 1861 **8**, 1965 **8**

De Maistre, LeRoy Leveson Laurent Joseph (Roy), artist (1894–1968), 1919 C

De Mestre, Prosper, merchant (1793–1844), 1818 **4**

De Mole, Lancelot Eldin, inventor (1800–1950), 1912 B

De Preu, Gerard, architect, 1982 A

De Rougemont, Louis. *See* Grin, Henri Louis

De Witt's Land (WA), 1801 **7**

Dead Men Rising (K. Mackenzie), 1951 D

Deakin, Alfred, Prime Minister (1856–1919), 1856 G, 1875 D, 1901 D, 1919 G; becomes Prime Minister, 1903 **9**; retains office at election, 1903 **12**; resigns over Arbitration Bill, 1904 **4**; second administration, 1905 **7**, 1908 **11**; forms "the Fusion", 1909 **5**; third administration, 1909 **6 8 12**

Deakin University (Geelong, Vic.), 1887 **11**, 1978 **5**

Dean, George, murderer, 1895 **6**

Dean, William F., balloonist, 1858 **2 12**

Deane, John Phillip, musician (1796–1849), 1822 C, 1825 C, 1834 C, 1836 C, 1837 C

Deane, Sir William Patrick, Governor-General (1931–), 1999 **2**

Death duties, 1898 **7**, 1977 **1**, 1981 **12**

Debt, Australia's gross foreign, 1986 F

Decimal currency, introduced, 1966 **2**. *See also* Banknotes; Coins

Deeds That Won the Empire (W. H. Fitchett), 1896 D

Deeming, Frederick Bailey, murderer (1853–92), 1892 **5**

Deer, introduced, 1803 F

Defamation legislation (NSW), 1958 **12**

Defence: batteries established in Sydney, 1788 A, 1791 A, 1801 A; SA and Vic. raise forces, 1854 *; royal commission on, 1858 **11**; Jervois-Scratchley reports, 1877 **6 7 12**; state establishments transferred to Commonwealth, 1901 **3**; Kitchener advises on, 1909 **12**, 1910 **2**; Anzus Treaty signed, 1951 **9**. *See also* Military forces; Naval defence

INDEX

Defence Act, 1903 **10**, 1904 **3**, 1905 **1**, 1909 **12**, 1939 **7**

Defries, Colin, aviator, 1909 **12**

Degraves, Peter, engineer (1778–1852); 1832 *, 1834 A

Dellit, Charles Bruce, architect (1898–1942), 1932 A

Demidenko, Helen (*née* Darville), author (1971–), 1994 D

Democratic Labor Party: origins, as ALP (Anti-Communist), 1955 **4 12**; formed in NSW, 1956 **9**; national party formed 1957 **8**; preferences aid Liberals, 1958 **11**, 1961 **7 12**, 1969 **10**; Qld affiliates to, 1962 **11**; gains balance of power in Senate, 1967 **11**

Democrats. *See* Australian Democrats

Demonstrations: against cost of living, 1917 **8**; against NT Administration, 1918 **12**; against volunteer workers in Melbourne, 1928 **11**; during President Johnson's visit, 1966 **10**; during Marshal Ky's visit, 1967 **1**; against street-march laws in Brisbane, 1967 **9**; against conscription, 1968 **7**; against Vietnam War, 1968 **7**, 1969 **7**, 1970 **5 9**; against Springboks, 1971 **7** E; against street-march regulations, 1977 **12**; anti-nuclear rallies, 1985 **3**. *See also* Riots, insurrections, etc.

Dengue fever, 1905 B

Denham, Digby Frank, Liberal Premier of Qld (1859–1944), 1911 **2**

Denham, Henry Mangles, naval officer, 1853 **2**

Deniehy, Daniel Henry, orator and writer (1828–65), 1853 **8**

Deniliquin (NSW), 1850 **3**

Denison, Sir Hugh Robert, businessman (1865–1940), 1922 **9**

Denison, Sir William Thomas, Governor of Tas. and NSW (1804–71), 1804 G, 1847 **1**, 1855 **1**, 1871 G

Denman, Thomas, 3rd Baron Denman, Governor-General (1874–1954), 1911 **7**, 1914 **5**

Dennis, Clara (Clare), swimmer (1916–71), 1932 E

Dennis, Clarence Michael James, poet and journalist (1876–1938), 1876 G, 1913 D, 1915 D, 1916 D, 1917 D, 1921 D, 1938 G

Dent, Bob, euthanasia recipient, 1996 **9**

D'Entrecasteaux Channel (Tas.), 1802 **1**, 1835 **4 7**

Derby (Tas.), 1929 **4**

Derby (WA), 1883 **11**

Deregulation: stockbroking, 1984 **1**; banks, 1984 **8**; domestic aviation, 1990 **10**; telecommunications, 1997 **7**

Derrick, Edward Holbrook, medical scientist (1898–1976), 1935 B

Derwent River (Tas.), 1793 **4**; Bass and Flinders at, 1798 **12**, 1799 **1**; Baudin explores, 1802 **1**; Bowen founds settlement on, 1803 **9**; bay whaling in estuary, 1806 *

Derwent Star and Van Diemen's Land Intelligencer (newspaper, Hob.), 1810 **1**

Descant for Gossips, A (T. Astley), 1960 D

Descubierta (Spanish ship), 1793 **3**

Destitute Board (SA), 1848 F

Dethridge, John Stewart, engineer (1865–1926), 1910 B

Development and Migration Commission, 1926 **7**

Devil's Advocate, The (M. West), 1959 D

Devil's Playground, The (film), 1976 C

Devitt, John, swimmer (1937–), 1960 E

Diamantina River (Qld), 1862 **4**

Diamond, Dick, playwright, 1953 C

Diamond, Michael, trap shooter, 1996 E

Diamonds, discovered in the Kimberley, 1978 B

Diana, Princess of Wales, 1983 **3**, 1988 **1**

Dibbs, Sir George Richard, Premier of NSW (1834–1904), 1834 G, 1885 **10 12**, 1889 **1**, 1891 **10**, 1894 **7**, 1904 G

Dibnah, Corinne, golfer (1962–), 1988 E

Dickens, Edward Bulwer Lytton, MP for Wilcannia (1852–1902), 1889 **2**

Dicks, David, lone sailor (1978–), 1996 **11**

Dickson, Sir James Robert, Premier of Qld (1832–1901), 1898 **10**

Dickson, John, engineer (1774–1843), 1815 B

Dictation test. *See* Immigration restriction

Dictionary of Australian Biography (P. Serle), 1949 D

Difficult Young Man, A (M. Boyd), 1955 D

Digger (word), 1917 F

Diggers (film), 1931 C

Dill, George, newspaper manager (1819–1901), 1862 **4**

Dimboola (play), 1969 C

Diphtheria, 1858 F

Diplomatic relations, 1988 **1**
  with China, 1941 **7**, 1972 **12**
  with Egypt, 1956 **11**, 1959 **11**
  with Japan, 1896 **3**, 1940 **8**, 1953 **1**
  with Unesco, 1978 **2**
  with United Arab Republic, 1959 **11**
  with USA, 1839 **1**, 1937 **5**, 1940 **1**
  with USSR, 1954 **4**, 1959 **6**, 1983 **4**

Diprotodon (marsupial), 1979 B

Dirk Hartog Island (WA), 1801 B, 1818 **9**

Disasters. *See* Adventure disasters; Air accidents; Bridge disasters; Fires, notable; Landslide at Thredbo; Mining disasters; Railway disasters; Road and level-crossing accidents; Shipwrecks and shipping disasters. *See also* Droughts; Floods; Storms

Discoveries and Surveys in New Guinea (J. Moresby), 1876 D

Discoveries in Australia (J. L. Stokes), 1846 D

INDEX

Du Cane, Sir Charles, Governor of Tas. (1825–89), 1869 **1**

Dubbo (NSW), 1849 **11**, 1966 **9**, 1996 **12**; zoo, 1977 B

Duchess of Bengal (ship), 1793 **4**

Duck Reach power station (Tas.), 1895 B

Dudley, Countess of, 1909 **12**

Dudley, 2nd Earl of (William Humble Ward), Governor-General (1867–1932), 1908 **9**, 1911 **7**

Duels: White-Balmain (first in Australia), 1788 **8**; Balmain–Macarthur, 1796 **2**; Paterson–Macarthur, 1801 **9**; Bannister–Wardell, 1826 **10**; Dumaresq–Wardell, 1827 **3**; Mitchell–Donaldson, 1851 **9**

Duff, Sir Robert William, Governor of NSW (1835–95), 1893 **5**

Duffield, Walter Geoffrey, astronomer (1879–1929), 1924 B

Duffy, Sir Charles Gavan, Premier of Vic. (1816–1903), 1816 G, 1871 **6**, 1872 **6**, 1903 G; promotes federation, 1857 **1**, 1870 **8**; Land Act, 1862 **6**

Duffy, Sir Frank Gavan, Chief Justice of the High Court (1852–1936), 1931 **1**

Dugan, Darcy Ezekiel, criminal (1920–91), 1980 **5**

Dugdale, Henrietta Augusta, feminist (1826?–1918), 1884 **6**

Duggan, Edmund, playwright (1862?–1938), 1907 C

Duhig, Sir James, Catholic Archbishop of Brisbane (1871–1965), 1871 G, 1965 G

Duigan, John, film director (1949–), 1987 C

Duigan, John Robertson, pioneer aviator (1882–1951), 1910 **7**

Duke of Clarence (ship), 1793 **4**, 1795 **5**

Duke of Edinburgh Study Conference, 1968 **5**

Dumaresq, Henry, government official (1792–1838), 1827 **3**

Dumaresq River (NSW–Qld), 1827 **5**

Dumont d'Urville, Jules Sébastien César, French navigator (1790–1842), 1826 **10 11**, 1839 **4**

Dunbar (ship), 1857 **8**

Duncan, George Ian Ogilvie, academic (1930–72), 1972 **5**

Dundas, Henry (Viscount Melville), UK Home Secretary (1742–1811), 1792 **7**

Dunera (ship), 1940 **9**

Dunlop, Sir Ernest Edward ("Weary"), surgeon and war diarist (1907–93), 1986 D, 1993 G

Dunlop, James, astronomer (1793–1848), 1821 **11**

Dunn, John, bushranger (1846–66), 1865 **1 5**

Dunn, Ross Anthony, Ananda Marga member, 1978 **6**, 1982 **10**, 1985 **5**

Dunolly (Vic.), 1869 **2**, 1871 **1**

Dunrossil, Viscount (William Shepherd Morrison), Governor-General (1893–1961), 1960 **2**

Dunstan, Sir Albert Arthur, Premier of Vic. (1882–1950), 1935 **4**, 1943 **9**, 1945 **10**

Dunstan, Donald Allan, Labor Premier of SA (1926–99), 1926 G, 1999 G; becomes Premier, 1967 **6**; forced to resign, 1968 **3**; Premier for second time, 1970 **5**; government re-elected, 1973 **3**, 1975 **7**, 1977 **9**; resigns, 1979 **2**

Duntroon (house), 1833 A. *See also* Royal Military College (Duntroon)

Durack, Dame Mary, author (1913–94), 1959 D, 1994 G

Durack, Sarah (Fanny), swimmer (1889–1956), 1912 E

Durack family, pioneers, 1883 **5**

Dusky Sound (NZ), 1792 **10**

Dust storms, 1983 **2**, 1994 **5**

Dusty, Slim. *See* Kirkpatrick, David Gordon

Dusty (F. D. Davison), 1946 D

Dutch New Guinea. *See* Irian Jaya

Duties. *See* Tariffs

Dutton Francis Stacker, Premier of SA (1818–77), 1842 *, 1863 **7**, 1865 **3**

Dutton, Geoffrey Piers Henry, author and editor (1922–98), 1922 G, 1998 G

Dutton, Henry Hampden, long-distance motorist, 1908 **6**

Dwyer-Gray, Edmund John Chisholm, Labor Premier of Tas. (1870–1945), 1939 **6 12**

Dyason Foundation, 1948 *

Dyer, Robert Neal, quizmaster (1909–84), 1909 G, 1948 C, 1957 C, 1971 C, 1984 G

Dysentery, 1824 F

Dyson, Edward George, author (1865–1931), 1906 D

Dyson, William Henry, artist (1880–1938), 1880 G, 1938 G

E

Eagar, Edward, emancipist lawyer (1787–1866), 1811 **7**, 1815 **5**, 1821 **10**

Eagle Farm (Bris.): racecourse, 1865 E; airport, 1925 *, 1931 *

Eardley-Wilmot, Sir John Eardley, Governor of Tas. (1783–1847), 1843 **8**, 1846 **4**, 1847 G

Earl Cornwallis (convict transport), 1801 **6 10**

Earl Spencer (convict transport), 1813 **10**

Earle, Augustus, artist (1793–1838), 1793 G, 1825 C, 1826 C, 1830 C, 1838 C, 1838 G

Earle, John, Labor Premier of Tas. (1865–1932), 1909 **10**, 1914 **4**, 1916 **4**

Early Closing Act: WA, 1898 **10**; NSW, 1899 **12**

Earth-Visitors (K. Slessor), 1926 D

Earthquakes and tremors: in Adelaide area,

INDEX

INDEX

Empire Theatre (Syd.). *See* Her Majesty's Theatre

Empire trade preference, 1932 **7**

Employers' Liability Act (NSW), 1897 F

Empress of Australia (passenger/car ferry), 1965 **1**, 1985 **6**

Emu (armed brig), 1812 **11**

Emu Plains (NSW), railway accident at, 1878 **1**

Encke's Comet, 1822 B

Encounter, HMS, 1913 **10**

Encounter Bay (SA), 1802 **4**, 1830 **2**, 1831 **4**

Endeavour (Cook's ship), 1969 **1**

Endeavour (fisheries research ship), 1914 **12**

Endeavour (ship), 1791 **7**

Endeavour Press, 1932 D

Endeavour Reef (Qld), 1969 **1**

Endeavour River (Qld), 1873 **9 10**

Enemy Within, The (film), 1918 C

English, Scottish and Australian Chartered Bank, 1893 **4**

Engravings, first in Australia, 1805 C

Enoggera Creek reservoir (Bris.), 1866 **7**

Enterprise (schooner), 1835 **7 8 10**

Entertainments tax, federal, 1942 C

Entomological Society of NSW, 1862 B

Environmental impact statements, 1973 F

Environmental Protection Authority (Vic.), 1971 F

Epidemics. *See* Acquired Immune Deficiency Syndrome; Bubonic plague; Influenza epidemics; Smallpox

Epping Racecourse. *See* Harold Park Paceway

Ern Malley hoax, 1944 D

Ernabella Aboriginal mission (SA), 1936 **12**

Erskine, James, military officer, 1817 **8**

Erskine, James Elphinstone, naval officer (1838–1911), 1853 D, 1884 **11**

Escape Cliffs (NT), 1864 **4**, 1865 **4 11**, 1867 **1**

Escape of the Notorious Sir William Heans, The (W. G. Hay), 1919 D

Eskbank Ironworks (Lithgow, NSW), 1875 **12**, 1894 **1**, 1900 **4**

Esky, 1961 B

Esmond, James William, gold discoverer (1822–90), 1851 **7**

Esperance (WA), 1893 **12**

Espérance (French ship), 1792 **4**

Esperance Bay (WA), 1792 **12**

Essential Services Act (Vic.), 1948 **1**

Esson, Thomas Louis Buvelot, author and playwright (1878–1943), 1910 C

Estate duty, 1979 **7**

Ether, first used in Australia, 1847 B

Ethnic radio and television, 1975 **6**, 1978 **1**

Eucalyptus (M. Bail), 1998 D

Eucalyptus oil, 1852 B

Eucla (SA), 1912 **11**

Eucumbene, Lake (NSW), 1958 **5**

Eugowra (NSW), gold escort robbery, 1862 **6**

Eureka Stockade, 1854 **11 12**, 1855 **2**

Eureka Stockade (film), 1907 C, 1949 C

European Vision and the South Pacific 1767–1850 (B. Smith), 1960 D

Euthanasia, voluntary, 1995 **5**, 1996 **7 9**, 1997 **3**

Evans, Ada Emily, first female law graduate (1872–1947), 1902 F

Evans, George Essex, poet (1863–1909), 1901 D

Evans, George William, explorer (1780–1852), 1802 **10**, 1805 **2**, 1809 **10**, 1852 G; discovers Warragamba River, 1804 **9**; surveys Jervis Bay, 1812 **4**; explores beyond Blue Mountains, 1813 **11**; discovers Lachlan River, 1815 **5**; accompanies Oxley, 1818 **5 7**

Evans, Harry J., geologist, 1955 **7**

Evans, Sir John William, Liberal Premier of Tas. (1855–1943), 1904 **7**

Evatt, Elizabeth Andreas, judge (1933–), 1976 **1**

Evatt, Herbert Vere, politician and judge (1894–1965), 1894 G, 1925 **5**, 1938 D, 1965 G; appointed to High Court, 1930 **12**; enters federal parliament 1940 **9**; and United Nations, 1945 **4**, 1948 **9**; and anti-Communist legislation 1950 **11**; opposition leader, 1951 **6**, 1960 **2**; and Petrov royal commission, 1954 **8**, 1955 **10**; attacks right-wing Vic. members of ALP, 1954 **10**; becomes Chief Justice, 1960 **2**

Eve, Richmond Cavill, diver (1901–70), 1924 E

Evening News (newspaper, Syd.), 1867 **7**, 1931 **3**

Everage, Edna *See* Humphries, John Barry

Everingham, Paul Anthony Edward, Chief Minister of NT (1943–), 1978 **7**, 1981 **9**, 1984 **10**

Evil Angels (film), 1988 C

Exchange rate: linked with sterling, 1931 **12**; nexus with sterling broken, 1967 **11**; dollar falls below parity with US dollar, 1982 **7**; dollar allowed to float, 1983 **12**; dollar collapses, 1985 **4**; dollar falls to all-time low, 1986 **7**; devaluations and revaluations, 1949 **9**, 1972 **12**, 1973 **9**, 1974 **9**, 1976 **11**, 1983 **12**

Excise Tariff (Agricultural Machinery) Act, 1907 **1**

"Exclusives", 1836 **4**

Executive Council, Commonwealth, 1901 **1**

Exeter (NSW), rail accident at, 1914 **3**

Exhibition Building (Syd.), 1870 **8** A

Exhibition Building (Melb.), 1879 A, 1880 **10**, 1901 **5**, 1901 **9**

Exhibitions
Adelaide, 1887 **6**
Brisbane, 1876 **8**

411

INDEX

F

Facey, Albert Barnett, author (1894–1982), 1981 D

Factory Acts, 1873 **11**, 1885 **12**, 1896 **7**

Fact'ry 'Ands (E. Dyson), 1906 D

Fadden, Sir Arthur William, Country Party Prime Minister (1894–1973), 1894 G, 1942 **10**, 1949 **12**, 1958 **3**, 1973 G; becomes CP leader, 1940 **10**; Prime Minister, 1941 **8 10**

Fahey, John Joseph, Liberal Premier of NSW (1945–), 1992 **6**, 1995 **3**

Faiman, Peter Leonard, film director (1944–), 1986 C

"Fair dinkum", term first printed, 1894 D

Fair Girls and Gray Horses (W. H. Ogilvie), 1898 D

Fairbairn, Sir David Eric, Liberal politician (1917–), 1969 **11**

Fairbairn, James Valentine, UAP politician (1897–1940), 1940 **8**

Fairbridge, Kingsley Ogilvie, social worker (1885–1924), 1912 **8**

Fairbridge Farm Schools, 1912 **8**

Fairfax, John, newspaper proprietor (1805–77), 1805 G, 1841 **2**, 1877 G

Fairlea Women's Prison (Melb.), 1982 **2**

Fairweather, Ian, artist (1891–1974), 1891 G, 1961 C, 1962 C, 1965 C, 1974 G; raft voyage, 1952 **5**

Faithfull, George, pioneer, 1838 **4**

Faithfull, William Pitt, pioneer (1806–96), 1838 **4**

Falkiner, R. S., inventor, 1921 B

Fall of the House of Usher (opera), 1965 C

Famechon, John, boxer (1945–), 1945 G, 1969 E

Family allowance, 1927 F, 1941 F, 1950 F, 1964 F, 1976 F

Family Colonization Loan Society, 1849 *, 1850 **9**

Family Law Act, 1975 **5**, 1976 **1**

Family Law Court, 1976 **1** F; Justice Opas shot, 1980 **6**; bombings, 1984 **3 4 7**

Fanfrolico and After (J. Lindsay), 1962 D

Fanfrolico Press, 1925 D

Fanny (convict transport), 1816 **1**

Fanny Bay Gaol (Darwin), 1883 A

Fantasy (painting), 1917 C

Far West Children's Health Scheme, 1924 *

Farm Cove (Syd.), farm at, 1788 **2 4**, 1789 F

Farmer & Co., 1881 A, 1923 **12**, 1961 **1**

Farmers and Settlers' Associations: NSW, 1893 *, 1911 **1**, 1913 **5**; SA, 1915 **12**; WA, 1913 **3**; form federal body, 1916 **9**

Farmhouse Creek wilderness area (Tas.), 1986 **3**

Farnell, James Squire, Premier of NSW (1825–88), 1877 **12**, 1878 **12**

Farquhar, Murray Frederick, NSW Chief Magistrate (1918–93), 1983 **7**, 1985 **3**

Farrell, John, poet and journalist (1851–1904), 1887 D

Farrelly, Bernard, surfer (1944–), 1963 E, 1964 E

Farrer, William James, wheat breeder (1845–1906), 1845 G, 1901 B, 1906 G

Fascist Party, declared illegal, 1940 **6**

Fatal Shore, The (R. Hughes), 1987 D

Fatal Wedding, The (film), 1911 C

"Fathers Day massacre", 1984 **9**, 1987 **6**

Fawkner, John Pascoe, pioneer (1792–1869), 1792 G, 1803 **4**, 1869 G; punished for helping convicts escape, 1814 **8**; and establishment of Melbourne, 1835 **7 10**; newspapers published by, 1838 **1**, 1839 **2**, 1840 **11**

Fearn, John, master mariner, 1798 **11**

Federal Aid Roads Agreement, 1926 **5**

Federal Bank of Australia, 1893 **1**

Federal Capital Commission, 1925 **1**

Federal Council of Australasia, 1883 **11**, 1886 **1**

Federal Court of Australia, 1976 **12**

Federal Hotel (Melb.), 1888 A

Federated Ship Painters and Dockers Union, royal commission into, 1980 **10**, 1981 **6**, 1982 **8**, 1984 **7 11**

Federation: C. G. Duffy promotes, 1857 **1**, 1870 **8**; Parkes advocates, 1867 **3**; Federal Council called for, 1883 **11**; Council meets, 1886 **1**; conference on Parkes's proposals, 1890 **2**; National Australasian Convention, 1891 **3**; Australasian Federation League founded, 1893 **6**; conference at Corowa, 1893 **7**; Hobart conference calls for draft constitution, 1895 **1**; enabling legislation enacted by colonies, 1895 **12**, 1896 **1 10**, 1899 **6**, 1900 **6**; People's Federal Convention, held, 1896 **11**; Federal Convention, 1897 **3 4 9**, 1898 **1**; referendums on, 1898 **6** F, 1899 **4 6 7 9**, 1900 **7**; amendments made to draft constitution, 1898 **8**, 1899 **1**, Constitution Act receives royal assent, 1900 **7**; proclaimed by Queen Victoria, 1900 **9**; Commonwealth proclaimed, 1901 **1**; WA proposes withdrawal from, 1906 **9**

"Federation" wheat, 1901 B

"Felix the Cat" (animated cartoon), 1917 C

Fellows, Warren, arrested for drug smuggling, 1978 **10**

Fellowship of Australian Writers, 1928 D

Felonry of New South Wales, The (J. Mudie), 1837 D

Felons' Apprehension Act: NSW, 1865 **4**; Vic. 1878 **11**

Felton, A. D., sculler, 1919 E

Felton, Alfred, public benefactor (1831–1904), 1831 G, 1904 C G

Female Eunuch, The (G. Greer), 1970 D

INDEX

INDEX

INDEX

Floods (continued)
WA: on Swan, 1830 **5**; on Fortescue, 1890 *
widespread, 1870 **12**, 1875 *, 1889 *, 1890 *, 1931 *, 1973 *
Floral emblem, national, 1988 **9**
Florey, Howard Walter, Baron of Adelaide and Marston, scientist (1898–1968), 1898 G, 1945 B, 1968 G
Fluoridation, 1953 F
Fly, HM corvette, 1842 **10**
Fly River (PNG), 1876 **5**
Flying Doctor Service, 1928 **5**, 1951 **6**
Flying Home (M. Lurie), 1978 D
"Flying Pieman". *See* King, William Francis
Flynn, Errol Leslie, film actor (1909–59), 1909 G, 1933 C, 1959 G
Flynn, John, minister and missionary (1880–1951), 1880 G, 1910 D, 1912 **9**, 1951 G; memorial complex, 1988 **10**
Flynn of the Inland (I. Idriess), 1932 D
Foley, Laurence (Larry), pugilist (1849–1917), 1871 E, 1879 E, 1883 E, 1917 G
Folger, Mayhew, US whaler, 1808 **2**
Follensbe (US ship), 1801 **1**
Follett, Rosemary, Chief Minister of ACT (1948–), 1989 **3**, 1991 **6**, 1992 **2**
Fonteyn, Dame Margot, English ballet dancer, 1964 C
Food preservation. *See* Canning; Refrigeration
Football: first recorded game, 1829 E
Australian Rules: first played, 1850 E, 1858 E; rules adopted, 1866 E; first premiership competition, 1870 E; Vic. Football Association formed, 1877 E; Victorian Football League formed, 1896 E; Brownlow Medal inaugurated, 1924 E; VFL Park opens, 1970 E; first Sunday matches in Vic., 1984 F; AFL formed, 1989 E
Rugby League: formed, 1907 E; Kangaroos tour, 1908 E, 1909 E; Super League, 1995 E, 1997 E; National Rugby League competition, 1997 E
Rugby Union: first club formed, 1864 E; Southern Rugby Union formed, 1874 E; first intercolonial match, 1882 E; first Australia–England test, 1899 E; first Australia–NZ Test, 1903 E; Wallabies win gold medal at Olympics, 1908 E; defections to League, 1909 E; Springbok tour, 1971 **7** E; Wallabies win grand slam, 1984 E; professional competition begins, 1996 E; Wallabies win World Cup, 1999 E
soccer: first club, 1880 E; NSW Soccer Association formed, 1882 E; Australian Soccer Federation formed, 1957 E; National Soccer League formed, 1977 E
Foot-racing, professional, 1869 E, 1878 E

Foott, Mary Hannay, poet (1846–1918), 1885 D
For Love Alone (C. Stead), 1944 D
For the Term of His Natural Life (M. Clarke), 1870 D, 1874 D; silent films of, 1908 C, 1927 C
Forbes, Sir Francis, first Chief Justice of NSW (1784–1841), 1824 **3 5**, 1834 **5**, 1841 G; and Legislative Council, 1825 **12**; and newspaper legislation, 1827 **4**
Forbes, John Woolcott, businessman, 1943 **8**
Forbes, Joseph ("Timor Joe"), 1839 **3**
Forbes (NSW), 1861 **9**, 1990 **8**
Forbes Act, 1834 **8**
Ford, Michelle Jan, swimmer (1962–), 1980 E
Ford, William, artist (*c.* 1820–*c.* 86?), 1875 C
Ford, William, prospector (1855–1932), 1892 **9**
Forde, Francis Michael, Labor Prime Minister (1890–1983), 1890 G, 1945 **4 7**, 1983 G
Forefathers (N. Cato), 1983 D
Forlonge, Eliza, grazier, 1831 **1**
Forlonge, John, grazier, (1783–1834), 1831 **1**
Forman, Colin Richard, pilot, 1977 **1**
Forrest, Alexander, explorer (1849–1901), 1879 **2**
Forrest, Sir John, explorer and statesman (1847–1918), 1847 G, 1869 **4**, 1870 **3**, 1918 G; crosses Gibson Desert, 1874 **4**; examines Kimberley district, 1886 **3**; becomes Premier of WA, 1890 **12**; Commonwealth minister, 1901 **2**; and "the Fusion", 1909 **5**; raised to peerage, 1918 **2**
Forrest Place (Perth), 1923 A
Forster, Sir Henry William, 1st Baron Forster of Lefe, Governor-General (1866–1936), 1920 **10**, 1925 **10**
Forster, William, Premier of NSW (1818–82), 1859 **10**, 1868 **10**
Fort Denison (Syd.), 1839 **11**, 1841 A, 1855 A
Fort Dundas (NT), 1824 **9**, 1829 **3**
Fort Macquarie (Syd.), 1817 A
Fort Mueller (WA), 1873 **10**, 1874 **1**
Fort Nepean (Port Phillip, Vic.), 1914 **8**, 1939 **9**
Fort Street School (Syd.), 1815 A, 1850 *
Fortescue River (WA), 1861 **5**, 1890 *
Fortitude (ship), 1849 **1**
Fortitude Valley (Bris.), 1849 **1**
Fortunate Life, A (A. B. Facey), 1981 D
Fortunes of Richard Mahony, The (H. H. Richardson), 1917 D, 1925 D, 1929 D
Forty Thousand Horsemen (film), 1940 C
Fossils: found by T. L. Mitchell, 1830 B; at Talgai, 1886 B; at Cohuna, 1925 B; Jervois skull, 1929 B; Keilor skull, 1940 B; stromatolites, 1954 B, 1993 B; at Lake Mungo and Kow Swamp, 1968 B; at Lightning Ridge, 1983 B; at Riversleigh

INDEX

INDEX

G

INDEX

INDEX

Gowrie, 1st Earl of (Alexander Gore Arkwright Hore-Ruthven), Governor-General (1872–1955), 1936 **1**

Goyder, George Woodroffe, surveyor and explorer (1826–98), 1826 G, 1865 **12**, 1898 G; founds Palmerston, 1868 **12**, 1869 **2**

Goyder's Line, 1865 **12**

Grace, William Gilbert, English cricketer (1848–1915), 1873 E

Grace Brothers, open first store, 1885 *

Gracetown (WA), 1996 **9**

Grafton (NSW), 1849 **6**, 1885 **3**; bridge at, 1928 A, 1932 **5**; Jacaranda Festival, 1935 *

Graham, John, wild white man (b. 1800?), 1833 **11**; rescues *Stirling Castle* survivors, 1836 **8**

Graham, William Franklin (Billy), US evangelist (1918–), crusades in Australia, 1951 **2**, 1968 **4**, 1979 **4**

Grainger, George Percy (Percy Aldridge), musician (1882–1961), 1882 G, 1894 C, 1903 C, 1925 C, 1961 G

Grainger, J., explorer, 1852 **5**

Grainger, John Harry, architect (1855–1917), 1902 A

Grainger & D'Ebro, architects, 1885 A

Gramophones, first in Australia, 1889 C

Gramp, Johann, wine-grower (1819–1903), 1847 *

Grand Days (F. Moorhouse), 1993 D

Grand Opera House (Syd.). *See* Tivoli Theatre

Granny Smith apple, 1868 B

Grant, James, navigator (1772–1833), 1800 **12**, 1801 **3 6**, 1803 D

Grant, Ron, athlete, 1981 E, 1983 E, 1986 E

Granville (Syd.), rail disaster at, 1977 **1**

Grape-growing: Busby imports vine cuttings, 1832 **8**; first vines planted in WA, 1832 *. *See also* Wine industry

Grassby, Albert Jaime, Labor politician and community relations commissioner (1926–), 1975 **10**

Gray, Charles, explorer, 1860 **12**, 1861 **2 4 9**

Gray, Edgar Laurence ("Dunc"), cyclist (1906–96), 1932 E

Gray, Robin Trevor, Liberal Premier of Tas. (1940–), 1982 **5**, 1986 **2**, 1989 **5 6**

Graziers. *See* Land settlement

Great Australian Bight, Eyre crosses, 1841 **2 4 6 7**

Great Australian Copper Mine, 1867 **5**

Great Australian Loneliness, The (E. Hill), 1937 D

Great Barrier Reef: wrecks on, 1791 **8**, 1836 **5**, 1846 **3**, 1875 **2**; and crown-of-thorns starfish, 1961 F, 1962 F; Marine Park, 1979 F, 1981 F

Great Britain, SS, 1852 **11**, 1854 **8**

Great Sandy Island. *See* Fraser Island

Great Synagogue (Syd.), 1878 **3**

Great White Fleet, 1908 **8**

Great World, The (D. Malouf), 1990 D

Greater Apollo, The (R. D. FitzGerald), 1927 D

"Greek conspiracy case", 1978 **3**, 1982 **6**

Greek Orthodox Church: first church built, 1898 **5**; Metropolis established, 1924 **3**

Green, Henry Mackenzie, literary critic (1881–1962), 1961 D

Green bans: first imposed, 1971 F; demonstrators arrested, 1973 **10**

Green Hills (NSW). *See* Windsor

Green Island (Qld), infested by starfish, 1962 F

Greens (political movement), 1989 **5 6**, 1998 **7 8**

Greenway, Francis, pioneer architect (1777–1837), 1837 G; arrives in Sydney, 1814 **2** A; appointed Civil Architect, 1816 **3**; given conditional pardon, 1817 **12**; dismissed, 1822 **11** works, 1813 A, 1816 A, 1817 A, 1818 A, 1819 A, 1821 A

Greer, Germaine, feminist writer (1939–), 1939 G, 1970 D

Greeves, Edward, Goderich ("Carji"), footballer (1903–63), 1924 E

Gregg, Sir Norman McAlister, ophthalmologist (1892–1966), 1941 B

Gregory, Sir Augustus Charles, explorer (1819–1905), 1819 G, 1848 **9 12**, 1885 **7**, 1905 G; crosses the north, 1856 **6**; searches for Leichhardt, 1858 **3 4 6**

Gregory, Dick, US comedian, 1970 **9**

Gregory, Francis Thomas, explorer (1821–88), 1858 **4**, 1861 **5**

Gregson, Thomas George, Premier of Tas. (1798–1874), 1857 **2**

Greiner, Nicholas Frank Hugo, Liberal Premier of NSW (1947–), 1988 **3**, 1991 **5**, 1992 **6**

Grenfell, John Granville, gold commissioner, 1866 **12**

Grenville, Catherine Elizabeth (Kate), author (1950–), 1985 D

Grey, Sir George, explorer and Governor of SA (1812–98), 1812 G, 1841 **5**, 1845 **10**, 1898 G; books by, 1839 D, 1841 D: exploration by, 1837 **12**, 1838 **3** C, 1839 **2**

Greycliffe (ferry), sinks, 1927 **11**

Greyhound racing and coursing: first open-field coursing meeting, 1867 E; first track meeting, 1927 E

Griffin, Thomas John Augustus, gold commissioner (1832–68), 1867 **11**

Griffin, Walter Burley, architect (1876–1937), 1876 G, 1912 A, 1920 A, 1924 A, 1937 G

Griffith, Sir Samuel Walker, legislator (1845–1920), 1845 G, 1883 **11**, 1920 G: and "continuous ministry", 1890 **8**, 1893 **3**; Chief Justice, 1903 **10**, 1919 **10**

H

INDEX

Hamersley Range (WA), 1861 **5**; iron ore discovered in, 1952 *

Hamilton, Edward William Terrick, NSW Agent-General (1809–98), 1863 **1**

Hamilton, Sir Robert George Crookshank, Governor of Tas. (1836–95), 1887 **3**

Hamilton (Vic.), 1851 **5**, 1949 **11**

Hamilton Hill (WA), first grapes grown at, 1832 *

Hammett, James, Tolpuddle Martyr, 1834 **8**

Hammond, Dame Joan Hood, singer (1912–96), 1912 G, 1996 G

Hampden, Viscount (Henry Robert Brand), Governor of NSW, 1895 **11**

Hampton, John Stephen, Governor of WA (1810?–69), 1862 **2**

Hancock, Langley George, industrialist (1909–92), 1909 G, 1952 *

Hancock, Tony, British comedian, 1968 **6**

Hancock, Sir William Keith, historian (1898–1988), 1898 G, 1930 D, 1988 G

Hand in the Dark, The (A. Cambridge), 1913 D

Hand That Signed the Paper, The (H. Demidenko), 1994 D

Handcock, Peter Joseph, army officer (1868–1902), 1902 **2**

Handicapped persons, sheltered workshops and employment allowance, 1967 F

Hang-gliding, 1968 E, 1972 E

Hanke, Henry Aloysius, artist (1901–89), 1934 C 1936 C

Hanlon, Edward Michael, Labor Premier of Qld (1887–1952), 1946 **3**, 1952 **1**

Hann, William, explorer (1837–89), 1872 **6**

Hannam, Ken, film director, 1975 C

Hannan, Patrick, prospector (1840–1925), 1893 **6**

Hanover Bay (WA), 1837 **12**

Hansard parliamentary reports, 1856 **11**

Hanson, Pauline Lee (*née* Seccombe), One Nation Party leader (1954–), 1996 **3**, 1997 **4**, 1998 **6 10**

Hanson, Raymond Charles, composer (1913–76), 1948 C

Hanson, Sir Richard Davies, Premier of SA (1805–76), 1857 **9**, 1860 **5**

Happy Dispatches (A. B. Paterson), 1934 D

Happy Valley (P. White), 1939 D

Harbinger (brig), 1801 **1**

Hard God, A (play), 1973 C

Harding, Jeffrey Stephen, boxer (1965–), 1989 E

Hardman, Damien, surfboard rider, 1988 E

Hardy, Francis Joseph, author (1917–94), 1917 G, 1950 D, 1975 D, 1994 G

Hare-Clark voting system, 1897 **1**, 1907 **11**, 1992 **7**

Hargrave, Lawrence, explorer and aeronautical pioneer (1850–1915), 1850 G, 1872 **2**, 1915 G; with d'Albertis in New Guinea, 1875 **5**; addresses Royal Society on principles of flight, 1884 B; invents rotary engine, 1889 B; experiments with boxkites, 1894 B

Hargraves, Edward Hammond, discover of gold (1816–91), 1816 G, 1851 **2**, 1855 D, 1891 G

Harland's Half Acre (D. Malouf), 1984 D

Harold, James, Catholic priest (1744–1830), 1800 **1**

Harold Park Paceway, 1927 E

Harp in the South, The (R. Park), 1948 D

Harpur, Charles, poet (1813–68), 1813 G, 1853 D, 1862 D, 1868 G

Harradine, Brian, senator (1935–), 1975 **8**, 1981 **8**

Harrington (brig), seized by convicts, 1808 **5**

Harris, Alexander, author (1805–74), 1805 G, 1847 D, 1849 D, 1874 G

Harris, John, pioneer surgeon and government official (1754–1838), 1790 **6**, 1801 **8**, 1803 F; and Kemp trial, 1803 **2 3**; allows Macarthur to remove stills, 1807 **3**; replaced as Naval Officer, 1807 **5**

Harris, Maxwell Henley, writer (1921–95), 1921 G

Harris, Rolf, entertainer (1930–), 1930 G, 1960 C

Harrison, Henry Colden Antill, Australian Rules football originator (1836–1929), 1866 E

Harrison, James, inventor (*c.* 1815–93), 1856 B, 1873 B

Harrower, Elizabeth, novelist (1928–), 1966 D

Hart, John, Premier of SA (1809–73), 1865 **10**, 1868 **9**, 1870 5, 1871 **11**

Hart, Kevin Charles ("Pro"), artist (1928–), 1928 G

Hart, Steve, bushranger, 1878 **4**

Hart, William Ewart, pioneer aviator (1885–1943), 1911 **12**, 1912 **6**, 1913 C

Hartigan, Patrick Joseph (pseud. John O'Brien), author and priest (1878–1952), 1921 D

Hartley (NSW), courthouse, 1833 A

Hartnett, Sir Laurence John, engineer (1898–1986), 1898 G, 1986 G

Hartwig, Rex, tennis player (1929–), 1953 E, 1955 E

Harvester judgment, 1907 **1 11**

Harvesters, invention of, 1884 B, 1913 B

Hashemy (convict transport), 1849 **6**

Haslem's Creek (Lidcombe, NSW), railway accident at, 1858 **7**

Hasluck, Nicholas, author (1942–), 1984 D

Hasluck, Sir Paul Meerna Caedwalla, writer, politician, and Governor-General (1905–93), 1905 G, 1949 **12**, 1977 D, 1993 G; becomes Foreign Minister, 1964 **4**; defeated for prime ministership, 1968 **1**; becomes Governor-General, 1969 **4**

INDEX

Hassall, Rowland, missionary (1768–1820), 1798 **5**, 1813 **5**, 1815 **12**

Hassall, Thomas, pioneer clergyman (1794–1868), 1813 **5**

Hasselburg, Frederick, discovers Macquarie Is., 1810 **7**

Hastings River (NSW), 1818 **9**

Hathaway, Marcia, shark attack victim, 1963 **1**

Hatton, Stephen Paul, Chief Minister of NT (1948–), 1986 **5**, 1988 **7**

Haunted Land, A (R. Stow), 1956 D

Hawdon, Joseph, pioneer (1813–71), 1836 **10**, 1838 **4**

Hawes, John Cyril (Friar Jerome), architect (1876–1956), 1916 A

Hawke, Albert Redvers George, Labor Premier of WA (1900–1986), 1953 **2**, 1956 **4**

Hawke, Robert James Lee, Labor Prime Minister (1929–), 1929 G; president of ACTU, 1970 **1**; president of ALP, 1973 **7**; wins preselection for seat in parliament, 1979 **10**; retires as ACTU president, 1980 **9**; enters parliament, 1980 **10**; becomes party leader, 1983 **2**; becomes Prime Minister, 1983 **3**; government re-elected, 1984 **12**, 1987 **7**, 1990 **3**; replaced by Keating, 1991 **12**

Hawker, Harry George, aviator (1889–1921), 1889 G, 1912 **10**, 1921 **7** G

Hawker (SA), railway reaches, 1880 **6**

Hawkesbury Agricultural College, 1891 **3**, 1989 **1**

Hawkesbury River (NSW): discovered, 1789 **6**, 1791 **5**; settlers on, 1794 **1**; Aborigines attack settlers, 1797 **7**, 1805 **4**; settlers kill Aborigines, 1799 **10**. *See also* Nepean River
floods on, 1795 **9**, 1799 **3**, 1806 **3**, 1808 **5** **7**, 1809 **5** **7**, 1817 **2**, 1830 **4**, 1831 **4**, 1867 **6**, 1952 **8**
railway bridges across, 1889 **5**, 1946 **7**
road-bridge across, 1945 A

Hawkins, Stephen, sculler (1971–), 1992 E

Hay, William Gosse, author (1875–1945), 1919 D

Hay (NSW), 1859 **10**

Hayden, William George, Labor politician and Governor-General (1933–), 1933 G, 1961 **12**; becomes Treasurer, 1975 **6**; elected ALP leader, 1977 **12**; replaced by Hawke as leader, 1983 **2**; becomes Governor-General, 1989 **2**

Haydock, Mary. *See* Reibey, Mary

Hayes, Attwell Edwin, journalist, 1829 **4**

Hayes, Catherine, soprano (1825–61), 1854 C

Hayes, Evie, entertainer (1911–88), 1947 C

Hayes, Sir Henry Browne, adventurer (1762–1832), 1802 **7**; arrested for unlawful assembly, 1803 **5**; shipwrecked, 1813 **2**

Hayes, Sir John, naval officer (1768–1831): surveys Derwent, 1793 **4**; founds New Albion, 1793 **10**

Hayes, John Blyth, Nationalist Premier of Tas. (1868–1956), 1922 **8**, 1923 **8**

Hayes, William Henry ("Bully"), adventurer and blackbirder (1829?–77), 1877 G

Hayllar, Tom, long-distance walker, 1976 E

Hayman Island (Qld), 1970 **1**

Haymarket Theatre (Melb.), 1862 C, 1871 **9**

Haynes, John, journalist (1850–1917), 1880 **1**, 1882 **3**

Hayward, Paul, arrested for drug smuggling, 1978 **10**

Hazzard, Shirley, writer (1931–), 1970 D, 1980 D

H. C. Sleigh Ltd, 1913 *

Head Station, The (R. C. Praed), 1885 D

Heales, Richard, Premier of Vic. (1821–64), 1860 **11**

Health insurance, criticized by Nimmo Committee, 1969 **3**. *See also* Medibank; Medicare

Hear the Train Blow (P. Adam-Smith), 1964 D

Heard Island, 1947 **12** B

Heart of Spring (J. S. Neilson), 1919 D

Heart transplant, first, 1968 **10**

Heat waves. *See* Temperatures, extreme

Heaton, Sir John Henniker, author (1848–1914), 1879 D

Hebe (ship), 1815 **8**

Heffron, Robert James, Labor Premier of NSW (1890–1978), 1959 **10**, 1964 **4**, 1978 G

Heidelberg Repatriation Hospital (Melb.), 1941 **3**

Heidelberg School, 1885 C, 1888 C, 1889 C

Heifetz, Jascha, US violinist, tours Australia, 1921 C, 1927 C

Heinze, Sir Bernard Thomas, musician (1894–1982), 1894 G, 1924 C, 1982 G

Hele, Ivor Henry Thomas, artist (1912–93), 1912 G, 1951 C, 1953 C, 1954 C, 1955 C, 1957 C

Helen Nicoll (ship), 1886 **12**

Heliport, Australia's first (Melb.), 1960 **12**

Helmrich, Dorothy Jane Adele, arts administrator (1889–1984), 1944 C

Helpmann, Sir Robert Murray, ballet dancer and actor (1909–86), 1909 G, 1964 C, 1968 C, 1986 G

Hely, Hovenden, explorer (1823–72), 1852 **2**

Helyer, Henry, explorer, 1827 **2**

Helyer River (Tas.), 1827 **2**

Henderson, Brian, TV newsreader (1931–), 1958 C

Henderson, Ronald Frank, academic (1917–), inquiry into poverty, 1972 **8**, 1975 **8**, 1976 F

Henley-on-Yarra regatta, first held, 1904 E

INDEX

INDEX

INDEX

Holmes à Court, Michael Robert Hamilton, businessman (1937–90), 1937 G, 1990 G, 1991 **4**, 1993 **12**

Holt, Harold Edward, Liberal Prime Minister (1908–67), 1908 G, 1960 **11**, 1967 G; becomes Prime Minister, 1966 **1**; increases forces in Vietnam, 1966 **3**, 1967 **9**; "all the way with LBJ", 1966 **6**; government re-elected, 1966 **11**; disappears, 1967 **12**

Holt, Joseph, Irish rebel (1756–1826), 1800 **1 9**, 1809 **6**, 1813 **2**, 1826 G

Holt, Joseph Bland, comedian and producer (1853–1942), 1876 C

Holtermann Nugget, 1872 **10**

Holy Trinity Church (Syd.), 1840 A

Holyman, Sir Ivan Nello, airline proprietor (1896–1957), 1932 **9**

Holyman, Victor, airline proprietor, 1932 **9**, 1934 **10**

Holyman's Airways, 1934 **10**, 1935 **10**, 1936 **7**

Homage to Garcia Lorca (music), 1963 C

Home of the Blizzard (film), 1913 C

Home of the Blizzard, The (D. Mawson), 1915 D

Homebush (Syd.), racecourse, 1841 E, 1842 E, 1860 E

Homesickness (M. Bail), 1980 D

Homestead Act (WA), 1893 **10**

Homosexual: Oppression and Liberation (D. Altman), 1972 D

Homosexuality: among convicts, 1846 **4**; law reform movement, 1970 F; decriminalization of, 1975 F, 1984 F, 1997 F; entitlements for same-sex partners, 1995 F

Honeysuckle Creek (ACT), space tracking station, 1967 B

Honours and awards, 1975 **6**, 1992 **10**

Hood, G., aviator, 1928 **1**

Hood, HMS, visits Australia, 1924 **2**

Hooker, Sir Joseph Dalton, botanist (1817–1911), 1859 B

Hoover Corporation, 1989 **12**, 1990 **12**

Hoover, Herbert Clark, US President (1874–1964), 1897 **5**

Hop. *See* Hopkins, Livingston York

Hope, Alec Derwent, poet (1907–), 1907 G, 1955 D

Hope, Louis, sugar pioneer (1817–94), 1863 B

Hope, Robert Marsden, judge (1919–99), 1983 **5**

Hope (US trading ship), 1792 **12**

Hopeful (schooner), 1884 **7**

Hopetoun, Earl of (John Adrian Louis Hope), Governor-General (1860–1908): 1900 **9 12**, 1901 **1**; Governor of Vic., 1889 **11**

Hopkins, Livingston York, cartoonist (1846–1927), 1846 G, 1883 C, 1927 G

Hopman, Henry Christian (Harry), tennis coach (1906–85), 1906 G, 1985 G

Horn Scientific Expedition, 1894 B

Horne, Donald Richmond, author anpolitical scientist (1921–), 1921 G, 1964 D, 1967 D

Horne, Richard Henry (Hengist), poet (1802–84), 1843 D, 1859 D

Hornet Bank station, 1857 **10**

Hornibrook Highway (Qld), 1935 **10**

Horse of Air, A (D. Stivens), 1970 D

Horse racing: first recorded meeting in Australia, 1810 E; Sydney Turf Club formed, 1825 E, 1943 E; Australian Racing and Jockey Club, 1828 E; Cornwall Turf Club, 1830 E; first meeting at Randwick, 1833 E; first meetings in Melbourne and Adelaide, 1838 E; first meeting at Flemington, 1840 E; St Leger first run, 1841 E; AJC founded, 1842 E; first meeting in Brisbane, 1843 E; first interstate meeting, 1847 E; first meeting at Ascot (Perth), 1848 E; WATC founded, 1852 E; Tas. Jockey Club founded, 1859 E; first meeting at Caulfield, 1859 E; Melbourne Cup first run, 1861 E; Brisbane Turf Club founded, 1861 E; Qld Turf Club founded, 1863 E; VRC founded, 1864 E; Adelaide Cup first run, 1864 E; first meeting at Eagle Farm, 1865 E; Sydney Cup and Brisbane Cup first run, 1866 E; Onkaparinga picnic carnival first held, 1876 E; totalizator sanctioned in SA, 1879 E; Canterbury Racecourse opens, 1884 E; Rosehill Racecourse opens, 1885 E; banned as wartime measure in SA, 1942 E; "magic eye" camera, 1945 E; off-course betting legalized in WA, 1954 **11**; TAB introduced, 1960 E; Trifecta introduced, 1974 E

Horses: exports of, 1816 **11**, 1843 **7**; numbers in NSW, 1849 F

Horsham (Vic.), 1850 **5**, 1949 **5**; railway reaches, 1879 **2**; level-crossing accident at, 1951 **2**

Horsley, Charles Edward, musician (1822–76), 1866 C

Hosking, John, mayor (1806–82), 1842 **11**

Hosking, John, teacher (1774?–1850), 1809 **1**

"Hospital Hour" (radio program), 1975 C

Hospital Saturday collection, 1894 F

Hospitals: portable hospital erected in Sydney, 1790 A; Rum Hospital built, 1810 **11**, 1811 A; Sydney Infirmary opened, 1845 **7**; training of nurses begins, 1868 **3**; managed and staffed by women, 1896 F; free hospital service begins in Qld, 1944 F. *See also names of specific hospitals*

Hotels and public houses: numbers in Sydney, 1810 F; oldest licensed house in Australia, 1825 **9**. *See also* Licensing and liquor laws
Bellevue (Bris.), 1979 A
Hero of Waterloo (Syd.), 1843 A

INDEX

I

INDEX

Irrigation: Chaffey Brothers and Mildura, 1886 **10**; Murrumbidgee Irrigation Area, 1906 **12**, 1910 **12**, 1912 **7**; Dethridge water meter, 1910 B

Irvine, Sir William Hill, Premier of Vic. (1858–1943), 1902 **6**, 1904 **2**

Irvinebank (Qld), 1907 **9**

Irving, John, first convict emancipated (d. 1795), 1790 **2**

Irwin, Frederick Chidley, Governor of WA (1788–1860), 1847 **2**, 1848 **8**

Isaac River (Qld), 1845 **2**

Isaacs, Sir Isaac Alfred, first Australian-born Governor-General (1855–1948), 1855 G, 1948 G; appointed to High Court, 1906 **10**; becomes Chief Justice, 1930 **4**; appointed as Governor-General, 1930 **11**, 1931 **1**; retires, 1936 **1**

Italians, on sugar plantations, 1891 **12**

Italy, trade sanctions against, 1935 **11**

It's Harder for Girls (G. Casey), 1942 D

Ivanov, Valeriy, Soviet diplomat, 1983 **4 5**

Ives, Joshua, musician, 1885 C

Iwasaki, Yohachiro, Japanese developer, 1979 A

IWW. *See* Industrial Workers of the World

J

Jabiluka (NT), 1982 **7**

Jacaranda Festival, 1935 *

Jack, Robert Logan, explorer (1845–1921), 1845 G, 1879 **8 11**, 1921 G

Jack, William, prospector, 1880 **4**

Jack Maggs (P. Carey), 1997 C

Jacka, Albert, soldier (1893–1932), 1915 **5**

Jackey Jackey (Galmahra), Aboriginal guide (d. 1854), 1848 **11 12**

Jackson, Marjorie, athlete (1931–), 1952 E

Jackson, Rex Frederick, Labor politician (1928–), 1984 **11**, 1987 **8**

Jackson, Samuel, architect (1807–76), 1846 A

Jails. *See* Gaols

James, Alfred Francis Phillip, journalist and publisher (1918–92), 1969 **11**, 1973 **1**, 1992 G

James, Brian. *See* Tierney, John Lawrence

James, Clive (Vivian), author (1939–), 1980 D, 1983 D

James, Florence Gertrude, feminist and author (1902–93), 1951 D

James, Frederick and Albert, cyclists, 1899 E

James, John Stanley (pseuds Julian Thomas, "The Vagabond"), journalist and author (1843–96), 1876 D

James, Sir Walter Hartwell, Premier of WA (1863–1943), 1902 **7**

James Cook University of North Queensland (Townsville), 1961 *

James Hay (ship), 1813 **3**

Jamison, Sir John, naval surgeon and pastoralist (1716–1844), 1830 **2**, 1835 **5**, 1844 G

Jamison, Thomas, pioneer surgeon (1745–1811), 1804 B, 1811 **7**

Japan: opens consulate in Townsville, 1896 **3**; bans imports of Australian goods, 1936 **6**; exports of iron ore to, suspended, 1938 **7**; Latham appointed minister to, 1940 **8**; war declared on, 1941 **12**; surrenders, 1945 **9**; occupation force in, 1946 **2**, 1951 **9**; peace treaty signed, 1951 **9**; first post-war ambassador, 1953 **1**; trade agreements with, 1957 **7**, 1963 **8**; Australia's best customer, 1966 F; Friendship and Co-operation Treaty with, 1976 **6**

Japanese prisoners of war, 1944 **8**

Japanese submarines: midget, in Sydney Harbour, 1942 **5**; sink *Iron Chieftain*, 1942 **6**; shell Sydney and Newcastle, 1942 **6**; sink hospital ship *Centaur*, 1943 **5**

Jardine, Alexander William, pioneer (1843–1920), 1864 **10**, 1865 **3**

Jardine, Douglas Robert, English cricketer, 1933 **1**

Jardine, Francis Lascelles, pioneer (1841–1919), 1864 **10**, 1865 **3**

Jardine, John, superintendent of Somerset (1807–74), 1863 **3**

Java: Australian troops in, 1942 **3**

Javacheff, Christo, artist (1936–), 1969 C

J. C. Williamson Ltd, 1920 C. *See also* Williamson, James Cassius

Jedda (film), 1955 C

Jeffcott, Sir John William, judge (1796–1837), 1837 **4**

Jehovah's Witnesses: established in Melbourne, 1903 *; declared illegal, 1941 **1**; hall bombed, 1985 **7**

Jenkins, John Greeley, Liberal Premier of SA (1851–1923), 1901 **5**, 1905 **3**

Jennings, Elizabeth Esther Helen (pseud. Essie Jenyns), actress (1864–1920), 1883 C

Jennings, Sir Patrick Alfred, Premier of NSW (1831–97), 1886 **2**, 1887 **1**

Jenolan Caves (NSW), 1848 F, 1866 F

Jenvey, Henry Walter, wireless pioneer (1851–1932), 1901 B

Jenyns, Essie. *See* Jennings, Elizabeth Esther Helen

Jerilderie (NSW), Kelly Gang raid, 1879 **2**

Jerome, Friar. *See* Hawes, John Cyril

Jersey, Earl of (Victor Albert George Child-Villiers), Governor of NSW (1845–1915), 1891 **1**

Jervis Bay (NSW): named, 1791 **8**; examined by Bass, 1797 **12**; surveyed by Evans, 1812 **4**; overland route to, 1818 **3**;

INDEX

first land sales, 1841 **6**; Naval College at, 1915 **2**; land transferred to Commonwealth, 1915 **9**

Jervois, Sir William Francis Drummond, Governor of SA (1821–97), 1877 **10**; reports on defences, 1877 **6 7 12**

Jervois Skull, 1929 B

Jevons, William Stanley, scientist and economist (1835–82), 1858 **10**

Jewell, Richard Roach, architect (1810–91), 1867 A

Jews: early services, 1817 *; synagogues in Sydney, 1842 **4**, 1844 **4**, 1878 **4**; first qualified minister, 1853 **6**

Jiang Zemin, President of China, 1999 **9**

Jimmy Brocket (D. Stivens), 1951 D

Jindivik target aircraft, 1952 B

Jindyworobak movement, 1938 D

Jinmium (NT), 1993 B

Joe Wilson and His Mates (H. Lawson), 1901 D

John Fairfax & Sons Ltd, takes over Associated Newspapers, 1953 **10**; placed in receivership, 1990 **12**. *See also Sydney Morning Herald*

John Flynn memorial complex (Cloncurry), 1988 **10**

John Lysaght Ltd, 1921 **4**

John Martin's department store, 1866 **10**

John Monash (G. Serle), 1982 D

Johnno (D. Malouf), 1975 D

Johns, Peter, lift manufacturer (1830–99), 1877 A

Johnson, Amy, British aviator (1903–41), 1930 **5**

Johnson, Arthur Ebden, architect (1821–95), 1874 A

Johnson, Frank C., publisher, 1923 D

Johnson, Gertrude Emily, opera singer (1894–1973), founds National Theatre Movement, 1935 C

Johnson, Gordon, cyclist (1945–), 1970 E

Johnson, Hewlett, Dean of Canterbury (1874–1966), 1949 **4**

Johnson, Jack, US boxer (1878–1946), 1908 E

Johnson, Lyndon Baines, US President (1908–73), 1966 **10**, 1967 **12**

Johnson, Richard, Anglican clergyman (1753?–1827), 1788 **7**, 1794 D, 1827 G; conducts first Christian service, 1788 **2**; receives land grant, 1793 **2**; opens Church school at Ryde, 1800 **7**; returns to England, 1800 **10**

Johns's Notable Australians, 1906 D

Johnston, George, soldier and pioneer (1764–1823), 1823 G; receives land grant, 1793 **2**; arrested and sent to England, 1800 **10**; returns to NSW, 1802 **10**; arrests Harris at Kemp court martial, 1803 **2**; and Castle Hill Rising, 1804 **3**; takes command of NSW Corps, 1804 **10**; and

deposition of Bligh, 1808 **1 2 7**; goes to England for trial, 1809 **3**; cashiered, 1811 **6**; returns to Sydney, 1813 **3**

Johnston, George Bain, riverboat captain (1829–82), 1855 **10**

Johnston, George Henry, author (1912–70) 1912 G, 1964 D, 1969 D, 1970 G, 1971 D; portrait of, 1969 C

Johnston, Robert, naval officer and explorer (1792–1882), 1821 **12**

Johnstone River (Qld), 1880 **6**

Joint Coal Board, 1947 **3**

Joint Defence Space Research Facility (Pine Gap, NT), 1966 **12**, 1967 B

Jolimont (Vic.), rail accident at, 1881 **8**

Jolley, Monica Elizabeth, author (1923–), 1982 D, 1986 D

Jonah (L. Stone), 1911 D

Jones, Alan, racing car driver (1947–), 1980 E

Jones, Alan Bedford, talkback radio host (1943–), 1999 **10**

Jones, Barry Owen, Labor politician (1932–), 1977 **12**

Jones, Sir Charles Lloyd, merchant and arts patron (1878–1958), 1916 C

Jones, David, merchant (1793–1873), 1793 G, 1838 *, 1873 G

Jones, Sir David Fletcher, businessman (1895–1977), 1920 **3**

Jones, Inigo Owen, meteorologist (1872–1954), 1872 G, 1923 B, 1934 B, 1954 G

Jones, Marilyn Fay, ballet director (1939–), 1939 G

Jordan, Henry, Qld Agent-General (1818–90), 1860 **10**

Jorgenson, Jorgen, mariner, explorer, and author (1780–1841), 1831 D, 1841 G

Jose, Arthur Wilberforce, historian and writer (1863–1934), 1863 G, 1899 D, 1925 D, 1934 G

Joshua Smith controversy, 1943 C

Journal of a Cruise among the Islands of the Western Pacific (J. E. Erskine), 1853 D

Journal of an Expedition into the Interior of Tropical Australia (T. L. Mitchell), 1848 D

Journal of an Overland Expedition in Australia (L. Leichhardt), 1847 D

Journal of a Tour of Discovery across the Blue Mountains in New South Wales (G. Blaxland), 1823 D

Journals of Expeditions of Discovery into Central Australia and Overland from Adelaide to King George's Sound (E. J. Eyre), 1845 D

Journals of Two Expeditions of Discovery in North-West and Western Australia (G. Grey), 1841 D

Journals of Two Expeditions into the Interior of New South Wales (J. Oxley), 1820 D

INDEX

INDEX

Kingston, Sir George Strickland, surveyor and politician (1807–80), 1836 **11**, 1839 A

Kingston (SA), railway reaches, 1877 **1**

Kinnear, Bobbie, runner, 1883 F

Kintore, Earl of (Algernon Hawkins Thomond Keith-Falconer), Governor of SA (1852–1930), 1889 **4**

Kipling, Rudyard, British author (1865–1936), 1891 D

Kirkpatrick, David Gordon (pseud. Slim Dusty), singer and song-writer (1927–), 1927 G, 1957 C

Kirner, Joan Elizabeth (*née* Hood), Labor Premier of Vic. (1938–), 1990 **8**, 1992 **10**

Kirribilli (Syd.), fire at, 1921 **12**

Kirribilli House (Syd.), 1854 A

Kirsova, Hélène (Ellen Wittrup), ballet dancer, (1910–62), 1940 C

Kirtley, John T., publisher, 1925 D

Kisch, Egon Irwin, Czech journalist (1855–1948), 1934 **11**

Kissing Point. *See* Ryde

Kitchener, Horatio Herbert, 1st Earl (1850–1916), 1909 **12**, 1910 **2**

Kitty (convict transport), 1792 **11**

Kiwi boot polish, 1906 *

Klim, Michael, swimmer (1977–), 1997 E

Knatchbull, John, murderer (1792?–1844), 1844 **2**

Kngwarreye, Emily Kame, artist (c. 1910–96), 1996 G

Knight, John George, architect (1826–92), 1856 A, 1858 A

Knight, Julian, gunman, 1987 **8**

Knites, Christopher, Greek Orthodox Metropolitan, 1924 **3**

Knopwood, Robert, clergyman (1763–1838), 1803 **4**, 1805 **12**, 1838 G; conducts first service: in Vic., 1803 **10**; in Tas., 1804 **2**

Knott, Frances (*née* Minnie Thwaites), baby farmer and murderer (*c.* 1868–94), 1894 **1**

Knox, Sir Adrian, Chief Justice of the High Court (1863–1932), 1919 **10**, 1932 G

Koalas: first observed, 1798 B; trapped in Qld, 1920 F, 1927 F; pelts exported from eastern states, 1924 F

Koch, Christopher John, novelist (1932–), 1958 D, 1978 D, 1985 D, 1995 D

Kokoda (Papua), 1942 **7 11**

Kokoda Front Line (documentary film), 1942 C

Konrads, John, swimmer (1942–), 1960 E

Kookaburra (aircraft), 1929 **4**

Koorinya (container ship), 1964 B

Korean War: RAN ships committed to, 1950 **6**; RAAF squadron goes into action, 1950 **7**; ground troops sent to, 1950 **7 8**; troops go into action, 1950 **10**; withdrawal of troops from North Korea, 1950 **12**; Australian forces capture Chisan, 1951 **3**; Chinese advance at Kapyong halted, 1951 **4**; Australians advance to the Jamestown Line, 1951 **10**; war ends, 1953 **7**; casualties, 1953 F

Kosciuszko, Mount (NSW), 1840 **2**; hotel at, 1909 A; National Park, 1944 F, 1998 **8**

Kow Swamp (Vic.), 1968 B

Krait (fishing vessel), 1943 **9**

Kramer, Dame Leonie Judith (*née* Gibson), academic (1924–), 1924 G

Krefft, Johann Ludwig Gerhard, zoologist (1830–81), 1870 B

Kreisler, Fritz, Austrian violinist (1875–1961), 1925 C

Kupang (Timor): Bligh at, 1789 **6**; Bryants at, 1791 **6**, *Pandora* survivors at, 1791 **9**; Flinders at, 1803 **3**

Kuttabul (ferry), 1942 **5**

Kwinana (WA), 1955 **1 2**

Ky, Nguyen Cao, Premier of South Vietnam, 1967 **1**

L

La Balsa (raft), 1970 **11**

La Boite Theatre (Bris.), 1972 C

La Mama (theatre, Melb.), 1967 C

La Pérouse, Jean-François de Galaup, compte de, French navigator (1741–88), 1788 **1 3**, 1792 **4**

La Trobe, Charles Joseph, Lt-Governor of Vic. (1801–75), 1801 G, 1875 G; arrives at Port Phillip as Superintendent, 1839 **9**; turns convict ships away, 1849 **6 8**; becomes Lt-Governor, 1851 **7**; resigns, 1853 **4**, 1854 **5**

La Trobe University (Melb.), 1964 **12**

Labor Call (newspaper, Melb.), 1897 **10**

Labor Council of New South Wales: origins in Eight Hour Extension Committee, 1869 **8**; first meeting as NSW Trades and Labor Council, 1871 **5**; sponsors member of NSW Parliament, 1874 **12**; promotes Labour Electoral Leagues, 1891 **3**

Labor Daily (newspaper, Syd.), 1922 **1**, 1924 **1**, 1937 **12**

Labor League of SA, 1874 **4**

Labor Party. *See* Australian Labor Party; Democratic Labor Party; Labour movement; Lang Labour Party; Non-Communist Labour Party

Labour Bureau, NSW, 1892 **2**

Labour movement: first "Labour" MPs, 1859 **8**, 1880 **11**; newspapers founded, 1890 **3**, 1891 **10**; United Labour Party formed in SA, 1891 **1**; Electoral Leagues formed in NSW, 1891 **3**, 1895 **5**; candidates win seats in SA, 1891 **5**, 1893 **4**; Progressive Political League formed in Vic., 1891 **5**; candidates win

INDEX

INDEX

INDEX

Longworth, William, swimmer (1892–1969), 1912 E

Lonsdale, William, administrator at Port Phillip (1799–1864), 1799 G, 1836 **9**, 1864 G

Looby, Keith, artist (1939–), 1939 G, 1984 C

Lord, Edward, officer of marines (1781–1859), 1822 **1**

Lord, Simeon, pioneer merchant and manufacturer (1771–1840), 1804 **11**, 1809 **12**, 1840 G; arrives at Port Jackson, 1791 **8**; acquires warehouse, 1798 **9**; buys Spanish ship, 1799 **4**; appointed auctioneer, 1801 **1**; joins Kable and Underwood, 1805 **1**; gaoled, 1807 **8**; establishes woollen mill, 1815 *

Lord Howe Island, discovered and explored, 1788 **2 3**

Lord Mayor, title conferred, 1902 **12**

Lord Melville (convict transport) 1817 **2**

Loring, William, naval officer, 1859 **3**

Lotteries, 1849 **1**
   Golden Casket (Qld), 1917 **6**
   NSW State Lottery, 1930 **12**, 1931 **8**; Opera House, 1958 **1**; Lotto, 1979 **10**; Instant, 1982 **11**; Oz Lotto, 1994 **2**
   Tattersall's 1881 **4**, 1895 **10**, 1896 **1**, 1902 **3**, 1954 **7**

Love Me Sailor (R. Close), 1945 D

Loveless, George, Tolpuddle Martyr (1797–1874), 1834 **9**

Loveless, James, Tolpuddle Martyr, 1834 **8**

Low, Sir David Alexander Cecil, cartoonist (1891–1963), 1891 G, 1963 G

Lowe, Douglas Ackley, Labor Premier of Tas. (1942–), 1977 **12**, 1979 **7**, 1981 **11**

Lowe, Nathaniel, soldier, 1827 **5**

Lower, Leonard Waldemere, humorist (1903?–47), 1930 D

Lower houses (state and territory). *See also* House of Representatives; Parliaments; Representative government
   ACT (Legislative Assembly), 1989 **3 5**
   NSW (Legislative Assembly), 1827 **1**, 1852 **12**, 1856 **3 5**, 1874 **2**, 1903 **11**, 1981 **9**
   NT (Legislative Assembly), 1974 **11**
   Qld (Legislative Assembly), 1860 **5**
   SA (House of Assembly), 1852 **12**, 1857 **3**
   Tas. (House of Assembly), 1852 **12**, 1856 **10 12**
   Vic. (Legislative Assembly), 1852 **12**, 1856 **10 11**, 1857 **11**, 1891 **10**, 1901 **5**
   WA (Legislative Assembly), 1890 **12**

Loyal Associations, 1800 **9**, 1801 **7**, 1803 **12**

Lucas Heights (NSW), nuclear reactor, 1958 B

Lucinda Brayford (M. Boyd), 1946 D

Lucky Country, The (D. Horne), 1964 D

Luhrmann, Baz, designer and film director (1962–), 1992 C

Lukin, Dean, weight-lifter (1960–), 1984 E

Luna Park (Syd.), 1935 C; fire at, 1979 **6**; closes, 1988 C

Lunacy Act, 1843 F

Lungfish (Qld), 1870 B

Lure of the Bush, The (film), 1918 C

Lurie, Morris, author (1938–), 1978 D

Lutheran Church: missionaries arrive at Moreton Bay, 1838 **3**; Kavel and SA settlers, 1838 **11**; founds Hermannsburg Mission, 1877 **6**; schools closed in SA, 1917 **6**

Lux Radio Theatre, 1939 C

Lycett, Joseph, pioneer artist (1774–c. 1825), 1814 **2**, 1824 C

Lyceum Theatre (Syd.), 1892 C, 1905 C, 1906 C, 1928 C; destroyed by fire, 1964 **2**

Lyell, Lottie (Lottie Edith Cox), actress (1890–1925), 1911 C, 1919 C

Lyell, Mount (Tas.), 1886 *; mine disaster, 1912 **10**

Lying-in Hospital (Melb.), 1858 **10**

Lynch, Sir Phillip Reginald, Liberal politician (1933–84), 1966 **11**

Lynd River (Qld), 1845 **5**

Lyne, Sir William John, Premier of NSW (1844–1913), 1844 G, 1899 **9**, 1900 **12**, 1913 G

Lyons, Dame Enid Muriel (*née* Burnell), Liberal politician (1897–1981), 1897 G, 1943 **8**, 1949 **12**, 1981 G

Lyons, Isaac, early teacher, 1809 **1**

Lyons, Joseph Aloysius, United Australia Party Prime Minister (1879–1939), 1879 G, 1932 **11**, 1939 G; Labor Premier of Tas., 1923 **10**; resigns from state parliament, 1928 **6**; elected to federal parliament, 1929 **10**; resigns from cabinet, 1931 **2**; votes against government, 1931 **3**; becomes opposition leader, 1931 **5**; becomes Prime Minister, 1931 **12**; forms coalition cabinet with Earle Page, 1934 **11**; attacked by Menzies, 1938 **10**; reconstructs ministry, 1938 **11**; dies suddenly, 1939 **4**

Lyrebird, 1798 B

Lyster, William Saurin, impresario (1828–80), 1861 C, 1870 C, 1880 C

M

Mabo, Edward Koiki, Aboriginal land rights activist (1936–92), 1992 **6** G

Macalister, Arthur, Premier of Qld (1818–83), 1866 **2 7 8**, 1867 **8**, 1874 **1**, 1876 **6**

Macalister River (Vic.), 1840 **1**

INDEX

Macarthur, Archibald, Presbyterian minister (d. 1847), 1822 **12**

MacArthur, Douglas, US soldier (1880–1964), 1942 **3 4**, 1943 **3**, 1945 **9**

Macarthur, Sir Edward, soldier and Lt-Governor of Vic. (1789–1872), 1790 **6**

Macarthur, Elizabeth (*née* Veale), pioneer settler (1766–1850), 1790 **6**, 1850 G

Macarthur, Hannibal Hawkins, pioneer pastoralist (1788–1861), 1805 **6**, 1822 **8**, 1843 **6**

Macarthur, James, pastoralist and politician (1798–1867), 1809 **3**, 1837 D

Macarthur, John, army officer, pastoralist, and public figure (1767–1834), 1820 *, 1834 G; arrives in Sydney, 1790 **6**; receives grants of land at Parramatta, 1793 **2**, 1794 **4**; appointed Inspector of Public Works, 1793 **2**; resigns, 1796 **2**; challenged by Balmain, 1796 **2**; clashes with Hunter, 1796 **9**; and merinos, 1797 **6**, 1800 **10**, 1805 **6**; fights duel with Paterson, 1801 **9**; goes to England for court martial, 1801 **11**; returns to NSW, 1805 **6**; granted land at Camden, 1805 **6 10**; and address of welcome to Bligh, 1806 **9**; and stills affair, 1807 **3 10**; and *Parramatta* affair, 1807 **6 11 12**; trial of, 1808 **1 2**; appointed "Secretary to the Colony" after Bligh deposed, 1808 **2**; goes to England with Johnston, 1809 **3**; ordered to remain in England, 1811 **6**; returns to NSW, 1817 **9**; appointed to Legislative Council, 1825 **12**; declared insane, 1832 **8**

Macarthur River (NT), 1845 **9**

Macartney, Frederick Thomas Bennett, bibliographer (1887–1980), 1940 D

Macartney-Snape Timothy John, mountaineer, 1984 **10**, 1990 **5**

McAuley, James Phillip, poet (1917–76), 1917 G, 1944 D, 1946 D, 1964 D, 1976 G; portrait of, 1963 C

McBride, William Griffith, medical researcher (1927–), 1961 B

McBrien, James, surveyor and discoverer of gold, 1823 **2**

McCabe, Stanley Joseph, cricketer (1910–68), 1910 G, 1932 E, 1968 G

Maccabiah Games, 1997 **7**

"McCackie Mansion" (radio show), 1947 C

McCallum, Francis ("Capt. Melville"), bushranger (1822–57), 1853 **2**

McCallum, John Neil, actor (1918–), 1918 G

MacCallum, Sir Mungo William, scholar (1854–1942), 1942 G

McClements, Lyn, swimmer (1951–), 1968 E

McCluer, John, explorer, 1791 **7**

McCluer Gulf (PNG), 1791 **7**

McCormack, William, Labor Premier of Qld (1879–1947), 1907 **9**, 1925 **10**, 1929 **5**; and Mungana Mines scandal, 1930 **7**

McCormick, Peter Dodds, composer (1834?–1916), 1878 C

McCrae, Hugh Raymond, poet (1876–1958), 1876 G, 1909 D, 1920 D, 1922 D, 1958 G

McCubbin, Frederick, artist (1855–1917), 1855 G, 1917 G; and Box Hill artists' camp, 1885 C, 1886 C; works, 1889 C, 1890 C, 1896 C, 1906 C

McCulloch, Sir James, Premier of Vic. (1819–93), 1863 **6**, 1864 **11**, 1865 **12**, 1868 **7**, 1870 **4**, 1871 **6**, 1875 **10**; and Tariff Bill, 1866 **1 3**; and Darling grant, 1868 **5**; introduces "gag" motion, 1876 **2**

McCullough, Colleen Margaretta, novelist (1937–), 1937 G, 1977 D

McDermott, Frederick, released from prison, 1952 **1**

McDonald, Bobby, athlete, 1887 E

McDonald, Bruce John, Liberal politician (1935–), 1981 **9**

McDonald, Sir John Gladstone Black, Country Party Premier of Vic. (1898–1977) 1950 **6**

McDonald, Roger, author (1941–), 1979 D

McDonald, William, murderer, 1963 **5**

McDonald Islands, 1947 **12**

Macdonald River (NSW), 1789 **6**

MacDonnell, Sir Richard Graves, Governor of SA (1814–81), 1855 **6**

MacDonnell Range (NT), 1860 **4**

McDowall, Valentine, television pioneer (1881–1957), 1934 B

Mace, Jem, English boxer, 1877 E

Mace, parliamentary, 1891 **10**

McEncroe, Francis Gerald, creator of the Chiko Roll (1909–79), 1951 B

McEwen, Sir John, Country Party Prime Minister (1900–1980), 1900 G, 1934 **9**, 1971 **2**, 1980 G; becomes CP leader, 1958 **3**; becomes Prime Minister, 1967 **12**; portrait of, 1971 C

Macfarlan, Ian, Liberal Premier of Vic., 1945 **10**

Macfaull, Charles, journalist (1800–1846), 1832 *, 1833 **1**

McGill, Linda, swimmer (1945–), 1965 E

MacGillivray, John, naturalist (1821–67), 1852 D

McGinness, Paul J., aviator (1896–1952), 1919 **8**, 1920 **11**

McGirr, James, Labor Premier of NSW (1890–1957), 1947 **2**, 1952 **4**

McGowen, James Sinclair Taylor, Labor Premier of NSW (1855–1922), 1895 **5**, 1910 **10**, 1913 **6**

McGregor, Kenneth B., tennis player (1929–), 1950 E, 1951 E, 1952 E

Macgregor, Sir William, Administrator and Governor (1846–1919), 1888 **9**

McHardy, Gregory Norman, criminal, 1981 **1**

McIlwraith, Sir Thomas, Premier of Qld (1835–1900), 1835 G, 1879 **1**, 1888 **6**,

442

1893 **3 8**, 1900 G; annexes New Guinea, 1883 **4**; and "continuous ministry", 1890 **8**

McInnes, William Beckwith, artist (1889–1939), 1921 C, 1922 C, 1923 C, 1924 C, 1926 C, 1930 C, 1936 C

McIntosh, Hugh Donald, entrepreneur (1876–1942), 1876 G, 1908 E, 1911 C, 1942 G

McIntosh, John Cowie, aviator (1896–1921), 1920 **1**

McIntyre, Ivor Ewing, aviator (1899–1928), 1924 **4**

MacIntyre, John, Phillip's gamekeeper, 1790 **12**

McIntyre, Margaret (*née* Edgeworth David), community worker (1886–1948), 1886 G, 1948 **9**

MacIntyre, River (NSW–Qld), 1827 **5**

McIvor goldfield (Vic.), 1853 **7**

Mack, Edward Carrington, independent MP (1933–), 1990 **3**

McKaeg, John, Baptist minister, 1831 **4**

McKay, A. F., Antarctic explorer, 1909 **1**

McKay, Claude Eric Ferguson, journalist (1878–1972), 1919 **3**

Mackay, Donald, anti-drug campaigner, 1977 **7**, 1986 **4**

Mackay, Donald George, explorer (1870–1958), cycles round Australia, 1900 E

McKay, Heather Pamela (*née* Blundell), squash player (1941–), 1941 G, 1962 E, 1976 E

McKay, Hugh Victor, harvesting machine inventor (1865–1926), 1884 B, 1907 **11**

Mackay, John, explorer (1839–1914), 1860 **3**

Mackay (Qld), 1862 **10**; damaged by cyclones, 1888 **2**, 1898 **2**, 1918 **1**

McKell, Sir William John, Labor Premier of NSW and Governor-General (1891–1985), 1891 G, 1939 **9**, 1985 G; Premier, 1941 **5**; Governor-General, 1947 **3**, 1953 **5**

Mackellar, Isobel Marion Dorothea, poet (1885–1968), 1885 G, 1908 D, 1968 G

McKellar, Michael John Randal, Liberal politician (1938–), 1982 **4**

McKellow & Ramsay, manufacturers, 1906 *

Mackennal, Sir Edgar Bertram, sculptor (1863–1931), 1863 G, 1893 C, 1902 C, 1925 C, 1926 C, 1929 C, 1931 G

McKenzie, Barry (comic-strip and film character), 1963 C

Mackenzie, Kenneth Ivo (Seaforth), poet and novelist (1913–55), 1913 G, 1937 D, 1951 D, 1955 G

Mackenzie, Sir Robert Ramsay, Premier of Qld (1811–73), 1867 **8**, 1868 **11**

Mackenzie, Stuart, sculler (1937–), 1962 E

Mackenzie, Sir William Colin, anatomist (1877–1938), 1924 B

Mackenzie River (Qld), 1845 **1** B

Mackerras, Sir Alan Charles MacLaurin, conductor (1925–), 1925 G

Mackie, Pat, unionist, 1964 **10**, 1965 **1**

McKie, Ronald Cecil Hamlyn, author (1909–91), 1974 D

MacKillop, Mary Helen, nun (1842–1909), 1842 G, 1866 *, 1871 **9**, 1909 G, 1995 **1**

McKinlay, John, explorer (1819–72), 1861 **7 9**, 1862 **4 5 8**, 1865 **9**

Mackintosh, Donald, sporting shooter (1866–1951), 1900 E

McLaren, John (Jack), author (1884–1954), 1926 D

McLarty, Sir Duncan Ross, Liberal Premier of WA, 1947 **4**

Maclay, Nicholas. *See* Mikluho-Maclay, N. N.

McLean, Allan, Premier of Vic. (1840–1911), 1899 **12**, 1904 **8**

Macleay, Alexander, scientist and official (1767–1848), 1843 **2**, 1848 G; Colonial Secretary, 1826 **1**, 1837 **1**; member of Legislative Council, 1825 **12**, 1843 **6 8**

Macleay, Sir William John, scientist and pastoralist (1820–91), 1820 G, 1874 B, 1875 B, 1891 G

Macleay River (NSW), 1818 **9**, 1863 **2**

Maclehose, James, author, 1838 D

McLeod, Donald John, bookmaker, 1906 **7**

Macleod, Euan, artist (1956–), 1999 C

McLeod, Tom, runner, 1851 E

McMahon, Charles, film director (1853–1917), 1907 C, 1908 C

McMahon, Gregan, actor and producer (1874–1941), 1874 G, 1911 C, 1920 C, 1941 G

McMahon, Sir William, Liberal Prime Minister (1908–88), 1908 G, 1988 G; elected to parliament, 1949 **12**; opposed by CP, 1968 **1**; challenges for leadership, 1969 **11**; Prime Minister, 1971 **3**; dismisses Gorton, 1971 **8**; replaced as party leader, 1972 **12**

McMaster, Sir Fergus, airline director (1879–1950), 1920 **11**

McMillan, Angus, explorer (1810–65), 1810 G, 1839 **5**, 1840 **1**, 1841 **2**, 1865 G

Macmillan, Harold, British Prime Minister (1894–1986), 1958 **1**

McNamee, Paul, tennis player (1954–), 1983 E, 1986 E

Maconochie, Alexander, prison reformer (1787–1860), 1837 **5**, 1839 D, 1840 **3**

McPhee, Sir John Cameron, Nationalist Premier of Tas. (1878–1952), 1928 **6**, 1934 **3**

MacPherson, John Alexander, Premier of Vic. (1833–94), 1869 **9**, 1870 **4**

McPherson, Sir William Murray, National Premier of Vic. (1865–1932), 1928 **11**

Macpherson Range (Qld), 1828 **8**

Macquarie, Lachlan, Governor of NSW (1762– 1824), 1824 G; appointed Governor, 1809 **5**; sails to NSW, 1809 **5 12**; takes over, 1810 **1**; and emancipists,

INDEX

INDEX

INDEX

INDEX

Prison boys arrive at Perth, 1842 **8**; outward migration to Chile, 1843 F; Britain resumes assisted migration, 1843 **7**; first assisted migrants to Moreton Bay, 1848 **12**; Lang's schemes, 1849 **1**; outward migration to California, 1849 **1**; Chisholm's scheme, 1849 *; to Port Phillip during gold rushes, 1852 **9** F; assisted migration to NSW resumes, 1906 *; number of arrivals, 1912 F; Empire Settlement Act, 1922 **5**; British settlers for WA, 1923 **2**; Big Brother movement, 1924 **9**; assisted migration from Britain resumes, 1938 **3**, 1947 **3**; refugees from Nazi Germany accepted, 1938 **7 12**; displaced persons from Europe, 1947 **7**; numbers of arrivals, 1948 F, 1949 F, 1955 F, 1959 F, 1970 F; assisted passages restricted to refugees, 1981 **5**; numbers of Asians increase, 1984 F. *See also* "Boat people"; Immigration restriction; Pacific Islanders; Refugees; *and entries under specific nationalities*

Migration Act, 1959 **6**

Mikluho-Maclay (Maklai), Nikolai Nikolaievich, scientist and explorer (1846–88), 1846 G, 1871 **9**, 1888 G

Milat, Ivan Robert, charged with backpacker murders, 1994 **5**

Mildura (Vic.), 1886 **10**, 1934 **8**

Mildura, HMS, 1891 **9**

Mildura Cultivator (newspaper), 1888 **5**

Miles, Beatrice, eccentric (1902–73), 1973 G

Miles, John Campbell, prospector (1883–1965), 1923 **2**

Miles Franklin Award: first awarded, 1957 D (*see under heading D each subsequent year for winners*): no award made, 1973 D, 1983 D, 1988 D

Military Board, 1905 **1**

Military colleges: Royal Military College (Duntroon), 1833 A, 1911 **6**, 1931 **2**; Australian Defence Force Academy, 1986 **1**

Military forces. *See also* Defence
British in Australia: marines with First Fleet, 1788 F; NSW Corps, 1790 **6**, 1792 **2**, 1796 **6**, 1809 **5**, 1810 **5** (*see also separate entry*); Macquarie's regiment (73rd) replaces NSW Corps, 1809 **5 8**; other imperial regiments, 1814 **2**, 1817 **7 8**, 1823 **8**; and Maori War, 1860 **4**; withdrawn from Australia, 1870 **8**
colonial: Loyal Associations, 1800 **9**, 1801 **7**, 1803 **12**; SA and Vic. raise volunteer forces, 1854 *; volunteer corps formed in Qld, 1860 **2**; and second Taranaki War, 1863 **8**; NSW raises permanent force, 1871 **5**; and Sudan War, 1885 **2 3 6**; and Boer War, 1899 **7 10**, 1900 **2 4 8**, 1901 **6**

Commonwealth: first battalion goes to South Africa, 1902 **2**; Defence Act provides for conscription, 1904 **3**; Military Board set up, 1905 **1**; Kitchener advises on, 1909 **12**, 1910 **2**; compulsory training introduced, 1911 **1**; force offered to Imperial government, 1914 **8**
Australian Imperial Force (1st AIF): recruiting begins, 1914 **8**; first troops leave from Albany, 1914 **11**; Australian and New Zealand Army Corps formed, 1914 **12**; mutiny and riot in Sydney, 1916 **2**; enlistments decline, 1916 **7** (*See also* Conscription); Australian Corps formed, 1918 **1**; Monash takes command, 1918 **5**; cricket team, 1919 E. *See also* World War I
peacetime training, 1921 **5**; replaced by voluntary system, 1929 **11**; Defence Act amended to allow conscripts to be sent to PNG, 1939 **7**
Australian Imperial Force (2nd AIF): 6th Division formed, 1939 **9**; sails for Middle East, 1940 **1**; troops recalled from Middle East, 1942 **2**, 1943 **2**; demobilization begins, 1945 **10**. *See also* World War II
militia in World War II: compulsory service reintroduced, 1939 **10**; call-up age extended, 1940 **7 12**, 1941 **12**; training period doubled, 1941 **2**; called up for full-time duty, 1941 **7 12**
Australian Women's Army Service formed, 1941 **8**
Australian Regular Army formed, 1947 **11**
Citizen Military Forces: re-established, 1948 **7**; liable for service anywhere, 1950 **9**
Royal Australian Regiment, 1950 **9**, 1965 **5**. *See also* Korean War; Vietnam War
National Service: introduced, 1951 **3**; ballot system for, 1957 **5**; scheme suspended, 1959 **11**, 1960 **6**; reintroduced with birthday lottery, 1964 **11**, 1965 **3**; conscripts sent to Vietnam, 1966 **3**; penalties for evading, increased, 1968 **5**; defiance of, 1970 **6**; ends, 1972 **12**
troops sent to Vietnam, 1962 **5 8**, 1965 **5**. *See also* Vietnam War
engineers sent to Sabah, 1964 **5**
and Malaysian Confrontation, 1964 **10**
women begin training alongside men, 1985 F
forces sent to Persian Gulf, 1990 **8**, 1998 **2**
peace-keeping force sent to Bougainville, 1997 **11**
peace-keeping force sent to East Timor, 1999 **9**

Military Hospital (Observatory Hill, Syd.), 1815 A

INDEX

Milk, free, for schoolchildren, 1950 F
Milk bar, first, 1930 F
Milking machines, 1892 B
Millard, W. J., runner, 1878 E
Miller, Alexander McPhee, author (1936–),
  1992 D
Miller, Sir Denison Samuel King, banker
  (1860–1923), 1912 **6**
Miller, Edmund Morris, bibliographer
  (1881–1964), 1940 D
Miller, George, film director (1945–),
  1979 C
Miller, Harry Maurice, entrepreneur
  (1934–), 1979 **2**
Miller, Henry, soldier, 1824 **9**
Miller, James William, murderer, 1979 **5**
Miller, John. *See* Lane, William
Miller, Dame Mabel Flora *née* Goodhart,
  Liberal politician (1906–78), 1955 **2**
Miller, William, athlete (1846–1939), 1883 E
Milliner, Bertie Richard, Labor politician,
  (1911–75), 1975 **6**
Million Wild Acres, A (E. Rolls), 1981 D
Millionaires, number in Australia, 1986 F
Mills, Bernard Yarnton, scientist (1920–),
  1953 B
Mills, Beryl Lucy, first "Miss Australia"
  (1907–77), 1926 **6**
Mills, Martin. *See* Boyd, Martin à Beckett
Mills Cross radio-telescope, 1953 B, 1965 B
Milner, Ralph, overlander, 1872 **3**
Milparinka (NSW), 1845 **1**
Minchin, William, Superintendent of Police
  (1774?–1821), 1820 **4**
Mineral boom, 1968 **5**, 1969 **9**, 1970 **1**
Mineral sands, 1976 F
Mineral Securities (Aust.) Ltd, 1971 **2**
Miner's Right, The (R. Boldrewood), 1890 D
Minerva (ship), 1800 **1**
Minerva Theatre (Syd.), 1939 C
Mini-golf, 1930 C
Minimum wage introduced, 1966 **7**
Mining disasters
  NSW
    Appin, 1979 **7**
    Bellbird, 1923 **9**
    Broken Hill, 1895 **7**
    Bulli, 1887 **3**, 1965 **11**
    Mount Kembla, 1902 **7**
    Newcastle, 1889 **6**, 1896 **12**, 1898 **3**
    Redhead, 1926 **1**
    Wyee, 1966 **10**
  Qld
    Box Flat, 1972 **7**
    Charters Towers, 1904 **10**
    Collinsville, 1954 **10**
    Mt Morgan, 1908 **9**
    Mt Mulligan, 1921 **9**
    Moura, 1975 **9**, 1986 **7**, 1994 **8**
  Vic.
    Creswick, 1882 **12**
    Wonthaggi, 1937 **2**

  Tas.
    North Lyell, 1912 **10**
  WA
    Agnew, 1977 **4**
    Bonnievale, 1907 **1**
    East Coolgardie, 1904 **5**
    Kalgoorlie, 1921 **12**
Miniskirts, 1966 F
Minogue, Kylie Anne, actress and singer
  (1968–), 1968 G, 1989 C
Minorca (convict transport), 1801 **12**
Minstrel (convict transport), 1812 **10**
Mint building (Syd.), 1811 A; as branch of
  Royal Mint, 1855 **5**; Infirmary and
  Dispensary, 1845 **7**
Minton, Yvonne Fay, singer (1938–), 1938 G
Mints: Sydney, 1855 **5**, 1927 **1**; Melbourne,
  1872 **6**, Perth, 1899 **6**; Royal Australian
  (Canb.), 1963 A, 1965 **2**
Miracle of Mullion Hill, The (D. Campbell),
  1956 D
Mirnyi (Russian ship), 1820 **4 5 9**
"Miss Australia" competition, 1926 **6**
Missionaries: Rowland Hassall and others
  from LMS arrive in Sydney, 1798 **5**;
  Marsden in NZ, 1814 **11**, 1815 **3**; Spanish
  at New Norcia, 1846 **2**, 1847 A; Lutherans
  at Hermannsburg, 1877 **6**; Chalmers killed
  at Goaribari, 1901 **4**
Missouri (US ship), 1801 **5**
Missouri, USS, 1945 **9**
Mitchell, David Scott, bibliophile
  (1836–1907), 1836 G, 1898 **10**, 1907 G
Mitchell, Helen Porter. *See* Melba, Dame
  Nellie
Mitchell, Sir James, Premier of WA
  (1866–1951), 1919 **5**, 1921 **3**, 1930 **4**
Mitchell, Dame Roma Flinders, judge
  (1913–2000), 1962 F, 1965 **9**, 1991 **2**
Mitchell, Sir Thomas Livingstone, explorer
  and Surveyor-General of NSW
  (1792–1855), 1792 G, 1830 B, 1838 D,
  1843 C, 1848 D, 1855 G; arrives in
  Sydney, 1827 **9**; becomes Surveyor-
  General, 1828 **5**; explores Bogan and
  Darling rivers, 1835 **3 5 7**; "Australia
  Felix" expedition, 1836 **3 6 7 8 9**; last
  expedition, 1845 **11**, 1846 **6 9**, 1847 **8**;
  and Philosophical Society, 1850 B; fights
  duel, 1851 **9**
Mitchell Library (Syd.), 1898 **10**, 1906 A,
  1910 **3**. *See also* State Library of New
  South Wales
Mitchell River (Qld), 1845 **6**
Mitchell River (Vic.), 1840 **1**
Mitsubishi Australia Ltd, 1980 **5**
Mittagong (NSW), iron smelting at, 1848 *
MLC Centre (Syd.), 1971 A
"Mo". *See* Rene, Roy
Mobile phones, 1987 B
Mockridge, Caroline, oldest Australian
  (1874–1987), 1987 **11**

450

INDEX

Murdoch, Keith Rupert, media proprietor (1931–), 1931 G, 1996 C

Murdoch, Sir Walter Logie Forbes, essayist and teacher (1874–1970), 1874 G, 1970 G

Murdoch, William Lloyd, cricketer (1854–1911), 1882 E, 1884 E

Murdoch University (Perth), 1973 **7**

Muriel's Wedding (film), 1994 C

Murphy, Arthur William, aviator (1891–1963), 1919 **11**

Murphy, Lionel Keith, Labor politician and judge (1922–86), 1922 G, 1986 G; elected to Senate, 1961 **12**; raids ASIO, 1973 **3**; leaves parliament for High Court, 1975 **2**; and *"Age* tapes", 1984 **2 3 10 12**; on trial, 1985 **4**, 1986 **4**; dies, 1986 **10**

Murray, ("Gelignite") Jack, rally driver (1910–), 1954 E

Murray, John, Liberal Premier of Vic. (1851–1916), 1909 **1**, 1912 **5**

Murray, John, naval officer (*c.* 1775–?), 1800 **11**, 1801 **11**, 1802 **7**; surveys Westernport, 1801 **12**; discovers and claims Port Phillip, 1802 **1 3**; examines King Is., 1802 **1**

Murray, Sir John Hubert Plunkett, administrator (1861–1940), 1861 G, 1904 **8**, 1907 **4**, 1940 G

Murray, Leslie Allan, poet (1938–), 1938 G, 1980 D, 1984 D, 1999 D

Murray, Robert William Felton Lathrup, journalist (1777–1850), 1828 **2**

Murray Bridge (SA), 1873 A, 1879 **3**

Murray Islands (Qld), 1836 **6**, 1992 **6**

Murray River (NSW–SA): discovered, 1824 **11**; Sturt on, 1830 **1 2**; navigated by steamer, 1853 **8**, 1854 **10**; floods, 1889 *, 1890 *; 1906 **7**; River Murray Agreement, 1915 **11**, 1917 **1**

Murray's Austral-Asiatic Review (magazine), 1828 **2**

Murrell, James, castaway, 1846 **3**, 1863 **1**

Murrumbidgee Irrigation Area, 1906 **12**, 1910 **12**, 1912 **7**

Murrumbidgee River (NSW): discovered, 1821 **4**; Sturt on, 1829 **11**, 1830 **1 3 4**; floods, 1852 **6**, 1853 **7**, 1891 **1 6**; riverboats on, 1857 **9**, 1858 **8**

Murwillumbah (NSW), fire at, 1907 **9**

Museums. *See* Art galleries and museums

Musgrave, Sir Anthony, Governor of SA and Qld (1828–88), 1873 **6**, 1883 **11**

Musgrave Ranges (NT), 1873 **7**

Musgrove, George, theatrical manager (1854–1916), 1854 G, 1880 C, 1882 C, 1916 G

Music college, Australia's first, 1883 C

Musica Viva, 1945 C

Musquito, Aboriginal guerrilla, 1823 **11**, 1824 **8**, 1825 **2**

Muswellbrook (NSW), 1833 **10**

Mutiny of the Bounty, The (silent film), 1916 C

MX missile tests, 1985 **2**

My Australian Girlhood (R. C. Praed), 1902 D

My Brilliant Career (M. Franklin). 1901 D; film of, 1979 C

My Brother Jack (G. Johnston), 1964 D

My Career Goes Bung (M. Franklin), 1946 D

"My Country" (D. Mackellar), 1908 D

My Crowded Solitude (J. McLaren), 1926 D

My Love Must Wait (E. Hill), 1941 D

Myall Creek massacre, 1838 **6 11**

Myer, Sidney (Simcha Baevski), businessman and retailer (1878–1934), 1878 G, 1911 **6**, 1934 G

Myer Emporium Ltd: merges with Farmer & Co., 1961 **1**; taken over by Coles, 1985 **8**

Myer Music Bowl (Melb.), 1959 C

Mynas: introduced, 1863 F

Mystery of a Hansom Cab (F. Hume), 1886 D; film of, 1925 C

Myxomatosis, 1950 B

N

Nabalco (North Australian Bauxite and Alumina Co.), 1971 **4**

Nabarlek (NT), 1970 **9**

NACC. *See* National Aboriginal Consultative Committee

Naked Island, The (R. Braddon), 1952 D

Namatjira, Albert (Elea), artist (1902–59), 1902 G, 1934 C, 1959 G; first exhibitions, 1938 C, 1945 C; granted citizenship rights, 1957 F; gaoled, 1958 **10**

Namoi River (NSW), 1827 **5**

Nancy, HMS, 1813 **2**

Naracoorte (SA), 1867 E, 1877 **1**

Narrative of an Expedition into Central Australia (C. Sturt), 1849 D

Narrative of an Expedition to Botany Bay (W. Tench), 1789 D

Narrative of a Survey of the Intertropical and Western Coasts of Australia (P. P. King), 1826 D

Narrative of a Voyage . . . in H.M. Vessel the Lady Nelson (J. Grant), 1803 D

Narrative of the Surveying Voyage of H.M.S. Fly (J. B. Jukes), 1847 D

Narrative of the Voyage of H.M.S. Rattlesnake (J. MacGillivray), 1852 D

Narre Warren (Vic.), 1842 **2**

Narrogin (WA), 1897 **6**

Narrows Bridge (Perth), 1959 A

Nash, James, discoverer of Gympie goldfield (1834–1913), 1867 **10**

Nashville. *See* Gympie

INDEX

Nathan, Isaac, musician (1790–1864), 1790 G, 1841 C, 1844 C, 1864 G; opera, 1847 C

Nation (magazine, Syd.), 1958 **9**, 1972 **7**

Nation Is Built, A (film), 1937 C

Nation Review (newspaper, Melb.), 1972 **7**, 1979 **10**

National Aboriginal Conference, 1977 **11**

National Aboriginal Consultative Committee, 1973 **11**, 1977 **11**

National anthem/song: competition for, 1973 C; "God Save the Queen" reinstated, 1976 **1**; national poll to choose, 1977 **5**; "Advance Australia Fair" proclaimed, 1984 **4**

National Australasian Convention, 1891 **3**

National Australia Bank, 1981 **10**

National Bank of Australasia, 1858 **10**, 1893 **4**, 1981 **10**

National Black Theatre, 1972 C

National Capital Development Commission, 1957 A

National Civic Council, 1957 **12**

National colours, proclaimed, 1984 **4**

National Council of Women of Australia, 1896 *

National Country Party of Australia, 1974 **3**, 1982 **10**, 1987 **4**. *See also* Australian Country Party; National Party of Australia

National Crime Authority, 1984 **7**, 1994 **3**

National debt, 1901 F

National Economic Summit, 1983 **4**

National Film and Sound Archives, 1984 C

National Fitness Movement, 1939 *

National Food Authority, 1991 B

National Front of Australia, 1978 **6**

National Gallery of Victoria (Melb.), 1864 C, 1869 **12**, 1904 C; and Sunday opening, 1883 C, 1904 F; new building, 1962 A, 1968 C

National Health and Medical Research Council, 1936 B

National Heart Foundation, 1959 **2**

National Institute of Dramatic Art, 1958 C

National Insurance scheme, 1939 **3**

National Labour Party, 1916 **11**, 1917 **2**

National Library of Australia (Canb.), 1909 D, 1960 **11**, 1968 A

National Literature Board of Review, 1968 D

National Museum (Melb.), 1854 B, 1869 **12**, 1899 B

National Mutual Life Association of Australasia, 1869 **8**

National Parks and Wildlife Service (NSW), 1967 F

National Party of Australia, 1982 **10**, 1984 **1**. *See also* Country Party of Australia; National Country Party of Australia; Nationalist Party

National Party of Australia (Qld), 1974 **4**; coalition with Liberal Party ends, 1983 **8**; governs in its own right, 1983 **10**

National Roads and Motorists' Association (NRMA), 1923 **12**

National Rugby League (NRL), 1997 E

National Safety Council, 1989 **3**

National Security Act, 1939 **9**, 1940 **6**, 1941 **1**, 1946 **12**

National Service. *See* Military forces

National Shipwreck Relief Society of NSW, 1877 **7**

National Standards Laboratory, 1938 B

National Tennis Centre (Melb.), 1988 E

National Theatre Movement, 1935 C

National Times (newspaper, Syd.), 1971 **2**, 1988 **3**

National Trust of Australia, 1945 F, 1965 F; NSW headquarters, 1815 A

National Welfare Scheme, 1943 **3**

Nationalist Party, 1917 **2 5**; becomes UAP, 1931 **5**

Nationalization: of airlines, attempted, 1945 **7**; of banking, attempted, 1947 **8 10**, 1948 **8**; of Qantas, 1947 **6**; of monopolies, referendums on, 1911 **4**, 1913 **5**

Native title, 1992 **6**, 1993 **12**, 1996 **10 11 12**, 1998 **7**

Native Tribes of Central Australia (Spencer and Gillen), 1899 B

Native Tribes of the Northern Territory, The (W. B. Spencer), 1914 B

Natural history societies, 1837 B, 1838 B

Naturaliste, Le (French ship), 1801 **5**, 1802 **3 4 9 11 12**

Naturalization. *See* Citizenship

Nauru: discovered, 1798 **11**; annexed by Germany, 1888 **10**; phosphate mining begins, 1906 *; Australian forces occupy, 1914 **11**; mandated to Australia, 1920 **12**; in World War II, 1940 **12**; UN Trustee-ship, 1947 **11**; becomes independent, 1968 **1**

Nautilus (ship), 1798 **5 10 12**, 1799 **5**

Naval Board, 1905 **1**, 1911 **3**

Naval defence: Australian station established, 1859 **3**; colonies allowed to maintain own naval forces, 1865 *; Auxiliary Naval Squadron formed, 1887 **12**, 1891 **9**; state forces transferred to Commonwealth, 1901 **3**; Naval Agreement negotiated with UK, 1902 **6**; Creswell appointed director of Commonwealth forces, 1904 **3**; warships ordered, 1909 **2 12**; independent fleet unit created, 1909 **7**; Naval Defence Act passed, 1910 **11**; RN establishments transferred to Commonwealth, 1913 **7**; Flinders Naval Base opened, 1920 **9**; Australia favours Singapore Naval Base, 1923 **10**

Navies, colonial: NSW, 1855 **4**, 1882 **1**; Vic., 1856 **5**, 1871 **4**; SA, 1884 **9**; Qld, 1885 **3**; transferred to Commonwealth, 1901 **3**

Navigation Act (Comm.), 1925 **7**

454

INDEX

INDEX

INDEX

Newman, Kevin Eugene, Liberal politician (1933–99), 1975 **6**
Newman, Mount (WA), 1969 **4**
News (newspaper, Adel.), 1923 **7**, 1992 **3**
News Limited, 1987 **2**
News Radio, 1994 **8**
Newsfront (film), 1978 C
Newspapers: Australia's first, 1803 **3** (*see also separate entry: Sydney Gazette*); first with front-page news, 1910 **7**; suppressed by censor, 1940 **5**, 1944 **4**; strikes at, 1944 **10**; Press Council established, 1976 **7**; last afternoon newspaper closes, 1992 **3**
Newton-John, Olivia, singer (1948–), 1981 C
Newtown (Syd.), battle over evictions at, 1931 **6**
Nicholas, George Richard Rich, chemist (1884–1960), makes aspirin, 1915 B
Nicholls, Sir Douglas Ralph, Governor of SA (1906–88), 1976 **12**, 1988 G
Nicholls, Jack ("Puttynose"), found dead, 1981 **6**
Nichols, Isaac, Sydney's first postmaster (1770–1819), 1791 **10**, 1799 **3 4**, 1809 **4**, 1819 G
Nicholson, Sir Charles, politician (1808–1903), 1857 B
Nicholson, William, Premier of Vic. (1816–65), 1855 **12**, 1859 **10**, 1860 **11**
Nicholson Land Act (Vic.), 1860 **9**
Nicholson River (NT–Qld), 1845 **8**
Nicholson River (Vic.), 1840 **1**
Nickel, 1966 **1**, 1969 **9**, 1970 **1**
Nicklin, Sir George Francis Reuben, Country Party Premier of Qld (1895–1978), 1957 **8**, 1960 **5**, 1963 **6**, 1966 **5**; retires, 1968 **1**
Nickol Bay (WA), 1861 **5** *
Nicolle, Eugene Dominique, refrigeration pioneer (1823–1909), 1861 B
Nielsen, Juanita Joan, publisher (1937–75?), 1975 **7**
Niemeyer, Sir Otto, British banker, 1930 **8**
Night on Bald Mountain (play), 1964 C
Night parrot, 1990 B
Niland, D'Arcy Francis, author (1917–67), 1955 D
Nile (convict transport), 1801 **12**
Nimmo Committee, 1969 **3**
Nimrod Theatre (Syd.), 1970 C
Nineteen Counties (NSW), proclaimed, 1829 **10**
1915 (R. McDonald), 1979 D
Nitschke, Philip, medical practitioner, 1996 **9**
Nobel Prize winners: W. H. and W. L. Bragg, 1915 B; Howard Florey, 1945 B; Sir Macfarlane Burnet, 1960 B; Sir John Eccles, 1963 B; Patrick White, 1973 D; John Cornforth, 1975 B; Peter Doherty, 1996 B
Noffs, Theodore Delwin (Ted), clergyman

(1926–95), 1995 G; opens Wayside Chapel, 1964 **4**
Nolan, Sir Sidney Robert, artist (1917–92), 1917 G, 1939 C, 1946 C, 1948 C, 1964 C, 1992 G
Nomad (aircraft), 1972 B
Non-Communist Labor Party, 1940 **4 9**, 1941 **3**
Noonan, Christopher, film writer and director (1952–), 1995 C
Norfolk (sloop), 1798 **6**; Bass and Flinders explore in, 1798 **10 11 12**, 1799 **1**; Flinders explores in, 1799 **7 8**
Norfolk Bay (Tas.), 1836 **3**
Norfolk Is.: settlement established, 1788 **2 3 10**; uprisings on, 1789 **1**, 1826 **9**, 1834 **1**, 1842 **6**, 1846 **7**; *Sirius* wrecked on, 1790 **3**; population, 1790 F; flax dressing on, 1793 **4**; plays performed on, 1793 C, 1794 **1**; population withdrawn, 1804 **9**, 1805 **11**, 1814 **2**; reopened as penal settlement, 1825 **6**; annexed to Van Diemen's Land, 1844 **9**; settled by Pitcairn Islanders, 1856 **6**; transferred to NSW, 1897 **1**; transferred to Commonwealth, 1913 **12**; given some self-government, 1979 **5**
Lt-governors and commandants: P. G. King, 1788 **2**, 1791 **10**; Robert Ross, 1790 **3**; John Townson, 1796 **10,** 1799 **11;** Joseph Foveaux, 1800 **6**; John Piper, 1804 **9**; T. A. Crane, 1810 **4**; Alexander Maconochie, 1840 **3**; Joseph Childs, 1844 **2**; John Price, 1846 **8**
Norm and Ahmed (play), 1968 C
Norman, Decima, athlete (1914–), 1938 E
Norman, Gregory John, golfer (1955–), 1955 G, 1986 E
Norman, Sir Henry Wylie, Governor of Qld (1826–1904), 1889 **5**
Normanby, Marquis of (George Augustus Constantine Phipps), Governor of Qld and Vic. (1819–90), 1871 **8**, 1879 **4**
Normanby River (Qld), 1872 **6**
North Australia, 1926 **6**
North Australian (newspaper, Darwin) 1873 **11**
North-West Cape (WA), US naval communications station, 1962 **5**, 1963 **5**, 1967 **9**
North-West Shelf (WA), 1971 B, 1984 **8**
Northam, Sir William Herbert, yachtsman (1905–88), 1964 E
Northcote, Henry Stafford, 1st Baron, Governor-General (1846–1911), 1904 **1**
Northcott, Sir John, soldier and Governor of NSW (1890–1966), commands BCOF, 1946 **2**
Northern Land Council, 1982 **7**
Northern Territory: annexed to SA, 1863 **7**; land sales, 1863 **11**, 1864 **3**; quarantined because of tick fever, 1897 F; taken over by Commonwealth, 1911 **1**; Gilruth

INDEX

INDEX

O'Farrell, Henry James, assassin (1833–68),
1868 **3**

Officer, Sir Frank Keith, diplomat
(1889–1969), 1937 **5**

*Official History of Australia in the War of
1914–1918, The* (ed. C. E. W. Bean),
1921 D

*Official Year Book of the Commonwealth of
Australia*, first issued, 1908 D

O'Flynn, Jeremiah Francis, Prefect Apostolic
of New Holland (1788–1831), 1817 **11**,
1818 **5**

Ogilvie, Albert George, Labor Premier of
Tas. (1890–1939), 1934 **6**, 1939 **6**

Ogilvie, William Henry, poet (1869–1963),
1869 G, 1898 D, 1963 G

O'Grady, John Patrick (pseud. Nino Culotta),
author (1907–81), 1957 D

O'Hagan, John Francis, song-writer
(1898–1987), 1922 C

O'Harris, Pixie (*née* Rhona Olive Harris),
artist (1903–91), 1903 G

Oil exploration, discovery, and production:
traces found at Lakes Entrance, 1924 **7**;
WAPET strike at Rough Range, 1953 **11**;
refinery at Kwinana, 1955 **2**; first
commercial oilfield (Moonie), 1961 **12**,
1964 **4**; offshore wells in Bass Strait,
1964 **12**, 1965 **2**, 1967 **5**; commercial
oilfield on Barrow Is., 1966 **5**; oil piped
from Bass Strait, 1969 **10**; discovered in
Cooper Basin, 1980 B. *See also* Gas,
natural

O'Keefe, John Michael, singer (1935–78),
1935 G, 1978 G

Old Bush Songs, The (A. B. Paterson, ed.),
1905 D

Old Days Old Ways (M. Gilmore), 1934 D

Old Government House (Parramatta),
1799 A, 1816 A

Old Melbourne Memories (R. Boldrewood),
1884 D

Old Tote Theatre (Syd.), 1963 C

Oldest Australian, 1987 **11**

Oldfield, William Albert Stanley, cricketer
(1894–1976), 1894 G, 1976 G

Olga, Mount (NT), 1958 F

Oliphant, Sir Mark (Marcus Laurence
Elwin), scientist and Governor of SA
(1901–), 1901 G

Olivier, Sir Laurence, British actor, 1948 C

O'Loghlen, Sir Bryan, Premier of Vic.
(1828–1905), 1881 **7**, 1883 **1**

Olsen, John, artist (1928–), 1928 G,
1961 C, 1968 C, 1973 C

Olsen, John Wayne, Liberal Premier of SA
(1945–), 1996 **11**, 1997 **10**

Olympic Games: first Australian
representative at, 1896 D; London,
1908 E; Stockholm, 1912 E; Amsterdam,
1928 E; Los Angeles, 1932 E; London,
1948 E; Helsinki, 1952 E; Melbourne,

1956 E; Rome, 1960 E; Tokyo, 1964 E;
Mexico, 1968 E; Munich, 1972 E;
Moscow, 1980 **5** E; Los Angeles, 1984 E;
Seoul, 1988 E; Barcelona, 1992 E;
Atlanta, 1996 E; Sydney, 1993 **9**, 1999 **1 2**

Olympic Theatre (Melb.), 1855 C

O'Malley, King, politician (1858?–1953),
1858 G, 1896 **4**, 1913 A, 1953 G

Ombudsman: state, 1972 **4**; Commonwealth,
1977 **7**; first female, 1985 **4**

O'Meally, John, bushranger, 1863 **10 11**

Omega navigational station (Vic.), 1982 B

Omeo (Vic.), 1839 **5**

On Our Selection (S. Rudd), 1899 D; stage
adaptation, 1912 C; films of, 1920 C,
1932 C

On the Beach (N. Shute), 1957 D; film of,
1959 C

On the Track (H. Lawson), 1900 D

On the Wool Track (C. E. W. Bean), 1910 D

One Day of the Year, The (play), 1961 C

One Nation Party, 1997 **4**, 1998 **6 10**

O'Neill, Eugene Patrick, union leader
(1874–1953), 1923 **3**

O'Neill, Susan, swimmer (1973–), 1996 E,
1998 E

Onkaparinga (SA) picnic race carnival,
1876 E

Onslow (WA), luggers wrecked at, 1892 **12**,
1909 **4**, 1995 **2**

Oodgeroo Noonuccal (Kath Walker), poet
and Aboriginal activist (1920–93), 1964 D,
1993 G

Oodnadatta (SA), 1919 **10**

Opals, 1872 **12**, 1889 *, 1903 **3**, 1915 **2**,
1989 *

Opas, David Louis, judge (1936–80), 1980 **6**

Open Learning (TV university), 1992 **3**

Opera: first composed in Australia, 1847 C;
Lyster's companies, 1861 C, 1870 C;
Cagli and Pompei company, 1871 C;
Melba–Williamson company, 1911 C;
Quinlan's company, 1912 C; National
Theatre Movement begun, 1935 C; NSW
National Opera Co. presents first season,
1951 C; Elizabethan Theatre Trust Opera
Co., 1956 C, 1969 C;
Sutherland–Williamson company tours,
1965 C; Australian Opera founded,
1969 C; Opera in the Park (Syd.) first
held, 1982 C

Operative Stonemasons' Society, 1853 **5**

Ophir (NSW), 1851 **4 5**

Opium, 1897 F

Opperman, Sir Hubert Ferdinand, cyclist and
politician (1904–96), 1904 G, 1924 E,
1928 E, 1931 E

Optus telecommunications network, 1992 B

Orange (NSW), 1846 **11**, 1946 **7**; railway
reaches, 1877 **4**

Orban, Desiderius, artist (1884–1986),
1884 G, 1986 G

INDEX

Orbital engine, 1970 B
Orbost (Vic.), 1885 **4**
Orchard, William Arundel, musician (1867–1961), 1903 C, 1908 C, 1923 C
Orchestras: Marshall-Hall's, in Melbourne, 1892 C; Melbourne Symphony, 1906 C; Sampson's, in Brisbane, 1907 C; Sydney Symphony, 1908 C, 1915 C, 1922 C, 1923 C; Hobart Symphony, 1923 C; ABC sets up, 1936 C; Queensland Symphony, 1947 C; Tasmanian Symphony, 1948 C; Melbourne Symphony, 1949 C; Adelaide Symphony, 1949 C; West Australian Symphony, 1950 C; AETT forms, 1967 C; National Training, 1967 C; Australian Chamber, 1976 C
Ord, Sir Harry St George, Governor of WA (1819–85), 1877 **11**
Ord river (WA), 1879 **2**, 1883 **5**; irrigation scheme, 1963 **7**, 1972 **6**
Ordell, Talone (William Odell Raymond Buntine), film maker (1880?–1948), 1927 C
Order of Australia, first awarded, 1975 **6**
O'Reilly, Alfonso Bernard, bushman (1903–75), 1937 **2**
O'Reilly, John Boyle, Irish revolutionary (1844–90), 1868 **1**, 1869 **2**, 1879 D, 1887 D, 1890 G
Organ, church, first in Australia, 1825 C
Organization for Economic Co-operation and Development, 1971 **6**
Oriental Banking Corporation, 1884 **5**
Orion (R. H. Horne), 1843 D
Ormiston (Qld), 1863 B
Ormond, Francis, philanthropist (1829–89), 1887 C
Ormsby, Lyster, deviser of surf reel, 1906 B
Orr, Sydney Sparkes, philosophy professor (1914–66), 1956 **3**
Orr, William, revue producer, 1954 C
Orton, Arthur, impostor (1834–98), 1871 **5**, 1873 **4**
Osburn, Lucy, pioneer nurse (1835–91), 1868 **3**
Oscar and Lucinda (P. Carey), 1988 D
O'Shanassy, Sir John, Premier of Vic. (1818–83), 1857 **3 4**, 1858 **3**, 1859 **10**, 1861 **11**
O'Shane, Patricia June, lawyer (1941–), 1976 F, 1981 F, 1986 **7**
O'Shea, Clarence Lyell, union leader, (1905?–88), 1969 **5**
OTC. *See* Overseas Telecommunications Commission
Ottawa Agreement, 1932 **7 11**
Otter (US ship), 1796 **2**
Otway, Cape (Vic.), 1800 **12**
Otway Range (Vic.), bushfires in, 1898 **1**
Our Antipodes (G. C. Mundy), 1852 D
Our Friends the Hayseeds (film), 1917 C
Outbreak of Love (M. Boyd), 1957 D
Ovens, John, soldier and explorer (1788–1825), 1823 **5**

Ovens River (Vic.), 1824 **11**
Over the Sliprails (H. Lawson), 1900 D
Overland (magazine), 1954 D
Overland Telegraph Line, 1870 **6 9**, 1871 **3**, 1872 **8**
Overlanders, The (film), 1946 C
Overlanding: Gardiner and Hawdon to Port Phillip, 1836 **10**; Bonney with first sheep, 1837 **3**; Hawdon and Bonney to Adelaide, 1838 **4**; Eyre to Adelaide, 1838 **7**; Sturt to Adelaide, 1838 **8**; Leslie to Darling Downs, 1840 **3**; Redford from Qld to Adelaide, 1870 **3**; Milner to NT, 1872 **3**; Duracks to Kimberleys, 1883 **5**
Overseas Telecommunications Commission 1946 **8**; opens first satellite station, 1966 B
Owen, Earl Ronald, microsurgeon (1933–), 1968 B
Owen, Evelyn Ernest, inventor (1915–49), 1941 B
Owen gun, 1941 B
Oxley, John Joseph William Molesworth, naval officer, surveyor, and explorer (1785?–1828), 1802 **10**, 1808 **11**, 1812 **10**, 1816 **12**, 1820 D, 1828 G; appointed NSW Surveyor-General, 1812 **1**; explores west of Bathurst, 1817 **4 7 8**; and journey to Port Macquarie, 1818 **5 7 8 9**; examines north coast, 1823 **10 11 12**; founds settlement at Moreton Bay, 1824 **9**
Oxley Memorial Library (Bris.), 1926 *
Oyster Bank (Newcastle), wrecks on, 1805 **3**, 1806 **4**, 1816 **1**, 1866 **7**
Oyster Bay (Tas.), 1789 **7**; Aboriginal tribe, 1832 **1**
Oyster Cove (Tas.), 1847 **10**, 1995 **10**
Oz (magazine, Syd.), 1963 **4**; found obscene, 1964 **9**; ceases publication in Australia, 1969 **10**
Oz Lotto, 1994 **2**
Ozone layer, 1987 F, 1988 F, 1998 F

P

Pacific Islanders: society for protection of, 1813 **12**; Ben Boyd employs, 1847 **4**; indentured to Robert Towns, 1863 **8**; legislation prohibits indenture of, 1885 **11**; importation ends, 1890 **12**; prohibition on importation removed, 1892 **4**; Commonwealth legislation ends importation, 1901 **12**; recruiting ceases, 1904 **3**
Pacific Islanders' Act, 1885 **11**
Packer, Sir Douglas Frank Hewson, media proprietor (1906–74), 1906 G, 1974 G; and Sydney Newspapers Ltd, 1932 **11**, 1933 **6**; yachts, 1967 E, 1970 E

INDEX

Parramatta (NSW): site of, discovered, 1788 **4**; farming at, 1789 **11** F, 1791 **2**; town laid out, 1790 **6**; name changed from Rose Hill, 1791 **6**; road to, 1794 *, 1811 **4**; St John's Church built, 1797 A, 1803 **4**; Old Government House built, 1799 A, 1816 A; first horse-race meeting held at, 1810 E; Female Orphan School at, 1818 **6**; Brisbane establishes observatory at, 1822 B; Lennox Bridge built, 1836 A; becomes a city, 1938 **10**. *See also* Female Factory

Parramatta (schooner), 1807 **6 11 12**

Parramatta, HMAS (destroyer), 1910 **11**, 1913 **10**

Parramatta, HMAS (sloop), 1941 **11**

Parramatta Marist High School, 1821 *

Parramatta River (NSW), 1789 **10**, 1793 *

Parsons, Richard, companion of Pamphlett, 1824 **9**

Paspalum grass, introduced, 1881 F

Passage, The (V. Palmer), 1930 D

Passing of the Aborigines, The (D. Bates), 1938 D

Passionate Heart, The (M. Gilmore), 1918 D

Passmore, John Arthur, philosopher (1914–), 1914 G, 1957 D

Pastoralist Association, NSW, 1844 **4**

Patch of Blue, A (E. Kata), 1961 D

Paterson, Andrew Barton, poet and journalist (1864–1941), 1864 G, 1895 D, 1905 D, 1917 D, 1933 D, 1934 D, 1941 G; first poem in *Bulletin*, 1886 D; and "Waltzing Matilda", 1895 C; portrait of, 1935 C

Paterson, Frederick Woolnough, Communist politician (1897–1977), 1944 **4**

Paterson, William, Lt-Governor of NSW (1755–1810), 1810 G; arrives in Sydney, 1791 **10**; discovers Grose River, 1793 **9**; replaces Grose, 1794 **12**; returns to UK on sick leave, 1796 **8**; returns to NSW, 1799 **3 11**; appointed acting Lt-Governor, 1800 **9**; arrests Johnston, 1800 **10**; founds settlement on Hunter, 1801 **6**; fights duel with Macarthur, 1801 **9**; and settlement at Port Dalrymple, 1804 **10 11 12**; transfers settlement to Launceston, 1806 **3**; and deposition of Bligh, 1808 **2 8 11**, 1809 **1 5**; sails for England, 1810 **5**

Patersonia (Launceston, Tas.), 1806 **3**

"Paterson's Curse", 1869 F

Patrick, Vic (Victor Patrick Lucca), boxer (1920–), 1920 G

Patrick Stevedores, 1998 **4**

Patrick White, A Life (D. Marr), 1991 D

Patrick White Award, 1973 D

Patriotic six, 1845 **10**

Patterson, Gerald Leighton, tennis player (1895–1967), 1919 E, 1922 E

Patterson, Sir James Brown, Premier of Vic. (1833–95), 1893 **1**

Patterson, Sidney Phillip, cyclist (1927–99), 1949 E, 1950 E, 1953 E

Paul, Evelyn Pauline ("Queenie"), entertainer (1895–1982), 1932 C

Pavilion theatre (Melb.), 1841 C

Paving the Way (S. Newland), 1893 D

Pavlova, Anna, Russian dancer (1885–1931), 1926 C, 1929 C

Pavlova (dessert), 1935 B

Payne, G. D., architect, 1910 A

Payroll tax, 1841 **7**, 1971 **9**

Pea Pickers, The (E. Langley), 1942 D

Peace Conference at Versailles, 1919 **1 6**

Peace Officers, 1925 **8**, 1960 **4**

Peacock, Sir Alexander James, Liberal Premier of Vic. (1861–1933), 1901 **2**, 1902 **6**, 1914 **6**, 1917 **11**, 1924 **4**

Peacock, Andrew Sharp, Liberal Party leader (1939–), 1939 G; enters parliament, 1966 **4**; resigns from cabinet, 1981 **4**; becomes party leader, 1983 **3**; replaced by Howard, 1985 **9**

Peacock, Lady Millie Gertrude (*née* Holden), Liberal politician (1870–1948), 1933 **11**

Peake, Archibald Henry, Liberal Premier of SA (1859–1920), 1909 **6**, 1910 **4**, 1912 **2**, 1915 **4**, 1917 **7**, 1920 **4**

Pearce, Alexander, convict, 1824 **8**

Pearce, Sir George Foster, Labor/Nationalist politician (1870–1952), 1921 **11**

Pearce, Henry Robert (Bobby), sculler (1905–76), 1928 E, 1930 E, 1932 E, 1933 E

Pearl, Cyril Alston, author (1906–87), 1958 D

Pearling: begins, 1861 *; fleets devastated by cyclones, 1875 **12**, 1881 **1**, 1887 **4**, 1892 **12**, 1894 **1**, 1908 **4**, 1910 **11**, 1934 **3**, 1935 **3**; Star of the West pearl found, 1917 *

Pearson, John, architect, 1910 A

Peat's Ferry (NSW), rail disaster at, 1887 **6**

Pedal radio, 1926 B

Pedder, Sir John Lewes, first Chief Justice of Tas. (1793–1859), 1824 **5**

Pedder, Lake (Tas.), 1972 F

Peddle, Thorp and Walker, architects, 1961 A

Pederick, Evan Dunstan, Hilton Hotel bomber, 1989 **9**

Pedley, Ethel Charlotte, author (1859–98), 1899 D

Pedorail (road wheel), 1907 B

Peebles, N. G., architect, 1909 A

Peel, Thomas, promoter of Swan River colony (1793–1865), 1828 **11**, 1829 **12**

Peel River (NSW), 1818 **8**

Pelletier, Narcisse, castaway, 1875 **4**

Pemulgwy, Aboriginal guerrilla, 1790 **12**, 1802 **6**

Pemulwy Koori College (Syd.), 1991 **2**

Penal settlements. *See also separate entries* Macquarie Harbour, 1822 **1**, 1833 **11**; Maria Is., 1825 **3**

462

INDEX

Moreton Bay, 1824 **9**, 1825 **2**, 1826 **3**, 1839 **5**
Newcastle, 1804 **3**
Norfolk Is., 1788 **2**, 1804 **9**, 1814 **2**, 1825 **6**
Point Puer, 1834 **2**
Port Arthur, 1830 **9**, 1877 **9**
Port Macquarie, 1821 **3**, 1830 **7**
Swan River, 1849 **1**, 1868 **1**, 1886 **3**
Penfold, Christopher Rawson, wine-grower (1811–90), 1844 *
Penicillin, 1943 B, 1945 B
Penola (SA), 1866 *
Pensioner Medical Service, 1951 **2**
Pensioner pharmaceutical benefits, 1951 **7**
Pensions: old-age, 1901 F, 1908 **7**, 1909 **7**, 1931 F; invalid, 1907 **12**, 1910 **12**, 1931 F; widows', 1926 F; service, 1936 **1**; means test for, 1969 F, 1973 F, 1975 F; assets test for, 1985 F
Penton, Brian Con, author and journalist (1904–51), 1904 G, 1934 D, 1936 D, 1951 G
Pentridge Gaol (Melb.), 1850 **12**, 1967 **2**
People's Advocate (newspaper), 1848 **12**
People's Federal Convention, 1896 **11**
People's Otherworld, The (L. Murray), 1984 D
Peppin family, sheep breeders, 1861 B
Perceval, John, artist (1923–), 1923 G
Perdon, George, long distance runner (1924–), 1975 E
Periodicals: Australia's first, 1821 **5**. *See also individual entries*
Perkins, Charles Nelson, Aboriginal activist and public servant (1936–), 1936 G, 1965 **2**, 1966 F
Perkins, Kieren John, swimmer (1973–), 1973 G, 1992 E, 1994 E, 1996 E
Perron, Marshall Bruce, Country Liberal Chief Minister of NT (1942–), 1988 **7**, 1990 **10**, 1994 **6**, 1995 **5**
Perry, Charles, Anglican Bishop of Melbourne (1807–91), 1847 **6**
Perry, Joseph Henry, film maker (1863–1943), 1900 C
Perseverance (ship), 1807 **1**, 1810 **7**
Persian Gulf, 1990 **8**, 1998 **2**
Perth (Tas.), 1821 **5**
Perth (WA): site of, chosen, 1829 **8**; first newspaper, 1833 **1**; Old Courthouse built, 1836 A; first theatrical performance in, 1839 C; constituted a city, 1856 **9**; Government House built, 1859 A; Town Hall opened, 1870 **5**; King's Park dedicated, 1872 F; Central Government Offices complex built, 1874 A; St George's Cathedral built, 1878 A; telephone exchange opens, 1887 **12**; railway station completed, 1894 A; Swan Barracks completed, 1898 A; electric trams begin running, 1899 **9**; Parliament

House built, 1902 A; University of WA established, 1911 **2**; War Memorial in King's Park unveiled, 1929 **11**; Causeway Bridge completed, 1952 A; Festival first held, 1953 C; Narrows Bridge completed, 1959 A; Concert Hall opens, 1973 C; new Art Gallery completed, 1979 A; new international airport opens, 1986 **10**; Superdrome sports complex completed, 1987 A; experiences highest temperature, 1991 **9**; metropolitan railway, 1993 **3**
Perth, HMAS, 1941 **3**, 1942 **3**
Perth Concert Hall, 1971 A, 1973 C
Perth Gazette and West Australian Journal (newspaper), 1833 **1**
Perth Modern School, 1910 *
Peter 'Possum's Portfolio (R. Rowe), 1858 D
Petermann Range (NT–WA), 1874 **3**, 1930 **7**
Peters, Frederick Augustus Bolles, ice-cream maker (1866–1937), 1907 **8**
Peters, Otto, merchant, 1866 **10**
Peters ice-cream, 1907 **8**
Petherick, Edward Augustus, book collector (1847–1917), 1909 **9**
Petrie, Andrew, pioneer and explorer (1798–1872), 1842 **5**
Petrie, John, building contractor (1822–92), 1886 A
Petrie, Thomas, pioneer (1831–1910), 1904 D
Petrov(a), Evdokia Alexeyevna, Soviet defector, 1954 **4**
Petrov, Vladimir Mikhailovich, Soviet defector (1907–91), 1954 **4**
Petrov royal commission, 1954 **4 5 8**, 1955 **9 10**
Petty, Bruce Leslie, cartoonist (1929–), 1977 C
Petty, Thomas, hotelier, 1836 **7**
Petty's Hotel (Syd.), 1836 **7**
Phantom Stockman (film), 1953 C
Phar Lap (racehorse): wins Melbourne Cup 1930 E; dies in California, 1932 E
Pharmaceutical Benefits Scheme, 1948 **6**, 1960 **3**
Philadelphia (US brigantine), 1792 **11**
Philharmonic societies: Sydney, 1833 C; Australian, 1844 C; Melbourne, 1853 C; Brisbane, 1862 C; Hobart, 1867 C
Philip, Prince, Duke of Edinburgh: opens Olympic Games, 1956 **11**; opens Commonwealth Games, 1962 **11**; opens Mint, 1965 **2**. *See also* Royalty in Australia
Philippoussis, Mark, tennis player (1976–), 1999 E
Phillip, Arthur, first Governor of NSW (1738–1814): arrives at Botany Bay, 1788 **1**; establishes settlement at Sydney Cove, 1788 **1**; commission as Governor read, 1788 **2**; explores Broken Bay, 1788 **3**; sights Blue Mountains, 1788 **4**; leads punitive expedition, 1788 **5**; captures Arabanoo, 1788 **12**; and difficulties with

INDEX

Phillip, Arthur (continued)
marine officers, 1789 **2 4**; discovers
Hawkesbury River, 1789 **6**; captures
Bennelong and Colbee, 1789 **11**; asks
permission to return to UK, 1790 **4**;
instructs Dawes to lay out Rose Hill,
1790 **6**; speared by Aboriginal, 1790 **9**;
returns to England, 1792 **12**; resigns,
1793 **7**; death, 1814 G, sculpture of,
1897 C
Phillip Is. (Vic.), 1928 E, 1989 E
Phillip Street Theatre (Syd.), 1954 C
Phillips, Arthur Angell, literary critic
(1900–1985), 1958 D
Philosophical societies: of Australasia,
1821 B; Australian, 1850 B; Adelaide,
1853 B; Victoria, 1854 B; Queensland,
1859 B; NSW, 1866 B. *See also* Royal
societies
Philp, Sir Robert, Premier of Qld
(1851–1922), 1851 G, 1883 **4**, 1899 **12**,
1903 **9**, 1907 **11**, 1922 G
Phoenician (clipper ship), 1849 **7**
Photography: first Australian photograph,
1841 B; first professional photographer,
1842 **12**; cartes-de-visite, 1863 F;
"pictorial" movement, 1909 C
Phylloxera, 1877 F
Piano, The (film), 1993 C
"Pick a Box" (quiz show), 1948 C, 1957 C,
1971 C
Pickworth, Horace Henry Alfred ("Ossie"),
golfer (1918–69), 1948 E
Picnic at Hanging Rock (J. Lindsay),
1967 D; film of, 1975 C
Picture of Sydney (J. Maclehose), 1838 D
Picturesque Atlas of Australasia, 1886 D
Piddington, Albert Bathurst, judge
(1862–1945), 1920 **11**
Pidgeon, William Edwin, artist (1909–81),
1958 C, 1961 C, 1968 C
Pigs, numbers in NSW, 1849 F
Piguenit, William Charles, artist
(1836–1914), 1836 G, 1901 C, 1902 C,
1914 G
Pilbara (WA), iron-ore discovery, 1961 **11**
Pine Gap (NT), 1966 **12**, 1967 B
Ping-pong, 1901 E
Pinjarra (WA): Battle of, 1834 **10**;
Fairbridge Farm School at, 1912 **8**
Pioneer Dairy Co. (Kiama, NSW), 1884 **6**
Piper, John, pioneer officer (1773–1851),
1792 **2**, 1804 **9**, 1814 **2**, 1818 E, 1851 G
Pipes (lampoons), 1803 **1**
Pitcairn Island: *Bounty* mutineers arrive at,
1790 **1**; last mutineer discovered at,
1808 **2**; community evacuated, 1856 **6**
Pitjantjatjara people, granted land rights,
1981 **11**
Pitt, William, architect (1855–1918), 1889 A
Pitt (convict transport), 1792 **2**

Pitt Street Congregational Church (Syd.),
1841 A
Pitt Town (NSW) 1810 **12**
Pizzey, Jack Charles Allan, Country Party
Premier of Qld (1911–68), 1968 **1 8**
Plains of Promise, 1841 **7**
Platypus, first observed, 1797 B
"Play School" (children's TV program),
1966 C
Playford, Thomas, Premier of SA
(1837–1915), 1887 **6**, 1889 **6**, 1890 **8**,
1892 **6**
Playford, Sir Thomas, Premier of SA
(1896–1981), 1896 G, 1981 G; becomes
Premier, 1939 **11**, ends record term, 1965 **3**
Plays and Fugitive Pieces in Verse
(D. Burn), 1842 C
Ploughman and Other Poems, The (P.
White), 1935 D
Plumier, El (Spanish ship), 1799 **12**, 1801 **1**
Poems and Songs (H. Kendall), 1862 D
Poetry Militant (B. O'Dowd), 1909 D
Poet's Home, A (C. Harpur), 1862 D
Point Cook (Vic.), flying school, 1914 **8**
Point Puer (Tas.) penal settlement for boys,
1834 **2**
Poker machines, legalized in NSW clubs,
1956 **7**
Polding, John Bede, Catholic Archbishop of
Sydney (1794–1877), 1835 **9**, 1836 **6**,
1837 *, 1842 **4**, 1877 **3**
Police
ACT: force formed, 1927 **9**
federal: Hughes forms force, 1917 **11**;
Peace Officers established, 1925 **8**;
Commonwealth Police Force, 1960 **4**,
1973 **3**; Australian Federal Police,
1979 **10**
native, 1842 **2**, 1883 **1**
NSW: convict night watch in Sydney,
1789 **8**, 1796 **11**; Macquarie's
reorganization, 1810 **10 12**, 1811 **1**;
Police Act regulations, 1833 F; brought
under one administration, 1862 **3**; and
phone tapping, 1984 **2**; royal
commission into, 1997 **3**
Qld, 1964 **10**; and demonstrators, 1967 **9**;
inquiry into, 1987 **7**
SA: commissioner dismissed, 1978 **1**
Vic.: strike, 1923 **11**
Police-Citizens Boys' Clubs, 1937 **4**
Policy and Passion (R. C. Praed), 1881 D
Poliomyelitis: Sister Kenny's treatment of,
1933 *, 1938 **1**; epidemics, 1937 **6**,
1938 F, 1949 *; deaths from, 1951 F;
immunization with Salk vaccine, 1956 **7**;
Sabin vaccine, 1967 **5**
Political Labour League, 1895 **5**
Polo, first played, 1875 E
Polynesian Labourers Act (Qld), 1868 **3**
Ponsford, William Harold, cricketer
(1900–1991), 1923 E, 1927 E, 1991 G

INDEX

INDEX

Power, John Joseph Wardell, art benefactor (1881–1943), 1943 C

Power of One, The (B. Courtenay), 1989 D

Power Without Glory (F. Hardy), 1950 D

Powers, Sir Charles, judge (1853–1939), 1920 **11**

Praed, Rosa Caroline (Mrs Campbell Praed; *née* Murray-Prior), novelist (1851–1935), 1851 G, 1881 D, 1885 D, 1902 D, 1935 G

Pram Factory (theatre, Melb.), 1970 C, 1981 C

Pratt, Steve, aid worker, 1999 **3**

Prell's Building (Melb.), 1885 A

Prelude to Waking (M. Franklin), 1950 D

Premier Permanent Building, Land and Investment Association, 1889 **12**

"Premiers' plan", 1931 **5**

Prendergast, George Michael, Labor Premier of Vic. (1854–1937), 1924 **7 11**

Presbyterian Church: first minister, 1822 **12**; and Australian College, 1831 **10 11**; Presbytery formed in Sydney, 1832 **12**; Synod of NSW, 1837 **12**, 1850 **4**; Synod of Australia, 1840 **10**; Synod of Eastern Australia, 1846 **10**; General Synod formed, 1864 *; General Assembly formed, 1865 9; Australian union, 1901 **7**; and Australian Inland Mission, 1912 **9**; buys Ernabella station, 1936 **12**; forms Uniting Church, 1977 **6**. *See also* Uniting Church in Australia

Presbyterian Ladies' Colleges: Melbourne, 1875 **2**; Sydney, 1891 **3**, 1916 **2**

Preservation Island (Bass Strait), 1797 **2 5 6**

Press Council, 1976 **7**

Preston, Margaret Rose (*née* McPherson), artist (1875–1963), 1875 G, 1927 C, 1963 G

Preston, William, soldier-explorer, 1829 **9 11**

Preston River (WA), 1829 **11**

Preston Stanley, Millicent Fanny, Nationalist/Liberal politician (1883–1955), 1925 **5**

Price, John, explorer, 1798 B

Price, John Giles, prison official (1808–57), 1846 **8**; murdered, 1857 **3**

Price, Thomas, Labor Premier of SA (1852–1909), 1852 G, 1905 **7**, 1909 **6**

Price control: during World War I, 1916 **3**; during World War II, 1939 **9**, 1948 **5 9**

Prices Justification Tribunal, 1973 **8**

Prichard, Katharine Susannah, author (1883–1969), 1883 G, 1921 D, 1926 D, 1929 D, 1937 D, 1969 G

Prickly pear: Board established, 1920 F; cactoblastis eggs released, 1926 F

Prime Ministers (chronologically, from Federation)
Edmund Barton, 1900 **12**
Alfred Deakin, 1903 **9**
J. C. Watson, 1904 **4**
George Reid, 1904 **8**
Alfred Deakin, 1905 **7**
Andrew Fisher, 1908 **11**
Alfred Deakin, 1909 **6**
Andrew Fisher, 1910 **4**
Joseph Cook, 1913 **6**
Andrew Fisher, 1914 **9**
W. M. Hughes, 1915 **10**
S. M. Bruce, 1923 **2**
J. H. Scullin, 1929 **10**
J. A. Lyons, 1931 **12**
R. G. Menzies, 1939 **4**
A. W. Fadden, 1941 **8**
John Curtin, 1941 **10**
F. M. Forde, 1945 **7**
J. B. Chifley, 1945 **7**
R. G. (Sir Robert) Menzies, 1949 **12**
Harold Holt, 1966 **1**
John McEwen, 1967 **12**
John Gorton, 1968 **1**
William McMahon, 1971 **3**
Gough Whitlam, 1972 **12**
Malcolm Fraser, 1975 **11**
R. J. L. Hawke, 1983 **3**
Paul Keating, 1991 **12**
John howard, 1996 **3**

Primogeniture, law of, 1862 F

Prince Alfred College (Adel.), 1869 **1**

Prince Alfred Hospital (Melb.). *See* Alfred Hospital

Prince Alfred Park (Syd.), 1869 **5**, 1870 **8**

Prince Edward Theatre (Syd.), 1924 C

Prince Henry Hospital (Syd.), 1881 **7**

Prince Henry's Hospital (Melb.), 1885 **10**

Prince of Wales (First Fleet transport), 1788 **1 7**

Prince of Wales Theatre (Syd.), 1855 C, 1863 C; destroyed by fire, 1860 **10**, 1872 **1**

Prince Regent River (WA), 1820 **6**, 1987 **3**

Princes Bridge (Melb.): first, 1846 A, 1850 **11**; second, 1886 A, 1888 **10**

Princess Margaret Hospital for Children (Perth), 1972 **10**

Princess of Tasmania (ferry), 1959 **10**

Princess Theatre (Melb.), 1886 C

Pringle, George Hogarth, doctor, 1867 B

Pringle, John Martin Douglas, journalist and essayist (1912–99), 1958 D

Printing: first in Australia, 1795 **11**; first book printed in Australia, 1802 D. *See also* Book publishing; Newspapers

Priscilla, Queen of the Desert (film), 1994 C

Prisoners of war: Australian, 1942 **2**; Japanese, 1944 **8**

Prisons. *See* Gaols

Privatization and demutualization: of Commonwealth Bank, 1991 **7**; of Qantas, 1995 **7**; of Telstra, 1997 **11**; of AMP Society, 1997 **11**; of Aust. Stock Exchange, 1998 **10**

Privy Council: first Australian member of, 1887 *; and bank nationalization, 1949 **7**; appeals to, abolished, 1967 **9**, 1975 **2**, 1985 **12**

Prize fighting. *See* Boxing

INDEX

Proctor, Lieut., naval officer, 1791 **7**

Prodromus Entomology: Natural History of the Lepidopterous Insects of New South Wales (J. Lewin), 1805 B C

Prodromus Florae Novae Hollandiae (R. Brown), 1810 B

Progressive Party (NSW), 1925 **8**

Progressive Political League, 1891 **5**

Prohibition, referendums on: NSW and ACT, 1928 **9**; WA, 1950 **12**

Propsting, William Bispham, Liberal Democrat Premier of Tas. (1861–1937), 1903 **4**, 1904 **7**

Prospect (NSW), 1801 **5**; reservoir, 1888 *

Prostitution: brothels legalized in Vic., 1984 F; in NSW, 1995 **11**

Protectionists, 1865 **8**, 1870 **6**, 1894 **7**; in first federal parliament, 1901 **3**

Protector (gunboat), 1884 **9**, 1900 **8**

Protestant Hall (Syd.), 1875 **11**, 1883 **3**

Proud, Geoffrey Robert, artist (1946–), 1990 C

Prout, John Skinner, artist (1805–76), 1805 G, 1842 D, 1845 C, 1876 G

Providence (convict transport), 1811 **7**

Providence, HMS, Bligh's voyage in, 1791 **8**, 1792 **9**, 1793 **8**; survey work in the Pacific, 1795 **8**

Provincial and Suburban Bank, 1879 **5**

Psychiatric institutions: at Castle Hill, NSW, 1811 *; Rydalmere, 1818 A; Gladesville, 1838 F; charges for patients abolished, 1948 F

"Pub With No Beer, A" (song), 1957 C

Public Lending Right, 1974 D

Public Service: Vic. Public Service Act, 1883 **11**; Commonwealth, established, 1902 **5**

Publishing. *See* Book publishing; Newspapers; Printing

Pugh, Clifton Ernest, artist (1924–90), 1924 G, 1965 C, 1971 C, 1972 C, 1990 G

Pugh, William, soldier, 1818 **10**

Pugh, William Russ, doctor (1805?–97), 1847 B

Pugin, Augustus Welby Northmore, architect (1812–52), 1850 A

Punch (magazine, Melb.), 1855 **8**, 1925 **12**. *See also Sydney Punch*

Pushes, 1846 F, 1893 F

Putland, Mary, daughter of William Bligh, 1809 **3**, 1810 **5**

"Pyjama girl", 1934 **9**, 1944 **3**

Pyramid Building Society, 1990 **6**

Pyrmont (Syd.): Bridge, 1858 A, 1902 A; power station, 1904 **7**; fire at, 1935 **9**

Q

Qantas: founded, 1920 **11**; first regular service, 1922 **11**; Qantas Empire Airways formed, 1934 **1**; Australia–England service, 1934 **12**, 1935 **2**, 1938 **7**; taken over by Commonwealth, 1947 **6**; inaugurates round-the-world service, 1958 **1**; receives its first 707 jet, 1959 **7**; pilots strike, 1966 **11**; headquarters building, 1969 A; and bomb hoax, 1971 **5**; acquires Australian Airlines, 1992 **9**; privatized, 1995 **7**

Qantas Empire Airways (QEA). *See* Qantas

Qintex (media company), 1989 *, 1994 **2**

Quadrant (magazine, Syd.), 1956 D

Quakers, 1832 **2**, 1887 **1**

Quarantine, 1852 **12**, 1854 **8**, 1909 **7**

Queen (Third Fleet transport), 1791 **9**

Queen Elizabeth (ship), 1941 **4**

Queen Mary (ship), 1940 **4**

Queen Victoria Building (Syd.), 1893 A, 1898 **7**

Queen Victoria Memorial Hospital for Women and Children, 1896 F

Queen Victoria Museum and Art Gallery (Launceston), 1887 A, 1891 B

Queen's Bridge (Melb.), 1890 A

Queen's Counsel, no more appointed in NSW, 1992 **12**

Queen's Theatre (Adel.), 1841 C, 1850

Queen's Theatre Royal (Melb.), 1845 C

Queenscliff (Vic.), 1901 B

Queensland: proclaimed a colony, 1859 **12**; parliament first meets, 1860 **5**; boundary moved, 1862 **6**; Constitution Act assented to, 1867 **12**; introduces free education, 1870 F; annexes islands in Torres Strait, 1872 **5**, 1879 **6**; naval forces, 1885 **3**; standardizes its time, 1895 **1**; abolishes Legislative Council, 1917 **5**, 1921 **10**, 1922 **3**; centenary celebrations, 1959 **8**; enacts harsh labour legislation, 1985 **3**; and daylight saving, 1990 **10**. *See also* Moreton Bay

Governors (chronologically, to Federation)
 Sir George Ferguson Bowen, 1859 **12**
 Col. Samuel Blackall, 1868 **8**
 W. W. Cairns, 1875 **1**
 Sir Arthur Kennedy, 1877 **7**
 Sir Anthony Musgrave, 1883 **11**
 Sir Henry Norman, 1889 **5**
 Baron Lamington, 1896 **4**

Premiers (chronologically, from foundation of colony)
 R. G. W. Herbert, 1859 **12**
 Arthur Macalister, 1866 **2**
 R. G. W. Herbert, 1866 **7**
 Arthur Macalister, 1866 **8**
 Robert Mackenzie, 1867 **8**
 Charles Lilley, 1868 **11**
 Arthur Palmer, 1870 **5**
 Arthur Macalister, 1874 **1**
 George Thorn, 1876 **6**
 John Douglas, 1877 **3**
 Thomas McIlwraith, 1879 **1**

INDEX

INDEX

INDEX

Rankin, Dame Annabelle Jane Mary, Liberal politician (1908–86), 1966 **1**

Rapotec, Stanislaus, artist (1913–97), 1997 G

Rason, Sir Cornthwaite Hector William James, Liberal Premier of WA (1858–1927), 1905 **8**, 1906 **5**

Rasp, Charles, discoverer of Broken Hill lode (1846–1907), 1883 **9**

Rasputin (musical), 1987 C

Rationing: petrol, 1940 **10**; ration books issued, 1942 **6**; butter and household drapery, 1943 **6**; meat, 1944 **1**; sugar ends, 1947 **7**; meat and clothing ends, 1948 **6**; petrol lifted and reimposed, 1949 **6**; petrol ends, 1950 **2**; butter ends, 1950 **6**

Rats of Tobruk, The (film), 1944 C

Rattlesnake, HMS, 1847 **7**, 1849 **10**

Raven, William, ship's master (1756–1814), 1792 **7 10**, 1794 **6**, 1799 **5**

Ravenswood (Qld), 1868 **10**

Rawlinson Range (WA), 1874 **1**

Raymond, W.E., astronomer, 1910 B

Raymond, Lord of Milan (E. Reeve), 1863 C

"Razor Gang" (Fed. govt.), 1981 **4**

Reaching Tin River (T. Astley), 1990 D

Read, Richard, artist (b. 1765?), 1822 C

Ready Mixed Concrete Co., 1939 A

Real Estate Bank, 1892 **2**

Receveur, Laurent, Franciscan priest and scientist (d. 1788), 1788 G

Recherche (French ship), 1792 **4**

Recherche Bay (Tas.), 1793 **1**

Recollections of Geoffry Hamlyn, The (H. Kingsley), 1859 D

Recollections of Squatting (E. Curr), 1883 D

Recruiting Officer, The (play), 1789 C

Red Cross. See Australian Red Cross Society

Red Pagan, The (A. G. Stephens), 1904 D

Red Rover (ship), 1832 **8**

Redcliffe (Qld), 1824 **9**, 1825 **2**

Redex trial, 1953 E, 1954 E. 1955 E

Redfern, William, pioneer surgeon (1774?–1833), 1833 G; arrives in Sydney, 1801 **12**; pardoned, 1803 **6**; given medical competence test, 1808 **9**; resigns from medical service, 1819 **10**; appointed magistrate, 1819 **11**; goes to UK to present petition, 1821 **10**

Redfern (Syd.), rail disaster at, 1894 **10**

Redford, Henry, overlander (1842–1901), 1870 **3**

Redheap (N. Lindsay), 1930 D

Redmond, John Edward, Irish politician (1856–1918), 1883 **2**

Reece, Eric Elliott, Labor Premier of Tas. (1909–99), 1958 **8**, 1959 **5**, 1964 **5**, 1972 **4**, 1975 **3**

Reed, Joseph, architect (1823?–90), 1854 A, 1855 A, 1863 A, 1867 A, 1868 A, 1873 A, 1879 A

Reed (Reid), William, ship's master, discovers King Is., 1798 *

Reedy River (play), 1953 C

Rees, Lloyd Federick, artist (1895–1988), 1895 G, 1950 C, 1988 G; portrait of, 1968 C

Reeve, Edward, dramatist (1822–89), 1863 C

Referendums, 1898 F

ACT: prohibition, 1928 **9**; hotel hours, 1955 **9**

Commonwealth: Senate elections, 1906 **12**; state debts, surplus revenue, 1910 **4**; trade and commerce, nationalization of monopolies, 1911 **4**; trade and commerce, corporations, industrial matters, trusts, nationalization of monopolies, railway disputes, 1913 **5**; conscription, 1916 **10**, 1917 **12**; extending wartime powers, 1919 **12**; commerce and industry, essential services, 1926 **9**; state debts, 1928 **11**; aviation, marketing, 1937 **3**; post-war reconstruction, democratic rights, 1944 **8**; social services, marketing, industrial employment, 1946 **9**; rent and price control, 1948 **5**; Communists and communism, 1951 **9**; nexus between houses of parliament, discrimination against Aborigines, 1967 **5**; prices and incomes, 1973 **12**; democratic elections, simultaneous elections, mode of altering Constitution, local government, 1974 **5**; Senate casual vacancies, territorial votes, retiring age for judges, simultaneous elections, 1977 **5**; simultaneous elections, interchange of powers, 1984 **12**; four-year parliamentary terms, fair and democratic elections, recognition of local government, trial by jury, freedom of religion, acquisition of property, 1988 **9**; establishing a republic, inserting a preamble into the Constitution, 1999 **11**

NSW: federation, 1898 **6**; prohibition, 1928 **9**; reform of Legislative Council, 1933 **5**; hotel hours, 1947 **2**, 1954 **11**; abolition of Legislative Council, 1961 **4**; new state, 1967 **4**; daylight saving, 1976 **5**; method of choosing MLCs, 1978 **6**; parliamentary term, MPs' pecuniary interests, 1981 **9**

NT: statehood, 1998 **10**

Qld: federation, 1899 **7**; abolition of Legislative Council, 1917 **5**; daylight saving, 1990 **10**

SA: federation, 1898 **6**

Tas.: federation, 1898 **6**; Wrest Point casino, 1968 **12**; dam site, 1981 **12**

Vic.: federation, 1898 **6**

WA: federation, 1900 **7**; secession, 1933 **4**; prohibition, 1950 **12**; daylight saving, 1983 **10**, 1991 **11**

Refrigeration: Harrison's processes, 1856 B, 1873 B; Nicolle's invention, 1861 B;

INDEX

Riley, Alexander, early official and merchant (1778?–1833), 1804 **6**, 1810 **11**, 1814 **12**, 1815 **5**

Ringarooma, HMS, 1891 **9**

Riots, insurrections, etc.: on Norfolk Is., 1789 **1**, 1794 **1**, 1826 **9**, 1834 **1**, 1842 **6**, 1846 **7**; Castle Hill Rising, 1804 **3**; Orangemen and Catholics in Melbourne, 1846 **7**, 1867 **11**; Eureka Stockade, 1854 **11 12**; Parliament House, Melbourne, attacked, 1860 **8**; "bread or blood" riots in Brisbane, 1866 **9**; at Circular Quay, Sydney, 1890 **9**; AIF troops in Sydney, 1916 **2**; "anti-Bolsheviks" in Brisbane, 1919 **3**; "Battle of the Barricades" at Fremantle, 1919 **5**; meatworkers in Townsville, 1919 **6**; returned soldiers in Melbourne, 1919 **7**; in Melbourne during police strike, 1923 **11**; on Adelaide waterfront, 1929 **1**; at Rothbury, NSW, 1929 **12**; at Newtown, Sydney, 1931 **6**; in Kalgoorlie and Boulder, 1934 **1**; in Bathurst Gaol, 1974 **2**. *See also* Demonstrations; Gold: goldfields, conflict on

Riou, Edward, naval officer (*c.* 1758–1801), 1789 **12**

Ripon regulations, 1831 **8**

Rippon Lea (Melb.), 1868 A

Risdon Cove (Tas.), 1803 **9**, 1804 **2 4 5 8**, 1995 **10**

Rising of the Court, The (H. Lawson), 1910 D

"Rising sun" badge, 1902 **2**

Ristori, Adelaide, Italian tragedienne (1822–1906), 1875 C

Ritchard, Cyril Joseph, musical comedy actor (1897–1977), 1946 C, 1977 G

Rites of Passage (opera), 1974 C

River Murray Commission, 1917 **1**

River transport: on Brisbane River, 1846 **6**; on Murray, 1853 **8**, 1854 **10**; on Murrumbidgee, 1857 **9**, 1858 **8**; on Darling, 1859 **1 2**, 1872 **11**. *See also* Ferries

Riversleigh cattle station (Qld), 1984 B

Riverview (Syd.): College, 1880 *; Observatory, 1908 B

Rivett, Sir Albert Cherbury David, scientist and administrator (1885–1961), 1885 G, 1926 B, 1961 G

Rivett, Rohan Deakin, journalist and author (1917–77), 1946 D

Road and level-crossing accidents: near Wodonga, 1943 **5**; near Hawkesbury River, 1944 **1**; at Horsham, 1951 **2**; at Boronia, Vic., 1952 **6**; bus at Cabramurra, 1973 **9**; death statistics, 1978 F; tour coaches on Pacific Highway, NSW, 1989 **9 12**; tour coach in Gold Coast hinterland, 1990 **9**; tour coach on Hume Highway, Vic., 1993 **11**; tour coach in Brisbane, 1994 **10**

Road from Coorain (J. Ker Conway), 1989 D

Roads: Sydney's first, 1788 **9**; Sydney–Parramatta, 1794 *, 1811 **4**; Sydney–Windsor, 1813 *; Sydney–Liverpool, 1814 **3**; over Blue Mountains, 1814 **7**, 1815 **1**; to Mrs Macquarie's Chair, 1816 B; Great Western Road, 1818 **1**; Hobart–Launceston, 1818 **5**; Hobart–New Norfolk, 1819 **6**; Richmond–Wallis Plains, 1823 **3**; Commonwealth aid for, 1923 **6**, 1926 **5**; Main Roads Board (NSW), 1925 **1**; Mt Isa–Tennant Creek military road, 1941 **4**; Darwin–Alice Springs, 1943 **6**; Sydney–Newcastle expressway, 1965 **12**; blockade by truck drivers, 1979 **4**; round-Australia, sealed, 1986 **9**; Adelaide–Darwin, sealed, 1987 **2**

Roaring Twenties, The (J. Lindsay), 1960 D

Robb, John, engineer (1834–96), 1890 A

Robb, Peter, writer (1946–), 1996 D

Robbery Under Arms (R. Boldrewood), 1882 D, 1888 D; melodrama, 1890 C; films, 1907 C, 1920 C

Robbins, Charles, naval officer, 1802 **11 12**, 1803 **1**

Robe, Frederick Holt, Governor of SA (1802–71), 1845 **10**, 1846 **3 7**, 1848 **8**

Roberts, Thomas William, artist (1856–1931), 1856 G, 1931 G; and Heidelberg School, 1885 C, 1886 C, 1888 C, 1889 C; paintings, 1886 C, 1890 C, 1891 C, 1894 C, 1895 C, 1927 C

Roberts, Violet and Bruce, released from prison, 1980 **10**

Robertson, George, Melbourne bookseller and publisher (1825–98), 1852 D

Robertson, George, Sydney bookseller and publisher (1860–1933), 1886 D

Robertson, Sir John, Premier of NSW (1816–91), 1816 G, 1860 **3**, 1868 **10**, 1870 **1**, 1875 **2**, 1877 **8**, 1885 **12**, 1886 **2**, 1891 G; coalition with Martin, 1870 **12**; coalition with Parkes, 1878 **12**; amending Land Bill defeated, 1882 **11**

Robertson, Louis Spear, architect, 1910 A

Robertson, Sir Macpherson, confectionery manufacturer (1859–1945), 1880 **6**

Robertson, R. J., naval officer, 1968 **2**

Robertson Land Acts, 1861 **10**

Robertson-Swann, Ronald Charles, sculptor (1941–), 1980 C

Robinson, Christopher Stansfield, Chief Judicial Officer of British New Guinea (1872–1904), 1904 **6**

Robinson, Clint, canoeist (1972–), 1992 E

Robinson, George Augustus, protector of Aborigines (1788–1866), guardian at Bruny Is., 1829 **3**; journey of conciliation, 1830 **1**; captures Aborigines, 1832 **1**; saved by Truganini, 1832 **9**; Chief Protector, 1838 **1**, 1841 **10**

INDEX

Rowley, Stanley Rupert, athlete (1876–1924), 1900 E

Rowley, Thomas, commander of Norfolk Is. (1748?–1806), 1799 **11**, 1800 **6**

Roxby Downs (SA), 1982 **6**

Royal Adelaide Golf Club, 1893 E

Royal Adelaide Theatre, 1846 C

Royal Admiral (convict transport), 1792 **10**, 1800 **10**

Royal Agricultural Society of NSW, 1822 **7**

Royal Agricultural Society of Vic., 1871 **11**

Royal Alexandra Hospital for Children (Syd.), 1880 **1**, 1906 **12**, 1995 **10**

Royal Arcade (Melb.), 1869 A

Royal Art Society of NSW, 1880 C

Royal Australian Air Force: origins, 1912 **9**, 1914 **8**, 1915 **4**; formed, 1921 **3**; Empire Air Training Scheme inaugurated, 1939 **10**; bombers attack Japanese landing force, 1941 **12**; College established, 1947 **8**; in Korean War and Malayan Emergency, 1950 **7**; squadron in Thailand, 1962 **5**; and F–111 aircraft, 1963 **10**, 1973 **6**; receives first Mirages, 1964 **1**; in Vietnam War, 1964 **7**; first female pilots, 1988 F

Royal Australian Naval College: opens at Geelong, 1913 **3**; moves to Jervis Bay, 1915 **2**; moves to Flinders Naval Depot, 1930 **6**; returns to Jervis Bay, 1958 **1**

Royal Australian Navy: origins, 1909 **2 7**, 1910 **11**; first ships, 1910 **11**, 1911 **4 10**, 1912 **4 5**; squadron enters Port Jackson, 1913 **10**; in World War I, 1914 **9 11**, 1915 **9**; in World War II, 1940 **7 11**, 1941 **3 5 6 11**, 1942 **3 4 5 6 8 9 12**, 1943 **5 6 7**, 1944 **10**; first air station commissioned, 1948 **8**; first aircraft carrier commissioned, 1948 **12**; in Korean War, 1950 **6 12**; *Voyager* disaster, 1964 **2**, 1968 **2**; *Sydney* takes troops to Vietnam, 1965 **5**; *Melbourne* collides with *Frank E. Evans*, 1969 **6**; fire at HMAS *Albatross*, 1976 **12**; ships sent to Persian Gulf, 1990 **8**. *See also* Naval defence; Navies, colonial

Royal Automobile Association of South Australia, 1903 **9**

Royal Automobile Club of Australia (RACA), 1903 **3**

Royal Automobile Club of Queensland, 1905 **5**

Royal Automobile Club of Victoria, (RACV), 1903 **12**

Royal Bank, 1842 **7**; 1849 **8**

Royal Bank of Queensland, 1893 **5**

Royal Canberra Hospital, 1997 **7**

Royal commissions: defence of NSW, 1858 **12**; Federation, 1870 **8**; Island Labour, 1885 **5**; sites for a national capital, 1899 **11**; basic wage, 1920 **11**; film industry, 1928 C; Mungana Mines sale, 1930 **7**; banking system, 1937 **7**; treatment of polio, 1938 **1**; "Brisbane Line", 1943 **7**; PNG timber leases, 1949 **1**; Communist Party, 1949 **5**; liquor laws in NSW, 1951 *; television, 1953 C; Soviet espionage (Petrov inquiry), 1954 **4 5 8**, 1955 **9 10**; organized crime (Moffitt), 1974 **8**; drug trafficking in NSW (Woodward), 1979 **10**; Painters and Dockers Union, 1980 **10**, 1981 **6**, 1982 **8**, 1984 **7 11**; drug trafficking (Stewart), 1981 **6**, 1983 **5**; Builders' Labourers Fed., 1981 **8**; Neville Wran and magistracy, 1983 **5 7**; security and intelligence agencies, 1983 **5**; British nuclear tests, 1984 **10**, 1985 **12**; Agent orange, 1985 **8**; Chamberlains' convictions, 1986 **2**, 1987 **6**; corruption in Qld police force, 1987 **7**, 1989 **7**, 1991 **10**; deaths of Aborigines in custody, 1987 **8**; WA government's commercial activities, 1990 **11**, 1991 **3 4**, 1992 **6**, 1994 **5**, 1996 **9**; into breach of power by WA Premier, 1995 **11**; 1997 **4**; into NSW Police, 1997 **3**

Royal George (ship), 1806 **10**, 1844 **11**

Royal Hospital for Women (Syd.), 1901 **11**

Royal Hotel (Syd.), theatrical venue, 1829 C, 1832 C, 1840 **3**

Royal Humane Society of Australasia, 1874 **9**

Royal Life Saving Society, 1894 *

Royal Melbourne Hospital, 1939 A

Royal Melbourne Institute of Technology, 1887 **5**

Royal Melbourne Women's Hospital, 1980 **6**

Royal Military College (Duntroon), 1833 A, 1911 **6**, 1931 **2**

Royal National Park (NSW), 1879 F

Royal Park (Melb.), 1854 F, 1861 F; zoo at, 1862 B

Royal Prince Alfred Hospital (Syd.), 1882 **9**

Royal Prince Alfred Yacht Club (Syd.), 1867 E

Royal Shipwreck Relief and Humane Society of NSW, 1877 **7**

Royal Societies: Tas., 1843 B; Vic., 1854 B; NSW, 1866 B; SA, 1880 B; Qld, 1884 B; WA, 1897 B

Royal Society for the Prevention of Cruelty to Animals (RSPCA), 1871 F, 1968 **5**

Royal South Australian Yacht Squadron, 1869 E

Royal Sydney Golf Club, 1893 E

Royal Sydney Yacht Squadron, 1862 E

Royal Tar (ship), 1893 **7 12**

Royal Veteran Company, 1823 **9**

Royal Victoria Theatre (Adel.), 1839 C, 1850 C

Royal Victoria Theatre (Hob.). *See* Theatre Royal

Royal Victoria Theatre (Launceston), 1845 C

Royal Victoria Theatre (Melb.), 1841 C

S

INDEX

INDEX

Seidler, Harry, architect (1923–), 1923 G, 1960 A, 1971 A
Select Committee on the Condition of the Working Classes of the Metropolis (NSW), 1860 **4**
Self-government. *See* Representative government
Sellers, Harry, pugilist, 1860 E
Senate: preferential voting for, 1919 **10**; proportional representation for, 1948 **5**; members increased, 1948 *; blocks supply, 1975 **10**; first woman president of, 1995 **5**. *See also* Parliaments
Sentimental Bloke, The (film), 1919 C; musical, 1960 C. *See also Songs of a Sentimental Bloke, The*
Seppelt, Joseph Ernest, wine-grower (1813–68), 1851 *
Serle, Alan Geoffrey, historian (1922–98), 1982 D
Serle, Percival, author (1871–1951), 1949 D
Serra, Joseph Benedict, Catholic prelate (1810–86), 1846 **2**
Service, James, Premier of Vic. (1823–99), 1880 **3 7**, 1883 **1**, 1886 **2**
Sestier, Marius, pioneer film maker and exhibitor, 1896 C E
Settlers and Convicts (A. Harris), 1847 D
Seven Little Australians (E. Turner), 1894 D
Seven Poor Men of Sydney (C. Stead), 1934 D
Seventh Day Adventists: first arrive in Melbourne, 1885 **6**; first church opens, 1886 **1**; Cooranbong college built, 1897 *; Sanitarium opens, 1903 *
73rd (Royal Highlanders) Regiment, 1809 **5 8**, 1810 **5**, 1812 **3**; officers kill settler, 1813 **7**; replaced, 1814 **2 4**
Sewerage: Melbourne connected to, 1898 **2**; Brisbane connected to, 1923 *
Sex shops, 1971 F
Seymour, Alan, playwright (1927–), 1927 G, 1961 C
Seymour (Vic.), 1844 **3**
Seymour Centre (Syd.), 1975 C
Shackleton, Sir Ernest Henry, British Antarctic explorer (1874–1922), 1908 **3**, 1909 **1**
Shah Hormuzear (ship), 1793 **2 7**
Shakespeare Memorial Theatre Company, 1949 C
Shallows (T. Winton), 1984 D
Shamrock (ship), 1841 **10**
Shannon River (Tas.), 1818 **10**
"Shark arm" case, 1935 **4**
Shark attacks: at Coogee (Syd.), 1922 **2**; in Middle Harbour (Syd.), 1963 **1**
Shark Bay (WA), 1801 **7**, 1954 B
Sharkey, Lawrence Louis, Communist Party chairman, gaoled, 1949 **10**
Sharman, James, boxing showman (1887–1965), 1912 E, 1971 E

Sharp, Cecil James, musician (1859–1924), 1889 C
Sharp, Martin Ritchie, artist (1942–), 1964 **9**
Sharp, Paul, crosses Simpson Desert on foot, 1983 **8**
Sharpe, Wendy, artist (1960–), 1996 C
Sharrock, Christine, murder victim, 1965 **1**
Shaw, George, zoologist (1751–1813), 1794 B
Shead, Garry, artist (1942–), 1993 C
Shearer, David, pioneer car builder (1850–1936), 1894 B
Shearers and shearing
  machines invented, 1868 B, 1872 B, 1877 B
  shearing records, 1892 **10**, 1965 F
  strikes, 1890 **9**, 1891 **1 2 3 5 8** D, 1894 **6 7 8 9**, 1956 **2**
  trade unionism, 1886 **6**, 1890 **1 8**
Sheep: imported from Bengal, 1792 **6**, 1793 **2**; merinos first imported, 1797 **6**; Macarthur brings back merinos of King George's flock, 1805 **6**; numbers, 1825 F, 1849 F, 1891 F, 1970 F; first overlanded, 1837 **3**; boiled down for tallow, 1843 **6**, 1849 F; Peppin merino developed, 1861 B; Corriedales introduced, 1882 F; blowfly becomes pest, 1903 F; Polwarth breed recognized, 1919 B; export of merino rams banned, 1929 **11**. *See also* Land settlement; Shearers and shearing; Wool
Sheepdog trial, first, 1872 E
Sheerin and Hennessy, architects, 1885 A
Sheffield Shield, 1892 E
Sheil, Ainslie Glenister Ross, surgeon, 1968 **4**
Shelbourne (Qld), 1848 **11**
Shellal Mosaic, 1917 B
Sheltered workshops, 1967 F
Shenandoah (Confederate cruiser), 1865 **1**
Shepparton (Vic.), 1855 **7**, 1949 **3**; railway reaches, 1880 **1**
Sherritt, Aaron, informer, 1880 **6**
Shiels, William, Premier of Vic. (1848–1904), 1892 **2**, 1893 **1**
Shiers, Walter Henry, aircraft engineer (1880–1968), 1919 **10**
Shifting Heart, The (play), 1956 C
Shine (film), 1996 C, 1997 C
Ship building: first vessels built, 1789 **10**, 1793 **7**; by Kable and Underwood, 1800 **7**, 1805 **4**; by Robert Campbell, 1807 **1**; *Governor Macquarie* launched, 1811 **10**; first steamer built, 1831 **3**; first warship built in NSW, 1855 **4**; at Whyalla (SA), 1941 **5**
Shipp, Gloria, first Aboriginal priest, 1996 **12**
Shipwrecks and shipping disasters. *See also under* World War I *and* World War II *for naval and merchant vessel losses*
  Admella, 1859 **8**
  Adolphe, 1904 **9**
  Alert, 1893 **12**

478

INDEX

INDEX

INDEX

Smiley (film), 1956 C
Smith, Alfred Louis, architect
(*c.* 1830–1907), 1874 A
Smith, Arthur Carrington, inventor, 1931 B
Smith, Bernard (Patrick) William, art
historian (1916–), 1960 D, 1984 D
Smith, Sir Charles Edward Kingsford,
aviator (1897–1935), 1897 G, 1907 **1**,
1935 **5** G; makes first flight across
Pacific, 1928 **5**; makes first non-stop
trans-Australia flight, 1928 **8**; makes first
trans-Tasman flight, 1928 **9**; founds ANA,
1928 **12**; flies to England, 1929 **3 6**;
completes circumnavigation of world,
1930 **6**; makes first east–west crossing of
Pacific, 1934 **10**; disappears, 1935 **11**
Smith, Eric John, artist (1919–), 1970 C,
1981 C, 1982 C
Smith, Francis Villeneuve, Premier of Tas.
(1819–1909), 1857 **5**
Smith, Frank Beaumont, film maker
(*c.* 1886–1950), 1917 C, 1921 C
Smith, Sir Gerard, Governor of WA
(1839–1920), 1895 **12**
Smith, Grace Cossington, artist (1892–1984),
1892 G, 1984 G
Smith, Jack Carington, artist (1908–72),
1963 C
Smith, James, prospector (1827–97), 1871 **12**
Smith, Sir James John Joynton, newspaper
proprietor (1858–1943), 1919 **3**, 1943 G
Smith, Joe, axeman, 1874 E
Smith, John McGarvie, bacteriologist
(1844–1918), 1918 B
Smith, Jonathan, pugilist, 1855 E
Smith, Joshua. *See* Smith, William Joshua
Smith, Sir Keith Macpherson, aviator
(1890–1955), 1919 **11 12**
Smith, Margaret. *See* Court, Margaret
Smith, Maria Ann (Granny Smith),
orchardist (1800–1870), 1868 B
Smith, Richard Harold, publisher and
adventurer (1944–), 1944 G; makes
round-the-world helicopter flight, 1983 **7**;
launches *Australian Geographic*, 1986 **1**;
reaches North Pole by helicopter, 1987 **4**;
flies round the world via poles, 1989 **5**;
crosses Australia by balloon, 1993 **6**
Smith, Robert Bowyer, inventor of
stumpjump plough (1838–1919), 1876 B
Smith, Sir Ross Macpherson, aviator
(1892–1922), 1919 **11 12**, 1922 **4**
Smith, Shirley ("Mum Shirl", *née* Colleen
Shirley Perry), social worker (1921–98),
1921 G, 1998 G
Smith, Sydney George Ure, artist and
publisher (1887–1949), 1887 G, 1916 C,
1949 G
Smith, William Forgan, Labor Premier of
Qld (1887–1953), 1932 **6**, 1942 **9**
Smith, William Joshua, artist (1905–95),
1944 C; portrait of, 1943 C

Smith, William Saumarez, Anglican
Archbishop of Sydney (1836–1909),
1836 G, 1890 **6**, 1897 **7**, 1909 G
Smith Family (welfare organization), 1922 *
Smithfield (Qld), destroyed by flood, 1879 **3**
Smith's Weekly (newspaper, Syd.), 1919 **3,**
1950 **10**
Smithy (film), 1946 C
Smoking, banned on public transport, 1977 F
Snedden, Sir Billy Mackie, Liberal Party
leader (1926–87), 1926 G, 1955 **12**,
1972 **12**, 1975 **3**, 1987 G
Snodgrass, Kenneth, army officer
(1784–1853), 1837 **12**
Snowfalls: in Sydney, 1836 **6**; heavy, in
eastern Australia, 1984 **7**
Snowtown (SA), 1995 **5**
Snowy Mountains (NSW), sighted by Joseph
Wild, 1820 **8**. *See also* Kosciuszko, Mount
Snowy Mountains Hydro-Electric Authority,
1949 **7**
Snowy Mountains Hydro-Electric Scheme,
1949 **7**, 1955 **2**, 1957 **6**; first major power
station begins operating, 1959 **5**;
completed, 1972 **10**
Snowy River (NSW–Vic.), named, 1834 **1**
Snugglepot and Cuddlepie (M. Gibbs),
1918 D
Sobraon (ship), 1867 **2**, 1891 **2**. *See also*
Tingira
Soccer. *See* Football
Social services, 1943 **3**, 1946 **9**, 1960 F;
reciprocal arrangements, 1943 **9**, 1953 **6**.
See also Family allowance; Funeral
benefits; Maternity allowance; Medibank;
Medical benefits; Medicare; Pensioner
Medical Service; Pensioner pharmaceutical
benefits; Pensions; Pharmaceutical Benefits
Scheme; Sickness benefit; Supporting
parent benefit; Unemployment benefit
Socialist (newspaper, Melb.), 1906 **4**
Socialist Party of Australia, 1971 **12**
Society for the Promotion of Fine Arts,
1847 C
Society of Friends (Quakers), 1832 **2**; open
Friends' School, 1887 **1**
Sodersten, Emil Lawrence, architect
(1900–1961), 1941 A
Solar energy, 1966 B
Soldier settlement, 1917 **1**
Soldiers of the Cross (film), 1900 C
Solid Mandala, The (P. White), 1966 D
Solomon, Albert Edgar, Liberal Premier of
Tas. (1876–1914), 1912 **6**
Solomon, Lance Vaiben, artist (1913–89),
1953 C
Solomon, Vaiben Louis, Premier of SA
(1853–1908), 1899 **12**
Somerset (Qld): settlement established,
1863 **3**, 1864 **8**; livestock overlanded to,
1864 **10**, 1865 **3**; settlement moved to
Thursday Is., 1877 **4**

481

INDEX

INDEX

South Australian Subscription Library, 1844 *
South Australian Theatre Company, 1965 C
South-East Asia Treaty Organization:
  created, 1954 **9**; first meeting, 1955 **2**;
  disbanded, 1977 **6**
South Esk River (Tas.), power station on,
  1895 B
South Head (Port Jackson): signal station,
  1790 A; lighthouse, 1816 A
South Melbourne Town Hall, 1879 A
South Pacific Commission, 1947 **2**, 1948 **5**
South Street competitions (Ballarat), 1891 C
Southerly (periodical), 1939 D
Southern Aurora (train), 1962 **4**; crashes,
  1969 **2**; combined with *Spirit of Progress*,
  1986 **8**
Southern Cloud (aircraft): lost, 1931 **3**;
  wreckage found, 1958 **10**
Southern Cross (aircraft): first trans-Pacific
  flight, 1928 **5**; first non-stop trans-Tasman
  flight, 1928 **9**; missing, 1929 **3 4**; flight to
  England, 1929 **6**; completes circum-
  navigation of world, 1930 **6**; develops
  engine trouble, 1935 **9**
Southern Cross (brigantine), 1920 **9**
Southwell, Harry, film director, 1920 C
Sovereign (ship), 1795 **11**
Soviet Union, diplomatic relations with,
  1954 **4**, 1959 **6**, 1983 **4**
Space tracking stations: Carnarvon (WA),
  1964 B; Honeysuckle Creek (ACT),
  1967 B. *See also* Joint Defence Space
  Research Facility
Spain and Cosh, architects, 1912 A
Spanish dollars, 1792 **11**, 1812 **11**
Spanish expedition, visits Sydney, 1793 **3**
Spanish prizes, 1799 **4 12**
Sparrows, introduced, 1863 F
Speak with the Sun (D. Campbell), 1949 D
Spears, Robert Adam, cyclist (1893–1950),
  1920 E
Spears, Steve J., playwright (1951–), 1976 C
Special Broadcasting Service (SBS), 1978 **1**
Specimens of a Dialect (L. E. Threlkeld),
  1827 D
Spedley Securities, 1989 **12**, 1990 **12**, 1994 **3**
Speedboat racing, 1950 E, 1977 E, 1978 E
Speedo swimsuits, 1928 *
Speedy (ship), 1800 **4**
Speight, Richard, Vic. railways commission
  chairman (1838–1901), 1892 **6**
Speke (convict transport), 1808 **11**
Spence, Bruce, actor (1945–), 1971 C
Spence, Catherine Helen, writer and
  reformer (1825–1910), 1825 G, 1854 D,
  1910 G
Spence, William Guthrie, labour leader
  (1846–1926), 1886 **6**, 1894 **2**
Spencer, Cosens, film exhibitor and producer
  (1874–1930), 1905 C, 1912 C
Spencer, John Brain, architect (1849–1930),
  1891 A

Spencer, Sir Richard, naval officer
  (1779–1839), 1833 **9**
Spencer, Thomas, billiard saloon proprietor,
  1851 E
Spencer, Sir Walter Baldwin, biologist and
  anthropologist (1860–1929), 1860 G,
  1899 B, 1901 B, 1914 B, 1927 B, 1929 G
Spencer Gulf (SA), 1802 **2**
Spencer Street Bridge (Melb.), 1930 **2**
Spencer Street Station (Melb.): lit by
  electricity, 1882 **6**; first electric lifts in,
  1923 A
Spender, Sir Percy Claude, jurist and
  diplomat (1897–1985), 1897 G, 1937 **10**,
  1985 G; initiates Colombo Plan, 1950 **1**;
  ambassador in Washington, 1951 **4**;
  president of International Court, 1964 **3**
Spessiva, Olga, Russian ballet dancer, 1934 C
Spirit of Progress (train), 1937 **11**, 1986 **8**
Spirits, traffic in: Grose instructed to
  prevent, 1793 **6**; distilling prohibited,
  1796 **1**, 1799 **2**; Paterson ordered to stop,
  1799 **3**; NSW Corps involved in, 1800 **1**
  10; King attempts to control, 1800 **10**;
  ships' cargoes rejected, 1801 **1 5**, 1803 **2**;
  Bligh attempts to control, 1807 **2**; and
  Rum Hospital, 1810 **11**, 1814 **12**; duty
  imposed, 1814 **12**
Spiritualism, 1878 F, 1920 F
Spitfire (warship), 1855 **4**
Spofforth, Frederick Robert, cricketer
  (1853–1926), 1853 G, 1878 E, 1879 E,
  1882 E, 1926 G
Spring Frost (painting), 1919 C
Squatters. *See* Land settlement
Squatter's Daughter, The (play), 1907 C;
  films of, 1910 C, 1933 C
Squire, James, early brewer (1755–1822),
  1795 **7**
Squires, Bill, boxer, 1908 E
Stadium Australia (Syd.), 1999 A
Stamp duties, 1865 *
Stamps. *See* Postal services
Standard Bank of Australia, 1893 **4**
Standards Association of Australia, 1922 B
Standfield, Thomas and John, Tolpuddle
  Martyrs, 1834 **8**
Stanley, Francis Drummond Greville,
  architect (1839–97), 1881 A, 1884 A
Stanley, Owen, naval officer and marine
  surveyor (1811–50), 1811 G, 1838 **10**,
  1847 **7**, 1850 **2**
Stanthorpe (Qld), tin discovered at, 1872 **3**
Stanwell Park (NSW), Hargrave experiments
  at, 1894 B
Stapylton, Granville William Chetwynd,
  surveyor (1800–1840), 1840 **5**
Starlings, introduced, 1863 F
State aid for education and religion: in
  NSW, 1826 **3**, 1833 **2**, 1836 **7**, 1862 **12**,
  1866 **12**, 1880 **2**; in SA, 1846 **7**, 1851 **8**;
  in Qld, 1860 **9**; in Vic., 1862 **6**, 1870 **6**;

INDEX

INDEX

Storey, John, Labor Premier of NSW (1869–1921), 1920 **3**, 1921 **10**
Stork (film), 1971 C
Storm Boy (film), 1976 C
Storms
  Gulf of Carpentaria, 1923 **3**
  NSW, 1950 **6**
    north coast, 1950 **1**, 1954 **2**
    Sydney, 1788 **2**, 1799 **6**, 1991 **1**
  NT
    Darwin, 1878 **1**, 1882 **1**, 1897 **1**, 1974 **12**
    Port Essington, 1839 **11**
  Qld
    Bowen, 1867 **3**, 1870 **1**, 1876 **2**, 1884 **1**, 1896 **1**, 1958 **4**, 1959 **2**
    Burdekin area, 1989 **4**
    Cairns, 1878 **2**, 1906 **1**, 1911 **3**, 1913 **1**, 1918 **2**, 1956 **3**, 1986 **2**
    Cooktown, 1907 **1**, 1913 **1**
    far north coast, 1899 **3**, 1934 **3**
    Ingham 1986 **2**
    Innisfail, 1906 **1**, 1911 **3**, 1913 **1**, 1918 **2**
    island resorts, 1970 **1**
    Mackay, 1888 **2**, 1898 **2**, 1918 **1**
    Port Douglas, 1911 **3**
    Rockhampton to Bundaberg, 1949 **2**, 1990 **12**
    south-east, 1974 **1**
    Townsville, 1867 **3**, 1870 **1**, 1896 **1**, 1903 3, 1956 **3**, 1971 **12**
  SA
    Adelaide, 1986 **12**
  WA
    Broome, 1910 **11**
    Carnarvon, 1960 **3**
    Eighty Mile Beach, 1887 **4**, 1908 **4**
    Exmouth Gulf, 1875 **12**, 1993 **3**
    north-west coast, 1881 **1**, 1894 **1**, 1908 **12**, 1935 **3**
    Onslow, 1909 **4**, 1995 **2**
    Roebourne, 1872 **3**; to Busselton, 1892 **12**
Story Bridge (Bris.), 1935 A
Story of Australian Art, The (W. Moore), 1934 D
Story of the Kelly Gang, The (film), 1906 C
Stow, Julian Randolph, author (1935–), 1956 D, 1958 D, 1963 D, 1965 D
Stow Memorial Church (Adel.), 1865 A
Strahan, Sir George Cumine, Governor of Tas. (1838–87), 1881 **12**
Strand Arcade (Syd.), 1891 A
Straiter, James, convict, 1822 F
Strangways, Henry Bull Templar, Premier of SA (1832–1920), 1868 **11**, 1870 **5**
Strathfield Mall massacre, 1991 **8**
Streaky Bay (SA): Eyre at, 1839 **8**; Stuart at, 1858 **8**
Street, Geoffrey Austin, politician (1894–1940), 1940 **8**
Street, Jessie Mary Grey (*née* Lillingston),

feminist and socialist (1889–1970), 1889 G, 1970 G
Street collections, 1894 F
Street lighting (oil), 1826 **4**, 1873 **6**. *See also* Electric light; Gas lighting
Street marches, in Qld, 1967 **9**, 1977 **9**, 1979 **9**. *See also* Demonstrations
Streeton, Sir Arthur Ernest, artist (1867–1943), 1867 G, 1888 C, 1890 C, 1891 C, 1893 C, 1896 C, 1907 C, 1928 C, 1943 G; and Heidelberg School, 1886 C, 1888 C
Stretch of the Imagination, A (play), 1972 C
Strickland, Shirley Barbara, athlete (1925–), 1952 E, 1956 E
Strictly Ballroom (film), 1992 C
Strike Me Lucky (film), 1934 C
Strikes and lockouts. *See also* Anti-strike legislation
  airline pilots, 1958 **11**, 1966 **11**, 1989 **8**
  bakers, 1884 *
  boot trade, 1884 **11**
  carpenters, 1840 **8**
  civil servants (WA), 1920 **7**
  coalminers, 1940 **3**, 1949 **6 8**; in NSW, 1861 **8**, 1873 **2**, 1909 **11 12**, 1916 **10**, 1929 **2 12**, 1944 **2**, 1945 **11**, 1948 **10**; at Newcastle, 1855 **5**, 1888 **8**, 1896 **4**
  copper miners (SA), 1874 **4**, 1891 **9**
  electricity workers (Qld), 1985 **2**
  general, 1912 **1**, 1917 **8 9 10**, 1976 **7**, 1979 **6**
  Maritime, 1890 **3 8 9 10 11**
  metal trades, 1946 **10**
  miners at Broken Hill, 1892 **7 9 10 11**, 1908 **12**, 1909 **1 3**, 1919 **5**
  newspapers, 1829 **11**, 1944 **10**, 1945 **11**, 1955 **6**
  over penal clauses, 1969 **5**
  railwaymen, 1903 **5**, 1948 **1**, 1950 **10**
  seamen, 1878 **11**, 1893 **7**, 1919 **5**, 1925 **6 7**
  shearers, 1890 **9**, 1891 **1 2 3 5 8** D, 1894 **6 7 8 9**, 1956 **2**
  steelworkers, 1945 **11**
  tailoresses, 1882 **12**
  tailors, 1840 **8**
  teachers, 1920 **7**, 1965 **7**
  timber workers, 1929 **2**
  tramwaymen, 1917 **8**, 1948 **1**
  wharf labourers, 1882 **11**, 1886 **1**, 1928 **9 11**, 1943 **3**, 1956 **1**, 1998 **5**
Stripper-harvester, 1884 B
Strong, Charles, minister of religion (1844–1942), founds Australian Church, 1885 **11**
Struggle for Europe (C. Wilmot), 1952 D
Strutt, William, artist (1825–1915), 1864 C
Strzelecki, Sir Paul Edmond de, explorer (1797–1873), 1797 G, 1840 **5**, 1845 D, 1873 G; names Mt Kosciuszko, 1840 **2**
Strzelecki Creek (SA), 1845 **8**
Strzelecki Track, 1870 **3**

485

INDEX

INDEX

New South Wales State Conservatorium of Music

Sydney Cove: settlement established at, 1788 **1**; livestock stray from, 1788 **6**, 1795 **11**

Sydney Cove (convict transport), 1807 **6**

Sydney Cove (ship), wreck of, 1797 **2 3 5 6**, 1798 **2**

Sydney Dance Company, 1965 C

Sydney Dispensary, 1826 **8**, 1845 **7**

Sydney Entertainment Centre, 1983 C

Sydney Football Stadium, 1988 E

Sydney Free Grammar School, 1825 **11**

Sydney Free Public Library, 1869 **9**

Sydney Gazette (Australia's first newspaper), 1803 **3**, 1825 **9**, 1827 **1**; printed on locally produced paper, 1820 **7**; censorship of, ends, 1824 **10**; ceases publication, 1842 **10**

Sydney Grammar School, 1830 **1**, 1857 **8**, 1867 **1**

Sydney Harbour: ferries on, 1807 **8**, 1842 **8**, 1847*, 1965 **1**; shipping disasters on, 1814 **5**, 1927 **11**, 1938 **2**; Japanese midget submarines enter, 1942 **5**

Sydney Harbour Bridge, 1923 A, 1932 **3**

Sydney Harbour Tunnel, 1988 A, 1992 **8**

Sydney Herald. See Sydney Morning Herald

Sydney High School, 1883 **10**

Sydney Hospital: first built, 1810 **11**, 1811 A; Lucy Osburn superintendent of, 1868 **3**; new hospital, 1880 A, 1894 **10**; first liver transplant at, 1968 **4**. *See also* Sydney Infirmary and Dispensary

Sydney Hospital for Sick Children. *See* Royal Alexandra Hospital for Children

Sydney Illustrated (J. S. Prout), 1842 D

Sydney Infirmary and Dispensary, 1826 **8**, 1845 **7**

Sydney Liedertafel, 1903 C

Sydney Mail (newspaper), 1860 **7**, 1882 D, 1938 **12**

Sydney Mechanics' School of Arts, 1833 **3**, 1879 *

Sydney Morning Herald (newspaper), 1831 **4**, 1840 **10**, 1841 **2**, 1842 **8**

Sydney Newspapers Ltd, 1932 **11**, 1933 **6**

Sydney Observatory, 1857 A, 1874 B

Sydney Opera House, 1957 A, 1959 A; Utzon resigns, 1966 A; opened, 1973 **10** A; mural and curtains, 1973 C

Sydney Punch (newspaper), 1864 **5**

Sydney Railway and Tramway Co., 1849 **10**

Sydney Repertory Theatre Society, 1920 C

Sydney Savings Bank, 1843 **6**

Sydney Showground, 1996 C

Sydney Sovereign, A ("Tasma"), 1890 D

Sydney Square, 1976 A

Sydney Stadium, 1908 E, 1970 E

Sydney Symphony Orchestra, 1908 C, 1946 C, 1947 C

Sydney Teachers' College, 1906 *

Sydney Town Hall, 1869 A, 1880 **2**, 1888 A, 1889 **11**

Sydney Tropical Centre, 1990 B

Sydney Turf Club, 1825 E, 1943 E

Sydney University. *See* University of Sydney

Syme, David, newspaper proprietor (1827–1908), 1827 G, 1856 **6**, 1908 G

Syme, Ebenezer, newspaper proprietor (1826–60), 1856 **6**

Synagogues, 1842 **4**, 1844 **4**, 1878 **3**

Syren (blackbirding vessel), 1868 **1**

T

TAA. *See* Trans-Australia Airlines

Table Talk (magazine, Melb.), 1885 **6**

Tahiti (steamship), 1927 **11**

Tait, Charles, film producer (1868–1933), 1906 C

Tait, J. and N., theatrical entrepreneurs, 1920 C

Tait, Robert Peter, murderer, 1962 **11**

Takeovers, company, 1984 F, 1985 **8**

Tales of the Convict System (P. Warung), 1892 D

Talgai skull, 1886 B

Tall Timbers (film), 1937 C

Tallow, 1843 **6**

Tamar, HMS, 1824 **8**

Tamar River (Tas.), 1798 **11**, 1804 **1**; settlement on, 1804 **11 12**

Tamworth (NSW), 1850 **6**, 1946 **7**; railway reaches, 1878 **10**; first town lit by electricity, 1888 **11**; Country Music Festival, 1973 C

Tangney, Dame Dorothy Margaret, Labor senator (1911–85), 1943 **8**

Tank Stream (Syd.), 1792 A, 1804 A, 1811 A

Tanunda (SA), Liedertafel, 1861 C; peace festival held in, 1871 **10**

Tarakan Is. (Borneo), 1945 **5**

Taree (NSW), 1854 **12**

Tariff Board, 1921 **12**, 1974 **1**

Tariff League of Victoria, 1859 **1**

Tariffs: import duty imposed, 1802 **6**; first tariff league formed, 1859 **1**; intercolonial conference on, 1863 **3**; Australia's first protective tariff legislation, 1866 **3 4**; intercolonial tariffs permitted, 1873 **5**; uniform, 1902 **9**; Commonwealth preferential, 1906 **10**; on agricultural machinery, 1907 **1**; duties increased, 1908 **6**, 1921 **12**; agreement with NZ on, 1922 **4**, General Agreement on Tariffs and Trade, 1947 **11**, 1963 **8**; reduced by 25 per cent, 1973 **7**

Taronga Park Zoo (Syd.), 1912 B

INDEX

Tarrant, Harley, pioneer motorist (1860–1949), 1904 E, 1905 E
Tarrant Motor and Engineering Co., 1901 B
Tarzan's Grip (glue), 1935 B
"Tasma". *See* Couvreur, Jessie Catherine
Tasman Bridge (Hobart), 1964 A; collapses, 1975 **1**; reopened, 1977 **10**
Tasman Empire Airways Ltd, 1938 **11**, 1940 **4**, 1954 **5**, 1961 **7**
Tasmania: explored by d'Entrecasteaux, 1792 **4**, 1793 **1 2**; explored by Bass and Flinders, 1798 **11 12**; circumnavigated, 1799 **1**, 1815 **12**; first settlements, 1803 **9**, 1804 **2**, 1806 **3**; first direct convict transport to, 1812 **10**; first free migrants, 1816 **9**; communication between Hobart and Launceston, 1818 **5**; first official census, 1841 F; name adopted, 1856 **1**; separated from NSW, 1825 **6 7 12;** numbers transported to, 1842 F; transportation to, ends, 1852 **11**, 1853 **5**; Norfolk Is. annexed to, 1844 **9**; apples exported from, 1849 *; postage stamps, 1853 **11**; representative government, 1855 **5 11**, 1856 **10 12**; time standardized, 1895 **9**; referendum on Federation held, 1898 **6**, adult male suffrage introduced, 1900 **4**, women gain the vote, 1903 **12**; and Hare-Clark voting system, 1907 **11**, 1998 **7**; free primary education introduced, 1908 **12**; homosexuality decriminalized, 1997 F

Governors (chronologically, to Federation)
Col. David Collins, 1804 **2**
Maj. Thomas Davey, 1811 **9**, 1813 **2**
Col. William Sorell, 1817 **4**
Col. George Arthur, 1824 **5**
Sir John Franklin, 1837 **1**
Sir John Eardley-Wilmot, 1843 **8**
Sir William Denison, 1847 **1**
Sir Henry Fox Young, 1855 **1**
Col. T. G. Browne, 1862 **6**
Charles du Cane, 1869 **1**
Sir Frederick Weld, 1875 **1**
Sir William Jervois, 1877 **10**
Sir George Strahan, 1881 **12**
Sir Robert Hamilton, 1887 **3**
Viscount Gormanston, 1893 **8**

Premiers (chronologically, from responsible government)
W. T. N. Champ, 1856 **11**
T. G. Gregson, 1857 **2**
W. P. Weston, 1857 **4**
F. V. Smith, 1857 **5**
W. P. Weston, 1860 **11**
T. D. Chapman, 1861 **8**
James Whyte, 1863 **1**
Sir Richard Dry, 1866 **11**
J. M. Wilson, 1869 **8**
F. M. Innes, 1872 **11**
Alfred Kennerley, 1873 **8**
Thomas Reibey, 1876 **7**

P. O. Fysh, 1877 **8**
W. R. Giblin, 1878 **4**
W. L. Crowther, 1878 **12**
W. R. Giblin, 1879 **10**
Adye Douglas, 1884 **8**
J. W. Agnew, 1886 **3**
P. O. Fysh, 1887 **3**
Henry Dobson, 1892 **8**
Sir Edward Braddon, 1894 **4**
N. E. Lewis, 1899 **10**
W. B. Propsting, 1903 **4**
J. W. Evans, 1904 **7**
Sir Neil Lewis, 1909 **6**
John Earle, 1909 **10**
Sir Neil Lewis, 1909 **10**
Albert Solomon, 1912 **6**
John Earle, 1914 **4**
Sir Walter Lee, 1916 **4**
J. B. Hayes, 1922 **8**
Sir Walter Lee, 1923 **8**
J. A. Lyons, 1923 **10**
J. C. McPhee, 1928 **6**
Sir Walter Lee, 1934 **3**
A. G. Ogilvie, 1934 **6**
Edmund Dwyer-Gray, 1939 **6**
Robert Cosgrove, 1939 **12**
Edward Brooker, 1947 **12**
Robert Cosgrove, 1948 **2**
Eric Reece, 1958 **8**
W. A. Bethune, 1969 **5**
Eric Reece, 1972 **4**
W. A. Neilson, 1975 **3**
D. A. Lowe, 1977 **12**
Harry Holgate, 1981 **11**
Robin Gray, 1982 **5**
Michael Field, 1989 **6**
Ray Groom, 1992 **2**
Tony Rundle, 1996 **3**
Jim Bacon, 1998 **8**

Tasmanian (newspaper, Hob.), 1827 **3**
Tasmanian Conservatorium of Music, 1964 C
Tasmanian Hydro-Electric Commission, 1929 *
Tasmanian Jockey Club, 1859 E
Tasmanian Journal of Natural Science, 1842 B
Tasmanian Museum and Art Gallery, 1863 A
Tasmanian tiger (thylacine), 1805 F
Tasmanian Workers' Political League, 1901 **10**
Tasminex NL, 1970 **1**
Tass, Nadia, film director, 1986 C
Tattersall's Hotel (Syd.), 1881 **4**, 1893 A C
Tattersall's Sweep, 1881 **4**. *See also* Lotteries
Tatura (Vic.), POW camp at, 1942 **9**
Tauchert, Arthur Michael, actor (1877–1933), 1919 C
Tauranga, HMS, 1891 **9**
Taxation: by representation, 1827 **1**; on newspapers, 1827 **4**, 1927 **1**; on wartime profits, 1917 **9**; increased to finance social services, 1945 **8**; avoidance schemes,

INDEX

INDEX

Tierney, John Lawrence (pseud. Brian James), author (1892–1972), 1950 D
Tiffin, Charles, architect (1833–73), 1865 A
Tilted Cross, The (H. Porter), 1961 D
Timbertop school (Vic.), 1966 **1**
Time, standard, 1895 **1 2 9 12**
Timeless Land, The (E. Dark), 1941 D
Times on Sunday. See National Times
Timor, 1942 **2**, 1952 **5**, 1999 **9**
Tin, discoveries, 1871 **12**, 1872 **1 3**, 1875 *, 1879 **6**, 1880 **4**
Tinaroo Creek (Qld), 1879 **6**
Tingira, HMAS (training ship), 1912 **4**. *See also Sobraon*
Tintookies (puppets), 1957 C
Tirra Lirra by the River (J. Anderson), 1978 D
Tivoli Theatre (Melb.), 1896 C, 1966 C
Tivoli Theatre (Syd.: 1, formerly the Garrick), 1893 C, 1896 C, 1899 **9**
Tivoli Theatre (Syd.: 2, formerly the Adelphi and the Grand Opera House, 1911 C, 1832 C, 1966 C
To Meet the Sun (R. D. FitzGerald), 1929 D
To the Islands (R. Stow), 1958 D
Toast to Melba, A (play), 1975 C
Tobacco, 1822 **8**, 1956 **1**; advertising of, banned on radio and TV, 1976 **9**
Tobruk, capture and siege of, 1941 **1 4**
Tocsin (newspaper, Melb.), 1897 **10**
Todd, Sir Charles, Postmaster-General of SA (1826–1910): constructs Overland Telegraph Line, 1870 **9**; wireless experiment, 1899 B
Tokens, as currency, 1849 *, 1852 **12**
Tollways, 1811 **4**, 1813 *, 1965 **12**
Tolmer, Alex, toymaker, 1957 E
Tolpuddle Martyrs, 1834 **8**, 1836 **3**
Tom, William, farmer (1791–1883), discovers gold, 1851 **4**
Tom Petrie's Reminiscences of Early Queensland, 1904 D
Tom Price, Mount (WA), 1962 **9**
Tom Thumb (boats), 1795 **2 10**, 1796 **3**
Tomato sauce, 1899 B
Tomorrow and Tomorrow (M. B. Eldershaw), 1947 D
Tompson, Charles, poet and public servant (1807–83), 1826 D
Tonkin, David Oliver, Liberal Premier of SA (1929–), 1979 **9**
Tonkin, John Trezise, Labor Premier of WA (1902–95), 1971 **2**
Toohey, John Leslie, judge (1930–), 1981 **11**
Tooheys Brewery (Syd.), 1870 *, 1985 **8**
Toongabbie (NSW), 1802 **6**
Tooth's Brewery (Syd.), 1835 **10**
Toowoomba (Qld), 1854 **6**, 1904 **10**
Topaz (US whaler), 1808 **2**
Torrens, Robert, colonization commissioner (1780–1864), 1835 **2**

Torrens, Sir Robert Richard, Premier of SA (1814–84), 1814 G, 1857 **9**, 1884 G
Torrens, Lake (SA), 1839 **5**, 1858 **3 5**; fills with water, 1989 F
Torrens River (SA), 1836 **11**; floods, 1851 **8**
Torrens system, 1858 **7**
Torres Strait, 1802 **11**; Bligh sails through, 1789 **5**, 1792 **9**; first merchant vessels pass through, 1793 **7**; Islands annexed to Qld, 1872 **5**, 1879 **6**
Torres Strait Islanders, 1793 **7**, 1988 **1**
Total wage, concept introduced, 1967 **6**
Totalizator, 1879 E; automatic, 1913 B, 1917 E
Totalizator Agency Boards, 1961 E
Tourmaline (R. Stow), 1963 D
Town Like Alice, A (N. Shute), 1950 D
Town planning, first national conference, 1917 A
Towns, George, sculler (1869–1961), 1901 E
Towns, Robert, pioneer merchant (1794–1873), 1794 G, 1846 **3**, 1863 **8**, 1873 G; founds Townsville, 1864 **7**
Townson, John, commandant on Norfolk Is. (1760–1835), 1796 **10**, 1799 **11**
Townsville (Qld), 1864 **7**, 1865 **10**, 1902 **12**; damaged by cyclone, 1867 **3**, 1870 **1**, 1896 **1**, 1903 **3**, 1971 **12**; Japan opens consulate in, 1896 **3**; strikers and police clash, 1919 **6**; sustains Japanese air raid, 1942 **7**; university established, 1961 *; sugar terminal fire, 1963 **5**; international airport, 1981 **2**
Trade: first foreign trading vessels, 1792 **11 12**; NSW Corps officers engage in, 1792 **10**; Campbell establishes business, 1800 **2**; protection against dumping, 1906 **9**; Empire preference, 1932 **7**; diversion policy, 1936 **5 6 8**; with Japan, 1936 **6**, 1938 **7**, 1957 **7**, 1963 **8**, 1966 F; free-trade agreement with NZ, 1965 **8**; free-trade agreement with APEC, 1994 **11**. *See also* Exports; Tariffs
Trade fair, Australia's first international, 1961 **8**
Trade Practices Act, Commonwealth, 1967 **9**, 1974 **10**
Trade unionism: convict attempt at organization, 1822 F; first trade association, 1829 *; United Operative Masons' Society formed, 1850 **11**; Melbourne Trades Hall Committee formed. 1856 *; legal recognition, 1876 *; intercolonial congresses held, 1879 **10**, 1886 **9**, 1888 **3**; unions sponsor MP, 1880 **11**; Australian Labour Federation formed, 1889 **6**; ACTU formed, 1927 **5**; Communist influence in unions, 1945 *; compulsory unionism, 1953 F; percentage of workforce unionized, 1954 F; Australia's largest union formed, 1972 **8**; voluntary unionism enforced, 1997 **1**.

492

INDEX

INDEX

Turrall, Jennifer Lynnette, swimmer (1960–), 1973 E
Turtle Beach (B. d'Alpuget), 1981 D
Tuxworth, Ian Lindsay, Chief Minister of NT (1942–), 1984 **10**, 1986 **5**
Twain, Mark (Samuel Clemens), US author (1835–1910), 1895 D
Tweed River (NSW), 1823 **10**
XXI Poems: Towards the Source (C. Brennan), 1897 D
Twenty Thousand Thieves (E. Lambert), 1951 D
Two Expeditions into the Interior of Southern Australia (C. Sturt), 1833 D
Two Thousand Weeks (film), 1969 C
Two-up, 1804 E
Two Years in New South Wales (P. Cunningham), 1827 D
Twofold Bay (NSW), 1797 **12**, 1818 *, 1926 *; Ben Boyd's interests at, 1843 * A, 1844 *
Twyborn Affair, The (P. White), 1979 D
Typhoid fever, 1905 F
Typhus, 1852 **12**
Tyranny of Distance, The (G. Blainey), 1966 D
Tyrrell, William, Anglican Bishop of Newcastle (1807–79), 1847 **6**

U

UAP. *See* United Australia Party
Ulladulla (NSW), 1870 **4**
Ullathorne, William Bernard, pioneer Catholic prelate (1806–89), 1833 **2**, 1838 **12**
Ulm, Charles Thomas Philippe, aviator (1898–1934), 1898 G, 1934 G; on first Pacific flight, 1928 **5**; on first trans-Australia non-stop flight, 1928 **8**; on first trans-Tasman flight, 1928 **9**; founds ANA, 1928 **12**; on flight to England, 1929 **3 6**; carries first Aust.–NZ airmail, 1934 **4**; killed in crash, 1934 **12**
Ultima Thule (H. H. Richardson), 1929 D
Uluru National Park (NT), 1958 F; title handed to Aborigines, 1985 **10**
Umberumberka Silver Mine, 1882 **11**
Unaipon, David. preacher, author, and inventor (1872–1967), 1872 G, 1929 D, 1967 G
Uncle Piper of Piper's Hills ("Tasma"), 1889 D
Under Aldebaran (J. McAuley), 1946 D
Under Capricorn (H. Simpson), 1937 D
Underwood, Jacky, outlaw, 1900 **7**
Underwood, James, shipbuilder and merchant

(1771–1844), 1791 **10**, 1807 **6**: partnership with Kable, 1800 **7**, 1805 **1 4**
Underwood, Joseph, merchant and ship owner (1779–1833), 1807 **6**
Unemployment, 1843 **8** F, 1930 **4** F, 1932 F, 1986 F, 1992 F
Unemployment benefit, 1945 F
Unemployment insurance. 1923 F
Unesco, ambassador to, 1978 **2**
Union Bank of Australia, 1951 **10**
Union Theatre Repertory Company (Melb.), 1953 C, 1955 C
Unionism. *See* Trade unionism
Unitarian Church, 1850 **6**
United Australia Party: formed, 1931 **5**; leadership changes, 1939 **4**, 1941 **8**, 1943 **9**; becomes Liberal Party, 1944 **10**, 1945 **2**
United Labour Party, 1891 **1**, 1893 **4**
United Nations Organization, 1945 **4 6**; Evatt president of General Assembly, 1948 **9**; Australia on Security Council, 1985 **1**
United Operative Masons' Society, 1850 **11**
United States of America: early trading vessels in Sydney, 1792 **11**, 1794 **7**, 1796 **2**, 1801 **1 5**; at war with Britain, 1812 **6**; privateers capture ships, 1812 **11**, 1815 **1**; first consul in Sydney, 1839 **1**; ships enter Port Jackson unannounced, 1839 **11**; attracts Aust. diggers to California, 1849 **1**; Confederate ship at Melbourne, 1865 **1**, visit of the Great White Fleet, 1908 **8**; visits of naval squadrons, 1925 **7**, 1941 **3**; withdraws Australia's most-favoured-nation concessions, 1936 **8**; Casey becomes Australia's Minister to, 1940 **1**; servicemen in Australia in World War II, 1941 **12**, 1942 **3 11**; atomic information agreement, 1957 **7**. *See also* ANZUS Treaty; Joint Defence Space Research Facility; North-West Cape
United Tradesmen's Society, 1874 **4**
Uniting Church in Australia, 1977 **6**
Unity (schooner), seized by convicts, 1813 **4**
Universities Commission, 1943 **2**, 1959 **4**
University of Adelaide, 1874 **11**; admits women, 1876 **3**; chair of music, 1885 C, 1897 C
University of Canberra, 1990 **4**
University of Melbourne, 1854 A, 1855 **4**, admits women, 1880 F, 1883 F; chair of music endowed, 1987 C; Conservatorium, 1895 C: bequest for biochemistry school, 1944 B
University of New England, 1938 **4**
University of New South Wales, 1949 **7**; NIDA established, 1958 C
University of Newcastle, 1951 **12**
University of Queensland, 1909 **12**; buildings, 1860 A, 1937 A

INDEX

University of Sydney, 1850 **10**, 1852 **10**; 1854 A, 1857 B; forms first football club, 1864 E; admits female students, 1881 F; Medical School opened, 1883 B; admits first female medical student, 1885 F; Power Bequest. 1943 C; first chair of Australian literature, 1961 D

University of Tasmania, 1890 **1**; and Orr case, 1956 **3**

University of Western Australia, 1911 **2**

University of Western Sydney, 1813 A, 1989 **1**

University of Wollongong, 1951 *, 1975 **1**

Unknown Industrial Prisoner, The (D. Ireland), 1971 D

Unknown soldier, 1993 **11**

Unlawful Associations Act, 1917 **8**

Unreliable Memoirs (C. James), 1980 D

Unsworth, Barrie John, Labor Premier of NSW (1934–), 1986 **7**, 1988 **3**

Up the Country (M. Franklin), 1928 D

Up the Murray (A. Cambridge), 1875 D

Upfield, Arthur William, author (1890–1964), 1890 G, 1929 D, 1931 D, 1964 G

Uranie, L' (French corvette), 1818 **9**, 1819 **11**

Uranium: discoveries, 1949 **8**, 1954 **7**, 1970 **9**; agreement on development at Radium Hill, 1952 **4**, treatment plant at Rum Jungle, 1954 **9**, Ranger mine, 1976 **11**, 1977 **5**, 1979 **1**; ALP policy on, 1977 **7**, 1982 **7**; government allows mining, 1977 **8**; unions' policy on, 1978 **2**; Roxby Downs deposit, 1982 **6**; at Jabiluka, 1982 **7**

Urquhart, Frederic Charles, police officer (1858–1935), 1884 **9**

Utzon, Joern, Danish architect (1918–), wins competition for Opera House design, 1957 A; resigns, 1966 A

V

Vaccination: smallpox, 1804 **5**; polio, 1956 **7**, 1967 **5**

"Vagabond, The" *See* James, Stanley

Valadian, Margaret, social worker (1936–), 1966 F

Valley of the Tweed, The (painting), 1921 C

Vampire, HMAS, 1942 **4**

Van Diemen's Land. *See* Tasmania

Van Diemen's Land Company, 1824 **5**, 1825 **6**, 1826 **10**, 1827 **2**

Van Diemen's Land Gazette and General Advertiser (newspaper, Hob.), 1814 **5**

Van Praagh, Dame Margaret (Peggy), ballet director (1910–), 1910 G, 1962 C, 1990 G

Van Wisse, Tammy, long-distance swimmer, 1996 E

Vancouver, George, navigator (1757–98), 1791 **9 10**

Vane, John, bushranger, 1863 **10 11**

Vareschetti, Modesto, miner, 1907 **3**

Vaucluse House (Syd.), 1827 A, 1911 F

Vaughan, Crawford, Labor Premier of SA (1874–1947), 1915 **4**

Vaughan, Roger William Bede, Catholic prelate (1834–83), 1877 **3**

Vaux, James Hardy, convict-adventurer (1782–1853?), 1801 **12**, 1819 D; returns to UK with King, 1807 **2**; transported second time, 1810 **12**, pardoned, 1820 **1**; absconds to Ireland, 1829 **4**; transported third time, 1831 **4**

Vegemite, 1923 B

Vendetta, HMAS 1941 **3**

Venus (brig), 1806 **6**

Venus (trading vessel), 1801 **8 11**, 1803 **2**

Venus, transit of, 1874 B

Verbrugghen, Henri Adrien Marie, musician, (1873–1934), 1915 C, 1922 C

Verdon, Sir George Frederic, Vic. Agent-General (1834–96), 1868 **12**

Verge, John, architect (1782–1861), 1828 A, 1832 A, 1835 A, 1861 G

Vernon Committee of Economic Inquiry, 1965 **8**

Verran, John, Labor Premier of SA (1856–1932), 1910 **4**, 1912 **2**

Verses, Popular and Humorous (H. Lawson), 1900 D

Vestey's meatworks, 1917 **4**

Viatel, 1985 B

Victa lawnmower, 1952 B

Victor Harbour (SA), 1839 **6**

Victoria: first postage stamps issued, 1850 **1**; separated from NSW, 1850 **8 11**, 1851 **7**; gold discovered, 1851 **7 8**; first Legislative Council, 1851 **9 11**; volunteer military force raised, 1854 *; first census, 1854 F; tax on immigrants imposed, 1855 **6**; responsible government granted, 1855 **7 11**, 1856 **11**; government railways established, 1856 **5**; naval vessels acquired, 1856 **5**, 1871 **4**; manhood suffrage granted, 1857 **11**; state aid to religion abolished, 1870 **6**; free, compulsory, and secular education introduced, 1872 **12** F; financial crisis, 1891 **8 12**, 1892 **1**; income tax introduced, 1895 **1**; time standardized, 1895 **2**; referendum on Federation held, 1898 **6**; contingent sent to Boer War, 1899 **7 10**, 1901 **6**; women given vote in state elections, 1908 **9**. *See also* Port Phillip district

Governors (chronologically from separation to Federation)
C. J. La Trobe, 1851 **7**

495

INDEX

W

INDEX

Wanderer (yacht), 1842 **7**, 1851 **10 11**
Wanderers soccer club, 1880 E
Wandering Islands, The (A. D. Hope),
  1955 D
Wangaratta (Vic.), 1849 **6**
War cabinet, 1939 **9**
War Census Act, 1915 **7**
War Cry (newspaper, Syd.), 1883 **3**
War Diaries of Weary Dunlop, The
  (Sir E. Dunlop), 1986 D
War memorials
  Adelaide, 1931 A
  Brisbane, 1930 A
  Canberra, 1925 **4**, 1941 A, 1954 A
  Melbourne, 1927 A, 1934 **11**
  Perth, 1929 **11**
  Sydney, 1927 **8**, 1929 C, 1932 A, 1934 **11**
War Savings Certificates, 1940 **3**
War service homes, 1919 **3**
War Precautions Act, 1914 **10**, 1917 **11**
Warburton, Peter Egerton, soldier and
  explorer (1813–89), 1813 G, 1873 **4 6 9
  12**, 1874 **1**, 1889 G
Warby, Kenneth, speedboat driver (1939–),
  1977 E, 1978 E
Ward, Edward John, Labor politician
  (1899–1963): and "Brisbane Line",
  1942 **10**, 1943 **7**; and New Guinea timber
  leases, 1948 **1**, 1949 **1**
Ward, Frederick, bushranger (1835–70),
  1870 **5**
Ward, Russel Braddock, historian (1914–95),
  1958 D
Wardell, Robert, journalist and advocate
  (1793–1834), 1824 **7 9**; founds *Australian*,
  1824 **10**; fights duels, 1826 **10**, 1827 **3**;
  tried for libel, 1827 **9**; shot, 1834 **9**
Wardell, William Wilkinson, architect
  (1823–99), 1858 A, 1868 A 1871 A
Wardley, Deborah Jane, pilot (1953–),
  1980 F
Wardrop, James Hastie, architect
  (1891–1975), 1927 A
Warragamba Dam (NSW), 1960 **10**
Warragamba River (NSW), 1804 **9**
Warramunga, HMAS, 1950 **12**
Warrego, HMAS, 1911 **4**, 1913 **10**
Warrego River (Qld), 1846 **6**
Warren, David, inventor (1925–), 1954 B
Warren, Guy Wilkie, artist (1921–), 1985 C
Warringah Expressway (Syd.), 1968 **6**
Warrnambool (Vic.), 1847 **1**, 1855 **12,
  1918 **4**; road race, 1895 E
Warrumbungle Ranges (NSW), 1818 **8**
Warung, Price. *See* Astley, William
Warwick (Qld), 1850 **7**; egg incident,
  1917 **11**
Washing machines, rudimentary, 1832 B
Washington conference on disarmament,
  1921 **11**, 1924 **4**
Washpool rainforest (NSW), 1985 F
Waste Lands Act, 1842 **6**

Watch Tower, The (E. Harrower), 1966 D
Watcher on the Cast-Iron Balcony, The
  (H. Porter), 1963 D
Waten, Judah, author (1911–85), 1952 D
Water supply
  Adelaide, 1860 **12**
  Brisbane, 1866 **7**
  Melbourne, 1857 **12**
  Morgan–Whyalla pipeline (SA), 1944 **3**
  Sydney, 1792 A, 1827 **9**, 1837 **6**, 1886 **11**;
    contaminated, 1998 **7**
  WA goldfields, 1902 **3**, 1903 **1**
Water under the Bridge (S. L. Elliott),
  1977 D
Waterhen, HMAS, 1941 **6**
Waterhouse, George Marsden, Premier of SA
  (1824–1906), 1861 **10**
Waterhouse, Henry, naval officer
  (1770–1812), 1795 **2 9**, 1796 **9**, 1800 **3**,
  1812 G; imports merinos, 1797 **6**
Waterhouse, Robert, bookmaker, 1984 E
Waterhouse, William Stanley, bookmaker
  (1922–), 1984 E
Waterloo (Syd.), 1818 B, 1820 **7**
Waterside workers, 1928 **9**; and Maritime
  Strike, 1890 **8**; refuse to load pig-iron for
  Japan, 1938 **11**, 1939 **1**; ban loading of
  Dutch ships, 1945 **9**; conflict with Patrick
  Stevedores, 1998 **4**
Watling, Thomas, artist (b. 1762), 1792 **10**,
  1794 C
Watson, John Christian (Johan Christian
  Tanck), Labor Prime Minister
  (1867–1941), 1867 G, 1901 **5**, 1907 **10**,
  1941 G; leads first federal Labor
  government, 1904 **4 8**
Watson, Mary Beatrice Phillips, "heroine of
  Lizard Is." (1860–81), 1881 **10**
Watson, Raymond Sanders, judge (1922–),
  1984 **7**
Watson, W. G., architect, 1883 A, 1892 A
Watt, Harry, film director (1906–), 1946 C,
  1949 C
Watt, Kathryn Anne, cyclist (1964–), 1992 E
Watt, William Alexander, Liberal/Nationalist
  politician (1871–1946): Premier of Vic.,
  1912 **5**, 1913 **12**; enters federal politics,
  1914 **6**; acting Prime Minister, 1918 **4**
Wattle (bot.), tannin extracted from, 1819 B;
  proclaimed as floral emblem, 1988 **9**
Wattle Day, 1992 F
Watts, John, architect, 1815 A, 1816 A,
  1820 A
Wau (PNG), 1943 **2**
Waugh, Mark Edward, cricketer (1965–),
  1990 E
Waugh, Stephen Rodger, cricketer (1965–),
  1990 E
Wave Hill station (NT), 1966 **8**, 1967 **3**,
  1975 **8**
Way Home, The (H. H. Richardson), 1925 D
Ways of Many Waters (E. J. Brady), 1899 D

INDEX

INDEX

INDEX

World War II, in Australia (continued)
Corps formed, 1942 **4**; Japanese midget submarines enter Sydney Harbour, 1942 **5**; SS *Iron Chieftain* and *Iron Crown* sunk off coast, 1942 **6**; Sydney and Newcastle shelled, 1942 **6**; ration books issued, 1942 **6**; air raid on Townsville, 1942 **7**; Women's Land Army established, 1942 **7**; air raid on Port Hedland, 1942 **7**; mass breakout at Tatura POW camp, 1942 **9**; "Brisbane Line" controversy, 1942 **10**, 1943 3 **7**; "Battle of Brisbane", 1942 **11**; women called up for war work, 1942 **12**; Boomerang fighter plane produced, 1942 B; SS *Iron Knight* torpedoed off NSW coast, 1943 **2**; conscripts become liable for overseas service, 1943 **2**; 9th Div. returns from Middle East, 1943 **2**; hospital ship *Centaur* sunk off Cape Moreton, 1943 **5**; air raid on Exmouth Gulf, 1943 **5**; butter and household drapery rationed, 1943 **6**; *Wallaroo* sinks off Fremantle, 1943 **6**; meat rationed, 1944 **1**; newspapers suppressed by censor, 1944 **4**; Japanese POWs break out at Cowra, 1944 **8**; brown-out restrictions removed, 1944 **9**; VE Day celebrated, 1945 **5**; demobilization begins, 1945 **10**
Mediterranean: Sydney sinks *Bartolomeo Colleoni* off Crete, 1940 **7**; Battle of Matapan, 1941 **3**; 6th Div. sent to Greece, 1941 **3**; troops withdraw from Greece to Crete, 1941 **4**; evacuation from Crete, 1941 **5**; *Waterhen* sunk, 1941 **6**; *Parramatta* sunk, 1941 **11**; *Nestor* sunk, 1942 **6**
Middle East: Australian forces capture Tobruk, 1941 **1**; Benghazi captured, 1941 **2**; Giarabub captured, 1941 **3**; 9th Div. relieves 6th Div. at Cyrenaica, 1941 **3**; Siege of Tobruk, 1941 **4**; Allies invade Syria, 1941 **6**; Damascus captured, 1941 **6**; armistice in Syria, 1941 **7**; Battle of El Alamein, 1942 **10**
Asia-Pacific region: German raiders sink ships off Nauru, 1940 **12**; RAAF bombers attack Japanese in Malaya, 1941 **12**; Rabaul bombed by Japanese, 1942 **1**; Australian troops engage Japanese in Malaya, 1942 **1**; Japanese bomb Salamaua, Lae, Madang, Bulolo, 1942 **1**; Rabaul falls to Japanese, 1942 **1**; Australian forces on Ambon surrender, 1942 **2**; Japanese bomb Port Moresby, 1942 **2**; Singapore falls; 15,000 Australians imprisoned, 1942 **2**; Australian force in Timor surrenders, 1942 **2**; *Perth* sunk, 1942 **3**; *Yarra* sunk, 1942 **3**; Japanese occupy Lae and Salamaua, 1942 **3**; Australian forces in

Java surrender, 1942 **3**; *Vampire* sunk, 1942 **4**; Battle of Coral Sea, 1942 **5**; Australian prisoners die in *Montevideo Maru*, 1942 **7**; Japanese land at Gona and occupy Kokoda, 1942 **7**; *Canberra* sunk, 1942 **8**; Japanese occupy Nauru, 1942 **8**; Japanese land at Milne Bay, 1942 **8**; *Arunta* sinks Japanese *RO33*, 1942 **8**; *Voyager* destroyed, 1942 **9**; Kokoda recaptured, 1942 **10**; *Armidale* sunk, 1942 **12**; Gona recaptured, 1942 **12**; Buna and Sanananda recaptured, 1943 **1**; Japanese attack on Wau repulsed, 1943 **2**; Battle of Bismarck Sea, 1943 **3**; *Hobart* torpedoed, 1943 **7**; Salamaua and Lae recaptured, 1943 **9**; task force in *Krait* sinks ships in Singapore, 1943 **9**; Finschhafen recaptured, 1943 **10**; Sattelberg recaptured, 1943 **11**; Shaggy Ridge occupied, 1944 **1**; Madang reoccupied, 1944 **4**; *Geelong* lost in collision, 1944 **10**; *Australia* damaged by kamikazes, 1944 **10**; Australian forces at Jacquinot Bay and Torokina, 1944 **11**; Australians land at Tarakan and capture Wewak, 1945 **5**; Australians land at Brunei, Labuan, and Sarawak, 1945 **6**; Balikpapan recaptured, 1945 **7**; Pacific War ends, 1945 **8 9**; peace treaty signed, 1951 **9**
Australian casualties, 1945 F
number of merchant ships damaged, 1944 F
World Weather Watch, 1968 B
Woronora Dam (NSW), 1941 **10**
Worrall, Henry, clergyman (1862–1940), 1906 **7**
Worrall, Thomas, convict, 1818 **10**
Wort Papers, The (P. Mathers), 1972 D
Wragge, Clement Lindley, meteorologist (1852–1922), 1884 B
Wran, Neville Kenneth, Labor Premier of NSW (1926–), 1926 G; becomes Premier, 1976 **5**; government re-elected, 1978 **10**, 1981 **9**, 1984 **2**; royal commission investigates, 1983 **5 7**; retires from politics, 1986 **7**
Wreck Reef, *Porpoise* aground on, 1803 **8 10**
Wren, John, sports promoter (1871–1953), 1871 G, 1953 G; sets up illegal tote, 1893 E; gains control of Stadiums Ltd, 1916 E; wife's libel action, 1950 D
Wrest Point Casino (Hobart), 1968 **12**, 1973 **2**
Wright, Edmund William, architect (1824–88), 1863 A, 1867 A
Wright, Judith Arundel, poet (1915–2000), 1915 G, 1946 D, 1949 D, 1959 D
Wright, Samuel, military officer, 1826 **12**
Wrigley, Henry Nelson, aviator (1892–), 1919 **11**
Wunderlich, Ernest (Henry Charles) Julius,

INDEX

manufacturer and music composer
(1859–1945), 1888 A
Wyatt, Joseph, theatrical manager
(1788–1860), 1838 C, 1855 C
Wybalenna Aboriginal settlement (Flinders
Is.), 1835 **1**, 1847 **10**
Wylde, Sir John, judge and constitutionalist
(1781–1859), 1816 **10**, 1817 **9**, 1822 **3**
Wylie, Aboriginal guide, 1841 **4 6 7**
Wyndham, George, wine-grower (1801–70),
1835*
Wyndham (WA), 1886 **3**; air raid on, 1942 **3**
Wynne Art Prize, first awarded, 1897 C
Wynyard Barracks (Syd.), 1792 A
Wyperfeld National Park (Vic.), 1909 F

X

Xavier College (Melb.), 1878 **2**
XPT (Express Passenger Train), 1982 **4**

Y

Yacht racing: Sydney–Hobart first held,
1945 E; Olympic Games wins, 1964 E,
1972 E; Admiral's Cup win, 1979 E;
rescues of round-the-world sailors, 1997 **1**;
Sydney–Hobart race disaster, 1998 **12**. *See
also* America's Cup
Yagan, Aboriginal guerrilla (d. 1833), 1831 **8**,
1832 **6**, 1833 **5 7**, 1997 **9**
Yallourn (Vic.), power station, 1921 **2**;
open-cut mining, 1924 **8**; briquette plant,
1924 **12**; bushfires at, 1944 **2**
Yan Yean (Vic.), water supply, 1857 **12**
Yanco (NSW), 1912 **7**
Yaralla (Syd.), 1899 A
Yarra, HMAS (destroyer), 1910 **11**, 1913 **10**
Yarra, HMAS (sloop), 1942 **3**
Yarra Glen (Vic.), 1838 *
Yarra River (Vic.), 1803 **2**, 1835 **8**; floods,
1839 **12**, 1849 **11**
Yarralumla (ACT), 1913 A
Yarrawonga weir (Murray R.), 1939 *
Yass (NSW), 1837 **3**, 1908 **11**
Yates, Alan Geoffrey, author (1923–85),
1951 D
Year Book Australia, first issued, 1908 D
Year My Voice Broke, The (film), 1987 C
Year of Living Dangerously, The (C. J.
Koch), 1978 D; film of, 1982 C

Yeldham, David Albert, judge (1929–96),
1996 **11**
Yemmerrawannie, Aboriginal, 1792 **12**,
1794 **5**
Yeppoon (Qld), tourist development at, 1979 A
York, Duke of, 1927 **3 5**
York, Mount (NSW), 1813 **5**
York Sound (WA), 1820 **6**
York Town (Tas.), 1804 **12**, 1806 **3**
Yorke Peninsula (SA), 1859 **12**, 1861 **5**
Yothu Yindi (rock group), 1991 C
You Can't See Round Corners (J. Cleary),
1947 D
Young, Cliff, marathon walker, 1983 E
Young, Florence Maude, actress and singer
(1870–1920), 1870 G, 1890 C, 1920 G
Young, Sir Henry Edward Fox, Governor of
SA and Tas. (1803–70), 1848 **8**, 1855 **1**
Young, John, building contractor
(1827–1907), 1882 A
Young, Sir John, Governor of NSW
(1807–76), 1861 **3**
Young, Lamont, geologist, 1880 **10**
Young (NSW): gold discovered at, 1860 **8**;
disturbances at, 1860 **12**, 1861 **6 7**
Young and Jackson's Hotel (Melb.), 1908 C
Young Desire It, The (K. S. Mackenzie),
1937 D
Young Lachlan (schooner), 1819 **2**
Young Men's Christian Association (YMCA),
1850 **12**, 1878 **11**
Young Women's Christian Association
(YWCA), 1880 *
Youth Hostels Association, 1939 *
Yuill, Brian, businessman, 1990 **12**, 1994 **3**

Z

Zeil, Mount (NT), 1872 **8**
Zélée (French ship), 1839 **4**
Zelman, Samuel Victor Albert (Alberto),
musician (1874–1927), 1906 C
Zigzag Railway (NSW), 1869 **10**
Zinc, 1904 B
Zoological societies: Melbourne, 1857 B;
South Australia, 1878 B; NSW, 1879 B
Zoology of New Holland (G. Shaw), 1794 B
Zoos
Adelaide, 1883 B
Dubbo (NSW), 1977 B
Melbourne, 1862 B
Perth, 1898 B
Sydney, 1849 B, 1879 B, 1912 B
Zoot suits, 1943 F